THE OXFORD ILLUSTRATED HISTORY OF

WORLD WAR II

The twelve historians who contributed to *The Oxford Illustrated History of World War II* are all distinguished authorities in their field. They are:

RICHARD BESSEL, University of York

PATRICIA CLAVIN, University of Oxford

DAVID EDGERTON, Imperial College London

DAVID FRENCH, University College London

ERIC GROVE, Liverpool Hope University

NICOLA LABANCA, University of Siena

STEVEN HUGH LEE, University of British Columbia

EVAN MAWDSLEY, University of Glasgow

RICHARD OVERY, University of Exeter

GEOFFREY ROBERTS, University College Cork

MICHAEL SNAPE, University of Birmingham

DAVID WELCH, University of Kent

THE OXFORD
ILLUSTRATED HISTORY OF
WORLD WAR II

Edited by
RICHARD OVERY

OXFORD
UNIVERSITY PRESS

OXFORD
UNIVERSITY PRESS

Great Clarendon Street, Oxford, OX2 6DP,
United Kingdom

Oxford University Press is a department of the University of Oxford.
It furthers the University's objective of excellence in research, scholarship,
and education by publishing worldwide. Oxford is a registered trade mark of
Oxford University Press in the UK and in certain other countries

© Oxford University Press 2015

The moral rights of the authors have been asserted

First Edition published in 2015

Impression: 1

Published in the United States of America by Oxford University Press
198 Madison Avenue, New York, NY 10016, United States of America

British Library Cataloguing in Publication Data
Data available

Library of Congress Control Number: 2014946123

ISBN 978-0-19-960582-8

Printed in Italy by
L.E.G.O. S.p.A.

EDITOR'S PREFACE

THE Second World War is now three generations away, the anniversary of its end in 2015 seventy years since the conflict formally ended. The war has left a long shadow across the second half of the twentieth century. Memorialization of its victims continues and popular fascination with its history is unabated. Unlike the Great War of 1914–18, the second conflict affected literally the whole world; it resulted in around five times as many deaths; and it was punctuated by remarkable moments of drama and sacrifice, all of which explains that persistent interest. The chronological distance from the war has, however, allowed historians to think differently about how to describe and define it, how to explain its course, and above all what subjects should now concern us when considering wartime experience. *The Oxford Illustrated History of World War II* follows a proud tradition in the Press in producing up-to-date and profusely illustrated volumes on a range of historical subjects. The current volume is designed to introduce a range of themes that are less commonly found in general histories of the war and which reflect current developments in historical scholarship. It is also designed to bring the war to life by presenting it in visual terms. The war was fought at a time when photo-journalism was at its zenith and colour film just coming into its own; the propaganda apparatus in every warring state produced leaflets and posters in profusion; official artists were organized even more than in the First World War to provide portraits of wartime life. There is of course an enormous wealth of material available to illustrate the war; the images chosen here are designed to accompany points raised in the texts and should be viewed with that in mind. My task as General Editor has been made easier thanks to the quality of the different contributions and the helpfulness and patience of the contributors during the editorial process. I am grateful to the team at Oxford University Press for all their help in turning this into a successful and visually attractive volume, in particular to Matthew Cotton, Kim Behrens, Kizzy Taylor-Richelieu, and Paul Simmons, who drew the maps. The result is, I hope, a fitting way to re-examine a conflict that with the passage of time remains a lived experience for only a few but which has become in the interval a vibrant example of living history.

RICHARD OVERY

Exeter and London, 2014

CONTENTS

List of Colour Plates ix
List of Maps xi

INTRODUCTION: TOTAL WAR—GLOBAL WAR 1
Richard Overy

1. THE GENESIS OF WORLD WAR 7
   Patricia Clavin

2. THE JAPANESE EMPIRE AT WAR, 1931–1945 35
   Steven Hugh Lee

3. THE ITALIAN WARS 74
   Nicola Labanca

4. THE GERMAN WARS 110
   Richard Overy

5. THE WEST AND THE WAR AT SEA 135
   Eric Grove

6. THE ALLIES FROM DEFEAT TO VICTORY 168
   Evan Mawdsley

7. FIGHTING POWER: WAR-MAKING AND MILITARY
   INNOVATION 202
   David French

8. ECONOMIES IN TOTAL WAR 232
   Richard Overy

9. FRONT LINE I: ARMED FORCES AT WAR 258
   Michael Snape

10. FRONT LINE II: CIVILIANS AT WAR 293
    Richard Overy

11. UNNATURAL DEATHS 322
    Richard Bessel

viii   *Contents*

12.   BRAINS AT WAR: INVENTION AND EXPERTS   344
      David Edgerton

13.   THE CULTURE OF WAR: IDEAS, ARTS, AND PROPAGANDA   373
      David Welch

14.   FROM WORLD WAR TO COLD WAR   402
      Geoffrey Roberts

Maps   433
Further Reading   455
Picture Acknowledgements   469
Index   477

LIST OF COLOUR PLATES

1. A French anti-Bolshevik poster from 1919 warning of the threat to capital, labour, and knowledge.

2. A Hungarian poster from 1919 welcoming President Wilson's Fourteen Points and hope for a just peace.

3. Kandy Commonwealth War Cemetery, showing tombstones for soldiers from the Madras Labour Unit and the King's African Rifles, 1944 and 1945.

4. Mother and child memorial statue, at ground zero, Nagasaki Peace Park, Japan.

5. Edward Bawden, painting of of an Italian partisan headquarters in Ravenna towards the end of the war.

6. A poster issued by the Italian Social Republic mocks the Allied claim to be liberating Italy while at the same time bombing its towns and killing an estimated 60,000 Italians.

7. A pre-war evening rally of the SS in Germany.

8. A German soldier armed with a flamethrower in the opening months of Operation Barbarossa, the Axis invasion of the Soviet Union.

9. A coastal convoy, probably between Southampton and the Thames estuary, seen from the barrage balloon vessel *Inverugie*.

10. One of the key naval aircraft of the war, a Grumman Avenger bomber, on the flight deck of an American escort carrier.

11. 'Jewish Plot against Europe!' In line with Nazi propaganda, an anti-Semitic Belgian collaborationist poster of 1942 depicts the British–Soviet alliance as part of the world Jewish conspiracy.

12. 'United we are strong', US Office of War Information poster (artist: Henry Koerner), 1943.

13. A German tank advancing towards Bordeaux in June 1940.

14. P-51 Mustang long-range fighter aircraft.

x *List of Colour Plates*

15. 'More Help for the Front', Russian poster.

16. A group of British Boy Scouts help to collect waste paper for the war effort at Balderston, Nottinghamshire.

17. The diversity of the Allied forces in Italy, 1943–45. French and Japanese-American troops at an artillery observation post on the French–Italian border.

18. A propaganda poster glorifying the exploits of the British Empire's African troops, in this case fighting against the Japanese in Burma.

19. A British poster from 1939 encouraging civilians to enrol in the quasi-military air-raid protection services.

20. A United States poster from 1942 aimed at encouraging housewives to make their contribution to the total war effort by preserving their own food.

21. After the bombing of Dresden in February 1945, dead bodies are burned at the Altmarkt near the Victory Monument (*Germaniadenkmal*).

22. A bus lies in a crater in the road in Balham in south London, the morning after a German air raid during the Battle of Britain.

23. A piston aero-engine, one of the most complex machines of the Second World War.

24. Sir Alexander Fleming, a pioneer researcher in antibiotic medicine, at his desk in 1929.

25. Paul Nash, *Battle of Germany*, 1944.

26. Mikhail Khmelko, *Triumph of Our Fatherland*, 1945.

27. Stalin, Churchill, and Roosevelt at Yalta in February 1945.

28. Truman, Attlee, and Stalin at Potsdam in August 1945.

LIST OF MAPS

1. Axis territorial expansion 1938–42   433
2. Japanese territorial expansion 1931–42   434
3. The German campaign in Poland, September 1939   436
4. German invasion in the West, May 1940   437
5. The Battle of Britain   438
6. Japan's campaigns in China 1937–45   439
7. Japan's advance in the Pacific War 1941–2   440
8. The Battle of the Atlantic 1943   442
9. Operation Barbarossa 1941   443
10. The bombing campaigns in Europe 1940–5   444
11. The war in Italy 1943–5   446
12. German defeat in the East 1943–5   447
13. The Holocaust in Europe 1941–5   448
14. The Allied invasion of France   449
15. The defeat of Germany in the West   450
16. The defeat of Japan in the Pacific War   451
17. The campaigns in Burma 1942–5   452
18. The Cold War division of Europe   453
19. The Korean War   454

Introduction

Total War—Global War

RICHARD OVERY

It is a commonplace that the Second World War was both global in extent and total in character. And yet with the passage of time since the end of the war in 1945 both of these realities seem more difficult to explain than they did at the time. That almost the entire surface of the earth, and the skies above, should be engulfed by war is an extraordinary, unique phenomenon. Even those nations that could remain neutral or were distant from the actual fighting were profoundly touched by war. Volunteers from neutral Spain went off to fight against 'Bolshevism' in Hitler's war on the Soviet Union; neutral Swiss banks stockpiled gold melted down from the dental fillings and jewellery of murdered European Jews; faraway Brazil declared war on Germany and Italy in 1942 and sent two divisions to fight in the last stages of the European war in northern Italy. From the Aleutian Islands in the northern Pacific Ocean to the jungle-coated island of Madagascar, from the deserts of North Africa to the harsh Arctic Ocean, states fought a desperate war for what they regarded as just causes. The sheer geographical scale of the war is a challenge to any history of the conflict, and demands its own explanation.

The geography of the Second World War was dictated by the ambitions of the aggressor states—Germany, Italy, and Japan (and the Soviet Union in 1939–40 in Poland and Finland)—in a world where global and regional security systems could no longer effectively function, as the opening chapter shows, either through the operation of self-restraint or through coercion. Each of these states pursued a number of distinctly separate wars to try to create new security regimes to protect and secure their international status. Although the ambitions of the three so-called 'Axis' states were confined to their own spheres of interest or 'new orders' in Europe, the Medi-terranean, and Asia (defined in the Tripartite Pact signed in Berlin in September 1940), the conflicts eventually coalesced into world war principally because of the global reach of the Western Allies—Britain, the British Commonwealth and Empire, and the United States—and the global nature of the aggregate threat that they perceived.

The territorial spread of conflict from the mid-1930s was literally world-wide. Italy fought wars against Ethiopia in 1935–6, in Spain to help Franco, briefly against France in June 1940 and then against the British Commonwealth in Africa, before invading Greece in October 1940 and opening a Balkan front. Germany began with a war against Poland on 1 September 1939 that grew immediately into a war with Britain and France; in February 1941 German forces set up a Mediterranean front; in June 1941 another war was launched against the Soviet Union, distinct from the war in the west; in December 1941 war was declared on the United States. Japan began aggression in China in 1931–2, escalated the conflict into full-scale war in July 1937, fought briefly against Soviet forces in 1938 and 1939 on the Manchurian border, and finally added a major conflict in the Pacific Ocean theatre against the United States, Britain, The Netherlands, Australia, and New Zealand. Though at times these aggressive wars were linked—for example, German help for the failing Italian army in North Africa and Greece—they were generally fought as separate contests, which is why they are dealt with in this volume as three sets of wars, one each for Japan, Italy, and Germany.

The geography of the war was also shaped by the search for economic security. Japanese aggression was largely fuelled by the belief that the resources of mainland China and South-East Asia were necessary to provide Japan's people with long-term economic benefits that could no longer be obtained from the conventional world trading economy. Hitler's war against the Soviet Union, for all its emphasis on a clash of ideologies, was supposed to engross the raw material and agricultural resources of Eurasia to support an economically independent and wealthy German imperial centre. Italy's war against British Commonwealth forces in Egypt had the Suez Canal and the oil of the Middle East as a probable prize. Since modern mechanized warfare, air war, and naval power all depended on oil, the modest oil resources of the aggressor states could only be reversed, so it was believed, by conquest. For the Western Allies, endowed with large merchant marines and navies, security meant keeping available distant sources of supply (particularly of oil) and defending long trans-oceanic trade routes that were essential to both the Allied war economies and to the pursuit of a global strategy. Both sides did what they could to deny resources to the other through economic warfare measures, bombing, or submarine war, with the result that warfare at sea and in the air spread out far beyond the fighting front.

Economic mobilization owed much to the necessity of securing new resources but it was also determined by the sheer scale of the fighting. Total war was a term used loosely at the time, suggesting a war without limits, involving the mobilization of economic, human, intellectual, and technical resources to their fullest extent. Since in the 1930s this was the prevailing view of what future large-scale war would look like, no major state could afford to risk war waged at any lower level of mobilization. The demands of total war were nevertheless not uniform. The United States with its vast resources and wealth mobilized only part of its economy and still out-produced all other nations. The Soviet Union was forced by the Axis invasion in 1941 to use everything available in the unoccupied zone to fight the war, even to the point of allowing the old or infirm to die rather than use up scarce food rations. The aggressor states mobilized their resources for some form of total war but the mobilization was always a gamble that swift military victory could be secured before the evident economic weight of the Allied powers could be brought to bear. When the hope for a quick victory evaporated, the gamble continued, but by 1943–4 it was evident that the resource base for the Allies, as long as it was used in militarily effective ways, would overcome Axis resistance. The turning of the tide was by no means automatic or predictable, but the chapters here on Allied victory at sea, in the air, and on the ground show how all three major Allies learned how to use their resources with growing operational and tactical skill.

Economic factors clearly mattered in explaining the nature and outcome of the war; if the German armed forces had captured the Caucasus oil, or Rommel and the Italians had captured the oil of the Middle East the war might well have taken a very different path. But economic factors explain only part of the reality of total war, which is why there are also chapters here on fighting power, the mobilization of science and technology, and the propaganda efforts made to sustain the commitment of the home front to the contest. The war witnessed dramatic changes in the organization of armed forces and in the scientific and engineering resources available to them. Biplanes were still in use in some air forces in 1939; by 1945 the jet age had already dawned. The use of radar was limited in 1939, chiefly by the early long-wave technology available; by 1945 short-wave centimetric radar, based on exploiting the wartime invention of the cavity magnetron, had revolutionized its use. Tanks were generally slow, small, and poorly gunned in 1939, but by 1945 the German Tiger and the Soviet IS-2 (Joseph Stalin) paved the way for the modern battle tank. Rockets, cruise missiles, and, most significantly, nuclear weapons were all in use by the war's end, anticipating the military stand-offs of the coming Cold War. How armed forces were used was also revolutionized during the war: the integration of air power with the operations of armies and navies transformed the latter's reach and strike capability, while the use of mobile forces eroded the old-fashioned infantry division and replaced it with motorized and mechanized divisions, self-contained and fast-moving. Success in planning and resourcing these changes played an important part in early Axis victories but also in the eventual success of the Allies.

By 1945 most servicemen were recruits from the civilian world rather than career soldiers or sailors and the organization of huge armed forces, numbering tens of millions, raised questions not only about how they were managed and resourced, but about how they could be policed, entertained, or comforted enough to keep them fighting. A chapter on the social and cultural history of the front line sets out to examine armed forces as social organizations, not just as fighting units. The other front line explored here is the home front. The issue of civilian commitment to war was also an integral component of the waging of total war, partly because of the extreme pressures exerted on civilian populations through bombing campaigns, state terror, strict limitation of existing freedoms, hunger, and displacement. When the European war came in 1939, states feared that city-bombing might bring about widespread civilian panic and demands for peace at any price. The German, Italian, and Soviet dictatorships monitored their populations daily with unscrupulous zeal to make sure that any sign of dissent could be quashed. At the same time every effort was made to ensure that the factors which had debilitated the war efforts in 1914–18—inflation, hunger, the black market, working-class unrest—would not do so a second time, even under extreme conditions. Demoralization at military failure was another matter. Every major state manipulated the news that its population could hear, developed sophisticated regimes of patriotic propaganda, undertook political warfare against its enemies, and tried to paint a picture of the war that masked the truth. When American pollsters carried out a survey among captured Japanese civilians on Saipan in February 1945, they found that a majority still believed that Japan would secure victory in the end. The propaganda and information war was a critical dimension of war-making and rightly has an entire chapter devoted to it.

Nevertheless, civilians did not just sustain the war effort because propaganda told them to do it. There had to be some sense that the cause was just and that the sacrifices imposed represented a necessary expedient to ensure victory. Civilians also had to find the means to help themselves in the face of bombing and other war-related hardships. Civil defence relied on millions of civilian volunteers who took many risks more usually associated with the armed forces, and suffered heavy casualties as a result. They did so not perhaps principally to defend some abstract principle, but to protect their families and the urban environment from destruction and to sustain a sense of home-front mobilization widely regarded as appropriate for a total war between whole societies. Popular commitment to war also rested on sentiments such as fear or revenge or anger, but year after year these were difficult sentiments to sustain. Victory became an end in itself, the means to ensure survival and to limit the existential threat posed by the enemy or the 'other'.

This also explains the harsh treatment meted out to all those who were deemed not to belong to the fighting community or who were believed to be subverting its struggle. In Britain and France in 1939–40 aliens were rounded up and interned; in the United States the Japanese Americans were sent into internal exile in specially-constructed camps; in the Soviet Union the habits of suspicion and denunciation continued to feed the GULag camps and labour colonies. The worst examples were to be found in the Axis states which used their territorial conquests as sites for extreme discrimination and violence. The 'enemy' now inside the conquered areas was defined as partisan or terrorist or subversive and subjected to savage reprisals. The chief enemy of the new German empire was deemed to be the Jew and almost six million European Jews paid for that cruel stigmatization with their lives. So too did hundreds of thousands of hostages, civilian prisoners and labourers, prisoners-of-war and political opponents. The patchwork of victims covers many different categories; the patchwork of perpetrators is less diverse. The killing was carried out by security agents, secret police forces, regular soldiers, and police militia using methods that were improvised and bloody—so bloody in the case of the genocide of the Jews that face-to-face killing was replaced in 1942 by factories of death, where the end product was piles of bone ash. These millions of victims suffered what is called here an 'unnatural death', one that would not have occurred but for the twists and turns of the war. Above all the victims suffered from the poisonous search for vengeance in systems that could see that the writing was on the wall and looked for someone to punish.

Victory for the Allies (or the United Nations as they called themselves from January 1942) did not end the violence and discrimination, and in some cases, principally in Eastern Europe, sustained it. The final chapter in the volume explores the complex and messy end to the conflict. The old empires faced a crisis precipitated by the Axis search for new empires. In Vietnam, Indonesia, India, and Burma it proved impossible to reimpose European rule and all were independent by 1954. In the Middle East the system of mandates from the League of Nations that had allowed Britain and France to dominate the region collapsed and independent Arab states emerged. They were challenged in 1948 by the unilateral declaration of an independent state of Israel by the Jews of Palestine, which resulted in the first Arab–Israeli war. In Eastern Europe old frontiers were restored or, in the case of Poland, shifted westward at the expense of Germans and Poles, to satisfy Soviet demands for former Polish territory in Western Ukraine. Insurgencies continued in the Baltic States, Ukraine, and Poland against the imposition of Soviet rule. These armed struggles continued down to the late 1940s. In Greece the end of Axis rule created the circumstances for civil war as nationalists and monarchists fought against the Communist partisans. All of these struggles took place against a tide of hardship—hunger, forced emigration, inflation, and expropriation.

The post-war crises did not provoke World War Three, as was widely feared in Europe, chiefly because the international order was stabilized around the reality of Soviet and American power and the weakness of a battered Europe and Asia. Germany and Japan were temporarily disarmed and never again posed a regional threat, their military and nationalist elites entirely discredited. In 1945 the victor states established the United Nations Organization in the hope that this would be a more effective factor for avoiding or controlling conflict than the League of Nations had been before the war. American contributions to reviving the world economy proved to be essential both materially and psychologically, though ironically it was war once again, in the Korean peninsula, that stoked the start of the extraordinary post-war boom in the non-Communist world after 1950. Under the shadow of the Soviet–American dual-power system both China and India began the long path to their later role as major powers. India and Pakistan gained independence in 1947 (though at the cost of a vicious religious conflict between Hindus and Muslims), while China became unified as a Communist state in 1949 at the end of a prolonged civil war. After more than a dozen years of violence, Asia achieved its modern political geography.

The Second World War and its confused aftermath brought to an end a long period in which economic and political modernization had encouraged the dissolution of old empires and political structures across the world, thrown up new forces of mass nationalism, and created the technical means to mobilize and arm vast military forces. The First World War was a symptom of those changes but its conclusion left many of the issues unresolved. Widespread economic instability, national resentments, anti-colonial struggles, and ideological confrontations followed in the wake of the first war, encouraging by the 1930s a wave of civil and international conflicts which merged together only later into what is now called the Second World War. The vacuum that had existed in the power relations of the 1930s was filled after 1945 by the two superpowers, but the harsh experience of war, with perhaps as many as 55 million dead, and millions more scarred physically and psychologically, was of itself enough to prompt a widespread acceptance of the new status quo and an aversion to the nationalism and militarism that had fuelled the belief that war was the only instrument to secure a better order. Self-restraint as much as mutual deterrence has kept the world from a third cataclysm.

1 The Genesis of World War

PATRICIA CLAVIN

THE origins of the Second World War lie in the First. But the route from the conflict of 1914 to 1918 to its successor was not as direct as it first appeared to the men and women who took up arms in 1939 within a generation of the first. In Europe, where most of the fighting had taken place, almost every family had a member who had been killed or wounded. Historians may now dispute whether the 'Great War' was the first-ever 'total war', a term coined at the time to imply the integration of organized combat and the societies, economies, and political systems that supported it, but everyone was touched by its effects.

Peace, though declared, was slow in coming. Officially, the armistice began on the eleventh hour of the eleventh day in November 1918, and it was then that the first estimate of the costs, that almost defied the imagination, could be made. Historians now put the number of war dead at been 9.4 and 11 million people, a figure that amounted to over one per cent of Europe's population in 1913. On average 5,600 men died for every day the war continued, and injured soldiers had some of the worst wounds ever seen. Approximately 755,000 British men and 1,537,000 German soldiers, for example, were permanently disabled in the war, and throughout Europe the care of disabled veterans posed an important challenge to post-war reconstruction. So did the destruction of homes, factories, and farm land to the tune of around $30,000 million in the war zones. It also had dramatic political consequences. The war shattered the Austro-Hungarian, Russian, German, and Ottoman Empires, and marked with them the declining role of the monarchy in history. At the same time, the locus of global and economic power moved firmly away from Western Europe to the United States, and saw New York displace London as the centre of world finance.

In the long run, the devastation wrought by the war impaired the ability of the Western powers to respond to the threat of another, potentially more destructive conflict, even as the leaders of Japan, Germany, and Italy actively prepared for it. More immediately, the 'Great War' provided the Russian Bolsheviks with the opportunity to launch a bid for power in November 1917, triggering a bitter civil war that brought renewed suffering to peoples of what was in 1924 to become the Union of Soviet Socialist Republics (USSR). The civil war shaped both the internal character of the Communist regime, and its foreign policy, which was born out of a deep suspicion and hostility to the powers that had supported the 'White Guard' fighting against the Red Army. These included the forces of

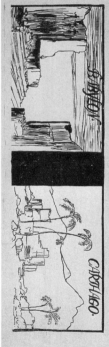
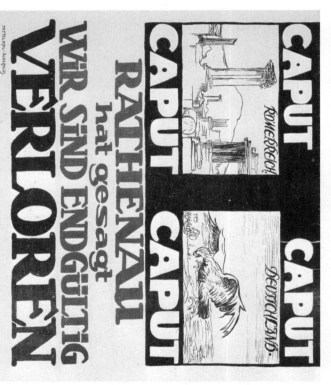

Under the banner headline, 'Global Empires and Global Nations can Fall', this poster anticipates Germany's defeat. It compares the collapse of Germany to that of the Roman empire.

For 'Italy—in the name of the dead!' This Fascist election poster from 1924 depicts Mussolini's party honouring the sacrifice of Italy's 900,000 dead and wounded in the war, while ready, with weapon in hand, to defend its national interests in the present and future.

the Allies and Associated Powers—notably the French and British Empires and Dominions, Japan, and the USA—but also, for portions of the civil war, the forces of Germany and Austria-Hungary too. The resultant antagonism was mutual. The successful Communist revolution inspired copy-cat risings in Hungary and Germany, as well as Communist movements around the world, and the ideology that sought to lead the urban working classes and, increasingly, impoverished peasants into revolution was a spectre that haunted relations between the USSR and the capitalist powers.

Conflict did not just continue along what had been called the Eastern Front after peace was declared. Political violence escalated dramatically in Ireland and China while, along the borders of collapsed states and empires in central Europe, men and boys who were formally demobilized continued to fight for the spoils of war. Much of this violence can be traced back to the dramatic eruption of revolution in Russia that by the end of 1917 saw the former territories of the Russian Empire engulfed in civil war. In 1918 an estimated 143 million people lived in the lands formerly claimed by the Tsar, but when the civil war ended in 1921 (but before the mass starvation began) the population had fallen to 134 million. Politics, too, was the continuation of war by other means. In parts of Europe and in Japan, the Great War facilitated the continued militarization of domestic politics, particularly in Germany, Austria, and Italy, where war veterans were a potent political force.

Most governments, whether old or newly-established, faced testing questions at home as a result of the promises made by those who governed between 1915 and 1918 to sustain the war effort, as did political parties which sought public support in

Women campaigned energetically for their political, social, and economic rights in the wake of the First World War. The picture shows peace delegates from countries that were designated 'enemy territories' who joined other members of the Women's International League for Peace and Freedom (WILPF) at the organization's second international congress held in Zürich in May 1919.

elections that were widespread at the end of the war. National politics now frequently turned on the issue of 'rights'. These included the right to vote independent of land ownership, especially for women; to greater representation by minority groups and colonized peoples; and to improved social rights, notably in the field of employment, housing, and social protection.

Legacies of the First World War

For the first four years after the First World War, then, peace was observed as much in the breach as in the making. The emerging language of rights around the world, and the sense of entitlement it represented, pointed to the profound changes underway between peoples and organizations that claimed to represent them. This posed a substantial, but not yet an insurmountable, challenge to international relations because the end of the war indicated common challenges and shared problems. But states largely sought to tackle these issues on a national basis in ways that generated ill-feeling between them. Despite the widespread and heartfelt desire for peace in 1918, the international co-operation that had distinguished the war effort, particularly among the victorious powers, gave way to narrowly defined self-interest; the internationalism of war gave way to the nationalism of peace. The change could be plotted in the gap that emerged between the US President Woodrow Wilson's famous 'Fourteen Points' that formed the basis for peace negotiations between January and November 1918, and the peace treaties signed at the Paris Peace Conference of 1919.

Wilson had aspired to a new diplomacy that would banish the dangerous practices of bilateral alliances and secret treaties that he believed led to war. His key to a flexible and 'healing' peace settlement was a new international organization, the League of Nations, which would work to resolve contentious issues between states after the preliminary work at Paris was done. As the short-lived American Under-Secretary of the League of Nations, Raymond Fosdick, put it in 1919, 'the hope of the situation—if there is any hope—lies in the League of Nations. Can the League, by exercise of its somewhat vaguely defined powers, either now or in the future, so soften the sharp edges of the treaty that, by gradual transformation, it can be made the basis of enduring peace?' In fact, despite lofty American claims to make the 'old' world conform to the ideas and values of the new, the genesis for this new intergovernmental organization to facilitate international arbitration was largely British, and Wilson's promise of self-determination merely reinvigorated and internationalized existing demands for self-government around the world. The USA's claim to world leadership was as tenuous as it was brief. Even as Wilson basked in his 'victory parade' around the capital cities of Europe in the run-up to the Paris Conference, his Democrat Party had lost control of Congress, and with it went US support for the new international order.

Not only did the US Congress reject the League of Nations, it failed to ratify the major multilateral peace treaties of Paris: the treaties of Saint-Germain-en-Laye with Austria, Neuilly with Bulgaria, Trianon with Hungary, and, crucially, the Treaty of

A striking image of President Wilson used to publicize US Independence Day of 4 July 1918 in Italy. Italy and the USA were presented as united in the cause of victory. But Wilson's disavowal of the terms of the secret Treaty of London of 1915 that had prompted Italy to join the side of the Triple Entente, resulted in a much less benign representation of Wilson, especially by Italian Fascists.

Versailles with Germany. (The USA signed separate bilateral treaties with these countries in 1921.) At the time, the Treaty of Versailles became rapidly associated with expectations that were frustrated by the peace. It came under vigorous assault from within Germany, especially from those on the right of the political spectrum who found it hard to accept that the Wilhelmine Empire had lost a war which, until the summer of 1918, it appeared to be winning. Their sense of grievance was bolstered by currency inflation, which had been sparked by the failed German war economy, but it was allowed to become a raging fire by the new Weimar Republic struggling to meet the demands made of it by German society, and the imposition of reparations by the allies. These were payments levied by the Allies for damages caused by the war. There had been no mention of any such indemnity in the 'Fourteen Points', and although such war tributes were common practice and had been levied by Prussia against France in 1871, the bitter pill was made all the harder to swallow because it was legitimated by the insertion of a 'war guilt' clause into the treaty. Although subtle in its drafting, a host of publicists and historians, in some cases supported by a special commission of the German Ministry of Foreign Affairs, set out to refute the claim that Germany alone had been responsible for the outbreak of war, an interpretation that none of the treaties actually made. A tidal wave of official documents, selected, edited, and when necessary falsified, followed.

This German attack was bolstered abroad by John Maynard Keynes's savagely brilliant book, *The Economic Consequences of the Peace*, published in 1919, excerpts of which were widely syndicated in the international press. His criticisms were supported subsequently in the memoirs and diaries of other participants at the Paris Peace Conference, and an official inquiry in the United States into the role played by munitions producers in the outbreak of the war. By the mid-1930s this critical view of the peacemakers helped to create the general consensus that the First World War was an accident for which no one power was accountable. As the British wartime Prime Minister, David Lloyd George, put it in his memoirs, 'nations slithered over the brink'. It was a perspective that undermined the credibility of the Paris Peace Settlement, and helped successive German governments to roll back the terms of Versailles.

The provisions of the treaty included a reduction in German arms and military forces, the dissolution of its navy, and the demilitarization of the Rhineland. It also gave up 27,000 square miles of territory containing around seven million people, and Germany's flirtation with empire was forcibly ended with the loss of overseas imperial territories in Tanganyika and South-West Africa, and in the Pacific. Closer to home, Germany returned Alsace-Lorraine to France, and watched on the sidelines as a strip of Western Prussia was used to provide a 'Polish corridor' to give the newly-independent Poland access to the sea. At the end of the corridor was the former Hansa trading city of Danzig, which was now given the status of Free City under the oversight of the League of Nations. After 1933, these terms were less the subject of international negotiation and more the opportunity for international assertion by Germany's National Socialist government, which used the pretext of treaty revision as the building block for their radical version of a racial empire.

Critical, too, to the prospects of peace was the principle of self-determination, vaunted by Wilson in the 'Fourteen Points'. This was the right of 'nations'—communities of people defined largely by which language they spoke—to choose their own form of government. For Wilson, and liberal nationalists in central and eastern Europe, such as the new president of the new Czechoslovak republic, Tomáš G. Masaryk, self-determination would enable the new republics to embed parliamentary democracy and 'stimulate endeavours to bring a renascence and regeneration in ethics and culture'. But the rich intermingling of language, history, religion, and culture in the region made Wilson's approach, at best, problematic. Minority groups had scant protection and ethnic tensions imperilled individuals' democratic freedom.

Alongside territorial losses imposed on Austria and Hungary—the latter joining Germany among the powers aggressively seeking to revise the peace—peoples and provinces were treated, in the words of Harold Nicolson, a British delegate at the conference, merely 'as pawns and chattels in a game'. The populous majority groups

Maryland's Best.

The Afro-American is the oldest, largest and newsiest weekly News-paper in Maryland.

VOL. XXVII. No. 15.

THE AFRO-AMERICAN, BALTIMORE, MD., FRIDAY, DECEMBER 20, 1918.

PRICE 5 CENTS

The Afro Is Issued Thursday at Six On Sale at News Stands Friday Morning.

THE AFRO AMERICAN

DuBOIS HANDS MEMORANDUM TO COLONEL HOUSE
HIGH WAGES PUT END TO GERMAN SCHEMES

N.A.A.C.P. HEAD ASKS INTER-NATIONALIZATION OF AFRICA.

Convention of Negroes of the World To Meet In Paris, During Peace Conference Interested Primarily In Democracy Here

FIVE BELL-BOYS TAKEN IN RAID

Sold Liquor to Men in Uniform at $3.00 per Half Pint. Federal Authorities Determined To Break Up Practice.

Negroes are Anglo-Saxons Says White Women.

TO DEDICATE NEW $100,000 Y.M.C.A. NEW YEAR'S DAY

McADOO CALLS HALT ON DIS-CRIMINATION.

Says He Object Is to Give Negro Working Conditions as Working Californian

NEWSPAPERS COMMENT ON DR. MOTON'S TRIP

INTELLIGENCE DEPT. SHEDS LIGHT ON WORK OF SPIES

"Small" Leaders of the Race Subsidized. Mexicans and Half-Breeds Used In The Work.

EBENEZER CHURCH BURNS MORTGAGE

FUNERAL OF ALFRED H. PITTS

Prominent Baltimorean Laid to Rest. Thousands Pay Tribute to Well-Known Nazarite. Interment in Laurel Cemetery.

won out, and ethnic minorities found themselves without the protection that larger empires had afforded. Self-determination, moreover, became the basis used by ethnic Germans who had never been resident in Germany, such as those in the Sudetenland newly incorporated into Czechoslovakia, to claim the right to join. In terms of European security, the new territorial configuration of Europe also presented Germany with a strategic advantage: where once it confronted mighty empires along its eastern frontiers, now it met only small querulous nation-states.

The 'winners' and 'losers' of the Paris Peace Conference did not match the winning and losing sides of the First World War. If territorial settlements had been made, as Nicolson claimed, on the basis of mere adjustments and compromises between the rival claims of states, Italy and Japan, both members of the victorious Allied powers, felt they had been subject to very shabby treatment. Italy had been promised the Dalmatian coast in the Secret Treaty of London in 1915, but when it was given instead to Yugoslavia Vittorio Emanuele Orlando, the Italian Prime Minister, stormed out of the Paris Conference in disgust. Within Italy, this treatment rankled among tens of thousands of young men, still intoxicated by patriotic fervour uncorked by war, and confirmed a widespread suspicion that Italy's centrist political parties could not meet their promises. As early as 1922 it helped to pave the path to power for Benito Mussolini, a ruthless and daring nationalist who made electoral and financial capital in the climate of frustration and political violence that engulfed Italy. His motto was *Tutto Osare* (Dare Everything), and his Fascist government became the first peacetime attempt to refashion politics and society to meet the organizational requirements of war. In the coming years, it was a trend mimicked by nationalist and authoritarian movements in Europe and in Asia. Japan's frustrations, too, were expressed in territorial terms. But its rancour with arrangements made at Paris exposed a more profound injustice in its failed attempt to secure 'Great Power' support for a clause endorsing racial equality in the covenant of the League of Nations. It was rejected by all the 'white' powers in Paris.

It is possible that some of the difficulties could have been ironed out by the League of Nations, as the delegates who put together the peace deals signed in Paris viewed their work as provisional, and although much is made of the fact that neither Germany nor the USSR were there at the start, Germany became a member in 1926 and the USSR in 1934. Yet in many ways, instead of ushering in a new diplomacy, the practices of the world's first intergovernmental organization replicated the world before 1914. There was certainly some truth in Nicolson's famous claim: 'We came to Paris convinced a new order was about to be established; we left convinced the old order had merely fouled the new.' The League of Nations was emphatically that: a league of *nations*, intended to reinforce the authority of member states not to challenge it. The primacy of state sovereignty was enshrined in the Covenant of the League, and in the organizational structures and institutional practice that emerged. The League presented a vision of the world where the unit that counted was the nation-state. Indeed the powers of its representatives were tightly prescribed by this principle, and by the need for unanimity among its members, or at least its most

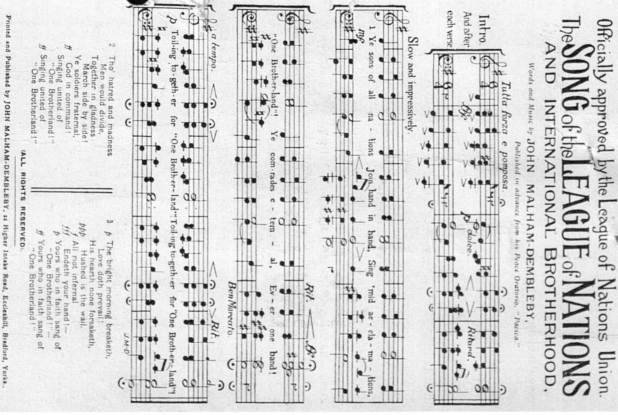

International enthusiasm for the League of Nations was often expressed in terms very similar to those of nationalism, including League of Nations stamps, flags and anthems. Written by Yorkshireman John Malham-Dembleby, this is one of three known anthems composed in honour of the organization.

powerful members, as a precondition of action. Over time, the League managed to effect some pioneering work in the fields of health, finance, and economics, and it did afford space for 'smaller states' to pursue some issues that were important to them, especially those for whom internationalism became a defining feature of their national identity, such as Ireland and Norway. But issues of race permeated the League as they did the rest of the world, and the membership of Asian and African countries was tokenistic at best.

The League reflected the established hierarchy of global power which, once the USA abandoned the organization, put Britain and France at the top. This blow was made all the more severe because US promises to support French security went with it, which prompted France in the 1920s to maintain resolutely that the Paris deliberations had determined the status quo. Nor was France reassured by British policy as the US action provided Britain with the opportunity to reassert the primacy of imperial security by taking a longed-for step out of Europe. Although it remained committed to the security of France's border with Germany, Britain feared becoming embroiled in French foreign policy and the republic's network of so-called Little Entente alliances with Poland, Czechoslovakia, Romania, and Yugoslavia. France courted these alliances in a forlorn attempt to contain any German ambitions for expansion along its eastern frontier. Instead, the French decision to establish mutual guarantees of struggling nations undermined the League, only serving to emphasize the potential mismatch in a conflict between a French nation of 40 million people and a Germany of 65 million.

The Search for Security

Into these testing circumstances came three big trends that dominated the history of international security and shaped the path to war. The first had a historical pedigree reaching back to the Treaty of Westphalia that ended the Thirty Years War in 1648, which stressed that the preservation of international peace and security was the provenance of the nation-state. As we have seen, this idea profoundly shaped the League of Nations, and was reflected in policies that equated national security with the extension of state powers over their peoples. The French Prime Minister Georges Clemenceau, le Père de la Victoire, never tired of declaring that he believed, above all, in well-secured borders. Many statesmen around the world shared this view, placing particular emphasis on having readily available and sufficient weapons, and trained soldiers, sailors, and increasingly airmen, to defend them. Indeed, it was precisely the thinking of these mere *Grenzpolitiker* (border politicians) that Hitler challenged. By contrast, he claimed that he was a *Raumpolitiker*, a 'spatial politician' who demanded that the world be reshaped to match his vision of the needs of National Socialist Germany.

Borders were not just increasingly fortified in physical terms. They were also protected by new bureaucratic practices. Although states everywhere had started to introduce immigration controls before 1914, barriers to the free passage of peoples, alongside new forms of documentation to monitor and control the movement of individuals, within as well as across countries, grew with alacrity during and after the First World War. The trend was facilitated by the introduction of passports, identity cards, and 'papers', giving states new powers of surveillance at home, while people labelled 'undesirable' or 'outsiders' were made to wear badges that echoed the practice of branding or tattooing slaves and criminals in the past.

States became obsessed with population. On the level of national defence this reflected their fear of the operational nightmare of a 'total' static war they had seen on the western front. This anxiety certainly spurred on those who advocated new types of armour, airpower, and elite and professional armies to generate a credible vision of more mobile forms of warfare. But men, women, and children, measured by their number and their 'quality', spoke to wider meanings of the term 'security' that had begun to emerge by the end of the nineteenth century. The second big trend was that security no longer meant simply protecting people and property against the threat of war—what political scientists would later call 'hard security'—but was now also related to the 'intactness' of the human body, defined in both racial and biological terms.

Not only did governments in Europe and Japan become vehemently pronatalist, seeking to ensure they had sufficient manpower to defend themselves in the future, but the development of genetic science added a potent biological component to states' interest in demography. A crude misrepresentation of Charles Darwin's founding work of genetics, *The Origin of the Species*, was especially influential, postulating that all human life was a struggle for survival in which the strong subjugated the weak. Particular human communities and minority groups had long been considered inferior, but what became known as Social Darwinism now gave this view a pseudoscientific basis on which to order the world. This was ethno-nationalism, which provided a means to rank nations and peoples abroad, and justified racist and eugenicist policies towards 'asocials', 'undesirables', and minority groups at home.

These ideas also reinforced notions of a global hierarchy. The Germans, for example, ranked themselves above the British and the French, just as Britain positioned itself above Germany and France, and so on. But while there was variation between nations on the details of their views, Northern Europeans (including those inside the United States) saw themselves generally above Mediterranean peoples. In Asia, the Japanese and Chinese had similar sorts of hierarchies, but they, like the Europeans and North Americans, were agreed that they were racially and culturally superior to the African continent and black people everywhere. Ethno-nationalistic ideas were particularly influential among nationalist, authoritarian, and Fascist political movements. These groups denied the legitimacy of the League of Nations, and saw international relations as the battle for survival in an anarchic world where nations had to assert themselves through power politics and the use of military force.

The third major feature of security was a stress on the economy. Like states' preoccupations with borders and population, economic security contained a number of facets. As early as 1899, Ivan Bloch, the Polish banker and railway financier turned

This illustrated menu from the International Press Association dinner at the League of Nations to honour the Locarno treaty is flanked by the 'angelic' foreign ministers who signed the deal. Alois Deso and Emery Kelen, internationally renowned caricaturists of Hungarian origin, produced gloriously inventive satires of the life and times of the League for more than fifteen years.

An early cartoon by the pre-eminent political cartoonist and satirist of the interwar period, David Low. A self-taught New Zealander, the moderately left-leaning Low captures here the frustrated expectations of the poorer members of British society following the peace of 1919.

Daily News.   December 20th. 1920.

THE WON'T-WAITS.   [From yesterday's "Star."

strategic analyst, predicted 'the future of war is not fighting but famine, the bank-ruptcy of nations and the break-up of the whole of social organizations'. The First World War demonstrated the power of his analysis, not simply in the effect of the British naval blockade on Germany, but in the degree to which adequate, reliable, and affordable food supplies shaped military and political outcomes everywhere. It was realized in the revolutionary cry of the Bolsheviks in 1917 for 'Peace, Bread, Land'.

The importance of food, and the land and sea from which to harvest it, to security was underlined in the interwar period by the development of nutritional science, which measured and defined hunger in new ways. It was not only soldiers who marched on their stomachs, as nutritional science underlined the importance of physical well-being for every facet of national defence. As the British Foreign Secretary Anthony Eden put it in November 1938, it was impossible to separate the question of national unity from that of the standard of living of the poorer sections of the population: if the government was to get the nation to fight in times of war, it needed to 'devote as much attention to the provision of housing, nourishment and sunlight as we do to the provision of arms'.

Developments, including the discovery of vitamins and the role played by minerals, widened and changed the meaning of 'hunger' from a phenomenon denoting a quantitative lack of food to one with a closer association with the new term 'malnutrition', which led to a fundamental redefinition of hunger in terms of the quality of diet and health, making it a biological condition amenable to a range of bio-medical and social-scientific forms of measurement and treatment. The League of Nations' Heath Organization set international standards for nutritional health, where British experts, notably the indefatigable Glasgow University trained nutritionist John Boyd Orr took a leading role. Imperial and security concerns dominated his work, and prompted him to report to the British Foreign Office in 1938 what he believed to be the large 'difference between the physique of the German youth and that of the ill-fed Scottish unemployed and poorly paid workers'. Boyd Orr was not the only one to be seduced by National Socialist self-aggrandizing propaganda about the Aryan master-race. In reality, workers in Germany were receiving less food than in Britain, and, crucially, the National Socialists did not just ration food according to gender and occupation, but did so according to race. Fascist, nationalist, and authoritarian political parties and governments wanted to improve the standard of living for men, women, and children they claimed as 'their own', but saw the resources from which such improvement would come as finite. Theirs was a struggle, potentially a war, for the 'right sort' of material, human and physical, that would raise living standards for

As the innocents of war, images of starving children, as in this picture of homeless children in Moscow in 1922, were used to elicit international sympathy to support campaigns for humanitarian aid. The First World War helped to fuel the development of the modern Non-Governmental Organization.

the chosen, and reduce them markedly for the ethno-national categories that were identified as the enemy. Food was a weapon of war first at home, and then abroad.

Food, and the territory from which to harvest it, connected to the genesis of the war in more immediate ways. Already in the 1920s, the plight of central European and the Danubian states became an exemplar for the interconnectedness of agricultural production, nutrition, health, economic stability, and international security. The fate of Romania, Yugoslavia, Bulgaria, Hungary, Austria, and Czechoslovakia was of particular concern (the last less because of the problems of its own agricultural sector than because it was imperilled by the vulnerability of the states around it). The League of Nations estimated that 'about a quarter of the 60 million peasants of eastern Europe do not produce enough to enable them to get enough bread to eat throughout the year' as a result of what was understood to be a vicious, persistent cycle of rural undercapitalization, under-productivity, underemployment, malnourishment, and pervasive misery. These countries were no match for the modern, industrial-scale food producers of North America, nor for the scale of Russian wheat sales overseas facilitated by collectivization of Soviet agriculture after 1927. Indeed, imbalances in the world's food supply and trade triggered an agricultural crisis that saw prices fall and tariffs rise, trends which particularly affected small-scale farmers in Europe and Asia.

During the 1920s, precious advancements in agricultural production achieved in the first two decades of the twentieth century had not just stopped but were being reversed. Such changes of fortune had more than economic and social consequences as they facilitated the rise of authoritarian governments in power. Although the relationship was by no means automatic, in Europe the agricultural crisis helped to produce a political climate that was conducive for right-wing political parties, many of whom, like the Hungarian Peasants Party, sought to address the concerns of the 'ignored' rural peasantry and pursue a revanchist foreign policy determined to challenge and reverse the inequities of the Paris Peace Settlement.

This authoritarian turn in central and eastern European politics helped to distance it from democratic Europe and the USA, which increasingly regarded governments there, with the 'noble exception' of Czechoslovakia, with suspicion and distaste. But if indifference had begun to characterize the attitude of the major powers, most striking was the changing position of France, whose Little Entente alliances were increasingly viewed as a liability rather than an indemnity. What these countries needed was access to international capital and markets, but there was only limited understanding that the world's wealthier powers had to facilitate this process. Although the League of Nations did what it could by, for example, attempting to raise capital on the international market, and arguing that these countries be granted preferential treatment in international trade, its powers were limited. The world's wealthier countries had yet to realize that their own security, especially when times were hard, would be advanced by helping those less fortunate than themselves.

In part, the impulse to extend financial and economic help to vulnerable countries was constrained because the fortunes of political parties and the legitimacy of every

These illustrations are part of a large collection of materials put together by the Hungarian government in the early 1920s bemoaning the loss of food and land as a result of the Treaty of Trianon of 1920. Is this 'what we're left with', challenged the League for the Territorial Protection of Hungary—fewer than two million cattle and four million farmers?

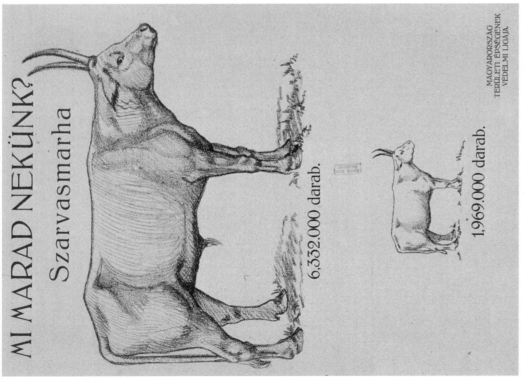

MI MARAD NEKÜNK?

Szarvasmarha

6,332.000 darab.

1,969.000 darab.

MAGYARORSZÁG
TERÜLETI ÉPSÉGÉNEK
VÉDELMI LIGÁJA.

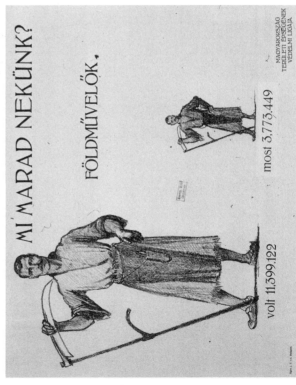

MI MARAD NEKÜNK?

FÖLDMŰVELŐK.

volt 11,599.122

most 3,773.449

MAGYARORSZÁG
TERÜLETI ÉPSÉGÉNEK
VÉDELMI LIGÁJA.

state was tied, far more than previously, to the prospects of economic stability and growth, and to the opportunities for employment. But governments struggled to match the expectation societies now had of them. During the First World War, states had become more involved in economic management than ever before, but once peace came, financiers and industrialists encouraged politicians to withdraw in order to allow market forces to heal the war-battered economies. But the problems of such an approach were laid bare immediately by the destructive impact of rapidly rising levels of inflation, unleashed by the war and exacerbated by the challenges of reconstruction without foreign aid. A potent combination of financial, political, and social pressures culminated in episodes of acute hyperinflation that devastated the successor republics of the Central powers, notably those of Austria, Hungary, Germany, and Poland. Austria descended into hyperinflation as early as October 1921, with a monthly inflation rate of 46 per cent, and unemployment running at over 33 per cent; in Hungary inflation grew by 33 per cent per month in 1923; and at its peak in the Weimar Republic in 1923 prices doubled every two days. Even in the comparatively stable setting of post-war Britain the rate of inflation stood at 15.4 per cent in 1920. The experience of inflation had a profound impact around the world. Governments now made currency stability the primary goal and their efforts centred on resurrecting the international gold standard, a fixed exchange mechanism, because it was widely believed it had facilitated the great expansion of the international economy in the nineteenth century. Between 1924 and 1929, forty-five countries joined the gold standard (most of the British Empire and Commonwealth joined in 1926).

The gold standard bound the fate of national economies more closely together. So, too, did the increase in international lending after 1924, which was essential to its reconstruction. But the period of stability and growth was only brief. Tariffs and quotas systems, employed on an unprecedented level during the war, were never abolished, despite the lofty aspirations to global free trade expressed in Wilson's 'Fourteen Points', and in the Covenant of the League of Nations. Instead, after 1920 levels of protection began to creep up, fed, in particular, by the crisis in global agriculture. By 1927, the impact of tariffs and quotas had become so severe that there was a World Economic Conference to address it, and it was in the context of these efforts to break through the economic deadlock that French Prime Minister Aristide Briand called for European political solidarity in his famous plan for a 'United States of Europe' presented at a meeting of the League Assembly on 3 September 1929. But within days of the announcement of the 'Briand Plan', the Dow Jones Industrial Average had peaked at a level it was not to reach again until 1954; a month later Briand was no longer in office, and the US Stock Exchange on Wall Street had crashed. Both events signalled an end to the fragile diplomatic and economic stability the world had enjoyed in the 1920s.

The Wall Street Crash both precipitated and reflected the rising economic and financial pressures. Already in 1928, as trade channels closed, financial pressures also were building. Asia and Europe, led by Germany, experienced a marked downturn in the levels of US and British investment. At the same time, the deflationary pressures of the gold standard exchange system exerted on countries whose currencies were overvalued (notably the German Reichsmark, the Italian lira, and British sterling) became especially acute. After 1929, the collapse of US market confidence also combined to increase the levels of state debt. As the United States descended into its greatest economic depression of the twentieth century, and elected Dr New Deal, President Franklin Delano Roosevelt, to combat it, Europe and Asia lurched in a new direction.

At the time, observers were in no doubt that the economic and financial crisis provided the nascent authoritarian, Fascist, and Communist movements with a path to power. In 1931 a series of banking crises swept through Austria, and then Germany, while a flight from the pound saw sterling abandon gold. Other currencies that had

'Improving the view', a cartoon from 1937 capturing German glee at the way Japan not only ignored the statutes, laws, and pacts organized by the League of Nations, but also exploited them. The Japanese solder tells the ailing figure of the League of Nations to pass up the latest document of protests: 'Bring it over here. It will be useful to help me increase my position.'

close ties to the British economy went with it, included Dominion and Empire territories and countries such as Denmark, which supplied most of the ingredients that went into the famous 'English breakfast'. Central European countries, including Germany, by contrast introduced tight exchange controls, which were to come in useful later when it came to directing their war economies, and made it hard for those who sought to flee the country to take their assets with them. Having spent most of the 1920s trying to join the gold standard, as an expression of national strength and determination to meet international standards, it reached its goal at the worst possible moment: January 1930. By December 1931, the pressures of international financial exposure were so great its finance minister, Korekiyo Takahashi, was forced to abandon it.

Japan's departure from the gold standard was another step in the reassertion of Japanese national and imperial concerns that reflected the violent battle of wills taking place between the country's Liberals, and the increasingly successful militarist Nationalist figures ranged against them. (Takahashi was one of many centrist and left-wing politicians who were murdered by their opponents in a trend that became known as 'assassination politics'.) A more dramatic moment had come three months earlier, in September 1931, with its invasion of Manchuria, which exposed the depths of Japan's insecurities and the powerful reassertion of models of empire that fed tensions between the USA, Britain, and France. The Japanese set up the puppet state of Manchukuo, and drafted plans to expand and integrate food and raw material production to meet Japan's needs. By 1934, confidently asserting these needs and attempted dominance over first China, and then the Pacific, the Japanese announced, in the 'Amau Doctrine', that China and East Asia was now Japan's sphere of interest.

The Fighting Spreads

The Western powers proved powerless to prevent or halt Japanese aggression. Their failure was most overt in the inability of the League of Nations to act effectively against a member that violated the rights of another, and in the failure of Anglo-American efforts to co-ordinate an effective response outside the League. But the shortcomings of diplomacy spoke to a wider challenge for peace: the reassertion of imperialism. International relations in the 1930s became characterized by what came to be called the division between the 'have' and the 'have-not' powers. The 'haves' were those believed to hold sufficient resources to sustain their 'security', exemplified by Britain, France, and the United States (rendered 'imperial' by the Monroe Doctrine and its extensive interests in central and south America), and the 'have-nots' were Japan, Italy, and Germany. Indeed, the legitimacy of the have-nots' claims were bolstered by measures taken to fortify the British Empire: it signed trade deals that gave preference to imperial producers in 1931, and a General Tariff Act that discriminated against everyone else in 1932. It also co-ordinated a new currency area, the sterling bloc, which the British Chancellor and after 1937 Prime Minister Neville Chamberlain saw as a project of imperial renewal.

Emperor Haile Selassie, leading with his cane in the centre of the photograph, arrives at Geneva airport in 1936 to plead with members of the League of Nations for help against Italian aggression. Selassie received no help from the League, which opted instead to lift trade sanctions against Italy.

In October 1935 Italy attacked Ethiopia in an overt echo of its nineteenth-century imperialist pretentions to make good its defeat at Adowa in 1896, and Mussolini's claim that 'if for the others the Mediterranean is a route, for us Italians it is a way of life'. There were many twentieth-century features to the war, notably Mussolini's pretext that Italian troops were on an anti-slavery crusade, and the deployment of modern weapons of war, terrorizing a largely unarmed people by air attacks and the use of chemical weapons. Ethiopian historians today estimate somewhere between 300,000 and 730,000 men, women, and children died during combat and under Italian rule. Mussolini's drive for dominance in the Mediterranean did not stop there. Delighting in the vocal but ineffective condemnation abroad, and the disquiet of the Royal Family, the army, and even party members at home, Mussolini launched with enthusiasm into supporting General Francisco Franco's military assault on the Popular Front government of Spain in July 1936. Unlike the calculated and controlled intervention of Hitler's regime, which used aid to Franco as the means to test and develop its capacity for air war, Mussolini committed his regime to far more than it could afford.

Italy's wars made it less not more secure, and prompted Mussolini to search for new means to bolster his regime. The Fascist 'master' now turned pupil, increasingly tying his fate, and that of his people, to National Socialist principles and objectives.

A Communist of Basque origins, Dolores Ibárruri Gómez is shown addressing a political rally. Nicknamed *La Pasionaria* (the Passion Flower), she came to symbolize Republican resistance against Fascism during the Spanish Civil War.

Alongside formal agreements—the Axis of November 1936; the Anti-Comintern Pact, which also included Japan, in December 1937; and the 'Pact of Steel' of May 1939—the Fascist regime now claimed Italian people were of the same Aryan stock as the German allies and introduced draconian anti-Semitic legislation. The growing imbalance of their respective fortunes, however, was laid bare by the fact that Italy began to send agricultural and industrial workers to the Third Reich: 37,095 in 1938 and 46,411 in 1939, with figures doubling year on year until 1941. When war came in September 1939, Mussolini, who had once declared, 'better to live one day like a lion than a hundred years like a sheep', had to prevaricate until 10 June 1940, when Hitler's victory in Europe appeared assured, and he believed he would no longer need to extend resources, either economic, military, or political, he no longer had to give.

The Axis and the Anti-Comintern Pact raised the spectre of full-scale co-operation between the world's most ambitious and militaristic powers, although in the 1930s it never extended to more than a loose understanding. But this axis now set the constellation of world diplomacy, and put these powers in opposition to the 'democracies' of Britain, France, and their allies, as well as the USA. The year 1936 was also when the pace of events quickened. With war raging in Spain and North Africa, and France mired deep in a political and financial crisis, Hitler took the bold but calculated move of cancelling the Locarno Treaties of 1925 which had guaranteed the borders of western Europe and were an essential precondition to Germany's entry into the League of Nations, and marching troops into the Rhineland. Remilitarizing Germany's industrial heartland was a calculated risk. Before it, Germany was vulnerable to foreign opposition. Afterwards, Germany had the economic and military base it needed to make it a formidable foe. Hitler had put German foreign policy ambitions at the forefront of the global diplomatic agenda, where they remained for almost a decade, helping to determine, to a degree, the conduct of British, French, and US foreign policy towards Italy and Japan.

It was easy to explain away the evident determination of Nazi foreign policy through the evident drive of its leader to address diplomatic grievances resulting from what he called *Der Schandvertrag* (the treaty of shame) of Paris. Certainly, his claims for restitution found a receptive audience abroad, and acclaim at home. First, he negotiated away, or defaulted on Germany's debts abroad, both reparations and the monies lent to stabilize it in the 1920s. Next, in December 1933, Hitler withdrew from international disarmament negotiations and rebuilt Germany's military base: in March 1935 he announced the existence of an air-force, reintroduced conscription, creating a peacetime army of thirty-six divisions and, with Britain's blessing in the Anglo-German Naval Agreement of June 1935, an expanded navy.

It was after the remilitarization of the Rhineland that German ambitions shifted outward. First came a claim for union, or *Anschluss*, with Austria and then the demand to include the ethnic Germans of the Sudetenland in Czechoslovakia and in Poland. It was then that the profound ideological component of Germany's security policies became clear. The desire to unite all Germans extended well beyond the

The Socialist Georges-Étienne Bonnet in tense conversation with the radical politician Édouard Herriot in 1936. Both men were anxious to avoid conflict with Germany, though it was Herriot's fellow party leader, Édouard Daladier, who as French Prime Minister took France to war in 1939.

revision of Versailles and was made yet more radical because Hitler believed the Reich's security was imperilled by the 'aggressive will founded on the authoritarian ideology of Bolshevism and world-wide Jewry'. The answer, as he put it, was 'in extending our living space, that is to say, expanding the sources of raw materials and foodstuffs of our people'. The USSR would be the ultimate stage in this quest for *Lebensraum*, but other territories in central and eastern Europe were important staging posts in garnering the resources Germany would need in what Hitler described in February 1939 as a 'people's war and a racial war'.

But for much of the 1930s the problem was turned on its head by Britain and France, which sought to use central and eastern Europe as a tool in Western efforts to contain, if not neutralize, the National Socialist threat. In the meantime, the USA stood aloof, the smaller powers of Europe largely stood on the sidelines, while the Soviet Union, keen to be involved, was excluded from the process, with explosive results. In a strategy known as 'economic appeasement', western European, and

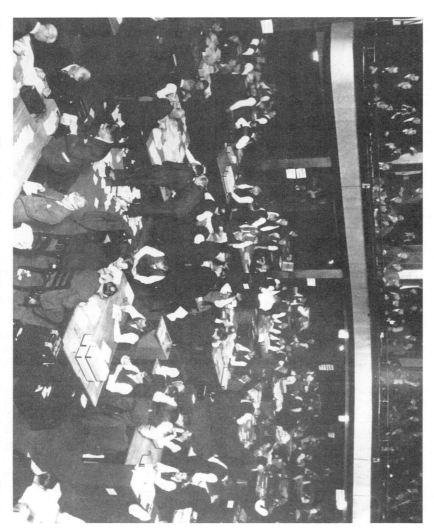

The scene is a counting office in the Saarland town of Püttlingen after the voting in the League of Nations plebiscite in 1935 to decide on the future of the territory. Although the Saarland, held under mandate by France and Britain, had become a sanctuary for German opponents of National Socialism after 1933, locals voted overwhelmingly to be absorbed into the Third Reich.

notably French, trade declined dramatically in eastern and southern Europe, and Germany was allowed to take over these markets. By 1936, for example, south-eastern Europe supplied 37 per cent of German wheat imports, 35 per cent of its meat, 31 per cent of its lard, 61 per cent of all the tobacco smoked in Germany, and more than 62 per cent of the bauxite needed for German industry. Over time, the trade deals that gave 'preferential access' to German markets for central and eastern European primary producers became increasingly oppressive and coercive. In the first known arrangement of this kind signed between Germany and Hungary in February 1934, for example, 90 per cent of Hungarian exports to Germany were paid for by deliveries determined by German industry, and only 10 per cent could be used by Hungary to buy raw materials and other goods of strategic importance. The terms were grossly disadvantageous, but when Hungary sought to break free or to negotiate a more favourable deal, bullying and default was Germany's answer.

In 1938, Hitler opened a new front in his bid for a *Grossraumwirtschaft* (large-area economy) under German control in ways that posed new questions about the ultimate intentions and implications of his foreign policy. His demand that Czechoslovakia's three million Sudeten Germans join a greater Germany also delivered Czech raw materials (bauxite, oil, and wheat) as well as its people, and again extended Germany's frontiers. Although a number of ministers in Britain and in France felt the price being demanded to avoid war was morally unacceptable, and public opinion in western Europe was also deeply uneasy, at a conference in Munich in September 1938, Beneš was forced to accept the transfer of the Sudetenland to Germany, as Britain's Prime Minister Neville Chamberlain (in)famously branded it 'Peace for our time'. Historians, too, have been deeply critical of the move. Chamberlain's determination to avoid war led him to bargain away the modern and well-equipped Czech army and the huge Skoda armaments factory whose output more than equalled that of all Britain's armaments factories put together.

The political costs were equally high. Once again, the USSR had been left out of negotiations that directly affected its security, as was Poland, which seized the terri-tory of Cieszyn (Teschen) in a vain attempt to bolster its position in response. France, embattled by political division and economic weakness—its economy experienced the worst effects of the Great Depression between 1934 and 1937—was forced to aban-don its ally, French Prime Minister Edouard Daladier felt a profound sense of shame, declaring, 'No, I am not proud. The Czechs are our allies, and we have obligations to them.' Within a month, he had instituted a policy of *fermeté* (firmness) in French foreign policy, and ordered a massive increased in rearmament spending, 93 billion francs against a 1937 level of 29 billion francs. The Munich Agreement also turned the US administration against the notion of further concessions to Hitler. Behind the scenes President Roosevelt did what he could to encourage Britain to face down Hitler in the face of determinedly isolationist public opinion, and a looming Presidential election, but US aid at this stage remained very limited.

The Munich Agreement turned the majority of public opinion in Britain and France firmly against making any further concessions to Hitler—Chamberlain received more

Prime Minister Chamberlain signs the Munich agreement. Standing at over 6 feet in height, Chamberlain's bent posture captures the moment when the British Empire appeared to prostrate itself before the Third Reich.

extended public acclaim in Germany than he did in Britain for his deal at Munich—and talk of British 'weakness' and 'betrayal' was rendered more bitter by news in November 1938 of the terrifying brutality of an assault against Germany's Jews on *Kristallnacht* and of a greatly accelerated programme of German rearmament. Then, in March 1939, came news that Hitler had invaded the rump of what remained of Czechoslovakia, while making renewed demands of Poland that included the return of Gdańsk (Danzig), a seaport which had been dominated by the Nazis since May 1933, and the right to establish transportation lines across the Polish corridor to East Prussia.

Hitler's appetite for eastern European territory seemed to grow with the eating, so why did Britain continue to feed him for so long? Certainly, the impact of a powerful Prime Minister determined to avoid war had a significant effect. But so did the arguments Chamberlain marshalled to his cause. Large swathes of public opinion, at home and abroad, were hostile to the use of war as an instrument of state policy in the wake of the First World War—a sentiment embedded in the popularly acclaimed Kellogg–Briand Pact of 1928. The anxiety of what a new war would visit upon the innocents was amplified by the spectacle of unprecedented violence against civilians in Ethiopia, Spain, and China. Indeed, in July 1937, in search of 'security', Japan went to war against China, although it did not declare it as such because that would have put it in contravention of US Neutrality legislation, and prevented Japan from purchasing war supplies from there.

The territory of 'Manchukuo' now served as Japan's industrial base for a war against China, although until 1941 the Japanese Empire continued to be heavily

Civilians around the world increasingly feared the prospect of aerial bombardment in war. Media images, such as this bombing of Canton in 1937, captured its horrific consequences for families and their habitat.

dependent on US strategic supplies, materials, and technology. Its battle for security defined by autarky pointed to the ways in which war would both join and divide the world in the future as Japan's expansion led to a series of border clashes with the USSR. In June 1937, Soviet and Japanese gunboats fought for control of the Amur river; in 1938 their armies contested strategic highpoints on the borders between Manchuria, Korea, and the USSR; and in the summer of 1939 General Georgii Zhukov surrounded and defeated a Japanese army of some 75,000 men, and launched his reputation as a daring military commander.

Japanese aggression, too, contributed to British 'appeasement', understood as a process of arbitration and negotiation at the time, and as the diplomacy of weakness and capitulation ever since. British security was dominated by the primacy of Empire. The irony was that the source of its world power status carried important liabilities. British military power was spread around the world to protect it, and it was sometimes stretched so thin that it had to tolerate aggressive expansionism so long as its own trade links with its Empire, and especially India, remained secure. Indeed, policing the Empire—India in political upheaval, the British mandate in Palestine in crisis—was a further drain on resources, while the 'White Dominions' (Australia, Canada, New Zealand, and South Africa) were becoming significant forces in their own right in the formulation of British diplomacy. In the end it was the global nature of the National Socialist threat in 1939, with Germany dominating all of central Europe, while its allies, Italy and Japan, menaced British interests in the Mediterranean and the Far East, that meant a reluctant Chamberlain, provoked too by the now considerable domestic opposition to appeasement in the British government and in wider society, seemed resolved to stand and fight.

The road to war was marked by discrete signposts, and critical moments when the fighting began. The escalation of tension between the Axis powers and Europe's remaining democracies reached one such new stage with the German invasion of Prague on 14–15 March, Mussolini's threat of war with France on 26 March, and Britain's guarantee of Polish security that followed, rounded off by Mussolini's invasion of Albania that prompted British guarantees to Greece and Romania, which together demarcated the lines of military engagement. War was now widely predicted, but there were still surprises, none bigger than the announcement of the Nazi–Soviet Pact in August 1939. Even senior members of the Politburo such as Lavrenti Beria, recently appointed head of internal security in the USSR, had no warning of what was coming. The Soviet Union had spent the 1930s positioning itself as the leading light of a global Anti-Fascist coalition, notably in the battle against Italian and German-backed intervention in the Spanish Civil War. Distrustful of the West, anxious to reinforce Soviet defences in the wake of its own internal battles, and greedy for territorial annexation of his own (the terms of an accompanying secret protocol gave Stalin a free hand in Finland, Estonia, Latvia, eastern Poland, and Romania), Stalin concluded a deal which remained an unlikely prospect until a couple of weeks before the pact was signed.

The Nazi–Soviet Pact should not have surprised the West. Britain and France, even in August 1939, never pursued an alliance with the Soviets with any degree of enthusiasm, and nor, by now, did such an alliance offer Stalin any great advantages. Poland found itself encircled by hostile powers, and Hitler waited for the news that Britain and France would abandon Poland in the way they had abandoned other European powers before it. Instead, France held firm and Britain sealed a formal alliance on 25 August—the day before Hitler had planned to launch his attack east—although Poland, justifiably, did not have very much confidence in allied plans for its defence. 'Operation Fishing' against Danzig began at 4.45 on the morning of 1 September. That evening in his regular 'Fireside Chat', US President Franklin D. Roosevelt told an anxious public, 'I cannot ask that every American remain neutral in thought. . . . Even a neutral cannot be asked to close his mind or his conscience', but there were few immediate signs the USA would abandon a foreign policy of neutrality. The British and French empires girded for war not only in Europe but in the Mediterranean and Far East, while the remaining European powers too did what they could to defend themselves. War in the west was formally declared at 11 a.m. on Sunday, 3 September 1939. The endemic crisis of global security under way for twenty years had reached its grim apotheosis.

2 The Japanese Empire at War, 1931–1945

STEVEN HUGH LEE

In the decade after 1931 Japanese government officials ordered a series of military campaigns across Asia which resulted in a conquest of the region unrivalled since the rise of the Mongol Empire in the thirteenth century. The war began in the autumn of 1931 when the Japanese leadership allowed the Guandong (Kwantung) army to expand the empire throughout Manchuria, China's north-east region; Chinese government resistance after the summer of 1937 resulted in a significant escalation of the fighting south of the Great Wall. The Nazi invasion of Poland and the onset of the European war in 1939 transformed Asia's devastating regional conflict into a war of global dimensions, even before American participation in the fighting. By 1940, at the time of the signing of the Tripartite Pact, Japanese and German officials shared the goal of overpowering the tottering liberal-capitalist international system and replacing it with an anti-Communist, anti-liberal, militaristic world characterized by insatiable colonial expansion and mass violence towards subject peoples. The reckless policies of the two regimes, combined with Allied resistance, especially in the Soviet Union and China, led to the eventual ruin of both empires, but not before the murderous policies of the Axis powers wrought a tremendous toll of suffering and dislocation around the world. China and eastern Europe were the two most ravaged areas of Eurasia, though the violence shattered social and familial relations across the globe. Recent estimates of the war's impact on the world's most populous country point out that up to twenty million Chinese perished and that almost 100 million became refugees, figures which are comparable to or surpass the impact of the German invasion of the Soviet Union. The Second Sino-Japanese War was more protracted than the Russo-German war, lasting from 1931 to 1945, with its most intense, cataclysmic phase enduring a little more than eight years, from July 1937 to August 1945. Although the war lasted longer in China than in other parts of Asia, the struggle had profound impacts on people throughout the continent. Perhaps even more than in Europe, the war in Asia destroyed the old political order. Indeed, the Second World War played a major role in overturning almost all of the continent's pre-war political systems (exceptions include Thailand, Malaya, and Hong Kong, though each was profoundly impacted by Japan's invasion of South-East Asia, and Mongolia) and brought to power a generation of politicians whose ideas and policies in most cases were opposed to the imperial or indigenous rulers who had previously controlled the destinies of colonies and countries that made up about half of the world's population. Unlike most of Europe after 1945, in Asia the war ignited further conflict, as revolutionaries and nationalists battled each other, challenged returning colonial troops, and replaced retreating imperial systems with newly established states. The Second World War was thus a crucial staging point for a long trajectory of wars in Asia, a number of which have remained unresolved to this day, and whose consequences are very much part of our twenty-first-century world.

Japan's Empire and the Roots of the Second World War in Asia, 1877–1931

The relationship between the two world wars is a significant theme in the historiography of the origins of the Second World War. From the point of view of Japan's war against China and the Japanese empire's 1940 alliance with Germany and Italy, the 1914–18 war left an ambiguous legacy. On one hand, the First World War seemed to highlight underlying differences between Germany and Japan. Diplomatically, for much of the early twentieth century, Japan had co-operated closely with Britain, the world's pre-eminent liberal empire. Japanese politicians were attracted to the alliance partly because it implicitly sanctioned Meiji diplomatic and military expansion since 1877 into areas previously under the suzerainty or control of the Qing dynasty: Okinawa and other Ryukyu islands, the Choson dynasty (Korea), and Formosa (Taiwan).

Children from Japan, Germany, and Italy meet in Tokyo to participate in the ceremonies surrounding the signing of the Tripartite Alliance, 17 December 1940. Japanese education minister Hashida Kunihiko, centre, holding crossed flags, and Mayor Okubo Tomejiro of Tokyo were among the sponsors.

The 1902 alliance also provided Japan with the security to limit Russian power in North-East Asia. Indeed, a case can be made that the Russo-Japanese war of 1904–5, more than the First World War, was a critical turning point for understanding the roots of Japan's war against China after 1931. In addition to occupying the southern half of Sakhalin island and establishing a Japanese protectorate over the Choson dynasty in 1905, the war with Russia led to Japan's acquisition of Russian holdings in Manchuria. The key strategic interests inherited by Japan, instrumental in understanding the origins of the Second World War in Asia, were the Russian naval base at Lushun (Port Arthur) and the nearby treaty port at Dalian (Dairen). The base and city were linked by the South Manchurian railway line, also acquired by Japan from Russia, which connected Port Arthur with Harbin in northern Manchuria.

The Anglo-Japanese alliance also meant that Germany and Japan were rivals during the Great War, when Japan forcibly incorporated Germany's Asian holdings into its imperial domains. By the war's end, Japan's new territories included the Marshall, Caroline, Palau, and Mariana islands in the South Pacific (minus Guam, which the Spanish ceded to America in the Spanish–American War of 1898), as well as the former German treaty port in Shandong province, Qingdao (Tsingdao). For more than a decade after the end of the war, Japan remained aligned to the Anglo-American powers, after 1922 through the series of naval arms limitation treaties agreed to at the 1921–2 Washington conference. In great contrast to Germany, which lost its empire in 1919, in the First World War Japan expanded its colonial empire. In this sense, the roots of Japan's involvement in the Second World War are, unlike the case of Germany, tied to the country's continuous history of empire and colonial expansion.

Imperial Germany, however, was a crucial political and military model for the Meiji oligarchs. The Japanese Prime Minister at the time of the Anglo-Japanese alliance, Katsura Taro, was an influential military figure who had studied German military bureaucracy and served as Japan's military attaché in Berlin in the latter 1870s. The First World War also heightened tensions between Japan and China, and China's self-appointed ally in the international system, the United States. These frictions were somewhat concealed by the Washington System treaties of 1921–2, but the war left a legacy of suspicion and conflict and established some of the reasons behind Japan's turn toward a more aggressive authoritarianism in the 1930s.

The Chinese government had also supported the Allied war effort in the Great War, and its leaders wanted to regain sovereignty over Shandong as well as access to that province's valuable economic resources. The warlord government in Beijing, however, was fractured and controlled only part of northern China. Warlords ran other areas of the country, and competed with each other for power and resources, with the result that China had no effective national government. Japan took advantage of this weakness in 1915 in putting forward its infamous 'twenty-one demands' to President Yuan Shih-kai, who rejected the most insidious of Japan's imperial claims on China.

After the Treaty of Versailles confirmed Japan's new Asian holdings, a major nationalist protest, the May Fourth Movement, erupted in China against Japan. The importance of the First World War in the wider history of the Second World War in Asia, then, partly lies in the nationalist movement it sparked in the republic.

The First World War also sharpened the ideological and material tensions between Japan and the USA. President Wilson's liberalism and the promise of democracy and self-determination especially irked more aggressive-minded Japanese officials like the vice-chief of the general staff, Tanaka Giichi, and the senior leader of Japan's militarist oligarchy, Yamagata Aritomo. Yet both governments joined European states after the war in regulating potential conflicts over Asia. At Washington, in December 1921, the big powers negotiated a series of naval arms limitations treaties and spheres of influence accords for Asia. Japan's top-ranking diplomats and naval commanders attending the conference, including its ambassador to the United States, Shidehara Kijiro, and Admiral Kato Tomosaburo, argued Japan's international position would be secured through co-operation with the European states and America. Particularly important was the perceived need to maintain the US market for Japanese goods and to access American investment and funds for post-war Japanese economic growth. The Washington System treaties replaced the Anglo-Japanese alliance while permitting Japan to retain its naval supremacy in the western Pacific and preventing the other powers from gaining additional exclusive spheres of influence in China. Japan agreed to respect China's sovereignty and all representatives acceded to a de facto open door in that country.

The Washington treaties were successful in maintaining the political status quo only as long as the Chinese political system remained fractured and divided. Japanese leaders' alienation from the agreements increased in the second half of the 1920s as the National Revolutionary Army (NRA) of Chiang Kai-shek's Guomindang (GMD) Party, based in the southern province of Guangdong, unified large parts of the country in a series of military offensives known as the northern expedition. Though the GMD remained highly factionalized, the Japanese government, and the military in particular, interpreted the offensives as a threat to the empire's strategic and economic interests. Key segments of army opinion, both in Manchuria and Tokyo, adhered to a total war ideology which posited that to win future conflicts Japan required access to substantial resources not available in the home islands. This group of army officers, influenced by studies of Germany's defeat in the First World War, coveted China's north-eastern region as the vital source of power needed to fuel their total mobilization strategies.

With the success of the northern expedition, long-held Chinese grievances found expression in sentiments of nationalism, anti-imperialism, and xenophobia. Foreign concessions came under condemnation and attack, for example, by striking workers, Guomindang supporters, and Communists. Japanese militarists responded by demanding more aggressive policies from the government in Tokyo. In late March 1927, after warlord and NRA troops attacked and looted international concessions in Nanjing, top-ranking Japanese military officers cited assaults against Japanese as

Chinese leader, Chiang Kai-Shek, along with President Franklin Roosevelt and Prime Minister Winston Churchill, at the 1943 Cairo Conference.

evidence of the failure of Foreign Minister Shidehara's 'weak' diplomacy and the need for a more militarily aggressive China policy. The Nanjing 'incident' contributed to the fall of the Japanese government and led to the appointment of Prime Minister Tanaka Giichi, a retired general who, in his role as vice-chief of staff during the First World War, was the person most closely associated with the notion of separating Manchuria from the rest of China. In the spring of 1928, anticipating the entry of the NRA into Shandong, Prime Minister Tanaka sent 5,000 Japanese troops from the Sixth Division to Qingdao, ostensibly to protect Japanese civilians and holdings in the province, but also as a symbol of Japan's determination to preserve its spheres of influence across China. The commander of the force unilaterally ordered his soldiers to the provincial capital, Jinan, where clashes occurred between the NRA and the Japanese infantry. On 1 May local time, Japanese shelling of the city caused hundreds of civilian casualties. Chiang was very concerned about an expanded military engagement with the Japanese, for while the 100,000 men under his command in the area could have won a tactical fight against imperial forces, the pressure on Japan to escalate the conflict might have been irresistible. He had recently initiated a bloody purge of his Communist allies and, placing his goal of unifying China ahead of fighting Japan, ordered most of his troops out of Jinan. Even so, several days later the Japanese attacked the remaining NRA troops. By the time the fighting ended, in a foreshadowing of the mass violence to come, Japanese soldiers had killed as many as 11,000 soldiers and civilians.

Japan's Invasion of Manchuria: Starting the Fifteen-Year War

The clash between Nationalist and Japanese troops in Jinan highlighted the agency of Japanese army officers to initiate military action of their own, in contravention of government policy. This tendency within the army reflected a weakness of Japan's 1889 constitution, Article 11 of which made the Emperor supreme commander of the Japanese military, thereby circumventing the Japanese Prime Minister and his cabinet. In the 1920s and 1930s, army officers learned to conceal aggressive militarism behind the formal constitutional authority of the Emperor. Unilateral army initiatives destabilized government and facilitated the rise of military officials within cabinet, their power checked mainly by factionalism within the army and navy establishments. Ultimately, however, Japanese governments themselves sanctioned the actions of insubordinate military officers, just as Tanaka had done in 1928. The most critical of these early decisions to support local military actions occurred in the late summer and autumn of 1931, when several officers of the Japanese Guandong army carried out a plot to expand Japan's sphere of influence in China's north-east to include all of Manchuria. Japanese soldiers secretly planted a bomb along a railway track in Shenyang (Mukden) located near barracks of the regional Chinese warlord's army. The Japanese military blamed the attack on Chinese 'bandits' and attacked the warlord soldiers. By early 1932 the Guandong army incorporated most of Manchuria into its zone of operations, and had established a regime called Manzhouguo (Manchukuo), or 'Manzhou State', nominally headed by the last Emperor of the Qing dynasty, Pu Yi. In the 1930s and 1940s the Soviet Union, right-wing and Fascist governments in Europe, and other puppet governments in China, recognized Manzhouguo. The invasion created an international crisis and led to Japan's exit from the League of Nations in March 1933, six months ahead of Germany's decision to leave the international body. The invasion of Manchuria represented the first major step, not yet irrevocable, in breaking with the Anglo-American liberal world order.

The 1931 conflict was essentially a colonial war over China's north-east, with Japanese troops fighting guerrilla and warlord armies. In Japan, public opinion strongly supported the Manchurian war. Popular media promoted what Louise Young calls 'war fever' among the population, laying the groundwork for the empire's further expansion in the latter 1930s. Newspaper companies used a novel technology, newsreels, to propagate the victories of the Japanese forces in Manchuria. These popular film shorts were shown not only in packed cinemas, but also in parks, department stores, and schools across the country. Live radio broadcasts included

Japanese people in Tokyo celebrating the fiftieth anniversary of the Constitution on National Day, also called Day of Empire, in front of the Yasukuni shrine, on 11 March 1938.

several dozen shows from the Yasukuni shrine, the Shinto place of worship for Japanese war dead. Magazines, books, postcards, roving exhibits, plays, public lectures, music, and song created new war heroes and eulogized past ones, in the process often sensationalizing the links between death and sacrifice. Films included *The First Step into Fengtian—South Manchuria Glitters Under the Rising Sun, Ah! Major Kuramoto and the Blood-Stained Flag,* and *The Yamato Spirit,* while jingoist songs such as 'Arise Countrymen', 'The Imperial Army Marches Off', and 'Attack Plane', played on the airwaves and in clubs and public places. According to one Japanese writer, as a result of the Sino-Japanese and Russo-Japanese conflicts, Japan had 'buried 100,000 souls in the Manchurian plain, and risked the fate of the nation to gain the rights and interests we now hold'. The 'victory prizes' had been 'won with the priceless blood and sweat of the Japanese race'. By the mid-1930s, Japanese civil society groups targeted Manchuria as a vast Japanese settlement colony, one which could help resolve long-term problems of poverty and dislocation in the domestic countryside. As a result of these groups' initiatives the Japanese government accelerated its public campaigns to populate Manchuria with Japanese citizens and drew up plans to settle some 20 per cent of Japan's farmers—one million people—in north-east China. Though the war with China eventually interfered with the project, about 300,000 Japanese had settled in the region by 1945.

The initial stages of the Manchurian conflict led to relatively easy Japanese victories but, by 1932, up to 300,000 guerrillas and volunteers fought against the incursion. The resistance included former warlord troops, peasants, supporters of secret societies, and members of the Chinese Communist Party (CCP). In Manchuria, many guerrilla fighters within the CCP were ethnically Korean, including the future leader of North Korea, Kim Il Sung. South of the Great Wall, Chinese businessmen, students, and civil society organizations like the Shanghai Anti-Japanese National Salvation Association also organized acts of resistance through street marches and successful boycotts of Japanese goods.

Japanese army officers in China countered the Chinese activists through covert actions designed to portray Japanese as victims of Chinese aggression. In late January 1932, in the aftermath of one staged incident in Shanghai that incited civilian violence, and despite efforts by Chiang to meet the ensuing Japanese ultimatum, Japanese troops engaged Chinese soldiers north of the international zone. The fighting soon escalated into a major conflict involving about 70,000 Japanese soldiers facing 60,000 Chinese troops. The six-week conflict, often poorly dubbed the Shanghai 'Incident', witnessed the aerial bombing of civilians and the flight of 230,000 refugees from the

Japanese Ministry of Overseas Affairs, 1927 propaganda poster encouraging Japanese settlement in Manchuria.

city. Chinese and Japanese casualties have been estimated at 11,000 and 9,000, respectively. Growing anti-Japanese sentiment in China had forced a reluctant Chiang to send reinforcements, but the Chinese leader wanted a diplomatic settlement, as did influential figures in the Japanese government who were concerned about the impact the conflict would have on the Japanese stock market and sales of Japanese bonds in the United States. Key members of the Japanese government had not yet given up on working out a means of accommodating the western powers to the new imperium. By March 1932, Chinese and Japanese officials had agreed to a truce and the fighting subsided.

The fighting ended in Shanghai, but between 1933 and 1937 the Guandong army, backed by the Japanese government, expanded its military operations into Inner Mongolia, and even north China south of the Great Wall. Chiang acquiesced to demands which permitted the Japanese to increase their sphere of influence, assert their sovereignty over Chinese territory, remove Chinese governors and mayors from power, and eject Chinese military forces from whole provinces. While some Chinese soldiers fought against Japanese advances, Chiang quelled the popular unrest which his policies helped to create. Instead of resisting the Japanese he dedicated China's military resources to defeating the Communists in the five encirclement campaigns against Mao Zedong's Jiangxi Soviet between 1930 and 1934. Military offensives against other Soviets around the country effectively decimated the Communist movement by 1935. The Communists in Jiangxi fled on the Long March, but with devastating consequences, as only about 7,000 of the 100,000 who had started the trek survived continuous Nationalist attacks, hunger, cold, and disease. In 1935 the exhausted revolutionaries created a new base in impoverished Yanan in Shaanxi province and brought together several Communist fighting forces to establish a small army of 20,000 soldiers.

On 1 August 1935, just prior to Mao Zedong's arrival in Yanan, the Communist International, backed by the Soviet Union, proclaimed a new strategy of establishing local anti-Fascist coalitions to fight the menace posed by Hitler, Mussolini, and their global allies. The policy came several months before the German and Japanese governments agreed to the Anti-Comintern Pact. For the CCP, the change in Soviet policy entailed a renewal of their 1924–7 united front with the GMD. Though Chiang went ahead with his plans to crush the Communists, he showed a willingness to negotiate a settlement with them, provided the agreement was along terms that placed the CCP army under the command of the GMD's Military Council. Representatives of the CCP and GMD reached a tentative agreement for an alliance but, without knowledge of these discussions, Manchurian warlord Feng Yuxiang kidnapped Chiang and attempted to convince him to end the civil conflict and create a government of national salvation to prosecute the war against Japan. The CCP leadership, which had previously co-operated with Feng in the kidnapping plot, received a communication from Stalin who reiterated to Mao that Chiang was crucial to the new united front. With this information, Feng released the GMD President, who had confirmed his commitment to the alliance as long as he retained his captors' military allegiance. While the second United Front broke down by 1941, Chiang, for the first time, committed Republican China to marshalling its human resources against Japan's imperial armies.

The War of Resistance

The Second Sino-Japanese War began in 1931, but Chiang's decision to confront Japanese militarism represented a turning point in the history of the conflict. In July 1937, Japanese troops stationed around the city of Beijing clashed with Chinese soldiers near Lugouqiao, the Marco Polo Bridge. Local commanders reached a settlement but Chiang refused to endorse it and ordered four divisions of his soldiers to Hebei province. In Tokyo, the government of Prince Konoe Fumimaro escalated the conflict by demanding an apology from the Nationalists for their anti-Japanese

Chinese civilians flee to Shanghai's international settlements, 1937. At the end of the war the Chinese government estimated there were still 42 million refugees in the country, many of whom had no home to return to.

activities. Believing that a military engagement with the Chinese would end quickly and teach the Republican government a lesson, Konoe ordered three divisions to China. On 28 July intensive fighting broke out in Beijing. These clashes began what the Chinese call the War of Resistance. After the Chinese President ordered 100,000 troops into the demilitarized area around Shanghai, Konoe publicly announced his decision to deal decisively with the 'atrocious Chinese army'. By the middle of August both sides had become engaged in a full-scale war.

Even more so than the First World War, the second global conflict of the twentieth century was a 'total war', involving the mobilization of hundreds of millions of the world's citizens and colonial subjects. The populations of northern and central China and eastern Europe were at the centre of the fighting, victims of genocidal actions carried out by Japanese and German military units in the war. Cities were particular targets of attack and destruction, as they represented centres of power, wealth, and culture which the Japanese and German invaders wanted to defeat, eradicate, or subjugate. In Shanghai, where the fighting lasted three months, between 500,000 and 700,000 Chinese soldiers confronted a smaller but better equipped Japanese force, supported by naval and air units. At the start of the fighting about 600,000 people fled the non-concession areas of the city. Half sought refuge in the international concessions, but neither the city authorities nor the 175 refugee camps

Nanjing Massacre Memorial Hall, with a severed head and a cracked city wall, with the bare stone on the right revealing the number of civilian casualties within the walls.

could begin to provide services for them. By the start of 1938 over 100,000 people had died on the streets of Shanghai as a result of starvation, disease, or exposure. The retreat of the Chinese army from Shanghai opened a path for the Japanese to march into the capital city of Nanjing. Along the way, the Japanese military committed atrocities against civilians, including the murder of eighty men, women, and children at Changzhou.

In November 1937 Nanjing's elite residents left, along with many others. Those with wealth could hire a boat to carry them upstream to Wuhan or Chongqing, the path pursued by the fleeing Nationalist government officials into China's interior. Japanese soldiers surrounded and shelled the city in mid-November. By this time, Chiang had started to receive shipments of weapons from the Soviet Union, and Russian pilots even flew some disguised Soviet fighter planes in an effort to defend the capital. The city's defences collapsed, however, and Japanese armies assailed the civilian population on 13 December, launching the infamous 'Rape of Nanjing', a six-week rampage of torture, rape, and slaughter. Conservative accounts of the deaths number about 50,000, based on German diplomat John Rabe's estimate of civilians who survived in the International Settlement Zone, while contemporary Chinese sources claim 300,000 deaths. The larger numbers do not indicate a massacre of 'worse' character. Events in Nanjing can be understood in the broader context of Japanese psychological warfare: to induce terror into local populations as a means of subjugating China and the Chinese. The massacres of civilians in Nanjing and elsewhere in China left indelible psychological scars on the population. By the spring of 1938 Nanjing and its people, or what was left of them, survived in a tortured land. About 80 per cent of the pre-war residents had fled the city, and of those that remained an equivalent percentage had no income. Many were widows, trying to feed their children. This kind of scene was repeated throughout eastern and central China in this era, but early in the resistance war many Chinese remained defiant and resilient.

The Japanese Central China Army next attacked communities upstream along the Yangtze, and to the north of Nanjing. About 300 kilometres north of the city, between the Yangtze and the Yellow Rivers, lay the city of Xuzhou, the site of a major five-month battle between Japanese and Chinese armies in the winter and spring of 1938. The fighting joined Japanese forces in north and central China for the first time, and was meant as a prelude to an offensive against the tri-city area of Wuhan. Nationalist armies were comprised of soldiers from warlord armies and their commanders, as well as troops whose primary loyalty rested with Chiang. Communist troops numbered approximately 100,000 at this stage of the war, but played only a minor role in the battles for control over central China.

In trying to stem the Japanese advance, Chinese military officials pursued a scorched earth strategy, one which resulted in a tremendous loss of life. In June 1938 Chiang ordered his army to break the dyke of the Yellow River in a desperate effort to prevent a Japanese army advance on the latest capital, Wuhan, and to allow 200,000 Chinese troops to escape to the south-west. The breaching of the dyke created another human disaster, flooding a huge area of flat land, and drowning and killing, by official accounts, some 800,000 people. At the height of the harvest season, the water destroyed crops, animals, homes, and caused millions to flee everywhere except eastwards, towards the Japanese. The war in central China in 1937 and 1938 resulted in the loss of one million Chinese soldiers, including injuries, and as late as 1945 there were still six million refugees living beyond the flood plain.

The population of Wuhan, like that of Nanjing and other cities located in the wake of the attacks, had grown significantly as a result of people fleeing the flood and the brutality of the violence. By July there were about 430,000 refugees in Wuhan; about 65,000 found a place in the city's 100-plus shelters, sponsored by the Chinese state, merchants' associations, missionary relief efforts, and the International Red Cross. Many of the refugees were child orphans—one orphanage in Wuhan included several hundred children who had fled Xuzhou—and special attention was paid to them by a group of prominent women in the city, including Song Meiling, Chiang Kai-shek's American-educated wife, and Shi Liang, one of China's first female lawyers and a prominent public defender in Wuhan in the 1930s. Politically active, Shi had been arrested and jailed in 1936 by Chiang's government for publicly advocating war with Japan. In the winter of 1938 these two women helped establish the non-partisan organization, Warfare Child Welfare Committee. Shi also created an organization dedicated to mobilizing women for the war effort and providing assistance to refugees. Lack of trained medical personnel was a major problem for soldiers and civilians alike, and malaria was rife amongst women and children, and a constant scourge to all soldiers in the war. Wuhan's relief system served as a model for the development of refugee and health services across the nation, and, later, for the social welfare systems of both the People's Republic of China and the Republic of China in Taiwan.

The breaching of the dyke did not prevent the Japanese advance on Wuhan, which they overran in October 1938, thus exacerbating China's refugee and human crisis, as millions continued to flee the war zone. Many refugees went further into the interior of the country, including Chongqing, the new wartime capital. Many people, however, continued to hope that the invading armies would be defeated and turned back. Civil society organizations immediately countered the invasion with efforts to mobilize the population against the invaders. Through newspaper stories, movies, travelling drama troupes, songs, and cartoons China's population attempted to create a national movement of resistance. For the first time in modern China, politics touched all areas of the country's cultural life. From Shanghai, groups of actors went to rural areas to mobilize the population. By the early 1940s there were some 2,500 such groups performing a wide range of street, commemorative, puppet, and teahouse plays in the interior of the country. By the late 1930s, the performers transformed a 1931 play entitled *Lay down Your Whip*, from one criticizing Chinese governmental corruption to an attack of the onslaught of Japanese imperialism and occupation. As one of the protagonists recounted: 'If we do not unite quickly to defend ourselves against Japanese aggression, we will soon meet the same fate as our countrymen in Manchuria'.

The emergence of Chinese resistance undermined Japan's ability to project violence, but after occupying Wuhan the Japanese advance slowed significantly, partly because the soldiers came up against the country's natural geographical barriers. Japanese armies did not pursue Chiang upstream along the Yangtze. Instead, they focused on establishing wartime governments in north and central China to displace Nationalist authority. The colonial dimensions of Japan's occupation policy were brought out most prominently through the search for Chinese collaborators and the creation of puppet regimes. These experiments failed, however, as Chinese collaborators, not surprisingly, did not gain the support of the local population. Japanese control over rural areas, weak to begin with because of the violence of the conquest and racism towards the Chinese, became even more tenuous when guerrillas began to operate in the eastern provinces. Within the confines of urban areas like Shanghai, small bands of guerrilla groups with ties to rural-based resistance movements conducted sabotage and assassinated collaborators and Japanese officials.

Between 1937 and 1940 the Communists rebuilt their armies. The Chinese Red Army, known after 1937 as the Eighth Route Army, expanded significantly in north China, especially in areas where the North China Area Army and the puppet Chinese soldiers had repeatedly attacked in so-called 'mopping up' terrorist operations, leaving the peasantry open to mobilization by Communist cadres. The high point of Communist military activity was the Hundred Regiments Campaign, undertaken in the autumn of 1940, when 400,000 troops of the Eighth Route Army attacked targets across five provinces, aiming especially at railway and mining infrastructure. The attacks achieved some limited short-term goals but resulted in 100,000 casualties, a significant Communist defeat. In central China, the war resulted in the creation in 1937 of a new Communist army, the New Fourth Army, ostensibly part of the NRA, but formally controlled by Communist leaders. The GMD attempted to limit the size of the Communist armies and to control their movements, while the Communists tried also to limit the expansion of Nationalist armies in central China. The Communist–Nationalist rivalry resulted in significant conflict, one underlined by the New Fourth Army Incident in January 1941 when Nationalist troops encircled a 9,000-person New Fourth Army unit and killed most of its soldiers, thus effectively putting an end to the Second United Front.

Military Authoritarianism in Japan

Japanese political and military elites shared a number of ideological predispositions with German Fascists, including anti-liberalism and anti-Communism. Like Germany, the Japanese government pursued a foreign policy of conquering neighbouring continental lands. Some Japanese policymakers studied the evolution of fascism in Europe, particularly Germany, and refined elements of Japan's state–society relations based on Fascist models. A number of state-based organizations, such as youth and women's groups, existed in Japan prior to the onset of the Sino-Japanese War, but in the 1930s, emulating Nazi models, the Japanese government expanded their size and made participation in them compulsory.

The substitution of autonomous organizations for ones controlled by the state was a characteristic of mass organizations in Germany, Italy, and Japan. In wartime Japan, but also colonial areas like Korea, these bodies were responsible for distributing food, employment, and other resources to the civil populations, so failure to join them would result in significant hardship. The organizations were anti-democratic, for they mobilized the population for state ends without allowing citizen input into policy. By pre-empting a civil society from developing, the regime reinforced the authoritarian character of the political system. The development of state-directed mass organizations was closely linked to German and Japanese efforts to establish an 'organic' or 'living corporate' society which would act according to objectives articulated by the state. In his book *Germany on the Rise* (1938), Japanese Minister of Commerce and Railways Admiral Godo Takuo praised Nazi labour laws for overcoming class conflict through their adherence to 'racial spirit'. Since both countries shared an anti-Communist mission, he argued, Germany's labour legislation could provide a model for Japan, as long as that model focused on the 'absolutist Japanese spirit'.

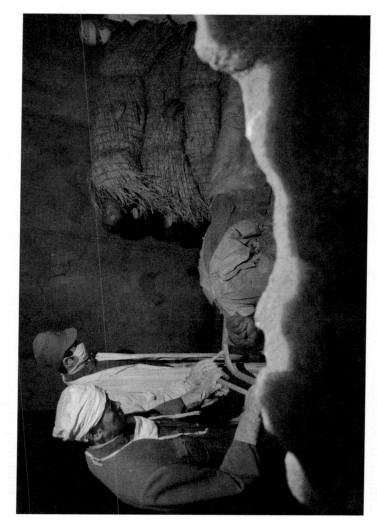

Japanese Unit 731 biological experiments on Chinese in Manchuria, as depicted in the Shenyang 9-18 Museum, the numbers in the museum name representing the month and day of the start of the Sino-Japanese conflict in 1931.

An important difference between the German and Japanese imperiums was that while the National Socialist party played a leading role in Germany, political parties almost ceased functioning in wartime Japan. The coercive power of the state was also different. In Japan there existed 'thought police', but not the kind of institutionalized and systematic state-perpetrated violence as occurred in Hitler's Germany. There were strong parallels between Japanese treatment of Koreans and Chinese, on the one hand, and German policies towards Poles and East Europeans on the other, but Japan did not create death factories like Belzec, Chelmno, or Treblinka. It did, however, pursue chemical warfare research and deadly biological experiments, especially through Force 731, located mainly in buildings across Manchuria. In 1936 the Japanese forced Chinese labourers to build a huge complex near Harbin for secret research into the effects of bacteriological agents on human captives, mostly Chinese, many of whom were Communists, but also Russians, Koreans, and other nationalities. A crematorium built at the site disposed of the bodies of the thousands of victims killed in the experiments. Another biological warfare station in Nanjing produced large amounts of chemicals used to poison wells and spread murderous diseases in central China. In the early 1940s, the Japanese established other bacterio-logical warfare facilities in South-East Asia.

Charismatic leadership was a defining characteristic of European fascism. Unlike Germany after the First World War, however, Japan retained its monarchy, embodied in Emperors Yoshihito and Hirohito. Ultimate political authority in Japan rested—in theory if not in fact—in a dynastic ruler who claimed to be descended from a sun goddess. For many of the ruling elite, the *kokutai*—the concept of national polity, based on the perceived cultural and political legitimacy of the Emperor—was the essence of Japanese politics. The cultural underpinnings of Hitler's public leadership were demonstrably different from Hirohito, whom the Japanese public never saw and whose voice was not heard until he announced Japan's surrender over the radio in 1945. In Japan, there was also no equivalent to the position of the Führer or *Il Duce*. Day-to-day decision-making authority was not centred in the power of one individual but in the collective decisions of the Japanese cabinet, the military, and bureaucracy. There were fifteen Japanese Prime Ministers during the Sino-Japanese War, and none came close to accumulating the power and authority of Hitler. Even one of the more powerful Japanese Prime Ministers of the period, the militarist general Tojo Hideki, was constrained by existing constitutional practices, especially the 'independent supreme command'. While the Nazis built the Third Reich on the ashes of Weimar and the Second Reich, Japanese politicians did not re-design the Meiji political system. Rather, they bolstered the existing political order with appeals linked to semi-religious mythologies of pre-modern Japanese history. A document produced by the govern-ment's cabinet planning board pointed out that 'since the founding of our country, Japan has had an unparalleled totalitarianism . . . an ideal totalitarianism is manifest in our national polity. . . . Germany's totalitarianism has existed for only eight years, but Japanese [totalitarianism] has shone through 3,000 years of ageless tradition'.

Japanese political thought was imbued with religious significance, especially in relation to Shintoism. By the time of the War of Resistance, government propaganda was closely linked to ultranationalist Shintoism, which affirmed Japanese purity and encouraged the belief that war helped to maintain a pure society. A 1937 publication of the Ministry of Education pointed out that Japan was unique in the world insofar as 'our country is a divine country governed by an Emperor who is a deity incarnate'. Since non-Japanese could never reach Japan's superior cultural level, 'justice' entailed the subordination of the colonial subjects and Chinese to their Japanese political masters. Similarly, 'stability' required the creation of an enduring hierarchy of authority based on inegalitarian and colonial or semi-colonial structures of power in which all subjects would find their 'proper place'. These ideas were critical starting points for Japan's so-called 'New Order in East Asia', announced by Prince Konoe in November 1938. The empire's concept of 'peace' was therefore closely tied to notions of subjugation.

The idea of purity reinforced the notion that the Japanese were also the leading race, not only of Asia, but around the globe. Some of the empire's soldiers viewed Germans as allies of convenience, to be tolerated, useful for battling Communists on conscious of Western racism against Asians, which encouraged the official tendency to criticize the contradictions of liberalism and yet also to look to Asia as a 'natural' Japanese sphere of influence. Thus Japanese propaganda in China emphasized that 'to liberate Asia from the white man's prison is the natural duty of every Asiatic! All of you Asiatics who have groaned under the yoke of the white man unite!' The propagandists accepted as natural the racism of their own rhetoric.

The idea that the Japanese were a morally superior race may have fuelled a sense of Japanese disillusionment with their Nazi allies. Some of the empire's soldiers viewed Germans as allies of convenience, to be tolerated, useful for battling Communists on the eastern front or for fighting the liberal European powers in Western Europe. Similarly, Japanese copies of *Mein Kampf* were heavily censored, with critical comments on the Japanese expunged from the book. In Germany, Hitler complained of his Japanese ally: 'The Emperor is a companion piece of the later Czars. Weak, cowardly, irresolute, he may fall before a revolution. My association with Japan was never popular. . . . Let us think of ourselves as masters and consider these people at best as lacquered half-monkeys, who need to feel the knout.' With both sides believing that their 'pure' race embodied the superior global culture, it is hardly surprising that Japan and Germany were unable to foster close collaborative policies during the war. For many Japanese leaders, however, the presence of a like-minded violent and revisionist power in Europe facilitated the goal of ridding the globe of Communism and the hegemony of the liberal Anglo-American powers.

Japan, the United States, and the Start of the Pacific War, 1940–1941

Like German empire-builders, Japanese planners sought to build an autarkic empire in territories contiguous to their homeland. This was part of an ideology of 'total war' advocated by a faction of army planners who demanded that Japan have under its direct territorial control the resources needed to prosecute war. This project, however, was complicated by Japan's perceived need for strategic materials from the United States and South-East Asia, which can also be viewed as the problem of managing enemies on land and at sea. Even as late as 1940 the Japanese government, headed by Admiral Yonai Mitsumasa (1880–1948), kept open the possibility of diplomatic co-operation with Britain and America; but hope for a *modus vivendi* was wishful thinking, given the entrenched positions of army officers in the government. By establishing Wang Jingwei's collaborationist puppet regime in north China in March 1940, the Yonai government further alienated those in the United States who demanded that Japan abandon its war against China. A Japanese offensive against Ichang in southern China in the spring of 1940 demonstrated the Chinese military's determination to continue the War of Resistance. The success of German armies in Western Europe in the spring of 1940 led the Yonai government successfully to pressure Britain and the new authoritarian Vichy regime in France to end their assistance to China through the Burma Road and across the Sino-Vietnamese border. As an army official observed on 4 July, 'we are aiming to put an end to seventy years' dependence on Britain and America commercially and economically'.

In the early summer of 1940 the Japanese army demanded a closer relationship with Germany, and forced Yonai, who had expressed reservations about a German alliance, to resign. Konoe Fumimaro returned to power, convinced of the need to overturn Anglo-American dominance in the international system. In Asia, an alliance with Germany would facilitate the expansion of the 'New Order', now to include Union. Government officials, including Foreign Minister Matsuoka Yosuke, hoped the alliance would either deter the Americans or fortify Japan's position against the Anglo-American powers should a trans-Pacific war become a reality. Later that month, the Japanese government threatened Vichy into allowing Japan's armies to occupy northern Vietnam. To acquire the resources needed to become relatively self-sufficient in wartime, including oil, tin, rubber, copper, and rice, the army now planned to invade and occupy all of South-East Asia. The logic of untrammelled territorial expansion soon led to war with West European colonial powers and America with its own colony in the region, the Philippines.

The European war remained at the forefront of President Roosevelt's strategic concerns, but South-East Asia blurred the distinction between the two theatres, as the British, French, and Dutch had substantial colonial interests in Malaya, Hong Kong, Singapore, Burma, Indochina, and Indonesia. South-East Asia was vital for American and European capitalism, and the prospect of a Japanese invasion of the region provided another reason for the Roosevelt administration to collaborate more closely with Britain. By late 1940 key US planners believed holding Singapore was critical, for the British naval control of those strategic seas kept South and South-East Asian resources open to liberal capitalist America. To deter the Japanese from advancing on the region, in the spring of 1940 Roosevelt ordered most of the US

Fleet, after completing annual exercises in the Pacific, to remain in the territory of Hawaii instead of returning to the west coast or being re-positioned in the Atlantic.

The Japanese economy between 1931 and 1941 had become increasingly dependent on America's precision tools, scrap iron, metals, and oil to fuel its weapons of war. American policymakers recognized Japan's need for US goods as a strategic weakness, and responded to the period bounded by Japan's expansion into the South China Sea and the tripartite pact—1938 to 1940—by imposing a series of economic restrictions and sanctions on the empire. These included airplanes and their parts, aviation fuel, and scrap iron and metal. Japanese officials criticized the sanctions, claiming US proclamations of maintaining an 'open door' hid America's own imperialist agenda. There was an element of truth in these accusations: the United States sought to assert its own sphere of influence in China and South-East Asia, thousands of miles from its western shores. The issue for the USA, however, was not the extension of trade or capitalism to Asia, but the manner in which the big powers negotiated this process, and leading figures in the Roosevelt administration, including Secretary of State Cordell Hull, China Hand Stanley Hornbeck, and Chief of Naval Operations, Admiral Harold Stark, did not want to allow Japan exclusive control over the resources of South-East Asia. Thus while Roosevelt believed that planning for war in Europe should take precedence over Asia, key officials were prepared to use force to stop the Japanese from expanding their New Order further into the South China Sea region. The military-economic rivalry between the Japanese empire and the liberal-imperialism of the Americans led to war in just over one year.

In late July 1941, in the wake of the Nazi invasion of the Soviet Union, the Konoe government succeeded in pressuring Vichy to allow Japanese troops to occupy southern Indochina. This increased threat to British, Dutch, and American colonial territory was designed to force the Dutch Indies to increase Japanese access to its raw resources, especially oil. In making the decision to foster the 'Greater East Asian Co-Prosperity Sphere', the Japanese government privately decreed that 'our Empire will not be deterred by the possibility of being involved in a war with Great Britain and the United States'. Imperial Japan now fully extended the notion of a New Order into the European and American colonial regions of South-East Asia. In early August the Japanese government issued an educational pamphlet entitled 'The Way of Subjects' which stated that 'An old order that has been placing humanity under individualism, liberalism and materialism for several hundred years since the early period of the epoch of modern history is now crumbling.' Japanese subjects were told to embrace the 'new order' that was 'in the making amid unprecedented world changes'. Roosevelt responded to the Japanese initiative against the Dutch Indies by freezing Japanese assets in the USA and embargoing Japanese access to aviation fuel. In the Department of the Treasury, Dean Acheson enforced the embargo with zeal, and succeeded in banning the export of all oil to Japan.

Even as Japan positioned itself to invade South-East Asia and the Western Pacific, Konoe hoped to avoid war with the USA. An earlier round of talks between Japanese ambassador to the US, Nomura Kichisaburo, and Secretary of State Hull had ended in

In 1958 President Dwight D. Eisenhower approved the creation of a memorial for the USS *Arizona*, sunk at Pearl Harbor, to honour and commemorate those members of the US Armed Forces who had died in the attack on 7 December 1941. In 1999, the US Navy parked the USS *Missouri*, the ship on which Japanese officials surrendered in 1945, parallel to the USS *Arizona*, emphasizing the US victory in war.

failure in June, but Konoe hoped for one last effort in the late summer. He agreed to prepare for war with the USA if the initiative failed. Neither side, however, would compromise. The USA demanded a Japanese withdrawal from Indochina and China. The Atlantic Charter, issued by Churchill and Roosevelt in August 1941, went further. The two leaders proclaimed that all peoples had the right to determine their government, a position which anticipated the eventual dismantling of Japan's overseas empire in 1945. Efforts to negotiate a *modus vivendi* only underlined the differences between the two empires. Konoe's failure led to a new government under Tojo Hideki, but it too failed to reach a compromise with America. By the end of November 1941, US Secretary of War Henry Stimson recorded that the US government needed to figure out how to manoeuvre Japan 'into the position of firing the first shot without allowing too much danger to ourselves'.

On 1 December 1941 Tojo Hideki's cabinet, meeting with the Emperor at an Imperial Conference, made the fateful decision to attack South-East Asia and the Western Pacific, including the US naval base at Pearl Harbor. During the discussions, the President of the Privy Council praised Japan's empire, noting that agreeing to American terms would have involved the loss 'in one stroke not only [of] our gains in the Sino-Japanese and Russo-Japanese wars, but also the benefits of the Manchurian incident'. Japan's existence was threatened and 'the great achievements of the Emperor Meiji would all come to nought, and . . . there is nothing else we can do. . . . This is indeed the greatest undertaking since the opening of our country in the 19th century.' The subsequent Japanese attack on Pearl Harbor on 7 December, far from causing the USA to think about suing for peace, ignited the most momentous big power war in history.

War and Occupation: South-East Asia

In late 1941, in conjunction with the attack on Pearl Harbor, the Japanese government ordered simultaneous assaults on Malaya, the Philippines, and Indonesia. By 6 May 1942, with the fall of Corregidor in the Philippines, the Japanese military controlled a huge swathe of land and sea as far west as the Burma–India border and the Andaman and Nicobar islands, south to Indonesia, the northern part of Papua and the Gilbert Islands, and northwards to Wake Island and some of the Aleutian chain. To the delight of Admiral Yamamoto Isakuru, the planner of the offensives, the territory had been acquired without the loss of a single Japanese battleship or carrier. The Japanese empire seemed to be on the edge of an immense victory against the Western powers.

The occupation of South-East Asia, while permitting Japan access to large quantities of natural resources, also extended the manpower of its empire to its limit. After December 1941, the Japanese shelved preparatory plans for an invasion of the Soviet Union. Some areas, like Vietnam, were occupied by a relatively small number of troops (30,000). Resistance to Japanese imperial rule, however, appeared in numerous areas, especially the Philippines, which attracted hundreds of thousands of guerrilla fighters. In Malaya, the pro-Communist Malayan Peoples' Anti-Japanese Army carried out attacks on the Japanese. During the Japanese invasion of Singapore, volunteers formed the Singapore Overseas Chinese Army, which included women recruits. In New Guinea, local populations worked with Australian and American soldiers, and in Burma the Anti-Fascist Organization (later the Anti-Fascist People's Freedom League) gained popularity in 1944 and 1945. In 1941 Ho Chi Minh travelled from the Soviet Union to Vietnam, stopping over at the CCP camp in Yenan before creating his own base along the Sino-Vietnamese border. The small Indochinese Communist Party sponsored the Viet Minh, an organization designed to attract widespread popular support, though it was also riddled with intrigue and dissension. Resistance groups sought and received aid from Force 136 of the British Special Operations Executive, as well as from the precursor body of America's Central Intelligence Agency, the Office of Strategic Services.

The Japanese ruled the region using South-East Asian politicians who had been active before the war. Many of those who collaborated—including lower level administrators or security forces—read like a *Who's Who* of post-Second World War political leaders: Phibun Songkhram, Sukarno, Suharto, Dato Onn, Tunku Abdul Rahman, Ne Win, U Nu, and Aung San. In declaring war against the United States and Britain on 25 January 1941 President Phibun of Thailand predicted: 'it is about time to declare war with the winner'. After 1943, as Japanese authority in Asia became more precarious, local leaders removed collaborators like Phibun from

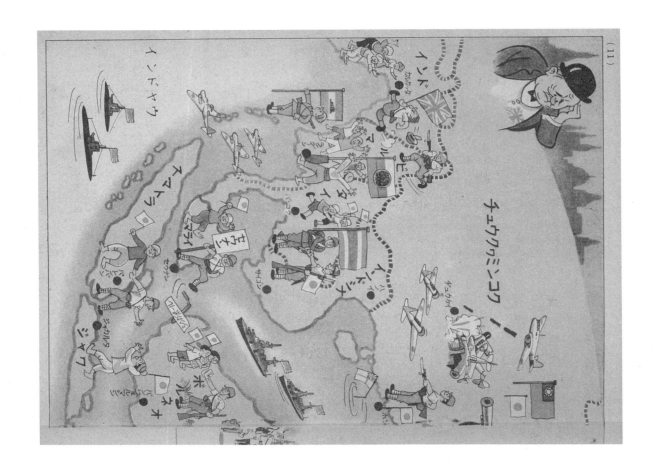

positions of authority, participated in acts of moral resistance (Tunku Abdul Rah-man), or switched allegiance (Aung San). The Japanese were careful to circumscribe the power of indigenous politicians and strictly controlled civil society organizations operating in urban centres. Prior to granting Burma a semblance of independence in August 1943, for example, the Japanese authorities demobilized the collaborationist

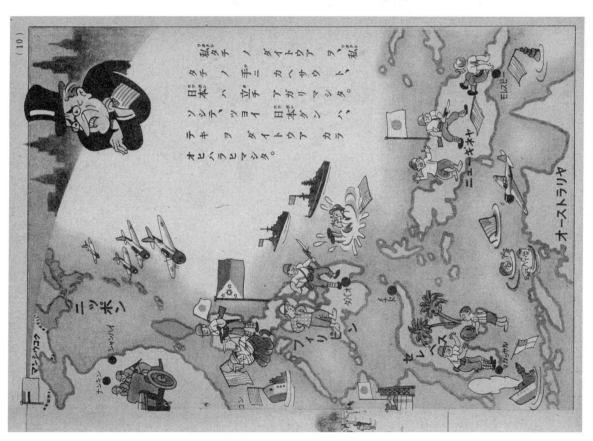

Japanese propaganda booklet from 1943 depicting South-East Asian peoples welcoming the victories of the Japanese soldiers while Roosevelt and Churchill look on in shock.

Burma Independence Army, cutting its size from 23,000 recruits to 5,000 and renaming it the Burma Defence Army.

Most of South-East Asia suffered greatly under the grossly misnamed Greater East Asia Co-Prosperity Sphere. The initial Japanese invasion, involving ground offensives, heavy shelling, and aerial bombing, had produced tremendous dislocation, fear,

US government poster rallying the Philippine resistance movement against the Japanese occupation. American wartime officials unwittingly promoted nationalist sentiment in the occupied American colony, which attained independence in 1946.

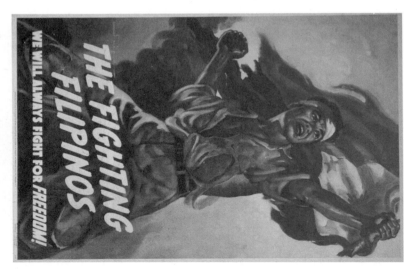

Participants from the Japanese empire at the Greater East Asia Conference, held in Tokyo in 1943 to underline Japan's commitment to the liberation of Asia from European and American colonialism. From left to right: Ba Maw (Burma), Zhang Jinghui and Wang Jingwei (China), Hideki Tōjō (Japan), Wan Waithayakon (Thailand), José P. Laurel (Philippines), Subhas Chandra Bose (India).

shock, and desperation. As in China, the Japanese military designed plans to induce terror into the population. In the week before Singapore fell, Japanese airmen dropped bombs filled with scrap metal, sulphur, and oil. After Singapore's defences collapsed, the occupiers ordered all men and boys between 8 and 50 to report to the Japanese police, the *Kempetei*. People were arbitrarily chosen for execution. Over three weeks in February and March 1942 tens of thousands of Chinese Singaporeans were killed in the infamous Sook Chin, or purification massacres, an example of ethnic cleansing.

POWs were similarly brutalized and murdered. In the Philippines, after the defeat of American commander Douglas MacArthur's troops in April 1942 on the Bataan peninsula west of Manila, the Japanese military force-marched American and Filipino POWs towards their prison camp. Abused, beaten, starved, and killed, thousands of Filipinos and hundreds of American soldiers died before arriving at the camp. The treatment of enemy soldiers was an extension of the abuses committed by the Japanese in China. Indeed, amongst the divisions serving Japanese Commander Homma Masaharu's Fourteenth Army in the Philippines, the Sixteenth had participated in the attacks on Nanjing, Xuzhou, and Wuhan. During the attack on Nanjing, the Sixteenth Division's then commander, Lieutenant General Nakajima Kesago, had written in his diary that the policy of the army was to kill all POWs upon capture. By 1941, the policy, it seems, was designed to extend their suffering. Bataan was infamous, but executions occurred in many areas across Asia. In Parit Sulong, Jahore, for example, during the Battle of Malaya in January 1942, the Japanese army committed summary executions of 150 Indian and Australian troops.

Hunger, disease, political persecution, arbitrary violence, forced labour, and exorbitant demands for resources characterized most areas of Japanese rule. Even so, the

Burmese refugees fleeing the Japanese invasion force, early 1942, highlighting the dramatic early military successes of the Japanese military in South-East Asia.

legacies of European colonialism produced collaborators willing to fight alongside Japanese soldiers. In February 1942 the Japanese began to recruit, amongst the 70,000 South Asian POWs captured in the Malayan and Singaporean campaigns, for the so-called Indian National Army (INA), created to subvert British rule in South Asia. The army was formed too late, however, to participate in the Japanese advance into Burma, which began with bombing runs in late December 1941, followed up by a land invasion at the end of January 1942. Burmese society was too disillusioned with British colonialism to put up much resistance to the invading armies. British armies retreated quickly, along with hundreds of thousands of refugees, many despairing for the safety of Assam or, even, Calcutta. By the spring of 1942 the Japanese military controlled Burma, had cut off supplies going to China from the Burma road, and had begun to bomb Calcutta. The Imperial Navy, having destroyed the British ships *Prince of Wales* and *Repulse* during the Battle of Malaya, easily ventured into the Bay of Bengal, their mobility limited only by America's strategic success during the Battle of the Coral Sea, which left Port Moresby and an important approach to Australia in Allied hands.

The Politics of Food in Wartime China and Vietnam

The war in Asia seriously disrupted food supplies and significantly exacerbated shortages caused by natural disasters. Famines are treated in Chapter 11 in the context of unnatural deaths caused by the war, but they are also an integral part of the political history of warfare in Asia, especially the growth of Communism in Vietnam and, to a lesser extent, China.

Famine struck China, most notably impoverished Henan province in 1942–3. The region had been cut off from transport networks by the Japanese army, which occupied forty-four of the province's 110 counties. The GMD controlled the western region of the province, the area hit hardest by the famine. Lack of rain and a locust attack in 1942 destroyed crops, and the province lacked the support systems, available in normal times, to assist the beleaguered population. The Japanese seized and held on to the grain, distributing only small, inadequate amounts to the Chinese. The Nationalist government also seized grain, and their relief efforts were hampered by a lack of political will, intransigent commanders, and corruption. Family members sold other family members into slavery, exchanged land for money or food, and turned to prostitution. Instances of murder and cannibalism occurred. The combined impact of starvation and warfare forced the Chinese population to turn to survival tactics. The social tragedy of war had consequences far beyond the Sino-Japanese conflict. In this context the CCP, offering an ideology of collective action as a means to live through the wreckage of societal norms, drew support from villagers. In East Henan the New Fourth Route Army fared poorly in 1942–3, but gained momentum following the partial withdrawal of Japanese troops from the region in the spring of 1944. Though the CCP also confiscated foodstuffs, an important factor in the growth of Communism in the area was Communists' ability to defend grain supplies from puppet and

GMD troops. Communist cadres also encouraged peasants to return to homes lost to flooding, loaned seed to farmers, and facilitated the cultivation of foodstuffs. The mobilization of the peasantry resulted in the nurturing of Communist-nationalist sentiment and a peasant political consciousness absent prior to the onset of the war. Ongoing conflicts between the Nationalists and Communists, however, limited the expansion of the New Fourth Route Army in central China, especially compared to the successes of the Eighth Route Army in north China. By 1945 the latter's army contained over a million soldiers who controlled an area comprised of almost 100 million people living across 800,000 square kilometres of land, while the former army grew to 310,000 in an area of 250,000 square kilometres inhabited by 34 million persons. In general, throughout the conflict Communist armies engaged in small-scale guerrilla warfare which resulted in comparatively few casualties.

The creation of local collaborating regimes, the growth of Communist base areas, and the failure of the Nationalists to stem Japanese expansion highlighted the complicated character of politics in China during the Second World War. There was effectively no national government as the territory which had comprised Republican China was occupied by warlords, Japanese and puppet troops, and Nationalist and Communist armies. These developments set the context for the Chinese civil war in the aftermath of the Japanese defeat in 1945. The Japanese war achieved exactly what the Japanese military sought to prevent: the rise of Communism in China.

In the northern part of the French protectorate of Tonkin, in Indochina, a famine that began in late 1943 and killed one million peasants was instrumental in the coming to power of the Vietnamese Communists. The Japanese ruled Indochina through Vichy bureaucrats for most of the war, though anti-Western feelings persisted. In July 1943, for example, Matsui Iwane, the former Commander of the Japanese Shanghai Expeditionary Force that had been responsible for massacres in Nanjing, told Vietnamese reporters in Saigon that the Japanese would liberate Asians from their British, American, and French colonizers. As elsewhere in Asia, and, to some extent, following the French colonial example in Indochina, the Japanese occupiers ruthlessly exploited the population, forcing them to switch rice production to industrial fibres like hemp or jute. After 1940, the French demanded that newly created emergency granaries be filled with rice at set prices. The policy resulted in the impoverishment of tenant farmers, setting the stage for their radicalization. At the same time that Matsui spoke in Saigon, Japanese soldiers established new bases in the north, forcing villagers to sell them rice at prices lower than market value. To meet Japanese demands, Vietnamese peasants sold their lands, bought rice on the market, and sold it back to the Japanese at one third the price. In this way, French and Japanese economic policies facilitated the onset of famine.

The fall of Paris in August 1944 and the defeat of Vichy France, combined with US aerial bombing against Japanese ships and transport systems in the South China Sea and mainland South-East Asia, placed significant pressure on Franco-Japanese relations. In 1944, French officials told the Japanese that they could no longer sustain Japan's demand for foodstuffs. Though the two sides subsequently worked out a rice-purchasing compact, in March 1945 the Japanese overthrew the French colonial regime, arresting Governor General Jean Decoux during the ceremony to sign the food agreement. Japanese officials released only small amounts of stored grain to the starving population and continued forcefully to take foodstuffs from Tonkinese peasants. The famine played a critical role in mobilizing support for the Communists, who seized the stored grain for the dying population. The new pro-Japan Vietnamese government, headed by Emperor Bao Dai and Premier Tran Trong Kim, a classical scholar unsuited for the position, fell quickly to the Vietnamese August 1945 Revolution.

Conscription, Forced Labour, and Slavery in the Japanese Empire

From 1942 onwards, to meet the strategic demands of an over-extended empire, Japanese politicians accelerated recruitment into the armed forces. The army, not including reserves, grew from just over one million soldiers in 1941 and 1942 to over 2.4 million by 1945. Although conscription had existed in Japan since 1873, in December 1943 the government lowered the draft age from 20 to 19 and extended the age of those serving from 40 to 45. The empire also targeted colonial subjects, especially Koreans and Taiwanese. In May 1942 authorities in Chosen (Korea) announced that conscription would be enforced in August 1943, with the first inductees integrated into existing imperial units in late 1944. Between 1938 and 1943, based on a voluntary system of recruitment, the colonial regime accepted 25,000 Koreans into military service, about a quarter of those who applied. In 1944 and 1945 another 110,000 Koreans were inducted into Japan's imperial army and navy. Most were stationed in Korea, Japan, and China. Korean colonial elites publicly supported conscription, but by the end of the war popular opinion tended to be cynical about the mobilization process, and evasion and desertion were means of resisting this coercive dimension of empire-building. In Formosa (Taiwan) the voluntary system, begun in 1942, generated several hundred thousand applications and some 4,500 recruits. Conscription, enforced in 1945, led to over 200,000 more enlistments, with almost half of the soldiers stationed beyond the borders of the island-colony. During the conflict, about 30,000 Koreans and at least 2,100 Formosans died.

The increased production of military goods in Japan, combined with the huge expansion of the area under Japanese control and the growth of the armed forces after 1942, led to worker shortages throughout the empire. Japanese government officials and agents managed manpower shortages partly through forced labour schemes. In north China, coerced labour mainly came from Chinese POW's, homeless people in cities, war refugees, and civilians captured during battle. The North China Area Army, for example, in its efforts to defeat Communist soldiers of the Eighth Route Army, captured about 100,000 civilians and sent them in the summer of 1942 to work in Manchuria. In various parts of north China, after destroying villages, the army forced former inhabitants to work in Japanese factories. Japanese soldiers even established a refugee camp in China in order to conscript its inhabitants. Between January 1941 and the end of the war in August 1945, three million workers laboured in factories and mines in north China while another 2.6 million were sent to work in other areas of the empire, including Manchuria and central China. During this time, one million Chinese laboured for the North China Area Army, building barriers, trenches, huts, and roads.

In South-East Asia, perhaps the most notorious instance of forced labour was the terrible suffering Asians and Allied POWs experienced in building the Thai–Burma Railway. Japanese soldiers beat, starved, and murdered the workers and thousands died of cholera and malaria. In June 1943, Japanese troops ordered that 250 victims of disease—men, women, and children—be burned alive in their living quarters. Of the 78,000 Malays who worked on the railway, almost 30,000 died. Recruiting initially involved deception and, later, force. As in China, conscripts included the homeless and refugees. In 1943 and 1944 up to 150,000 people died building the railway, which Allied planes began to bomb in the summer of 1944. Once the railway was completed, many of the POWs were sent to work in Japan.

Within the empire, about one million Koreans were also recruited or forced to work as labourers or sexual slaves for the Japanese war machine. Between 1939 and 1945, 724,000 Koreans, male and female, went to Japan to work. They took on positions in a wide variety of industries, including chemical, textile, metal, and construction, but

Chinese comfort woman interrogated in Rangoon, Burma, at the end of the war. Burmese women were also recruited for comfort stations, and in some cases Burmese auxiliary troops as well as Japanese soldiers and, occasionally, civilians were allowed to exploit them for sex.

the majority were miners. In 1939 Koreans accounted for 6 per cent of Japanese miners, but by the end of the war the 128,000 Korean miners in Japan represented about one-third of the industry's labourers. On the northern island of Hokkaido, where Koreans made up over 40 per cent of mining employees, they earned wages far below their Japanese counterparts, toiled under slave-like conditions, experienced beatings, lynchings, and torture for running away, working slowly, or even not understanding employers' demands. One guard at a Hokkaido mining company argued that 'bond labourers and Koreans are not human beings. Even if one or two of them die, there is no time for funerals for them. Make them work hard and quickly.' Koreans who were caught fleeing the mine were 'flogged with a hide whip or were hung from a beam and a fire lit under them so that they choked from the smoke until they lost consciousness'.

Korean women were also lured from the peninsula under false pretences and forced to provide sex for the imperial troops serving throughout Asia. The so-called 'comfort women', a euphemism for sexual slavery, came from many parts of the wartime empire, including mainland China, Taiwan, the Philippines, Indonesia, and Malaysia. The majority of the roughly 90,000 women forced into prostitution were ethnic Koreans. Many of the women who ended up working in camps alongside the Japanese Imperial Army were tricked into believing that they would work in Japan or overseas for good wages and in good working conditions. Some were literally kidnapped by soldiers and shipped overseas. In some cases, girls were sold by families desperate for money to buy food or to pay debts. By the end of 1942, 280 of the 400 Japanese sex stations were located in China, but 100 were scattered around South-East Asia, with ten in the Pacific theatre and another ten on Sakhalin. The women often found out about their inhuman living environment only when they arrived at a 'comfort station'. In one case, a girl was tricked into leaving Korea for work in a brush factory in Japan. She ended up in the South Pacific on an island in the Palau chain, where she initially resisted being raped, but was beaten and bayoneted into submission.

These forms of violence were linked to the racism underpinning Japanese colonialism in Asia and to notions of masculinity which degraded women and treated them as sexual slaves. That these stations were part of the military's policies throughout Asia reflects how abuse was institutionalized within the military setting, and how little concern there was for the means and conditions under which the women were forced to serve soldiers. As with other forms of exploitation and torture during the war, the horrific experience left lifelong scars on its victims.

The Oceanic War, 1942–1945

American naval assaults on Japanese-held territory came from two directions. In the south-west Pacific, General Douglas MacArthur, based in Australia, directed his forces into New Guinea, the Philippines, the Ryukyus, and southern Japan. From Hawaii, Admiral Chester Nimitz's fleet crossed the central Pacific from Wake Island to Saipan and Iwo Jima. Heading north, they met with MacArthur's forces at

American propaganda poster emphasizing exterminationist violence against Japanese soldiers, 1944. Such posters were part of the sensationalist reporting of 'Japanese barbarism' after 1943.

Okinawa in the Ryukyus, where they were to co-ordinate the invasion of the home islands, beginning with Kyushu.

The strategic and military history of the Pacific War is described in greater detail in later chapters. This section will focus on the cultural and racial dimensions of the conflict, for the struggles for the Pacific islands were characterized by an intense hatred between the Japanese and Americans, fuelled by racism on both sides. Between 1942 and 1945 the American media portrayed the Japanese as unique in the scale of their brutality and desire to kill. Japanese wartime atrocities received significant attention in the news and radio, and the public became particularly incensed over Japanese killings of American POWs, including the pilots who had participated in the 'Doolittle' air raid against Tokyo in the spring of 1942. Only when the public learned of the horror of the Nazi concentration camps in the spring of 1945 did they come to recognize the scale of German atrocities in Europe. Public opinion polls in the USA indicated that about 10 per cent of Americans believed the Japanese should be exterminated or annihilated. Such genocidal attitudes were encouraged by officials like Admiral William Halsey, commander of American forces in the South Pacific, who infamously encouraged his troops to 'Kill Japs, kill Japs, kill more Japs'. In a 1945 poll, 25 per cent of US soldiers fighting in the Pacific stated their main goal was to kill as many Japanese as they could. Another poll taken by a US magazine in December 1945 suggested that almost a quarter of all Americans had wanted to use many more atomic bombs against Japanese targets.

In Japan, the state paid some lip service to its alliance with Germany, telling its propaganda officers not to depict the war with the United States in racial terms. At the same time, the government continued to tie the creation of the new world order to a holy 'total war', the goal of which was to create 'eternal world peace', one linked to Emperor Jimmu's creation of Japan almost three millennia earlier. A document produced in 1943 by the Ministry of Health and Welfare outlined a colonization scheme that would have seen 14 per cent of the Japanese population permanently living overseas as settlers of the new imperium. At times the report accepted German war aims, including Nazi policies towards Jews, but in other places suggested that Japan aimed at global cultural and racial hegemony. The Japanese empire would take on a 'leading position in the creation of a new world order' and under Japanese authority, 'all peoples of the world' would assume their 'proper place'. The 'cooperative body' to be forged in war 'would place the whole world under one roof'.

Such policies were formulated even as the Allied powers began to penetrate the empire's defences. The Japanese began to lose control over their oceanic empire after the battle of Midway in June 1942 and the start of the struggle over Guadalcanal in August. In Japan, the population felt increasing material deprivation, now interpreted by some commentators as an 'emaciated endurance', something that could be experienced as a virtue. By 1943, driven to desperation, Japanese propaganda encouraged the population to become more tough, as sacrifice, war, and mass death became seen as a way to further purify, not only the nation, but the world. It was in this context that the military formed suicide squads of pilots, whose missions involved the purging of pollution and impurity. By contrast, the Anglo-American enemy became associated with demons, monsters, and bestial devils. A popular magazine in 1944 ran a headline labelled 'This is the Enemy! The Bestial American People ... Beat the Americans to Death.' Americans in particular were depicted as without humanity, only interested in base instincts like sex and conquest. News reports highlighted US racism against Japanese and African-Americans and described acts of Americans killing babies, intent on destroying 'the divine state of Japan'.

Final Offensives: China and South-East Asia, 1944–1945

In the spring of 1944 Japan's armies in Burma initiated a major military offensive in northern Burma against British forces in Kohima and Imphal. The main goal of the *U-Go* (Operation C) campaign was to invade India, and, with the assistance of the Indian National Army of 40,000 soldiers, trigger an uprising against British rule. A successful operation against the British would also create a base in north-western Burma which could be used for a possible invasion of Yunnan province. The military planning for the *U-Go* offensive originated in an imperial conference in September 1943 in Tokyo which called for a strategy of local offensives against the Allies in India and China and significant naval victories over the United States in the Pacific. The overall objective was to force the USA into peace negotiations while driving India and China out of the war altogether. Such a plan was highly unrealistic, given the growing military and economic capacity of the Allies against Japan. By 1945 the USA had

Indian engineers and labourers construct a wooden bridge over a shallow stream or *chaung* during the allied advance to Rangoon, April 1945.

effectively abandoned China as a major theatre of operations and concentrated its aerial attacks on Japanese targets from Pacific Ocean bases, especially those acquired in the Marianas in 1943. Japan's determination to continue fighting had devastating consequences, not only for Japanese society, but also for millions of others in Asia who remained under its 'New Order'.

The Japanese commander of *U-Go*, Lieutenant-General Mutaguchi Renya, had led the regiment at the Marco Polo Bridge fighting in 1937 that began the War of Resistance. To justify *U-Go*, he wrote in his diary that, 'if I...can exercise a decisive influence' on the war, '[I] will have justified myself in the eyes of our nation'. By 1944, however, the Japanese and Indian armies were significantly weakened by disease and shortages of food and medicine. They lacked mechanized transport and attack vehicles. Though the Japanese almost overran Kohima, the British armies were huge, now numbering almost two million men across the region. Hundreds of thousands of others played critical supporting roles as labourers. Some of those who died in the fighting were later buried at the Commonwealth War Memorial Cemetery in Kandy, Ceylon, not far from where Lord Mountbatten had moved his South-East Asia Command Headquarters in April 1944. Minority groups were hired as labourers—some 200,000 Nagas, for example, worked as porters in Assam—but later they also alerted the British armies to Japanese encampments and defensive strongholds in Burma. At Kohima, British tanks played a decisive role, and key support from Indian and Nepalese troops (Punjabis and Gurkhas) turned the conflict in favour of the British. The battles were as grim and infused with racist violence as those in the Pacific war. One British Commander recalled: 'We had experienced fighting the Japs in the Arakan, [with them] bayoneting the wounded and prisoners.... They had renounced any right to be regarded as human, and we thought of them as vermin to be exterminated. That was important—we are pacific in our nature, but when aroused we fight quite well.'

Collectively, the battles at Imphal and Kohima in the spring of 1944 were the most devastating for the Japanese during the entire war in their toll on troops. Of the 85,000 Japanese who participated in the battles, 30,000 died, half of these of disease and starvation. Soon Chinese, Burmese (Kachin), and American soldiers began their own offensive in the north, and by August 1944 Japanese power in northern Burma had collapsed. The Allies controlled the skies and their air forces bombed Japanese positions throughout the country. The air raids killed many civilians and destroyed towns and cities, including Rangoon, which British armies occupied in early May 1945.

As Allied offensives ravaged Burma, Japanese armies continued to devastate large parts of China. The *Ichi-Go* (Number One) operation, launched in conjunction with the offensives in Burma, was the biggest military action ever undertaken by the Japanese army, and brought much of southern and central China under Japanese control by February 1945. The military offensive was designed to establish a rail and land corridor between North-East and South-East Asia in the event oceanic communications between those regions was lost to the Americans, to defeat

A destitute boy in the Poor People's Refuge in Changsha, 1944. The huge offensives of the Japanese army at the end of the war created tremendous suffering across Asia.

Chiang's armies, and to destroy American air bases in southern China which had launched attacks on the empire in South-East Asia and the East China Sea. For these purposes, the China Expeditionary Army mobilized 500,000 soldiers in early 1944 and carried out two major campaigns which lasted into early 1945. Although the Japanese soldiers captured US air bases throughout southern China, the American Fourteenth Air Force relocated further inland and replaced medium-range bombers with B-29 long-range bombers capable of flying over 5,000 miles. From Chengdu, for example, as early as June 1944, B-29s started to attack the southern home island of Kyushu.

The *Ichi-Go* offensive had a tremendous social and political impact on China. The initial attacks in central China occurred while the population still suffered from famine. Chinese soldiers were poorly fed and paid. Shortages of food and medicine led to malnutrition, disease, and death. Poor transport systems resulted in devastating losses. A Red Cross survey indicated that because of lack of food and transport, 80 or 90 per cent of new recruits perished before even reaching their military unit. The *Ichi-Go* battles also resulted in significant battlefield losses for the Chinese army, which suffered some 750,000 casualties in nine months of fighting. These factors seriously impacted the post-war ability of Chiang's armies to defeat the Communists in the Chinese Civil War.

The Japanese military co-ordinated the *Ichi-Go* offensives with operations in South-East Asia, specifically Operation *Sho-Go* (Victory) in the Philippines. The broader and unrealistic purpose of *Ichi-Go* was to enable the Japanese to launch an offensive from the southern Philippines in 1946 with the intention of taking back the

The battle for Manila, which lasted for one month, from 3 February to 3 March 1945, resulted in the widespread destruction of the city and casualties on a par with the devastating firebombing of Tokyo.

initiative in the Pacific War and forcing the USA into a negotiated peace. In October 1944, as General MacArthur's forces landed on Leyte island in the Philippines, the Japanese navy lured Admiral Halsey's Third Fleet northward in a desperate attempt to defeat the Seventh Fleet near the Philippines. The ensuing Battle of Leyte Gulf on 23–25 October, the largest ever naval engagement, decimated the Japanese fleet, which lost four aircraft carriers, effectively eliminating it as a significant strategic factor for the remainder of the war.

Despite America's successes at sea, the struggle for the Philippines continued until the Japanese surrender in August. One of the most devastating battles for the islands occurred in Manila, which American soldiers began to reach in early February 1945. The local Japanese naval commander refused to recognize an order from the army allowing Manila to be a 'free city' and told his 17,000 soldiers to fight Americans and Filipino guerrillas inside the city. In the ensuing battle, much of Manila was razed to the ground, with Japanese soldiers blowing up buildings and shooting, bayoneting, and raping Filipinos. American artillery attacks showed a complete lack of concern for

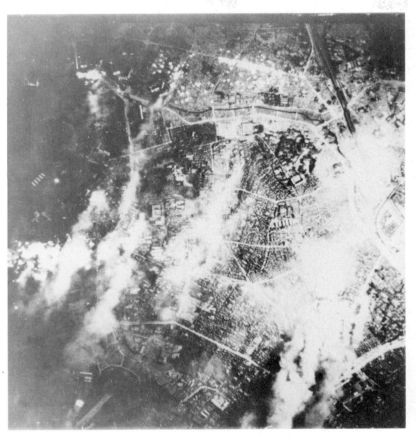

American firebombing of Tokyo, 'Operation Meetinghouse', on 9–10 March 1945, the deadliest non-atomic aerial bombing of the war, anywhere in the world. The attack launched America's saturation bombing campaign against Japanese cities, and Japanese began to execute US airmen who were captured on subsequent raids.

civilians. For every six deaths caused by Japanese assaults, another four were caused by American artillery, used indiscriminately in the capital. The commander of the 37th Infantry Division that was largely responsible for the shelling, Robert S. Beightler, stated that his soldiers 'plastered the Walled City until it was a mess', creating a 'churned up pile of dust and scrap' out of stately government buildings. America's bombers had also done 'some pretty fine alteration work on the appearance of Berlin and Tokyo', and he wished 'they could see what we did with our little artillery on the Jap strongholds of Manila'. Beightler viewed his actions in terms of saving US soldiers' lives, a position which helped to create another battered, decimated, and broken population, with as many as 100,000 deaths in a city of 700,000 inhabitants.

The End of the War with Japan

American and Allied racism and feelings of retribution against Japan and Germany played a fundamental role in shaping the policy of unrestricted bombing that occurred in Europe and Asia. At the beginning of the War of Resistance, President Roosevelt articulated the horror he felt about Japanese bombings of Chinese cities. In the autumn of 1937 the Department of State criticized Japan on the basis that 'any general bombing of an extensive area wherein there resides a large population engaged in peaceful pursuits is unwarranted and contrary to principles of law and of humanity'. In the UK, the British Air Force began its incendiary bombings of Germany in 1941. By the summer of 1943 the British Minister of Information, Brendan Bracken, asserted that the allies would 'bomb, burn and ruthlessly destroy' Germany and Japan. Though the United States Air Force initially practised 'precision' bombing in both Europe and Asia, they abandoned the practice in early March 1945, when Curtis LeMay's XXI Bomber Command, based in the Marianas, used napalm and incendiaries to firebomb Tokyo. The raid on the night of 9–10 March killed over 80,000 civilians and destroyed over a quarter of a million buildings. The bombing raids continued to the end of the war. To destroy the enemy the Anglo-American political and military leadership had come to believe they needed to commit mass killings.

The Japanese reluctance to surrender was indicative of the military's insensitivity to the suffering going on throughout the empire. Roger Dower has suggested that by 1944 and 1945 elements of Japanese military and society were prepared to expose the population to the 'supreme sacrifice' of extermination in order to preserve the state's honour and purify the collective body. The unwillingness of some of the military to negotiate peace can be gleaned from the diary of the deputy chief of staff, Kawabe Torashiro, the planner of Japan's defence of the homelands, Operation *Ketsu-Go* (Decisive). On 9 August 1945, several days after the explosion of the atomic bomb over Hiroshima, and upon learning of the Soviet entry into the war, Kawabe wrote that 'we should not consider seeking peace'. In order 'to save the honour of the Yamato race, there is no other way but to keep fighting . . . I don't like to think about peace and surrender. Whatever the outcome we have no choice but to try.'

As the single most devastating weapon to be used in the Second World War, the atomic bomb has often been considered the central factor in getting the Japanese government to surrender unconditionally to the Allies. Historian Tsuyoshi Hasegawa, however, has argued that the entry of the Soviet Union in the war against Japan, and not the explosion of atomic bombs in Hiroshima and Nagasaki, was decisive in convincing the Emperor and military to accept unconditional surrender. Although the dropping of the atomic bomb on Hiroshima had had a significant impact on Hirohito, the Emperor had been especially conscious of the Soviet threat to his power. In February 1945 former Prime Minister Konoe Fumimaro wrote to the Emperor that Japan should not be worried by a defeat by the Anglo-American powers since 'public opinion in America and England has not gone far enough to destroy the *kokutai*'. Instead, Japan should be concerned about 'a Communist revolution that might accompany defeat'. Saving the *kokutai*, argued Konoe, required the Emperor's active intervention to contain the military. The danger of external threat and domestic upheaval significantly shaped the Emperor's ideas, as he manoeuvred until the very last to preserve as much of his authority as possible. On 9 August the Emperor told his closest advisor that because of the Soviet entry into the conflict in Asia 'it is necessary to study and decide on the termination of the war'. As Hasegawa has pointed out, preserving the Emperor's position now involved blaming the military for the war. Fear of a Soviet political role in the post-war occupation of Japan, however, now led much of the military leadership reluctantly to agree to the American government's terms for ending the conflict. On 14 August, the Emperor told the Japanese cabinet of his decision to accept unconditional surrender, and the next day a recording of his surrender speech was played at noon to the Japanese public.

The dropping of the two atomic bombs were war atrocities, committed by a liberal empire and by a President bent on retribution against the Japanese. As Hasegawa and others have argued, the sense of victimization that has accompanied Japanese understandings of the war has also prevented the government from accepting full responsibility for its own actions in the conflict. The destruction of Japan and Germany at the end of the war was brought on by the American and Allied war machines, but, even more, by the Japanese and German leaderships themselves.

3 The Italian Wars

NICOLA LABANCA

Italy at War, and National Stereotypes

On 10 June 1940 Benito Mussolini, the Fascist 'Duce' and Prime Minister, proclaimed in ringing tones before a mass gathering of Italians that Italy was entering the war alongside its ally, National Socialist Germany, against the liberal democracies.

Combatants on land, sea and in the air.

Blackshirts of the revolution and of the legions.

Men and women of Italy, of the Empire and of the kingdom of Albania....

We are taking the field against the plutocratic, reactionary democracies of the west, which have at all times obstructed the forward march, and often undermined the very existence of the Italian people.... A people of forty-five million souls is not truly free unless it has free access to the ocean....

The laws of Fascist morality state that when we have a friend, we march alongside him to the end. This we have done and we shall do with Germany, with her people, with her victorious armed forces.... We raise our voices to salute the Führer, the leader of our great German ally.

Italy, proletarian and Fascist, has risen to its feet for the third time, strong, proud and united as never before.

There is a single watchword, categorical and binding on all.

It is already spreading and setting hearts on fire from the Alps to the Indian Ocean: victory! And victory shall be ours....

This declaration enabled Fascist Italy to escape from an awkward situation. When Germany had launched its war in 1939 Mussolini was unprepared militarily but anxious to declare himself on the side of Hitler's Germany and not of the democracies, and so had declared Italian 'non-belligerence', not neutrality. This had had immediate and unwelcome consequences for him. On the one hand, the fact that he had not immediately entered the war alongside the Reich had renewed the old prejudice about Italy as a country of traitors, who never entered (or finished) a war with their own allies; on the other hand, it revived the stereotypes of Italians failing to fight or, if they did, of being useless or a liability to their ally.

It is possible to ignore stereotypes and prejudices if they are not considered to be the material of history; and yet they are a force in history, even though they are also a threat to historical research. They affected even the Duce, who was always anxious not to be regarded as the ruler of a country of pizza eaters, card sharps, and mandolin players. The blanket bans he imposed on the Italian press, as early as the war in Ethiopia, on publishing innocuous photographs of soldiers playing cards or musical instruments, are still preserved in the archives; for the Duce, Fascist Italy must be the Italy of 'eight million bayonets' and nothing else. Stereotypes and anti-Italian prejudices had an effect not only abroad, among allies and enemies alike, but also within the country and in the mind of its dictator.

The history of the Italian wars, or of Italians at war, between 1939 and 1945 is far more complex than stereotypes or anti-Italian prejudices; and yet such prejudices still survive in the memories of those who took part, in many popular books, and even in some academic studies.

Images or Complex Reality

It cannot be seriously maintained, for example, that Fascist Italy's war was superfluous or a liability for its German ally. The Reich and the German armed forces could not contemplate acting entirely alone. Even if Hitler and the German military command did not have confidence in the effectiveness or capacity of Italian combat forces,

Mussolini and Hitler meet in Munich in 1940 after the Italian declaration of war on Britain and France on 10 June when France was close to defeat.

Berlin needed Rome to contain the British forces in North Africa, and also to provide occupation forces in the Balkans, Russia, and elsewhere.

The enemies of Fascist Italy also sometimes overstated the weakness of Rome as the soft underbelly of the Axis. It is true that Fascist Italy was in the end the first of the Axis powers to withdraw from the war, but it was some time before this happened. In North Africa, too, although the British were well aware of the difficulties and inadequacies of Italian armaments, it took three years for them to beat the Italians (aided by the Germans), and some Italian units fought in a way which took London and Washington by surprise.

Finally and most important, the Second World War in Italy did not end with the Fascist war. Following the collapse of the regime on 25 July 1943, and the subsequent armistice in September later that year, Italy was a divided nation. Hundreds of thousands of soldiers remained under arms with the 'Kingdom of the South', that part of Italy which remained loyal to the monarchy, with a government headed by Marshal Pietro Badoglio under British and American control. The regular combat units of the Kingdom of the South fought under various names: Combat Groups, the First Motorized Group, the Italian Liberation Corps. Equally valuable and necessary to the Anglo-American forces was the logistical and support role played by the Italian Auxiliary Divisions.

Above all, part of the Italian population responded to the call of the Anti-Fascist parties in German-occupied Italy, taking to the mountains or in other ways making life difficult for the German occupiers and their weak Neo-Fascist allies in the Italian Social Republic established under Mussolini's rule in October 1943. Contrary to the myth of Italians as non-fighters, these intrepid and public-spirited Italians waged a resistance war which, with the exception of Yugoslavia, had few equals in Nazi-occupied Europe, fighting for two years in difficult conditions as the retreating German forces committed appalling atrocities and massacres against the civilian population and these so-called 'bandits'. Other Italians from the small Kingdom of the South, under Anglo-American control, fought in the reconstituted Italian armed forces, in principle alongside the resistance although numerous obstacles made this difficult.

It is necessary to explain the image of Italian soldiers throwing down their arms and returning home on hearing the news, on 8 September 1943, that the armistice had been signed; such an image cannot be seen as representative of a people and a country and their participation in the Second World War. By the same token, we can no longer accept the reassuring image of the 'decent Italian' or of 'Italians as decent people' in wartime: during the Fascist war Italian troops, like their German counterparts, were guilty of war crimes linked to the ideology of the regime that had sent them to fight in the African colonies, in the Balkans, and in the Soviet Union. Seventy years after the end of the conflict, the images both of what happened on 8 September 1943 and of 'Italians as decent people' must be fundamentally re-examined.

The Years of 'Peace': From One World War to Another

Mussolini's rhetoric in 1940, while profoundly Fascist, was not entirely without foundation.

Italy was unified as a country only in 1861; it was a young country and was economically backward. Its industrial development is conventionally reckoned to have taken off only at the end of the nineteenth century, and it was not until 1958, on the eve of the 'economic miracle', that industry surpassed agriculture in terms of production. This explains why Italians were both proud and surprised to find themselves among the victors at the end of the First World War.

The Versailles conference of 1919 had to deal with a situation which was very different from that of 1914. Italy was still 'the least of the great powers', but the list of such powers was much shorter following the defeat and disappearance at the end of the war of four empires, those of Russia, the Ottomans, Germany, and Austria. Their disappearance gave Italy a greater status as one of the four victorious powers.

The reality was that liberal Italy had emerged from the world war greatly weakened and divided. As early as 29 October 1922 the king called on 'the knight' Benito Mussolini to form a government ('knight' in this context being used purely as a courtesy title, since the new head of the government was not an aristocrat). On 3 January 1925, the Duce threw off the mask and established a regime which, in domestic Italian politics, was totalitarian, anti-democratic, and destructive of liberty. At the level of international politics, however, the Great War had transformed Italy's role in relation to the other European powers; the years which followed, up to the formation of the 'Four-Power Pact' of 7 June 1933 between France, Great Britain, Germany, and Italy, reflected the greater role played by Rome on the international stage. The revisionist foreign policy of Fascist Italy—anti-pacifist, colonialist, expansionist, and bellicose—can only be understood within this changed strategic framework.

Unfortunately for Mussolini, Italy's international position changed once more in 1933 with the rise to power of Adolf Hitler in Germany, which in itself represented a radical reduction in the country's status. Far from stopping Mussolini's dictatorship in its tracks, this development prompted a further radicalization of the bellicose policy of Fascism.

Radicalization

Early demonstrations of the warlike policy of the regime were the Corfu incident of 31 August–1 September 1923, and the stubborn refusal to return the islands of the Dodecanese, which Italy had occupied in 1912 during the Turkish–Italian war with an undertaking to relinquish them at the conclusion of hostilities, but which it always refused to give up. Another pointer was provided by the substantial colonial campaigns in Somalia and above all in Libya in the 1920s. When Mussolini came to power

Italy's control over these African colonies was effectively confined to the coast; the Fascist regime launched elaborate and ruthless military operations into the interior to bring them fully under its control.

It was, however, the attack on Ethiopia in October 1935 that clearly demonstrated Fascist Italy's intention to defy the League of Nations and the peace settlement established at Versailles, in its quest for international success after Hitler's rise to power in Germany. While it was taken for granted that a modern European state like Italy would overcome a traditional African state like Ethiopia, the campaign nonetheless produced some surprises: international military observers, such as J. F. C. Fuller, were amazed that it could take almost half a million men and seven months of combat in order to win an African war.

Fascist Italy did not stop there. In 1937 it intervened in support of Francisco Franco's coup in Spain, promising to commit 50,000 'volunteers' to help Franco against the democratic republic (although in reality they were conscript troops without Italian uniforms, and as late as spring 1939 they numbered only 28,000), together with 764 aircraft and 5,700 airmen between 1937 and 1939. Italy also launched a series of submarine operations against the British in Spanish Mediterranean waters. More broadly, the war planning of the Italian armed forces had already for some years been based on the supposition of a clash not only with their traditional enemy the French, but also (in the case of the navy) with the Royal Navy. This radicalization in foreign policy was accompanied by a comparable development in internal affairs: autonomously and without any prompting from Germany, the regime set up a system of institutional racism, first in the African colonies in 1937 and then, in 1938, with a policy of anti-Semitic racism in Italy itself.

In short, Fascism was becoming radicalized, both internally and in its external affairs. It lacked the disruptive power of German Nazism because the economic strength and the military readiness of the two countries were so different, but nonetheless Fascist Italy represented a clear threat to the European order by the end of the 1930s.

Preparation for War?

In the second half of the 1930s the threat posed by Fascism was still political and strategic rather than military; but in practical military terms, too, Italy was no longer to be underestimated. France had 86 divisions at its disposal, while Great Britain before the war had just over 300,000 men under arms, of whom more than half were Indian troops needed for the defence of India itself. Against this background the 73 divisions which Fascist Italy declared itself able to deploy could, if ranged alongside the 103 divisions of Hitler's Germany, have altered the military balance of Europe. The military situation reflected what was already apparent at a political level: that while Fascist Italy alone, especially before 1933, did not have the political strength to revise the international settlement established at Versailles, if allied with Germany it was capable of challenging Europe. Neither of the Fascist powers was prepared for a long war, but in a short conflict they could constitute a dangerous threat to the European democracies; and it was clear from the military doctrines of their armed forces—Italy's 'guerra di rapido corso' ('rapid course war') and Germany's *Blitzkrieg*—that this was the kind of war that Rome and Berlin had in mind.

Many observers and advocates of appeasement were prompted to emphasize the weaknesses in the military edifice of Fascism, of which there were many. At the end of the 1930s the armed forces of the regime were severely weakened by the consumption of armaments in the Ethiopian and Spanish wars. The Italian arms industry was not able to provide the Fascist state with the armaments it demanded, and for which in any case the country did not have the necessary resources. The wars in Ethiopia and Spain cost Italy at least 60 billion lire, against a national budget of 20–25 billion lire in the years before 1939, and 42 billion in 1939 itself, the year before Italy entered the world war. This level of expenditure meant that Italian rearmament lost momentum and fell behind schedule.

This weakness was compounded with Mussolini's reluctance to countenance any real co-ordination between the separate armed services. General Pietro Badoglio was the Chief of General Staff, but he did not have sufficient staff to carry out this role, and it was not clear that he would be the supreme military commander in case of war. There was a Supreme Defence Committee, but it met too rarely and it played no part in national military planning. For too long under the Fascist regime the posts of Secretary of State and the Chiefs of Staff of each of the armed services—in other

Italian tanks were poor in quality in comparison with the other major combatants. Here in 1939 Italian tanks take part in a pre-war exercise.

Mussolini with Marshal Pietro Badoglio at the San Bernardo pass in 1940 during the Italian attack on France. Badoglio later replaced Mussolini as Prime Minister in July 1943.

words, the senior political and military positions respectively—were held by the same person, a serving officer, with no political oversight. This meant that each of the armed services made its own preparations for war without necessarily co-ordinating with the others, with consequences made all the more serious because military planning had traditionally not looked much beyond immediate requirements.

Moreover, prevailing over all this was the vagueness and superficiality of Fascism, which for all its rhetoric of technological modernity never gave the country more than a veneer of militarization. It was revealing that, in the age of tanks, bombers, and aircraft carriers, the preferred slogan was that of 'eight million bayonets'.

For all these reasons international observers were sceptical, Italy's German allies were anxious, and the Italian military chiefs were convinced in 1939 that the country's armed forces would not be ready for war until 1942—as the service chiefs told Mussolini, who even wrote as much to Hitler. The chief of army staff reckoned that, of the 73 divisions at his disposal, 19 were ready for action, 32 could optimistically be defined as effective, and the others were simply incomplete, in other words not in a fit state to go to war. And yet everyone underestimated the extent to which, when it came to fighting a war not on its own but in coalition, Fascist Italy could have a significant effect—Mussolini hoped it would be a decisive effect—on the fate of Europe.

All these elements may have been in the Duce's mind when he declared to the Italian people that 'non-belligerence' was at an end and that the Fascist regime was entering the war alongside its National Socialist ally. He had no way of knowing whether the war would be short or long, European or worldwide; still less could he have imagined that he was signing the regime's death warrant, and his own.

The Fascist War: A Gamble

Fascism was not modest in its ambitions; scholars have characterized them as a project, or rather a set of ideas, for a 'New Mediterranean Order', on the analogy of Hitler's dream of a New European Order. The Tripartite Pact of September 1940 between Germany, Italy, and Japan clarified what the three Fascist powers already had in mind, a sharing out of areas of influence between them. Fascist Italy aspired to control the Mediterranean and part of the Balkans (although here it would be competing with Germany) and to play a leading role in Africa and the Middle East.

Mussolini contemplated extending his control to take in Corsica and Tunisia at the expense of France, and also compelling France to accept some adjustments to its frontier with Italy. He planned next to build on the Italian commercial presence in the Balkans, starting with Albania and taking in Croatia and Greece, not to mention Montenegro, and even setting his sights on parts of Turkey. There were also ideas of expanding towards Egypt and the Suez Canal, and more vaguely in the direction of the Middle East. In the case of Spain he considered a possible hegemony rather than conquest, especially after the consolidation of Franco's regime. The combined effect of all these objectives would be to give Italy control over a large part of the Mediterranean and the countries around its shore, at the expense of France and Britain. It was true that there was a source of friction in the Balkans, but all in all the plan was complementary to the Nazi project for continental Europe.

But did Italy have the military strength to carry out such a plan, and did the preparation of its armed forces match these strategic goals? The navy, under Admiral Domenico Cavagnari, was preparing for—or was resigned to—a clash with 'perfidious Albion'; but it lacked both aircraft carriers and radar, and its submarine fleet, although large, was not without problems. The army, under General Alberto Pariani, had planned for a war on two fronts, against France and against Yugoslavia, but it was hoping that these plans would not be put to the test; its doctrine of 'rapid course war' aimed to beat British tanks in North Africa, but even there it had more bayonets than armoured vehicles, and Italian tanks were light and lacked radio communications. The air force, finally, had been the pride of Fascist propaganda and of its chief, Italo Balbo; but it was geared much more to propaganda stunts such as transatlantic flights than to military operations, either strategic bombing as conceived by Giulio Douhet or tactical operations in collaboration with the infantry.

In short, leaving propaganda aside, the clear impression was that the Fascist government's aims were much more ambitious than the military means at its disposal. Above all, were Italians ready to fight? The Fascist regime, especially in the 1930s, had set up courses in military culture in schools, and had made Italian youth take part in military parades. It had increased the fully funded and trained strength of the army to 544,000 men by 1939. It had hugely expanded the military arm of the Fascist party, the so-called Voluntary Militia for National Security (Milizia volontaria di sicurezza nazionale, MVSN). On 1 June 1940 the army numbered 1.1 million men, the navy 170,000, and the air force 100,000. The Fascist militia had 310,000 men, with 40,000 in the blackshirt battalions. But all this amounted to no more than a warlike façade, more rhetorical than effective, rather than a genuinely professional approach to the armed forces. The regular forces could not be given the training they needed because of a lack of modern equipment, because Italy did not have access to sources of oil (fuel being essential for mobile, 'rapid course' warfare), and because of shortfalls in funding. Among the officers, too, many were not equal to the task of achieving the regime's aims.

Finally and perhaps most important, in the late 1930s the regime faced a crisis in its relations with the country as a whole. Fascism lost the support of some sections of the bourgeoisie, and the mass of the population no longer identified with it. It was for this reason that Mussolini did not proclaim a general mobilization in June 1940; he did not want to alarm public opinion or to put its loyalty to the test. The 'eight million bayonets', then, did not exist: just over half this number were called up, a figure much lower than liberal Italy had been able to mobilize for the First World War even though the Italian population was larger in the early 1940s than it had been in 1915–18.

Italian soldiers with their bicycles reviewed by Mussolini in the Val d'Aosta in June 1940 before the assault on southern France.

Attack and Occupation

The months following September 1939 were a period of frantic activity by the regime. It would be many months if not years before Italy had armed forces ready for a prolonged general war; but Mussolini's hope was for a quick war. Many Italians, and some subsequent historians, have regretted his entry into the war in 1940, but it would be more accurate to describe it, in the words of the historian Giorgio Rochat, as an 'enforced intervention'. If Mussolini wanted to preserve any degree of prestige, if Fascist ideology had any substance, if the alliance with Germany was not to be renounced, he had no choice but to enter the war.

The first manoeuvre was the attack on France, launched on 21 June 1940. By the time Italian troops crossed the frontier the French government had already left Paris (10 June) and had sought an armistice with Berlin (17 June). The Italians were surprised to encounter resistance from French forces; moreover, they found themselves facing a campaign for which they were unprepared. Italian planning had long envisaged a defensive campaign in the Alps, but while they were able to advance along the coast, fighting was difficult in the mountains, and was not helped by the failure to co-ordinate air attacks, which were meant to bomb the French defences, with troops on the ground. The only definitive result of the action was the seizure of Corsica.

Italian troops riding into battle on their bicycles during the brief summer campaign against France in which the Italian army was pinned down on the French frontier by firm defence.

Unfortunately for Mussolini, the war did not end in the summer of 1940. The Italian intervention against a France which was already on its knees allowed Mussolini to impose some conditions on France and to occupy a small part of its territory. It did not give Italy a place at any European peace conference, since no such conference took place; rather it plunged the country into a world war which exposed its lack of military preparation.

In France, meanwhile, the Italian forces were transformed into an army of occupation; by November 1942 their numbers in the south of France had increased from a few thousand men to nearly 150,000, with an additional 80,000 in Corsica. To this extent they provided support for Germany, which was able to concentrate on occupying the larger and richer northern part of France. The Fascist regime tried to extract resources and industrial production from the zone which it occupied, but it did not always do so in a co-ordinated or effective way. Corsica, however, was subjected to a harsh occupation intended to ensure that Italy kept control of an island of strategic importance for the control of the Mediterranean and the defence of the Italian mainland, and to guard against the danger of local resistance. The seizure and occupation of France, therefore, immediately tied up substantial Italian forces, although the French front always remained a secondary one.

Albania, Greece, and the Balkans

Altogether more decisive for Italy was the war on the Balkan front, where the Fascist government had been intriguing for decades, penetrating Croat, Serb, and Albanian political movements. It is too often forgotten that Italy invaded Albania as early as May 1939, six months before the German invasion of Poland.

Following his intervention in France, and while the news from the African fronts (as we will see later) was not good, Mussolini decided to invade Greece. The date chosen was 28 October 1940, the anniversary of the Fascist March on Rome in 1922. The army chiefs, including Badoglio (who was dismissed), opposed the invasion but accepted the Duce's political decision. The invasion on 28 October soon proved to be a disaster, with the Italian army incapable of breaking through the Greek army's resistance despite continuous reinforcements of men. The Italians were once again defeated by mountain warfare and its logistical problems; the high number of frostbite victims tells its own story. The stalemate was broken only on 6 April 1941, when German and Bulgarian forces attacked Yugoslavia and Greece to protect their rear for the projected Axis attack on the Soviet Union; in the face of this onslaught, the Greek forces surrendered or withdrew to Crete, and Germany and Italy then divided the occupation of the Balkans between them.

The few months of Italy's substantially failed conquest of Greece cannot, however, erase the memory of the long years of Italian occupation in the Balkans. From the spring of 1941 to the summer of 1943 Italian forces played a valuable role for Berlin, committing 30–35 of their 65 available divisions to the occupation of the Balkan lands. Some areas were directly annexed to Italy: Slovenia, the Dalmatian coast,

Albania, and Kosovo. Others were controlled in the face of strong Anti-Fascist resistance; this was the case in Montenegro and Greece. The Germans retained a small zone of control, comprising part of Slovenia, Serbia, Thessalonica, and Crete, while the rest was under the rule of the Axis allies Croatia, Bulgaria, and Hungary. It is hard to see this situation remaining acceptable to Berlin and Rome if they had won the war, but these were nonetheless important military gains by the Fascist allies—albeit as occupying forces rather than as conquerors.

The Italian occupying force of 600,000–650,000 men was a heavy burden on these territories, not least because the land was poor and the occupiers were disorganized. It was difficult for the occupiers as well because they had to contend with the Yugoslav resistance movements, which were among the strongest in Nazi-occupied Europe. The Italian command did occasionally assert its independence, as when the Nazi authorities asked for Jews to be rounded up: Italy failed to comply, or complied only belatedly, more as an assertion of some degree of national autonomy than to defend Jewish lives. The Italian occupiers made extensive use of internment camps, where living conditions were extremely harsh. Aspects of this occupation still remain to be studied, but it is clear that the image of 'Italians as decent people'—in contrast to the German occupiers—cannot be sustained.

The Collapse of the Empire

In the winter of 1940–1, at the same time as Italy was failing to achieve a break-through in Greece, another defeat which was in the last resort inevitable was unfolding in East Africa.

In 1935–6 a concentrated propaganda campaign had underpinned Fascist aggression against Ethiopia, and since then a vague but ambitious concept of the Empire had been promoted in Italy. The conquest of Ethiopia, a country which was both very large (at more than a million square kilometres, it was almost four times the size of Italy) and very rich (albeit difficult to exploit), made Italy no longer just a kingdom but an Empire—a status confirmed by the occupation of Albania. All Italians, Fascism proclaimed, should now think 'at the level of the Empire'; they should consider themselves 'empire-builders'. It was the Italian Empire that had declared war on the democracies in June 1940.

In 1940–1 the reality did not appear to bear out this propaganda. After the meagre results in France and the frustration of Italian plans in Greece, between January and May 1941 Italy lost its empire in East Africa. The Italian forces there were not large—they numbered 180,000 in June 1940—and consisted mainly of colonial troops; but they collapsed under the assault of British Commonwealth forces who were far fewer in number but more up-to-date. The last pockets of Italian resistance held out until November, when their position was hopeless, but the empire was effectively lost by the spring of 1941. The regime did its best through censorship to limit the negative effect of the loss of East Africa on public opinion, and the strategic situation meant that Rome was unable to provide support for its troops in the field, who were

A primitive experimental Italian tank at Gondar in Italian East Africa in 1940. The East African Empire was quickly lost to a British Commonwealth invasion.

therefore left on their own. But the defeat of 1940–1 nonetheless sounded a clear alarm bell on the military effectiveness of Italian units and their commanders.

It could not be said that this strategic defeat was unforeseen, for any attempt to resupply Italian East Africa from Italy itself was blocked by the British stranglehold on the Suez Canal. But its impact on popular opinion in Italy was much greater than has generally been thought. What was more, the loss of Italian East Africa meant that for the first time Italian soldiers had the demoralizing experience of being taken prisoner.

A Central Front

East Africa was ultimately a side-show; what made the collapse there much more serious for the Fascist regime was the lack of success on the Mediterranean and North African fronts. North Africa should, in any case, have been the real focus of Italy's war, if Fascism was serious about putting into practice its project for a New Mediterranean Order. There were grounds for hope in Rome, since after December 1941 the United Kingdom was committed in theatres ranging from the Middle East to Japan, and so could send only limited reinforcements to its forces in Egypt. Italian success in the Mediterranean and North Africa would mean controlling the sea communications between Italy and Libya and breaking through the defence of Egypt, opening the way to Alexandria and the Suez Canal.

Italy was heavily committed on this front. In the army alone, the 90,000 soldiers deployed there in 1939 had grown to 170,000 in 1940, to fall to around 140,000 at the time of El Alamein. To these should be added the men from the other armed forces, so that the navy had to provision a force of around 200,000 men, not counting the Germans. The 'battle of the convoys' in the stretch of sea between Sicily and Libya was one which may have seemed to promise little military glory, but was strategically vital. The number of convoys increased from around 90 in 1940 to 350 in 1941, 550 in 1942, and 450 in the winter and spring of 1943. The great majority of convoys got through, but the level of materials lost increased from 7 per cent to 30 per cent, and losses of vital fuel supplies grew from 6 per cent to 71 per cent.

The Italian navy had already suffered several humiliating defeats: at Punta Stilo on 9 July and Capo Spada on 19 July 1940, at Taranto on 11–12 November 1940, Capo Teulada on 27 November, and Capo Matapan on 27–29 March 1941. It tended, nonetheless, to exercise great caution in deploying its capital ships, since it knew that the state of Italian industry meant that they could not be replaced. Moreover, the navy lacked aircraft carriers, its ships did not have radar, and its submarines had neither ASDIC nor sonar. Defending communications with Libya in the 'battle of the convoys' was already a heavy burden on its resources. What was more, the British intelligence services began decrypting Italian messages at an early stage of the conflict; indeed the impact of intelligence on the Italian war can hardly be overstated.

The army was in any case unprepared for fighting a modern desert war, the doctrine of 'rapid course war' notwithstanding. Its tanks were too few, too light, and had inadequate firepower, and the infantry did not have the training, the armaments or the tactics for fighting in such a theatre. Their commanders learnt quickly, and some of them put what they had learnt into practice, as was demonstrated by the successes in the spring advance towards Sollum and above all by the advances the following year towards El Alamein; not all the successes before the defeat of 1942 were achieved by the Germans. But the fact was that the Italian troops were superior only in numbers. When the Germans under Erwin Rommel arrived in February 1941, more or less at the insistence of Hitler despite Mussolini's wish for the war in North Africa to be exclusively Italian, the mood in the ranks changed. The Italian contribution to the war, however, was subordinate to that of Germany; nor was the course of the campaign immediately reversed, not least because of the difficulty of supporting the Italian and German troops fighting in North Africa. The risks of crossing the Mediterranean with Malta solidly in British hands remained high. On the other hand, despite these Italian weaknesses, any grounds for excessive optimism on the British side should not be overstated: it took more than three years for Britain to overcome the Italian and German resistance in Egypt and Libya.

Thus the front in the Italian, German, and British fighting moved back and forth three times. The Italians initially reached Sidi Barrani on 13 September 1940, then

Italian soldiers in North Africa near the Egyptian town of El Alamein in 1941. This was later the site of a heavy Axis defeat in November 1942.

German Field Marshal Erwin Rommel discusses operations with Italian commanders during the Axis campaign to capture Egypt and drive on to the Suez Canal. Though larger in numbers, the Italian army now played a secondary role to the Germans.

British Commonwealth prisoners of war in Italian North Africa in 1941. Thousands were sent on to camps in Italy.

were driven back by the British to El Agheila on 9–12 December. The Italians and Germans responded with an advance as far as Sollum (23 March–15 April 1941), but the British counter-attacked once more from Egypt, reaching Agedabia and El Agheila (18 November–31 December). The Italo-German response penetrated as far as El Alamein (21 January–30 June 1942) and Alam El Halfa (30 August–5 September), then once again to El Alamein (23 October–4 November). At this point, however, the Commonwealth forces broke through in an unstoppable advance from Sidi Barrani to Tobruk and Benghazi, and from Sirte to Tripoli and on to the Tunisian border (9 November 1942–4 February 1943). From here the Italian and German forces, while continuing to fight a tough rearguard action, were forced to surrender in Tunisia on 13 May. Clearly, then, it was a protracted campaign, and North Africa was by no means as easy for the British as East Africa had been.

It was the defeat on the North African front that sealed the fate of Italy's war and of the Fascist regime, not only because of the huge losses in terms of personnel—by the end of the war more than 400,000 Italian prisoners were in British hands, a large part of them captured in the battles in East and North Africa—but also because defeat on this front marked the failure of the whole Fascist programme.

From Parallel War to Subaltern War: Russia

Long before the final collapse, however, a fundamental change had transformed the strategic framework of Italy's war. In June 1940 it was still possible for Mussolini to hope that, in a short-lived conflict, an Italian 'parallel war'—parallel, that is, with the

German war—would suffice to give Italy a place at the table at the peace negotiations. The war, however, became more and more protracted. Hitler's Germany was expanding but was not achieving complete victory, either against British resistance in the west or against the Soviet Union in the east. On the contrary, decisions taken in Berlin and Tokyo prompted the entry into the war, on 7 December 1941, of the United States of America, the greatest industrial and financial power of the time. In these same months, as we have seen, the experience of the Italian armed forces, despite some moments of valour, was substantially one of failure, in Greece and in East and North Africa. Added to this, the Italian peninsula, with its lack of raw materials and strategic needs—coal, petroleum, rubber—was becoming more and more dependent on its more powerful German ally. For all these reasons, Mussolini's was increasingly what Giorgio Rochat has called a 'subaltern war':

The war of 1941–43 can be described as a 'subaltern war' because it was totally dependent on German decisions. In reality Italy's war was already subordinate to Germany's in 1940, and the hope of victory was dependent on the success of German arms; but the 'parallel war' left a margin—or rather an illusion—of autonomy which was lost in the winter defeats [of 1941].

The clearest and most dramatic example of Fascism's subordinate war was its participation in the German attack on the Soviet Union.

Berlin had kept Rome completely in the dark about its plans for an attack on Russia, and the Germans did not want commanders or troops in whom they had no confidence. Mussolini did not intend the Fascist role in the war to be a subordinate one, as is clear from his insistence on having a significant Italian presence in the eastern campaign; he succeeded in sending first an armoured corps of three divisions (62,000 men) and then an army of more than six divisions (170,000 men), and the military chiefs provided them with the best equipment at their disposal. The Italian troops did not always take part in the conquest of new territory, but rather fulfilled a valuable role for the Germans in defending and occupying the territory overrun by German forces, allowing them to be concentrated on the front line.

Even the best equipment at the Italian commanders' disposal was not, however, enough to compensate for such serious errors as deploying the Alpine troops, trained for mountain warfare, to fight on the Russian plains, or the failure to provide them with adequate motorized transport, compelling them to exhausting deployments on foot. Nor did it suffice to withstand, in the winter of 1942–3, the powerful Soviet offensive of 'Operation Little Saturn' and the later offensive of Ostrogorsk-Rossosk.

The Italian troops were thus condemned to a disastrous retreat for which they were completely unprepared, and in which they had very little help from their German allies, who were concerned almost exclusively for themselves. Italian losses were huge: of 150,000 men, 85,000 were missing and 27,000 wounded. The image of the retreat from Russia had a devastating effect on support for the regime; moreover a large proportion of Italian prisoners died in forced marches or subsequently in Russian camps.

Italian forces on the eastern front in Russia. Mussolini decided in 1941 to send an expeditionary force but it took catastrophic losses and was poorly equipped.

Disengagements

The overall position of Fascist Italy in the Second World War in the early months of 1943 was, in short, extremely critical on all fronts: retreating in disarray from Russia and North Africa, the empire in East Africa already lost, and reduced to the role of an occupying force in France and the Balkans. In the latter, moreover, the Yugoslav resistance had worn down the Italian units and had forced them to engage in a harsh counter-insurgency campaign. It is hardly surprising, therefore, that the position of the regime at home was increasingly weak.

The king, who for years had put his faith in Mussolini as the 'man of destiny', feared that the Duce was dragging the country and the monarchy itself into the abyss. The military chiefs began finally to despair of the succession of defeats, the consequence of both the armed forces' lack of preparation for a long war fought on so many fronts, and of the dispersal of their forces among Mussolini's many war aims. Popular opinion, despite the stifling effect of the dictatorship and war censorship, was increasingly alienated from the regime; in March–April 1943 a major workers' strike paralysed the big factories in the north of the country, in defiance of the wartime atmosphere and of Fascism. Many of the industrialists themselves, in fact, were severing their ties to the regime—a process made easier by the fact that Mussolini had not instituted a general industrial mobilization, just as he had not introduced general conscription, in marked contrast to the liberal ruling class in 1915–18. Thus alongside the principled Anti-Fascism of the pre-war years there now grew up a kind of wartime Anti-Fascism, fed by the news of defeats which succeeded in filtering through despite official propaganda.

What was more, in the Second World War the field of combat was not confined to soldiers; the development of aerial warfare meant that the civilian population came directly under fire. It is true that in the early years of the war Anglo-American bombing was not especially intense and did not affect the whole country; bombers flying from the British Isles could only strike the industrial cities of the north, but the southern ports such as Naples could only be bombed by planes from Egypt, Malta, the Middle East, and Cyprus. It was only in the spring and summer of 1943 when the Italians had been driven out of Libya that the rest of the Italian peninsula came within easy reach of Anglo-American planes. But despite the technical difficulties facing the British and Americans, what made a strong impression on the Italian population was the complete failure of the regime's air force and of its anti-aircraft defences, which were unable to provide any significant defence against attack from the air—and this after years of propaganda extolling Fascist Italy's air power. Excessive faith in the air force's offensive capacity, a central tenet of Douhet's theories, had led Rome to underestimate the need for anti-aircraft defences.

Taken together, therefore, the inadequacy of government assistance on the home front, the absence of a general mobilization, the crumbling morale in the Fascist party and in the regime, the concern of families for the fate of their fighting men, the news received from prisoners of war: all these demolished the Fascist regime from within, at the same time as its Anglo-American and Soviet adversaries were combating it militarily. In particular, the anxiety felt by families whose loved ones were prisoners of war should not be underestimated; around 700,000 men were already held prisoner by this time, over five continents: Asia (India), Africa (Kenya, South Africa, Egypt), Australia, the Americas (the USA), and Europe (Great Britain, the Soviet Union).

Not surprisingly, the Anti-Fascists who had been exiled abroad since Mussolini's rise to power, or who had faced great difficulties at home at the time of the success (albeit short-lived) of the Ethiopian war, now re-emerged: Communists, socialists, the few but influential militants of the 'Action Party' (Partito d'azione, a left-wing group embodying the principles of the pre-war 'Justice and Freedom' movement), Catholics, and also moderate liberals and conservatives, were all gathering strength. Wartime Anti-Fascism was now added to all these.

Downfall

As internal support for the regime crumbled, the Anglo-American pressure continued unabated. The Italian units on the outlying islands of Pantelleria and Lampedusa surrendered on 11–12 June, and American and British units landed in Sicily on 9 July. The invasion force was substantial: the initial expeditionary force was made up of three British, three American, and one Canadian division, totalling around 160,000 men, but within a few weeks this had grown to just under half a million. Since there was no way of seeing how they could be repulsed, Mussolini and the rest of the country watched, with contrasting emotions, the approaching end of the regime.

As the military situation developed, the plotting and fragmentation of the regime intensified. Some elements at the top of the Fascist party nurtured the illusion of a Fascism without Mussolini. Circles within the armed forces contemplated seizing power and ridding themselves of the dictator who had led them into so many humiliating defeats, or at least supporting his opponents. Some leaders of industry signalled unequivocally that they would be open to support the clandestine Anti-Fascist movement. At the centre of all these intrigues was King Victor Emmanuel III, who was anxious to save the monarchy and the country from ruin or at least to limit the damage.

At the same time, however, Germany acted, as much for its own defence as for that of its ally, and this was to be an important element in the years that followed. An Anglo-American conquest of Italy, quite apart from the enormous emotional impact it would have on the war in Europe, would leave German cities even more at the mercy of enemy air attacks, which were already inflicting heavy losses on the civilian population in the Ruhr-Rhineland and in Hamburg. Already in the spring of 1943, therefore, Germany had implemented Operation Alaric (an ominous name from

Italian soldiers and civilians in the Italian-occupied Balkans found themselves prisoners of the German army following the Italian armistice on 8 September 1943. Thousands were killed or died later in labour camps in Germany.

Italy's point of view, later renamed Operation Axis) to increase the presence of its troops in Italy, so that they would be ready to take over strategic points in the country, if necessary against the opposition of their ally, whom they evidently no longer trusted.

It was this complex web of secret activity, while Italian soldiers were still fighting and dying, that led to the overthrow of Fascism after more than twenty years in power. In the night of 24–25 July 1943 the Duce was outvoted in the Fascist Grand Council, the supreme body of the Fascist Party, and on the afternoon of the 25th the king had Mussolini arrested by the military police and replaced him with a government led by General Pietro Badoglio. The author of the military campaign of Vittorio Veneto in 1918 (but who had shared some responsibility for the defeat of Caporetto in autumn 1917), of the colonial campaigns of reconquest in Libya in the 1920s and of the war in Ethiopia, Badoglio had been Chief of the General Staff until his dismissal for his opposition to the war in Greece. The armed forces now hoped to guide a defeated Italy in the transition from Fascism to post-Fascism.

Forty-Five Difficult Days

This was the beginning of one of the most contested and difficult phases of Italy's war.

The armed forces had undoubtedly been a source of strength in the change of regime that the country was undergoing. But in July 1943 the army had perhaps 3 million men (in addition to 500,000 new conscripts) still under arms in Europe, fighting alongside their German 'allies'; 700,000 were prisoners of war; and there were perhaps as many as 2½ million in Italy itself, either in training, regrouping after the defeats in North Africa, or retained to maintain public order in the dying days of the regime. An immediate change of sides by the new government could have put many lives at risk. Above all, from the point of view of the forces and the monarchy, it would have given enormous political weight to the Anti-Fascists, at the expense of the military and the royal court. It was clear in the days immediately after 25 July that the country had no desire for war; cities up and down the country were flooded with spontaneous popular demonstrations celebrating the fall of Fascism, tearing down the symbols of the regime from public buildings, and rejoicing at what they wrongly believed to be the end of the war.

For all these reasons, the king and Badoglio declared that 'the war continues' and Italian forces were ordered to continue combat against Britain and the United States. In reality, secret contacts were made to negotiate an armistice, and on 6 September an order was prepared instructing the forces to fight against the Germans. But the public position taken by the king and the military chiefs had the surprising effect of earning simultaneously the distrust of the country at large because of the continuation of the war; the suspicions of the Anti-Fascists because they did not see Badoglio as a reliable supporter; the low opinion of Hitler and the German forces because everything led them to expect an imminent 'betrayal'; the discomfort of the armed forces because no clear orders were given (such as an order for the forces fighting abroad to return home); and the distrust of their Anglo-American adversaries because the new government was slow to make its position clear.

This period of uncertainty lasted exactly forty-five days: until, that is, General Eisenhower announced on the radio on 8 September 1943 that Italy had signed an armistice with the Allies. The announcement was made in breach of an agreement with Badoglio, who wanted the news to be published several days later, and was followed after a few hours by an embarrassed radio statement from Badoglio himself. On the same day the king, the court, and the senior armed service chiefs abandoned Rome, the national capital, for a capital in the south—to maintain institutional continuity, it was claimed; to save their own skins by leaving the country to its fate, said their critics. The armistice changed Italy's status from that of an enemy country to a 'co-belligerent', a novel and ambiguous term used by the British and Americans and by Italians in the Kingdom of the South in the vain attempt to redefine themselves as allies instead of enemies.

The total secrecy surrounding the process of detaching the king and Badoglio's supreme command from the German alliance, and the accompanying lack of any orders to the troops in the field or within the country, left the Italian forces at best to follow the dictates of their own conscience. No serious orders or guidance on how to behave were given to commanders or officers, who were left not knowing what to say to their troops or to the country. Italy descended into chaos. The German Operation Alaric, in contrast, provided detailed instructions on what to do in such circumstances, and German units immediately moved onto the attack: arms and strategic positions were to be seized, 'traitors' disarmed and arrested, and Italian soldiers who attempted armed resistance were to be shot.

Some Italian units did not disband, and responded with armed resistance to German attacks: this happened at Porta San Paolo in Rome, in Piombino on the Tuscan coast, and on the Greek island of Cefalonia. In the latter, the strategic importance of controlling the island, the armed reaction of the Italian troops, and the imbalance between the weak German garrison and the substantial presence of the Italian Acqui division, prompted the Germans on 23–28 September 1943 to disarm the Italians and kill several thousand of them in cold blood. (Recent research has questioned the figure of 9,500 traditionally given for this massacre, but has confirmed that at least 2,000 soldiers were shot after they had surrendered and been taken prisoner following several days of fighting; a further 3,000 perished in the wreck of a ship intended to take them to the Greek mainland, on which they had been crowded without any possibility of escape.) Other units disbanded themselves, with officers and men evading arrest by the Germans; some of these attempted to return home, while others took to the mountains and joined those who had obtained or seized arms in the first groups of the Anti-Fascist resistance. Others again, especially those fighting abroad who had no means of escape, were disarmed by the Germans and taken prisoner; a few of those in the Balkans joined the Yugoslav resistance against which they had previously been fighting. More than a million men were disarmed in the space of a few days.

A German tank and Waffen-SS soldiers stand guard outside the cathedral of Milan in autumn 1943 when Germany occupied northern and central Italy following the Italian armistice.

Meanwhile, four days after 8 September a German parachute group rescued Benito Mussolini from his imprisonment at Campo Imperatore, in the Gran Sasso massif in the Abruzzi, and took him to Munich and then to Hitler's Wolf's Lair at Rastenburg in East Prussia. On 23 September, while Rome was still unoccupied, a Neo-Fascist Italian Social Republic was set up at Salò on Lake Garda, with Mussolini as its head, in opposition to the king and Badoglio.

The establishment of the new regime was both the last action of the Fascist war and a clear signal that the transition away from Fascism would not be purely political but would involve a military confrontation between Neo-Fascists on the one hand, and on the other the monarchy, the government in the south, and Anti-Fascists of all kinds. The presence of German troops on Italian soil, moreover, made it clear that the country would become a battleground.

As Italy suffered the humiliation of occupation, division, and civil war, the Italian wars continued.

The War of Liberation: From the South

At the end of September 1943 Italy was a country divided in two, with what remained of the Kingdom of Italy, the king, Badoglio, and the military chiefs in the south, and Mussolini and the Italian Social Republic (RSI) in the north. But real power lay in the hands of the Anglo-American command in the south, and of the forces of the Reich in the north; the Italian unity which had been achieved in the Risorgimento eighty years earlier appeared to be at an end. There now began a period of civil war, with Italians divided, in the words of Claudio Pavone, between two occupations (the Allies and Germany) and three governments (a kingdom in the south, a collaborationist republic in the north, and a clandestine Anti-Fascist resistance in the north, close to the government in the south).

It would be mistaken, however, to claim that Italians no longer fought after 8 September. Clearly conditions were such that it was no longer possible to form large armies; it should be borne in mind that 1.3 million former combatants were now prisoners of war. But for many Italians the war went on, in the war of liberation from Nazi and Fascist occupation, which was a regular war as well as a guerrilla campaign.

The regular war continued for the units that fought for the Kingdom of the South, authorized by the Allied Military Government of Italy (AMGOT) and the Military Mission Italian Army (MMIA), whose numbers were initially small but steadily increased. At first these included only a few hundred Italians, in the 'First Motorized Group' set up on 26 September 1943, then six thousand in the 'Italian Liberation Corps' (22 March 1944), eventually developing into the five divisions, totalling

Prince Umberto, heir to the Italian throne, together with Italian soldiers now serving in 1945 with Allied forces against their former German ally.

Italian auxiliary labour helping the Allied forces in 1944. The Allied armies relied on tens of thousands of Italians to provide supporting services for the fighting front.

50,000 men, of the 'Combat Groups' (31 July 1944). The war continued, too, for the Italians enlisted as Auxiliary Troops, by the end of the war numbering 195,000 men, who were much sought after by British and American commanders as they enabled them to concentrate their own forces on the Italian campaign while leaving more menial tasks to the Italian auxiliaries; it was no coincidence that the MMIA was opposed to the conversion of the auxiliary troops into combat units.

It would be wrong to underrate the importance of the role played by these regular troops, on whom the Kingdom of the South depended to strengthen its legitimacy as a co-belligerent. They were often inadequately equipped and armed, were poorly motivated, had been too long under arms, and were commanded by officers who had not always grasped the profound transformation that the country was undergoing. When they did not desert, however, they fought with conviction for the liberation of their country.

The war continued, too, for the civilian population—in the north, clearly, but in the rest of the country as well. As Italy was progressively liberated by British and American troops, by the regular forces of the Kingdom of the South and, from Rome northwards, by the small but determined and significant forces of the Anti-Fascist resistance, liberation was accompanied by the experience of peace—though not entirely. Many families still lived with the anxiety of having men under arms or as prisoners. The resumption of normal life was beset with difficulties in a country that had gone through the turmoil of war and had been bombed and mined. The civilian population still bore the wounds of total war, such as the communities which had been the victims of atrocities and massacres committed by the retreating German forces. There were cases where even the British, French, and American forces had committed acts of violence against the population, including rape and a range of other crimes; these were clearly not on a comparable scale to the Nazi and Fascist atrocities, but it was disturbing that these crimes were committed by 'liberators' who were supposedly fighting for higher values of civilization and democracy.

The war, in short, continued, and the Italian campaign appeared to run into the ground. How was it that such a powerful military force, which had defeated the Fascist regime, was not able to liberate the Italian peninsula? Technical factors—the difficulty of making progress over the rugged mountainous terrain of the Apennines, or the harsh winter of 1943–4—are a valid but not a sufficient explanation. The fact is that once the strategic goal of eliminating Germany's strongest ally from the war had been achieved, the Italian campaign was no longer of primary strategic importance for the Allies, especially after the fall of Rome on 4 June 1944, the landings in Provence on 15 August, and the earlier Normandy landings on 6 June. From the point of view of Washington and London, it was enough that a few German divisions were tied down in Italy; the final liberation of the country was no longer their chief problem but a

The United States Fifth Army enters Rome on 4 June 1944, seen here by the Colosseum in the city centre.

largely Italian concern, for the government in the south and the Anti-Fascist resistance in the centre and the north.

Resistance

The genuinely new element in the Italian wars between 1943 and 1945 was not the regular forces fielded by the Kingdom of the South alongside its new 'allies', important though they were; much less was it the smaller and badly led forces of Mussolini's Italian Social Republic (RSI), discussed below. What was truly new were the hundreds of thousands of Italians, men and women alike, who took up arms against the German invaders and their Neo-Fascist collaborators.

Anti-Fascist resistance movements arose throughout Nazi-occupied Europe, in varying forms and with varying results; but nowhere else in Europe, with the exception of Yugoslavia and the occupied part of the Soviet Union, was the resistance as strong and as militarily effective as in Italy. The Italian resistance owed its strength partly to the support of the Kingdom of the South and especially of the Allies, who launched missions in its support and provided it with arms and strategic direction. Many of the Italian soldiers disbanded on 8 September, and many other young men, who were unwilling to comply with the compulsory conscription introduced by the RSI, took to the mountains and boosted its numbers. But there is no doubt that the main credit for organizing the resistance, in the mountains and the cities alike, went to the Anti-Fascist parties which had re-emerged in 1940–3 after twenty years of repression by the Fascist regime had failed to destroy them. The majority of partisans belonged to military formations affiliated to the political parties of the left. But the political strength of the Italian resistance was ultimately due to its success in bringing together all the opponents of Fascism and creating the greatest possible degree of unity among them, from the most radical (Communists, socialists, the Action Party) to the most moderate (Catholics, liberals, conservatives), who were all united in opposing, in different ways, the RSI and the return of Fascism.

It is always difficult to put a figure on the size of the resistance forces, not least because larger or smaller figures were given at different times in the post-war period. In Italy after 1945, those recognized as partisan combatants ('partigiani combattenti') numbered 185,000, and active supporters ('patrioti') 115,000; casualties were put at 28,000 fallen and 21,000 wounded or disabled. These figures, while they may not be precise, indicate the scale of those involved—a minority, of course, but substantial nonetheless. The number of partisan bands and their local territorial roots help to explain how the resistance war in Italy was not simply one of sabotage and ambushes but of full-scale pitched battles. There were even fully developed, if short-lived, partisan republics, often in peripheral areas, where the resistance administered territory that it had liberated. The military and political strength of Anti-Fascism was evident in the last days of the Nazi occupation, in the spring of 1945 in the north (but as early as summer 1944 in Florence), when the resistance launched a full-scale insurrection in cities still occupied by the Nazis, before Allied forces arrived in

Thousands of Italians died in the last weeks of the war and the first weeks of peace as a result of the final fierce armed struggle between partisans and Fascist collaborators.

strength. The decisive role played by resistance forces in the liberation of cities such as Milan, Turin, and Genoa, and their independent installation of their own men in the main civic offices (such as mayor and prefect) before British and American troops arrived, were signals by the Italian Anti-Fascists that the country which Fascism had led to defeat and division was not wholly reliant on external help as it rose from the ruins.

Clearly the Italian resistance could not have liberated the country on its own, and equally clearly the support of the Allies was critical in maintaining it. There were disappointments, such as the Allied 'Alexander communiqué' of 13 November 1944 inviting the partisans to stop fighting, if not actually to disarm, or the demobilization of the partisan bands, prematurely in the view of the partisans themselves, once hostilities against the German enemy were at an end. But their achievements remained—militarily in their role in wearing down the occupying forces, and politic-ally in their identification of a new local governing class who could be called on to replace the Fascists and Neo-Fascists.

The unusual scale of the Italian partisan resistance in Europe has led recent historians to extend its definition to include not just the Italians who engaged in guerrilla warfare (the *maquis*) but also the regular soldiers of the Kingdom of the South, the troops abroad (especially in the Balkans) disbanded on 8 September who joined the forces fighting against Nazism, the Italian Military Internees who did not rally to the RSI (of whom more below), and in general all those in the population who

102 *Nicola Labanca*

impeded, obstructed, or opposed Nazism and Fascism, by civil and unarmed resistance as well as by taking up arms.

This broader definition clearly means that the term 'resistance' loses the military and combat role traditionally associated with it; on the other hand it does justice to the struggle against Fascism which, while not universal, was certainly very widespread and deep-rooted in Italy.

In the North

What of the forces opposing the resistance and the Allied armies? The German divisions commanded first by Field Marshal Albert Kesselring and then by General Heinrich von Vietinghoff were very substantial, deployed both in fighting on the front and for internal security. They increased from just over 200,000 in the summer of 1943 to over 440,000 by the spring of 1945, an indication of the fierceness of the fighting against the Allies and the Italian Anti-Fascist resistance which obliged the Germans to occupy the country.

No occupying power can survive without collaborators, and the collaboration of the Salò republic also extended to the military sphere. Unfortunately for Mussolini and his Minister of Defence, Rodolfo Graziani, the number and effectiveness of the RSI's military units were somewhat deficient. Official publications spoke of 15,000 officers and 239,000 men, not including conscripts; in addition there were 140,000

A reprisal against anti-Fascist resistance in 1944. Resisters were victimized by the German occupiers and by Italians still loyal to Mussolini's Italian Social Republic.

men in the 'National Republican Guard' (GNR), a kind of police force. But these were propaganda figures; in September 1944 the GNR had fewer than 50,000 men, untrained and badly led. The Italian forces of the Neo-Fascist RSI were used primarily for internal security, since the German commanders had no confidence in them as fighters on the front.

The troops of the RSI were thus left to maintain public order behind the front line, and to carry out the dirty work against the resistance. Moreover, Graziani never managed to impose order on the different components of the RSI's 'army'—small regular units which were inadequately armed and trained, a chaotic collection of fanatical Neo-Fascist gangs committed to counter-insurgency, and the 'black brigades', a politicized military force of 30,000 men.

An indication of the lack of support for the RSI among the population of central and northern Italy is given by the fact that the attempt to impose conscription in the territory it controlled, even with the threat that those evading the draft would be shot, may well have succeeded in driving more young men into the mountains to join the resistance than into its own ranks.

Anomalous Prisoners: The Italian Military Internees

Another indicator of the Italians' marked lack of support for the occupying German troops or for the RSI is the history, still hardly known outside Italy, of the Italian Military Internees or IMIs. It will be recalled that more than a million Italian soldiers were disarmed by the Germans on 8 September 1943. Of these, perhaps 200,000 eluded capture, and some 94,000 transferred from the ranks of the militia to units of the RSI. Approximately 750,000 were sent to prison camps. It was, however, embarrassing for the Reich to refer to these Italians as prisoners, especially once the RSI had been set up with Mussolini reinstated as its head; they were therefore designated 'Italian Military Internees', a title which had the added advantage for Berlin of removing them from the oversight of the International Committee of the Red Cross. Hitler and Mussolini offered these IMIs the opportunity to return to Italy if they would support the RSI and join its armed forces. This offer was reinforced by the extremely harsh conditions in the prison camps, reflected in the fact that some 40,000 IMIs perished in them before the end of the war.

It is a fact of primary importance for the military and political history of these years that the overwhelming majority of IMIs refused to collaborate with Nazism and Neo-Fascism, preferring to remain as forced labourers in the camps rather than joining the RSI. Perhaps as many as 110,000 did accept the offer, though some of these took to the mountains to join the resistance once they were back in Italy. But the refusal of the great majority of IMIs was an extraordinary popular vote against Fascism which radically weakened the prospects of the RSI both politically and militarily.

To this should be added a further fact from across the Atlantic. As noted above, a further 700,000 Italian soldiers were held as prisoners of war by the Allies. They too were offered the opportunity to co-operate with the Anglo-American war effort, contrary to the Convention on Prisoners of War. The overwhelming majority—

perhaps more than two-thirds of the 50,000 held in the USA—chose to co-operate; the others remained interned in 'Fascists' camps'.

These two situations—of the IMIs in German hands and of those who co-operated in the hands of the Allies—were very different, yet their convergence is remarkable. Despite twenty years of Fascist propaganda and Mussolini's attempts to construct the 'New Man', Fascism had failed to establish itself sufficiently in the allegiance of Italians. Taken together, and in conjunction with the numbers of the regular forces of the Kingdom of the South and of the partisans in the resistance (numbers which are relatively small given the conditions prevailing in the country), but nonetheless much larger than that of men under arms for the RSI), they already pointed to the direction in which Italy would travel in the post-war period.

In the light of these facts, it cannot be said that the liberation of Italy was achieved solely through the military advance of the Allied forces, decisive though this was.

A Divided Country and Nazi Massacres

The Italian wars of 1943–5 were not, however, confined to soldiers under arms; in a total war the civilian population was also, in its own way, involved as a combatant, chiefly through bombing. The bombing war saw a reinforcement of the division between the north and south of the country. Air raids were directed more intensely at the cities and communication lines in the north; the figures for the war as a whole show at least 60,000 Italian victims of bombing, a substantial proportion of all Italian casualties of the war. Civilians were also exposed to the violence of the German and Fascist counter-insurgency. In particular, as German forces retreated in the face of the British and American advance they sought to eliminate any threats from immediately behind the front line, and there were many examples of full-scale massacres of unarmed civilians: 23 victims at Caiazzo on 13 October 1943; 143 victims at Pietranieri di Roccaraso, 21 November; 335 dead at the Ardeatine Caves in Rome, 29 March 1944; 173 at Civitella Valdichiana, 29 June; 560 at Sant'Anna di Stazzema, 12 August; 770 at Marzabotto, 29 September 1944; etc. Not all of these were places where there had been previous Resistance activity which might allow the crimes of the Wehrmacht in Italy to be defined as reprisals; and in any case the rules of war always forbid actions against unarmed civilians. It was rather a strategy and a form of warfare which the Wehrmacht had already practised on the eastern front and in the Balkans, which German and Italian historians have defined as 'war on civilians'.

Life in the south, in contrast, was difficult because of the strange situation, halfway between peace and war, in which that half of the country lived, under Allied control behind the Allied lines in the Italian campaign. Here women bore the brunt of the responsibility for caring for the elderly and for children while continuing to work and to hunt for food. Yet in spite of all these difficulties, in spite of the suffering caused by Allied bombing, and in spite of the German massacres which could have led to divisions in the communities where they had been carried out, support for Anti-Fascism remained solid in both the north and the south.

Insurgency and Liberation

After the liberation of Rome on 4 June 1944 and of Florence on 11 August, the Anglo-American advance in the Italian campaign lost its momentum. It seemed that breaking through the German 'Gothic Line' north of Florence would require more forces than Washington and London were prepared to devote to Italy. In the winter of 1944–5 it was left to the effect of bombing and Resistance activity to wear down the German forces in the peninsula, while elsewhere the Soviet advance in the east and the second front in Normandy in the west were beginning to produce the desired results for the Allies.

In the spring of 1945, however, the situation changed. The German forces were much weakened and the Allied advance in Italy began to progress again, across the plains on the Adriatic side of the country though more slowly in the mountainous terrain in the centre and on the western coast. Bologna was liberated on 21 April as the Combat Groups of the Kingdom of the South entered the city, opening the way for an advance along the Po valley. This set the context for the liberation of Genoa, Milan, and Turin—the three cities of the Italian 'industrial triangle'—by the resistance: Genoa and Milan on 25 April and Turin on 28 April, in a co-ordinated military operation which came to be defined as an insurrection. The first Anglo-American troops entered the cities on 26 April, 29 April, and 1 May respectively. In effect, this meant that the liberation of Italy was achieved with the military collaboration of the Italians themselves, something which could not be said of Germany and to a far greater extent than in occupied and divided France. In this regard too, the Italian wars were complex.

This made an enormous difference politically, and it also helps explain why the Italian republic still celebrates 25 April as the date when the war came to an end, rather than 2 May, when representatives of the German forces formally surrendered to the Allies at Caserta, or 7 May when the Germans finally capitulated to Eisenhower.

Of course the war against Germany and Mussolini's Neo-Fascist regime in Italy would have had no chance of success without the intervention of the Allies. But it was a success which Italians fought for with whatever arms they had at their disposal: the partisans in the mountains and in the cities; the regular troops of the Kingdom of the South; the soldiers who joined the resistance in other countries; the Italian Military Internees who refused to support the republic of Salò; and the civilian population with various forms of civil and unarmed resistance. It is hard to maintain, in a war of such complexity, that Italians did not fight.

Post-War Memories: The War Continues

When the guns finally fell silent the legacy of Italy's involvement in the conflict was far from straightforward. Matters were made even more complex, if that were possible, by the beginnings of the Cold War.

A ruined apartment block in Rome, part of the extensive damage done to Italian cities throughout the war by extensive Allied bombing.

In the 69 months that the conflict lasted—72 up to the bombing of Hiroshima and Nagasaki—Italy had been for 9 months a non-belligerent ally of Nazi Germany, and then for another 39 months its ally in arms, first in a parallel and then in a subaltern war; then the country had been split in two, for another 21 months of fighting between Anti-Fascists and Neo-Fascists. It is hard to see how such a complex legacy could be recalled in future years without multiplying the wounds that had been opened during the conflict itself.

Once the war was over, from the Yalta conference onwards, Italy aligned itself with the western Allies. The peace treaty of 10 February 1947 imposed harsh military terms on Rome, but politically the treatment of Italy was different from that of Germany and Japan; Italy was important for western control of the Mediterranean. The decision by Rome in 1949 to join NATO (even though the Atlantic Ocean was nowhere near the Italian peninsula) brought an alleviation of the terms imposed in 1947; but it was only in 1955 that Italy was accepted as a member of the United Nations.

Meanwhile, in domestic politics the Communist party and the left, strengthened by the prestige they had gained in the war of liberation, received a higher share of the vote

than anywhere else in western Europe: 31 per cent in 1948 (in an electoral pact with the Socialists), 22 per cent in 1953, 25 per cent in 1963, rising to 34 per cent in 1976. When the Communists were excluded from the national coalition government in February 1947, it was clear to everyone that the Cold War had begun; their links with the Soviet Union and the suspicions of the Cold War made it impossible for the Communists to find other parties to share their political platform. After 1947, it was not until 1996 that the (now former) Communists returned to coalition government. This post-war political context clearly made it harder still to arrive at any form of consensus regarding the complexities of the war of 1939–45.

The Fascist war of 1940–3 was generally therefore passed over in silence. It was recalled in the polemical memoirs of generals and the painful recollections of veterans, but there were few monuments to the fallen; it was more usual to see elliptical and ambiguous plaques on church façades 'to the fallen of all wars'. The war of liberation was naturally much more widely commemorated, although with the left in opposition the resistance was celebrated much less than one might expect today. The IMIs were almost completely forgotten; they had after all been prisoners, and they had initially been fighting for Fascism. The regular units of the Kingdom of the South had been too small-scale to inspire popular rhetoric although they were recognized in official commemorations. Only the Neo-Fascists had any nostalgia for the soldiers of the RSI. In the changed climate of the Cold War, a significant number of those who had fought in the resistance were even prosecuted, notwithstanding that the liberation and the restoration of national self-respect had begun with the resistance movement. The recollection of a complex war was itself complex.

Added to this was the fact that, in Italy as almost everywhere else, the numbers of dead in the Second World War were smaller than they had been in the first; and whereas in the First World War Italians had fought on a single front, the Italian wars of 1939–45 were fought on many different fronts. For this reason as well as on ideological grounds the veterans' organizations were divided, and this too made it harder for posterity to do justice to the complexity of the war.

The tensions which arose within the military were of a different kind. On the one hand, how could the dead in the regular (Fascist) war be forgotten? But on the other hand, how should they be commemorated, now that Italy was a democracy? How should all the soldiers who abandoned their uniforms on 8 September 1943 and went to join the resistance be remembered now that, in the climate of the Cold War, the resistance seemed to be remembered only by the Communists and the left? What was the appropriate way of commemorating the soldiers massacred on Cefalonia, now that Italy and Germany sat together as members of NATO? (It is significant that many of the criminal files opened in Italy relating to the German massacres of 1943–5 were set aside, and many of the perpetrators never came to trial.)

And yet, as Italy progressed from post-war reconstruction to the economic miracle, there were hundreds of thousands of widows, orphans, and war wounded, and dozens of communities that had witnessed massacres, for whom the war was far from over.

From Memoir to History

It is difficult if not impossible, in the brief space available here, to impose any kind of order on the enormous flood of memoirs, diaries, and published and unpublished autobiographies, dealing with the Italian wars. What is beyond doubt is that changes in the political climate in Italy influenced the ways in which the wars of 1939–45 were remembered.

At the height of the Cold War, when Italy had a series of governments of the centre, it was the regular war that was the most popular; but in the Sixties with the coming to power of the centre-left, officialdom was receptive to memories of the resistance and these were widely commemorated. As a general rule, the polarized positions of the Cold War led to rival celebrations of different aspects of the Italian wars of 1939–45, with each side forgetful of the other's memories. More recently, during the twenty years dominated by the right-wing politician Silvio Berlusconi, publishing the memoirs of a partisan or a member of the resistance appears once again to have acquired significance as a political gesture in addition to a contribution to the historical record.

In contrast, there has never been a period when prisoners of war have been well received. The IMIs, for instance, went on silently publishing their memoirs for decades, but it was only in the 1980s that they received any public recognition—which had the effect of stimulating memories which had previously remained buried or unpublished. The choices they made have recently been once again the subject of discussion, and are now considered simply as 'human resistance' or 'escape from the war' rather than as a popular vote against Fascism. Today's collapse of ideologies evidently also extends to the memories of a war fought seventy years ago.

In short, the memory of the Second World War seems still to be a source of division among Italians. Indeed, it is a source of division between Italy and other countries: as recently as 3 February 2012 the International Court of Justice at The Hague, the principal judicial organ of the United Nations, was required to give judgment in cases involving the imposition of forced labour on the IMIs and German atrocities in Italy, two subjects which continue to divide Italy (and also Greece) from Germany.

It was inevitable that Italian historical studies of the Italian wars should reflect all these currents. That Italian research in contemporary history has strong connections with politics is well known, and divisions were inevitable in the study of such a complex war, and one moreover which laid the foundations of the post-war democratic republic. That said, historians have fulfilled a civic as well as a historiographical function in seeking to give an ordered account of Italian participation in such a complex war. In carrying out their research, in reconstructing forgotten episodes, their aim has not been simply to establish hierarchies of importance among the various fronts, the various experiences, the various phases, and the various actors in the war. In doing so they have, in a sense, fulfilled a contemporary political and public role as well as a purely scholarly one, because the object of their investigations has been the very origins of democracy and the Italian republic.

In the course of this mission, historical research has often had to combat a threefold and insidious adversary: the tendencies to minimization, to victimization, and the myth of 'Italians as decent people'.

The country as a whole faced a difficult process in coming to terms with Fascism, and more than once historians have warned against the temptation to minimize the extent of Italy's participation in the Second World War. There have been 'alternative history' novels which have imagined that Fascism could have survived the war if it had stood apart from it; but Italy was not Spain, and by 1940 Mussolini was too closely tied to Hitler.

Another recurrent tendency in Italy is to see the country as a victim. Links of cause and effect can be loosened or even inverted in memory; Italians, who for a long time were forces of occupation if not of conquest, prefer to recall themselves as victims of occupation, bombing, imprisonment, and massacres, and to lament their fate. Here sound historical research can serve to recall what is too easily forgotten about the nature of the Fascist state and its wartime policies.

Above all, however, public perception is still dominated by a thinly veiled myth of 'Italians as decent people'. Yet in Libya, in Ethiopia, in the Balkans, and in the Soviet Union, Italian troops were perpetrators of brutal acts of war; and it is hard to forget the widespread violence of the 1943–5 civil war, violence which the Fascist regime had preached for the previous twenty years. The fact is that brutalization was as much part of the Italian wars as of any other, even if it was these same wars which made possible the birth of the first true democracy the country had known.

4 The German Wars

RICHARD OVERY

In February 1945, reflecting to his circle on the imminent defeat of German forces in Europe, Hitler claimed that he had been Europe's last hope. 'She proved incapable of refashioning herself by means of voluntary reform,' he continued. 'To take her I had to use violence.' Hitler saw himself echoing the fate of Napoleon, always hoping for peace but compelled by circumstances to keep on fighting. This was characteristic of Hitler's view of the world: wars were forced on him by the obstinacy, ill-will, and ambitions of others. In reality, the German wars waged between 1939 and 1945 were all the product of deliberate aggression on Hitler's part. Violence was indeed central to his vision of re-shaping Europe in Germany's image.

A case could be made to argue that any German government in the 1930s might have increased the pressure to allow Germany to rearm and have continued step-by-step to undo many of the restrictions imposed by the 1919 Treaty of Versailles. But the evidence of caution on the part of the army leadership and German conservative nationalists in the 1930s, faced with Hitler's demands for risky aggression, makes it more likely that a Germany without Hitler would have tried to assert its position as a major economic and political player without recourse to war, as indeed happened in the 1950s. Hitler represented, as he well understood, all the inarticulate resentment built up among broad sections of the German public against the military weakness and economic malaise imposed, so it was argued, by the richer and more heavily-armed Western states. He represented, too, the wide popular hatred for Communism and fear of the consequences of the Russian Revolution for the rest of Europe, and a narrower constituency that blamed all these things on the Jews. The National Socialist Party (NSDAP) depended for its eventual electoral success and Hitler's appointment as chancellor in January 1933 on the ability to mobilize this diverse and disgruntled constituency.

Hitler and German Foreign Policy

The radical nationalism unleashed in 1933 by a genuine mass movement encouraged the military and conservative elites to join forces with Hitler to try to restrain the revolutionary impulses in the movement, but in doing so they created a situation in which it was difficult to withdraw from the compact made with the dictatorship. When the conservative banker and economics minister, Hjalmar Schacht, tried to restrain arms spending in 1937 he was sidelined and two years later sacked as president of the central bank. Hitler's foreign policy and eventual aggression was possible only because of the mass support for re-militarization, anti-Communism, and the penalization of German Jews among the active NSDAP enthusiasts, and because the German elites, whose own ideology coincided in important respects with that of the new regime, colluded with the creation of a modern armed forces and a programme of economic recovery whose core was a large-scale military build-up at the expense of satisfying consumer wants.

It has never been entirely clear what kind of aggression Hitler contemplated in the 1930s. His foreign policy was directed towards overturning the restrictions of Versailles and if possible revising the post-war territorial settlement by negotiation or threat. The re-militarization of the Rhineland in March 1936 and the *Anschluss* with Austria in March 1938 were risks taken in the hope that war would be avoided. The rearmament of Germany was undertaken in a hurry and it was based on the idea that Germany had to become proof to enemy blockade and able to organize and resource a war effort from within. The measure of German military build-up was the extensive re-militarization of Stalin's Soviet Union, where war production by the late 1930s dominated the new industrial economy and made the Soviet Union, on paper, the most heavily armed state in the world. The Second Four-Year Plan, established under the air force commander-in-chief Hermann Göring, in October 1936 was predicated on fear that the Red Army would become too powerful and would menace Europe with 'Jewish-Bolshevism'. The plan laid the foundation for a programme of heavy industrial expansion—chemicals, machinery, synthetic oil and rubber, iron and steel—and for greater agricultural self-sufficiency, both of which were essential to waging some kind of major war in the 1940s. By 1939 almost one-quarter of the German national product was devoted to military purposes, a level of commitment that could hardly be maintained for any length of time. Hitler seems to have favoured a major war, as he told his military and party leaders, at some point in 1942–4, but against whom and with what object was not made clear.

Hitler was strongly affected by the idea that war was valuable in itself. He had a crude Darwinist view that the human world mirrored the struggle in nature which allowed only the fittest to survive. War was a test of that fitness, and the only means in Hitler's view to reassert Germany's destiny as the nation and culture best fitted to reinvigorate Europe and to hold at bay the Soviet threat and the malign influence of vulgar Americanism. No doubt there were many younger Germans brought up in the Hitler Youth and army service who shared this vision of redemptive conflict, but perhaps a large majority of Germans even in 1939 did not want a real war against the enemies of 1914, however strong the sense of resentment at the way Germany had been treated. When war with Britain and France broke out on 3 September 1939, neutral pressmen could see how startled and depressed the German crowds had suddenly become. The so-called 'bloodless victories' from 1936 onwards— reoccupation of the Rhineland, union with Austria, occupation of the Czech Sudeten areas in October 1938 and of Bohemia and Moravia in March 1939—suited a

The German training ship *Schleswig Holstein* opens fire on the Westerplatte fortress in Danzig at the start of the German–Polish war, 1 September 1939.

population anxious to revive Germany's great power status, but they were welcomed because they were achieved short of war. In spring and summer 1939 it is clear that Hitler wanted to provoke a war with Poland once the Polish government had rejected any basis for negotiating the future of the former German city of Danzig and the Prussian territory granted to Poland in 1919. But it is not clear that he wanted that war to develop into a second world war, and the decision to reach an agreement with the Soviet enemy with the signing of the Molotov–Ribbentrop Non-Aggression Pact on 23 August 1939 showed that Hitler gambled on Western timidity and uncertainty when faced with a solid bloc of dictators, and expected to be able to 'blood' his young army in Poland without risking more.

Once the decision for war with Poland was finally taken in late August 1939, Hitler set himself on a path from which there was no real prospect of turning back. Only surrendering German gains in a humiliating climb-down, or a German political coup to replace him (which army and conservative leaders toyed with in autumn 1938 and again in 1939), would have reversed German policy. Hitler had little idea of how his war would unravel or who his enemies might eventually be. In October 1939 he offered the West the prospect of peace if they would accept German–Soviet domination of Poland, but was brusquely rejected. The war fuelled itself on the success or failure of German arms. This planless war certainly had something in common with Napoleon's imperialism, as Hitler later realized. War had to be fought to destroy British and French power in Europe; only once that had been achieved was it possible

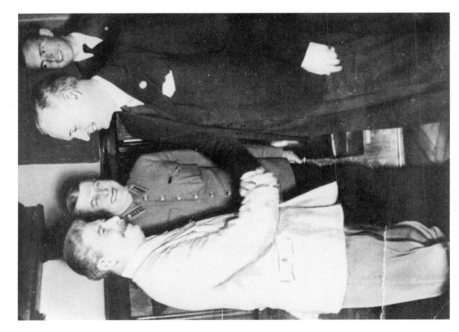

The German foreign minister, Joachim von Ribbentrop, signing the second treaty between the Soviet Union and Germany on 28 September 1939. The agreement sealed the division of Poland between the two dictators, Stalin and Hitler.

to think through any larger project for a German-dominated Europe and come to terms with the awkward alliance with a Soviet Union growing stronger every month.

Germany Alone

It was a war fought at first in isolation. Germany's allies did not rally to the German cause. Mussolini's Italy was not prepared for a major conflict and Italian military leaders rejected a joint war effort. Mussolini declared 'non-belligerence'. Japan was occupied with a major military confrontation with the Red Army on the Manchurian border when the Polish crisis emerged and had as yet no intention of inviting British or American armed retaliation in the Pacific theatre. German forces, rearmed but not yet fully modernized, faced the combined weight of French, British, and British Commonwealth military and economic strength, which explains Western confidence that a long war of attrition (three years was the planning target) would wear Germany down again as in 1914–18 and result in Western victory. German military leaders were far from confident that aggression against the West in 1940 was going to succeed but

Ethnic Germans in the Polish city of Łódź greet German soldiers after the rapid Blitzkrieg victory over the Polish army. The city soon became the site of a major Jewish ghetto.

Hitler insisted on it. In the end a variation of the 1914 Schlieffen Plan was drawn up: large German forces would attack through The Netherlands and Belgium directed at the French army and the British Expeditionary Force (BEF) on the Flanders plain while a second major strike force, composed of most of the new German armoured divisions, would negotiate a way through the Ardennes forest, strike the French army at its weakest point, and push the mobile force rapidly towards the English Channel, trapping all the British forces and an important part of the French army. The plan contained a high element of risk for generals who could recall how close German victory had come in 1914 before it was snatched away on the Marne, but it also contained the possibility of a spectacular success. Hitler's war-making over the next four years was characterized by the gambler's urge to keep on playing however loaded the dice might appear to be.

Hitler's ambitions were not, like Mussolini's, based on bombastic over-assessment of the capability of the German military. The Polish campaign in September 1939 is often overlooked in military terms as the outcome of an asymmetrical conflict, but Polish armed forces were large and preparations for defence extensive. German operational planning and the introduction of effective combined arms combat using ground vehicles, tanks, and aircraft produced a comprehensive victory in a little over three weeks. There were lessons to be learned from the conflict but the Western Allies failed to learn them. Further evidence of Germany's revived military capability was shown in April 1940 when Hitler, alerted to British ambitions to mine waters around

Hitler and the chief of his headquarters, General Wilhelm Keitel, examine a Polish armoured train in the aftermath of the lightning German victory against the Polish army and air force in September 1939.

Norway and Denmark to prevent the passage of iron-ore supplies and to bottle up the German fleet, sent a small expeditionary force north at short notice. The result was, like Poland, a tribute to combined arms combat and the first example of a major amphibious operation in the war. Though the cost to the German navy was high, Denmark was occupied with scarcely a fight on 9 April and Norway was effectively captured at the end of two weeks of combat. A small Allied expeditionary force remained in northern Norway, short of aircraft and supplies, fighting a rearguard action until forced to retreat in June. By this time Hitler had launched his gamble in the west when German forces moved forward into The Netherlands and Belgium on 10 May 1940.

The risks taken in the invasion in the west proved in the end to have been worthwhile because the campaign resulted in the most decisive German victory of the war, won in just five weeks of fighting against forces armed with more tanks, more divisions, and air forces (had they been fully combined) not much smaller than the German air force. Dutch and Belgian resistance was swept aside quickly and by

May 15 The Netherlands had surrendered. The Belgian army as in 1914 retreated westward to meet up with the British and French but this time no fixed defensive line could be established and the Belgian king surrendered on 28 May. The German plan worked on the assumption that the Allies would see the invasion through Belgium as the chief threat, and indeed British and French forces pushed rapidly forward across the Flanders plain to hold up what they thought was the chief axis of attack. In the Ardennes forest Colonel General Ewald von Kleist's XXX army group assembled the German Panzer divisions, including a corps led by the tank expert Lieutenant General Heinz Guderian. Their deployment was not secret, since Allied aircraft could see the long lines of vehicles, but the Allies simply failed to appreciate how much German strength was concealed in the forest. On 13 May Guderian led the armour out of the woodland and swiftly across the River Meuse, pushing rapidly through north-east France behind the BEF and the French First and Ninth Armies. By 19 May the tanks had reached Abbeville on the coast. Four days later the British chiefs-of-staff decided the battle was lost. Vigorous counter-attacks from within the trapped Allied pocket held up the final defeat and allowed some 338,000 British and French troops to be evacuated from Dunkirk, but the defeat was complete. The French army faced collapse, trapped between the defence of the fixed Maginot Line and the need to regroup to save Paris. The capital was abandoned on 11 June and the French army retreated south. On 10 June Mussolini declared war and began a limited invasion across the Italian–French border. On 17 June the new Prime Minister, Marshal Philippe Pétain, sued for an armistice. By 22 June von Kleist's corps had reached the Spanish frontier south of Biarritz.

Tank General Heinz Guderian watches as a French standard is burnt following the German triumph in the Battle of France in June 1940.

The German victory had many explanations. The German decision to concentrate the mobile divisions in one powerful punch completely unhinged the more defensive Allied line; the use of massed aircraft to achieve local air supremacy and to support the ground forces transformed the nature of modern battle; the element of surprise, when the tank forces burst out from the Ardennes, kept the French army off balance for long enough to secure room for effective large-scale manoeuvre. The Allies also helped in their own defeat. The British sent a small expeditionary force with little experience at mobile warfare, but retained most of their aircraft at home to defend the British Isles, leaving the smaller French air force to absorb the German attack. The French scattered their aircraft across France to defend vital centres, making the Allied air force at the front weaker still. French strategy had been predicated on holding the fixed border defences of the Maginot Line, leaving many units and tanks tied up away from the main battle area. The German armed forces had spent much of the inter-war period planning innovation to avoid the mistakes of the Great War; the Allies had won the war and still thought in terms of fixed fronts and the war of attrition that had ended with victory in 1918.

The defeat of France and Britain transformed the possibilities open to Hitler, but also presented him with imponderable questions now that Germany, against the expectations of many among the German political and military leadership, dominated the whole of continental Europe, together with Mussolini's Italy in the Mediterranean. It is sometimes argued that Hitler now decided to turn east against his real enemy, Soviet Communism, but it is clear from the evidence that in the weeks following victory in the west he was very uncertain about how to proceed. He hoped that Britain would reach an agreement, leaving him to control Europe while Britain kept its wider imperial role, and in a Reichstag speech on 19 July he made an oblique offer to Britain to be reasonable and come to terms. At the same time he ordered the armed forces to prepare for a possible invasion of southern England in the early autumn—Operation Sea Lion—which was to take place if the military conditions were sufficiently propitious. While these preparations were under way the German army leadership suggested a possible move against the Red Army. Taking advantage of the war in the west, the Soviet regime had taken over complete control of the Baltic States, pressured Romania into handing over the Bukovina territory, and was clearly looking towards the Balkans and the Turkish Straits as an area of Soviet interest. The German army, now fully mobilized and basking in its operational successes, thought that a swift blow against the Soviet army would put Stalin in his place and secure the eastern border of the new German order in Europe. Hitler was impressed by the Soviet threat and also inclined to see the resources of the Ukraine and western Russia as a possible area for German 'living space' (*Lebensraum*). On 31 July, even while the preparations for Sea Lion were under way, Hitler called together his military chiefs and told them that he planned an annihilating blow against the Soviet Union, to be launched in the late spring of 1941. This was not yet a firm strategic

Hitler and Italian foreign minister Galeazzo Ciano sign the Tripartite Pact in September 1940. The treaty allocated world spheres of influence to the three Axis states, Germany, Italy, and Japan.

decision, any more than Sea Lion, but it showed that victory in the west had opened up for Hitler truly Napoleonic visions of imperial grandeur, impelled forward by the apparent invincibility of German arms.

Historians have often argued that Sea Lion was never a serious option because the contest with the Soviet Union was the centrepiece of Hitler's world view, traceable back to the passages in *Mein Kampf* on the need for territory in the east. Nothing was so clear-cut. Sea Lion rolled forward, dependent on the capacity of the German navy to protect the vulnerable convoys as they crossed the Channel, but above all dependent on the creation of an aerial shield over the invasion forces that would keep the Royal Navy at bay and repel any residual threat from the Royal Air Force. The invasion and defeat of Britain was a decision for high stakes, because it really would transform the balance of power. Dates for invasion were found in mid-September, when there would be favourable tides. Large-scale exercises were conducted and equipment adapted to amphibious operations. The German air force was supposed to do what it had done so successfully in Poland and France—attack the enemy air force, its sources of supply and production, and eliminate it as a threat.

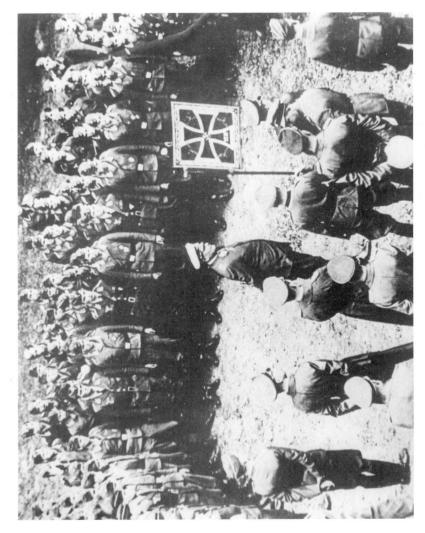

Reich Marshal Hermann Göring addresses German pilots during the Battle of Britain in the late summer of 1940. Air supremacy was regarded as essential to German plans to invade southern England.

In early August Göring ordered a week of devastating air attack designed to knock out the RAF and so create the conditions for invasion. Poor weather postponed the opening day—Eagle Day (*Adlertag*)—until 13 August, but the weather failed to improve and not until 18 August was the systematic campaign, the 'England Attack', finally launched. So sure was the air force of success that pilots' reports and casual photo-reconnaissance suggested that by late August the RAF was beaten, with no more than 200–300 aircraft and a declining stock of pilots. The apparent success persuaded Hitler to approve the next stage of the campaign, a destructive attack on military and economic targets in London to create panic in the capital as a prelude to invasion, now set for 15 September.

The Battle of Britain, as it has come to be known, was not won in August and Fighter Command actually grew stronger in aircraft and pilots as the battle went on. The damage inflicted on the German air force in the first two weeks of September made it clear that air supremacy had eluded him and Hitler postponed Sea Lion yet again. Finally on 19 September he directed that preparations should be scaled down and three weeks later Sea Lion was postponed indefinitely until more propitious

A building blazes in the British city of Manchester following heavy raids in December 1940 at the height of the German 'Blitz' against British trade and industrial targets.

conditions for invasion could be created in 1941 or 1942. All through this period the campaign against the Soviet Union was at the planning stage, directed by General Friedrich Paulus (later the defeated commander at Stalingrad), but no firm decision had been taken. Instead, Hitler continued to explore ways of forcing Britain to abandon the war to free his hands for the war in the east. The direct way was to impose an air–sea blockade on Britain in order to cut off food, oil, and raw material supplies (and a growing quantity of American military production). The war at sea waged by submarine and aircraft brought damaging levels of shipping loss through 1940 and 1941. Submarine production expanded rapidly and large groups of sub-marines, the 'Wolf Packs', led by Admiral Karl Dönitz, tracked down ships sailing singly, or convoy stragglers. The war in the air, known in Britain as the Blitz, was directed at British ports, oil installations, warehouses, flour mills, and storage depots, as well as the industries supporting aircraft and aero-engine production. The air attacks on British cities have often been painted as deliberate terror attacks, but Hitler vetoed these in favour of more strategically important blockade targets and 86 per cent of German bombs fell on ports and their associated stores. Hitler did not believe that British morale would crack because of bomb attack, but he did hope that the combined pressure of bombing and submarine war might create conditions in which an isolated Britain would see sense and seek peace.

Though it is tempting to see the months after the collapse of Sea Lion as a prelude to the great war of annihilation to be waged in the east, German strategy in the winter of 1940–1 was focused on finding indirect ways of defeating Britain, with whom Germany was at war, rather than preparing for the war against the Soviet Union, to

Hitler meets the Spanish dictator, General Francisco Franco, at the town of Hendaye, on the French–Spanish border. Hitler could not persuade Franco to join the Axis war effort.

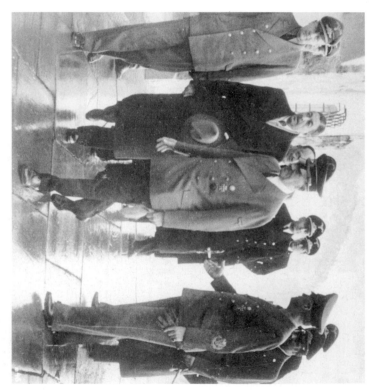

Adolf Hitler meets the Yugoslav foreign minister, Alexsandar Cincar-Marković, in February 1941 to try to cement an agreement between the two countries prior to the invasion of the Soviet Union.

German tanks use a rail line as an avenue of advance during the brief campaign in Greece in April and May 1941. Hitler needed to stabilize the Balkans before he could launch the invasion of the Soviet Union.

German paratroops prepare to board a Junkers Ju52 transport aircraft before flying to Crete in May 1941 to capture the island from the British and Greek defenders.

whom Germany was still tied by treaty. The indirect strategy favoured by the German navy and by Göring was to isolate British forces in the Mediterranean, seize Gibraltar with Spain's acquiescence, and join Italy in a drive to the Suez Canal, all the while isolating Britain from any political role in Europe. The Spanish dictator, Francisco Franco, refused to commit support for Operation Felix, a German plan to take Gibraltar, when he met Hitler at Hendaye on 23 October. Mussolini refused the offer of German help in Libya against British Commonwealth forces in Egypt, but German hopes for indirect pressure on Britain did not disappear. Following Italy's declaration of war on Greece on 28 October 1940 (for which Hitler had not been forewarned) and the disastrous campaign that followed, German pressure to help in the theatre finally paid off. In February 1941 German forces under Major General

Erwin Rommel were sent to North Africa (Operation Sunflower) to support Italian forces and he immediately began to drive the British back towards the Suez Canal. The confused state of the Balkans, thanks to Mussolini's failing war on Greece and the uncertain support of Yugoslavia for the Axis, prompted further German planning for intervention here, which finally resulted in the invasion of Yugoslavia on 8 April 1941. Yugoslav capitulation came ten days later, to be followed by a German invasion of Greece, whose army surrendered on 23 April. British forces sent to help the Greeks were routed. Evacuation to Crete of 50,000 British Commonwealth and Greek forces prompted Hitler to order a successful, if costly, paratroop operation against the island, and Britain was forced in late May into yet another humiliating evacuation. The indirect approach, however, only had the effect of widening Germany's military responsibilities while bringing Britain no nearer to the conference table.

One of the key arguments Hitler used to persuade his generals and party leaders that invasion in the east was necessary was the assumption that the Soviet Union represented Britain's last hope in Europe. Soviet defeat would hasten a British capitulation. In this sense the British and Soviet strategies were not alternatives but complementary. If Britain did not finally see sense, Hitler suggested, then heavier bombing and an invasion could be mounted at some point in spring 1942. There were, of course, other compelling arguments for war against the Soviet Union: despite the Non-Aggression Pact, convinced National Socialists saw Moscow as the heart of world Communism and the international Jewish conspiracy, a permanent threat to Europe's future; Soviet military and political pressure in Eastern Europe and Scandinavia challenged the idea of a German-dominated region and the economic interests of the German 'New Order'; Soviet armed forces were engaged in a colossal arms race that would soon turn the Soviet Union into a military superpower (a judgement that was indeed close to the truth). The issue of timing, however, was all-important, because German military intelligence judged that the Soviet colossus was not yet prepared to wage effective modern war and that Communism was inherently corrupt and incompetent. Defeat of the Soviet Union was likely in 1941 (and most senior officers, victims of hubris after the rapid defeat of France, assumed a campaign in the east of no more than a few weeks), and this would pave the way for defeat of Britain using the large new resources made available from the territories of the east.

The final decision rested with Hitler, and although historians have searched the archive for evidence of exactly when he irrevocably decided on war in the east, the decision is elusive. On 10 November 1940 the Soviet Foreign Minister, Vyacheslav Molotov, arrived in Berlin to discuss extending the Pact, and his request for further concessions to Soviet interests in Bulgaria and Turkey certainly confirmed Hitler in his view that Soviet ambitions in Europe would clash with his own. But when the army leaders, Field Marshal Walter Brauchitsch and Colonel General Franz Halder, went over the plans for the Soviet invasion with Hitler early in December 1940, his response seemed non-committal, though he approved the planning. But two weeks later, on 18 December 1940, he published Directive No. 21, 'Operation Barbarossa', whose purpose was '*to crush Soviet Russia in a rapid campaign*' (italics in original). Even then it would have been possible to postpone or cancel the decision, since many directives had been issued, including Sea Lion, which had led nowhere. Popular opinion in Germany, which the dictatorship monitored closely, was not wholeheartedly committed to continuing the war. Secret police reports found that the high point of popular enthusiasm following the defeat of France was not sustained once it was clear Britain would not abandon the conflict and as RAF bombers, night after night, raided western German cities. The war against the Soviet Union was a gamble not only that Soviet defeat would pave the way for an end to the war with Britain, but that German armed forces could present the German public with a second stunning victory and allay popular anxieties about a long-drawn-out conflict.

Perhaps all these considerations played some part in Hitler's final decision to go ahead with the invasion. By February 1941 the blockade of Britain had clearly not succeeded and Hitler was sceptical that bombing would achieve anything decisive. 'We'll deal with them later,' he told Göring, 'if the stubborn Churchill fails to see sense.' The bombing continued because it pinned British forces down in mainland Britain and prevented them from playing a fuller role in the Mediterranean or threatening German preparations against the Soviet Union. In the months leading up to Barbarossa Hitler's ideological arguments for war with the Jewish–Bolshevik enemy hardened, perhaps to avoid seeing the war as a product of mere strategic, great power calculation. In a meeting with his senior generals in March 1941 he told them that the war was to be a war of annihilation, destroying the Soviet system, and pushing the remnants of the Russian people back into 'Asiatic Russia'. The campaign

A crashed German Junkers Ju88 bomber in the Suez Canal, September 1941. Air power played an important part in the desert war but the Luftwaffe was always outnumbered.

gradually assumed in Hitler's mind the dimensions of a world-historical contest between Europe and Asia, Aryan and Jew.

The 'Barbarossa' Gamble

To give weight to the idea of a crusade against Bolshevism, Germany's Axis allies were persuaded to join the campaign. The four million troops that launched war along the whole Soviet border on 22 June 1941 were composed of Romanians, Slovakians, Hungarians as well as Germans; they were joined four days later by Finns as co-belligerents, and in July by three Italian divisions sent by Mussolini as a token gesture in the fight against Communism. Hitler also fixed the terms in which the battle against Communism would be fought. The German army and security forces (Gestapo, police, Security Service (SD), and Heinrich Himmler's SS) had already indulged in regular atrocities against the Polish population from September 1939, murdering alleged partisans and terrorists and large numbers of the Polish national and cultural elite; in the so-called 'criminal orders' issued by Hitler's headquarters—they were not, of course, regarded as criminal by Hitler—the military and security services were given licence to kill out of hand all Communist officials, Jews in Soviet state service, military commissars, and anyone deemed to pose a security threat to German forces.

The Barbarossa campaign was based on a series of overlapping operations designed to bring German forces to the 'AA-Line' from Archangel in the Soviet Arctic to Astrakhan at the mouth of the Volga in the far south of Russia. Three main army groups, North, Centre, and South, would drive respectively towards Leningrad, Moscow, and the southern Ukraine; the object was to pierce the Soviet frontier defences rapidly, encircle and annihilate the Red Army units, and then to advance on the major cities, destroying what was left of Soviet resistance on the way. The army chief-of-staff, Franz Halder, thought it would be over in six weeks, the army commander-in-chief suggested four weeks; Hitler gave the campaign four months with decisive victory by October. The attack when it came, despite numerous and precise intelligence warnings passed on to Stalin, was a complete shock to the Soviet forces in the path of the invasion. Although on paper the balance of tanks and aircraft favoured the Soviet Union (11,000 tanks against 4,000 Axis, 9,100 aircraft against 4,400) they were technically inferior to Axis equipment and deployed in small packets rather than concentrated as they were in the 21 armoured divisions and three air fleets devoted to the German campaign. The opening weeks seemed to confirm German optimism. The army groups pushed on rapidly, Army Group North reaching the outskirts of Leningrad by late August, Army Group Centre reaching far into the Ukraine (Kiev fell on 15 September), and Army Group South, a mix of German and Romanian contingents, capturing Odessa on 16 October. Within four weeks more than two million prisoners were netted and nine-tenths of Soviet tanks destroyed. Almost all the Soviet aircraft in the west to oppose the invasion were knocked out. On 6 September Hitler issued Directive No. 35 (Operation Typhoon) which ordered Army Group Centre to advance on Moscow, seize the capital, and eliminate all remaining Red Army opposition. On 4 October Hitler returned from his new headquarters, the Wolf's Lair in Rastenburg, East Prussia, to tell an audience in Berlin that he had returned from 'the greatest battle in the history of the world'. The Soviet dragon, he announced, was slain and 'would never rise again'.

For Hitler and his cohort of anti-Semitic party leaders, the campaign in the Soviet Union involved two wars, one waged against the Red Army but a second one waged against the Jews. This war had a long pedigree, for Hitler and many of his closest supporters subscribed to the myth that the German Jews had been responsible for stabbing the German army in the back in 1918. In his early speeches in the 1920s he identified the critical struggle facing Germany as the fight 'between Jew and German'. In a speech to the Reichstag on 30 January 1939 he announced that in the event of a world war, engineered for German destruction by world Jewry, it would be the Jews who would be destroyed, not the Germans. In his reflections on the war in the spring of 1945 he told Martin Bormann that there never before had there been a war 'so exclusively Jewish'. Defeat, he concluded, would mean 'that we have been defeated by the Jew'.

This warped world view lay behind the orders issued before Barbarossa to murder Soviet Jews in state service, and to single out Jewish prisoners of war for death, and to encourage the German security forces and the German army to equate 'partisan' and 'Jew'. By autumn 1941 permission was given to murder not only male Jews but

Men from a German *Einsatzgruppe* shoot Jewish women in a pit somewhere on the Eastern front in the late summer of 1941. By 1942 more than a million Jews had been killed in executions like this.

women and children too. By 1942 more than 1.4 million Jews had been killed in the Soviet area in so-called 'wild' killings. The war against the Jews was fuelled by Hitler's belief that the Atlantic Charter agreed by Roosevelt and Churchill at a meeting in August 1941 gave evidence that a truly global war was now a reality and that the Jews of Europe should pay for American involvement. Most historians date the decision for systematic genocide, if there was one, from mid-December 1941, a few days after Germany had declared war on the United States on 11 December. The declaration has usually been explained as a simple recognition of reality after months in which American naval vessels had been helping in the Battle of the Atlantic and a stream of American equipment had been supplying the British, but it also makes sense in terms of Hitler's fantastic notions about the influence of 'world Jewry', who allegedly pulled the strings of the Roosevelt and Churchill puppets. The coming of a real global war in December 1941 was swiftly followed by the operation of the first death camps, the expulsion of German Jews to the east, and, from the late spring, the systematic round-up and deportation of Jews in Western Europe to their deaths or forced labour. The bizarre logic of anti-Semitism explains why heavily armed security agents and policemen were used to murder unarmed men, women, and children in the name of a war against Germany's mortal enemy. 'We were on the defensive,' claimed Robert Ley, head of the German Labour Front, and a leading party anti-Semite, to his interrogators at Nuremberg after the war.

This second war, the war against the Jews, was played out side-by-side with the drive to destroy the Red Army in the last months of 1941. The German armed forces, and Hitler, expected Soviet resistance to crumble after suffering more than five million casualties. The forces opposing Army Group Centre as it launched 'Typhoon' on 15 September 1941 were indeed small, and despite the rain, mud, and cold, German soldiers were in sight of the Kremlin spires by early December. As it turned out there were sufficient Soviet reserves drawn from the eastern Soviet Union (in case of a Japanese attack in the rear) to halt the German offensive and drive the German army back from Moscow to a fixed defensive line. The German army and air force had also suffered heavy losses and the long supply lines were difficult to operate in deteriorating weather. The Moscow failure was a turning point of a kind because it ended any prospect of the quick victory army leaders had hoped for and the possibility of returning to the war against Britain with Russia defeated. With the declaration of war on the United States, Hitler created the worst possible strategic situation by adding to the list of German enemies the world's largest economy and potential military superpower. This situation did not immediately signal the end of the German wars, since the initiative for offensive action still lay with the German side, but the course of the war in 1942, except for the savage one-sided war against the Jews, showed that the German effort to construct a European New Order had reached the limits of the possible.

The Path to Defeat

During 1942 German expansion reached its fullest extent. In the two years since victory over France, German officials, businessmen, policemen, and party bosses had set about establishing German imperial rule in Europe. The long-term plan in the West and Scandinavia was to set up puppet regimes sympathetic to Germany and to compel them to accept a German-centred trade and financial system, with the Reichsmark as the central currency. In Eastern and South-Eastern Europe a more colonial form of rule was envisaged, with German administrators ruling a population denied any form of political or cultural self-expression, providing cheap labour for the German 'Large Area Economy' (*Grossraumwirtschaft*). This involved destruction of local culture— for example in Poland university professors were murdered or sent to concentration camps—and systematic expropriation of land and resources not only from Jews, whose property was forfeit everywhere, but from ethnic Czechs and Poles to make way for German colonizers. The programme for remodelling the ethnic and economic pattern of the region, expressed most clearly in the General Plan East (*Generalplan Ost*) ordered by Heinrich Himmler, head of the SS and also in 1939 made special commissioner for the defence of 'Germandom', involved a great deal of administrative and logistical effort even while the war was going on. Hope for a German victory, unlikely as it now seemed, kept German officials active throughout the New Order working on projects that had little prospect of realization.

The German war effort was far from over, whatever setbacks it faced. The war economy expanded continuously and the quality of German weapons constantly improved. Research on nuclear weapons was advanced but lacked Hitler's support. Work on rockets and cruise missiles, which Hitler did encourage, resulted in the V-weapons unleashed finally in 1944. The Tiger tank and the turbojet-engine Me262 did not turn the tide of war, but showed that German science and engineering were the equal or more of the enemies Germany faced. Manpower for a war on three fronts was an issue and in the end some 17 million men (and some women) were mobilized from the Greater German area, but only because by 1944 almost eight million foreign workers and prisoners of war had been compelled to take up work in Germany. By 1944 around one-third of all armaments workers were foreign, many of them women from Poland and Ukraine. Millions more Germans—women, youths, older men—volunteered for work in German civil defence against the mounting threat of bombing, first by RAF Bomber Command, then from January 1943 by the US Eighth Air Force in Britain as well. The bombing war turned the German home front into a fighting front too; by the end of the war at least 350,000 had lost their lives and half the urban area in the principal cities was turned into rubble.

The year 1942 was, however, the turning point. In the submarine war in the Atlantic more than 5 million tons of shipping was sunk in 1942 for the loss of 32 submarines; but a combination of better intelligence, new forms of 'centimetric' radar, fast escort groups of anti-submarine vessels for convoys, and the introduction of very long-range aircraft all produced a situation where the Allied navies could impose an

A German submarine and its crew on their return to Kiel harbour in November 1939 following a voyage in search of British shipping.

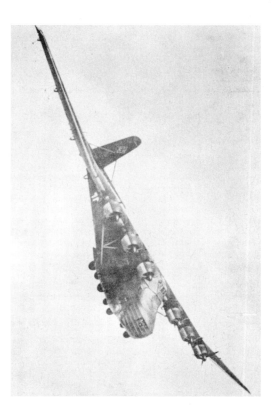

A Messerschmitt 'Gigant' transport aircraft used to bring essential supplies to Field Marshal's Rommel's forces in North Africa. Shortages of fuel and ammunition were a constant problem.

insupportable level of attrition on the German submarine force. Between January and May 1943, 73 submarines were lost and on 24 May Admiral Dönitz withdrew the 'Wolf Packs'. Though submarine production continued at a high level, the war in the Atlantic was too risky and had to be abandoned. In the Mediterranean German aircraft were used to neutralize the British air and sea bases on Malta in the spring so that supplies could flow to Rommel and the Afrika Korps for a campaign to capture Egypt and the Suez Canal. Hitler never seems to have accepted the full value of a Mediterranean strategy, since more German divisions and aircraft in North Africa might well have opened the way to seizure of Middle East oil. As it was, Rommel drove British Commonwealth forces back across the Egyptian border at Alam Halfa and captured the port of Tobruk by June 1942. This was as far as Axis forces would get. The British and Americans realized how important for their global war effort the retention of Egypt was and large forces and equipment poured into the Middle East theatre. A German–Italian thrust at Alam Halfa in August was repelled, and in late October 1942 the British Eighth Army under command of General Bernard Mont-gomery scored a decisive and hard-fought victory at El Alamein which ended any prospect of Middle East oil falling to the Germans and Italians.

The oil that Hitler wanted was to be found in the rich Caucasus oilfields in the southern Soviet Union. In spring 1942 the German line held against further Soviet offensives and in the early summer the Axis armies were ready for renewed cam-paigns. Hitler remained confident that the Soviet Union could still be defeated in 1942; since he had appointed himself commander-in-chief of the German Army in December 1941 there were limited prospects for his senior commanders to challenge the strategic option Hitler chose. After capturing the Crimean port of Sevastopol in early June 1942, Army Group South, supported by the bulk of the German air force in the east, was directed in Operation Blue to capture the Caucasus oilfields and to cut the Volga River at Stalingrad, seizing the river route and capturing Astrakhan. The risks seemed smaller then than they do with hindsight, since much of the Red Army was defending the northern line in front of Moscow where Stalin and his military leaders expected the main thrust to come from. The south was more weakly held and the strategic consequences of seizing Soviet oil and cutting off trade from the south would have had potentially disastrous consequences for the Soviet war effort. The principal problem was one of geography: holding and exploiting an area so large with only one army group relied on the rapid collapse of all Soviet resistance.

Operation Blue opened, nevertheless, with startling successes. So rapidly did Ger-man and Axis forces move south-east across the Don steppe that Hitler divided his army group in two, the Sixth Army under General Friedrich Paulus to move towards Stalingrad and cut the Volga, the First Panzer Army under Field Marshal von Kleist to move south to seize the oil. The southern thrust reached as far as the oil town of Maikop but was halted by the mountainous terrain and stiff Red Army resistance. The easterly offensive reached the Volga and the suburbs of Stalingrad on 23 August; by mid-September Paulus was ready to launch what he assumed would be the rapid seizure of the city itself. The story of what followed is well-known. Stalingrad was

A signpost at Stalingrad set up by the besieging army warns Germans not to enter the zone out of curiosity. The battlefield was dominated by snipers who shot at anything that moved on the enemy side.

shelled and bombed into ruins and the 62nd and 64th Soviet armies used them as defensive strongpoints from which it was difficult in the landscape of rubble to find them, or to deploy aircraft and armour effectively. The city battle became a harsh war of attrition instead of the rapid cutting of the Volga that Hitler had envisaged. In November, with both sides exhausted, the contest ground almost to a halt. On 19–20 November the Red Army launched surprise counter-offensives against the long enemy flanks stretching across the steppe, Operation Uranus, and the Axis front crumbled. Paulus was cut off in the Stalingrad pocket and the initiative passed to the Soviet side. At the end of January Paulus was forced to surrender. Over 330,000 soldiers had been trapped in the pocket and few survived.

Stalingrad and El Alamein did not end the war but they shifted the balance of the conflict so that the 'German Wars' became wars of defence against operations waged by the enemy. The initiative now lay with the Allied powers, who could decide on the point of engagement. After January 1943 there were sudden German counter-strokes, aggressive defensive operations and local successes, but the main shape of the war was dictated by the enemy. For Hitler the change did not bring him any nearer the idea of abandoning the struggle, since German forces were still far away on distant battle-fields, but like Napoleon he had to gamble that the Allies might fall out among themselves, or might find the cost of a long-drawn-out war against a skilled opponent too much to bear. It was certainly true that the alliance of Communist Russia, capitalist United States, and imperialist Britain was an unlikely combination, but the Allies were united in the view that the German wars were the most dangerous of all the Axis threats and that the Hitler dictatorship had to be destroyed as the precondition for any post-war order. Hitler assumed that only the presence of Jews in all three enemy states could explain their determination on unconditional surrender, announced at the Casablanca Conference in January 1943, and every effort was made by the genocidal apparatus now in place to ensure that the war against the Jews would at least be won. Mass murder continued unabated down to the autumn of 1944, when the Red Army began to approach the extermination centres, but tens of thousands more Jews died in the remaining concentration camps and the death marches to the German interior.

The slowness of the German retreat, which ended only in May 1945 with the complete destruction of German resistance and the occupation of all German territory, can be explained by the same operational, technical, and fighting skills displayed in the period of German victories. The German armed forces, even under massive numerical pressure, and starved of air support once fighters were withdrawn to contest the bombing, were formidable opponents on all fronts. Why the German armed forces kept fighting and the home front continued to support the war effort are important questions. A loose network of senior German officers and civilian sympathizers tried to assassinate Hitler on a number of occasions because they believed he was leading Germany to destruction, but the principal attempt, on 20 July 1944, when a bomb exploded under the table at which Hitler was sitting in his headquarters, was a failure. Secret police reports indicated that there was genuine horror at the attempted coup and relief that Hitler had survived. For the German people and armed forces, options by 1944 were extremely narrow. After the experience of Versailles it was widely assumed that Allied vengeance this time would be even worse, resulting perhaps in the dismemberment of Germany and the eradication of German culture, the emasculation of the German economy and the collective punishment of the German people for supporting the war. The propaganda regime of Joseph Goebbels played on the idea that Germany was struggling to save European civilization from Allied barbarism, but many ordinary Germans no doubt made their own mind up that the future after defeat would be terribly bleak.

The options were narrow in other senses too. Any sign of dissent or defeatism was harshly treated in a dictatorship which behaved in increasingly lawless ways against its own people. Continued participation in the war effort also brought rewards, since the state and the party were the source of food rations, welfare, evacuation schemes, and, for bomb victims, of compensation and rehabilitation. Confronting the state's decision to continue fighting promised only the most negative of outcomes. Moreover inside Germany by 1944 were more than eight million forced labourers and prisoners who were kept under control only by harsh discipline, but whose presence was a permanent threat to the native German population. There seems little doubt that given a free choice most Germans would have opted to end the war, but there were no free choices in 1944–5 and only the prospect of an unknown fate after unconditional surrender. Some sense of the paradoxes facing German soldiers and civilians, fighting a war that was evidently going to be lost, for a system they had applauded but now feared, can be found in a conversation between German prisoners in Italy, secretly recorded by local Allied intelligence officers:

What have we really got out of life? Born in the middle of the war, children during the inflation, to school in the depression, our lives regimented for the last ten years by Nazism and the army, and now prisoners. What sort of life is that? Isn't it better to live in a free country where you can vote for a different government whenever you please? It isn't freedom we are fighting for now; it is for a lost cause.

Most accounts of the last year of the German war highlight the fatalism and apathy evident among much of the population, which awaited defeat with an understandable mixture of apprehension and relief.

For Hitler the war could only be fought to a final end. Given his chiliastic view of the world, complete victory or complete defeat were the only possibilities. As late as April 1945, with total defeat only weeks away, he told Bormann that this war could 'only be settled by the total destruction of one side or the other'. He was horrified that Germany was going to be dismembered and the German people exposed to the 'savage excesses of the Bolsheviks and the American gangsters'. But true to his vision of war as a product of the universal struggle of the German people against the Jew he argued that his success in eradicating the Jew from Germany would mean that in the long run Germany would once again emerge supreme. While the real war for which he was uniquely responsible was bringing the Red Army to storm the government quarter of Berlin in the last days of April 1945 and completing the utter destruction of German military power in the rest of Europe, the war against the phantom Jewish conspiracy in Europe was the German war Hitler claimed to have won.

5 The West and the War at Sea

ERIC GROVE

ONE of the most important statements made by that great maritime strategist Sir Julian Corbett was that since men live on land and not at sea wars are usually decided ashore. The Second World War was no exception. Nevertheless, his definition of a maritime conflict as one where the sea is a principal factor also characterizes the Second World War. Any world war must be maritime. The earth as seen from space is a blue planet. Most of it is covered by water. Moreover, water remains the most efficient if not always the fastest mode of transport. An ability to use the sea is therefore a vital, if not decisive, advantage for any global coalition such as the self-styled 'United Nations' of the Second World War.

The importance of the sea in the Pacific War is given away by its title; with much of Japan's army locked up in mainland Asia, its conflict with the United States was all about the projection of maritime power, first Japan's conquest of the 'Southern Resources Area' of the 'Great East Asian Co-Prosperity Sphere' and then the American counter-attack that brought the USA to the gates of Japan, threatening annihilation if the Empire did not surrender.

The sea was no less important in the war against Germany. Despite appearances, the Third Reich was chronically short of resources. The Hitler regime always had to make difficult choices on priorities for scarce raw materials and fuel. The war was intended to *create* a self-sufficient superpower that could take on the USA as more of an equal. This could only be done by dominating a continental land mass, without necessarily a direct challenge to the great sea powers of the west. Indeed, Hitler saw an association with the erstwhile greatest of those sea powers, the British Empire, as a natural thing, not least on racial grounds. The Anglo-German Naval Agreement of 1935 had demonstrated Germany's willingness to accept 35 per cent naval inferiority, a fleet sufficient to deal with France and Poland, in return for a British move towards Germany and away from France. The British also benefited; they could, hopefully at acceptable cost, concentrate against Japan, by now their Empire's clearest danger. Moreover the agreement encouraged the Germans to build 35 per cent of British strength in all kinds of ship, rather than adopting a more radical approach based on commerce raiders both submerged and on the surface. A German fleet 35 per cent of British strength in all categories could be more easily dealt with by the balanced British fleet.

Despite this agreement, Britain soon mended its fences with France, with which it co-operated in the attempted containment of Germany. As relations with Britain deteriorated after Munich, Hitler dreamed about building a battle fleet to rival the British Empire's. The German naval high command jumped at the chance and presented the ambitious 'Z' plan that was adopted on 27 January 1939. This looked forward to a German fleet in 1945 of 10 battleships, four aircraft carriers, three battlecruisers, 15 pocket battleships, 56 cruisers, 158 destroyers and torpedo boats, and 249 submarines (U-boats). All this required a greatly increased infrastructure. For a moment the *Kriegsmarine* was top of Germany's industrial priorities. After a violently anti-British speech by Hitler at the beginning of the month at the launch of the battleship *Tirpitz*, the Anglo-German Naval Agreement was denounced on 28 April 1939.

The demand for resources of all kinds to meet the 'Z' plan was totally unrealistic, especially if an army and air force were needed for warfare on land, and not all resources were available for the armed forces, given the German economy's requirement for increased exports. In July the twelve new improved pocket battleships, a design that was proving troublesome, were cancelled. The beginning of the war marked the end of Germany's naval ambitions. The necessary concentration on the army and the Luftwaffe meant the 'Z' plan was a dead letter. The German fleet in 1939 was in no position seriously to challenge Britain's fleet that could concentrate its strength against Germany, given Hitler's inability to create a coalition of his potential allies, Italy and Japan.

Japan was especially concerned by Germany's entente with the USSR, but the Molotov–Ribbentrop Pact did undermine, at least to an extent, the ability of superior Allied sea power to inflict as much damage through economic blockade as had been done in the First World War. Germany, however, was in no position seriously to threaten the merchant ships that kept the Allied war effort going. Britain owned 18 million tons of shipping and could augment this from foreign sources. Despite its reductions in capacity before the war and its relatively inefficient methods, the British shipbuilding industry could replace about a million tons of losses a year and additional ships could be built overseas. The Germans calculated they would need to sink over seven million tons of shipping per year, 600,000 tons per month, to force Britain to come to terms. This would require an operationally deployed fleet of about 100 U-boats in the Atlantic, out of a total force of three times that figure. This was more than the U-boat flotilla anticipated in the 'Z' plan, and the pre-war shortages of raw materials had not gone away. Submarines did not just require steel but their electrical underwater propulsion systems demanded imported copper and rubber insulation. Less than sixty U-boats were actually available at the beginning of September 1939, of which 32 had sufficient endurance for Atlantic operations. As usual German plans were ambitious, with almost 660 new submarines planned by 1943, but actual production in the first nine months of the war was a mere 20.

The Attack on Shipping

The German navy had failed to learn the fundamental lesson of the First World War: that their U-boat offensive had been neutralized by convoy. It seems it actually wanted the British to *introduce* convoy as the disruption in deliveries thus caused seemed the most fruitful way to reduce shipping delivery rates. This was a clear sign at the outset of hostilities of the desperation of Germany's naval position and the perceived inability of its maritime forces, notably the small U-boat flotilla, to sink enough ships. In the event a U-boat sank the *Athenia* on the day the war broke out. The submarine commander had thought he was attacking an armed merchant cruiser, but the attack on a civilian liner led the Royal Navy to think, wrongly at this stage, that it was a sign of unrestricted submarine warfare. The Admiralty, which, contrary to common belief, had not neglected anti-submarine warfare pre-war, had decided that unrestricted warfare would trigger the introduction of convoy in the Atlantic approaches to the United Kingdom. This prevented the U-boats from inflicting serious damage on shipping. Of the 49 convoys sailed from Halifax, Nova Scotia to Liverpool from September 1939 to the end of March 1940 only three convoys lost a single ship each and only one was to a U-boat. The other two were mined, this weapon posing a significant threat in this early stage of the war until the firing rules of the German magnetic mines were learned and counter-measures taken. The 46 convoys sailed from Freetown, Sierra Leone to Liverpool over the same period lost but a single ship.

The convoy was the key to the safe and timely arrival of merchantmen; most lost no ships at all. This one is viewed from the air escort whose provision all the way across the Atlantic was the vital factor in the defeat of the U-boat in 1943.

The story was the same with the outward-bound convoys. The U-boats naturally concentrated on those ships which still sailed unescorted and were able to sink in the six months up to the end of March 1940 a total of some 222 Allied and neutral ships of almost 765,000 tons; another 430,000 tons were lost to mines. This was nowhere near the estimated 600,000 tons per month needed for serious effect.

The German surface fleet created some disruption but only sank a trivial 63,000 tons at the cost of one of its few major units, the pocket battleship *Admiral Graf Spee*, defeated by three British cruisers which she had chosen, against orders, to fight. Damaged, she was deluded into scuttling herself, thinking that heavier Allied units were at hand. German ships took risks at their peril on oceans dominated by their enemies. Hitler was moved to rename *Graf Spee*'s sister ship *Deutschland* when she returned from her disappointing first raiding cruise. The ship was given the name *Lützow*, originally allocated to the unfinished cruiser that was given to the USSR to help cement the Nazi–Soviet pact. The Führer could not risk a ship with the national name being sunk; it was symbolic of the German naval weakness that would contribute to its downfall.

It got worse for the German fleet in April. Hitler was rightly concerned at Germany's dependence on Swedish iron ore. The Reich depended on foreign supply for more than half of its iron ore and over 80 per cent of these imports came from Sweden. These had to come through the port of Narvik in winter, and although the Baltic routes were reopening for the summer, Hitler was (rightly) convinced that the Allies were planning an operation to cut off Germany permanently from the Norwegian route. The entire German navy was thus committed to a daring multi-pronged amphibious campaign which, with the help of the Luftwaffe in partially neutralizing the superior British fleet, scored a great success. The price, however, was cripplingly high. Germany's newest heavy cruiser *Blücher* was sunk, as were two light cruisers, and ten of her latest destroyers. Debilitating damage was inflicted on Germany's only two battleships, *Scharnhorst* and *Gneisenau*, and on *Lützow*, now classified as a heavy cruiser. By summer the German navy was down to an effective force of the heavy cruiser *Hipper* (also damaged off Norway but now repaired), two light cruisers, and four destroyers.

This was a particular problem as Germany was now in the totally unexpected position of considering an invasion of Britain. Her concentration on land and air forces had been vindicated by a victory against the Allies in France and the Low Countries in May–June 1940 that was unexpected in its decisiveness for both sides. The fact that the Royal Navy was able to evacuate the forces trapped around Dunkirk, however, boded ill for further German conquest beyond the coast of continental Europe. France's armistice took the French fleet out of the strategic equation and the panicky British response of attacking its capital ships at Mers-el-Kébir in North Africa, with only limited success but heavy loss of life, risked bringing France's numerous and powerful cruisers and destroyers into the lists against Britain, exactly what was required to cover an invasion. Happily the anti-German instincts of the Vichy regime prevented such a disastrous outcome.

To carry their threatened invasion force across the Channel the Germans spent the summer of 1940 gathering a large number of barges which they hoped to tow across the Channel by tugs. The speed of this improvised armada would be so slow that at times the invasion fleet would be going backwards against the tide. The barges full of troops would spend hours crossing the Channel, including a considerable period at night. The barges had no naval escort or cover. The large number of British destroyers deployed on the east coast backed up by small anti-submarine sloops capable of firing depth-charges would have had no trouble in sinking (or just swamping) these sitting ducks. The British ships were supported by cruisers based on the Humber and the fleet's most powerful capital ships in the Firth of Forth. All Germany's few surviving surface units could do was act as decoys. Operation Sea Lion was a totally impractical plan.

The German alternative was the 'Eagle Attack', the attempt to knock out the RAF, whose apparent failure was used as an alibi to postpone 'Sea Lion', much to the German navy's relief. This has created the misleading impression that the air battle was a preliminary to invasion. The Luftwaffe could have done little to stop the massacre of the German army as it crossed the Channel. It could not attack any ships at night, nor British ships among the invasion fleet. With no German naval gunfire support available it would have had to support the troops ashore. In the event, the Luftwaffe really wanted air superiority to coerce Britain into coming to terms by bombing alone, something it singularly failed to do. Britain held out by commanding the surrounding narrow seas, and the loss of the barges from normal trade probably inflicted more economic damage than RAF Bomber Command at this stage of the war could ever have done.

As the Germans planned the invasion of the Soviet Union both the Luftwaffe and the German navy tried to wear down Britain's resistance by attacking its cities and its shipping. The conquest of France had greatly enhanced the potential of the small number of U-boats available, a mere 25, which were now capable of a much shorter transit time into the Atlantic. The British had to concentrate all shipping into the north-west approaches as far away as possible from the new threat. In August, they also began a new series of convoys for the slow ships that had not been allowed in convoy so far and which, sailing independently, had been the U-boats' major victims. This put a considerable strain on resources of escort vessels, as convoy escort required the same type of ships, notably destroyers, as were necessary to guard against invasion.

The U-boat commanders had a potential answer to convoys, packs of multiple U-boats using their surface mobility under radio direction to concentrate against convoys and attack at night. Such tactics had been attempted unsuccessfully but were in any case unnecessary at first as the large number of independent sailings provided such rich pickings. Losses of independents to U-boats shot up from eight in May to 44 in June, although they were reduced to 27 in July. Convoy losses however also increased from two in May to 11 in June.

The larger number of ships in convoy encouraged the adoption at last of the Wolf Pack. The small number of available escorts sometimes could do little to stave off the danger. In September HX 74 was attacked by five boats which sank 12 ships. In October one of the new slow convoys suffered a very serious pack attack, almost half the 35 ships in convoy SC7 being lost. The pack then moved on to HX 79, sinking 10 out of 49. Total losses in convoy in October were 32 plus 13 stragglers. Germany was also able to put to sea that month the pocket battleship *Admiral Scheer*, which had been out of the war because of engine trouble and a subsequent long refit. She struck lucky on 5 November and found HX 84, from which she sank six ships and the escorting armed merchant cruiser *Jervis Bay* that bravely covered the convoy as it scattered.

Yet how significant was this in damaging Britain's shipping and supply situation? At no time did shipping losses come anywhere near the 600,000 tons a month that the German Commander of Submarines, Vice-Admiral Karl Dönitz, thought he needed. The total sunk in the North Atlantic in October was 286,000 tons, less than half the required figure and that was the peak figure in 1940. Most convoys lost no ships at all. Only 15 of the 40 HX convoys run between June 1940 and the end of December lost any ships. Even the slow SCs lost ships from only five of the 17 sailed by the end of 1940. This might have been the U-boats' 'Happy Time' but they were far from achieving their objectives. Hitler had talked of increasing the priority of U-boat production and building 25 per month but the steel allocations were soon returned to the army preparing for its adventures in the east. From June 1940 to March 1941 U-boat production averaged only seven per month and numbers at sea in the North Atlantic in January 1941 were a mere eight.

U-boats were not, however, the only threat. As *Admiral Scheer* continued her wide-ranging voyage the Germans put to sea the cruiser *Hipper* and the battleships *Scharnhorst* and *Gneisenau*, the latter pair working together. They proved generally unable to inflict serious damage on convoys thanks to powerful defences, including old battleships. Only *Hipper* scored a significant convoy success, sinking seven of the 19 ships of a slow Sierra Leone convoy that had not yet picked up its escort. The Germans had also begun to use long-range Focke-Wulf 200 'Condor' aircraft (a modified airliner design). At the end of February 1941 these aircraft scored their greatest success, sinking eight from the 41 ships in OB 290; two more were lost to a U-boat.

Churchill was rattled. The passage of the Lend Lease act in the USA (which became law on 1 March) promised North American supply if shipping could be safeguarded. The German threat was not the only problem. The disruption of ships being put into convoy compounded by congestion in inefficient west coast ports caused shortages of imports. The main problem, however, was ship repairing. Overloaded ships in heavy weather on routes for which they had not been designed were subject to serious damage and ships obtained from overseas often required considerable work before they could be used. In February 1941 no less than 2.6 million tons of British-controlled shipping was under repair or immobilized waiting for repair, over six

Flour is seen here stockpiled in a Liverpool warehouse. Bread was never rationed in wartime Britain, a major victory for Allied command of the sea and the organization of Allied shipping.

times that month's total allied and neutral losses. The dry cargo component of this repair total was equivalent to a quarter of Britain's importing fleet. When the Prime Minister declared the Battle of the Atlantic as Britain's main preoccupation on 6 March he put emphasis on a 'concerted attack ... upon the immense mass of damaged shipping now accumulated at our ports'. Such efforts, as well as preventing losses to German forces, constituted 'the crux of the Battle of the Atlantic'.

That battle was won over the rest of 1941. It started well for the British. With the invasion threat diminished, sufficient convoy escorts were back in place and operating in better-trained groups. They were also beginning to be fitted with early radar. One such group was escorting convoy HX 112 when it was attacked by a pack that included two of Germany's finest 'ace' captains. It lost five ships but at the cost of three U-boats including those of both 'aces'. A few days earlier perhaps the most famous of the U-boat captains, Günther Prien, who had sunk the battleship *Royal Oak* in the British base of Scapa Flow in 1939, had his boat so heavily damaged attacking OB 293 that it later sank with all hands. All the German major surface units were back in port by the end of March.

March was a peak month for sinkings in the North Atlantic (almost 325,000 tons). As losses fell, the repair situation was improved by measures such as diversion of labour, double day shifts, and special lighting that allowed night shifts. By July 1941, when Atlantic losses were less than 100,000 tons, the lowest figure since May 1940, the amount of tonnage tied up in repair had come down to 1.6 million.

The Germans tried a decisive moral blow in May when they sent out their most powerful battleship, *Bismarck*, now fully worked up, accompanied by the newest heavy cruiser *Prinz Eugen*. The battleship would engage and sink the old battleship escort while *Prinz Eugen* gobbled up the convoy. Such a massacre or two, it was hoped, coupled with some the heaviest bombing yet, might just cause Britain to see sense before all was turned against the Soviet Union. The mission started well with the battle group sinking the pride of the British fleet, HMS *Hood*, and driving off Britain's newest but unready battleship, *Prince of Wales*. The *Bismarck*, however, suffered damage that forced the mission to be abandoned. Her weak anti-aircraft batteries allowed her to be crippled by carrier-based aircraft and she was pounded into a wreck by the battleships *King George V* and *Rodney*. The *Prinz Eugen* took refuge in Brest with *Scharnhorst* and *Gneisenau* where they had been immobilized by bombing. This was the last time German surface ships operated against North Atlantic convoys. *Lützow* tried a final breakout in June but was torpedoed and seriously damaged by an RAF Beaufort. The German surface fleet had been successfully contained.

The campaign against the U-boats was transformed in Britain's favour over the summer, despite an increase in their numbers. One factor was intelligence. Up to now the Germans had held the intelligence advantage. A number of captures now allowed British code breakers to read U-boat signals and this, together with other radio intelligence, allowed ships concentrated in convoys to avoid Wolf Packs. Faster merchant ships that, at significant cost, had been routed independently to improve shipping productivity were put back in convoy. The convoy system itself was extended in June and July to give anti-submarine escort for the entire North Atlantic voyage. This was enabled by the crash growth of the Royal Canadian Navy. Corners were cut in training but the mere existence of escorts gave sufficient security against the still limited U-boat threat. There were also technological improvements; new microwave surface search radar was a quantum leap in capability against surfaced U-boats.

August 1941 saw the beginning of American participation in the maritime war. At the Atlantic Charter meeting the USA agreed to take over responsibility for the Western Atlantic, including the escort of convoys which contained American ships that had been sent to Halifax to make these convoys clearly 'American'. This allowed the transfer of some Canadian escorts to reinforce the British, although slow convoys normally remained a Canadian responsibility in the western area. The US ships began escort and convoy support operations at the beginning of September.

This happened to be the last relatively bad month. Although it did its best, a badly equipped and trained Canadian escort group could not prevent a dozen U-boats sinking 15 out of SC 42's 65 ships. This was an isolated success, however, despite an increase in operational U-boats to 80 in October as increased production finally had an impact. From June 1941 to the end of the year no HX convoy lost a single ship and only five out of 25 SCs, which lost 39 ships in all, equivalent to a single relatively small convoy. In tonnage terms losses fell from almost 185,000 in September to just over 50,000 in November and December. The U-boats had been decisively defeated; their overall productivity in terms of shipping sunk to total boats at sea never recovered. At the end of 1941 they were transferred to apparently more productive business, to defend Germany's vital Scandinavian iron ore supplies and to reverse a deteriorating situation in the Mediterranean. By the middle of December only five U-boats remained in the North Atlantic, an extension of the new deployment to the Mediterranean.

The war in the Mediterranean had begun in June 1940 with the declaration of war by an Italy anxious not to be left out of the fruits of France's defeat. Italy had a powerful fleet but, its overseas supplies cut off, was desperately short of fuel. This hobbled the Italian navy's activities for the entire war. The British were able to confirm their advantage by a carrier air strike on the Italian naval base at Taranto in November 1940 that halved Italian strength in capital ships. In night action the Royal Navy was also able to outfight a fleet unprepared technologically for such engagements.

When the Italians invaded Egypt in September 1940, Churchill was tempted to authorize a full-scale North African campaign. This provided morale-boosting British victories at considerable cost in shipping capacity, most supplies having to go round the Cape. Germany came to Italy's rescue and some German leaders toyed with the idea of a Mediterranean strategy, but this was unlikely, given Hitler's Soviet priority. In 1941 German air power in the shape of the specially trained Fliegerkorps X was able to do much to neutralize a British Mediterranean fleet whose carriers' immature anti-air warfare capabilities were unable even to protect themselves. This safeguarded Axis Mediterranean maritime lines of communication and enabled Rommel to counter-attack in March 1941.

Churchill had mistakenly withdrawn forces from North Africa to aid Greece, also invaded by the Italians. The Germans came to their assistance here too to clear the southern flank for their eastward offensive. British sea power could only withdraw British forces first from Greece and later Crete. The Royal Navy's successful defence of the latter island was neutralized by an airborne invasion compounded by mistakes by the Imperial land command ashore. The casualties were such that Hitler never again attempted such an operation, but the maritime evacuation proved equally expensive for the British as they were assailed again from the air. Merchant shipping losses were also grievous. In April 1941 more ships were lost in the Mediterranean than in the Atlantic, pushing monthly losses through Dönitz's magic 600,000 tons for the first time in the war. It was worse in May with 325,000 tons lost in the Mediterranean, although this was mitigated by reduced Atlantic losses.

The Germans could do little, however, to prevent British consolidation of their position in Syria, Iraq, and Ethiopia, which meant that Middle Eastern oil could be securely obtained and safely transported. Securing the Indian Ocean also meant that Roosevelt could allow American ships directly to support the British in the Middle East despite restrictive Congressional legislation. This did something to mitigate the shipping situation. The invasion of the Soviet Union also took German air assets away from the Mediterranean, allowing Britain to reassert command of the theatre. The British were able fully to exploit Malta with the deployment of cruiser and destroyer striking forces that fatally disrupted Axis communications, massacring entire convoys. For most of the war there were more supplies in Tripoli than could be transported forward to the Axis forces. This was not the situation in late 1941. Rommel was forced to retreat and the Germans to reallocate their U-boats to retrieve the situation. The North African campaign may have been expensive in shipping but it also diverted U-boats from the main shipping routes, thus consolidating British victory there.

The British maritime blockade was working better than many have since thought. Although German production increased that was not the case in the occupied territories, whose economies, at best, stagnated. Starved of fuel, Germany's conquests sank back into the nineteenth century as far as transport was concerned, with disastrous consequences for the supply of such products as milk. In 1941 the Germans were forced to consider a still greater emphasis on horses for the army's transport requirements. Truck drivers were given only minimal training, with disastrous results when the Eastern campaign opened, and even after that, with German forces at the gates of Moscow, Germany's leading truck manufacturer had to shut down for a period because of insufficient fuel even to check the fuel pumps!

These problems, it was hoped, would be solved by conquests and colonization in the east, and the great campaign began on 22 June 1941. The Soviet Union was soon the recipient of Anglo-American aid which came by sea, at first largely in American ships and almost entirely via the Arctic ports, despite their infrastructural limitations. Ships had to be taken out of service to be modified for the Arctic conditions, compounding shipping shortages. Even at this early stage, however, the aid was significant. Heavily armoured British-supplied tanks played a significant role in replacing the catastrophic losses of Soviet armour and in helping turn the tide at the gates of Moscow.

The Two-Ocean War

December 1941 was the key month of the entire war as it saw Japan attack both the USA and the British and Dutch Empires and Germany declare war on the USA. Japan had little choice but to go to war if it was to hang on to its existing conquests. It was dependent on supplies of fuel brought in from overseas, notably from the East Indies. These were purchased with dollar assets subject to American control. After Japan's move into southern Indochina in the summer of 1941 those assets were frozen. It became clear that the USA was demanding an unacceptable total withdrawal from both post- and pre-1937 conquests in China. There seemed to be a maritime alternative.

In the mid-1930s Japan had withdrawn from the naval arms control system and raced ahead with a naval build-up. This was in a context of attempts to exploit

The British battlecruiser *Repulse* escorting troop ships shortly before her sinking by land-based Japanese navy torpedo bombers in December 1941. British reinforcement of Singapore in 1941 was too little, too late.

technological superiority to make up for the inferior numerical strength resulting from the Washington and London treaties. By 1941 the Japanese navy had the best torpedoes in the world, the best-equipped naval air arm (with a unique long-range land-based naval air striking-force to back up a powerful carrier force), and was building the largest battleships ever. Its older ships were fully modernized. This superior capital had to be cashed in soon, as Germany's victory over France had stimulated the USA to embark in 1940 on the rapid construction of a 'Two-Ocean Navy', that would be impossible to counter. It was now or never.

So the Japanese planned an ambitious series of landings covered by surface forces and land-based air power to take British and Dutch South-East Asia, and the Philippines that dominated the sea route in between. Admiral Yamamoto, the commander of the Japanese Combined Fleet, thought the USA could be shocked into acquiescence by a surprise attack on the American battlefleet, which Roosevelt had forward deployed at Pearl Harbor as a supposed deterrent. He had an instrument to do so: the carrier strike-force of six ships and 350 aircraft. Even if it only sank one battleship, the Admiral thought the shocked Americans would soon cry 'Enough!' For an officer who had served in the USA this was a grave misjudgement.

The Americans were anticipating war and waiting for the first shot, though they did not expect it to come at Pearl Harbor. The administration's attempts to prevent an early clash that might have seemed a provocation to opponents of war in Congress prevented reconnaissance in the direction from which the attack occurred and encouraged the commanders in Hawaii to reduce the level of alert. On 7 December this

A view taken three days after the Pearl Harbor attack from the capsized battleship *Oklahoma* of the USS *Tennessee* (left) and the USS *West Virginia* (right) with *Arizona* visible in the background. The *West Virginia* was returned to service in 1944; *Oklahoma* and *Arizona* were the two total battleship losses of the raid.

allowed the Japanese, despite faults in executing the attack, to achieve relatively good results in terms of its basic objectives, blowing up one battleship and capsizing another, and leaving three others sunk at their moorings. Many aircraft were destroyed (to prevent an air counter-attack) but, crucially, all carriers were away reinforcing American island bases in the expectation of war. This was much to the chagrin of the Japanese airmen, who, despite intelligence to the contrary, had distorted the original plan in order to attack the carrier anchorage on the off-chance one might be present.

The Americans were indeed shocked, but not into acceptance of Japanese expansion. Instead they were roused to an anger that would only be stilled by Japan's total defeat. Roosevelt could not have wished for a better result politically although strategically, in the short term, the situation was dire. The USA was forced to use its aircraft carriers as capital ships, despite the carriers' limited ability to defend themselves from air attack given their lack of adequate fighter control. They did however carry more aircraft than any other carriers and could engage in long-range strikes. Their dive bombers made them formidable opponents for Japanese carriers, cruisers, and destroyers but their lack of an adequate torpedo bomber limited their ability against enemy battleships. There was little to prevent Japanese land-based aircraft quickly dispatching with torpedoes the two capital ships sent east by the British as a

The work required to repair the damaged battleships after the Pearl Harbor attack can be gauged from this view of the USS *West Virginia* being patched up to sail back to the USA for a complete rebuild. With a transformed appearance she was back in action before the invasion of the Philippines and led the line at the world's last battleship v. battleship engagement during the Leyte Gulf battle.

deterrent, while Japanese surface forces annihilated the scratch multinational squadron put together to defend the East Indies.

The Japanese attack on the United States was welcomed in Berlin. The USA was already effectively in the war against Germany. In November, in addition to escorting convoys (a destroyer was sunk on this duty on 31 October), the US navy sent a battle group to guard the Denmark Strait against a possible break-out by a surface unit indicated by intelligence sources. This was the most likely path to the Atlantic and other commitments meant only one British battleship was available, and it could not provide sufficient cover alone. No German ship appeared, but it would have created an interesting situation if it had. In the event, encouraged by the prospect of a withdrawal of US naval forces to the Pacific and the promise of rich pickings in independent shipping off the American coast (as well as a possible Japanese declaration of war against the USSR), Hitler declared war on the USA.

The U-boats were unleashed in American waters and results were indeed catastrophic for Allied shipping. The Americans did divert warships to the Pacific and, as a result, did not introduce convoy in their own waters. According to American naval doctrine, the main purpose of convoy escorts was not to ensure the safe and timely arrival of the merchant ships but to sink U-boats. Ignoring British experience, the US navy held that badly escorted convoys were worse than none. The results were disastrous. Allied and neutral shipping losses in the whole North Atlantic shot up to

472,000 tons per month in the first half of 1942, and the global average was almost 700,000. In June losses in the North Atlantic alone passed Dönitz's 600,000 tons, the only time they did so during the war. Yet, as British and Canadian ships replaced US ships in the escort groups, convoys sailed unscathed; no HX lost a ship in this period and only one SC, and that only one ship. This was despite the fact that relevant German codes could once again not be read from February 1942.

The Battle of the Central and Eastern Atlantic remained won; it was now accompanied by a massacre of undefended ships in the Western Atlantic, which spread to the Caribbean in May as U-boat fuel tankers increased the range of the smaller standard German submarines. Numbers of unescorted ships sunk by U-boats climbed in June to 121, largely in American waters. The US navy finally began to run coastal convoys in May and, as the system spread, losses at last came down. The belated introduction of convoy in US waters was, at best, a remarkable act of faith in the capacity of the American shipbuilding industry to replace losses. It is perhaps also noteworthy that in the first half of 1942 the net loss of British major dry cargo ships was 496 while the American fleet's net *gain* was 326 vessels.

Shortage of shipping constrained Japan's strategic options after its initial successes. The unwillingness of the USA to come to terms forced Japan to consider its choices. The one with the most potential was to turn west and complete the destruction of the British Empire by an offensive into the Indian Ocean. Taking Ceylon would have destabilized India and been a stepping stone to Madagascar and cutting the Allied

In spring 1942, WS17 with 31 ships was the largest troop convoy so far sent from Britain to the Indian Ocean to reinforce India and the Middle East against the Japanese threat. This view, taken from the British cruiser *Hermione*, shows the section of convoy that sailed under escort from Freetown to South Africa.

supply line to the Middle East. There were, however, neither the ships nor the troops for such an initiative and, when the Japanese carrier striking force was sent on a flank protecting raid against Ceylon in April, the British Eastern Fleet of five old and mostly unmodified battleships and three inadequately equipped carriers operating from a secret atoll base—and keeping out of harm's way—was able to survive largely unscathed. Only a small carrier and two cruisers sent to Ceylon to prepare for an operation to safeguard Madagascar were sunk. Churchill, for obvious reasons, called it 'the most dangerous moment' of the war. Even a major defeat at sea of the fleet would have been an unbearable burden for his government following the loss of Singapore, but the need not have worried. Japan could do little more, and Madagascar was partially occupied in a model amphibious operation early the following month.

The other two Japanese options were to go south-east to prevent Australia being used as a base for a counter-attack, or an attack on Midway Island to threaten Hawaii and draw out the American carriers to their destruction These were beginning to mount raids, one of which, using army medium bombers, hit Japan itself. It was decided therefore first to safeguard the position in the south, where Port Moresby, the capital of New Guinea, was still holding out, and then go for a decisive battle that would surely at last cause the Americans to lose their nerve.

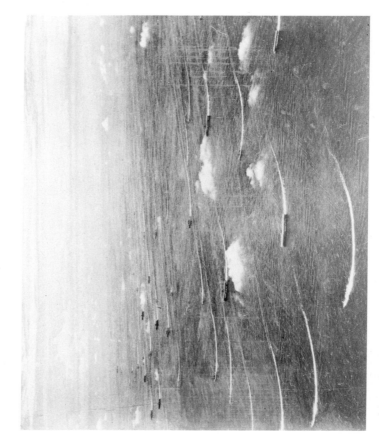

The power of the US Pacific Fleet in 1944 is demonstrated by this view of two Carrier Task Groups operating together. Each consists of two to three fleet carriers and two light carriers plus escorts. Four such Groups constituted a formidable task force.

These plans failed miserably. The battles of Coral Sea and Midway demonstrated both the vulnerability as well as the power of carriers before effective radar fighter control. The Americans lost two carriers and the Japanese five, with two others effectively disabled. Without his carriers Yamamoto withdrew his Midway invasion fleet. Although his battleships were not vulnerable to the US carriers (whose torpedo bombers had been shot out of the sky), his cruisers and destroyers were. Moreover there were land-based aircraft at Midway to consider and the Japanese admiral, mirror-imaging his own navy's capabilities, was concerned about the dangers he thought they still posed to his surface ships without carrier air cover.

Midway was the high-water mark of Japanese expansion. The Americans now began a maritime 'offensive defensive' in the Solomons which drew the Japanese into a series of battles in which both sides suffered heavy losses of ships, aircraft, and skilled personnel, especially pilots. The USA could afford this attrition; Japan could not. As the 'Two-Ocean Navy' began to come on stream in 1943 it was clear that the Japanese gamble had failed.

Defeating the U-Boat

Despite the preoccupations of its navy in the Pacific the USA was still committed to a strategy of 'Germany First'. This meant that American forces had to begin to cross the Atlantic in substantial numbers to prepare for the assault on mainland Europe which

The British Cunard liner *Mauretania* in Liverpool on a trooping voyage. A new ship, she had barely begun her career when she was diverted to wartime duties transporting British Empire and American troops. Note the degaussing coil along the side to neutralize magnetic mines.

the US army saw as the centrepiece of its strategy. Operation 'Bolero', as this process was known, was moving around 20,000 personnel a month from the USA to the UK by the summer of 1942. In the second half of the year the liners *Queen Mary* and *Queen Elizabeth* were put on this run, having previously been used to move troops between Australia and the Middle East A total of a quarter of a million Americans had arrived in the United Kingdom by the end of the year.

In the summer of 1942 the Germans moved back to trying to interdict mid-Atlantic shipping as the spread of the convoy system drove them out of American waters. There was now no alternative to taking on the convoys and for nine months a second Battle of the Atlantic took place, largely in the mid-Atlantic gap beyond the range of shore-based air cover. Numbers of operational U-boats steadily rose from 140 in July to almost 200 in October. The German surface fleet was now completely out of the picture in these waters, the ships at Brest having fled northwards under heavy escort through the Channel in February 1942.

The code-breaking advantage lay with the Germans until the end of the year but, despite some battles, most convoys in late 1942 got through unscathed. Only three HX convoys suffered any loss and only one, HX 212, lost a significant number of ships, five out of 43. Predictably the SCs were less lucky; SC 94 lost a third of its thirty ships and SC 107 no less than 15 of its 41. The westbound ON 154 was almost as bad with 13 lost out of 45, but these were isolated failures. From July to December out of 24 SC convoys 17 lost no ships at all and out of 47 ON convoys only nine suffered losses. The escorts could usually cope. They were now equipped with ship-borne high-frequency radio direction-finding equipment (HFDF or 'Huffduff') that capitalized on the U-boats' transmissions that were a necessity for pack attacks. The less well equipped and trained Canadians were at a disadvantage and the two worst battles were against these groups. Delicately, at the beginning of 1943 they were withdrawn for training and re-equipping.

The Germans were still far from winning. In June 1942, facing likely Allied shipbuilding capacity of 10 million tons per year, Dönitz increased his sinking objectives to 900,000 tons per month. Despite the losses of 1942 the amount of dry cargo shipping available to Britain was almost the same at the end of 1942 as it had been in 1939 and there were more tankers than there had been before the war, standard designs aiding mass production. This helped safeguard oil supplies. In 1942 Britain imported 10 million tons of oil from its overseas suppliers, five times the amount of oil Germany obtained from its main supplier, Romania.

Allied shipbuilding in 1943 was even worse than Dönitz expected. US merchant shipbuilding increased from 5.5 million tons in 1942 to no less than 11.5 million tons in 1943. In terms of load carrying weight dry cargo capacity, deadweight tonnage, the USA built in 1943 the same amount as the entire British dry cargo fleet at the beginning of the year. Mass production techniques were utilized with prefabrication and welding. It took an average of six weeks to produce one 1,000 deadweight ton Liberty ship and three were produced a day at peak production; eighteen yards produced 2,751 such ships over the whole war. Over 1942–3 the British Empire added another 4 million tons. Similar ships to the Liberty (which was in any case of British design) were built in both Britain and Canada. The Canadian industry's efforts were particularly impressive, the number of its slipways expanding fourfold by 1943.

The Germans never attained their enlarged objective for the number of merchant ships sunk. In only two months in the second half of 1942, August and November, did monthly losses in the North Atlantic exceed 500,000 tons. South Atlantic losses did suddenly triple to almost 150,000 tons in October because of the need to support the first amphibious offensive (see below), forcing unescorted ships to take their chances with the U-boats. In November 1942 total global shipping losses peaked again at over 800,000 tons but they were never as great again. The Rome–Berlin–Tokyo axis just could not sink enough ships.

Despite—and because of—chronic fuel shortages, Hitler made his bid for secure oil supplies in the summer of 1942 with a land offensive into the southern USSR. As the campaign became diverted into the battle for Stalingrad the Allied maritime threat to his flanks prevented deployment of sufficient forces to give security against Soviet counter-offensives. The major raid on Dieppe by British and Canadian forces in August was a tactical fiasco but it caused Hitler to keep forces in France that might have made all the difference in the east. Hitler lived at the armed forces headquarters, OKW, which was responsible for all fronts except Russia. This meant that threats to the maritime flanks had particular salience to the Führer. The British, with their instinct for peripheral maritime strategies, pressed for such diversions from the US army's main priority of reopening a western front in Europe. They were right to do so.

The mass-produced Liberty ship was a major factor in the Allies' capacity to exploit the world ocean. Here is one in convoy RA64 from the Kola Inlet to Loch Ewe in February 1945. Two merchant ships were sunk from this convoy plus two escorts; one U-boat was destroyed.

Hitler's sensitivity about his maritime flanks meant that he felt forced to guard a massive maritime perimeter as well as redeploy forces to deal with maritime threats as they arose. This prevented him from concentrating sufficient forces in Russia.

Instead of a major assault in France the Allies decided to mount an invasion of North Africa to defeat the Axis once and for all in this theatre. The Mediterranean and North African war had been raging throughout 1942. German submarines and Italian human torpedoes had neutralized the major units of the British squadrons at each end of the Mediterranean at the end of the previous year. The Germans once more laid siege to Malta from the air, and rather than being an offensive base the island became an Imperial 'fortress' which could not be allowed to fall. As Rommel advanced in North Africa, extending the reach of Axis air power, the island had to be supplied from the west. The USA provided tankers to major convoy operations. These culminated in the huge 'Pedestal' convoy in August when virtually the entire available British fleet was committed to the relief of the island. British carriers helped fight off Axis attacks, although the slowly maturing techniques of fighter control were eventually swamped. It remains a matter of dispute how far the aircraft and submarines based in the island contributed to the supply problems of the Axis forces as they extended their lines of communication into Egypt, but it was certainly true that the shipping sustaining and re-equipping the British army had a much greater capacity and security. When the Eighth Army eventually attacked at Alamein this maritime superiority was expressed in a numerical and logistical strength that no amount of German skill could counter.

The Allies now planned to exploit their dominant sea power to assault the Axis position in North Africa from both ends. An attack in the Western Desert would be combined with a major maritime invasion, Torch, to capture French North Africa. This began on 8 November 1942. US landings against Morocco were projected directly across the Atlantic, despite the submarine threat. In the event the landings diverted U-boats from the merchant shipping routes without interfering with the invasion. The British landed in Algeria. France effectively re-entered the war as a result, although at the price of the larger part of its fleet at Toulon that was scuttled to stop it falling into German hands as Vichy France was occupied.

North Africa did not work out quite as the Allies had hoped. The Germans and Italians held out in Tunisia until May 1943 and the campaign made a major contribution to a growing shipping crisis. It took time for the new ships to come on stream and Allied co-operation became strained as the Anglo-American stock of ships had to be allocated between different priorities. The price was paid in the Indian Ocean where Allied plans for a major operation to retake Burma had to be abandoned and civilian supply shipping so seriously curtailed that famine gripped Bengal and millions died. The Bolero transatlantic transport operation also faltered for a while but the major priorities, maintaining Britain as a forward base, achieving victory in North Africa and expanding the Mediterranean campaign to an invasion of Italy, and supplying the Soviet Union and the US navy's war against Japan in the Pacific went ahead with little hindrance.

Allocation of shipping was the major crisis of 1943, but in parallel the U-boat war rose to a peak. Numbers of operational U-boats went through the 200 mark at the beginning of the year. The result was a series of major convoy battles as the packs made their supreme effort, especially in the mid-Atlantic where air cover was still not available. This again was a matter of allocation. The Allied high command considered that the shipping situation was not serious enough to make maritime patrol a priority, and they preferred to use the long-range bombers needed over the Atlantic to bomb Germany instead. The new escort carriers also went elsewhere to support the amphibious offensive.

The proportion of Atlantic shipping lost in convoy increased from 58 per cent in December 1942 to 67 per cent in January and 84 per cent in March. Although the Allies had regained their ability to read the signals of the German U-boats at the end of 1942, the speed at which they could do so slowed down in March 1943 and the 70 deployed U-boats regained an intelligence advantage. In early March all convoys were intercepted, and over half were attacked, preventing over 20 per cent of the ships that set out in the first three weeks of the month making a safe and timely arrival. For perhaps the only time in the war the 'Battle of the Atlantic' looked like its post-war legend.

Doubts began to be expressed about the continued utility of convoy but, in retrospect, the overall situation does not look so dire. Of the nine slow and vulnerable SC convoys that sailed between January and March 1943 only three suffered losses, eight out of 61 ships, seven out of 57, and eight out of 51; only a third of the convoys lost any ships and the worst lost barely over 15 per cent. Of the 11 fast HX convoys sailed in the same period only three lost ships, HX 229 suffering the worst loss of any such convoy in the war, 12 out of 38; the other two convoys lost only seven between them. HX 229 was an isolated disaster that caused morale to wobble, not a typical U-boat success. Losses in the North Atlantic in March did indeed spike to almost 475,000 tons but this was substantially less than even Dönitz's earlier 600,000. Global losses that month were less than 700,000, nowhere near Dönitz's revised figures. And losses would never be as serious again.

A war of attrition was being fought in the Atlantic, and the Germans, not the Allies, were losing. A new series of slow outward-bound convoys was begun in March. The second lost two out of 18 ships but ONS 5 in April lost 11 out of 42. This was, however, at a cost of seven U-boats, with two more lost by accident, more than half of the pack engaged. More surface escorts were being allocated in support groups that, thanks to renewed rapid reading of German codes, could be sent to endangered convoys. Enough escort carriers and long-range aircraft were belatedly made available to close the gap and well-trained escort crews had the radar and direction-finding technology to defeat the submarines. May was a disastrous month for Dönitz as 41 submarines were sunk, smashing themselves against a convoy system that had finally matured; only 163,000 tons of Allied ships were lost. The Germans tried to make a comeback with new weapons later in the year but to little effect. After May 1943 for the rest of the war only three out of over a hundred HX convoys and four out of over fifty SC convoys lost any ships at all and none more than two.

Sea Power and Allied Victory

With the Atlantic link secure and better organization of available shipping the Allies could continue their offensive against the European Axis. In July 1943 Sicily was invaded in an operation that deployed over 1,600 British war and merchant ships, 945 American, and 31 from the European allies. This investment of Allied sea power had an enormous overall impact on the war. The Germans had begun their major 'Zitadelle' offensive against the Kursk salient in the east and were inflicting highly disproportionate attrition on their enemies. With his southern flank threatened and British deception operations threatening attacks from Sardinia to the Balkans, Hitler at OKW felt constrained to call off this operation so that vital formations (notably the SS

Panzer forces which had been massacring Soviet armour around Prokhorovka) could be transferred in order to protect his southern flank. Never again would the German ground forces be deployed in such strength against the Red Army.

Without Allied maritime diversion of German forces, the Soviet army, always suffering hugely disproportionate casualties, might well have faced defeat. Western supplies were also of crucial importance for the Red Army and, except for most of the US-built aircraft, they had to come by sea. The Arctic convoys were joined by routes through occupied Iran and the Soviet Far East as Japan appeased Stalin and did nothing to stop the flow of ships to Vladivostok, as long as they bore Soviet flags.

The Arctic route remained the most dangerous as it had to run the gauntlet of the forces Hitler had massed in Norway to guard the vital iron ore lifeline. These included the remaining heavy units of the German fleet as well as U-boats and aircraft. When used in synergy these could massacre almost entire convoys, but at the end of 1942, when convoy escort and supporting forces drove off one of his cruisers and a pocket battleship, Hitler ordered his surface fleet scrapped. Dönitz, appointed to command the whole navy, managed to maintain a fleet in being but the battleship *Tirpitz* was neutralized by midget submarine and air attacks and *Scharnhorst* sunk in the last ever British battleship v. battleship action at the end of 1943. Indeed the Arctic convoys became as much bait to draw out German assets to their destruction as a supply channel and an important political token of Western support.

In the event only 7 per cent of the almost 4 million tons of supplies sent on the Arctic route failed to get through. Over 4 million tons went through Iran and more than the other two routes combined came via the Pacific. The Japanese insisted this not include war material, so this was the main artery carrying food (Khrushchev, Stalin's successor, said the Soviet army could not have operated without SPAM processed meat), clothing, telephone cable, aluminium, and railway equipment (which the Soviets had almost stopped producing themselves). Many non-combat motor vehicles also went through the Pacific. Transport was perhaps the greatest single Lend Lease contribution to the Red Army's fighting power. Over 500,000 American-built vehicles were sent to the USSR, almost 78,000 jeeps, and over 350,000 trucks. By 1945 two-thirds of the Red Army's wheeled transport was American-manufactured. 22,800 American, Canadian, and British armoured vehicles went via Iran and the Arctic, providing the USSR with 16 per cent of its total force. Western tanks, Stuarts and Valentines, often substituted for interior Soviet light tanks, and the reliability of the Sherman, the most numerous single type, was valued. US armoured personnel carriers were the only such vehicles the USSR deployed. The shipping effort was considerable. In the American shipping 'budget' for the first half of 1945 some 2 million deadweight tons of ships were allocated to supplying the USSR, over four times the US tonnage allocated to sustain the UK and almost half of the tonnage allocated to supporting the US army in Europe.

The route to the USSR via Iran was made easier by the opening of the Mediterranean. The allies moved from Sicily to the Italian mainland in September 1943 in two landing areas. This caused Italy to change sides and surrender its fleet. The Germans

The sheer extent of Allied amphibious capability is shown by this view during the Normandy landings of a flotilla of large infantry landing craft with smaller landing craft in the foreground. The LCI(L)s are American-built as are the three smaller landing craft vehicle and personnel (LCVPs) in the forefront; the Assault Landing Craft (LCA) in the left foreground is British-designed.

were, however, able to respond and the Allied armies were soon bogged down. An attempt was made to turn the German flank by a seaborne assault at Anzio in January 1944 but with disappointing results. Planning for this operation also revealed the problems in providing sufficient numbers of landing craft to service all strategic options.

One of the most remarkable features of the maritime war was the development and production of different types of landing craft and larger landing ships. Passenger ships were converted so that they could land infantry in small assault landing craft while larger tank and infantry landing craft were built along with ocean going Landing Ships Tank (LSTs), the origins of today's roll-on roll-off ferries. Britain played a large part in designing these ships but most were built in the USA. Britain received 115 tank landing ships under Lend Lease and 220 large infantry landing ships; over a thousand of each type were built in America. Nevertheless UK facilities (including a converted furniture factory close to an inland waterway) were not idle, building over 2,000 assault landing craft as well as 450 tank landing craft.

These ships and craft gave strategic maritime mobility to modern armies but there were not enough, especially as they were as essential to the American maritime offensive against Japan as they were to the projection of Allied power against Germany. Given the decision finally to open a new Western Front in France in the summer of 1944, Operation Overlord, the planned move of landing craft and ships back to the UK had to be diverted to provide the assets for Anzio. They were eventually sent home in April. The Indian Ocean had again paid the price. The South-East Asian Command

British Fleet Air Arm Corsair fighters prepare to take off to support the British Pacific Fleet's attack on the oil refineries at Palembang in January 1945 which reduced Japanese oil supplies by over a third.

had to give up half its amphibious capability to support the Mediterranean operations, causing its ambitions both for landings in the Andaman Islands and then on the Arakan coast of Burma to be abandoned. It was ironic that the newly appointed Supreme Allied Commander South-East Asia, Lord Louis Mountbatten, should find his options constrained by shortages of the landing vessels that he, as Chief of Combined Operations in London, had done so much to create and build up. His appointment showed what Churchill might have expected, a maritime campaign across the Bay of Bengal, but, given other and overriding priorities, there were just not enough specialist amphibious vessels. What shipping was available in theatre had to be used to support operations ashore—and stave off another famine.

The scope and global reach of the sea power of the 'United Nations' was never better demonstrated than in June 1944. Simultaneously two of the largest maritime offensives ever seen were carried out on opposite sides of the world. In Europe Operation Neptune, the naval side of 'Overlord', placed an army ashore on the beaches of Normandy. This was the last time an operation of global stature was commanded by the Royal Navy in the person of Admiral Bertram Ramsay and his largely British staff. Most of the ships were also British; only 30 per cent were American. The scale of the operation was immense: almost 6,500 ships and craft including almost 1,100 warships from battleships downwards, over 4,000 landing ships and craft, and over 1,250 merchant ships.

American troops come ashore from American-operated large infantry landing craft on 6 June, the first day of the Normandy landings. Constructed to British Admiralty requirements to take advantage of American production facilities, over a thousand of these vessels were built for American service, some operated by coast guard rather than naval crews.

The Luftwaffe had been defeated over Germany by the USAAF's strategic offensive, which was a potent demonstration of the synergy of air and sea power. It used fuel, ground crews, ammunition, and other supplies brought by sea and could not have been carried out without Allied maritime dominance. Allied warships and land-based air forces covered and supported the landings by bombarding the shore and defeating what limited naval opposition was put up. As the Normandy beach head was used to sustain and reinforce the initial landings, both over the beaches and using two 'Mulberry' artificial harbours, the Germans were reduced to manned torpedoes and explosive motor boats, a sign of naval desperation. One of the Mulberries was wrecked by a storm but, nonetheless, by the end of June almost 90,000 vehicles had been landed for each of the major allies. Even more were scheduled, but it was enough for the scale of advance actually achieved by the Allied armies; supplies were not the limiting problem. The limited initial advances however did nothing to prevent the diversionary impact of Allied maritime power affecting the Eastern Front. With some of Germany's best armoured forces facing the Western Allies, the decisively depleted Wehrmacht was crushed in the Red Army's summer offensive.

As the ships deployed for the Normandy beaches another, amphibious force set sail for the Marianas. It was covered by perhaps the most powerful battle fleet the world had yet seen, the Fifth Fleet with four carrier task groups and a battleship task group.

This image of the Normandy beaches shows the maritime logistics that sustained the Allied armies after the invasion in 1944. From right to left is a coaster beached and unloading waiting for the tide, a tank landing craft, and, just in view, a tank landing ship.

The Two-Ocean Navy was now in being. After grinding down the Japanese in the Solomons the Americans had moved to a two-pronged maritime offensive, with MacArthur's forces in the south moving through the Bismarcks and along the northern coast of New Guinea and Admiral Nimitz's central Pacific drive through the Gilberts and the Marshalls. This latter was a masterpiece of maritime logistics with the front line backed up by a mighty fleet train of naval auxiliaries and merchantmen. Naval construction battalions were able to turn uninhabited atolls into bases and suitable island lagoons became some of the greatest naval anchorages in the world.

In June 1944 this capability was unleashed on Saipan. After air strikes from the 15 American main carriers and bombardment by some 15 battleships, eight from the main fleet and seven from the amphibious force (most of the latter survivors of Pearl Harbor), the landings went in. The amphibious force alone consisted of over 550 ships, including its own dedicated air support component of eight escort carriers. This was sea power on the grand scale.

Inter-war planners had always seen the area of the Marianas as the scene of the great Japanese–American showdown. The Japanese fleet now obliged. The pre-war officers had expected a clash of battleships but this engagement was between aircraft carriers, the emergent capital ships. The American carriers were now mature platforms deploying almost a thousand high-performance torpedo bombers to sink battleships, dive bombers to sink carriers, and fighters to command the air. The latter were part of an air warfare system based on radar, systematic plotting, and experienced fighter direction officers to allocate the effective Hellcat fighters to engage incoming raids.

Given its limited resources Japan had done well to assemble a carrier fleet of nine ships, but these were a heterogeneous collection of one new fleet carrier, two Pearl Harbor veterans, two converted passenger liners, and four converted auxiliaries. They carried mainly a new generation of strike aircraft, but the fighters remained only slightly modified versions of the same 'Zeros' with which Japan had started the war. Crucially, attrition had taken its toll and fuel shortages had prevented the new pilots, who made up most of those available, attaining the quality of their better-trained opponents. Outnumbered around two to one, the Japanese suffered a crushing defeat. Their initial carrier strike was massacred in what the Americans called a 'turkey shoot'. American submarines and a carrier air strike sank three Japanese carriers. The Battle of the Philippine Sea was the end of the Japanese carrier air arm as an offensive force and a truly decisive defeat. The rest of the Japanese fleet, including the two super battleships, withdrew, and the Marianas fell, to become a forward base for the strategic bombing of Japan, carried out by the army and army air forces but sustained by sea supply.

The poor quality of Japan's aircrew was a result of the Japanese failure to counter the American campaign against its shipping that was increasingly cutting off the Empire from its vital overseas sources of supply. The Japanese merchant fleet began the war with 6.4 million tons of ships. It then began a downward spiral, to less than 6 million tons by the end of 1942, less than 5 million in 1943, and a catastrophic drop of almost a half to 2.6 million tons by the end of 1944. Shipbuilding increased from around a quarter of a million tons per year before the war to 1.1 million tons in 1943 and 1.6 million in 1944 but it could not keep up with losses. The submarine was the main killer. After problems with defective torpedoes were cured, US submarines sank 1.3 million tons of shipping in 1943 and 2.4 million in 1945. Unlike the British the Japanese never organized an effective convoy system. Convoys were only belatedly introduced and inadequately escorted when they were. A culture that stressed the sea as a medium for knightly combat missed the point of what the mundane objective of any maritime strategy must be: the safe passage of shipping.

Japanese imports plummeted. Imports of coal dropped from around a million tons per month to around half that by the late summer of 1944, iron ore imports fell from over 400,000 tons in April 1943 to 31,000 in September 1944. Oil imports, which had peaked to 740,000 tons in the second quarter of 1943, slumped to 304,000 in the second quarter of 1944 and 178,000 in the third. No wonder Japan kept its surviving and still powerful surface fleet of battleships and heavy cruisers based near to the East Indies oilfields, which in 1944 were still producing over 1.5 million tons of oil per quarter.

When the Americans decided to co-ordinate their two offensives and land in the Philippines (Taiwan had been the original Nimitz objective) the Japanese committed their fleet in a typically elaborate plan to use their remaining operational but relatively empty carriers to decoy the US carrier groups in order to allow their surface fleet to destroy the landings in Leyte Gulf. The plan almost worked but the Japanese lost their

nerve in the face of an aggressively handled escort carrier force which the Japanese mistook for the main fleet. They retreated, having lost heavily to no purpose. The battle was notable for the last gunnery action between battleships, the loss of the super battleship *Musashi*, whose inadequate AA armament was incapable of preventing about nineteen hits by torpedo bombers, and the first use of Kamikaze (Divine Wind) aircraft as manned missiles. Japan was outdoing Germany in her desperation at sea.

The Third Reich thought it had one last chance to turn the tide at sea following the clear defeat of the U-boats in 1943. By 1944 radical new submarines were about to appear. The main focus was on boats that would use large capacity batteries to be faster under water than on the surface. They could make 17 knots under water, older U-boats just over seven. Streamlined, they would also be optimized to use the snorkel (refitted also to standard boats) to cruise fast on diesels at periscope depth. Two classes were planned, one medium-sized sea going, one small coastal.

Producing these boats in the conditions of the Third Reich in 1944 was another matter. Speer, the Minister of Armaments, thought the new boats could be rushed into service and rapidly produced, using inland steel manufacturers each producing pre-fabricated sections. These would then be transported to dockyards for completion to be transported again to three assembly yards. It was hoped that the first new boat would be ready in time for Hitler's birthday in April 1944 and that production would soon ramp up to 30 a month by the autumn. The first was duly 'commissioned' on

A prefabricated section of an advanced Type XXI German U-boat found after the war. The failure of this form of construction using dispersed facilities in a pre-computer world was a major factor in the abject failure of a programme upon which so many German hopes had been set.

time, but she was only a shell displayed for propaganda purposes and although 80 more came along by the end of the year, none was fit for service.

Design problems had to be overcome and shortages of materials forced desperate compromises on things such as the copper wiring layout, which made the boats dangerous to operate (post-war navies were reluctant to use captured examples without major modification). The hull sections were not produced accurately enough to fit together; the boats leaked and much time had to be taken to prove the integrity of the hulls. A boat might be built in about three months but it needed four more months of repairs. Allied air forces were strewing mines in the Baltic areas used for trials and training, seriously holding up both. Bombing also interrupted the internal rail and canal systems on which the construction plan depended.

Eight of the smaller, more easily produced boats were deployed operationally in the coastal game of cat and mouse to which the older U-boats had been reduced. They sank six ships (two after the war in Europe had ended) and none was lost or even detected. Two of the larger boats were sent on patrol but they sank no ships before being told of the surrender; it was far too little far too late. The Allies were very concerned about the prospect of the new submarines threat but it is highly doubtful if these new boats could have changed the course of the war, given that overwhelming Allied maritime superiority that lay at the heart of many of the problems the Germans had faced in building the submarines on time.

Despite having to use the beaches of Normandy for much longer than expected before the port of Antwerp was belatedly opened after an amphibious landing on Walcheren at the mouth of the Scheldt in early November 1944, there were no real problems in landing enough supplies to keep the Allied armies moving once the break-out occurred. The scale was massive. A month after D-Day some 3·4 million tons of merchant shipping was engaged in supporting operations in north-west Europe, two-thirds of it British-controlled. From July 1944 to May 1945 over half a million vehicles crossed the Channel, almost 57,000 in tank landing craft, almost 259,000 in tank landing ships, and 252,000 in mercantile motor transport ships.

Concerns about supplies, however, strengthened American arguments to open a southern front in France which would allow the use of Toulon and Marseilles. Much against British wishes, therefore, landings took place along the French Riviera in August, Operation Dragoon. By early 1945 it was planned to use about 1·35 million

The first coaster to enter Antwerp at the end of November 1944 after the belated opening of the Scheldt estuary. The failure to capture rapidly the maritime approaches to this vital port created significant logistical problems for the Western Allies.

deadweight tons of American shipping on this route to supply US and French forces, compared with 4.6 million tons moving supplies directly to north-west Europe. Germany was being inexorably squeezed to defeat on both sides by Allied maritime power. As the Third Reich contracted, the Allied blockade bit with a new intensity. The new German jet fighters of which much was expected were delayed by shortages of raw materials and when they did come into service they had insufficient fuel even to taxi, having to be hauled, like much of the German army, by horses that could eat the main domestically produced fuel, fodder.

Japan was also facing ruin. There was some recovery in imports in late 1944 but not much and not for long. During 1945 the Japanese mercantile marine lost another 1.5 million tons, more than half its remaining much-reduced strength. By this time other agencies than submarines were doing most of the damage. The mining of Japanese waters by long-range aircraft took a deadly toll and held up what shipping was left. From May to July 1945 submarines sank some 97,000 tons of civilian shipping, mines over twice that amount, almost 200,000 tons. The result was the almost complete interdiction of the shipping upon which the Japanese economy depended. After the first quarter of the year oil imports to Japan ceased. Stocks of aviation fuel that had totalled almost 500,000 tons at the start of the war were reduced to 78,000 in January 1945 and 17,000 in August; stocks of heavy oil from 3.6 million tons in 1941 to just 4,000 in August. Monthly coal imports remained at about half a million tons until May but were less than 300,000 tons by June. After a final spike to over 71,000 tons in April 1945 iron ore imports were just over a mere 1,000 tons in July. After erratic ups and downs, rubber imports had ceased completely by the beginning of 1945 and the import of non-ferrous metals that had usually been over 200,000 tons per month in better days was reduced to 30,000 tons in June.

Yet Japanese culture prevented the truncated and paralysed Empire from facing facts. American B-29 bombers systematically destroyed Japan's cities, a campaign aided by the capture of Iwo Jima in a major amphibious operation using almost 500 ships, to provide a diversion airfield and escort fighter base. The offensive then moved on to Okinawa in late March, by which time the maritime power being projected against Japan had become truly 'Allied'. The British chiefs-of-staff had overruled Churchill's imperial instincts and subordinated the interests of the Empire in the Indian Ocean to the perceived need to be with the main American fleet at the end of the direct offensive against Japan. The defeat of the German and Italian surface fleets had allowed a major force to be formed in the Indian Ocean in 1944 which was then sent on to Australia to create the 'British Pacific Fleet' (BPF). The Indian Ocean maritime campaign continued but it remained low priority and the operation to recapture Malaya and Singapore was finally executed without opposition when the Japanese surrendered.

The BPF was the most powerful fleet Britain had deployed yet, with four well-stocked fleet carriers, but given British aircraft priorities most of the aircraft were Lend Lease and the four carriers formed but a single task group by American standards. Senior figures in the US navy had not wanted the British to appear as they doubted the British ability to provide sufficient logistical shipping to project the BPF over Pacific distances and did not want their ally interfering with their private revenge for 7 December 1941. Nevertheless political pressure dictated that the BPF be accepted as a whole 'Task Force'; US fleet support was provided as required when British shipping, as predicted, proved inadequate.

The British were given a flanking role in the Okinawa campaign, attacking the continuation of the archipelago to the west protecting the Fifth Fleet from the Japanese army and air forces based in Taiwan. Both these aircraft and navy formations from Japan made the largest Kamikaze attacks of the war, which strained the efficient air defences of both nations' carriers and caused serious damage to the American ships. The British carriers, designed with armour at a time when aircraft could provide little defence, suffered less severely. Despite the damage they inflicted, the suicide pilots could do little to stem the Allied tide. Japan's situation was also demonstrated dramatically when some of the last fuel available to the Japanese navy was loaded into the surviving super-battleship *Yamato* for a one-way mission that, thanks to US carrier aircraft, barely got out of sight of land.

By the summer Japan was prostrate. Over half the remaining Japanese merchant ships were desperately carrying food from mainland Asia to try to stave off complete starvation. The Allied fleet prowled off the coast, adding their weight of carrier air strikes and gunnery bombardment to the strategic air assault on the home islands. The

The end of both the battleship and the ocean-going career of the Imperial Japanese Navy. The super battleship *Yamato* is assailed by hundreds of US carrier-based aircraft on her attempted one-way mission to Okinawa on 7 April 1945. Hit by perhaps thirteen torpedoes and at least nine bombs she rolled over and sank, exploding as she did so, taking with her over 3,000 of her ship's company.

last time a British battleship fired its guns in anger was to destroy a musical instrument factory making aircraft propellers. It seemed there was no alternative to an amphibious invasion that would be ruinously expensive on both sides. Then a B-29 bomber from the Marianas fuelled by sea and carrying a nuclear bomb that had come to Tinian in a US navy cruiser began the process of Japanese surrender. There could have been no more potent example of the synergy of air and sea power. Western maritime dominance—in its widest sense—had finally triumphed.

Maritime power had been fundamental to the war's outcome. The Western effort was predicated on control of the oceans without which no serious operations could be mounted at all. Even the Eastern Front was fundamentally affected by maritime power diverting German strength and enabling Soviet forces to prevail against a qualitatively superior opponent able to inflict highly disproportionate attrition. Britain and the United States had the world's largest navies and merchant marines and they used these to dominate the global field of conflict, combining their operations with land-based air power. The war at sea also involved imposing or overcoming maritime blockade, a central feature of the Allied war effort which contributed massively to the eventual defeat of the Axis. The sea was also the supply lifeline for the Allies, enabling them to hold the entire global battlefield together and to supply large quantities of vital goods to the Soviet Union, as well as shipping their own men and materials around the world. On a watery planet only dominant sea powers could prevail in a global conflict, and, for the second time in thirty years, they did.

6 The Allies from Defeat to Victory

EVAN MAWDSLEY

Introduction

How did the Allies come to prevail in the Second World War? The subject is a very large one and the space available limited; as a result this chapter will be mainly about Britain, the USSR, and the USA, and will focus on events in Europe. Little will be said about Allied naval campaigns and maritime logistics, as they are covered elsewhere; effective control of the seas was, however, both crucial to Allied victory, and a task to which Britain and America devoted huge resources.

Unlike three other contributions to this volume, the present chapter is not about the conduct of the war by one country, where the conflict might be said to have been fought in a 'national interest', or at least in the interests of one ruling elite. It was indeed a strange and strained 'alliance'. The members did not have a common set of political objectives—beyond the cardinal one of completely overthrowing German power. Two new partners joined in 1941, but only with great reluctance, and only under direct attack by Germany or Japan. The leading states of the 'United Nations', Britain and America on one side, and Communist Russia on the other, had been bitter ideological enemies before June 1941. Their ways would part almost as soon as Germany and Japan were defeated; World War was quickly followed by Cold War.

The three major Allies also did not have one conception of how to achieve victory. They fought the war in very different ways, achieved different effects, and paid different costs. Indeed at one or another point between 1939 and 1945 the leaders (and much of the population) of each of the states involved were content to have the others do all or most of the fighting for them. While Britain and America co-ordinated their conduct of the war closely from 1941 onwards, there was little practical combined planning with the Russians (there was, however, considerable one-sided co-ordination on the logistics side, in the form of Lend Lease).

Failed Alliance: 1939–1940

Before the 'Grand Alliance' of December 1941 there was the Anglo-French Alliance of 1939. When the 'European War' began on 3 September the question at hand seemed straightforward: how could Britain and France defeat an aggressive German state intent on establishing hegemony over central Europe. Various attempts, in the form of appeasement, rearmament, even co-operation with the USSR, had been made to deal with German ambitions between 1933 and 1938. The European democracies concluded from the 1939 Danzig crisis and the German invasion of Poland that further diplomacy was impossible, and—to Hitler's considerable surprise—they went to war.

Stalin and the Russian government stood aside that September. The Soviets had in the past taken a strong stand against their extreme ideological enemies in Berlin. Moscow also entertained, however, a fear that the British and French wanted to manoeuvre it into a German–Soviet war; the USSR would act as the cat in the fable that pulls the chestnuts from the fire for the monkey and gets its fingers burned. Stalin chose to deal with the autumn 1939 crisis through a policy of appeasement, coupled with a continued large-scale rearmament programme. The non-aggression pact and territorial 'deal' suddenly offered to the Soviets by Ribbentrop in August 1939 were accepted. As a result the strategic position of the USSR seemed greatly to have improved; Moscow gained control of a wide buffer of territory stretching from the Baltic States to the borders of Romania. The Soviet government now expected a protracted 'Allies versus Germany' war in the west, a conflict which would weaken both sides, and one in which the Red Army could intervene—at a favourable moment.

The United States also was not involved. The transatlantic republic had had little direct involvement in the growing European tensions of the 1930s. Although the Roosevelt Administration opposed Nazism and all it stood for, a powerful isolationist sentiment both in Congress and in public opinion at large was opposed to any intervention. In any event, aside from a powerful navy the USA had weak standing armed forces; with the effects of the Great Depression still being felt, even the potential of economic 'weapons' was limited.

Britain and France, the two leading countries which did take a military stand against Nazi aggression in September 1939, had closer views on how to defeat Germany than Britain and Russia would have in 1941, or Britain would have with either of its partners in 1942–5. The military planners in London and Paris hoped to prevail by continued military preparation and by smothering Germany through economic warfare. The war would be a long haul, as their advantages of population and economic power were gradually translated into superior military strength. Britain and France certainly hoped to avoid casualties on the scale of 1914–18. They could do nothing to help Poland. The British expectation had initially been to provide the naval and economic side of the war effort, while the French army faced the frontiers of the Reich. Once the war began, however, the British Empire had agreed to commit a significant number of army divisions to supporting the French on the Continent.

Any Allied military initiative was to be confined to the edges of German territory, in Scandinavia or the Balkans. Britain possessed an independent Royal Air Force (RAF), whose leaders were strongly committed to a doctrine of 'strategic' bombing. The air weapon, however, could be used only with great restraint, at least in the initial stages of the war, in order to avoid retaliatory attacks on French and British cities. The

Allies did consider action in neutral Norway to block the supply of Swedish iron ore to Germany, but the Wehrmacht beat them to the punch in April 1940. Unfortunately the Germans wanted a short victorious war, and they possessed an army and air force that were nearly able to bring about that result.

The Allies did make plans to deal with a possible German offensive in the west in 1939–40. They understood the significance of the neutral Low Countries as a place of great strategic value to both sides. Belgium was also the most likely avenue of German advance, in view of the prepared French defensive position on the border further south (the Maginot Line). The Allies' most significant—and fatal—planning decision was to respond to a German strike into the Low Countries by occupying as much of Belgium as possible. The Germans invaded the Netherlands, Belgium, and Luxembourg on 10 May 1940. The French and British armies moved into southern Belgium, and they were then trapped by the famous Panzer drive from the Ardennes due west to the Channel. Many Allied troops were successfully evacuated through Dunkirk and elsewhere, but they had lost their heavy equipment and much of their fighting value. The second phase of the campaign, fought from the Somme to Paris, was largely a Franco-German affair, and lasted until the French signed an armistice on 22 June.

The fall of France had another very difficult consequence for the 'Allied' cause—now for the moment the cause only of the British Empire and sundry 'governments in exile'. Fascist Italy entered the war on Germany's side. In effect—in geographical terms at least—Mussolini's action doubled the original strategic problem, by extending the war to the Mediterranean.

Troops of the BEF enter neutral Belgium from France. As the Germans invaded Belgium, the Allies drove north to block them and occupy as much of the country as possible. This rash manoeuvre helped to cause the Dunkirk fiasco.

What happened next demonstrated the importance of the British Empire as the catalyst of the final victorious alliance. The formation and survival of the Churchill government was a development of the greatest moment. The new Prime Minister not only opposed any thought of compromise with the victorious Third Reich, but was also more prepared than his predecessor Neville Chamberlain had been to make use of economic help from outside the Empire, especially from the United States. In truth the British government did not perceive that it was in a desperate situation, or even an unprecedented one, after June 1940. The overall state of affairs could be seen as a stalemate between the British Empire and the Third Reich (with Italy as Germany's junior partner), rather than an end-game in which an isolated Britain was fighting for its life.

Fortunately the Germans could not end the stalemate. Their immediate military threat to Britain was not an overwhelming one, thanks to the great superiority of the Royal Navy. Invasion of the British Isles was never taken seriously by the German navy in 1940. The attempt to mount an operational air campaign in the summer of 1940 (the 'Battle of Britain') was unsuccessful, as a result of the limited means available to the Luftwaffe and a well-integrated British air defence system. The Empire, meanwhile, was beyond the reach of Germany and its partners. In the Mediterranean the threat of Fascist Italy was checked at the end of 1940, after remarkable successes by British forces. The Italian navy was crippled by the torpedo-bomber attack on Taranto, and the Italian army suffered a humiliating defeat in Libya, in which the British took 130,000 prisoners.

The British, on the other hand, also could not bring an end to the stalemate. A land campaign against the Third Reich was unthinkable; the small British army was hardly about to challenge the victorious Wehrmacht on the Continent. The ground forces of the British Empire had only the most limited contact with the Germans, and only on the periphery, in Greece and Libya. 'Economic warfare' remained the cornerstone of British policy, but it was now substantially more difficult. The Third Reich had gained direct control of the economic resources of much of western and central Europe. Resource-rich neutrals like Romania had changed sides. The compliant neutrality of the Russians gave Germany access to an even larger resource base, and indeed a transit route to Asia.

Nevertheless the Royal Navy's blockade—now of the ports of all of western Europe—continued after June 1940. The military planners in Whitehall did consider the prospects for strategic bombing by the RAF and the development of popular resistance in the occupied populations. Both would take much time to develop. Both were based on false assumptions about the extent to which the German economy and political system were already under strain.

The Soviet government, for its part, was both surprised and alarmed by the fall of France. Moscow's approach in 1940–1 to this problem was still one of appeasement, coupled with military preparations. The latter were very considerable. Soviet factories produced, on average, 250 tanks, 1,250 artillery pieces, and 800 combat aircraft a month in 1939–41. (The comparable monthly figures for Germany in 1940 and 1941 were 225 tanks, 590 guns (over 75mm), and 885 aircraft.) The USSR now took a unilateral view of its security, and the favoured policy was expansion of its own frontiers, and deployment of military forces into the newly-annexed Baltic states and eastern Poland. Stalin was in direct control of Russian policy (including intelligence assessments), and he assumed that even if Hitler felt strong enough to attack the USSR, he would not do so before the British Empire had been knocked out of the war. Fighting a two-front war, Stalin believed, would be suicidal for Germany; it was a prediction which would turn out to be correct, but only after the USSR had paid an extremely heavy price.

Like the British, the Soviet leaders thought in terms of an eventual 'war of machines', as an alternative of the bloody stalemate of 1914–18, although in their case the underlying concept was mechanized offensive warfare with very large ground forces. The key concept was known to the Red Army as 'deep operations' (*glubokie operatsii*; in the West this is sometimes termed, less accurately, 'deep *battle*'). The idea had been developed and fostered by Red Army leaders like V. K. Triandafillov and M. N. Tukhachevskii in the late 1920s and 1930s. To a remarkable extent it had been converted into military hardware during Stalin's Five-Year Plans. Infantry, armour, airborne forces, artillery, and tactical aviation were to be employed to mount a powerful blow which impacted near simultaneously throughout the enemy's entire depth to disintegrate his defensive system. The war was thought of in terms of 'operations' conducted through a depth of 150 miles and lasting 30 to 45 days. Enthusiasm for the concept was reinforced by the evidence of Panzer successes in 1939–40. The final

Red Army T-26 tanks on parade in 1936. The USSR was the first state to rearm; the build-up of strength in the 1930s and the development of armoured doctrine was crucial for survival in the Second World War.

version involved creation of powerful armoured formations—'mechanized corps' (two tank divisions and a motorized division—comparable to a German *Panzergruppe*). A large number of these were in the process of formation (but far from combat-ready) in 1940–1. The Soviet concept of a future war was neatly expressed in a propaganda song from 1938: 'We will smash the enemy on enemy territory | Scant the bloodshed, but mighty the blow!' (*I na vrazh'ei zemle my vraga ragromim* | *Maloi krov'iu, moguchim udarom!*).

The United States dealt with the unpleasant fact of German control of central and western Europe in a different way. Unlike the USSR, America had the great good fortune not to be *directly* threatened. And as a liberal democracy the government in Washington had to pay heed to considerable popular sentiment that still opposed involvement in overseas wars. Drastic defensive measures were taken, however, following President Roosevelt's call for US army and navy air forces totalling 50,000 aircraft (May 1940), the 'Two-Ocean Navy' programme (July 1940), and the introduction of conscription (September 1940).

The Roosevelt Administration established America as the 'Arsenal of Democracy', hopefully enabling Britain—and later the USSR—to fight the Axis without direct US involvement. The Lend Lease programme was enacted in March 1941. British cartoon by Leslie Illingworth.

THE WAY OF A STORK

While Soviet neutrality in 1939–41 leant towards Nazi Germany, that of the United States leant very much towards the British Empire. Beyond historical and political ties, it was certainly in America's interests to keep the British Empire in the war. In his 'Arsenal of Democracy' speech (December 1940) President Roosevelt outlined a situation where America got the best of both worlds, battling with the Nazi menace but avoiding direct combat. The United States undertook to provide a great amount of military equipment under the Lend Lease programme (approved by Congress in March 1941). American ships began escorting Atlantic convoys in the autumn of 1941, and there was important sharing of intelligence and technology. In the spring of 1941 secret staff 'conversations' (ABC-1) were held in Washington to lay out a common strategy. It was agreed that Hitler's Third Reich was the most likely and dangerous common enemy. 'Germany First' would remain the theoretical basis of the strategy until May 1945.

The British–Soviet Alliance

On 22 June 1941 Hitler launched his great surprise attack on the USSR, Operation Barbarossa. The British–Russian alliance, thrown into existence by the invasion, was the start of a second partnership against Hitler, and one that would eventually destroy his empire. Nevertheless the new alignment had no immediate operational significance. The British, as they had in past centuries in their dealings with Continental allies, promised to provide matériel (and would do so), but they still did not intend to dispatch any significant body of troops onto the Continent. (And in any event the war planners in Whitehall were not at all certain that Soviet resistance would continue for more than a few months.) The contribution of the British to the common effort would take the form of bombing factories and blockading ports. Any action of the Empire's ground forces would be on the extreme periphery of the 'European' theatre. In particular the British took advantage of the preoccupation of the Wehrmacht in Russia and the revealed weaknesses of the Italians in the Mediterranean. Considerable hopes were placed on an offensive, Operation Crusader, launched into eastern Libya in November 1941.

The Red Army, for all its innovations in military theory, had lacked a realistic military strategy in the months before 22 June 1941. There had been war plans which involved offensive ground and air operations into German-occupied territory in the event that the Third Reich began (or appeared to be about to begin) operations against the USSR. These plans were more vigorous and immediate than anything the French and British staff had had in mind in 1939–40. They were certainly unrealistic in the summer of 1941, but the plans were never put to a test. The Wehrmacht achieved overwhelming tactical surprise on the morning of 22 June, and the Red Army was quickly so embattled that there were few positive decisions to make.

Various factors explain the very poor showing of the Red Army in the first campaign of the war. It was caught by surprise. The forward deployment of mechanized and air formations, a legacy of the 'deep operations' concept, actually exposed

'Our cause is just. The enemy will be defeated!' This poster, from the earliest days of the German invasion, quotes Molotov's speech of 22 June 1941; it exemplifies an ill-judged faith in reckless counter-attacks.

those forces to devastating attack. A combination of a murderous purge of the senior officer corps in 1937–8 and the very rapid expansion in the next three or four years badly shook the coherence of the army's organization. German troops, on the other hand, were better trained and more experienced. For all their calamitous defeats, however, the 1941 campaigns did demonstrate the successes of the Soviet pre-war armaments programme and the potential of the Red Army's reserve and mobilization system. In contrast to France, the geography of even European Russia provided its defenders with extraordinary defensive depth. After one final—and truly catastrophic—defeat in October 1941 the Germans were finally stopped two months later at the Battles of Rostov (in south Russia) and Moscow.

This turn of events was extremely important for the eventual outcome of the war. With the failure to defeat the Red Army in one sudden campaign Hitler's Wehrmacht lost its only chance for a rapid and complete victory. Furthermore, although the battles of the summer and autumn of 1941 were highly successful in gaining territory and killing or capturing Soviet soldiers they were won at a very high cost, compared to the fighting of 1939–40. Wehrmacht losses (deaths) before Barbarossa had been 102,000 (including 50,000 in the period of the French campaign). German losses in the east in the period between 22 June and the end of November 1941 were 262,000. (In early December 1941, when Hitler spoke secretly to the Nazi leaders about the

European Jews, he justified their mass killing as revenge for 160,000 [*sic*] German 'victims' who had been 'sacrificed' in the Russian campaign.)

The Grand Alliance

The Japanese attack on Pearl Harbor on 7 December 1941 and Hitler's ceremonial declaration of war on the USA four days later were, in the long term, events of the greatest significance. It has even been argued that the defeats in Asia in 1941–2 had a worse effect on the global war effort and prospects of the British Empire than did the fall of France in 1940. In immediate operational terms, moreover, the entry of America had a markedly negative impact. The flow of weapons and supplies from the 'Arsenal of Democracy' was now diverted from British and Soviet forces fighting the Germans to American forces which were embattled in the Pacific or were undergoing formation in the USA itself.

But the essence of the war did change in December 1941, and not only because America was bought into the conflict. With the Battles of Rostov and Moscow the Barbarossa campaign in Russia could now be seen to have failed. The possibility the Wehrmacht might achieve an 'operational' solution to Germany's strategic dilemma of a stalemated two-front war—a rapid battle of annihilation against the entire Red Army—no longer existed. All-out American support, and the continuing Russian-front demands on the Wehrmacht, meant that there was even less of a danger than before of Britain being invaded, bombed into submission, or forced to sign a capitulation. Equally, the failure of the Wehrmacht's Blitzkrieg strategy meant that Germany was now engaged in a long-term war of attrition, fought on two fronts, against opponents which were far more powerful in demographic and economic terms.

The question for all the Allies in the winter of 1941–2 was not how they could survive—they were going to—but how they could prevent a stalemate, and roll the Axis back from the gains that they had already made—out of the mid-Pacific and South-East Asia, out of the western regions of the USSR, out of France and the Low Countries, out of the Balkans, out of North Africa. (The only region where the Axis was to make a significant new advance after March 1942 was in the Caucasus.) Nazi Germany had now achieved the most extreme aspirations of Wilhelmine Germany in 1914. Control over large parts of continental Europe put Germany in a strong position to withstand a siege war. The supply of food and iron ore was no longer a strategic problem (although the supply of oil was more problematic). The control of the advanced economies of occupied western Europe should have been an advantage. Even the more economically backward parts of the continent which were under German control provided fresh labour; this could be used to substitute for Germans who were being mobilized into the Wehrmacht or the war industry of the Reich.

Stalin, for his part, was overly optimistic. He believed in the winter of 1941–2, after the Soviet successes in the Battle of Moscow, that the course of the war could be rapidly transformed. There would be a comprehensive counter-attack all along the front, from Leningrad to the Crimea, fought by the Red Army on its own. Grave setbacks had been suffered by the Russian forces in 1941, but like the British in the summer of 1940, Stalin was confident of his country's underlying strength and the weakness of his enemy. Although the Russian forces had suffered extremely heavy losses in the summer and autumn of 1941, the assumption was that the Wehrmacht, too, had lost heavily and was on its last legs; it certainly seemed to lack reserves. There was also the Napoleonic prototype of the retreat from Moscow in 1812, which Soviet propaganda made much of. Some of Stalin's public pronouncements in the winter of 1941–2 were aimed at unseating the 'adventurist' Hitler regime in favour of a more realistic nationalist regime led by the army.

In the end, however, the effect of these winter operations in Russia was to wear out *both* sides, and the campaign was more costly to the Red Army than to the Wehrmacht. German losses (dead) in the east in the 'crisis winter' from December 1941 through April 1942 (inclusive) were another 200,000 men—far from an insignificant number—but Red Army losses were three or four times as great (the Russian statistics include 619,000 'permanent' losses—killed, fatally injured, captured, and missing—in the period from January to March 1942). The only territorial gains were an advance of a hundred miles in central Russia, and a tenuous foothold on part of the Crimea. From hindsight, the consolidation and regrouping of the Red Army would have been a wiser course of action.

The last Russian push was the Kharkov offensive of May 1942, which—after the Germans mounted successful counter-attacks—had the net result of dislocating the Red Army's position in the South. The full-scale German Operation Blue—what historians sometimes call Hitler's 'second campaign'—began in south Russia in

A lend lease US M3 light tank used to tow a Soviet howitzer. Captured by the Germans at the Battle of Kharkov, May 1942.

the following month. The Panzers quickly pushed the defenders back east beyond Rostov and Voronezh, and then drove towards Stalingrad and the Caucasus.

At least there were none of the huge encirclements which had been such a prominent feature of 1941. The scale of the German attack was also different from 1941, as it was concentrated on the southern part of the Russian front. After the losses of the first year of the war, and as their front line ballooned out, German forces had to rely heavily on supporting troops from the minor Axis partners—Italy, Hungary, and Romania. The Red Army successfully held the line in the north and centre of European Russia, around Leningrad and in front of Moscow. The fighters of the Red Army were now more experienced, and better equipped than they had been in the previous winter. Lend Lease aid was still extremely limited in 1942 (certainly compared to Soviet production of basic military equipment), but it was beginning to arrive. Offensive war was as costly for the Wehrmacht in 1942 as it had been in 1941. In the period from May to November 1942 (inclusive)—the Stalingrad counter-offensive began on 19 November—the Red Army inflicted losses of 269,000 on the Germans. (Wehrmacht losses on all other fronts were 44,000.)

In the spring of 1942 came the first inter-Allied discussion of strategy against the Axis involving all three major partners, Britain, the United States, and the USSR. Probably this was a time when disagreements were greatest. The Combined Chiefs of Staff (CCS) structure was created, but this took in only the British and the Americans. Russian involvement in overall strategy was at a diplomatic level. Soviet military strategy, it must be said, was substantially more coherent than that of the United States or the British Empire. This was partly the result of structural factors (in Russia the ground forces were bureaucratically all-powerful, with no independent air force and a small coastal navy). It also stemmed from strategic and geographical realities: the Russians were literally fighting for their lives, and on only one—albeit long—front.

Belligerent Britain and neutral America had largely seen eye to eye in the spring of 1941, with the ABC-1 and 'Germany First' strategy. 'Official' American strategy in early 1942 was that of the US Army, which proposed an Allied cross-Channel operation for mid 1943 (codenamed Roundup) or even a smaller emergency effort in late 1942. Believers in a concentration of force, the American generals favoured a direct approach across the Channel. Since, unlike the Russians and the British, the Americans had no ground forces engaged in active operations in Europe, few specific interests, and only one serious historical precedent (April 1917 to November 1918), they could begin with a blank sheet of paper and follow simple logic.

The British, in contrast, were eager to avoid a bloody—and possibly unsuccessful—head-on operation in France. Not only had Britain's armies suffered enormous casualties fighting there in 1914–18, but they had already been ejected across the Channel once in the current war, from Dunkirk in 1940. Churchill and his generals favoured continuing peripheral operations in the Mediterranean, 'closing the ring' around German-occupied territory, and otherwise putting an emphasis on blockade and aerial bombardment. In the end they were able to get their way in the debates with the Americans. This came about partly because of better British staff work, and partly because any landing operation in 1942 or early 1943 would have had to be carried out mainly by troops from the British Empire.

Staff disagreements between Marshall and the head of the British army (Chief of the Imperial General Staff) General Sir Alan Brooke were only resolved in June 1942; President Roosevelt and Prime Minister Churchill agreed to carry out a major landing operation in North-West Africa, which was garrisoned by forces of the French collaborator government in Vichy. Originally codenamed Super-Gymnast, the operation was later given the more inspiring designation Torch.

This decision to start the campaign in North Africa was an extremely portentous one. It was driven partly by a desire to mount a successful operation in the general area of Europe in the late autumn of 1942 (and before the US Congressional elections on 3 November 1942). Torch generally met those criteria, and more (although it missed the election date), and it probably eventually distracted more German troops than any feasible alternative action could have done. It was, however, the beginning of a chain of events that delayed the cross-Channel landing until 6 June 1944.

There were other proposed strategies for defeating Germany at this time. In both Britain and America the visionaries of strategic air power continued to believe that the war could be won by the bomber alone. In late 1940 and 1941 this had been largely theoretical speculation, as the RAF lacked the means to mount serious attacks, and there was not even agreement on which targets to hit. In 1942 for the first time the RAF bombing campaign was beginning to achieve some results. Air Marshal Arthur Harris took over Bomber Command in February 1942 as a single-minded advocate both of the strategic use of the RAF, and of the specific strategy of attacking large urban areas and German morale, rather than specific economic targets. He made his mark especially with the 'thousand bomber' raid (Operation Millennium) against Cologne in May 1942. Churchill, too, was an enthusiast for the bomber (although not as the sole means for winning the war); in his correspondence with Stalin the Prime Minister made much of the damage directly inflicted on Germany by this and other air raids.

The leaders of the US Army Air Forces (USAAF) also believed that the war could be won by air power, although they were arguing for a different kind of air power, 'precision' daylight raids targeting against specific sectors of the economy. In 1942 this was even more 'theoretical' than the RAF approach, because the USAAF were unable to mount attacks even on the edges of German territory. The American targets were in occupied territory; even in the last three months of 1942 RAF Bomber Command dropped over seven times the weight of bombs that the new British-based US 8th Air Force did.

The expectation of Allied attacks did lead to a gradual build up of the air defences of the Reich. Germany had devoted a high proportion of its expenditure on armaments to the construction of aircraft and (to a lesser extent) anti-aircraft artillery, both before and during the war. However the actual achievements of the Allied bomber forces fell a long way short of the aims of their advocates.

In America another body of opinion, led in the high command by Admiral King (Chief of Naval Operations) and others, favoured an all-out war with the Japanese. Arguably the USA began to go against the spirit of the agreed 'Germany First' strategy when its forces started offensives in the Solomon Islands and New Guinea in August 1942. The American naval victory in the Battle of Midway in June had, after all, ended any prospect of a further Japanese thrust west toward Hawaii or south (towards Australia) from the mid-ocean perimeter the Imperial forces had already conquered.

To be sure, this focus on Japan was not wilful 'navalism'. The US navy was still legitimately, at least until the end of 1942, concerned about the trans-Pacific lines of communication to Australia. Out of necessity American servicemen had been fighting the Japanese rather than the Germans for the first eleven months of the war. Continuing the campaign against Japan provided a role for the huge navy (currently under

'But westward, look! The land is bright!' Stalin and Molotov in the Kremlin, Churchill, in his letters to them, repeatedly stressed that the RAF night-bombing campaign was a war-winner; he hoped this would lessen their demands for a land invasion. British cartoon by Leslie Illingworth.

The US Army Air Force hoped that 'precision' day attacks on key German factories could inflict decisive damage. The heavy losses of unescorted B-17s in the August 1943 Schweinfurt raid led to the temporary abandonment of the strategy.

construction) which was scheduled to become available at the end of 1943, and in 1944. For this fleet no serious opponent now remained afloat in Europe, thanks to the efforts of the Royal Navy. All the same, in a sense the attitude of Admiral King justified Hitler's expectation, at the end of 1941, that the embroilment of the USA in the Pacific would be a good thing for the German cause, as it would divert forces and resources from Europe.

The Soviet involvement in Allied strategy-making took the form of diplomatic notes and some high-level meetings. Since the autumn of 1941, even before Hitler declared war on the USA, the Soviets had been requesting some kind of action on land in western Europe—what came to be known as the 'Second Front'. When Soviet Foreign Commissar Molotov visited Washington in June of 1942 it was publicly announced that there was 'full agreement' about a second front. In London, however, there had been no such commitment. Just as the British turned down American proposals for a cross-Channel invasion, so they turned down the requests of the Soviets.

In August 1942 Churchill took the extraordinary step of flying to Moscow to explain the Torch strategy to Stalin. There would, he explained, be no Second Front in Europe in 1942. Furthermore, because of the need to assemble merchant ships and escorts for the planned North African landings, shipments to North Russia were to be reduced (convoy PQ 17 had suffered very heavy losses in early July). The British leader nevertheless indicated that a 'very great operation' would be mounted by the Americans and British in 1943. It is unlikely that Stalin and Molotov can actually have

Although this late war poster by the veteran American illustrator James Montgomery Flagg suggests that the war against Japan was an afterthought, American global strategy was influenced from the time of Pearl Harbor by a popular desire for revenge. President Roosevelt and the US Army high command accepted that Europe was the most important theatre, but from early 1942 a high proportion of US combat forces and shipping were sent to the Pacific.

By July 1942 a 'second front' in Europe was being openly discussed. Churchill (and his senior commanders) were, in reality, unenthusiastic about a costly cross-Channel invasion and preferred peripheral attacks in the Mediterranean or Norway. British cartoon by Leslie Illingworth.

British convoy PQ 18, September 1942, bound for North Russia; a merchant ship explodes. German attacks were so effective that the British abandoned the Arctic convoys for most of 1943.

expected a serious second front to begin in Europe in 1942, although the failure of the western Allies to attack 'as promised' could be used in propaganda and diplomacy. To their own population the Soviets could excuse continuing retreats, and in correspondence with the Allies they could gain leverage to ensure the maximum flow of Lend Lease supplies.

Stalin had good reason to feel aggrieved. In June 1942 183 German divisions were deployed in Russia and Finland, and only three were in action in North Africa (there were also 42 German divisions on occupation duty in western Europe and Scandinavia, and five in the Balkans). The losses actually inflicted on the Wehrmacht by the Red Army (269,000) in the summer and autumn of 1942 were six times those the Germans had suffered elsewhere (44,000). In terms of Allied *losses* the disparity between East and West was very much higher.

Despite these inter-Allied frictions three striking operations were carried out in Europe and North Africa in November 1942, which did clearly mark another turning point in the struggle against German hegemony. Of the three the least important was perhaps El Alamein (even though General Montgomery's victory was the greatest purely British land battle of the war). The British position in the eastern Mediterranean had not been under serious threat, even though the German–Italian forces in North Africa had achieved major territorial gains in the spring and summer of 1942, driving some distance into western Egypt. Alamein was also not a new strategic initiative, but rather a continuation of see-saw battles of the last two years.

Operation Torch, the second pivotal operation, began against weak opposition in Morocco and Algeria. It was outside Europe proper and did not initially engage any German troops. The intensity of the fighting, at least in the early stages, was much lower than at Alamein. Nevertheless Torch radically changed the Allied position in Africa, ensuring that Montgomery's success in Egypt would not be followed by another setback. It would eventually lead (in 1943) to the isolation and surrender of all German and Italian forces in their last North African redoubt, Tunisia. Some 270,000 Axis troops were captured in May 1943, along with their German and Italian commanders, General von Arnim and Field Marshal Messe. (The scale of the Allied victory was increased by Hitler's foolhardy decision to reinforce Tunisia with a considerable number of fresh troops.)

Torch also demonstrated the feasibility of Allied large-scale amphibious landings (the equivalent of six Allied divisions was landed in North Africa), and the limited ability the Germans had to interfere with them; for the first time in the war the western Allies achieved a large-scale surprise. And the strategic consequences were immense. The victory now covered an entire theatre of operations, it provided better bases for air attacks on Italy and southern Europe, and it eased the use of the Mediterranean by Allied shipping. Finally, the opportunity now beckoned for knocking Hitler's main European partner out of the war.

The Battle of Stalingrad was both more impressive and more important than either Alamein or Torch. The Stalingrad surrender (2 February 1943) came three and a half months before the final surrender in Tunisia, so it was psychologically more of a turning point. Although comparable numbers of Axis troops were put out of action in

After Alamein and Operation Torch the battles in Tunisia lasted longer than they might have. They constituted, however, the first successful British–American land campaign. British Cartoon by Leslie Illingworth.

Stalingrad and Tunisia, more were killed by Allied action (as opposed to surrendering) in the Russian battle, and a higher proportion were German; more than twice as many German divisions were destroyed.

Stalingrad also demonstrated a factor that would dominate the remaining years of the war: growing Soviet mastery of 'operational art'. In western popular imagination the Battle of Stalingrad is about urban, building-to-building fighting and suicidal Soviet resistance. In fact the Red Army carried out a very wide-ranging operation with a great deal of skill. Paulus's German Sixth Army was pinned in Stalingrad while Soviet mobile forces were secretly moved into attack positions far from the city. The Red Army then mounted a carefully co-ordinated, two-pronged, counter-attack against the weak flank divisions on either side of the Sixth Army. They quickly

February 1943: German prisoners after the Battle of Stalingrad. The destruction of the German Sixth Army was the turning point of the Second World War.

1943: *The Axis in Retreat*

Allied—or at least British and American—strategic planning pushed ahead rapidly at the beginning of 1943. The end of 1941 had seen the creation of a *potential* war-winning alliance. In the course of 1942 the British, Russians, and Americans had deployed forces that stopped any further advance by the Axis anywhere (except China), and began the actual process of 'roll back'. The Allies had ceased simply to react to emergencies. They were no longer lagging behind in the arms race, quantitatively or qualitatively. A significant amount of US forces were now available in Britain and North Africa. It remained to be seen, however, whether the Axis powers could successfully resist an Allied counter-offensive by making use of the large economic space (*Grossraumwirtschaft*) and resources that they had taken control of between the spring of 1940 and the autumn of 1942.

The Casablanca Conference (11–24 January 1943) was a British–American summit; Stalin declined to attend, largely on practical grounds. The meeting is famous for a declaration demanding 'unconditional surrender' of the Axis powers, but this announcement, on balance, had little impact on events. Churchill and Roosevelt, and their senior military chiefs, made the far more important decision that the next step would be continuing operations in the Mediterranean, initially against Sicily. Most important, a cross-Channel invasion in 1943 was essentially ruled out—although it was agreed that such an attack was definitely to take place in 1944. The problem—and one reason why the cross-Channel invasion was delayed for two years—was that such a massive and decisive operation was regarded as possible only when the weather conditions were favourable. In north-west Europe this meant the period from May to September. If the seasonal weather 'window' was missed, there would be a delay of seven months.

At the next meeting of Roosevelt, Churchill, and their senior military staffs (the CCS), the Trident Conference in Washington in May 1943, the decisions made at Casablanca were confirmed. It was agreed that the cross-Channel invasion would take place in May 1944—not 1943. Another operation would be mounted in the Mediterranean after Sicily, but one from which experienced divisions would be withdrawn to Britain in the late autumn to prepare for the cross-Channel invasion. Meanwhile—and not altogether logically—the CCS accepted that American operations in the Pacific were to be expanded with a dual advance, one thrust into the South Pacific and a new one into the Central Pacific. It was left to the President to communicate to Stalin that the promised cross-Channel invasion would now not occur in 1943. The

encircled the city, preventing a break-out of the German forces there or a break-in of reinforcements. The end result was the surrender of a German field army of 22 divisions and the capture of a recently-promoted field marshal. The Stalingrad campaign was also of great strategic importance. It prevented the Germans cutting the important Volga transport artery, and it put paid to all of Hitler's hopes for an advance into the oil-rich Caucasus.

Soviet dictator, with some justification, protested at a second broken promise, and in many respects this was the low point of inter-Allied strategic relations.

It took some time for the three Allies to exploit their successes of late 1942. The Axis forces in Tunisia did not surrender until May 1943. In Russia after Stalingrad Field Marshal von Manstein was able to organize counter-attacks which recaptured Kharkov in March 1943. A second Russian attempt at comprehensive encirclement operations in the early months of 1943, including offensives at Leningrad and Moscow and an operation to trap the German army group in the Caucasus, was only partially successful; Stalingrad was the one great victory. But then, in the late spring of 1943, Stalin was prevailed upon by his generals to wait for the Germans to make the next major move.

The big German tank attack at Kursk (Zitadelle) and the Allied invasion of Sicily (Husky) both occurred in early July 1943. The coincidence was not planned; the start of Zitadelle was delayed by Hitler, and Husky was delayed by enemy resistance in Tunisia. The campaign in Sicily was not a complete Allied military success, as the Germans were able to extract most of their forces from the island. Politically, however, it was very important, as it led to the collapse of Mussolini's government and the disintegration of the Italian armed forces. Husky was followed in September 1943 by two landings in the southern part of the Italian mainland, the most important being at Salerno (Avalanche).

Hopes of quickly occupying the whole of Italy were thwarted, as the Wehrmacht raced into the country, disarmed the Italian army, and created a strong defensive position between Naples and Rome. This incomplete Allied success was the product partly of rugged Italian geography and the skill of the German defenders, but it also had to do with the compromise nature of the whole Italian campaign; by the autumn the Allies were already withdrawing some of their best troops in readiness for the 1944 cross-Channel landing. The Italian campaign absorbed many Allied resources and was a strategic dead end; the Alps blocked any further advance into the vitals of the Third Reich. On the other hand by June 1944 the Germans, now fighting without a major ally, had had to move 27 divisions into Italy, and another 25 into the Balkans, especially to Yugoslavia and Greece, to replace the Italian garrisons there.

Red Army losses at Kursk were actually considerably higher than those of the Wehrmacht. Nevertheless, despite a concentration of Panzer formations the attack failed to penetrate the layered defences in the Kursk 'bulge'. The Germans were unable either to trap the Soviet forces there or to weaken the Red Army so thoroughly that it would be unable to take the offensive in 1943.

Kursk was in fact followed by a sustained Soviet counter-offensive, in effect a new phase in the war. The Wehrmacht had been greatly weakened by its losses on the Russian front in 1941, 1942, and early 1943. The motley forces extracted by Hitler from his satellites in early 1942 to flesh out Axis strength in the vast Russian front line were no longer available; they had been among the first formations to be destroyed in the previous winter.

Meanwhile the Red Army had now shown itself to be much more capable. After two years of the most bitter defeats imaginable, in which the Russian forces lost 6,750,000 personnel (and about 40,000 tanks and 20,000 aircraft), the USSR was finally able to put into the field a first-class army. It was a powerful modern offensive force, based on the pre-war concept of the 'deep operation'. Such actions had originally been intended to take place in enemy territory, instead of starting deep in European Russia, but the tactical principles were the same. From the top down the Red Army was better, and more realistically, led. Stalin awarded himself the rank of Marshal after Stalingrad (although not before two key military professionals, Zhukov and Vasilevskii, had been promoted to this rank). Churchill once publicly described Stalin as 'a warrior leader … whose authority enables him to combine and control the movements of armies numbered by many millions upon a front of nearly 2,000 miles and to impart a unity and concert to the war direction in the east'. Churchill was engaging in rhetoric (and he probably secretly envied his Soviet counterpart's power to override his generals). But, aided at the *Stavka* (GHQ) in Moscow by Zhukov, Vasilevskii, and the General Staff, Stalin had genuinely developed into an effective supreme commander of a large and complex military machine.

'When they call us D-Day Dodgers—which D-Day do they mean, old man?' Some of the British press accused the troops in Italy of shirking the main battles in France. British cartoon by 'Jon' (W. J. P. Jones).

The Red Army was not simply a crude battering ram, achieving its ends through unthinking self-sacrifice, 'human wave' tactics, and draconian punishment (although those elements existed). The spearhead forces of the Red Army were now technologically as advanced and effective as those of the Germans, and a good deal more effective in practice than those of the western Allies. 'Guards' forces, first so designated in 1941, had developed into a military elite. The *bronetankovye* (armoured) forces in general were given preferential treatment in equipment and personnel, and by February 1944 the main strategic thrust in the Ukraine included five 'tank armies'. Massive but flexibly structured 'frontal' air formations were organized from early 1942, partly on the basis of German practice; these 'air armies' provided effective domination of the airspace over the long battle line, and immediately in front of it.

The Russians benefited from the transfer of Luftwaffe forces to the Mediterranean from late 1941. Also to their advantage, from the second half of 1943, was the redeployment of German fighters and dual-purpose (anti-tank/anti-air) artillery to homeland air defence, as the British–American bomber campaign gathered pace. However the greater factor was Soviet aircraft production, which emphasized 'tactical' aircraft—short-range fighters and attack aircraft (Lend Lease provided a significant but small portion of these forces). The Luftwaffe had concentrated some 2,050 aircraft for Zitadelle, against which the Soviets could deploy two air armies with nearly 2,200 aircraft. By the end of 1943 2,600 combat Soviet aircraft were supporting just the advance across the Ukraine, and the grand total of forces available to the Red Army air force on all fronts and in the air defence (*PVO*) system (and in the supply and training pipeline) included 16,900 fighters, 8,800 strike aircraft (*shturmoviki*), and 6,800 (medium) bombers.

Soviet attempts to use airborne forces failed (notably for the Dnepr River crossings), but otherwise the Red Army demonstrated exceptional and sustained mobility. Self-propelled artillery had now been developed on a very large scale. The Red Army had 404,000 motor vehicles at the start of 1943, 496,000 a year later, and 621,000 on 1 January 1945. A large role here was played by Lend Lease heavy trucks, perhaps the most important single contribution of Allied military supply. The Red Army, for example, received 3,800 big Studebaker trucks in 1942, but 34,800 in 1943 (and 56,400 in 1944).

Soviet mobile reserves were now thrown into the Orel operation (codenamed Kutuzov) in July–August 1943 and the Briansk–Kharkov operation (Rumiantsev) in August. These offensives swept away the German positions north and south of the Kursk bulge. The whole German position in southern Russia had now been blasted wide open. This period of the Kursk defensive battle followed by Soviet summer counter-offensives, from July to September 1943, saw the most lethal fighting of the entire war, if measured by Soviet casualties. Red Army permanent losses—killed in action, died from wounds or disease—totalled 688,000; a further 116,000 were listed as missing or POWs. Wehrmacht deaths in the east for this same period, enumerated using a different methodology, were 188,000. However calculated, and whatever the exact figures, they were much lower than those for the Russians, but the heaviest in 1943 since January (the worst Stalingrad month).

Out of this maelstrom of blood five Soviet army groups advanced in parallel across the Ukrainian steppe. Half-hearted—and unrealistic—German attempts to create an *Ostwall* defensive line on the Dnepr and elsewhere proved untenable. During the autumn of 1943 and early spring of 1944 the offensive took the Red Army forward, without major pauses, to the western borders of the Ukraine. The Germans did (narrowly) avoid major operational encirclements in the Ukraine and elsewhere, but according to Russian figures 334,000 Axis troops were captured between July 1943 and June 1944. Liberation (or re-conquest) of the western borderland regions of European Russia, with a population of tens of millions, also provided fresh—if politically problematic—personnel for the Red Army. The Soviet drive only halted in April 1944, as a result of a combination of over-stretched supply lines, the weather, and the natural obstacles of the lower Dnestr River and the Carpathian Mountains. Nearly all of this fighting was still within the territory of the USSR (1941 borders); the Red Army only reached 'foreign' territory, the north-east corner of pre-war Romania, on 7 April 1944.

German army losses in the east were rapidly accumulating, and this more than anything else determined the course of later events, including the D-Day landings in June 1944. As Churchill colourfully put it in a radio address in March 1944, 'the guts of the German Army have been largely torn out by Russian valour and generalship'. It is hard to disagree with this assessment. In the ten months from July 1943 to April 1944 (inclusive) the Wehrmacht lost 1,360,000 personnel killed in the east (compared to 250,000 for all three services in other areas; the largest share was in Italy).

When Hitler and the German high command reviewed the strategic position in the autumn of 1943 they did place priority on their western defences rather than those in the east. The German border was about 250 miles from the Channel coast, but 600 miles from the Soviet front line at Kursk. Furthermore, the western Allies would have to execute a complicated amphibious operation which could conceivably suffer defeat. Throwing this landing force back into the sea would have a devastating political effect in the United States and Britain. This would be just the kind of operational victory that had served the German cause so well in the past; in overall command of the forces in the west were leaders who had actually achieved such successes, von Rundstedt (in France and the Ukraine) and Rommel (in North Africa). But the German high command had not anticipated the new potency and mobility of their opponents in the east; the rules of the game had changed. In any event it proved impossible to move a significant number of divisions to France.

The operations of the British and American armies in the autumn of 1943 and the following winter were less successful. The landings in Sicily and southern Italy did demonstrate growing mastery of amphibious war on a large scale and against an active opponent (which had not been the case in the confrontation with the Vichy French in Operation Torch). Nevertheless once safely ashore the Allied armies had great trouble breaking through the German defences (the Gustav Line) across the

Stalin, Roosevelt, and Churchill at the Tehran Conference, November–December 1943. This was the first time the three Allied supreme leaders met together, and they agreed military strategy for the following year.

narrow Italian boot. The last major landing of the campaign, at Anzio/Nettuno in January 1944 (an attempt to turn the western flank of the German position), was unsuccessful, as the Allied forces were penned up for four months within a confined 'bridgehead'.

The Casablanca Conference, back in January 1943, had also confirmed the role of strategic air power as a major element of British and American strategy for defeating Germany. The 'Combined Bomber Offensive' (CBO), as it was formally termed, paired two different air strategies. The British continued area-bombing of cities at night, and the Americans prepared to attack point targets by day. By the end of 1943 average monthly tonnage dropped by Allied heavy bombers based in Britain had risen to 20,300 tons, compared to 3,400 tons at the end of 1942. (The bomber campaign was still predominantly a British undertaking; even in the last three months of 1943 Bomber Command dropped twice as many bombs as did the American 8th Air Force.)

It has recently been argued that the so-called Battle of the Ruhr, mounted by RAF Bomber Command in the spring and summer of 1943 against a key region for coal, steel, and sub-components, played a critical role in slowing the growth of German armaments construction. Air Marshal Harris's bombers also succeeded in killing a large number of German civilians, especially in the attacks on Hamburg in July–August 1943. But German weapons output continued to rise, the morale of German city-dwellers did not crack, the British and American bomber production was itself swallowing great resources, and the aircrew were suffering high casualties. The attempts by the Americans to mount daylight raids deeper into Germany in the late summer of 1943 proved, for the moment, unsustainable. They were very costly to the attacking side, due to the vulnerability of unescorted bomber formations to defending fighters. Although the Americans continued to use the rhetoric of precision bombing, the European weather forced their B-17s and B-24s to carry out much of their bombing 'through the clouds', which, even with radar aids, was essentially blind bombing of target areas. The Germans did have to put many resources into Reich air defence. This change, however, only occurred in the autumn of 1943 after the tide of the war had turned in the east. Prior to that 40 per cent of Luftwaffe strength had been based in the east, 30 per cent in the west, and 15 per cent in the Mediterranean.

Meanwhile, the conduct of the war against Japan had slipped further away from the 'Germany First' agreements of 1941. The Americans had continued their advance in the South Pacific even after securing the Australian Supply line. More important, they began (as agreed at the May 1943 Trident Conference) on a parallel offensive across the Central Pacific from the Gilbert Islands to the Marianas and the Philippines. In addition it certainly made sense to keep the Japanese off balance by throwing a rapid offensive across the Pacific before they could adequately fortify their defensive perimeter. The Americans also devoted lavish resources to the crash development programme of a new—and very long-range—heavy bomber, the B-29 Superfortress, which was not required in Europe.

It was at this point in the war that the planners in Washington decided to limit the overall combat strength of the US army. At the beginning of 1943 General Marshall had still been planning in terms of an army of 120 to 125 divisions by June 1944. However, manpower was required to raise supply troops and for the B-29 bomber programme. The projected final strength of the army was reduced to 90 divisions (about 60 of which would be in Europe). The US army 'activated' 38 divisions in 1942, but only 16 in 1943; some 17 divisions were sent overseas in 1942, but only 13 in 1943. (By way of contrast the Red Army order of battle at the start of 1945 would comprise 32 tank corps and mechanized 'corps'—comparable to armoured divisions—and 473 infantry divisions.)

1944: Decisive Allied Offensives

The western Allies informed the Russians that the cross-Channel landing (Overlord) would take place on May 1944 (it was later delayed for a month). Both sides carried out grand offensives in June and July. This was the closest the British and Americans, on the one side, and the Soviets, on the other, came to co-ordinating major operations. The conclusive arrangements had been made six months earlier, at the Tehran summit (Eureka). Marshal Stalin attended the first of the 'Big Three' conferences, and made a direct contribution to agreeing strategy for the whole alliance. In effect he supported President Roosevelt against Churchill, who proposed a further postponement of Overlord in favour of continued Mediterranean operations. (Although not strictly a quid pro quo, Stalin agreed that the USSR would join the war against Japan after Germany was defeated.)

The first of these two great operations, the 6 June 1944 Normandy invasion, finally brought British and American troops back into north-west Europe, thirty-one months after the United States entered the war. Overlord was a huge operation. General Eisenhower had drafted a press statement to cover the eventuality that the Allied assault divisions were driven back into the sea. The landings at Salerno and Anzio in 1943–4 had demonstrated the potential of German counter-attacks and the danger of invasion forces being bottled up in the beachhead. The coastal defences in Normandy were considerably more developed than those that had been encountered anywhere else on the periphery of Europe. But this did not mean that D-Day was a desperate gamble. The Wehrmacht had only 60 divisions under the command of C-in-C, West (von Rundstedt), covering all of France and the Low Countries. Only 22 were Panzer or motorized; many of the remainder were regular infantry, but 24 were 'static' (coast defence) divisions. In contrast there were, in June 1944, 186 divisions in the east (including 51 in Army Group Centre), 12 in Norway, 27 in Italy, and 25 in the Balkans.

Everything did not go according to plan on 6 June and the days that followed, but the situation was only critical on one of five beaches (Omaha). It was important that D-Day was not a baptism of fire for all of the invading troops, which might have been

US troops on Omaha Beach in Normandy, June 1944. This shows the scene after the bloody assault landings, with the arrival of LSTs and other supply ships.

the case had the landing been attempted in 1942 or even 1943. Six of the 13 Allied divisions that came ashore in Normandy on D-Day or immediately afterwards had gained combat experience in North Africa or Italy. Clever deception planning made the German command think the main weight of the landings would fall in the Pas de Calais area, east of Normandy. Short-range aircraft operating from Britain were able to isolate the bridgehead area from German troop movements; the French resistance also played its part in inhibiting enemy action. The ingenious Mulberry artificial harbours, floated in modules from Britain, ensured that supplies and initial reinforcements could be brought in until a port was captured.

The Russian contribution to this dual attack began on 22 June 1944, eighteen days after D-Day. Operation Bagration took place in Belorussia, north of the Ukraine. The front line here had been relatively stable in 1943, although Hitler had permitted German Army Group Centre to make a number of pre-planned withdrawals. The Russians, like the western Allies, proved adept at masking their intentions; the Germans expected an offensive to come in the western Ukraine. Hitler had demanded a rigid defence based on 'fortified places', but these were very quickly surrounded and then swept away. German Army Group Centre was effectively destroyed, and the later part of the battle consisted of the pursuit of the scattered remnants. By the end of July the Red Army had re-captured all of Belorussia and occupied the southern part of the Baltic States; it did not stop until it approached the Vistula River in central Poland. The Germans were also surprised that the Red Army was able to continue its advance, for as far as 300 miles, without a significant pause.

T-34-85 tank in Minsk, July 1944. The destruction of German Army Group Centre in Operation Bagration, and the rapid Soviet advance across Belorussia, was a larger battle than the one in Normandy.

Bagration cost the Red Army 125,000–150,000 'permanent losses', compared to 30,000 British and American troops killed in Normandy up to the time of the breakout from the Normandy bridgehead in late July. More telling, however, was the relative impact of the two fronts on the Wehrmacht. The German forces lost 589,000 killed in the east in June, July, and August 1944, compared to 157,000 for all three Wehrmacht services in other areas. Bagration was followed in August by the Soviet Iasi–Kishenev operation, which led the Bucharest government to desert the Axis unexpectedly, and in turn to the rapid collapse of the German position in Romania. The Russian claim to have captured 200,000 German prisoners in this period (in Belorussia and Romania) is plausible. The total number of Axis troops claimed captured by the Russians in the whole second half of 1944 was 949,000.

Nazi Germany was not defeated in 1944. After D-Day the Allies were held for some weeks in the area close to the beaches, but then the liberation of most of France was achieved very quickly. The Germans had burned out their defending forces in Normandy and now had to pull what was left rapidly back to the former border defences of the Siegfried Line. The Allied drive was then slowed by supply problems, following delays in winning control of a major port in the Low Countries. General Eisenhower, who had now taken overall command of the campaign, decided on a cautious approach to the German frontier. He moved his three army groups to the east on a broad front, rejecting a more concentrated blow proposed by the British Field Marshal Montgomery. In December 1944 the Germans were even able to carry out a major counter-attack against the Americans in the Ardennes in Belgium, leading to the so-called Battle of the Bulge.

The Russians, for their part, had been halted on the Vistula before Warsaw in August. Like the British and the Americans they had supply problems. In addition the frontage which the German army had to defend was significantly shortened as it stumbled back into Poland; its flanks were now anchored in East Prussia to the north and in the Carpathians to the south. The Soviet command was also concerned with completing the capture of the Baltic region, partly bypassed by Bagration; Riga was only captured after heavy fighting in mid-October. Meanwhile the unexpected defection of Romania had suddenly opened a route for the Red Army into the Balkans and the Danubian countries. Soviet mobile forces thrust forward into Bulgaria, and north-eastern Yugoslavia. A major new campaign began in Hungary in October 1944 (which was brought to a halt by the need to besiege Budapest).

It was only in the autumn and early winter of 1944 that the western Allies began to inflict heavy losses on the ground forces of the Wehrmacht, comparable to what the Red Army had been doing for most of the war. Between September and December 1944 the Wehrmacht lost 293,000 personnel killed in the east, which—for the first time in the war—was slightly less than half of its total losses. Nevertheless the share that can be attributed to the main American and British ground forces fighting in France and the Low Countries was still less than those caused by the Russians in the east; the 'non-eastern' element of Wehrmacht losses (306,000 out of 599,000) included German navy and air defence losses, as well as those suffered in Italy.

The effect of the Allied heavy bomber offensive in 1944 was much greater than in the previous year. Average monthly tonnage dropped at the end of the year by RAF Bomber Command and the US 8th Air Force had increased to 275,000 tons, four times greater than the tonnage dropped at the end of 1943 (the British share was still significantly larger than that of the Americans for every month except February 1944). Many of the missions in the spring and summer were 'diverted' to preparing and supporting Overlord, rather than attacking industrial targets in Germany. But the Allied strategic bombing effort was now more potent: the British night bombers had developed effective new tactics and been provided with electronic navigation and target-finding aids. The American deployment of large numbers of long-range escort fighters made deep daytime 'penetrations' into Germany possible. The success achieved by the escorts in air-to-air combat was more effective in reducing the Luftwaffe fighter forces than was the bombing of the aircraft factories. In the autumn of 1944 the loss of territory in France and the Low Countries seriously disrupted the air-defence system of the Reich.

Many historians argue that the bombing campaign only began to have a telling effect on the enemy's war-making capability with the successful American attack on German synthetic oil installations in May 1944. It may well be that in the last months of the war the bombing campaign did cause paralysis to the war economy of the Third Reich. (For the first time, monthly tonnage dropped by RAF Bomber Command and the US 8th Air Force was about equal, with the Americans slightly ahead.) But rather than saying that the strategic bombing offensive made possible the Normandy landings, it was D-Day and the rapid liberation of France that enabled the greatest 'success' of the bombers, allowing them to cause devastating damage—at Dresden and elsewhere—but not having little effect on the outcome of the war.

1945: The Defeat of Nazi Germany

The year 1945 began with the stabilization of the western front, after the containment of the German Ardennes counter-offensive. While the US army in February–March 1945 made slow progress through the fortified and defended Rhineland, the Russians launched ambitious new deep operations. The most momentous was the Vistula–Oder operation of January and February, which was even more successful than Bagration in Belorussia. In Poland the Russians had been held on the Vistula River since August 1944; now they were thrown into action towards the west. Stalin, still in Moscow, had put himself in direct command of three army groups; his role matched that of Eisenhower in the west. The core of this thrust, Marshal Zhukov's 1st Belorussian Army Group, began its part of the offensive on 14 January 1945. Within three weeks it had advanced nearly 300 miles west to the Oder River, and was only 50 miles from Berlin.

The Soviet plan incorporated a second stage, in which the 1st Belorussian Army Group would have taken Berlin (by the end of February). This ultimate deep operation was thwarted by a variety of factors, including the unexpected strength of German resistance, supply problems, the winter weather, and—especially—concern about surviving German strength in Pomerania and East Prussia (on the northern flank of the attack). But Marshal Konev's 1st Ukrainian Army Group had made a similar rapid advance to Zhukov's south, and was soon in a position to surround the important industrial region of Silesia.

The British and Americans moved on towards western Germany. The methodical Rhine crossing planned by Montgomery in the north was pre-empted by the unexpected American capture of an intact bridge over the Rhine at Remagen (7 March) and by the development of another American bridgehead further south. The prepared crossing (Plunder-Varsity), when it came on 23 March, was followed within two weeks by the encirclement of an entire German Army Group in the Ruhr, and the end of any serious resistance in the west.

The last period of the war, and the certainty of imminent victory over Germany, revived latent tensions between the Allies. On the whole, however, both sides were careful to avoid an open break. Churchill's trip to Moscow in October 1944 (the Tolstoy Conference) had set out rough and ready 'spheres of influence' between Russian and Britain, at least in the Danubian lands and the Balkans. The summit

Operation Plunder: British troops crossing the Rhine in Buffalo amphibious tractors, 24 March 1944. The Americans had already succeeded in crossing the strategic river further upstream.

In April 1945 Churchill and some American commanders urged racing the Russians to Berlin in order to gain influence in Central Europe. The Red Army began so close to the German capital that the western armies could not have reached it first. American cartoon by Vaughn Shoemaker.

meeting at Yalta in the Crimea in February 1945 seemed to offer acceptable agreements, especially regarding the future treatment of Germany, and the borders and government of Poland.

However, the successful American and British Rhine crossings, and the evident disintegration of German resistance in the west, alarmed Stalin. He moved forward the start-date of the planned advance from the Oder bridgeheads to Berlin. This now took the form of a race between the army groups commanded by Marshals Zhukov and Konev. Despite unrealistic advice by Prime Minister Churchill and some of the British and American field commanders that Berlin be made the objective of the western Allies, Eisenhower decided to continue to direct his main effort into Bavaria, to end any last-ditch Nazi defence there. The unexpected death of President Roosevelt on

12 April, in any event, made even more unlikely any sudden change of Western strategy. But taking account of the starting points of the respective armies at the beginning of April and their relative strength (and, of course, the location of Berlin in eastern Germany), there can be little doubt that under any circumstances the Red Army would have reached the German capital first.

The final four months of the war, the so-called 'final battles' (*Endkämpfe*), saw Wehrmacht deaths calculated to have been as high as 1,400,000. Available figures do not divide these between east and west, but the Russians again faced the heaviest fighting. Contrary to modern conventional wisdom their highest losses (and presumably the highest losses of the Wehrmacht) were not so much the battle for the city of Berlin itself but rather the extremely heavy fighting in East Prussia, which between January and April 1945 cost the Russians 126,000 personnel as 'permanent losses', 40 per cent more than the whole of what they called the 'Berlin operation' (which, in turn, took in much more than just the city of Berlin). On the western side, some 15,000 US troops were killed in the Battle of the Bulge, and then heavy fighting took place in the Rhineland, which turned out to be the costliest US army campaign of the war; 40,000 US troops were killed. But only 10,000 US troops fell in action in Germany east of the Rhine from late March to the end of the war.

Conclusion

This overall interpretation of how the Allies came to prevail over their enemies, and to move from defeat in June 1940 to victory in 1945 leaves less to chance than do the views of some other historians. As soon as the 'grand alliance' was assembled in December 1941 the most likely outcome was Allied victory. It was from that time on nearly inconceivable that Britain, the USSR, or the USA would suffer complete defeat. I even find it difficult to see how, after December 1941, Germany, Italy, and Japan could have fought their enemies to a stalemate, exhausting them and preserving their 'new order'. A deadlock could only have come about had the Allies fallen out, and this was an eventuality on which the desperate leaders of the Third Reich (and later of Imperial Japan) placed their hopes. But the governments in London, Moscow, and Washington were also fully aware of this potential danger. In view of the extraordinary character of the Nazi regime and the appalling nature of its past actions they were convinced that the safest course was to hold firm—for the moment—to the alliance. A compromise peace, even with a (hypothetical) post-Hitler regime, would have been politically impossible in Britain and the USA, and practically impossible in the USSR, given the extent of Soviet territory under occupation from 1941 onwards.

The intention here is not to forget the courage of the combatants and the great sacrifices made. Nor is it to belittle the skill of individual commanders, or to ignore the high drama of events. The war, however, was not won by 'miraculous' victories, uniquely talented commanders, nor even by brilliant use of intelligence (from Ultra and other sources). That does not make the victory of British, Russian, and American forces any less legitimate.

Could the Allied victory have been won sooner or at lower cost? An armchair general might well argue that the Allies, as a collective, *did* fight a 'sub-optimal' war against a very dangerous enemy. The Soviet Union and the United States both delayed in entering the conflict. Even when Britain had two very powerful allies Churchill and his generals held back what might have been a decisive return to the Continent in 1943. The massive strategic air campaign distorted British and American production as much as it did German war industry. The United States diverted very large resources to the Pacific, which was—in the abstract and in terms of agreed strategy—a secondary theatre.

On the other hand the British and Americans did fight a capital-intensive 'war of machines' that well suited their resources and interests. In absolute terms the 'great generation' paid a heavy price. But the western Allies emerged from a fierce global war with a victory achieved at *relatively* low human cost—relative to losses in the First World War and relative to the losses of the Third Reich and the Soviet Union. Their economies were in many respects stronger than they had been in the 1930s (certainly relative to their erstwhile opponents). It was the British and Americans, ironically, who achieved the Soviet pre-war ideal of 'smashing the enemy on enemy territory' and achieving this with mighty blows and at a comparatively low cost in their own spent blood.

The population of the Soviet Union, civilians and military, paid the highest price. The war also had a crippling—and enduring—effect on the Russian economy. The Soviet victory had several long-term outcomes. It fused Russian nationalism and Soviet Communism, and legitimized for a time the Communist dictatorship as the saviour of the Soviet people. It ensured, for what it was worth, forty-five years of Soviet control over Eastern Europe. But the actions of the Red Army and the sacrifices of the Soviet people also destroyed the monstrous threat posed by Nazi Germany.

Sea power was an essential feature of the victory in Europe (and, of course, central to the Pacific war). It provided a powerful economic weapon, and it enabled the British and Americans to choose when and where to fight. Britain and the United States enjoyed an advantage in the strength of their navies and merchant marines, relative to their enemies; this maritime dominance was facilitated by industrial and geographical advantages, and a lengthy head start.

Going beyond that element, however, was the Second World War in Europe essentially a ground war or an air war? On both sides, and from beginning to end, there was a belief in the effectiveness of strategic 'air power'. The aeroplane was without doubt an essential feature of success in the Second World War. All the major states devoted a very large proportion of their war effort (measured in terms of government expenditure, usage of steel, aluminium and other raw materials, or number of workers employed) to aircraft production. A distinction needs to be made, however, between planes which provided—essential—direct support to the operations of armies and navies, and those intended to have an independent war-winning role. The strategic bombers did not achieve a 'decisive' role in Europe. Even in 1943 when they began to inflict serious physical damage on German cities and transport they were unable to stop the growth of war production. The dislocation of German transport and the interruption of fuel supplies came about only from the autumn of 1944, after the western Allies had secured their bridgehead in Normandy and after the Russians had thrust their forces into Poland and the Danube basin. At that point in the war, the German achievement of marginally more production would have made no difference to the outcome.

Air-power enthusiasts sometimes argue that the Germans lost the war because they failed to develop an independent long-range bomber force, and instead tied their air force to a ground-support role. In point of fact, the leaders of the Luftwaffe did at various points before and during the war take very seriously the role of their own service as a war-winner. More important, however, this supposedly flawed model actually applies very closely to the Soviet experience. In the USSR the air force was not an independent service like the Luftwaffe or the RAF, and there was virtually no wartime production of heavy bombers. Russian factories turned out just 91 modern four-engined bombers (TB-7/Pe-8 type), compared to over 50,000 produced in Britain and the United States.

Nazi Germany could only be defeated by invasion and occupation. The centrality of 'boots on the ground' in warfare is something of a cliché, but it certainly was the case for Germany in 1939–45. Hitler's Third Reich was a totalitarian state whose political and military elites were incapable of effecting a negotiated exit from the war; both groups were in any event unacceptable to Germany's enemies. Broken-backed fighting continued in Germany for some days even after Soviet tanks had cleared the centre of Berlin. For all of the Allied governments 'regime change' was an essential outcome. In the background, too, was the experience of the previous great European war and the consequences of ending that conflict—in 1918—without the invasion or full occupation of Germany. The bombing campaign was not going to destroy the Hitler regime or German militarism.

The land campaign in Russia played a much greater role in wearing down the Wehrmacht and the German war economy that supported it than did the bomber offensive. Armies prevented the Third Reich, after June 1940, from successfully extending its perimeter to a Eurasian resource zone (*Grossraumwirtschaft*) which would have given it the mineral and food resources required for autarkic superpower status. Armies had to fight their way to Poland and Romania, and the Allies had to begin ground operations in France and the Low Countries, before 'occupied' Europe could cease to provide Germany with a powerful resource base. Armies, too, had to drive across the Rhine and the Oder, into Greater Germany and on to the very centre of the Reich, before the Nazi regime and the Wehrmacht would stop fighting and victory could be achieved.

7 Fighting Power

War-Making and Military Innovation

DAVID FRENCH

Introduction

THE Second World War was won by the big battalions. However national power is measured, be it in terms of gross national product, size of population, numbers of men and women mobilized and put into uniform, or numbers of divisions, aircraft, and ships that put into the field, the Allied forces enjoyed an overwhelming superiority over the Axis powers that was in the end decisive. The argument that the final outcome of the war was determined by 'brute force' has not gone unchallenged, though it remains unanswerable. But along the way there were many instances when David gave Goliath a bloody nose.

The rapidity and completeness of the German victory in France in 1940 led many contemporary observers to believe that the Germans owed their success to the fact that they had enjoyed an overwhelming numerical superiority. In fact on the ground the combined Allied and German armies were evenly matched. The Germans fielded 142 divisions compared to a combined total of 144 French, British, Dutch, and Belgium divisions. The French army actually had 3,254 tanks, compared to the Germans, who had only 2,574. It was only in the air that the Germans enjoyed a slight margin of superiority. The Luftwaffe had 2,570 aircraft in the theatre, compared with an Allied total of 2,200.

The Axis powers were not alone in sometimes being able to turn the tables on a more numerous enemy. Between December 1940 and February 1941 the 36,000 men of Lieutenant General Sir Richard O'Connor's British and Commonwealth Western Desert Force advanced 500 miles across Egypt and Libya and, at a cost of only 2,000 casualties, killed or captured over 110,000 men of the Italian 10th Army. However, a year later the tables were painfully turned on the British and Commonwealth forces by the Japanese. Between December 1941 and February 1942 Japanese forces advanced nearly 600 miles down the length of the Malay peninsula. In February 1942, even though the defenders outnumbered the 35,000 men of Lieutenant General Yamashita's 25th Army by more than two to one, Singapore, Britain's bastion in the Far East, fell within days of the Japanese launching their attack.

German tanks and motorized infantry advancing through France in May 1940.

Japanese troops capturing a British airfield in Malaya, December 1941.

There was a common theme running through each of these cases. One side won, and the other lost, because the winners could maintain a higher tempo of operations than the loser. The winners were able to gather information about the situation on the battlefield, make their plans, issue their orders, and execute them, more quickly than their opponents. The result was that the cohesion of the losing side began to crumble. The German adoption of Blitzkrieg tactics was a classic example of this in practice. German doctrine was not a revolutionary break with past practices. In the 1920s the German army had taken a hard look at the lessons of the First World War. They then evolved a war-fighting doctrine that blended past practice with new weapons. In 1917–18 the German army had developed combined arms tactics, which saw infantry, artillery, and combat engineers working together as integrated teams. Now they incorporated into that mixture tanks, radios, and tactical air power, while at the same time they continued to decentralize command decisions, so that officers actually in contact with the enemy could exercise their initiative to seize and exploit any fleeting opportunities that presented themselves.

In 1940 this doctrine succeeded because their enemies allowed them to work. The French and British had also developed their own tank forces, but they did not marry them to the kind of flexible doctrine that enabled the Germans to exploit their potential to the full. Instead they opted for much more managerial command and control systems in which information had to pass from the front line to the rear, and orders then had to pass from the rear to the front. The result was that the Germans always seemed to be a day's march ahead of their enemies. What that meant in practice for the losers was explained by a British staff officer who was evacuated from Dunkirk in June 1940. 'Decisions had to be made so very quickly,' he wrote on his return to Britain, 'and so often could not be confirmed on the basis of the information coming in. Because of these armoured vehicles, the general moves the Germans made were so quick and where you may have a stable situation in the morning, by 7 o'clock or 8 o'clock in the evening, if you did not act and do something, the situation might be irretrievably lost.'

In the Far East the Japanese could conquer Malaya, capture Singapore, and then advance through Burma to the frontier of India because their opponents also made mistakes. At the strategic level the British worked on 'best case' assumptions. The First World War had been a devastating experience for them, and the lesson they drew was that in future all powers would base their strategic plans on rational calculations. This implied that because the Japanese could not hope to prevail in a war of attrition against Britain and the USA, its leaders would not be so stupid as to attack their Far Eastern possessions. But they were also impeded in assessing Japanese intentions by that country's strict military secrecy laws, and the chaotic planning apparatus of the Japanese government and armed forces. It was difficult for the British to predict that the Japanese would begin their southwards expansion in December 1941 because it was not until as late as October that the Japanese cabinet itself agreed that it was essential to occupy the British and Dutch colonies in South-East Asia.

Consequently, with their forces stretched elsewhere fighting the Germans and Italians, the British gave the Far East a low priority. They starved it of military resources, and many of the formations that they did send were under-strength and poorly trained. But it was also the case that they did not make the best use of what they had. The British believed that the landward defences of Singapore were assured because the Malayan jungle was impenetrable. It was for the British, whose army was trained and equipped to fight a highly mechanized war using masses of motor transport. But that meant they were road-bound, and the Japanese were able to use their air superiority to block their road movements. Contrary to post-war British accounts, the Japanese had no training in jungle warfare, but they did have a secret weapon. Bicycles made them more mobile than the defenders, and their simple tactical doctrine, pinning the defenders in front, outflanking them through the jungle, and establishing a blocking position behind them, proved sufficient time and again to unnerve poorly trained British and Indian troops and cause them to withdraw.

But what was a weakness in Malaya was a strength in North Africa. O'Connor's force was entirely motorized, unlike the Italians, whose forces consisted largely of marching infantry, and he possessed more and better tanks than the Italians. The British were also better trained than their opponents, and they had even rehearsed the opening moves of the offensive before they mounted it. Italian doctrine also put too much emphasis on fire at the expense of movement, and their lack of motor transport meant that they could neither mount rapid counter-attacks to support their isolated forward positions, nor withdraw out of reach of the British. They therefore dug in, and, rather as the Japanese were able to do in Malaya, the British were able to isolate and then overcome each of their fortified positions one at a time.

A column of Italian prisoners captured by the British Western Desert Force during their assault on Bardia, Libya, in January 1941.

'Brute force' may, therefore, explain the final outcome of the war. But it can only offer a partial explanation for its course. Explaining success and failure at the level of battlefield engagements has to go beyond a bean-counting approach. It requires an acknowledgement that armed forces exist to generate fighting power, and that fighting power was the product of the interaction of three elements. It had an intellectual component. Armies, navies, and air forces had to have a realistic doctrine that set out the fundamental ideas about how they should be organized, trained, and equipped to go about their business of fighting. It had a physical component, for they had to have enough men who were properly trained to fight; they had to have enough equipment of the right quality; and they had to have enough logistic support in the shape of supplies of essentials such as food, medicines, fuel, ammunition, and spare parts, to enable them to keep their fighting men in the field for long enough to get the job done. Finally, fighting power had a moral component. Soldiers, sailors, and airmen had to believe that they were part of a team with a common goal, and that together they were pursuing a cause for which it was worth fighting and perhaps dying.

Equipment

The Axis owed a good deal of their initial successes in the first part of the war to the fact that they had begun to mobilize their manpower and economies several years earlier than their opponents. Consequently in 1939–41 they had larger stockpiles of equipment and trained manpower than their enemies, although in the case of the Italians much of it was obsolescent. But by 1942–3 Allied war production had decisively overtaken that of the Axis powers in every important field. In 1943, for example, the USA produced 38,500 tanks and 54,100 combat aircraft, the British produced 7,500 tanks and 21,200 aircraft, and the USSR produced 24,100 tanks and 29,900 aircraft. The Axis powers could not match this. Italy's industrial base was so small that in the whole period between 1940 and 1943 it produced only 4,152 tanks and 10,389 aircraft. Japan's industrial base was slightly wider and in 1943 it produced 13,400 aircraft, but only a mere 800 tanks. Germany had the most extensive industrial infrastructure of all the Axis powers, but in 1943 it still only managed to manufacture 10,700 tanks and 19,300 aircraft. In the second half of the war, with their economies being squeezed by Allied air attacks and naval blockades, neither Germany nor Japan could make good equipment lost at the front. The result was that as the war continued the Axis armed forces underwent a process of de-modernization. That meant, for example, that by the end of the war German Panzer divisions had on average only about one-sixth of the tanks they had possessed in 1939.

But even if the Germans or Japanese had been able to produce more equipment, it is doubtful if they could have used it. Tanks, trucks, and aircraft ran on oil. The Allies had access to vast stocks. The Axis powers did not, and oil proved to be the Achilles heel of the Axis war effort. In the Pacific, American submarines and aircraft sought out and sank the oil tankers bringing supplies from Japan's overseas empire to the home islands. By 1945 virtually no supplies got through to Japan. In Europe, by

One of the United States Navy's submarines that was responsible for crippling the Japanese mercantile marine in the Pacific War.

1943–4, the Allied strategic air forces were mounting a growing number of attacks against both the Romanian oilfields and the synthetic oil production plants upon which Germany depended for its supplies. The result was that by the final year of the war German operations were handicapped at almost every turn by shortages of fuel.

To some extent quality could compensate for a lack of quantity. If tanks are taken as just one example, German Panzer divisions in North Africa enjoyed a marked advantage because many British-built tanks, such as the Crusader, were notoriously mechanically unreliable and frequently broke down. The American-built Sherman tank which equipped American and most British armoured divisions from 1943 onwards were much more reliable. They had been designed with one role in view, exploiting a hole in the enemy's front that had already been made by the infantry. Their comparatively thin armour meant that they could travel fast, but in the enclosed countryside of Normandy it also made them easy prey for the heavier German Panther and Tiger tanks. The latter had been developed as antidotes to the surprise discovery that the Germans made in 1941–2 that at least two marks of Soviet tanks, the T-34 medium tank and the KV-1 heavy tank, were considerably superior to their own vehicles. But the Panther and Tiger had their own vulnerabilities. Not only were they prone to breakdown, but their high petrol consumption made them vulnerable when Allied fighter-bombers destroyed the lorries carrying the petrol they needed. In Normandy many were abandoned by their crews when they ran out of petrol.

The story of tank development during the Second World War illustrated a larger truth. Armies in combat developed a dialectical relationship. Improvements in design by one side served only to encourage the other to redouble its own efforts to produce something better or to find other ways of nullifying the enemy's advantage. In general, and measured in terms of weapon for weapon, German mortars, machine-guns,

Soviet T-34 tank at the Battle of Kursk in July 1943.

Hiroshima after the dropping of the first atomic bomb in August 1945.

artillery, and anti-tank guns, were probably more destructive than their American and British counterparts, although in the T-34 the Soviets undoubtedly possessed the war's best medium tank. In 1944 the Germans began to bombard London with unguided cruise missiles, the V1 'flying bomb', and the world's first ballistic rockets, the V2. However, that did not mean that the western Allies always lagged behind in terms of technologies. The British enjoyed a clear advantage in the way in which they developed specialized armour to perform a variety of engineering tasks on the battlefield, from mine clearing to bridge-laying. They also employed new technologies in the shape of proximity fuses fitted to anti-aircraft shells to destroy a large number of V1s, and the new turbojet Gloster Meteor fighters were able to knock others off their course. But it was not until the Americans exploded two atomic bombs over Japan in August 1945 that one of the belligerents was able to deploy a weapon that was so far in advance of anything that its enemies possessed that it gained a really decisive technological advantage.

Logistics

Tanks, aircraft, and warships were the kinds of glamorous pieces of equipment that have always attracted popular attention. But if armies, navies, and air forces were to be able to fight, they also had to have sufficient spare parts and maintenance personnel to repair equipment when it broke down, they had to be able to provide fighting units with food and ammunition, they had to keep their men healthy, and, in the case of the German, Soviet, and Japanese armies, their horses fed. Front-line soldiers of all armies often regarded logisticians with a certain disdain, but the Axis forces allowed that mindset to spill over into how they organized their armies, with results that were, in the long term, catastrophic.

The idea that the German army was the acme of modernity was a carefully cultivated propaganda myth. It did have a spearhead of mechanized and motorized divisions, but most German soldiers marched on foot, and most German transport was dragged along by horses. It had a logistical system that could just about cope with operations in western Europe, with its short distances and good road and rail communications. What it could not do was cope with the much greater distances, and the much less developed road and railway systems, that it confronted in Russia and North Africa. The Wehrmacht went into Russia in June 1941 with about 3,600 tanks, but more than 700,000 horses, and with totally inadequate stocks of winter clothing. When the campaign was not over before the onset of winter, horses and men froze, and vehicles stopped because their engines could not cope with the cold. The Japanese attempt to invade India from Burma in 1944 betrayed a similar willingness to ignore logistics, with the result that when their advance was stopped at Imphal and Kohima their troops literally starved.

Not surprisingly, it was those belligerents with the biggest industrial economies and the best access to international trade which were best able to provide the necessary wherewithal to support their men at the front. The British and American armed forces

German troops using horse-drawn transport making their way towards Hamburg to surrender to British forces in May 1945.

both had more men in the rear supplying and maintaining their fighting troops than they had in the front line. In the American army the ratio between active combatants and support troops was 1:4. But access to sufficient resources by itself did not necessarily give one side or the other a significant advantage. Adequate resources had to be married to a culture of command that ensured that senior officers recognized the real importance of providing good logistics and administration. This could boil down to such mundane matters as sanitary discipline, as the contrasting experiences of Axis and Allied troops in North Africa in 1942 showed. In the year up to El Alamein, sickness rates in the German Afrika Corps were three times higher than they were in the 8th Army. The most important causes of sickness were dysentery and diarrhoea. They could not be prevented by vaccinations or inoculations, but they could be prevented by officers who insisted that their men carefully bury all human and food waste to prevent flies and germs polluting supplies of food and water. The British did this, and the Germans and Italians did not, and they paid the price in terms of manpower lost to the front. The gap between medical provision in the Far East was even wider and more significant. The Japanese, willing to accept what were by western standards extremely high casualty rates, made only minimal provision for sick and wounded soldiers. By contrast the British and Americans put increasing amounts of effort into their medical services in order to conserve the lives of their soldiers, and to ensure that sick and wounded men returned to the front line with the least possible delay.

But even the western powers, who by 1944 enjoyed a material abundance undreamt of by the Axis powers, were sometimes brought up short by their inability to provide their forward troops with what they needed. The Anglo-American break-out from Normandy in August and September 1944 was halted less by German resistance, and more by the fact that the Allies did not have enough transport to bring forward the petrol they needed to maintain the momentum of their advance.

Morale

The third element of fighting power, morale, was dependent on numerous factors, but one of the most important was how soldiers were selected and trained to perform their roles, and that in turn was a product of differing doctrines that dictated how armed forces ought to go about their business of fighting. The Germans, Italians, and Japanese believed that weapons alone would not produce victory. War was a struggle that would ultimately be decided by the will to win of the leaders and men of the opposing forces. The Soviets expected to fight a costly war of attrition involving both masses of men and machines, and they were willing to pay the human cost of doing so. It was therefore logical that the Germans, Italians, Japanese, and Soviets should ensure that their front-line units received their fair share, and sometimes more than their fair share, of the best men available.

The British and Americans did not ignore the importance of morale, but the First World War had taught them that fighting by relying on willpower and manpower would produce the kind of huge casualty lists that were no longer acceptable in a democracy. They therefore looked for a cheaper way of winning, and opted to rely on machinery rather than willpower and manpower. They wanted to maximize the firepower and mobility of their forces by employing the greatest possible quantities of the most sophisticated weapons. As a corollary to their doctrine, they assigned their highest quality manpower to their air forces and navies, and their armies had to make do with what was left. Front-line service in ground combat units in both the British and US armies tended to be the preserve of the young, the ill-educated, and the socially disadvantaged.

Once personnel had been selected, they had to be trained. All armed forces put their recruits thorough a process of basic training. It did not just impart physical fitness, an acceptance of military discipline, and an understanding of how to use weapons. It was also intended to weld individuals into small groups of men who would have the mutual confidence they would need to work together and fight together on the battlefield. Men who had gone through the shared hardships of basic training would not, or so the military authorities hoped, run away under fire, because if they did they would be letting down their mates. But problems arose when these carefully nurtured primary groups began to break down on the battlefield under the weight of heavy casualties. The Soviet and German armies tried to overcome this problem by keeping divisions in combat until their front-line soldiers had been exhausted. They then withdrew them and replaced losses en masse with new groups of men who had trained together. The Americans also kept their divisions in combat indefinitely, but posted reinforcements to them as individuals. The result was that when replacements arrived at the front line they found themselves fighting alongside strangers, and without the friends who might have helped them to cope better with the psychological and physical strains of combat. The British regimental system fell somewhere between the American system on the one hand and Soviet and German systems on the other. In theory recruits were posted to their local regiment where they would serve amongst men from the same county or city. But by 1942–3 the system was collapsing. There had been too many casualties, and there were too few men of military age to replace them from the same locale. It therefore became increasingly common for British soldiers to be posted between units to fill gaps in their establishments regardless of their local affiliations.

It is difficult to determine the extent to which morale gave one side or the other a decisive advantage in fighting power. The war in Russia was fought with a bitterness that was rarely replicated in the west. The grim fate that awaited prisoners encouraged soldiers on both sides to continue fighting beyond a point at which their counterparts in France, Italy, or North Africa might have surrendered. But equally important was the fact that both German and Soviet soldiers thought that they were engaged in a struggle for the survival of their people that could brook no compromise. Just in case they forgot that fact, both armies imposed a ferocious disciplinary system to punish backsliders. The German army executed between 16,000 and 18,000 men for desertion in the course of the war. The Soviets are reported to have executed 13,500 of their own men during the battle of Stalingrad alone. Even so, Soviet morale did sometimes sag. About 5.25 million Soviet soldiers did not fight to the bitter end, but were taken

Russian Cossacks serving with the German army in 1943.

prisoner. Nor was support for the regime universal, something demonstrated by the fact that by the end of the war between about 80,000 and 100,000 Soviet nationals were serving in the Wehrmacht.

The Japanese were imbued with ideas similar to those of the Germans about the issues at stake in the war. Japanese military culture demanded that every soldier, sailor, and airman must be prepared to sacrifice his life for the Emperor. Retreat or surrender brought eternal dishonour. Their morale was sustained by a system of strict discipline that could involve officers and NCOs physically chastising their subordinates in ways unlike anything seen in Western armies. The result was that Japanese soldiers in both the Pacific and Burma theatres frequently fought on until they were annihilated. On the battlefield that translated into the fact that by 1944 the Japanese, who were by then desperately short of effective anti-tank weapons, were resorting to suicide attacks during which soldiers with explosives strapped to their backs tried to blow up allied tanks.

The attitude of British, Commonwealth, and American soldiers was more varied. They believed that they were the victims of unprovoked assaults by their enemies. They were engaged in a war for a morally just cause, so everywhere they could use the language of freedom and liberation to justify their actions. But the degree to which they were imbued with a real hatred of their enemies varied. Shortly after El Alamein, Field Marshal Sir Bernard Montgomery, the commander of the victorious 8th Army, complained in a private letter that 'The trouble with our British lads is that they are not killers by nature . . .'. Most British and Commonwealth soldiers found it difficult to work up any high emotions about the Italians. The Germans occupied an intermediate position. In Crete some Australians likened shooting German paratroopers to duck shooting. But most Western Allied troops regarded killing them not as a pleasure, but as a necessary job they had to do before they could return home. The SS were regarded with opprobrium, often because of their callous treatment of Allied prisoners, and Germans and Italians who tried to surrender in the heat of battle were sometimes shot down when they did so. But the treatment meted out by the British and Americans in the west to those who did succeed in getting their surrender accepted was generally as humane as the circumstances of the battlefield allowed.

Before 1941 Americans had a stereotyped attitude towards the Japanese that was a mixture of ignorance tempered by racial contempt. Once the war started the surprise nature of the Japanese attack on Pearl Harbor, coupled with reports of the barbaric manner in which the Japanese treated Allied wounded and prisoners, reinforced these pre-war stereotypes. The Japanese came to be seen as alien and repulsive, and the Americans believed that the only way to defeat them was to kill them. Their own behaviour meant that they had forfeited all rights to mercy. At times, the fact that few unwounded Japanese prisoners fell into Allied hands owed at least as much to the unwillingness of Allied troops to take prisoners as it did to the unwillingness of the Japanese to surrender.

Innovation in Wartime

Between the autumn of 1939 and the middle of 1942 the Axis powers were victorious in Eastern and Western Europe, North Africa, and in the Far East. However, in a series of battles in 1942 and 1943, at Stalingrad and Kursk on the Eastern Front, El Alamein in the Middle East, at the Coral Sea and Midway in the Pacific, and along the convoy routes in the North Atlantic, the Allied powers first contained the advance of the Axis forces, and then began to drive them backwards. The outcome of the Second World War was decided by attrition. But the Allied powers owed their success not just to the fact that their factories and shipyards could ultimately out-produce those of their enemies. The margin of material superiority they enjoyed during the battles of 1942–3 was significant, but it was not as significant as it was to become in 1944–5. They also won because they were willing to change their doctrines, and to learn how to use the tools with which they were provided in increasing abundance in more effective ways than in the past.

Military innovation can take two forms. It can constitute what today is called a 'Revolution in Military Affairs', that is, changes that are so far reaching in their implications that they recast the ways in which societies can generate military power. The Second World War did not experience such a change until the dropping of two atomic bombs on Hiroshima and Nagasaki in August 1945 ushered in a new age of warfare. The major innovations in the conduct of military operations seen in the Second World War were on a lesser scale. The use of combined arms tactics, Blitzkrieg operations, strategic bombing, carrier and submarine warfare at sea, amphibious operations, electronic warfare (most notably radar and signals intelligence), were all innovations that had first been seen during the First World War. During the Second World War military innovations took the form of refining and developing these techniques.

Historians and social scientists have not been able to produce a single, simple reason why armed forces innovate. In September 1939 the Wehrmacht overcame Poland in a campaign that lasted barely a month, but the Germans did anything but rest on their laurels. They quickly gathered after-action reports, analysed what they had done right, but also self-critically looked at what had gone wrong. Their conclusions were that, although their basic tactical concepts did not need changing, the rapid expansion of the army since 1935 meant that many units were not fully trained. They therefore embarked on an intensive training programme during the winter of 1939–40 that prepared the army for the campaign against the Western Allies in the spring of 1940.

But more usually defeat was the mother of innovation, although defeat by itself was rarely sufficient to promote positive changes. Armies, navies, and air forces were large and hierarchical bureaucracies. Everything that we know about bureaucracies suggests that they are not good at innovation. The essence of bureaucracy is the routine repetition of the same actions. Innovation was, therefore, foreign to their nature. An external shock, such as a major defeat, might initiate a move towards changing the ways in which organizations went about conducting their business. But more was needed if the process was to reach fruition. Someone had to take an honest look at what had gone wrong. That entailed not only understanding how one's own forces had operated, but also gathering and analysing information about what the enemy had done. Someone had to analyse how the organization could avoid repeating its past mistakes, but also determine how it should act so as to succeed next time around. Future success would probably need more or different resources, and these had to be provided. The men who were going to do the fighting then had to be trained in how to operate their new equipment and in the new ways of fighting. Finally, if future success was to be institutionalized, mechanisms had to be put in place to ensure that this virtuous circle could be repeated. Perhaps the outstanding example of this process was the transformation of the Red Army and Air Force that began in 1942 and which by 1943–4 had made them more than a match for their opponents.

Intelligence

An understanding of how the enemy worked, what his forces were capable of doing, and what they were likely to do in the future, was fundamental to the process of innovation, just as it was to the maintenance of a higher tempo of operations. In general, the Allies were more adept at collecting, analysing, and utilizing intelligence than were the Axis powers. The German and Japanese intelligence communities suffered from common two defects. They consisted of too many agencies who competed rather than co-operated, and the raw information they produced was all too often twisted to support preconceived theories about their enemies. But perhaps even more important was the widespread illusion that intelligence just did not matter. Battles were decided not by knowledge of the enemy, but by the determination of each soldier to conquer, and the Germans and Japanese were convinced of their innate superiority in all aspects of warfare. The Japanese believed that their enemies lacked the kind of martial spirit that they themselves possessed in abundance, and that would always allow them to prevail even if their enemies were better armed. Consequently there seemed little point in gathering information about them. Thus the Japanese General Staff did not establish a special section devoted to analysing intelligence about the US army until 1942. Equally catastrophic was the way in which German intelligence officers vastly underestimated both the size of the Soviet armed forces in 1941, and their ability to resist the German invasion.

Poor intelligence did not always produce failure. Had the Japanese forces advancing through Malaya in December 1941 known that the British outnumbered them by a considerable margin, they might not have acted with such boldness, and might not have captured Singapore. Conversely, Japanese plans to advance into Assam in 1944 were based on the false assumption that the British and Indian troops facing them were no better prepared to fight than they had been in 1941. Nor was accurate intelligence always a battle-winner. Stalin had ample warnings of German preparations to invade Russia in 1941, but chose to ignore them. He may have believed that

Hitler would not behave so irrationally as to try to conquer the USSR with armed forces that were so numerically inferior to the Red Army. He may have thought that German preparations were a ploy to force him to negotiate. He may have thought that Hitler would not be so stupid as to embark voluntarily on a two-front war, and he may even have trusted Hitler to keep his word and fulfil his treaty obligations, just as Stalin himself had done.

Soviet battlefield intelligence was also poor in 1941, but by 1943 had improved by leaps and bounds. The Soviet forces devoted increasing resources to it, relying in particular on aerial reconnaissance, signals intelligence, and reports from partisans operating behind enemy lines. Signals intelligence for example, enabled the Soviet forces prior to their counter-offensive at Stalingrad to identify the location of weak and vulnerable Romanian formations, and to direct their thrusts against them. Signals

A Type 1 Enigma coding machine.

intelligence played an equally vital role for the Americans and British. In the Pacific it enabled the Americans to predict with accuracy the Japanese attack on Midway in June 1942 in time for US aircraft carriers to be in position to ambush the Japanese fleet. In the Atlantic the breaking of the German 'Enigma' codes enabled the British Admiralty to plot the positions of U-boats and to route their convoys away from them. Nearer to home British scientific intelligence reduced the effectiveness of the German night bombing campaign of 1940–1 by detecting the existence of radio beams that the Luftwaffe used to direct its bombers onto their targets, and then to 'bend' them so that the bombers dropped their loads on open ground.

The maintenance of a higher tempo than the enemy could also be secured if he could be persuaded to tie down men and resources against a non-existent threat. It was here that the ability of British code breakers to crack the supposedly completely secure German machine codes provided the Western Allies with an invaluable advantage. It enabled the British to arrest every German agent who landed in Britain, to turn many of them against their erstwhile masters, and to use them to feed false information to the German intelligence services. That ability, combined with the creation of dummy forces consisting of fake tanks and aircraft, and generating fake radio signals, formed the basis of a gigantic deception programme that persuaded the Germans that the Western Allies could field far larger forces than was in fact the case. In 1944 this culminated in 'Operation Fortitude'. It persuaded the Germans that the Allied landing in Normandy was a feint, and encouraged them for several weeks to hold back divisions in the Pas de Calais that might have been put to far better use further west.

Innovation on the Eastern Front: The Red Army

For a very long time Anglophone historians wrote as if the Second World War in Europe had been decided in the west. But in fact after the Axis powers invaded the USSR in June 1941 the Germans never deployed less than two-thirds of their army on the Eastern Front, and it was there that the key to the eventual Allied victory lay. If Stalin's forces had not learnt how to contain, and then destroy, the bulk of the Wehrmacht, the outcome of the war would have been very different. That the Soviets were able to effect a transformation of their forces that took them from abject defeat in 1941 to the gates of Berlin by May 1945 was all the more remarkable when seen against the background of their pre-war history. By the time Stalin's purges of the Soviet armed forces had ended in late 1938, 35,000 officers had been murdered, including 90 per cent of all generals and 80 per cent of all colonels. The poor performance of the Soviet armed forces during the Russo-Finnish Winter War of 1939–40 showed up the effects of this, and efforts to set things to rights had begun before June 1941. But in truth the German invasion hit the Soviet forces when they were still in a state bordering on chaos.

That the Soviets were able to survive at all was due in the first instance to their willingness to absorb massive casualties. They mobilized about 34.5 million people, including several million women, and the Red Army suffered about 8.6 million fatalities. Soviet doctrine, which insisted on defending every inch of ground, played into Hitler's hands in the opening stages of the war. It enabled the Wehrmacht to surround and capture about 3.8 million Soviet soldiers in the first five months of the campaign. This was the unpromising background against which the Red Army embarked upon a process of reform which transformed its organization and modernized its doctrine.

At the very top Stalin surrounded himself with a group of competent and talented officers, and then listened to, and acted on their advice. The grip of political commissars over the armed forces was relaxed, and officers were encouraged to use their initiative more than in the past. The Red Army that was almost swept aside by the Wehrmacht in 1941 possessed large numbers of tanks, most of which were obsolescent, but it was fundamentally an infantry force. Reformed and reorganized in 1942, it moved from being a human-intensive to a capital-intensive organization. Troops were issued with new, better, and more robust equipment in the shape of T-34 and KV-1 tanks, self-propelled artillery, and multi-barrelled rocket-launchers. But the Soviets did not merely equip their forces with more, newer, and better weapons. The Soviet General Staff took a hard and objective look at the past performance of their forces, analysed what had gone wrong in the battles of 1941 and 1942, and embarked on a programme to put this right. Tank and mechanized corps, brought together in tank armies, became the cutting edge of the Soviet army. Specialized personnel such as tank crews and junior officers underwent a programme of intensive training, so that everyone knew what he was supposed to do. Casualty rates dropped as better training meant that Soviet forces were increasingly adept at practising combined-arms tactics. In 1941 Soviet forces had suffered from poor communications, which made combined-arms co-operation exceedingly difficult. By 1944 this problem had been overcome, in part at least due to massive deliveries of communications equipment under the Anglo-American Lend Lease programme. The result was that at Stalingrad and Kursk the tank and mechanized corps were able first to punch holes in weak points in the enemy's positions, and then to advance deep into their rear areas. There they linked up to trap the enemy in pockets, and annihilated him. It was a measure of the improved efficiency of the Red Army that whereas in 1941 the Germans had lost one tank for every seven Soviet tanks they destroyed, by 1944 the ratio was down to one to one.

Innovation on the Western Front: The US Army

The American army in the west underwent a similar process of reform. In February 1943 the American II Corps, the first major American ground force to come into combat against Axis forces in the west, suffered a humiliating setback at the hands of the Germans during the battle of the Kasserine Pass in Tunisia. But only eighteen months later, in the summer of 1944, the same American army took the lion's share in the liberation of France and inflicted a decisive defeat on the German armies in the west. This apparently almost miraculous turn-around was the product of two things.

Not only could the American economy, once it had been mobilized, produce weapons in unparalleled quantities, but the US armed forces were able to learn quickly from past mistakes and put them right. On the ground the process had actually begun even before America entered the war. When field exercises in 1941 showed that the army's first armoured division had too many tanks and too few infantry the army was quick to transform its armoured divisions into balanced combined-arms formations that resembled in many ways the German Panzer divisions. But, unlike the Germans, American industry could produce so many tanks, trucks, and self-propelled guns that every division in the American army in Europe was fully motorized, and even infantry divisions had their own organic tank battalion.

Kasserine was the first occasion when the new army went into action, and given the rapid expansion of US ground forces, which had more than tripled in strength in the preceding year, mistakes were inevitable. The American army did not win in Normandy or in the Ardennes because it could pit overwhelming numbers of lavishly equipped troops against an exhausted Wehrmacht. It was hampered throughout the north-west European campaign by the War Department's decision to limit the army to 90 divisions, by the inefficiencies imposed on it by its replacement system, and by the inexperience of many of its units and formations. But just what the mature system could do was seen during the American army's break-out from Normandy in August 1944. By 1944 both the British and American armies had learnt how to employ their artillery en masse, but with a flexibility that the Germans could not match. After the German defenders had been pounded by an overwhelming weight of shells and bombs, well-equipped infantry divisions broke through the crust of their defences, creating a gap which the armoured and motorized infantry divisions of General George Patton's 3rd Army could exploit all the way to Paris and beyond.

Even so, significant weaknesses remained. In the European theatre divisions remained in combat for months without relief. Heavy casualties and difficulties in integrating replacements degraded the tactical efficiency of many infantry units. This was less of a problem in the Pacific theatre. There was usually a hiatus of several months between one amphibious landing and the next. That gave commanders ample time to rest and retrain their troops. In the west the technical inferiority of American tanks in tank-versus-tank actions remained a constant throughout the war and, like the British, the American army never really solved all of the problems of tank-infantry co-operation. However, the ability of both the British and American armies to combine formations of fighter bombers operating in a close air support role with their ground forces went far towards cancelling this weakness.

But the successes of the Allies on both the Eastern and Western Fronts in the second half of the war was not entirely due to their ability to develop or modify their doctrines and organizations so as to use their weapons and equipment more effectively. They were also helped by German mistakes. The Wehrmacht's early successes had owed a good deal to its own doctrine of devolving decision-making downwards, of giving commanders a mission and allowing them to carry it out in their own way. However, beginning in the winter of 1941–2, when Hitler had ordered his commanders on the

Eastern Front to remain in place in the face of the Soviets' winter offensive, the initiative allowed to subordinate commanders was gradually narrowed. In the autumn of 1942, Hitler insisted that Army Group commanders would not be allowed to order a retreat without his explicit permission. By early 1945 he was interfering in the work of mere divisional commanders. That played into the hands of the Allies, for it meant that time and again German forces found themselves pinned to the spot, only to be ground down by Allied artillery, air power, and tanks. To that extent the Allies' material superiority counted in their favour because the Germans acted in ways that allowed them to reap the maximum advantages from it.

Carrier Warfare and Amphibious Operations

The key to Japanese successes in the first six months of the Pacific War was the fact that the Imperial Japanese Navy possessed a force of aircraft carriers equipped with long-range aircraft which were superior to anything that their enemies had. But beginning in the middle of 1942 the United States navy was able to commit a growing number of carriers to the Pacific War that carried more and better aircraft than most of their Japanese counterparts, and, because they were equipped with radar, they could direct their aircraft more effectively than could the Japanese. Initially Japanese and American carriers fought each other and then, once American carrier aircraft had effectively destroyed Japanese naval aviation during the Battle of the Philippines Sea in June 1944, the Americans could direct their own naval air power against Japanese

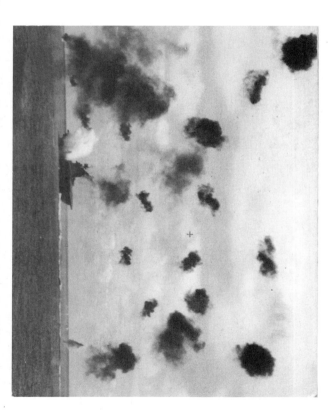

The US Navy's aircraft carrier *Yorktown* under air attack during the Battle of Midway in June 1942.

surface ships and assist their own land forces in their operations against Japanese-held islands.

In the inter-war period the Japanese, the British, and the Americans had all given some thought about how to conduct opposed amphibious landings. Recent precedents were not encouraging. The British landing at Gallipoli in 1915 had ended in abject failure. The landing forces had barely got beyond the beaches, the entire operation stalled, and after several months of stalemate, the troops had to be humiliatingly evacuated. The British did little more than think about the problems involved, and when their pre-war preparations were put to the test in Norway in 1940 they were shown to have done too little and too late. The Japanese did better and, albeit against weak opposition, in 1941–2 they achieved some spectacular successes, such as at Hong Kong, Luzon, Malaya, Guam, the Solomons, and the Dutch East Indies. But they also had some notable failures. During the campaign in the Philippines in 1942 the Americans repulsed no fewer than four separate Japanese amphibious landings.

Expelled from the Continent in 1940, Churchill established a Directorate of Combined Operations to think through the problems involved in landing on a hostile shore, and to prepare the necessary equipment for the day that the British could return

A Sherman Firefly tank coming ashore from a Landing Ship Tank in Normandy on 7 June 1944.

to north-west Europe. Working together, the British and Americans developed, and the Americans built, a whole family of specialized amphibious assault craft, ranging from large Landing Ship Tank, able to carry a squadron of tanks, to smaller craft capable of depositing a platoon of infantry on shore. Thanks to these preparations within three weeks of D-Day in June 1944 the Allies had managed to land over 850,000 troops, 148,000 vehicles, and 570,000 tons of supplies in Normandy.

Only the Americans possessed an independent service, in the shape of the US Marine Corps, that was specifically designed and equipped to carry out large-scale amphibious operations. In the 1920s and 1930s the American armed forces knew that one day they might have to project American military power across the Pacific, and to do that they would have to establish a series of forward operating bases along the island chains that led to Japan. In the 1930s the US navy and Marine Corps conducted a series of trials and exercises that enabled them first to identify, and then overcome, the practical problems involved. It only required the outbreak of war to make available to them the necessary resources to put their preparations into practice. By the end of the war the US Marine Corps had grown into two amphibious corps of six divisions, with its own integrated air force, although it remained dependent on the US navy's carrier aviation for air support during the assault phase of each landing. The Marines had become experts in integrating the operations of amphibious assault craft, naval gunfire, and close air support, with their own infantry. But the fact that both the fleet and the Marines could 'hop' from one Japanese island fortress to another also owed a great deal to the creation of a fleet train of logistic support ships that could either provision vessels underway at sea or in an anchorage.

The War in the Far East: Slim and the 14th Army

The Japanese had begun the war convinced that they could deal a knock-out blow to their enemies and their early victories had left them with no reason to question their most fundamental belief that the spiritual bravery of their own troops would more than counterbalance their opponent's material superiority. Conversely the early defeats that the British suffered in Malaya and Burma in 1941–2 which threw them onto the strategic defensive also gave them every incentive to study their enemy more carefully. Knowledge and understanding of what the Japanese could do and how they might do it was essential so that they could make the optimum use of the exiguous forces that they had available.

The trauma of the fall of Singapore and Malaya convinced the British that their own forces would require extensive re-equipping and retraining before they could match their enemies. They quickly revised their pre-war image of the Japanese. Their morale and discipline were of the highest order, and even when confronted by overwhelming odds they seemed to prefer to fight on until they were killed rather than surrender. The problem confronting the British was how to defeat such an enemy at an acceptable cost. The army in India had been trained to fight lightly armed guerrillas on the North-West Frontier of India, or German or Soviet mechanized

Troops of 5th Indian Division loading a jeep into a Douglas Dakota transport aircraft.

forces advancing through Afghanistan or the Middle East. It needed to be almost entirely retrained to fight the Japanese in the jungles of Burma. In India the army therefore established a centre to analyse Japanese tactics, and its assessments were fed into the training programmes of troops destined for the Burma front. The failure of the first Arakan campaign in 1942–3 demonstrated that overwhelming firepower alone would not deliver victory. By 1943–4, the British had developed flexible and effective methods for analysing lessons and disseminating them to front-line units. The British–Indian army created its own training programme, which was kept constantly updated, to prepare troops about to go to Burma for the rigours of jungle warfare, and it disseminated a common doctrine through *The Jungle Book*. Troops developed counter-measures to overcome the Japanese habit of outflanking and infiltrating around and behind their positions. They learnt to hold their ground when outflanked or surrounded, and to rely on supplies delivered by air when they were cut off.

The 14th Army's success, under the leadership of Sir William Slim, in containing and then destroying the Japanese forces advancing towards India in the twin battles of Imphal and Kohima in the spring of 1944 underlined the success of the reformation of the British–Indian forces in the India–Burma theatre. With only enough logistics support to last for a couple of weeks, General Mutaguchi's 15th Army advanced towards Imphal in the confident expectation that the British–Indian defences would quickly collapse, and that he would be able to capture all the supplies he needed. But his opponents did not collapse. When they were surrounded they dug in, fought back, and were reinforced and supplied by air. The Japanese, by contrast, were bereft of food and ammunition. When their infantry received little artillery support they were

British and Gurkha troops advance on the Imphal to Kohima road in April 1944.

reduced to making suicidal frontal assaults. Their failures, together with hunger and disease, culminated in the disintegration of the 15th Army, and that in turn enabled Slim to mount a counter-offensive in 1945 that brought about the collapse of the entire Japanese defensive system in Burma.

The War at Sea: The North Atlantic

Examples of such reversals of success and failure were not confined to operations on land. Between 1940 and 1942 the balance of advantage between the German U-boat fleet and the Allied navies in the North Atlantic also swung back and forth until, in the spring of 1943, it shifted decisively against the Germans.

The U-boats enjoyed their first 'Happy Times' in the winter of 1940–1. The fall of Norway and France in the spring and summer of 1940 gave the Germans access to Atlantic ports, and from then they were able to send forth groups of U-boats to operate in Wolf Packs against Allied merchant shipping. Attacking at night and on the surface in order to avoid the convoy escorts' underwater detection devices, they were able to overwhelm the often feeble defences and inflict severe losses on the convoys. Their second period of greatest successes came in the first half of 1942, following the entry of the USA into the war. The British had shared with the Americans the fruits of their hard-won experience on convoying, only to see their advice ignored.

Ultimately, however, the Allies prevailed. They owed their success to several factors. The Germans made mistakes. They underestimated the tonnage they would have to sink in order to force Britain to surrender, and although they increased the size of their submarine fleet, the Allies were able to take effective counter-measures in time to forestall them. The British adjusted their economy so that they could survive, and continue to fight, on about half the imports they had received before the war. The building capacity of American shipyards meant that the Allies did not just produce enough merchant ships to make good losses from enemy action. They could also actually increase their total tonnage, so that whereas in 1941 the Allied merchant fleet could carry 45 million tons deadweight, by 1945 it could carry 68 million tons.

At sea the British had employed convoys to protect their merchant ships in 1917–18, and the Americans followed suit after their own horrendous losses in the first part of 1942. The Allies built more anti-submarine naval craft, and when they were finally able to equip them with an array of scientific devices such as radar and sonar (a device that detected submerged submarines), the escorts could detect U-boats whether they attacked on the surface and at night, or below the waves. Scientific operational research suggested better ways of engaging the enemy, and new weapons, such as the forward-firing hedgehog mortar, provided better ways of destroying U-boats once they had been detected.

American factories also produced enough very-long-range aircraft, most notably the B-24 Liberator, so that by early 1943 the mid-Atlantic air gap was beginning to be plugged. Henceforth convoys could be shadowed across the whole of the Atlantic. Aircraft were important because, even if they could not destroy U-boats, they could force them to submerge, and once submerged submarines were too slow to keep pace with their prey. Finally, in June 1941 British code-breakers had succeeded in cracking the radio codes used by the U-boat fleet. Although they lost access to German messages between February 1942 and early 1943, for as long as they could read them, they could plot the position of waiting Wolf Packs and try to route convoys away from them.

The convoy battles reached a climax in the spring of 1943. By then the Germans had so many U-boats at sea that it was not possible for the convoys to be routed around them. But the Allied escorts knew where they were, and finally they had the ships, aircraft, detection devices, and weapons to destroy them. The U-boats were drawn into a battle of attrition that they could not win. In the first five months of 1943 the *Kriegsmarine* lost nearly 100 U-boats in the Atlantic, including 47 in May alone. At the end of the month Grand Admiral Dönitz, the commander-in-chief of the German navy, acknowledged defeat and withdrew his boats from the Atlantic.

Strategic Bombing

The Germans mounted the first strategic air campaign of the war in the west when, in the summer of 1940, the Luftwaffe began to attack Britain. Initially they conducted a counter-force strategy, targeting RAF airfields and aircraft factories, only to encounter the world's first integrated air defence system. Radar stations that could detect incoming aircraft at some distance from the coast were linked by telephone lines to a system of control rooms that plotted the position of the raiders and used radio to

U-210 attacked and sunk by HMCS *Assinboine*, 6 August 1942.

direct the operations of squadrons of Spitfires and Hurricanes to intercept them. RAF Fighter Command was, therefore, able to inflict an unacceptably high loss rate on the German air force. The Luftwaffe was compelled not only to switch its tactics, from daylight raids to night operations, but also its strategy. Counter-force operations went out of the window, to be replaced by attacks on ports, food stocks, silos, ships, and aero-engine factories in the hope that their destruction would bring London and other major cities to a halt and force the British to sue for peace. Civilian morale sagged in the winter of 1940–1, but it never collapsed.

RAF Bomber Command began the war believing that its twin-engined bombers could survive in daylight over German air space. They were quickly disillusioned when German day-fighters shot their most modern aircraft out of the sky in the autumn of 1939. The RAF then switched to night-time raids against precision targets such as railway marshalling yards and individual factories, whose destruction, the Air Marshals hoped, would cripple Germany's ability to make war. But in July 1941 Bomber Command was issued with a new directive. It was ordered to devote the majority of its operations to attacking German cities in a quest to undermine the

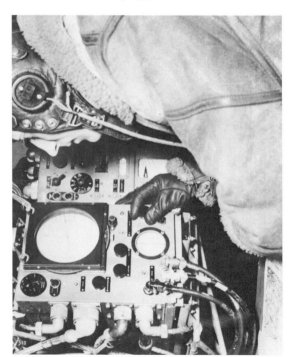

The cathode ray tubes and controls of an H2S set in an RAF bomber.

morale of factory workers. A month later a report prepared in the Cabinet Office discovered that only a third of RAF aircraft were dropping their bombs within a 5-mile radius of their intended targets. Towns and cities seemed to be the smallest target that the RAF could hit at night. Consequently, in February 1942 the new head of Bomber Command, Sir Arthur Harris, was told that attacking German cities was now his overriding priority. Area bombing, Harris explained in October 1943, would enable Bomber Command to bring about 'the destruction of German cities, the killing of German workers, and the disruption of civilised community life throughout Germany'. To enable his crews to do so Harris also oversaw the introduction of new navigation aids such as 'Gee', 'H2S', and 'Oboe', and he created an elite Pathfinder Force within his command whose job was to fly in advance of the main bomber force, and to find and mark the targets for them.

By 1943 Bomber Command had been joined by the USAAF in a combined bomber offensive, but the two air forces did not apply the same tactics. The USAAF refused to draw the same lessons that the British had taken from the opening weeks of the war, and persisted in believing that their bombers could fight their way to their targets protected only by their own machine guns. They were similarly convinced that if they could operate in daylight they could avoid the problems that the British had faced in hitting precision targets, and that their aircraft would be able to bomb with pinpoint accuracy. By late 1943 experience had proven them wrong. In August and October 1943 the losses that the US 8th Air Force bombers suffered over Schweinfurt forced its commanders to reassess their methods. They stopped mounting deep penetration raids inside Germany while they decided how to nullify the impact of the German fighter defences. The British persisted with their existing methods for a further five months. Between November 1943 and March 1944 Bomber Command tried to wreck

Berlin from end to end and, Harris hoped, win the war. In fact he nearly succeeded in wrecking Bomber Command. His belief that chaff, strips of metal foil dropped by his aircraft, would blind the German radar proved to be illusory. Over a five-month period Bomber Command's casualties exceeded 1,100 aircraft, more than its entire front-line strength, and a rate of losses it simply could not sustain.

The Luftwaffe had thus managed to force the Western Allies to call a temporary halt to their bomber offensive. It was the Americans who found a way to reverse the situation when their leaders accepted that if losses were to be reduced to a sustainable level, their bombers would have to be escorted all the way to and from their targets by single-engined fighters capable of out-performing the best aircraft that the Luftwaffe could put up against them. Their willingness to abandon the dogma that the unescorted bomber would always get through worked. In February 1944 the USAAF mounted a series of attacks on German aircraft factories. When the Luftwaffe's fighters rose to defend them, they discovered that the Americans had developed a new long-range fighter, the P-51 Mustang, and lengthened the range of their existing P-38 and P-47 fighters, by fitting them with large drop-tanks. American bombers could now be escorted by relays of fighters all the way to and from their targets, and those fighters could inflict an unsustainable rate of attrition on the German fighter force. In air-to-air combat US long-range fighters shot down their opponents in a ratio of 3:1. The Germans could make good their losses of equipment, but they could not make good their losses of trained pilots. That problem became even worse when, in April, the USAAF switched its attacks to the German petro-chemical industry, and so deprived the Luftwaffe of the aviation fuel it needed to train new pilots.

In the spring of 1944 the bomber fleets were switched to support the Normandy invasion, but when the Allies were safely ashore the demise of the Luftwaffe opened the way for Harris to recommence his night attacks. But this time his bombers were also accompanied by long-range escort fighters that could intercept German night-fighters before they found their prey. Harris reluctantly accepted that he would have to divert some of his resources from area bombing, and in fact Bomber Command dropped a greater tonnage of bombs on petro-chemical targets than the Americans did. The USAAF continued to insist that it was conducting a campaign of precision bombing. But it was not, for most of its bombs fell outside their intended target areas. Indeed by the autumn of 1944 studies suggested that, using their latest electronic navigation and bombing aids, RAF bombers operating at night were more likely to hit their targets than large formations of USAAF bombers flying in daylight, but relying on visual bombing techniques and handicapped by the often cloudy weather over western Europe.

Bomber Command dead numbered 55,463 dead in the European theatre, while the USAAF's fatalities were about 30,000. They killed approximately 355,000 Germans, injured many more, flattened many German towns and cities, and ultimately they denied the Germans the oil and transport resources they needed to continue the war. But their successes came too late to do more than contribute to the Allied victory.

1. A French poster from 1919. After the Bolshevik Revolution in Russia in 1917 other belligerents were spooked by the Red Threat. Hostility to Soviet-style Communism was also a way of shoring up national support for an increasingly unpopular war. The loss of labour, capital, and know-how would spell ruin.

2. A Hungarian poster from 1919. Woodrow Wilson's 'Fourteen Points' resounded around the world. The language of self-determination raised expectations in colonial territories that would be frustrated. Here, it is Hungarian expectations of Wilson's call for a 'just peace' that would be dashed by the outcome of the Paris Peace Conference.

3. Kandy Commonwealth War Cemetery, showing tombstones for soldiers from the Madras Labour Unit and the King's African Rifles, 1944 and 1945.

4. Mother and child memorial statue, at ground zero, Nagasaki Peace Park, indicating the date and time of the dropping of the second atomic bomb on Japan. The majority of the victims of the bombing were women, children, and senior citizens.

5. A 1945 painting by the British war artist Edward Bawden of an Italian partisan headquarters in Ravenna towards the end of the war, when partisans fought to liberate Italian cities from German occupation.

6. A poster issued by the Italian Social Republic mocks the Allied claim to be liberating Italy while at the same time bombing its towns and killing an estimated 60,000 Italians.

7. An evening rally of the SS in Germany in 1939. The National Socialist Party's elite units played a key part in the programmes of murder, extermination, and deportation that followed the German armies through Europe.

8. A German soldier armed with a flamethrower in the opening months of Operation Barbarossa, the Axis invasion of the Soviet Union.

9. A coastal convoy, probably between Southampton and the Thames estuary, seen from the barrage balloon vessel *Inverugie*, a Sheerness-based member of the Channel Mobile Balloon Barrage Flotilla. The coastal convoys around Britain provided a vital part of the interlocking network that allowed the Allies successfully to exploit their global command of the sea.

10. One of the key naval aircraft of the war, a Grumman Avenger bomber, is seen on the flight deck of an American escort carrier. In combination with the Hellcat fighters seen in the background these machines were the backbone of the forces that destroyed the Japanese navy and the Japanese naval air arm.

11. 'Jewish Plot against Europe!' In line with Nazi propaganda, an anti-Semitic Belgian collaborationist poster of 1942 depicts the British–Soviet alliance as part of the world Jewish conspiracy.

12. 'United we are strong', US Office of War Information poster (artist: Henry Koerner), 1943. After December 1941 the Allies had a clear numerical superiority. Axis hopes that the enemy alliance would fall apart were destined to be dashed. The Allied guns fired in unison.

13. A German tank advancing towards Bordeaux in June 1940.

14. P-51 Mustang long-range fighter aircraft.

15. A Russian poster declares 'More help for the Front'. The mobilization of Soviet society for the economic war effort was total and ruthless.

16. A group of British Boy Scouts help to collect waste paper for the war effort at Balderston, Nottinghamshire. Recycling was an essential way to expand scarce resources for war production.

17. The diversity of the Allied forces in Italy, 1943–45. French and Japanese-American troops at an artillery observation post on the French–Italian border.

ASKARI WETU WASHINDA WAJAPANI
Smash the Japs!

18. A propaganda poster glorifying the exploits of the British Empire's African troops, in this case fighting against the Japanese in Burma.

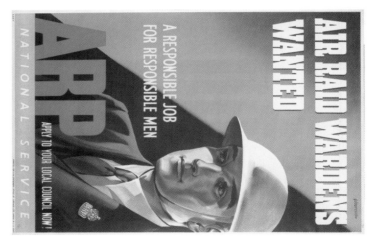

19. A British poster from 1939 encouraging civilians to enrol in the quasi-military air-raid protection services. Despite the appeal to men, over 300,000 women had volunteered for full-time or part-time service by the summer of 1940.

20. A United States poster from 1942 aimed at encouraging housewives to make their contribution to the total war effort by preserving their own food. In the Second World War the Home Front also meant the home.

21. After the bombing of Dresden in February 1945, dead bodies are burned at the Altmarkt near the Victory Monument (*Germaniadenkmal*).

22. A bus lies in a crater in the road in Balham in south London, the morning after a German air raid during the night-time Blitz. During the raid on the night of 14 October, a bomb had exploded on Balham High Street, destroying part of the tube station underneath.

23. A piston aero-engine, one of the most complex machines of the Second World War.

24. Sir Alexander Fleming, a pioneer researcher in antibiotic medicine, at his desk in 1929. Penicillin was widely used with Allied armies towards the end of the war to prevent wound infection.

25. Paul Nash, *Battle of Germany*, 1944.

26. Mikhail Khmelko, *Triumph of Our Fatherland*, 1945.

27. Stalin, Churchill, and Roosevelt at Yalta in February 1945. This was the second meeting of the wartime Big Three, the first summit having taken place at Tehran in November 1943. At the time Yalta was hailed as a great success for the Soviet–Western entente but has since been criticized for conceding too much to Stalin.

28. Truman, Attlee, and Stalin at Potsdam in August 1945. Roosevelt died in April 1945 and was replaced by his Vice-President, Harry Truman. Winston Churchill participated in the first half of the Potsdam conference but withdrew when he lost his position as Prime Minister following the announcement of the results of the July 1945 General Election. His place at Potsdam was taken by the new Prime Minister, Clement Attlee, leader of the victorious British Labour Party.

B-17 Flying Fortresses of the US 8th Airforce on a raid over Berlin, 6 March 1944.

Strategic bombing was based on the assumption that modern industrial economies were inherently fragile edifices, and that the weakest points in a nation at war were its economy and the morale of its civilian population. If they could be attacked directly, both the enemy's means and his will to fight would be destroyed. But the German economy contained far more slack than the Allies realized. German fighter production, for example, did not peak until September 1944, and the German people proved to be at least as resilient under bombardment as the British had been in 1940–1. The bombers could not, as some of the pre-war exponents of strategic bombing had hoped, win the war without the need to employ large ground forces.

The USAAF was equally willing to innovate during its strategic air offensive against Japan. In November 1944 the fall of the Mariana Islands enabled the Americans to base squadrons of B-29 Superfortresses within range of the whole of Japan for the first time. Initially they mounted high-level daylight raids. But when these proved to be ineffective and their losses mounted, they shifted to low-level night-time attacks, and in March 1945 they abandoned precision attacks in favour of dropping incendiary bombs over wide areas of Japanese cities. By the end of July 1945 almost every town and city of any size in Japan had been attacked and burnt out, and Japan's economy had effectively ground to a halt. Three hundred thousand people had been killed, half a million injured, and 8.5 million people had been made homeless. Some civilian and military leaders could read the writing on the wall, and thought that surrender was the only possible option left to them. But most of the military leadership disagreed. They were not overridden until, following the dropping of two atomic bombs and the entry of the USSR into the war against Japan, the Emperor himself insisted on surrender.

Conclusion

The Germans, Italians, and Japanese did not have a high opinion of their British or American opponents. (The Germans developed a much higher opinion of the Red Army.) Man for man, they insisted, they simply could not match the fighting qualities of the ordinary Japanese or German soldier. In August 1944, in the middle of the Normandy campaign, a German intelligence officer reassured his own men that 'Tommy is no soldier'. But in reaching such a conclusion, he was missing the point. No matter how highly developed were the martial qualities of their soldiers, sailors, and airmen, it would avail the Axis powers little if they did not have the equipment and supplies they needed to fight, and the replacements they needed to make good their casualties.

But the fact that by the second half of the war they possessed more and better equipment was not the complete answer to why the Allies won. Military organizations are always likely to have flawed doctrines in peacetime. Soldiers, sailors, and airmen, unlike other professionals, have no way of constantly and realistically testing and refining their doctrines short of actual combat. What was critical to success or failure was their ability and willingness to spot the flaws in what they were doing once the shooting had started, and then to put them right. The Allied powers did not win the

American B-29 Superfortress bombers at the base of XXI Bomber Command in the Marianas in 1945.

war just because they were able to mobilize an overwhelming mass of men and equipment. They also won because their soldiers, sailors, and airmen developed, to varying degrees, the skills they needed to make good use of the weapons and supplies at their disposal. Without their ability to do that, without the willingness of their armed forces to suffer often horrendous losses and learn from their past mistakes, understand what their enemies were trying to do, and find ways to nullify their efforts, the eventual outcome of the war might not have been different. But its duration would certainly have been prolonged, and the casualties they suffered would have been even higher. It was because they were more able and willing to change and adapt to new ways of fighting that they were able, to echo the title of Sir William Slim's account of the Fourteenth Army's campaign in Burma, to turn defeat into victory.

8 Economies in Total War

RICHARD OVERY

Few lessons of the Great War of 1914–18 were as important as the realization that modern industrialized warfare could only be fought successfully if the national economy was as fully mobilized for war as it reasonably could be and, if possible, prepared in advance for the contingency. Economic staying-power had many components, and was dependent on a wide variety of strategic, political, and social choices, but none of the combatant powers in the Second World War could afford to ignore the economic reality behind their war-making. Indeed for the major aggressors, Japan, Germany, and Italy, the war itself had a strongly economic core. Waging war was supposed to provide new resources and potential markets; victory was intended to make their populations richer and to overturn the existing balance of commercial and financial strength in their favour.

Wartime economies had to be able to do a number of things at once: to provide weapons and equipment to fulfil the requirements of the armed forces; to maintain an adequate supply of food and commodities for the civilian population; to distribute labour between the competing demands of military, industry, and agriculture; and to find the finances to fund conversion to total war without a damaging level of inflation. Financial stability was all-important because in the First World War problems in raising funds had eroded the value of currencies, stimulated labour demands for wage increases, and encouraged a widespread black market. These were complex requirements and they had to be met under conditions in which military circumstances and emergencies, the effective operation of blockade, or the prospect of heavy bombing from the air all threatened to undermine national efforts to create an effective war economy, capable of solving the problems of wartime mobilization and distribution.

The Pattern of Economic Mobilization

Unsurprisingly, the economic experience of the different major combatant powers varied widely. The three Axis states, Germany, Italy, and Japan, had begun in the 1930s, well before the onset of world war in 1939, to gear their economies more fully to the possible needs of war, partly by bringing important areas of economic policy and industrial production under state control or supervision, partly by controlling trade and instituting programmes of self-sufficiency (or 'autarky'). As a major industrial economy with large resources, Germany had many advantages over the other

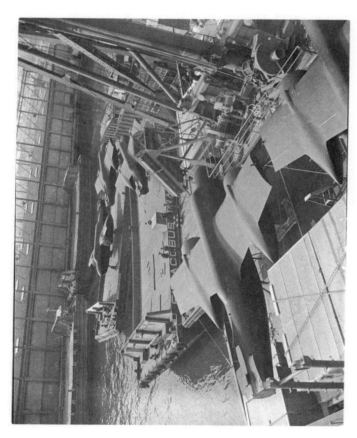

Bomber sections being loaded onto ships in New York Harbor prior to transport across the Atlantic. The United States had to ship adequate supplies across thousands of miles of ocean, a remarkable logistical achievement.

Axis states. In 1936 a Second Four-Year Plan was launched under the direction of the air force chief, Hermann Göring, which was designed to increase agricultural self-sufficiency, control trade, wages, and prices closely, and set up programmes of industrial development in synthetic products (oil, textiles, rubber) in which Germany was deficient. The German economic base was expanded by absorbing Austria, the Sudeten areas of Czechoslovakia, and then the Czech lands themselves in March 1939. War against Poland in September 1939 had the additional advantage that it brought the Polish coal, steel, and machinery industries under German control and additional farmland to feed the German people in wartime. The war economy was never based just on Germany.

In 1939 the German central bank and the finance ministry developed plans to regulate the macroeconomic performance of the economy in wartime to ensure that consumption did not compete for the resources needed to support military output and to restrict wage and price increases. The economics ministry appointed a so-called 'Committee of Professors' to advise on ways to avoid inflation and curb inessential spending. The German experience after 1939 was very different from the First World War when price increases, falling real wages, and a flourishing black market had undermined the domestic economy. This time, inflation was suppressed, the diversion of resources to war on a large scale was carried out in the first years of the conflict, savings were diverted to fund the issue of war bonds, and the black market was dealt with by widely publicizing the execution of the first black marketeers as a deterrent to the rest of the population.

Japan and Italy faced rather different problems. The Japanese economy was potentially fragile, dependent on imports for food and raw materials, and above all reliant on overseas supplies of oil, essential for the operation of the Japanese air force and the large Japanese navy. It was technically up-to-date in a number of key areas but its motor industry was very underdeveloped and the early attempts to construct synthetic substitutes for key materials lagged far behind the German example. A programme of 'autarky' began in 1936 on an ambitious scale but it could not be realized in full because by 1937 Japan was already heavily engaged in war in China, a conflict that absorbed manpower, finance, and resources which could have been used for the more effective modernization and expansion of Japanese industry. Japanese output of steel, for example, reached a peak of just under 7 million tons in 1943, where Germany produced 30 million tons that year and Britain 13 million. Japanese coal supply was a mere 66 million tons at the peak in 1940 against German maximum output of 347 million tons in 1943. High reliance on trade made Japan vulnerable to blockade, and indeed it was American limitation of scrap iron exports and freezing of Japanese overseas assets in 1941 that prompted Japan to go for all-out war against the Western powers.

Italy was the weakest of the three Axis states in terms of war potential. Like Japan, Italy had been fighting wars from the mid-1930s, first the conquest of Ethiopia and then intervention in Spain on the side of Franco's nationalist rebels. These conflicts also absorbed resources needed to build up Italian war economic potential to match Mussolini's growing imperial ambitions. Italy was short of almost all core materials for war (though it had extensive supplies of hydro-electric power), and unlike German and Japanese industry was geared much more to small-scale specialist industry rather than large-scale output. Italian coal supply in 1940 was 15.8 million tons, output of steel a puny 2.2 million tons. Italy, like Japan, had a large and inefficient agricultural sector; in 1941 there were only 3.8 million employed in industry against more than 13 million in Germany and 8.7 million in Britain. Even then, Italian industrial performance in the Second World War was lower than it had been in the First; shortages of raw materials, poor overall planning, and financial crisis meant that industrial production declined from a peak in 1940 to around one-fifth lower by the time of Mussolini's fall from power in 1943. The hope that Italy's weak resource base might be compensated for by seizing assets abroad never materialized. The oil under the Libyan desert remained hidden there while Italian forces proved too weak to be able to seize the Suez Canal and gain access to the oil of the Middle East. For a country reliant on imports, the most damaging problem was the loss of merchant shipping to British air and sea power. By the end of the war some 64 per cent of Italy's merchant fleet lay at the bottom of the Mediterranean. This outcome was only exceeded by Japan, where the merchant fleet declined from some 5 million tons in 1942 to 670,000 tons three years later.

The situation for the Allied powers fluctuated a good deal over the wartime period and differed widely between them. Britain, though committed to preserving the peace in the 1930s, nevertheless began planning for a possible war from 1934 onwards. Economic rearmament was an important part of that planning. Reserve factory capacity was built (the so-called 'shadow factories'), stocks of food and raw materials built up, and manpower allocation—unique in peacetime—was begun with the National Service Act of 3 September 1939 and completed with a supplementary act in December 1941 for conscripting women. Britain had many obvious economic advantages: a large manufacturing base, the largest trading network in the world and a merchant marine of over 20 million tons to support it, substantial domestic resources of iron ore and coal, and the support of the Commonwealth and Empire, where much of the world's copper, rubber, tin, and cotton was produced. As the war loomed in 1939 the government established boards to oversee the macroeconomic direction of the war economy, to avoid financial crisis, inflation, and the collapse of Britain's purchasing power abroad. Senior academic economists were drafted in as advisors, including John Maynard Keynes, who became a consultant with the Treasury. Most of these objectives could be met by an unprecedented degree of state control of economic variables, tight regulation of the labour market, limited rationing of consumer goods, and higher taxation. At its peak, Britain's military effort consumed 55 per cent of national income, yet without seriously destabilizing the overall operation of the wartime economy or reducing living standards too far.

London's Marble Arch is decorated with banners encouraging Londoners to 'Dig for Victory'. Producing extra food in gardens and parks was seen as an essential way to supplement rationed goods.

Workers shovel the waste material from the production of beet sugar so that it can be used by farmers as feed. The wartime economy depended on the recycling and exploitation of all possible material resources.

Two problems, however, the British government was unable to solve: British trade was subject to prolonged assault by enemy aircraft and submarines between 1940 and 1943, and although trade lines were kept open and stocks of vital food and materials built up, the volume of British trade declined steadily, from 68 million tons of imports in 1938 to only 26 million in 1941. The enemy blockade never achieved its aim, but the war against the submarine was an essential battle to win. In January 1943 Britain was down to just two months' supply of oil. The second problem was payment for overseas supplies. Since Britain could no longer export more than a fraction of the goods sent abroad before the war, much of what was needed from the Americas had to be paid for by liquidating overseas assets or using up scarce foreign currency or dollar deposits. By the end of 1940 these resources were almost at an end and only the generosity of the United States and Canada in supplying goods without payment, or extending substantial loans, prevented Britain's war economy from serious crisis in 1941. As it was, there were limits to British war production and output failed by 1944–5 to match the productive effort of Germany, the United States, or the Soviet Union.

The Soviet situation was different from that of any other combatant power. During the 1930s the Communist regime pioneered, at high social cost, the construction of a large industrial economy and a more efficient agriculture. Fear of 'imperialist capitalism' prompted the Soviet government to embark from 1932 on a large programme of military production which meant that by 1939 the Soviet armed forces were, on paper, the largest in the world. The Soviet air force, with more than 10,000 aircraft, was twice the size of its German opponent in 1941, though the superiority of German models and German pilot training compensated for the wide difference in numbers. It was fear of Soviet economic potential and military strength that prompted high levels of rearmament in Germany in the 1930s and was one of the reasons for launching Operation Barbarossa on 22 June 1941, before the Red Army grew too strong. Preparing a war economy in the Soviet Union was a quite different question from preparations in capitalist states with large private industrial sectors. The Soviet planning apparatus of the era of Five-Year Plans in the 1930s could easily be adapted to war because it already controlled physical use of resources and labour and had no serious financial problems in a command economy. Labour unrest, which might have presented a problem as resources were pushed into armaments and living standards and working conditions deteriorated, was tightly monitored by a security apparatus that sent millions of potential working-class and peasant opponents to the GULag labour camps or the labour colonies during the 1930s.

What undermined the Soviet war effort dramatically was the rapid seizure by Axis forces of the areas of the western Soviet Union (and the Ukraine in particular) where much of Soviet heavy industry was located and a large part of the annual grain surplus produced. By the end of 1941 two-thirds of Soviet productive capacity was in German hands, though much was destroyed before the area was abandoned, and 2,600 enterprises moved eastward with 16 million workers and their families. None of this could disguise the degree of crisis. Soviet coal supplies were cut from 151 million tons in 1941 to 75 million in 1942; steel output fell from 17.9 million tons to 8.1 million. In 1943 Germany and the German 'New Order' in Europe produced four times the amount of steel forged in Russia. The remarkable fact is that the Soviet Union, from its shrunken industrial base, produced more aircraft, more tanks, and more artillery pieces than the richly-endowed German enemy. The explanation lies in the willingness of Stalin's government to subordinate everything to the military effort, so that all industry worked for the war at the expense of any consumer production. Workers got rations if they worked for the war effort, but other Soviet citizens had to rely on their family or else eke out a living from thousands of allotments created so that additional foodstuffs could be grown. Living standards and working conditions were primitive and inadequate but the Soviet workforce continued to turn out masses of sturdy and increasingly sophisticated weapons, buoyed up from late 1942 by news of continuous victories as their productive effort helped to turn the tide against the Axis.

The United States was the exception to all the other war economies. In the 1930s the level of military expenditure and output was tiny compared with the rearming European and Asian states. In 1938 Japan produced almost twice as many aircraft as the United States. But America was a sleeping giant, with the world's largest industrial economy, rich raw material resources (including oil), and abundant agricultural produce. It also had a large labour force, much of it unemployed or underemployed in the 1930s following the 1929 depression, which could be made available for war. In

The crew of the British vessel HMS *Belfast* in Russia on convoy duty with Lend Lease supplies to the Soviet armed forces and people. The northern route to Archangel and Murmansk was dangerous and hazardous for the men involved.

1938 there were 44 million employed in all sectors, by 1943 there was a wartime peak of a little over 65 million. The existence of unemployed resources of capital, industrial capacity, and manpower meant that the United States could begin to rearm and then develop, from 1942, a giant war economy without the risk of high inflation or the problems of labour allocation found elsewhere, and without extensive central state direction. Even at the peak of the war effort only 45 per cent of the American economy was committed to military spending, by which time the figure for the German 'New Order' economy was 70 per cent and in Britain 55 per cent. This was made possible because GNP expanded by 87 per cent between 1938 and 1944, a remarkable expansion that allowed the economy to satisfy at one and the same time the demands for military output, the needs of allies, and the requirements of domestic consumers.

It proved necessary to increase the scope of state intervention (against much resistance) in order to bring about the conversion to war as rapidly as possible, but American industrial practices—large firms, mass production methods, high engineering standards, professional management—meant that private initiative as much as state control was a driving force of American war production. The United States produced two-thirds of all Allied supplies during the war, including 297,000 aircraft, 193,000 artillery pieces, 86,000 tanks, and 2 million trucks. American shipyards turned out 8,800 naval vessels, sixteen to every one produced by Japan. All of this

'Liberty' ships lined up in a California dockyard. The brainchild of the industrialist Henry Kaiser, almost 3,000 of the mass-produced vessels were launched during the war.

could be done while sustaining generous consumption levels by the standards of other states (though rationing, particularly of petrol, was introduced for a number of products) and raising income levels for the workforce. Average calorie intake was higher in 1944 than it had been in 1938, a situation enjoyed by no other warring population. Better food and higher incomes were particularly important for the poorer sections of American society, hit hardest by the depression, but now able to share high standards with the better-off. Though historians have argued that the idea of wartime boom years can be exaggerated, by comparison with the decade of economic crisis that preceded it, the boom seemed real enough.

Economic Collaboration

The entry of the United States into the war in December 1941 also helped to improve the economic fortunes of the other Allied fighting powers, first because the American government made a commitment, already enshrined in the Lend Lease Bill passed by

Congress in March 1941, to supply goods without payment to states engaged in the war against Germany and Italy, second because the American navy and air forces limited German and Japanese economic performance with bombing and blockade. Britain was the chief beneficiary of the generous supply programme, receiving $30 billion of aid, two-thirds in the form of military equipment and weapons, 15 per cent of it in food and agricultural supplies. The Soviet Union was also provisioned from summer 1941 onwards with a flow of food, vehicles, communications equipment, and raw materials, eventually reaching a total value of $10.6 billion. Generous though these supplies were, and vital for the continued belligerency of both states, Lend Lease only involved 4 per cent of the United States' domestic output between 1941 and 1945. The flow of aid was also substantial from Canada, with loans of 4 billion Canadian dollars and a flow of aircraft and vehicles to Britain's war effort that could be had on credit. In return Britain supplied the United States and Canada with facilities and equipment in Britain or with scarce regional resources (oil, for example, for United States forces in North Africa came from British supplies in the Middle East). Reciprocal aid resulted in a total transfer of $5.6 billion worth of services and material to the United States over the period 1941–5.

The willingness of the Western Allied states to share their resources was an important component in eventual Allied victory, though it was calculated that the Soviet Union gave its allies no more than $2 million worth of reciprocal aid. The

Sub-machine-guns sent under the United States Lend Lease scheme are unloaded at a port in Britain in March 1942. Two-thirds of the aid came in the form of military equipment.

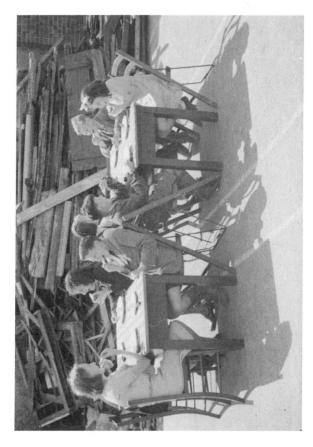

A group of British schoolchildren in 1941 eating Lend Lease food in the ruins of their school, hit by bombing.

Soviet war effort relied heavily on Lend Lease because the supply of food, materials, and equipment allowed Soviet industry to concentrate production on finished weapons. The 363,000 trucks supplied to the Soviet Union exceeded total German production throughout the war; Lend Lease supplied 58 per cent of Soviet aviation fuel and 53 per cent of explosives, and 1,900 rail locomotives against just 92 produced in the Soviet Union. The Soviet military communications system was transformed by the supply of telephones, telephone wire, and front-line radios. Though the Soviet position after the war was to play down aid from the imperialist West, Khrushchev recalled in the 1960s that Stalin had several times remarked that without the aid the Soviet Union 'could not have continued the war'.

This collaboration was in evident contrast to the Axis states. Germany supplied goods to Italy only grudgingly and gave priority in the transfer of machinery and raw materials to firms in German-occupied Europe which were working for the German armed forces. When radar and anti-aircraft guns were sent to Italy in 1942 they were allocated to German units based in the peninsula—which on occasion fired at Italian aircraft if they strayed into the path of the guns. German supplies of coal and steel were agreed after difficult negotiations, but only in return for a more generous flow of agricultural products and 'voluntary' labour the other way. Italy ended up subsidizing the German war effort at its own expense. Between Japan and the Axis partners in Europe there was little mutual assistance. Japan sent rubber supplies to Germany across the Soviet Union in 1940 and the first half of 1941; details of technical equipment and industrial processes were sent by air or submarine to Japan late in the war, but otherwise economic aid was, to all intents and purposes, non-existent.

Rails for the Soviet Union being loaded onto goods wagons in Iran. The southern Lend Lease route through Iran was operated by American soldiers and engineers. The Soviet Union got much of its wartime railway equipment from the West.

The Production of Weapons and Equipment

The principal test of any war economy, and even more so in a condition of total war, is the capacity to produce military equipment in sufficient quantities to meet strategic requirements and of a sufficient quality to match the technical threshold enjoyed by the enemy. Here the performance of the different warring states varied widely, as Table 8.1 shows.

These contrasts at one level were, of course, due to the differing endowments of resources, labour, or finance. It was impossible for Italy and Japan with their more limited resources to compete on equal terms with the other major industrialized economies. By 1943 the Ford Company of America was producing more military equipment than Italy. But levels of military output were also affected by the different ways in which the production of military equipment was managed and by the nature of the war being fought, which in general determined both the kind of weapons and goods to be produced and in what quantity. For example, the high toll taken of Allied shipping in the Atlantic convoys forced Britain and the United States to devote extensive capacity to building new cargo ships. The United States constructed 21

Table 8.1 Military Output of the Major Powers 1939–1944

	1939	1940	1941	1942	1943	1944
I. Aircraft						
Britain	7,940	15,049	20,094	23,672	26,263	26,461
United States	5,836	12,804	26,277	47,826	85,998	96,318
Soviet Union	10,382	10,565	15,735	25,436	34,900	40,300
Germany	8,295	10,247	11,776	15,409	24,807	39,807
Japan	4,467	4,768	5,088	8,861	16,693	28,180
Italy	1,750	3,257	3,503	2,821	2,024	–
II. Major Vessels						
Britain	57	148	236	239	224	188
United States	–	–	544	1,854	2,654	2,247
Soviet Union	–	33	62	19	13	23
Germany (submarines)	15	40	196	244	270	189
Japan	21	30	49	68	122	248
Italy	40	12	41	86	148	–
III. Tanks						
Britain	969	1,399	4,841	8,611	7,476	5,000
United States	–	c.400	4,052	24,997	17,565	17,565
Soviet Union	2,950	2,794	6,590	24,446	24,089	28,963
Germany	c.1,300	2,200	5,200	9,200	17,300	22,100
Japan	c.200	1,023	1,024	1,191	790	401
Italy	(1940–3)	1,862 tanks, 645 self-propelled guns				

Note: Major vessels excludes landing craft and small auxiliary boats. Tank figures for Germany and the Soviet Union include self-propelled guns.

million tons of shipping in three years as a result not only of ship losses, but also because of the demand for landing craft and escort vessels for the large amphibious operations in the Pacific theatre, in the Mediterranean, and for the invasion of France in 1944.

Germany and the Soviet Union, on the other hand, had exceptionally high losses of men and equipment throughout the long war on the Eastern Front, while Germany had to provide weapons for fronts in southern Europe and in the air war against the bombing threat. The scale of losses forced the German industrial economy to find ways to speed up production in 1943 and 1944 to meet the demands of the front, and to simplify and rationalize production methods. The Soviet Union was prodigal with its weaponry, expecting high losses as an inevitable result of the nature of Red Army operational practice and the urgent demands from Stalin for offensive action. Soviet industry produced in large quantities to cope with the high loss rates, not just because the armed forces were very large. With better prospects that weapons could survive longer in battle, both states might have mobilized at a lower level of production. Without the direct and indirect consequences of bombing, German industry could certainly have responded to the demands for replacement weapons more flexibly than proved to be the case.

The German war economy has always excited greater historical interest than those of other powers. This is chiefly because of the effort by the British and American bomber forces critically to undermine German war economic performance and the ambiguous efforts to measure the effects of the campaign once the war was over. The post-war bombing surveys concluded that Germany had not been fully mobilized for war in 1939–41 and that this fact explains how production could go on expanding to reach a peak in September 1944 despite ever heavier bombing. More recent research has rejected this view and shown how the Hitler regime sought large-scale mobilization from the start of the war, and indeed that the higher production in 1943 and 1944 reflected a prior commitment to large investment programmes which finally bore fruit only later. Of one thing there seems little doubt: the resources available for German production of weapons were very much larger than the resources available to any enemy until the entry of the United States, but the level of military output remained well below what that resource base might have allowed. The Soviet Union produced more aircraft, tanks, and guns than Germany even though it had substantially smaller resources of steel, coal, and aluminium. German conquests brought most of continental Europe into the German economic orbit, and although there was a price to pay in occupying such a wide area, much of this price was paid by the occupied states themselves, while perhaps as many as 20 million additional workers in occupied Europe worked for the German war effort in some capacity or other.

There are a number of explanations for the German failure to match resources to output long before the onset of bombing. The most important factor was the way in which the war economy was organized, in clear contrast to the organizational practices of the Allied powers. In the Soviet Union the war economy was directed by the central Defence Committee, chaired by Stalin, which met every day of the war. Military and civilian chiefs met together, issues and problems were identified, and action ordered from the top. Because of the development of physical planning methods under the Five-Year Plans, it proved possible to institute a flexible central planning apparatus, run by the young economist Nikolai Voznesensky, head of the Gosplan organization. He and his staff drew up schedules for monthly, quarterly, and annual output of each class of weapon. Alongside these were the balance sheets of the main factors of production to make sure that the supply of machine-tools, labour, and materials matched the production targets. The system was often challenged by unanticipated problems, but the Defence Committee would act at once to try to resolve any difficulty (and in all too many cases punish those responsible).

A portrait of the Soviet economist Nikolai Voznesensky. As head of the Gosplan state planning agency, he played an important part in organizing the Soviet system of mass production.

In Britain the War Cabinet and Defence Committee kept a close watch on economic issues, but the question of matching resources and labour to the needs of war industry was solved by setting up two executive bodies, the first the Lord President's Committee under Sir John Anderson, which oversaw general economic policy, and the second a Production Executive led by Ernest Bevin, the trade union leader and Minister of Labour and National Service. The second was eventually turned into the Ministry of Production in 1942. The system was designed to identify and eliminate bottlenecks and shortages, like the Soviet one, and although it did not work perfectly, it did supply a formal, centralized structure in which civilians played a major part in organizing the production of equipment for the armed forces. Only in the United States did Roosevelt fight shy of creating a fully centralized war economic apparatus. The War Production Board set up in January 1942, chaired by the Sears-Roebuck vice-president Donald Nelson, oversaw the allocation of contracts and controlled the supply of some essential materials but there were many examples of poorly planned factory construction, misallocation of resources, and administrative waste. These problems were disguised first by the sheer wealth of American resources, second by the go-getting production culture which encouraged entrepreneurs and managers to produce what they could, at high speed and in large quantities, even at the risk of duplicating their efforts.

In Germany the nature of the dictatorship militated against a centralized and co-ordinated system. Hitler gave up cabinet meetings by 1938 and there was no defence committee or national body which brought together civilian ministers and senior

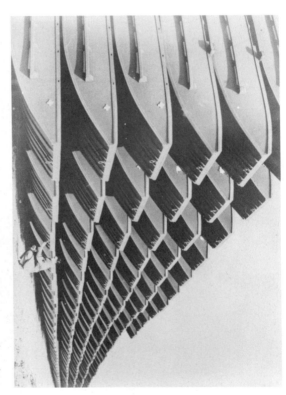

Pontoons piled up for use in Operation Overlord, the invasion of France in June 1944. American suppliers were able to produce almost unlimited military supplies free from any threat of aerial attack.

officers concerned with war production. The Supreme Headquarters was a primarily military institution; economic problems were left to individual ministries, where the permanent state secretaries tried to supply an alternative 'cabinet' system by regular meetings of their own. Major decisions about the scale of war production or the allocation of resources or the cutbacks in the civilian economy rested in the end with Hitler, even if the policies were worked out at ministerial or military level. The absence of any single forum in which resources and labour could be matched to the military programme, or any central plan for the economy, might have resulted in a more disastrous outcome if local initiatives had not overcome the absence of central direction. The German economy had a great many resources and a world-class scientific and engineering base to work with, and left to themselves German industrialists and bankers achieved a great deal in rationalizing and organizing production and managing the larger economic picture.

They were hamstrung in the early years of war by the excessive interference of the military, which had a large and technically-informed establishment dedicated to monitoring and directing the production of weapons and the allocation of resources. The Economics and Armaments Office, headed by Colonel General Georg Thomas, operated a nationwide system of Armaments Inspectorates whose personnel thought that they should have responsibility for the military war economy. The military preferred to control the number and quality of weapons themselves; they disliked the idea of crude mass-production of standard weapons, and as a result the German armed forces had hundreds of different models of aircraft, vehicles, and guns and complicated systems of maintenance, store-keeping, and modification. Only in 1944

Workers at the Berliner Maschinenbau at Wildau producing locomotives for the German communications system. Air attack undermined the transport network and eventually led to the collapse of German military industry.

did it prove possible, at the insistence of a new civilian apparatus set up under Albert Speer, Hitler's pet architect and from February 1942 Minister for Armaments and Munitions, to concentrate production on a narrow range of proven models and shed the wasteful dispersion of effort on the latest technology or tactical requirement. Anti-tank weapons were reduced from 12 models to one, vehicles from 55 to 14, aircraft from 42 (not counting numerous variants) to an eventual priority figure of just five. Even then it was impossible to reverse other strategic decisions encouraged by the military researchers, including the 'Vengeance Weapons', the A-4 rocket (or V2), and the Fieseler 76 cruise missile (V1), which ate up precious resources in 1944 for little military value but appealed to Hitler's uncritical longing for new weapons that might turn the tide of war.

Of course mere quantities of production did not necessarily translate into effective battlefield performance, nor did economies with more effective and centralized administrative structures avoid production crises. The introduction of the heavy bomber into the RAF was held up during the war because of the technical inadequacy of the preferred models. The Avro Lancaster was created by accident rather than design when two additional engines were added to the poorly-performing Manchester. RAF demands for large numbers of bomber aircraft could not be met until the bombing campaign was nearing its end. The introduction of the long-range fighter with drop

A British factory in the Midlands producing Covenanter tanks for the British army. Put into production in 1939, these were plagued with technical problems and were declared obsolete in 1943.

fuel tanks was held up for months in 1942–3 because of the failure to push through with sufficient urgency a production programme for disposable tanks. The United States Sherman tank was fast and versatile and produced in tens of thousands, but it was outclassed entirely by later models of German tanks and easily destroyed by German anti-tank weapons. Much Allied weaponry had technical defects which required costly repairs or modifications. Even though Allied forces greatly outnumbered the Axis in terms of ships, aircraft, vehicles, and guns, the enemy possessed enough high-quality matériel to impose high loss rates and a heavy economic cost for their eventual defeat.

The Home Front Economy

The second major problem confronting every warring state was the distribution of manpower between the differing requirements of military, industry, and agriculture. At the same time, states had to find ways to avoid inflationary pressures, control

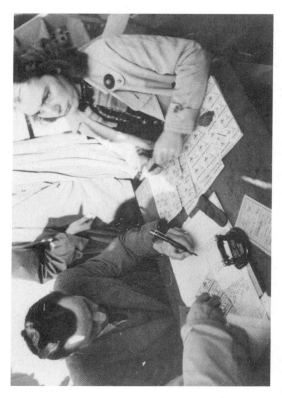

A German official distributes ration cards to women who have been bombed out of their houses. Strict food rationing began in Germany from the very first days of the war.

wages, and maintain a sufficient supply of food and consumables to keep the work-force committed to the war effort. The balance sheet of labour was easier in economies with a cushion of spare or unemployed resources. In the United States large numbers of unemployed could be brought into the rural and industrial workforce or mobilized into the armed forces. The decision was taken not to create massive armed forces (total mobilization into the services even at the peak was only 11.4 million men and women, most of whom were not actually fighting), but to focus energies on producing large quantities of weapons and equipment for the American armed forces and for those of the Allies.

The expansion of the war economy made necessary the recruitment of labour in areas with high unemployment and their transfer within the United States, particularly to the western seaboard, the north-east, and the industrial belt in Illinois and Mich-igan. Since there was continued prejudice against using American Blacks on any scale for military service, many of the new male workers were from the black communities of the American south. The demands for industrial labour also led to a rapid increase in female employment, rising from 14 million in 1940 to 19.4 million in 1944, a participation rate of 36 per cent of all women of working age. Almost all of this increase was voluntary. There was no compulsory civilian recruitment, though a nationwide propaganda campaign encouraged men and women to take up war work, including the famous campaign based on 'Rosie the Riveter' that appeared all over America on posters, in newspapers, even in the form of a popular song. The flood of new workers owed much to the long period of depression; new opportunities and high and regular wages were seen as a bonus to be collected as long as the war was

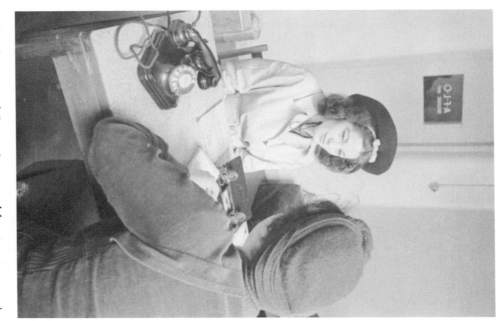

being fought. Civilian consumption in the United States increased by 13 per cent in real terms during the war, while it declined, often sharply, everywhere else. The inflationary pressures and rising prices generated by high state spending were eventually compensated for by rising earnings and extensive overtime and bonuses, since wage rates were pegged at the level of September 1942. One result of the wartime pressure to work harder and accept longer hours was regular work stoppages to protest pay or conditions. These were in defiance of an agreement made at the start of the war between the American unions and the government that there would be no official stoppages. There were instead 14,471 unauthorized wildcat strikes during the war, including a major strike of coal and anthracite workers in the American north-east which finally prompted Congress, ignoring Roosevelt's veto, to pass legislation in 1943 giving the government the right to take over production during a strike if it threatened national security.

The situation among the other major warring powers was dictated by the reality of severe labour shortages. In Britain, Germany, and the Soviet Union labour was compulsorily allocated to war work because without compulsion the balance between the needs of the military and the requirements of the home economy would not have been met. In Britain there were sufficient unemployed workers to cushion the immediate demand for labour in 1939–40, but arbitrary recruitment of skilled workers into the armed forces led to growing shortages. The military took 5.5 million men and almost half a million women during the war, but among those recruited in the first wave of conscription were skilled workers who had to be returned to the home economy because of labour shortages. By the end of 1941, Ernest Bevin had used the Essential Work Order to protect 6 million workers in 30,000 firms from military call-up, more than 40 per cent of the male workforce. He instituted a Register of Employment which made it possible for the first time in British history to track the movements of the entire workforce. As in the United States shortages of labour were met by recruiting additional women into the workforce, an increase from 5 million to 7 million over the war period. In the vehicle and aircraft industries female workers made up 36 per cent of the workforce by 1943. In the first year of war little effort went into curbing inflation and as a result wage rates lagged behind price rises. Rationing was not yet extensive and as a result there was regular labour protest; strikes cost 3.7 million working days in 1940. In July 1940 Bevin set up the National Arbitration Tribunal with trade union co-operation and the strike wave died down over the following years, due partly to the operation of arbitration, partly to the introduction of a broader rationing scheme, better amenities at work (including canteens and crèches), and rapid increase in earnings because of overtime, longer hours, and bonus schemes. Consumption per head fell by 13 per cent, but real weekly earnings increased by 80 per cent over the same period, with much of the addition siphoned off into war savings. This was a favourable level of sacrifice compared with the experience of continental Europe.

The situation in the Soviet Union was among all the Allies the most adverse. The loss of territory and of a population of around 60 million following the Axis invasion cut the potential Soviet workforce from 87 million in 1940 to 54.7 million in 1942, almost half of whom worked on the land. The level of industrial employment failed to reach the 1940 figure again throughout the war, partly because by the end of the conflict some 34.5 million men (and women) had been recruited into the armed forces. Of these almost 9 million were killed or died, and many of the rest were wounded, often many times (though some injured men could be brought back to work in industry). The crisis was coped with because the regime insisted that anyone who could work would work, including young teenagers and the old, while penalizing those who were too old or debilitated by giving them no ration cards. Work for the war effort meant survival and for many Soviet workers the factory became the source of warmth and one square meal a day. Since the level of male conscription was so high, the essential workforce was found among Soviet women and youths. By 1945 80 per cent of all rural workers were women, and 51 per cent of all industrial workers.

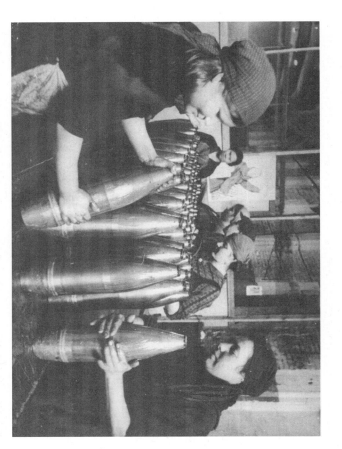

Russian women greasing artillery shells at a Soviet factory. Women by 1945 made up more than half of the Soviet workforce, in agriculture more than four-fifths.

The British minister for national service, Ernest Bevin, enjoys a canteen meal with workers in a war factory. Better conditions for workers were seen as a necessity to keep them productive.

Young people also formed an important part of the workforce, compelled to work long hours in arduous conditions. One 15-year-old girl in a factory in Cheliabinsk ('Tankograd' after the tanks it produced) was crippled by burns from drops of hot metal on her legs and feet, but when she tried to recover at home the foreman found her and dragged her back to her lathe. There was no prospect of labour protest, and living standards mattered only to the extent that labourers could still work in all weathers and with shrinking supplies of food without physically collapsing. By 1943 output for the civilian consumer had declined by more than half, while defence output increased an estimated fourfold. The Soviet war effort was made possible only by imposing severe sacrifices, and a high death rate, on the civilian population.

For Germany and Japan the war also imposed extreme demands on the workforce, though in both cases the war economy had access to foreign labour resources, which could be exploited more ruthlessly than the domestic population. Half of the Japanese workforce, like that of the Soviet Union, was engaged in agriculture, and provided a high proportion of the approximately 10 million men conscripted into the armed forces. From 1939 compulsory labour allocation was adopted and by 1945 over 6 million workers had been assigned to war-related industries, as well as 320,000 labourers from Korea and China. The female workforce increased by less than a million, from 12.7 million in 1940 to 13.2 million in 1944, but many women were directed into war industry from the consumer sector; from summer 1943 the government authorized the employment of schoolchildren and suspended all education from middle school upwards, bringing an additional 3.4 million into the workforce. For new sources of labour, conditions deteriorated over the course of the Pacific War as the American blockade cut off food supplies. Most workers subsisted on a shrinking ration of rice and only half the normal quantity of vegetables. Prices for non-rationed goods trebled over the war and real incomes fell to only 70 per cent of the pre-war level. Great efforts were made to sustain the output of armaments, which rose steadily over the war period at the expense, here too, of the civilian population.

The German war economy benefited from the territorial expansion of the Reich in the late 1930s and early 1940s because the overall population increased from 69 to 96 million in 'Greater Germany' and greatly expanded the potential workforce. Nevertheless mobilization into the military right from the start of the war reached exceptionally high levels and in the end some 17 million men (and some women) were drafted. The native industrial workforce declined from 10.8 million in 1939 to 7.6 million in 1944, most of it redistributed into war work. As in other countries the proportion of women working was high, partly as a result of the structure of German agriculture. Millions of small peasant holdings were left to be worked by women once the men had been conscripted; by 1944 two-thirds of native German workers on the land were women. In industry women moved out of consumer sectors to take up work in engineering and the basic materials sector. By 1944 one half of the native German workforce was female, much of it subject to compulsory registration and allocation. Married women were not directly conscripted, though many did work, but most women in Germany not in full-time employment were recruited into part-time work, or the large volunteer welfare organization, or into civil defence roles.

No doubt more women would have been compelled to take up full-time work or work for longer hours (though women could be required to work more than 50 hours a week), but the German war economy had direct access to a large pool of labour in the occupied territories as well as camp prisoners and millions of prisoners of war. The high levels of mobilization of the native German population led to severe shortages of labour as early as 1941. Some European labour was attracted by the prospect of higher wages or regular work, so not all the foreign labour in Germany was present at the point of a gun, but by 1942, when Gauleiter Fritz Sauckel was made Plenipotentiary for Labour Supply, there was a serious need to supplement the existing German workforce. By 1944 there were almost 9 million foreign workers, prisoners, and POWs working in Germany. In some of the major armaments sectors up to two-thirds of the workforce were foreign, many of the workers women conscripted in Ukraine, Poland, or Belorussia. Millions more were drafted into farm work. The high losses of German manpower inflicted at the front in 1944 and 1945 made it imperative for the regime to find ways to make the workforce more productive by rationalizing work practices, increasing the length of shifts, and (for German workers) providing social payments and generous bonuses.

The Japanese industrial city of Osaka burnt out by American incendiary bombing in the summer of 1945. Bombing was seen as a form of economic warfare designed to limit what Japan could produce.

Wage and price controls in Germany worked well over the war period, unlike the experience in the First World War, but this owed much to the capacity of the regime to extract food and consumer goods at the expense of the occupied populations, and the ruthless expropriation of Jewish assets, goods, and clothing from across the continent. For the native German population strict rationing was imposed from the very first day of the war and pressure to consume was suppressed by increased taxation and saving schemes that were voluntary in name only. Per capita consumption fell by 30 per cent between 1938 and 1944, though the poor quality of goods and the adulterated and limited diet meant in effect even lower standards. For camp prisoners and forced labour, food supplies were so poor that tens of thousands died of the effects of malnutrition and disease. With the onset of heavy bombing from 1943, living conditions deteriorated still further with long treks to evacuation destinations, local shortages of food, and the widespread destruction of housing. By early 1945 some 9 million had left the major cities and many of the smaller ones. In the last weeks of war, as the Allies closed in, most of the workforce found themselves either displaced or unemployed; in Japan the last months of the war saw the same chaos descending as Japan's industrial cities were systematically reduced to ashes, forcing millions to flee to the countryside.

The International Economy

The commitment to large-scale war production completely distorted the functioning of the world economy. The structure of international payments and trade broke down, to be replaced by regional trade in the areas under German and Japanese control, and by a residual trade between the Allied states that operated alongside the goods supplied under the Lend Lease agreements. Once it was evident that the Allies would eventually defeat the Axis, British and American economists and politicians began to explore the future prospects for reconstructing the world trade and payments system after the war and physically rebuilding and replacing what had been lost or damaged. The eventual losses from the effects of war were enormous in Europe and Asia. Capital markets were overburdened by the costs of the conflict, or in the case of Germany and Japan collapsed altogether with the coming of peace; trade was hampered by the crisis in transport and shipping brought about by wartime destruction; agricultural revival suffered from shortages of machinery, chemical fertilizers, and vehicles; the housing stock in Germany and the Soviet Union was completely inadequate for the surviving population. In anticipation of the likely post-war difficulties, delegates from the self-styled 'United Nations' assembled at Bretton Woods in New Hampshire in July 1944 to discuss a plan drawn up by the US Treasury Secretary, Henry Morgenthau, to establish new international institutions to govern world trade, currency transactions, and the worldwide demand for reconstruction credits.

The result was a series of agreements that shaped the development of the post-war world economy. In an effort to escape from the economic nationalism and beggar-my-neighbour policies of the 1930s, which American leaders blamed for creating the crisis

A post-war market in the Tiergarten in Berlin in 1945. Germans had to barter what they could to provide a minimum of food and provisions.

of war in the first place, the 'United Nations' signed a General Agreement on Trade and Tariffs (GATT) to govern trading practices, and agreed to establish an International Monetary Fund to help individual states cope with payments or financial difficulties, and to fund an International Bank for Reconstruction and Development, which was the forerunner of the World Bank. The United States was the driving force behind the new initiatives, and the revival of the world economy did depend critically on the willingness of the world's richest country (whose territory had remained physically untouched by the war) to accept the responsibility for ensuring that the rest of the world could overcome the worst effects of wartime dislocation. The exception here was the area occupied by the Red Army in Europe, where recovery was based instead on the institution of command economies based on Soviet experience in state planning. The slow pace of recovery in the rest of Europe led the American Secretary of State in 1947, General George Marshall, the former army chief-of-staff, to inaugurate a European Recovery Program (Marshall Aid) which stimulated the still limited revival of the economy in Italy, Germany, France, Britain, and the Low Countries, which between them took $9.9 billion out of the estimated $12.7 billion finally allocated by the ERP. By the early 1950s all those areas assisted by American aid had surpassed the economic performance levels of 1938.

The economic balance of the war was self-evidently negative with huge losses of manpower, widespread physical destruction, the loss of wealth, and persistent low living standards. The conviction in the 1930s that economic rearmament was essential to prepare for total war was a self-fulfilling prophecy, and one whose ultimate costs could not be foreseen. It was nevertheless the case that the war would not have been won by one side or the other without large-scale economic mobilization. Italy at the wartime peak only devoted 23 per cent of its GNP to the war effort and was unable to prosecute effective overseas campaigns or to defend the homeland against Allied attack. It was not inevitable that the balance of resources would always preclude an Axis victory, as the brief triumph over the French and British Empires in 1940–1 showed. In 1941, before American entry to the war, and with the Soviet loss of the whole of the productive western areas, the balance favoured the Axis. By 1943 the balance was clearly with the Allies, but victory depended on being able to use those resources effectively in terms of battlefield performance, maintaining domestic support for the war effort, and keeping the Grand Alliance of the British Commonwealth, the United States, and the Soviet Union together. One caveat in assuming that economic resources will always in the end determine the outcome remains the Eastern Front, where despite a vast inferiority in key industrial materials—but endowed with a regime able to extract the harsh maximum from its people—the Soviet Union out-produced Germany and its conquered areas by a wide margin.

9 Front Line I

Armed Forces at War

MICHAEL SNAPE

In the Second World War an unprecedented number of men and women were drawn into the armed forces of the belligerent states. The Soviet Union conscripted over 34 million, more than twice the number that had served in the Russian army in the First World War. A further 17 million served in the Wehrmacht and, given the numbers mobilized by China, the United States, the British Empire, Italy, France, and Japan, it is likely that the global figure was in the region of 100 million. In individual societies, the extent of this military mobilization could reach staggering proportions; the number of those who passed through the Wehrmacht amounted to well over one fifth of Germany's entire population on the eve of war. However, these armed forces varied enormously in terms of their capabilities, their composition, and their cultures. For example, by 1945 there was a vast gulf in all three respects between the USAAF (United States Army Air Forces) and the Chinese Nationalist army. The former represented a force of enormous technological and organizational complexity that was capable of delivering atomic destruction across vast oceanic distances; the latter, on the other hand, represented an ill-fed, ill-trained, and ill-equipped peasant host that had essentially been in retreat since 1937. Furthermore, differences of this kind could be marked between and within the individual armed forces of a single state. In contrast to the Italian army, on Italy's entry into the war in June 1940 the *Regia Marina* was a modern and well-balanced naval force that was manned by a comparative elite. Similarly, in the victorious Red Army of 1945 there was a huge disparity between the quality of its front-line troops (especially in its tank formations) and those in its support echelons. Nor did total war have the effect of creating armed forces that were a representative cross-section of the societies that produced them. The specific personnel requirements of individual armed forces and a raft of other factors—cultural, legal, political, and ideological—also influenced their composition. Nevertheless, all bore the heavy imprint of their own societies and were subject to varying degrees of change in response to the urgent demands of war. This chapter explores these themes with reference to their recruitment and composition, their capacity for waging modern war, their training and indoctrination, their connection with civilian society, their culture, religion, and criminality.

Recruitment

Given the perceived totality of the Second World War, it is easy to assume that the burden of military service was ubiquitous and that its weight was borne more or less evenly. This is very far from being the case, as the example of the British Empire and Commonwealth serves to illustrate. The Indian army, which after the British army was the largest of the Empire's armed forces, numbered 2.5 million men in August 1945 and was the largest all-volunteer army in the world. For their part, Australia and Canada were originally wary of sending their troops overseas to be slaughtered in a replay of the First World War. Hence there was a critical distinction between volunteers and conscripts in the Australian army, with only the former being eligible for service overseas with the Australian Imperial Force. Conversely, conscripts, who comprised the bulk of Australia's Citizen Military Forces, were eligible only for home defence. Unfortunately for these much-derided 'Chocos' ('Chocolate soldiers'), home defence included that of the Australian territory of Papua and the Australian mandate of New Guinea, which meant they played a major role in the gruelling New Guinea campaign that commenced in March 1942 and ended only with the surrender of Japan. In Canada, which had opted for a similar system of 'limited liability', attempts in 1944 to send home-service conscripts overseas to replace losses among the all-volunteer Canadian units in Europe unleashed a political storm and resulted in a large-scale mutiny in the 15th Infantry Brigade at Terrace in British Columbia.

Where more demanding systems of military conscription prevailed these were less than all-embracing under normal circumstances. The needs of individual societies and

A rifleman of the Indian army, Egypt, 1940. In the Second World War, the British Indian army eventually grew to be the largest volunteer army in history.

economies meant that there were many occupational exemptions, even for able-bodied adult males. In Fascist Italy, university students could defer military service until the age of 26, a privilege that led to a 100 per cent increase in student enrolments from 1940 to 1943. In the United States, where agricultural workers comprised almost a quarter of the male workforce, local draft boards granted such a lavish number of deferments to this favoured occupational group that its members comprised only 15 per cent of the draftees inducted in 1942. Even in Germany, as late as May 1944 more than 6 million men remained in reserved occupations. Besides the claims of essential workers, the Anglophone democracies (unlike France) also recognized the right to some kind of exemption from combatant service on conscientious grounds, scruples that risked the death penalty or a concentration camp in Germany. For political or ideological reasons, entire regions, nationalities, and racial groups could also be spared the full demands of conscription. In the United Kingdom, the six counties of Northern Ireland were spared conscription and the resistance of Francophone Canadians to an unlimited war effort did much to complicate and inflame the vexed issue of conscription in Canada. In Germany, Nazi anti-Semitism meant that full-blooded Jews had been excluded from the Wehrmacht since 1936. Despite its chronic shortage of manpower, incremental steps were taken to purge the ranks of the

Black American GIs at a Red Cross field unit in the Philippines, 1944. The endemic racism of society ensured that the US armed forces were essentially segregated throughout the war.

Wehrmacht of its German-Jewish 'crossbreeds' during the war years and as late as 1944 a decree was issued that ordered the discharge of its remaining 'Quarter-Jews'. For black Americans, however, racial discrimination was much more a question of partial exclusion. While the US army, navy, and Marine Corps remained segregated, the navy refused to accept any black conscripts, or even wartime volunteers, until December 1942. Furthermore, all three services largely restricted their black personnel to labouring and support duties throughout the war.

It is also important to emphasize that no belligerent state—not even China or the Soviet Union—had an endless supply of manpower and that the dividing line between civilian and soldier was often blurred as a result. Communist field armies in China had a symbiotic relationship with a militia system created in areas controlled by the Chinese Communist Party (CCP). This provided them not only with trained reinforcements but with supplies and medical care. When the need arose, militia units also served alongside Communist regulars in conventional operations against the Japanese. In the Soviet–German war, the rapid German advances of 1941–2 ensured that fugitive bands of Red Army soldiers formed the trained nuclei of numerous partisan groups, while the mass deployment of ad hoc divisions of workers' militia, especially in the defence of Moscow and Leningrad in 1941, also served to confound any neat distinctions between soldiers and civilians on the Eastern Front. The growing Allied threat to Germany's eastern and western borders in the autumn of 1944 likewise prompted Hitler to create the *Deutsche Volkssturm*, a national militia organized by the National Socialist Party in which all males between the ages of 16 and 60 were liable to serve. Despite their limited training and equipment, *Volkssturm* units played a critical role in the last-ditch defence of Breslau, Berlin, and other towns and cities in eastern Germany, and suffered tens of thousands of casualties in the process.

In considering the different demands made on armed forces personnel in the Second World War it should be emphasized that a vast number of military personnel had a comparatively quiet and risk-free war. At the end of the war in Europe, more than one third of the US army was still in the States and, in the highly mechanized armies of the western democracies, vast numbers were routinely employed in maintenance and support duties even in active theatres of war. Only a small minority of soldiers in a US, British, or Canadian infantry division even belonged to its infantry units. Under these circumstances, the precise definition of a combat soldier proved surprisingly elusive and it is clear that merchant seamen, to say nothing of many civilians in the towns and cities of Great Britain, were exposed to far greater danger from enemy action than were a great many British and American service men and women, who could find themselves in the position of cheering civilians from the sidelines. The occupational distinctions and glaring numerical disparity between support and front-line personnel were even more apparent in the air forces of the belligerent states, often equating to the basic dichotomy between ground crew and air crew. After years of expansion under Göring, by 1942 the Luftwaffe numbered nearly 2 million men and yet was chronically under-strength in terms of front-line aircraft. With the deterioration of Germany's position on the Eastern Front later that year, the army's manpower needs meant that 200,000 extraneous Luftwaffe ground crew had to be combed out and, at Göring's insistence, formed into separate Luftwaffe Field Divisions. Lacking the necessary training, leadership, and equipment, these hapless formations put in a predictably poor performance against the resurgent Red Army.

The fate of the Luftwaffe Field Divisions underlines the fact that the armed forces of the Second World War had very specific technical requirements and that the skills of their personnel were not easily transferable. During the Second World War, the naval and air forces of the major belligerents deployed the most complex weapons systems yet produced by industrial societies. In comparison with battleships, submarines, fighters, and strategic bombers, even modern tanks and artillery were distinctly 'low tech'. In itself, this fundamental fact had major implications for the composition of contemporary armed forces. For example, the U-boat arm of the *Kriegsmarine* contained a high proportion of sailors from the landlocked, industrial, and metalworking regions of the Ruhr and central Germany. Besides their technical requirements, matters of prestige also helped to generate a better class of recruit for the Royal Navy and the RAF. While the Royal Navy had always stood higher in national esteem than the British army, the creation of an independent air force in April 1918 produced still more competition for the latter in the Second World War, especially given the mournful legacy of the trenches, the sheer excitement of aviation, and the comparatively progressive ethos of the RAF. Under the British system, those who volunteered before being called up could join the service of their choice and even conscripts were allowed to express a preference. Significantly, the army suffered from an embarrassing scarcity of volunteers while the Royal Navy and the RAF had a telling surplus of conscripts hoping to join them. In common with the Royal Navy, the US navy and the *Regia Marina* also attracted a high proportion of volunteers and could take their pick of the conscripts required to make up any shortfalls. In the pre-war years, such was the standing of the Imperial Japanese Navy (IJN) that it accepted conscripts only to ensure that its influence and interests were maximized in Japanese society, an important consideration given its bitter rivalry with the Imperial Japanese Army (IJA). Despite its subsequent and increasingly one-sided battle with the US navy in the Pacific, the popularity of the IJN proved enduring and two-thirds of its inductees were volunteers even in 1945.

While navies and air forces proved more attractive to volunteers and could cream off more skilled and educated conscripts, the impact of mechanization triggered a proliferation of specialities in many armies during the inter-war years. In the Second World War, and in order to meet their increasing technical needs, the highly mechanized British and US armies developed a raft of personnel policies and aptitude tests that served to ensure that their infantry units had the lowest priority in the allocation of desirable recruits. In total, the British army came to recognize over 500 individual trades and specialities, and the number and quality of its ordinary riflemen suffered accordingly. When, because of a serious manpower shortage, men from the RAF and Royal Navy were transferred to the army in 1945, their instructors were impressed by their comparative quality. The same situation also came to prevail in the US army.

Sailors man an anti-aircraft gun on a Free French destroyer, an illustration of the sheer variety of the war's many forces-in-exile.

Here, racial segregation, a policy of placing soldiers in roles that most closely corresponded to their civilian jobs, and the results of the Army General Classification Test meant that infantry squads were disproportionately composed of unskilled, disadvantaged, and patently disposable whites. While it has been said that 'hicks, micks, and spics' made up the bulk of American infantry squads, the Nazi ideal of *Volksgemeinschaft* ('community of blood and destiny') and the priorities of the German army's personnel policies meant that there was a more even representation of German society in its front-line units. Unlike the British and American armies, the needs of the racial community demanded equality of sacrifice from all social classes and a ruthless determination to maximize its 'teeth to tail ratio' served as an effective brake on the expansion of its support units.

German infantrymen shelter behind a wall at Stalingrad, 1942. Nazi ideology—and sheer necessity—served to minimize the proportion of support troops in the German army.

Social Structures

Whether they relied on volunteers, conscripts, or a mixture of the two to feed their lower ranks, the armed forces of all the belligerent states were ultimately led by a relatively small cadre of long-service professionals. However, their social background varied considerably from nation to nation, and even from service to service. In terms of the social profile of the German army, one of the most radical effects of the war was the transformation of its officer corps. Long the preserve of the nobility and of the wealthier middle classes, the socially levelling implications of *Volksgemeinschaft* and the practical demands of a war for national existence saw the wholesale promotion of battle-hardened veterans from the ranks, with eight former NCOs even reaching the rank of general. Unencumbered by social conventions inherited from the Prussian and imperial armies, the smaller Waffen SS proved to be an even better vehicle for promotion and three of its former rankers, including Hitler's one-time chauffeur, Sepp Dietrich, also became general officers. In this respect, the relative meritocracy of Germany's ground forces came to resemble that of their ultimate nemesis, the Red Army. Created as a new type of armed force that was controlled by the Communist Party and dedicated to the service of workers and peasants, by 1939 the combined effects of the Russian civil war and of Stalin's purges had produced a generation of Red Army generals who were more distinguished for their political reliability than for their command of the finer points of strategy, operations, and military administration. Nevertheless, the better generals of the Red Army survived the further winnowing of the war years, their success underlining the limited opportunities available to their social peers in other armies. Whereas aristocrats continued to dominate the very highest reaches of the German army throughout the war, the two Marshals of the Soviet Union responsible for the capture of Berlin in April 1945, namely Georgy Zhukov and Ivan Konev, were both the sons of peasant families and had served in the ranks of the Russian army in the First World War.

There was no prospect for such promotion and distinction in other, peasant-based European armies such as those of Italy and Romania. Like the Red Army, both were heavily reliant on their predominantly rural populations for their manpower, but the effects of two decades of Soviet education policy meant that illiteracy remained a much greater problem among Italian and Romanian conscripts than among Russian. While this factor limited promotion from the ranks and hindered the efficiency of their NCOs, both armies were also dominated by a corps of professional officers whose innate social and political conservatism was not tempered by a sense of paternalism or *noblesse oblige*. Quite apart from the social and cultural gulf that lay between officers and other ranks in the Italian and Romanian armies, the privileges that attended rank in both armies were obvious and excessive. If Rommel was critical of the poor example set by Italian officers in this respect, Kesselring wryly noted that he could enjoy better meals at an Italian officers' mess than he could at his own headquarters. While Romanian officers also lived in considerably more comfort than their men, Romania's archaic military code also entitled them to flog unruly subordinates. All this contrasted not only with the example of soldierly egalitarianism set by the German army but also with the ethos of the MVSN, Italy's Fascist militia, which sent many blackshirt legions and divisions to fight alongside the *Regio Escercito* (Royal Army).

If these disparities took their toll on morale in the Romanian and Italian armies, they also stood in striking contrast to the situation that prevailed in the IJA, another army that was heavily dependent on peasant soldiers. In Japan, a very different view of the nation's peasantry was taken by its right-wing military establishment. Given the cultural and political dangers posed by industrial and urban growth, the IJA's increasing number of urban recruits was viewed with mounting suspicion in the inter-war years. Instead, it was Japan's peasantry, indoctrinated by a highly militarized and nationalistic state education system that had all but eradicated illiteracy, which was thought to provide the best soldier material. Despite the fact that the authority of an officer was regarded as a direct extension of the divine authority of the Emperor, and notwithstanding the severe physical violence that characterized training and discipline in the IJA, there was remarkably little social distance between officers and other ranks. By the 1920s, only one-fifth of the IJA's officers were drawn from the former samurai class, and the sons of small landowners, and even shopkeepers, were well represented among them. Furthermore, and in marked divergence from normal European practice, officers were not forbidden from socializing with their men. Indeed, a strong mutual attachment between junior officers and other ranks seems to have been a key component in the formidable cohesion and combat performance of the wartime IJA.

Social tensions also affected the armed forces of the United Kingdom and the United States. Standing in the long shadow of the Somme and Passchendaele, embracing a less deferential type of soldier, and reflecting the class tensions that were rife in British society, the British army was especially troubled by this problem. Indeed, its litany of defeats from 1940 to 1942 led to unprecedented criticism of its traditional officer class, then personified in the absurd cartoon figure of Colonel Blimp. In order to allay rampant suspicion of endemic, class-based discrimination in the selection of prospective army officers, a system of War Office Selection Boards was introduced in April 1942 for the purpose of selecting officer cadets from the other ranks. While these boards promoted transparency, objectivity, and a greater sense of fairness, they signally failed to achieve anything like a social revolution. Former public schoolboys continued to be greatly over-represented among British army officers and they comprised more than a third of their number over the course of the war. The Royal Navy was no less conservative in social terms, despite its technical needs. Deeply reluctant to commission experienced, pre-war sailors from the lower decks, the senior service showed the same preference for comparative novices from the middle and upper classes. Consequently, there were the same bitter complaints of institutionalized class prejudice in the selection of the Royal Navy's temporary officers, who comprised nearly 90 per cent of its officer corps by 1945. Even in the new and comparatively progressive RAF, whose losses demanded a greater pragmatism in the selection of its pilots, class distinctions were still widely felt, being reflected, for example, in the invidious dichotomy between its pilot officers and sergeant pilots.

Despite the egalitarian and meritocratic image of the United States, the situation seems to have been little better in the US army and navy. Here the graduates of the two great service academies of West Point and Annapolis very much set the tone and dominated the senior ranks. While they may not have come from America's wealthiest families, they were at least sufficiently well connected to have secured congressional and senatorial nominations to their academies, and were sufficiently educated to have passed the competitive entrance exams. Despite the exponential wartime growth of the officer corps of the US army and the US navy, this was not accompanied by a major shift in their social composition. In the US army, whose officers were already thirty times more numerous in 1943 than in 1941, nearly 90 per cent were high school graduates and more than half had spent some time at college. If such backgrounds were fair indicators of comparative privilege, the US navy proved to be even more socially exclusive. During the war, fewer than one in five of its new officers were commissioned from the lower decks, while the vast majority passed muster on the basis of a college education or a respectable background in business.

Foreign Legions

Although a system of conscription held sway in the major belligerent states, the opportunities offered by the crisis of a world at war could create armed forces that were surprisingly heterogeneous. In the case of the RAF, nearly 40 per cent of its airmen were volunteers from across the wider British Empire. In Bomber Command, which also had Polish, French, and Commonwealth squadrons in its order of battle, a policy of mixing aircrews was the norm throughout the war and its implications were far reaching. For example, far more Canadians were killed while serving in the other squadrons of Bomber Command than with its all-Canadian No. 6 Bomber Group. Furthermore, no fewer than 800 West Indians, in addition to several West Africans, flew in the RAF from 1943, thereby demolishing a pre-war colour bar to enlistment. A chronic shortage of trained manpower also served to overcome racist inhibitions in the Wehrmacht, its immense accumulation of starving and often disaffected Red Army POWs ensuring that it eventually made use of millions of Soviet citizens as *Hilfswillige* ('voluntary helpers'), and as *Osttruppen* ('eastern troops') in a plethora of discrete *Ostlegionen*. Theoretically, the German army's 'type 44' infantry division was composed of no fewer than 1,400 *Hilfswillige* out of a total strength of 12,770. However, the German army was outdone in this regard by the Waffen SS. Far from remaining an Aryan racial preserve, from 1943 it opened its ranks to an array of distinctly 'non-Germanic' groups, including Russians, Albanians, and Ukrainians, who formed their own SS divisions. If these developments underlined tensions that were inherent in Nazi ideology, and in Nazi policy towards the occupied peoples of Eastern Europe, a similar inconsistency was evinced by the Japanese, who subjected their despised Korean subjects to conscription from 1942, though these largely served in labour and rear area units.

For a mixture of ideological and opportunistic reasons, neutrals could also be well represented in the armed forces of belligerent states. Despite the implicitly anti-British neutrality of Eire, nearly 40,000 Irish men and women volunteered to serve in the British armed forces, even helping to form an all-Irish infantry brigade that served with distinction in Italy. Likewise, in an echo of the celebrated *Escadrille Lafayette* of the First World War, before Pearl Harbor scores of American aviators volunteered to serve as fighter pilots in the three Eagle Squadrons of the RAF, and for the American Volunteer Group (or 'Flying Tigers') of the (Nationalist) Chinese air force. While these proved a valuable asset in terms of their technical expertise and propaganda value, in the 'Winter War' of 1939–40 the Finnish army was substantially reinforced by thousands of anti-Soviet volunteers from Sweden, Norway, Denmark, and Hungary. Finally, and although Franco's Spain remained ostensibly neutral, the ideological alignments of the Spanish Civil War were reflected in the Second World War. These

included the presence of the 'Blue Division' (the German army's 250th Infantry Division) on the Eastern Front from 1941 to 1943 and the large number of Spanish Republican refugees who served in France's metropolitan army of 1940, and in the legendary Foreign Legion and Zouave regiments of its *Armée d'Afrique*.

Women in the Military

A further factor that points to the divergence between the composition of civilian societies and that of their armed forces lies in the presence (or otherwise) of women. In general terms, the armed forces of the Second World War remained overwhelmingly male in composition and the role of women within them has been seen as emblematic of the dominant cultural and ideological values of their respective societies. Viewed from this perspective, the unusual figure of the female combatant has been largely identified with the experience of the Red Army and with the relative equality enjoyed by women in the Soviet Union. Prior to the outbreak of war, women already comprised 40 per cent of the Soviet Union's industrial work force and received the same pay as their male equivalents. Women also comprised more than 40 per cent of students in higher education and more than half of the students in the Soviet Union's technical and professional schools. Although exempt from conscription until 1939, young Soviet women were also very active in *Osoaviakhim*, the state-sponsored Society for the Promotion of Defence, Aviation, and Chemical Development, acquiring

A female radio operator of the Red Army. No nation matched the Soviet use of female soldiers as both combatants and non-combatants.

flying and shooting skills as well as medical training. As a result of their involvement, by 1941 the Soviet Union had already accumulated a substantial reserve of women trained in various military skills that could be utilized to repel the German invasion. Comprising around 8 per cent of the Red Army by the end of 1943, hundreds of thousands of women served as anti-aircraft gunners and signallers, while also performing a variety of front-line roles. By the end of the war, Soviet women had served as combat aviators, tank crew, machine-gunners, and, most famously of all, as snipers. In fact, given the innate savagery of the war on the Eastern Front, non-combatant status was fundamentally illusory and even female medics and drivers were trained in the use of firearms.

However, while much has been made of the uniqueness of the Soviet situation, and of German and Allied reactions to the Red Army's front-line women soldiers, this level of female integration was as much a function of sheer necessity as it was of Communist ideology. Significantly, such was the sense of national vulnerability in conservative and Catholic Poland that the compulsory military training of young Polish women, which included the use of firearms, had commenced in 1937. While National Socialist ideology was fundamentally resistant to the same degree of female mobilization, exalting motherhood and placing a prime emphasis on '*Kinder, Küche, Kirche*' ('Children, Kitchen, and Church'), shortage of manpower and military necessity once again served as the catalyst for dramatic practical change. German women were initially recruited into the Wehrmacht only as nurses and auxiliaries (nicknamed '*Blitzmädchen*') in order to release men from clerical and similar duties. However, with the increasing weight of the Combined Bomber Offensive, from 1943 up to 100,000 women were recruited into the Luftwaffe as *Flakwaffenhelferinnen* (Anti-Aircraft Auxiliaries) whose task was to crew searchlight and anti-aircraft positions. Although ideological concerns still dictated that women should be prevented from actually firing anti-aircraft guns, a taboo that had been reinforced by contact with the Red Army's detested 'gun women', in November 1944 an allowance was made that women in regions under threat from the Soviets should be trained in the use of arms. As the situation deteriorated, in February 1945 Hitler even sanctioned the creation of an all-female infantry battalion for the defence of the Reich is only now becoming clear. By the end of the war, female anti-aircraft auxiliaries were not only allowed to fire their own guns but had been sent into action to stop Soviet tanks. Similarly, from the summer of 1944 numerous female army auxiliaries and civilians appear to have taken up arms on both the Western and Eastern Fronts.

For the Western Allies, their disconcerting encounters with female German snipers in Normandy seemed to suggest an utter perversion of roles—namely that their troops were being fired upon by the *French* girlfriends of German soldiers. In the case of the Anglophone democracies, which were more conservative than the Soviet Union in terms of gender roles and never had to suffer the wholesale invasion of their home soil, the role of women in their armed forces was correspondingly more restricted. Although significant numbers of women were recruited into the British armed forces (nearly 450,000 nurses and female auxiliaries were serving by June 1945) their primary role was to release much-needed manpower for other duties by undertaking a wide variety of non-combatant roles. Ultimately, around eighty different trades were recognized in the British army's Auxiliary Territorial Service and, from 1941, its members were increasingly drawn into an anti-aircraft role in 'mixed' anti-aircraft batteries. However, even in this capacity they were forbidden by the terms of the Royal Warrant that had created the ATS in 1938 from actually firing an anti-aircraft gun. Routinely exposed to enemy action, and even deployed to Europe in 1944, ATS gunners formed part of a highly complex system of fire control in which the question of who pulled the lanyard was of much more symbolic

Flotsam of defeat. German female prisoners with a British lance corporal of the Auxiliary Territorial Service. Although they did not usually serve in a combatant role, women played an invaluable part in the armed forces of both belligerents.

importance than practical significance. Nevertheless, the British army was never hard pressed enough to diverge from the terms under which the ATS was founded by conceding an official and unambiguous combatant role to women. If this was true of fortress Britain, the US army had even less reason to accord women a front-line role. Following the ATS precedent, in 1942–3 nearly 400 women of its Women's Army Auxiliary Corps (or Women's Army Corps from 1943) were trained in the United States for anti-aircraft duties. Despite the evident success of their training in a mixed environment, the US army's chief-of-staff, George C. Marshall, decided to abandon the experiment. Besides the considerable weight of conservative civilian opinion and the legislative changes that would be required to allow women to undertake a combatant role, the key issue was once again that of military necessity—or lack of it. The fact was that the United States was under no significant aerial threat, that it had enough men to serve its stateside anti-aircraft batteries, and that a much greater priority was to release potential combat soldiers from administrative duties.

Preparedness and Training

The formative relationship between armed forces and their parent societies was also reflected in their preparedness and training for the ordeal of the war. In this respect it has already been noted how the relative economic and cultural backwardness of Italy and Romania had a major and limiting impact on the effectiveness of their armies in particular. Nevertheless, in global terms Nationalist China provides the most extreme example of how a society's inherent economic, cultural, and political problems undermined the performance of its armed forces. The generally parlous condition of Nationalist armies during the Sino-Japanese war should not obscure the fact that the Nationalist government had been laying the foundations for a protracted conflict with Japan for several years before the Marco Polo Bridge incident of July 1937. In addition to the drafting of successive defence plans, its measures had included a new

Nationalist troops at a Chinese military academy, 1944. Their smart appearance belies the generally wretched condition of the Nationalist armies.

system of conscription and the political and military training of China's small number of high school students. However, given the weakness of China's industrial base, especially in its interior, it proved impossible to properly feed, train, and equip a Nationalist army that mustered 5.7 million men by 1941. Even in the initial campaigns of the Sino-Japanese war, the crack units of the Nationalist army had lacked radios, artillery, and motor vehicles, and throughout the conflict it remained heavily reliant on foreign aviators for air support. While the Japanese largely succeeded in cutting China's supply routes through the capture of its coastal cities, the overall value of the American Lend Lease aid that began to arrive from 1941 was sorely diminished by rampant corruption, factional infighting, and by the infrastructural problems that plagued its onward distribution. Starved of supplies, and increasingly drawn into a renewed if undeclared civil war with their Communist rivals, Nationalist forces proved adept at alienating China's peasantry in order to survive, a problem that played a large part in unravelling Chiang Kai-shek's guerrilla strategy against the Japanese. Given the enormous human, material, and territorial losses sustained in the opening stages of the conflict, and their inexorable retreat from China's relatively developed littoral into its vast and backward hinterland, the quality of Nationalist forces inevitably declined. Whereas the national literacy rate stood at around 20 per cent on the eve of war, illiteracy rates grew to 90 per cent among Nationalist conscripts, a factor that depressed the educational levels of their junior leaders and general standards of technical proficiency.

Nevertheless, pre-war military experience and education tended to produce greater dividends for more developed societies. Separated by only a generation, the lessons of the First World War and, for the Soviet Union, of the Russian civil war, exerted a major influence on the conduct of the Second World War. A great many generals had seen front-line service as junior officers and even NCOs in the First World War and their experience often had a formative influence on their reputations and styles of command. Lieutenant General Sir Bernard Freyberg, who commanded the 2nd New Zealand Division in North Africa and Italy and who led the defence of Crete in 1941, was a much-wounded national war hero who had won the Victoria Cross on the Somme in 1916. Field Marshal Bernard Law Montgomery, Freyberg's superior for part of the war, had likewise been wounded as an infantry officer on the Western Front and, like Freyberg, was determined to minimize casualties and to sport an informal style of command for the benefit of his citizen soldiers. In tactical terms, Montgomery's characteristic caution and his preference for the carefully planned set-piece battle clearly betrayed the legacy of 1914–18. Although this contrasted with the trademark opportunism and élan of Montgomery's arch-rival, Erwin Rommel, in his solicitude for the lives of his soldiers he was in fact no different from many other German generals (such as von Leeb and von Kleist) with comparable experience of the First World War. The personal and professional legacy of the First World War was, of course, very widely felt among men of their generation and this no doubt added to the military potential of the British Home Guard and the German *Volkssturm*, whose ranks were leavened by large numbers of veterans of the previous war.

In terms of the routine military training of civilians, an important distinction should be made between what have been termed 'volunteering' and 'mobilizing' societies. The former, which included the Anglophone democracies, eschewed conscription and in peacetime maintained professional, all-volunteer armed forces. At times of crisis, these could be supplemented by various categories of reservists and by public-spirited, defence-minded citizens embodied in part-time organizations such as the United Kingdom's Territorial Army and the United States' National Guard. In addition to this, elements of military training were unevenly diffused via uniformed youth organizations and through attendance at a relatively small number of elite schools. In contrast, mobilizing societies practised general or universal conscription and could promote the military training of their youth through state schools and state-sponsored schemes and organizations. The latter system was characteristic of such totalitarian or autocratic states as Nazi Germany, Fascist Italy, Japan, and the Soviet Union, but was also shared to some extent by authoritarian states such as Poland, Romania, and Yugoslavia and by democracies such as France, Finland, and Belgium.

The merits of these systems, as revealed in the cauldron of the Second World War, have been the subject of some debate. With the Wehrmacht often billed as the *ne plus ultra* of fighting power (wrongly, in this author's opinion), much has been made of the military and ideological training acquired through membership of the Hitler Youth (compulsory from 1940), of the Reich Labour Service, and, ultimately, of the

A Finnish ski patrol, January 1940. The military preparedness of Finland helped to demonstrate the inadequacies of the vast but lumbering Red Army during the so-called 'Winter War', November 1939–March 1940.

Wehrmacht itself. Similarly, the remarkable resilience and adaptability of the Soviet war effort can at least in part be attributed to the fact that, on the eve of war, more than 70 per cent of men aged between 23 and 35 had already passed through the Red Army. Furthermore, military training in skills ranging from first aid to parachuting had been widely available for more than a decade through the activities of *Osoaviakhim*, whose pre-war membership ran into millions. Nevertheless, it is easy to exaggerate the benefits of such pre-war training as the requirement to undertake it often exceeded the means to provide it. In the Soviet Union, limited resources had placed a ceiling on the numbers of men who could be drafted each year. Elsewhere in pre-war Europe, conscription meant that mobilizing societies often accumulated large reserves of manpower that were poorly trained and motivated and which strained the state's ability to equip them. Furthermore, their existence could hinder technical and tactical innovation. On mobilization in September 1939, France possessed an army that numbered just under 5 million and which was widely regarded as the best in the world. However, in reality, and as the catastrophic campaign of May–June 1940 went on to demonstrate, the French army was overly reliant on its infantry and on its doctrine of the *bataille conduite* ('methodical battle'). Furthermore, it lacked flexible communications for a mobile war, an effective tactical doctrine for mechanized warfare, and the numerous *poilus* of its reserve divisions often proved to be woefully unprepared for the demands of the modern battlefield. Nor were these problems confined to the French army. Despite the lustrous fighting reputation of the IJA, and a system of conscription that dated back to 1873, the large numbers of reservists it committed to the war in China were notorious for their low morale, poor discipline, and criminal propensities. In the course of its six-year sojourn in northern China, the 37th Division lost hundreds of its soldiers to psychological breakdown, 7,000 were taken prisoner, and as many as a hundred appear to have deserted to the CCP's 8th Route Army (it may be significant that there were many recruits from Okinawa and the coal-mining and industrial areas of northern Kyushu in its ranks). Even at the height of its success, training as well as equipment in the much-vaunted German army often proved deficient. Prior to the invasion of Poland, it lacked training in fighting in wooded or urban terrain and the months of the Phoney War were dominated by remedial instruction. Still, in the ensuing campaign in the west, German infantry tactics were often judged to be clumsy and wasteful even by their French adversaries. In the hard fighting on the River Somme and River Aisne in June 1940, German infantrymen seemed content to simply fling themselves at enemy strongpoints, with predictable consequences.

A tendency to overstate the military capabilities of mobilizing societies was already evident during the war. This can be illustrated by the reputation for jungle-fighting prowess which the Japanese acquired from their avalanche of conquests in South-East Asia and the Pacific in the months after Pearl Harbor. In fact, the IJA had next to no prior experience of jungle fighting and its early successes largely arose from its heavy tactical emphasis on bold offensive action and rapid manoeuvre, a formidable doctrine when employed against ill-trained and unsteady opponents. As events were to show, the IJA's capacity to wage war effectively in jungle areas was fatally under-mined by supply problems and by Japan's high-handed neglect of logistics per se. In its Asia–Pacific war, it seems quite possible that more Japanese soldiers starved to death than were killed by enemy action. Still, improvements in Allied training also played their part in overturning the myth of Japanese invincibility in the jungle. After the British retreat from Burma, one of the key achievements of General Sir William Slim in restoring the battered confidence of his polyglot 14th Army lay in a new emphasis on intensive training in jungle warfare, training that was undertaken in India and which did much to raise morale in its own right. While Montgomery also famously demon-strated the morale-boosting effects of ongoing, in-theatre training in his preparations for the second battle of El Alamein in 1942, both examples serve to underline the critical importance of adequate time, resources, and training cadres in providing effective training. This lesson was also learned the hard way by the German army and, as late as 1944, it aimed to provide even its humble infantrymen with between twelve and fourteen weeks of basic training. However, sufficient time and resources were not always available, even to the Anglo-Americans. Although training in the US army steadily improved with the passage of time, benefiting from lessons learned in North Africa, Europe, and the Pacific and from greater resources that eventually included hundreds of different training films, it was inevitably subject to the irresist-ible demands of the wider war. In January 1945, for example, the period of training for armoured personnel in the United States was cut to only fifteen weeks, whereas their German counterparts could still expect a period of twenty-one. Furthermore, and for American replacements in the later war period, months spent in transit to their assigned units served to blunt the edge of their stateside training. As they were likewise ultimately dictated by the vagaries of war, training programmes proved extremely variable in the Red Army. With the revival of the Red Army's fortunes in 1943, a Soviet tank officer could expect his (or her) training to last for a year. In contrast, and as it pushed westwards in 1943 and 1944, the Red Army not only incorporated former partisans but also large numbers of conscripts from the Ukraine and Belorus-sia. In the case of these so-called 'booty troops', training could last for as little as ten days before they were pitched into action.

If Hew Strachan has argued that soldier training was as much about raising morale as about imparting specific military skills, this argument bears much less weight in the more technical realms of naval and aerial warfare. As in the German navy of the First World War, the U-boat arm proved by far the most potent asset of the *Kriegsmarine* and, despite extremely heavy losses, the emphasis on the intense training of its U-boat crews never diminished. In keeping with established practice, prospective crews were trained on their boats while they were still under construction, and as late as 1944 it was common for U-boats to spend nine months in trials and training before their first operational cruises. Nevertheless, and as the outcome of the Battle of the Atlantic revealed, by the summer of 1943 such methodical practice could neither overcome nor even emulate the greatly increased human, technological, and material resources that the British, Canadians, and Americans were now able to commit to anti-submarine

Soviet troops in a celebratory mood—a picture that aptly captures the ethnic diversity of the Red Army.

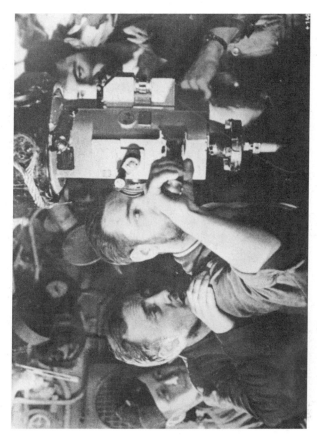

A U-boat operation in progress. An enduring system of intensive training helped to account for the formidable proficiency of Germany's submarine arm.

warfare. By the end of the war, 80 per cent of all operational U-boats had been lost and U-boat crews had suffered a higher proportion of fatal casualties than any other branch of the Wehrmacht.

As in the struggle against the U-boats, and in combination with improved technology and superior production levels, effective if heavily improvised training also accounts for the establishment of Anglo-American aerial dominance over the Axis powers. In this respect, both the British and the Americans were able to expand their air training capacities through remarkably effective wartime expedients. Overcoming the practical problems of flight training in the dangerous skies and changeable climate of the United Kingdom, the RAF secured the aircrew it needed for a vastly expanded force through the Empire Air Training Scheme (later the Commonwealth Air Training Plan). Under this programme, most of its aircrew were trained in the clearer and safer skies of Canada, Australia, India, South Africa, and Rhodesia. In development from the outbreak of war, by 1943 the RAF had access to 333 flight training schools, more than half of them overseas. In total, more than 300,000 of its aircrew passed through them during the war years, with less than a third being trained in the United Kingdom. The scale of the scheme and the number of trained volunteers it was able to feed into operational training units, another useful wartime innovation, helped to keep standards of training relatively high, and it was not unusual for an RAF pilot to be in training for as long as eighteen months. The aviators of the United States army and United States navy enjoyed similar advantages of clear air space and plentiful training resources. The USAAF, which by 1941 aimed to train 30,000 pilots a year in addition to other aircrew, contracted dozens of civilian flying schools to instruct its trainee pilots in the rudiments of flying and, after this primary training instruction, passed them through basic, advanced, and transitional courses. In aggregate, the various stages of essential flight training usually took the best part of a year. Nevertheless, between July 1939 and August 1945 nearly 200,000 pilots graduated from the USAAF's advanced flying training schools in addition to the tens of thousands of graduates produced by its navigator, bombardier, and gunnery schools.

In comparison with such massive and successful improvisation, aircrew training in the Luftwaffe and in the separate naval and army air forces of Imperial Japan was an increasingly threadbare affair, a problem that proved to be both a cause and symptom of their decline. As early as 1940, the Battle of Britain revealed the inability of the Luftwaffe to generate an adequate flow of trained aircrew for sustained operations, if only to replace its own casualties. Indeed, until 1942 its pilot training programme had scarcely diverged from its peacetime curriculum, including such key essentials for aerial combat as skiing and dancing. By 1943, however, a serious shortage of fuel and high attrition rates in the skies over Germany, Russia, and the Mediterranean led to a significant reduction in training hours. Still, if the number of Luftwaffe fighter pilots trained in 1943 was double that of 1942, even this advance was scarcely sufficient to cover that year's losses. By 1944, Luftwaffe pilots in training were completing only half the flying hours of their British and American

A Japanese pilot prepares for a sortie. Due to heavy losses and inadequate training, the competence of Japanese fliers declined sharply over the course of the war.

equivalents, often in obsolescent machines, and the Luftwaffe was losing almost as many aircraft to accidents as it was to enemy action. In air-to-air combat over Europe American fighter pilots were shooting down their German opponents in the ratio of 3:1. In October 1944 the American fighter ace Chuck Yeager destroyed five German fighters in a single aerial action: two he shot down, two crashed into each other, while the fifth flew into the ground. In the Pacific, US navy pilots, the beneficiaries of a training programme every bit as thorough as their army equivalents, eventually established the same ascendancy over the Japanese. Though aviation training in the IJN was more demanding than that in the IJA, during the 1930s both placed a supreme emphasis on the quality rather than the quantity of their aircrew. Already battle-hardened in China by the time of Pearl Harbor, growing fuel shortages and very heavy losses among experienced Japanese aviators in 1942–3 took their inevitable toll in the longer term. By 1944, it was even apparent that the IJA and IJN had been wrong-footed by their own elitism, and that their hurriedly expanded and abbreviated training programmes were incapable of training aircrew in sufficient numbers and to the standard required to stem the American onslaught. Instead, the deterioration of aviation training was repeatedly exposed in desperately one-sided engagements with US navy and Marine Corps fliers. Most notorious of these was the so-called 'Great Marianas Turkey Shoot' of June 1944, an episode in which almost 300 Japanese planes were shot down at the cost of only twenty American planes lost in action.

Culture

As the nationwide controversy over the commissioning of officers in the British armed forces serves to illustrate, service men and women were liable to reflect the tensions, needs, and concerns of wider civilian society. In relative terms, very few of them were career soldiers, sailors, or airmen and the war years were for the most part experienced as an unwelcome aberration. As civilians in uniform, home links were usually cherished and nurtured, typically through mechanisms of home leave and through a flow of correspondence maintained by elaborate military postal systems. However, their effectiveness and viability depended on numerous variables including personal circumstances, organizational priorities, and the general course of the war. The armed forces of Allied governments in exile were, of course, in exile themselves (and, it often transpired, not only for the duration of the war). Poland's vast wartime diaspora of refugees, deportees, and prisoners of war resulted in Polish troops fighting in Norway,

Mail being unloaded at a British army post office in the Western Desert, 1941. Reliable postal services were one of the many ingredients of good military morale . . .

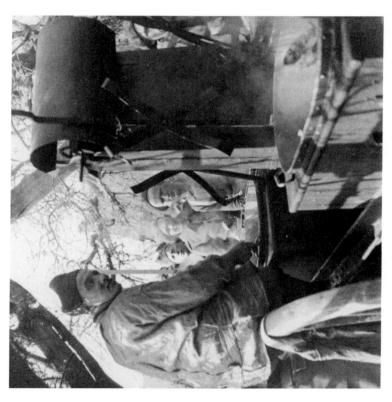

... as, indeed, were decent rations. Polish soldiers-in-exile at a field kitchen in France during the Phoney War period, 1939–40.

France, North Africa, Italy, the Low Countries, and also with the Red Army on the Eastern Front. Four hundred Polish officers helped train Britain's West African forces, while Poles conscripted into the Wehrmacht and captured in north-west Europe were widely enlisted to fill the ranks of General Maczek's 1st Armoured Division. The extent and degree of such displacement was a far cry from the experience of the Anglo-American armed forces, though here again there were inevitable variations in the strength of home ties between those who remained at home, those who were sent overseas, and those for whom capture could involve an intense and protracted experience of isolation. Even before the United States entered the war, senior officers in the US army had taken note of a disconcerting tendency for their soldiers to stop at isolated farms during stateside manoeuvres in order to phone home, a habit they deplored as 'unwarlike'. Nevertheless, this preoccupation with home was incurable; by 1943 the average GI was receiving fourteen items of mail a week and it was largely to ease the logistical strain that V-mail was introduced in 1942, a technique whereby letters were photographed before transmission overseas and then reproduced on lightweight photographic paper for delivery. In addition to their mail, the ubiquitous welfare and recreational activities of the American Red Cross and United Service

Organizations (USO) also helped to bring a reassuring taste of home to America's far-flung GIs. Likewise, according to Field Marshal Montgomery, the British soldier was basically happy so long as he received his mail, his newspapers, and copious quantities of tea. However, the British armed forces also went to great lengths to cultivate collective regional and local ties. While the army's much-vaunted system of county regiments had strong historical foundations, the government's Warship Week campaign of 1942 sought to foster equivalent links with the Royal Navy. Britain's towns, cities, and even businesses were called upon to raise funds with which to adopt their own ship.

However, it was a painful truth that exposure to home did not always benefit military morale. Just as the mail could bring unsettling news to their Anglo-American counterparts (not least in the form of the dreaded 'Dear John . . .'), the effects of the Combined Bomber Offensive rendered personal correspondence and the experience of home leave distinctly double-edged for many German soldiers. Conscious of the devastation being wrought on Germany's towns and cities by British and American bombing, in a telling case of role reversal senior army commanders urged German soldiers to write home in order to bolster the morale of their civilian friends and relations. Though large amounts of correspondence flowed between Red Army soldiers and their homes throughout the war, this was often erratic and could be greatly complicated by the extent of German occupation and the severity of Red Army censorship. Still, the westward advance of the Red Army beyond the borders of the Soviet Union not only liberated Soviet territory but enabled Soviet civilians to share in the condign looting of the Red Army. From December 1944 all Red Army soldiers in good standing were entitled to send at least one parcel home per month, varying in weight from 5 kilos for privates to 16 kilos for generals. The carriage of these parcels was given high priority and they were protected from pilfering, mishandling, and delay by severe penalties. Although it put considerable strain on fragile rail and distribution systems, the ensuing influx of goods and foodstuffs helped to raise morale and even enhance survival on the devastated home front. However, and despite this belated gesture of Stalinist magnanimity, the natural concern of Red Army soldiers for their families had in fact been used to coerce them for much of the war. In August 1941, Stalin's notorious Order No. 270 had stipulated a raft of punishments for the families of those soldiers and commissars who failed in their duties. These included arrest for the relatives of those who deserted and the removal of state benefits for the families of those who surrendered.

Beneath a carapace of dress, terminology, and functions that were often quite alien from civilian experience, their human composition nevertheless ensured that the culture of most armed forces remained highly civilianized. In this respect, the new medium of radio furnished an additional and unprecedented means of keeping service personnel at home and overseas in the orbit of civilian society. In the case of the United States, from 1942 the Armed Forces Radio Service was primarily responsible for overseas broadcasting to service personnel. Most of its programmes were commercially produced, only their advertising being deleted, and they offered a miscellany of news, sports, popular and classical music, comedy, and drama. By January 1940 the

BBC had already launched a dedicated Forces Programme for the benefit of British forces in France. Eventually, its lighter and more attractive schedules drew a larger military and civilian audience than the Corporation's comparatively drab Home Service. With the arrival of hundreds of thousands of GIs, the Forces Programme mutated into the General Forces programme which carried an even lighter and more varied mix of British, American, and Canadian productions. If British and American programming thus closed the gap between military and civilian audiences, then the same was also true of Radio Moscow. Notable for its initial failure to even broadcast the news of Barbarossa, in time Radio Moscow emerged as a powerful cohesive force in the Soviet Union. While broadcast readings from the correspondence of civilians and Red Army soldiers were a wartime staple, its most popular programme bridged the home and fighting fronts by seeking to reunite estranged family members.

The underlying civilian identity of most armed forces personnel was reflected in other leisure pursuits. Through their correspondence with the home front, literate Red Army soldiers revealed a remarkable and characteristically Russian taste for poetry and its composition. For their part, in literary matters the Anglo-American armed forces reflected the varied tastes and liberal norms of their own societies. If the appeal of comic books exceeded that of all other literature, their appetite for superior reading material still did much to promote the popularity of the paperback book. In Great Britain, demand from the armed forces helped to expand the list of Penguin titles from eighty-seven in 1941 to around 700 in 1945, and Penguin even created its own Forces' Book Club. Furthermore, the format and content of their own magazines and peri-odicals, which ranged from the in-house products of individual ships, stations, and units to high-end publications for mass circulation, conformed to civilian styles and reflected civilian interests. In fact, when *Yank* commenced publication in June 1942, the staff of this celebrated and ubiquitous weekly magazine reassured its readership that it was 'not G.I. except in the sense that we are G.I.'. While *Yank* duly served up a rich diet of cartoons, home news, sport results, and pin-up girls, organized recreation in the American armed forces also had a distinctly civilian flavour. Indeed, it was the responsibility of the US army's expanding Special Services organization to support *Yank*, to facilitate USO camp shows, and to ensure the accessibility of sports gear, films, theatre equipment, and post exchanges.

The essentially civilian culture of the British armed forces was also reflected in the contents of a range of service weeklies and dailies such as *Blighty*, *Reveille*, *Union Jack*, and *Crusader*. While the NAAFI (Navy, Army, and Air Force Institute) was but one of several providers of canteens and clubs where the comforts of civilian life could still be enjoyed, an endless stream of ENSA (Entertainments National Service Associ-ation) shows played at home and overseas, if not always to appreciative audiences. Under greater ideological and material constraints, the Wehrmacht also recognized the benefits of familiar leisure activities in promoting a general sense of loyalty and wellbeing. In an echo of the efforts of *Kraft durch Freude* (Strength-through-Joy), and in imitation of work already undertaken in Reich Labour Service camps, the Wehrmacht organized thousands of theatre artists into mobile theatrical troupes, with

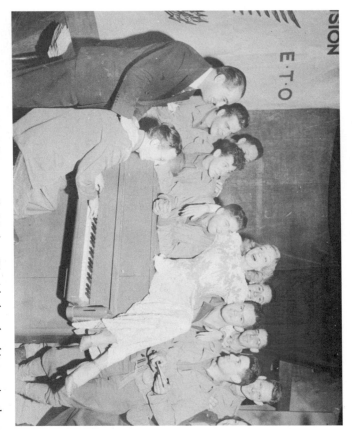

Somewhere in Europe, the anti-Nazi German exile Marlene Dietrich does her bit to raise the morale of American GIs.

14,000 entertainers serving in 1942 alone. The war also produced a proliferation of forces' newspapers such as *Mitteilungen für die Truppe*, *Sud Front*, and the lavishly illustrated *Signal*, which was circulated throughout occupied Europe in up to twenty foreign editions. Nevertheless, and however it was packaged, Nazi ideology enjoyed nothing like the appeal of American popular culture, whose GI ambassadors went by the million to Europe, North Africa, Asia, and the Pacific. America's cultural penetration of European societies was, of course, well under way before the war, with Nazi sensibilities being ruffled by the popularity and racial provenance of jazz. Still, America's well-paid and lavishly-resourced citizen soldiers greatly advanced this developing process. While enjoying the attractive guise of allies and liberators in most of western and southern Europe, GIs imported their music, their films, their language, and a seemingly endless supply of commodities and consumer goods—all of which cemented the cultural ascendancy of the United States in war-torn Europe. This process was also in evidence in the Pacific theatre, where American material abundance did much to foster 'cargo cults' in various parts of Melanesia.

Religion

Religion was yet another indicator of the fact that, to a greater or lesser extent, armed forces reflected the cultural character of the societies that produced them. Due to a now largely discredited chronology of the secularization of Western cultures and

A British soldier rests beneath a crucifix, Holland, 1944. The desecration of the adjoining church indicates how the religious dimensions of the Second World War have been greatly underestimated.

societies, religion per se has received scant attention in studies of the armed forces of the Second World War. Nevertheless, its importance was often obvious and ubiquitous. The Japanese armed forces were, institutionally at least, permeated with the cult of Japan's god-emperor and animated by the imperatives of *kokutai*, their sense of sacred uniqueness and superiority over other peoples. While their standard battle cry of *Banzai* was an acclamation of Japan's living god, a Japanese survivor of the battleship *Musashi* ruefully noted the punctilious care with which the Emperor's portrait was removed as it foundered during the battle of Leyte Gulf. According to General Sir William Slim, commander of the largely Indian 14th Army in Burma, the Indian soldier had three loyalties—to his religion, his regiment, and his officers in that order. The army of British India had long been highly attuned to the religious sensitivities of its multi-religious, multi-ethnic, and multi-lingual soldiers and great care was exercised, even on the battlefields of the Second World War, to ensure that these were not offended. As late as April 1945, for example, a British officer serving with the 6th Bengal Lancers in Italy was careful to consult his regiment's senior Indian officer on the appropriate practices to be observed when burying its high-caste Hindu dead. The importance of religion to Indian soldiers was also evident in action. In the cacophony of the fighting for Lone Tree Hill near Imphal in 1944, a Hindu officer of the Rajputana Rifles noted the distinctive battle cries raised by his Hindu and Muslim soldiers as they mingled with those of the Japanese. However, other imperial soldiers in the Burma campaign also experienced the war in religious terms. Although one Muslim soldier of the 5th Gold Coast Regiment regretted the war in religious terms. Although one prayer, he still claimed that he and his African co-religionists understood their struggle with the Japanese in terms of a jihad. Remarkably, the war itself had a major impact on the traditional religious profile of the Royal West African Frontier Force, whose battalions saw service in Italian Somaliland and Burma and which numbered almost 100,000 by 1942. Due to the heightened technical demands of the war, the regiment's recruiters evinced a strong preference for literate products of Christian mission schools. Consequently, the proportion of Christians in its ranks increased from only 2 per cent in 1939 to nearly 50 per cent by 1945.

Whether they were West African animists in Burma or American Presbyterians in Europe, service personnel of all nations and backgrounds evinced the same tendency to seek supernatural or divine protection through the possession of religious artefacts serving as talismans. Even prospective Kamikaze pilots, though assured of their godlike status and future repose at the Yasukuni Shrine, clung to their protective talismans, which even included Bibles as well as the more traditional *senninbari*, a good-luck sash sewn by well-wishers. However, the significance of religion as a motivating factor even in Western armed forces should not be underestimated. The demands of total war and the accompanying imperatives of cultural mobilization meant that religious language and symbolism were often well to the fore, being intended to have a profound and inspiring cultural resonance. For example, and apparently at the instigation of Thierry d'Argenlieu (a Catholic priest, friar, naval officer, and reputedly 'one of the greatest minds of the twelfth century'), the Gaullist Free French rallied to the Cross of Lorraine. Although a symbol of that disputed French province, the Cross of Lorraine had also been closely associated with the Catholic League in France's sixteenth-century wars of religion. While many of France's leading clergy sought an advantageous accommodation with the Vichy regime, some prominent Gaullists continued to draw inspiration from a very different and uncompromising strain of Catholic patriotism. Under the command of General Philippe Leclerc, a conspicuous case in point, one of the first ceremonies to be held by the Free French 2nd Armoured Division on its arrival in the United Kingdom in 1944 was a public mass in honour of St Joan of Arc. For their part, the British armed forces also drew deeply on their nation's rich religious heritage. In a striking departure from the anodyne and comparatively secular precedents of the First World War, in the war against Nazi Germany the British army made extensive use of a crusader's cross motif, variations of which became the insignia of its 1st, 2nd, and 8th Armies and of Montgomery's 21st Army Group. Montgomery himself, the son of an Anglican bishop and the brother of a serving army chaplain, routinely invoked the Almighty in language redolent of the King James Bible and the Book of Common Prayer in his famous public messages to his troops. In a similar vein, the Old Testament proved a rich source of inspiration in all but christening some of the RAF's most famous operations, notably Gomorrah (the firebombing of Hamburg in 1943), Jericho (the bombing of Amiens prison in 1944), and Manna (the dropping of food supplies into occupied Holland in 1945).

It is, however, important to emphasize that the use and force of this language and symbolism was by no means dependent on a strong churchgoing culture. In this regard, the case of the remarkable and pragmatic rehabilitation of Russian Orthodoxy in the Soviet Union from the outbreak of the Soviet–German war affords the best example of how a powerful and essentially historic fusion between religious faith and national identity was harnessed in the overriding interests of winning the war. Through the reopening of churches and the revival of church life, the effects of this policy were largely to be found behind the lines, but the Red Army was by no means unaffected by this phenomenon. Marshal Fedor Tolbukhin, who captured Vienna in 1945, had long been suspected as a covert believer, but numerous signs of a recru- descent if unchurched faith were also widely apparent among the rank and file of the Red Army. Furthermore, and thanks to the donations of the faithful, the T-34s of an entire Soviet tank brigade were emblazoned with an Orthodox cross, while Orthodox priests even blessed Soviet tanks as they rolled off the assembly lines. Although Nazi Germany's struggle with the Soviet Union was often billed in neo-crusading terms, for conflicting ideological reasons the Nazi regime proved much less willing to promote religion in the Wehrmacht. In contrast with the Anglophone democracies, which made generous and even mandatory provision for religious observance in their armed forces, only a thousand or so chaplains appear to have ministered to the 17 million men who passed through the Wehrmacht, usually in the army as the more Nazified Luftwaffe and Waffen SS disdained such provision. Still, a widespread need for the consolations of religion could obtain even under these circumstances. In terms of Nazi ideology, one of the Third Reich's more problematic war heroes was Oberst Werner Mölders, a recipient of the Knight's Cross and the first ever fighter ace to achieve a tally of more than 100 aerial kills. However, Mölders was a devout and demonstrative Catholic and, following his death in November 1941, his religious convictions were widely portrayed as being in conflict with the Nazi regime and with its euthanasia programme in particular. Likewise, beleaguered German paratroopers at Monte Cassino in 1944 had scant use for noxious Nazi anticlericalism as there appears to have been a strong and consistent demand among them for the ministrations of army chaplains.

Propaganda

A further extension of civilian norms and attitudes can be seen in the manner in which armed forces disseminated their wartime propaganda. The Red Army, of course, maintained its pre-war political systems, it being the task of its *politruki* (commissars) to promote Communist ideology and activity and to monitor deviant behaviour even down to platoon level. Despite early disasters and a fair measure of ideological backtracking, the course of the war from 1943 came as the party's supreme vindication and the Communist Party reaped the fruits of victory in a surge of soldiers' applications for Party membership. Pointedly eschewing the tainted, Red Army model of the meddling, gun-toting commissar, in the German army the task of realizing the Nazi vision of the political soldier was in hand from the reintroduction of conscription in 1935, and was allotted to its officers in 1938. Accordingly, Nazi ideology and rhetoric coloured the orders and pronouncements of the army's senior commanders throughout the war but, standing as they did at the very heart of the idealized *Kampfgemeinschaft* (or 'battle community'), it was the army's junior officers who were mainly responsible for promoting the National Socialist world view through their example and direct instruction. Although this onus was not confined to the army (one U-boat ace, Wolfgang Lüth, claimed to gather his crew at regular intervals in order to enlighten them as to the deeper nature and significance of the war) the ultimate test of the system came in the context of the Soviet–German war. With the deterioration of Germany's situation in the winter of 1943–4, the ideological mission of the army's officer corps was intensified with the publication of a standard booklet entitled *Wofür kämpfen wir?* (What do we fight for?), and by the introduction of party-trained *Nationalsozialistische Führungsoffiziere* (National Socialist Leadership Officers). The task of these new functionaries was to assist the officer corps in what was deemed to be their 'spiritual' work.

In contrast with the Red Army and the Wehrmacht, to say nothing of the IJA and IJN, the armed forces of the relatively liberal and unwarlike Anglophone democracies have been portrayed, then as now, as sadly deficient in ideological motivation. Illustrated by a tacit internal consensus that the war was an unpleasant job that had to be done, and by their preference for surrender rather than self-immolation, this disposition was a cause for concern among their commanders and was observed and even despised by their adversaries (and most notably, in the matter of surrender, by the Japanese). Even after the victory of El Alamein, Montgomery wrote ruefully that 'The trouble with our British lads is that they are not killers by nature; they have got to be so inspired that they will want to kill, and that is what I tried to do with this Army of mine.' As early as 1942 the US army also recognized the need to engender a higher sense of purpose among its soldiers and enlisted its Information and Education Division, along with the Hollywood director Frank Capra, to explain America's war aims through a series of seven training films entitled *Why We Fight*. Although this series presented the war as a straightforward global clash between good and evil, a post-war survey concluded that its impact on its intended audience had been minimal. Still, this discourse on the generally poor motivation of Anglo-American servicemen in comparison with that of their German, Soviet, and Japanese equivalents is confounded by an obvious evidential anomaly. Despite the long shadows cast by calamities such as the fall of Singapore, the Philippines, and Tobruk in 1942, no

Not fighting to the last man. Waffen-SS troops with their diminutive British captor, Normandy 1944.

Anglo-American forces surrendered in numbers remotely comparable to those witnessed by the Red Army in 1941, by the Wehrmacht from 1943, or even the IJA in Manchuria in the summer of 1945. Ultimately, and beneath the ideological posturing and bombast, the overriding human instinct for self-preservation was common to all armed forces.

Criminality

Quite apart from strategic and officially sanctioned violations of the accepted rules and conventions of war, such as unrestricted submarine warfare and the indiscriminate bombing of civilians, it is easy to discern the influence of entrenched civilian attitudes in a seemingly endless litany of wartime atrocities. Given their profound racial contempt for the Chinese, and the abiding threat of partisan activity, Japanese soldiers soon strained and broke the bonds of discipline in their treatment of the Chinese civilian population in the Sino-Japanese War. Most notoriously demonstrated in the protracted 'Rape of Nanking' in the winter of 1937–8, the widespread practice of murder, rape, torture, and pillage that became habitual for the IJA in China eventually elicited a protest from the Emperor's brother and resulted in the promulgation of a 'Code of Battlefield Honour' in January 1941. Intended as a remedial measure, in practice this code seems to have been honoured more in its breach than in its observance. A lethal cocktail of racism and fear, especially of partisan activity, was also the catalyst for a host of Wehrmacht atrocities in Europe. In Poland the German army was deeply implicated in the murder of Polish civilians from the start of the European war. For example, on 4 September 1939 General Walter von Reichenau ordered that three Polish hostages be shot for every German soldier killed. In the campaign against France in 1940, black African POWs were particularly vulnerable to the murderous corollaries of Nazi racial ideology, with hundreds of Senegalese soldiers being shot out of hand after surrendering.

Senior army commanders were also key contributors to Hitler's war of annihilation against the Soviet Union. Besides disseminating Hitler's murderous *Kommissarbefehl* (Commissar Order) of March 1941, they took in their stride the planned starvation of the Soviet population and made careful provision for collective reprisals and the summary shooting of civilians. In contrast, but in keeping with the nature of the campaign, they made very little provision for accommodating and feeding Soviet POWs. Within this framework, and along with the *Einsatzgruppen*, the German army was fully complicit in the murder of hundreds of thousands of Jews and other Soviet civilians, often under the exculpatory guise of anti-partisan operations. Furthermore, around 2 million Soviet POWs died in Wehrmacht custody during the first six months of the Soviet–German war, largely through disease, exposure, and malnutrition. However, such conduct was not a Japanese or German preserve, as neither the Italians nor the minor Axis powers lagged very far behind in perpetrating war crimes (that is, breaches of the accepted rules of war) or crimes against humanity (such as the genocide, deportation, enslavement, and repression of civilian populations). Despite being credited for standing aloof from the Holocaust, Italy's armed forces were very much involved in both. During their invasion and occupation of Abyssinia (1935–41) they bombed Red Cross facilities, used phosgene gas and other chemical weapons, and systematically terrorized the Abyssinian population, executing 30,000 civilians in 1937 in reprisal for the attempted assassination of the Italian viceroy Rodolfo Graziani. For its part, the Romanian army was responsible for the war's largest single massacre of Jews following the capture of the fiercely defended port of Odessa in October 1941.

If, in aggregate terms, the Axis armed forces generally outdid their Allied counterparts in the commission of war crimes and crimes against humanity, the gap between them was not necessarily wide. Following its invasion of eastern Poland in September 1939, the Red Army was an accessory to the NKVD in the murder of thousands of Polish POWs and in the expropriation and deportation of over a million Polish citizens. Moreover, this proved to be but one of several wartime deportations of entire ethnic groups by Stalin's regime. As part of its vengeful advance westwards, in 1944–5 the Red Army not only practised licensed looting on an enormous scale but was also responsible for the rape of hundreds of thousands of girls and women in Romania,

American GIs shot by their German captors, Luxembourg, 1944. Although by no means unknown in Western Europe, such atrocities were dwarfed by the scale of Germany's routine mistreatment of Soviet prisoners of war.

Hungary, and Germany. However, such conduct was by no means unknown among the forces of the Western Allies. In the course of the Italian campaign of 1943–5, the Moroccan *goumiers* of General Alphonse Juin's French Expeditionary Corps ran amok and committed dreadful crimes against Italian civilians. In the words of a senior French officer, these irregular soldiers recruited from among Berber tribesmen 'lived only for brigandage and war'. True to this reputation, in 1944 they were responsible for the rape of thousands of Italian civilians of all ages and both sexes, their rampage being checked only by a spate of exemplary executions.

Spontaneous war crimes were also committed by the Anglo-Americans, who could not fail to recognize that the accepted rules of war were often discarded in a combat environment. Apparently incited by General George S. Patton's exhortation to show no quarter to their enemies during the invasion of Sicily, American troops of the 180th Infantry Regiment shot dozens of Italian and German POWs out of hand after heavy fighting for the airfield at Biscari in July 1943. If the killing of enemy POWs was a minority practice in Europe, the same cannot be said of the American war against Japan. In this context, the reluctance of the Japanese to surrender, and the unwillingness of American soldiers and marines to take prisoners, greatly complicated the task of intelligence gathering. Among Americans in the Pacific (though not, it would seem, among British Empire troops in the Burma campaign) this visceral hatred of the enemy frequently spilled over into the mutilation of corpses and into the practice of taking Japanese body parts—especially skulls—as souvenirs. American attitudes and behaviour were partly caused by exposure to Japanese brutality but they were also influenced by a longstanding racial and cultural disdain for the Japanese and other Asians, a prejudice that underpinned severe pre-war restrictions on Asian immigration into the United States. The weighty issue of war crimes, moreover, should not be allowed to obscure the lesser forms of criminality in which Anglo-American personnel were often involved. Denied the official sanction enjoyed by their Red Army counterparts, looting if not rape was still commonplace, and not only in Germany. Furthermore, an abundance of military supplies of all kinds led to widespread pilfering, racketeering, and exploitation against a backdrop of infrastructural devastation and civilian destitution.

Conclusion

The armed forces of the Second World War were as diverse as the societies that produced them. However, this diversity went beyond obvious national and cultural differences and, by dint of their specific needs, was detectable between and even within the individual armed forces of a particular state. In terms of their personnel, armed forces were not simply militarized cross-sections of particular civilian societies. In addition to the effects of voluntary systems of recruitment, the presence of large numbers of foreign volunteers could create organizations that were quite distinct in terms of their composition from the societies they existed to defend, as was the case with the RAF, the German army, and even the Waffen SS. Furthermore, and because of a host of cultural, political, ideological, and military considerations, systems of conscription differed greatly in terms of their scope and severity, as the glaring contrast between Canada and the Soviet Union serves to illustrate. If societal norms and conventions helped shape the human composition of armies, navies, and air forces, then civilian culture could also permeate them as well. Despite the militaristic pretensions and trappings of so many societies in the inter-war years, their armed forces were overwhelmingly composed of civilians-in-arms, men and women who were often reluctant warriors at best and who hoped to return to their peacetime existence as soon as possible. This phenomenon was as true of Japanese soldiers in China as it was of Italian soldiers in North Africa. While, under such circumstances, home ties were cherished rather than discarded, new technologies, and especially the radio, could reinforce these bonds to an unprecedented degree. Beyond the personal preoccupations of service personnel, the imprint of civilian society also had a fundamental bearing on their ability to wage modern war, being reflected in the gender roles, social structures, cultural pursuits, religious beliefs, political indoctrination, and criminal propensities of all armed forces. Thus, and amidst the massive demands of a total war, it was in their mentalities and cultures rather than in their composition that armed forces most closely reflected the belligerent societies of the Second World War.

10 Front Line II

Civilians at War

RICHARD OVERY

THE Second World War began and ended with the bombing of undefended civilians. On the hot Saturday afternoon of 14 August 1937, the first bombs fell on Shanghai, killing 1,000 civilians. In the words of a reporter, as the fumes slowly lifted, he saw how 'Heads, legs, arms lay far from smashed masses of flesh ... Dead in his tracks as he had been directing the corner traffic lay the corpse of a Chinese policeman with shrapnel through his head.' The carnage was the work of three light bombers, part of a Chinese squadron which had been ordered to attack a Japanese cruiser in the harbour. It was a tragic error, committed by the Chinese Nationalists at the start of the battle for control of China's most important city. The Japanese began to bomb too, as the battle for Shanghai raged on into October and November, deliberately burning sections of the city to the ground and inflicting large-scale casualties. Almost exactly eight years later, an American B-29 Superfortress bomber, the *Enola Gay*, flew across the Japanese port city of Hiroshima to drop the first atomic bomb, killing at one blow an estimated 70,000 people. Unlike the First World War, the Second involved civilians, voluntarily and involuntarily, in a new front line far from the fighting fronts in which civilians had to learn to cope with extreme violence. Bombing was the most obvious manifestation of the civilian front line, but it was only one part of the wartime experience of civilians caught in the coils of a total war.

The concept of 'total war', elaborated in the inter-war years, endorsed the view that in any future conflict national war would be fought between whole populations and not just the fighting services. Those who produced arms, drove trains, ploughed the fields, or ran the bureaucracy were regarded as contributors to the national war effort, and as such legitimate objects of war. National governments also viewed their own societies that way. Mobilization of labour resources, personal wealth, and essential supplies transformed the home fronts temporarily into large war camps in which all citizens were supposed to share in the hardships and sacrifices that total war required of them. The national community became an exclusive zone, committed to the search for national victory. Those deemed not to belong to that community were rounded up and deported or sent to camps, or, in the most extreme case of the European Jews, exterminated. Civilians were given little opportunity to protest their inclusion in the

Chinese dead in the Nationalist capital of Chonquing following Japanese air raids in 1939. Civilians were in the front line almost everywhere thanks to the advent of the bomber.

warring community. Only when the state collapsed or fragmented did civilians find themselves on a new front line of civil conflict either through armed resistance to the occupying power or in a state of civil war between rival ideological factions. By the end of the war in 1945 there were millions of civilians across Europe and Asia with guns in their hands alongside the organized armed forces.

Civil Defenders

Of all the direct threats to the civilian way of life, bombing was the most extreme and ubiquitous during the war. Almost every major city (and a great many smaller towns) in Europe and eastern Asia experienced bombing at some point during the war. This was a reality widely expected in the 1930s, when all major states adopted programmes of what became known as civil or civilian defence. This was not entirely a novelty since primitive air-raid precautions were taken in the First World War to cope with the early bombing raids by German bombers and airships and the British bombing of Germany. Yet the idea that civilians should volunteer in large numbers to organize home front defences against the threat of bombing transformed the nature of popular commitment to the war effort and gave civilians a real sense that they were on a new and unpredictable front line of civilian war. When the British Home Secretary,

British men volunteers for the Home Guard, set up in 1940, parade with broomsticks instead of rifles, which were in short supply. German authorities announced that they would shoot any Home Guard they caught if they landed.

Herbert Morrison, reflected in 1945 on the large civil defence forces he had been responsible for, he described them as a 'citizen army' composed of 'rank-and-file warriors', men and women alike.

Civil defence served many purposes besides preparing sections of the community for the work of rescue and welfare in the wake of bombing raids. It imposed social discipline through the regular routines of air-raid drills and the blackout. Failure to observe the regulations on air-raid protection usually involved a fine or even imprisonment. In Germany and the occupied territories of Western Europe, in Italy, Britain, and the Soviet Union, the regular blackout, compulsory fire-watching against incendiary attack, and the maintenance of domestic air-raid shelters all gave a daily reminder to citizens of their responsibility to the community during wartime. Civil defence training, which extended even to schoolchildren, mimicked the training enjoyed by the regular forces, and encouraged civil defenders to identify themselves directly with the war effort. In Germany civil defence personnel were given uniforms, helmets, and badges even before the war broke out. In Britain the onset of war found many civil defence members with little more than an armband and a helmet, but, following widespread protests, they became a uniformed force, even one allowed to join the three armed services in parades and pageants. Above all, civil defence gave ordinary citizens a front-line experience not very different from the regular military

British civil defence personnel demonstrate the use of the gas mask. By the outbreak of war masks had been distributed to the entire population.

front line. Heavy bombardments, the search and rescue of casualties, the hunt for body-parts, the risks and dangers to which they were exposed in every raid, required the same level of discipline and courage expected of the front-line fighter, and brought regular death and disablement to the citizen-soldiers.

The numbers involved in the civil defence effort were enormous. In the Soviet Union and Germany, participation in the national air defence associations was not compulsory, but it was regarded as a community obligation for all those in a position to take part. The German *Reichsluftschutzbund* (Reich Air Defence League) had 13 million members by the outbreak of war; the Soviet *Osoviakhim* (Society for Assistance to Defence) had 15 million members by 1933, when the air threat to the Soviet Union was minimal. The members of these organizations were given training sessions in fighting incendiary and chemical weapons, in supervising the creation of domestic air-raid rooms, and first-aid. From their ranks were selected the officials and workers who ran the formal air-raid protection services. In the Soviet Union in 1944 there were 747,000 full-time air-raid protection personnel, supported by 2.9 million people in urban 'self-defence' units, to help with rescue and fire-fighting. A staggering total of 71 million Soviet citizens were given rudimentary training in anti-gas warfare and rescue work. In Germany there were 1.5 million civilian office-holders in the air defence system, while 22 million had been given training in all aspects of air-raid protection, almost one-quarter of the population. There were 3,400 training schools for civilian defenders in Germany, where courses were given on fire-fighting, anti-gas protection, first-aid, and civil defence leadership.

The figures for participation in other countries were more modest, but nevertheless significant. In Britain a vigorous campaign of recruitment for civil defence personnel was undertaken from 1938 onwards. By 1940 there were over one million paid or part-time civil defence workers as well as 193,000 auxiliary fire-fighters. As fire-watching and incendiary training became compulsory, the figures for those engaged in some aspect of civil defence increased to 1.86 million by the end of 1943 together with an estimated 4 million additional fire-watchers and auxiliary civil defenders. In urban areas each street was supposed to organize its own self-protection group with a regular rota of fire-watching responsibilities. In France, a system of 'Passive Defence' was set up in the 1930s obliging all urban communities to create an air-raid protection service and to train the necessary personnel. This system was sustained by the German occupiers and the Vichy regime after French defeat in June 1940 because of the persistent bombing of French targets by the Allied air forces, but the numbers engaged in civil defence were always too small for the tasks expected of them, partly because the French Vichy regime, no longer in a state of war, was reluctant to mobilize civilians or to pay the costs of an effective civil defence structure. In Italy, too, the numbers directly involved in civil defence were much smaller than in Britain or Germany. The National Union for Anti-Aircraft Protection (UNPA) could call on only 150,000 members in 1939, not all of whom were effective civil defenders, and when war broke out in June 1940 against Britain and France, many UNPA members abandoned the organization. To keep the rest available, the Fascist regime defined them as 'mobilized civilians' in August 1940, giving a formal military status to the urban home front.

Civil defence was not confined to the areas of Europe within easy reach of bomber aircraft. In the United States a Civilian Defense Office was set up in May 1941 under the Harvard law professor, James Landis. The threat to American cities and factories was expected to come either from Japan against the west coast or from German aircraft, perhaps catapulted from submarines, bombing the east coast. The whole panoply of air-raid wardens, blackout regulations, and fire-watching was introduced once war came in December 1941, though later on the absence of any clear threat led to relaxation of the blackout rules to a state known as 'dim-out', with subdued lighting. The introduction of civilian defence measures in the United States made clear the nature of civilian responsibility in modern war. 'Modern war is not confined to battle lines,' wrote Landis. 'It is all the arms, resources and production of one people against all the arms, resources and production of another.' Civilian defence, continued Landis, was 'a military assignment'. Air-raid precautions were also introduced in most parts of the far-flung British Empire, including Hong Kong, which was

Schoolchildren in Los Angeles are given rudimentary instruction in civil defence in December 1941 following the Japanese attack on Pearl Harbor. Though never bombed, Americans kept up civil defence preparations for much of the wartime period.

the most immediately threatened. In New Zealand, air-raid defence was organized under the Emergency Precautions Service, set up in March 1942 following the introduction of similar regulations in Australia after Pearl Harbor. This service again covered the whole range of post-raid emergency aid necessary for community defence. A warden service was set up on the basis of six wardens for every 500 people, with additional guards for factories and offices, though New Zealand was, like the mainland United States, never actually attacked from the air.

Mobilization for civil defence was socially inclusive. A significant proportion of those recruited to home defence were women, a fraction of them children. In Germany the shortage of male civil defence workers once the war had started made it imperative to recruit women and around 200,000 of the Air Defence League officials were female. In Britain women were encouraged to join from the start, many of them as first-aid or welfare workers, but as shortages of male manpower developed, they became air-raid wardens and even fire-fighters. By the summer of 1940 there were

An air raid precautions post in the British colony of Hong Kong in 1941. Civil defence preparations were made throughout the British Empire to guard against sudden air attack.

over 151,000 full-time or part-time women civil defence workers, sharing all the hardships of the men under the hail of bombs and prompting a re-evaluation of conventional gender roles. Over the course of the war 618 of them were killed or seriously injured, together with 102 female welfare workers. In addition to women in civil defence, there were large welfare organizations which were run by women to supply post-raid food, shelter, information, and comfort. The British Women's Voluntary Services for Air Raid Precautions (WVS), set up in 1938, had over a million members during the war; the National Socialist People's Welfare (NSV) in Germany had 15 million members, a large majority of them women. Both organizations during the war helped to organize the temporary relief of the bombed out. Children, too, found themselves in the front line. In Britain young boys were used as bicycle messengers between air-raid posts; in the Soviet Union youngsters from *Komsomol*, the Soviet youth organization, organized rescue squads or were posted on rooftops to watch out for and, if necessary, to extinguish incendiaries; schoolchildren in Germany were given regular talks and demonstrations about the different kinds of bomb and how to cope with their effects.

In Germany the recruitment of women and young people into the air defence system became urgent as millions of younger and over-age men were drafted into the armed forces at exactly the time, in 1943–5, when the bombing reached a peak. They were engaged not only in post-raid assistance and welfare, but even in manning

Berliners clear up a street in the aftermath of an RAF bombing raid in November 1940. The German population was expected to work collectively to combat the after-effects of bombing raids. More than 22 million joined the Reich Air Defence League.

the anti-aircraft batteries that sprang up all over German territory. The female *Luftwaffehelferinnen* (Air Force Auxiliaries) were recruited for a wide range of tasks, including work at the batteries, and although they were not explicitly allowed to fire the guns, on occasion local commanders turned a blind eye. For boys drafted in as *Flakhelfer* (anti-aircraft auxiliaries), there was less choice and thousands found themselves aged 14 or 15 manning anti-aircraft equipment originally designed for regular air-force troops. Nowhere did the demands of total war on the home front impinge so heavily on civilians as in Germany and by the end of the war over 350,000 of them had been killed. To demonstrate the link between military fighting front and civilian home front, civil defence personnel who were killed had an iron cross printed next to the death announcement, as soldiers did; civil defence personnel could also win the real Iron Cross for exceptional bravery on the home front battleground. In Britain too, civil defence workers who were killed on duty were given a formal funeral, with a coffin covered with the Union Jack and a solemn military-style procession to the funeral.

For the many millions of civilians who did not actively participate in civil defence, the wartime experience of hours spent in shelters listening to the bombs fall and smelling the sour odour of burning flesh and buildings was a vivid and traumatic reminder of the home front war. This was an experience shared across the warring world between 1937 and 1945, from the poorly constructed shelters in Chinese cities subjected to occasional Japanese raids, to the giant purpose-built Flak-towers constructed in Berlin, Hamburg, and Vienna, capable of housing 10,000 people each under metres of solid concrete. The pattern of shelter provision and the experience of sheltering varied widely between the different combatants. The cost of every shelter programme was very large and the decision was made in most countries under threat that the sheltering population should be decentralized as far as possible to their own homes. This resulted in an uneven distribution of shelter opportunities based largely on social geography. The working-class tenements and houses in British cities were

Londoners shelter under railway arches in the city's East End during the nine-month 'Blitz' on the capital. Though notoriously unsafe, they were regarded as better than many of the purpose-built shelters.

unsuitable for the garden shelters—Andersons—and had few cellars or basements. As a result working-class communities, the ones repeatedly attacked during the Blitz of 1940–1, relied more on public shelters or improvised sanctuaries, particularly the London Underground system. Middle-class families were more likely to live further from the bombed areas, and to have a garden or cellar in which a shelter could be constructed. Even then most shelters, private or public, gave scant protection from a heavy raid. Knowledge of how little protection the public shelters gave encouraged many to abandon shelters altogether and surveys found that around 50 per cent of people did not bother to seek refuge during raids. The result was an exceptionally high death rate in relation to the weight of bombs dropped, 43,000 people in nine months of bombing, around one fatality per ton of bombs.

In Germany, propaganda for the creation of the 'bomb-safe room' began in the late 1930s and by the start of the war millions of basements under large apartment blocks or cellars in individual houses had been converted into improvised shelters with reinforced roofs, gas-proof doors, and a lightly-bricked escape shaft connecting one shelter to another. Sheltering was compulsory and shelter discipline was respected more than it was in Britain. Only when massive incendiary strikes set whole city centres on fire did the shelter become a mixed blessing. Thousands were killed in domestic basement shelters by carbon monoxide poisoning or overheating, or, like the burned bodies in the Hamburg firestorm of July 1943, reduced to piles of ash. Life in the shelter was monotonous and exhausting, a regular reminder of the civilian front line. The experience provoked less evident psychiatric breakdown than the authorities in Britain and Germany had anticipated, but civilians under fire, like soldiers at the front line, nursed the psychological damage in private. Propaganda in the Blitz emphasized that 'Britain can take it', while German propaganda later in the war played on the idea of a sombre 'community of fate' bound together in a spirit of sacrifice. This left little room for social action to protect the victims of bombing, though there were regular examples of temporary panic or demoralization, even of more direct protest, such as the occupation of the London Savoy Hotel in September 1940 led by East End Communists. Only in Italy, where shelter provision was rudimentary and anti-aircraft defences feeble, did bombing prompt protest against the shelters of the rich, or the lack of post-raid food and aid. Here the idea of the civilian 'home front' made little sense for a population disillusioned with Mussolini's failed war, and then, after September 1943, held hostage by the German occupation.

War Comes to the Home Front

The life of civilians on the home front was affected by more than bombing, since many millions across the warring populations did not directly experience aerial attack. The demands of large-scale war transformed the distribution of the population in response to the imperatives of the war economy, and brought millions of women and youths into the industrial workforce. Regimes of forced labour in Japan and in German-occupied Europe transported millions of workers away from their homelands. The high financial cost of the war, greater by far than the overall cost of the First World War, imposed severe restrictions on personal wealth and the pattern of consumer spending. Buying war bonds was not compulsory but propaganda programmes highlighted the patriotic duty of the citizen to contribute financially to the war effort and to forgo the pre-war pattern of consumption. To ensure that consumers saved more and spent less, the output of consumer goods was restricted and key articles of clothing, petrol for vehicles, and above all food were rationed, even in the resource-rich United States.

It is difficult to generalize about the way the war affected the supply of food, medical care, and welfare because the experience changed over time according to the fortunes of war, and differed fundamentally between the more prosperous communities in Britain or the United States, both able to dominate world trade routes and to avoid direct invasion, and the poorer regions of Asia and Europe which were exploited for their resources by the occupying powers. The reality for almost all the territories involved in the war, except the United States and the British Dominions, was a decline in the standard diet, either measured in calorific terms, or in terms of the variety and range of foodstuffs available. In German-occupied Europe average calories per day of rationed food varied in 1943 between 1,920 in the Czech lands to 855 in the Polish 'Government-General'; but even in Germany itself, the beneficiary of extensive supplies from the conquered lands, average calories were only 1,980. The vast armed forces consumed far more per day than the civilian populations since their wellbeing was seen as a strategic necessity. As the war went on, food consumption continued to decline and the rationed supplies became more restricted. Britain enjoyed a better diet and more plentiful supplies thanks to overseas trade, the support of American Lend Lease consignments, and the decision to expand domestic agriculture. In the United States, food consumption went up for many poorer Americans who now had access to regular rationed goods and higher incomes. In both the Western democracies health for the civilian population tended to improve as unemployment disappeared and an emphasis was placed on foodstuffs that could sustain war work effectively.

The situation was very different in the Axis powers and their occupied areas, and for the population of the Soviet ally. In Germany rationing began from the first day of the war and for city-dwellers access to fruit, fish, fresh vegetables, and meat declined rapidly. The diet became a monotonous round of substitute (*ersatz*) food and drink, potatoes, and occasional supplies of meat, margarine, and dried fish. The rural population was expected to provide more of its own supplies, and evidence suggests they generally ate better. The ration was reduced step-by-step over the war period, but never as low as in the First World War, thanks to the import of large supplies from the occupied territories. French agriculture, for example, contributed 2.4 million tons of wheat, 891,000 tons of meat, and 1.4 million hectolitres of milk. Dutch and Danish farmers prospered on supplying eggs, bacon, and dairy products to the German market, both countries together supplying by 1943 more food (in terms of value) than any other occupied territory, though average calorie intake of rationed food in

An American woman buying meat from a butcher in Chicago in 1945. Although some foodstuffs were rationed in the United States, many Americans were better fed by the end of the war than they had been at the start.

The Netherlands was only 1,765 per head. In France, post-war calculations suggest that only one-quarter of the population had adequate access to food, chiefly the French peasantry, while 55 per cent living in urban areas found access to food irregular and limited. In much of the German-occupied area the ration entitlement did not mean that the food would actually be available, and for most urban dwellers the search for food, from shop to shop, or on the black market, came to dominate daily life.

In the Soviet Union the problem of food supply was at its starkest. The German invasion in summer 1941 captured the rich 'bread basket' of the Ukraine which supplied a large proportion of the Soviet Union's food surplus. Standards of food consumption were low even before the war, particularly for the peasant population, which had been forced into collective farms in the early 1930s and now relied on meagre handouts from the farm and anything they could grow themselves. The war had an immediate impact on the farms as men left for the army and horses were requisitioned; tractor output fell from 18,500 in 1940 to a mere 416 three years later. By 1944 three-quarters of the male workforce on the farms had gone and women and children were left to pull the ploughs themselves when there was no petrol for the tractor and no horses remaining. The product of the farms went chiefly to feed the army or the industrial workforce. Work was the only way to earn entitlement to adequate food rations, and dependants, young and old, had to live off what they could grow or borrow from those in work. Rationing was introduced in July 1941, 700

French civilians queuing for food under the German occupation. Large quantities of wheat, milk, and meat were sent to Germany, leaving French townspeople short of essential rations.

calories for children and the elderly, 4,000 calories for miners. Those not engaged in heavy labour got around 1,900 calories, just enough to sustain their work. To supplement the diet, factories introduced canteens that served a guaranteed hot meal once a day, while allotments were made available to workers outside the city where they could grow anything extra they wanted, a total of 16 million by 1944. Food was used as a punishment or a reward. Rations were cut for workers found guilty of minor derelictions. To secure extra rations workers were invited to donate blood for injured soldiers, earning an extra ration card and 500 grammes of butter or sugar. An unknown number of Russians died of starvation during the war, some the victims of German operations, including an estimated 700,000–800,000 during the Leningrad siege, others the victim of neglect or isolation.

At its most extreme, the wartime supply of food proved quite inadequate to sustain life. This was not always the result of deliberate deprivation, but of poor communications, or the failure of the harvest or poor storage facilities. But in most cases, starvation was the result of the policy of the occupier or a particular set of military circumstances. The Greek famine in the summer and winter of 1941 was provoked not only by German seizures but by the British blockade that denied Greece access to American wheat. By November rations for the population of Athens had fallen to 183 calories a day and thousands died a slow wasting death. Churchill was finally forced to allow shipments of food into Greece, but hunger persisted in a region with poor

A Ukrainian peasant woman collecting sunflower seeds for the German occupiers. The Soviet population under German control faced chronic hunger while food went to feed German troops and horses.

facilities for raising agricultural productivity. An estimated half a million Greeks died from starvation and hunger-induced diseases. In China, Japanese policies of slash and burn left millions facing starvation in the middle years of the war, while by the end of the conflict the Japanese population itself faced imminent starvation as supplies of food from overseas dried up in the American sea blockade. In Bengal the distortion of the market for food as a result of the war, combined with a poor rice harvest in 1942/3 and a British failure to release the shipping space necessary to transfer food surpluses, resulted in the death of at least 2 million people, probably substantially more. Here, remote from the main theatres of combat, the war was still capable of imposing on local communities a wartime crisis of catastrophic proportions.

The problem of food supply was exacerbated by the large-scale movement of people throughout the war. Displacement and dispossession were major factors for millions of civilians caught up in the crossfire of the war and in many cases resulted in additional pressures on existing food supplies. There were many factors influencing population movement, some of it voluntary, most not. In the Soviet Union the rapid advance of German forces led to the transfer of 16 million workers and their families from their path to the distant industrial centres in the Ural Mountains or central

Russia, placing an additional strain on the food supply system. Some evacuation occurred in combat zones, particularly at the start of the war, but was generally only temporary. Other mass evacuations occurred in the path of the oncoming Red Army in 1944–5, but the factor that influenced evacuation most was the bombing of European and Asian cities. The pattern of evacuation varied according to the intensity of the bombardment and the policy preferences of the regime. In France and Britain extensive plans were made before the war to move the vulnerable urban population—women, infants, young children, the elderly and disabled—to rural or small town destinations. In Germany, the regime gambled on the effectiveness of anti-aircraft defences and air-raid protection and kept the population where it was, though from 1940 limited evacuation of children was encouraged from the major cities. But only when forced by heavier raids in 1943 was a formal programme instituted of mass evacuation away from the major industrial targets to areas beyond bombing range or into suburban and rural areas closer to the cities. Some of the evacuation was voluntary, as civilians anxious about bombing moved to live with families in the countryside. In Japan and Italy, with large peasant populations, this was the commonest form of evacuation.

Whether voluntary or organized, evacuation posed major social problems. The urban populations found it difficult to adjust to life in the countryside, while rural dwellers deplored the alleged criminality and delinquency of the evacuees, or regarded them with disdain because they worked hard on the land while evacuees did little. The rationing system was complicated by the mass movement of the population and the need to supply food and welfare to more remote localities. Tension between evacuees and hosts was one of the reasons that many evacuees returned home to face the dangers of the urban front line, but many returned because they preferred familiar, if dangerous, surroundings or because they wanted to reunite families. In Britain 1.4 million were evacuated in September 1939, but by January 1940, with no sign yet of a bombing campaign, 900,000 had returned home. Once the Blitz started evacuation expanded, but at its peak never reached the level it had been at the start of the war. In France the early evacuations carried out at the start of the war were largely abandoned following defeat in June 1940, but started again when Allied bombers began to target French inland cities in 1942. The schemes were complicated by the reluctance of French city families to send their children away and by the insistence of the German occupiers that the men stay to carry on working in regions from which they wanted the rest of the population to move. Wives moved away unwillingly, and then tried to return despite the German threat to cut off their rations. The improvised evacuation of up to 1.2 million people by 1944 created numerous difficulties for rural areas where little preparation had gone into finding billets or supplying additional food. Italian evacuation, which increased steadily after German occupation in 1943 as Allied aircraft hit the cities of the north and centre of the country, was also a largely improvised affair. City populations decamped to the surrounding rural area, since no region was immune from bombing. By 1944 an estimated 2.28 million had fled the bombs. They were regarded by the authorities as a potential source of social protest,

British children on their way to their evacuation destination in the autumn of 1939. A total of 1.4 million vulnerable children and mothers were evacuated in the early months of the war, though many soon returned.

and distrusted by their hosts because the evacuees' one priority was to find food, in competition with those they came to live with.

Evacuation became a large-scale phenomenon in Germany and Japan, where the city-bombing offensives were larger and more destructive. In Germany a scheme of official evacuation began only in April 1943, beginning with the cities in the Ruhr-Rhineland. The preference of the regime was to relocate people close to the city boundary, in suburban areas or neighbouring villages, because this kept the work-force close to their place of work and was less disruptive to the rationing system. Large-scale evacuation threatened to destabilize the regime and every effort was made to prevent unorganized evacuation, where the evacuees could not be properly monitored or fed. Rising casualty rates in 1943, however, made a larger evacuation programme of children, mothers, and the infirm to more distant destinations essential and by the end of the year there were 3.2 million refugees from the bombing, a fraction of them workers who were moved to dispersal sites to keep production going.

In 1944 and 1945, the remorseless hail of bombs made evacuation unavoidable, both organized and voluntary, and the regime found itself trying to control as far as it could an exceptionally mobile population. By January 1945 there were 8.9 million evacuees sheltering in small towns and villages all over Germany; even here there were dangers as the Allied air forces roamed freely over German territory, flattening small towns and strafing vehicles. In Japan the peak of evacuation also reached 9 million by the end of the war, but here evacuation was a sudden and unexpected response to the onset of American fire-bombing of Japanese cities in March 1945. Evacuation as in Germany was a mix of formal programmes and flight from the cities, and here too it imposed a sudden additional burden on farming communities where food was already in short supply. Near famine conditions in Japan by the end of the war left the refugees from bombing especially vulnerable.

Civilians were also moved in large numbers as either internees or deportees, a direct result of wartime policies. One of the motives was fear of a so-called 'fifth column'. The phrase had been used by the Nationalist general Emilio Mola during the Spanish Civil War to describe the supporters of his cause active inside the walls of besieged Madrid, but it quickly became common currency in the late 1930s to describe any group identified as a potential threat to internal security. This led during the war to the internment or deportation of whole ethnic groups who were deemed by definition to be a threat. In France 'aliens' and Communists, many of them Jews who had fled from German persecution, were rounded up and put in concentration camps in 1939 and 1940, where they suffered extreme levels of deprivation. Between September 1939 and May 1940, 87 camps were set up, housing around 20,000 internees. Following French defeat, many were handed over to the Germans, making it clear that they had never been a serious threat to the French war effort. In Britain, a popular panic about 'fifth columnists' in the summer of 1940 led to the round-up and internment of Germans, Austrians, and Italians resident in Britain, many of whom had lived there for decades. A large proportion of them were also Jewish refugees from Hitler's Germany. Around 70,000 were imprisoned or placed under supervision in conditions equivalent to a prisoner of war, but widespread protest led to a relaxation of the regulations and by autumn 1941 there were only 5,000 still in custody. In North America there was a similar fear of a Japanese 'fifth column'. In Canada around 22,000 Japanese-Canadians, mainly from the Pacific West Coast, were interned, and in the United States 110,000 Japanese-Americans, two-thirds of them American citizens, were rounded up from the West Coast states and deported to eleven camps in the interior. They were compelled to sell their property and forced to live behind barbed wire in wooden barracks, with one room per family. When in 1943 the War Relocation Board tried to recruit the young Japanese men as soldiers, a quarter refused to obey the mobilization orders and were sent to an inhospitable camp in the California desert.

Internment and deportation were nevertheless much harsher under the dictatorships. In the areas of Japanese conquest 131,000 European and American civilian internees were forced into camps, where they were given poor food and scant medical assistance. Almost 15,000 died during the war. In the Soviet Union whole populations were shifted from their homes and deposited with almost no resources in remote parts of Siberia or central Asia. In 1940 and 1941 almost one million Poles were deported

Japanese-American children on their way to deportation centres in the western United States. The government insisted on moving 110,000 Japanese-Americans from the West Coast areas to purpose-built camps in the interior.

from the Soviet zone of Poland. Finns and Koreans were moved from frontier areas in the west and far east because they too were deemed a security risk. In August 1941 the Soviet government authorized the compulsory movement of 1.5 million citizens of distant German descent—the so-called Volga Germans—who were described by Stalin as 'saboteurs and diversionists'. By January 1942 800,000 German-Russians had been shipped east, the men to forced labour, the women and children to fend for themselves. Of the forced labourers, 175,000 died. In 1943 and 1944, in the belief that the peoples of the Caucasus region had helped the German army in its offensive towards Stalingrad, Stalin ordered their deportation further east, a total of 970,000 people. In total around 3 million Soviet citizens were deported in harsh conditions, most to so-called 'special settlements', where they were forced to undertake tough manual labour and to live in whatever rough homes they could assemble from local materials or dig into the ground.

There were few enemy aliens living within German territory and the early internments at the start of the war were directed at Communists and socialists, who were moved into concentration camps to ensure that they would not constitute a potential 'stab-in-the-back' of the German war effort. In the German conquests in Europe internment and deportation were undertaken not simply from fear of a 'fifth column', but as part of a grander plan for the ethnic and economic reconstruction of the German 'New Order'. In the conquered areas Hitler ordered Heinrich Himmler, head of the SS and from October 1939 'Plenipotentiary for the Protection of

Germandom', to gather together the ethnic German elements in Eastern Europe, even from allied or satellite states, so that a solid core of German racial stock could be constructed from whom colonizers and administrators would be chosen for the new German empire. The plan was to move 650,000–740,000 Germans scattered across the east back to a new Germanized homeland in Poland. Poles and Czechs were thrown off their farms to make way for German settlers. In 1941 Himmler authorized the drawing up of General Plan East in which it was proposed that following German victory over the Soviet Union, four-fifths of all Poles, 75 per cent of Belorussians, and 64 per cent of Western Ukrainians were to be deported to Siberia. The deportations and planned food deprivation were expected to reduce the population by 31 million. In the event the grotesque plans for the new empire failed to materialize except for the specific policy to eliminate the Jewish and gypsy populations of Europe and the enforced hunger in a number of captured Soviet cities. The Jews were regarded as a

A Dutch Jewish family in Amsterdam preparing for deportation to the east in 1942 where most deportees were killed in extermination centres in Poland.

vast 'fifth column', working not only to undermine the German racial and cultural inheritance but to aid the enemies of Germany through a worldwide Jewish conspiracy. The deportation and extermination of the Jewish population was finally authorized in late 1941, though large-scale killings had already been conducted in Poland and the occupied Soviet Union by the *Einsatzgruppen* of the SS. The story of the subsequent genocide is told more fully in the following chapter.

The circumstances of war also promoted another form of mass deportation to serve the interests of the German occupying power. Severe shortages of labour in Germany led to a large-scale programme of forced labour recruitment throughout the German-dominated area. The exact number of foreign workers transported to Germany during the war is not known with certainty. Official figures show around 7 million by 1944, but there were high death rates (an estimated 2.5 million labourers died during the war). Estimates of the total number of Europeans deported for labour vary between 12 and 13.5 million. Very few of these impressed workers were allowed to return home, and most enjoyed an existence, unless working on German farms, not very different from that of internees, except that they were paid a wage and generally fed better. The conditions varied widely between the tough treatment of Polish and Soviet labourers, and the more lenient treatment of those from Western Europe. Although Dutch workers were compelled from March 1942 to accept work in Germany, more than 180,000 had moved voluntarily to work there in 1940 and 1941, and even after the introduction of compulsion, some 94,000 were able to return to The Netherlands during 1942–4. In France, with a large industrial workforce, recruitment proved difficult and, when compulsion was introduced with the *Service du Travail Obligatoire* (STO), many workers simply disappeared into hiding. French businessmen found all kinds of ways to demonstrate that their workers were indispensable and in 1943 it was decided that German orders could be fulfilled better by workers staying in France rather than moving them to the Reich. Over the war some 1.2 million French workers were sent to Germany, but in autumn 1944 there were only 646,000 left. In Italy too, following the compulsory deportation of surrendered soldiers in September 1943, the German occupiers opted to exploit the remaining labour reserves where they were in the hope that this would increase the supply of war goods from Italy more efficiently. Deportation nevertheless remained a permanent threat in the areas under German rule, a further invasion of the civilian sphere alongside the menace of internment, the problems of evacuation, and the constant search for food.

Civilian Wars

The exceptional wartime experience imposed on all the warring and occupied populations might have been expected to provoke civilian resistance. In the First World War, the pressures of wartime exigencies provoked revolution in Russia and accelerated the collapse of the domestic war effort in Germany and the Austrian Empire. The reliability of their own civilian population faced with the unprecedented demands of total war was always a consideration for every government. Yet in the Second World

War, even in the Soviet Union, where wartime conditions were at their most debilitating, the home front did not totter or collapse. Instead, states faced with defeat exhibited a remarkable capacity to secure the continued allegiance of the home population. Resistance from civilians, when it came, was prompted among populations in the occupied territories where insurgency and civil war turned millions of civilians into actual combatants.

The survival of the home front under extreme pressure has a number of explanations. In the first place, the terms in which the war was presented to the public were also extreme. The alleged threat of national extinction or fears for the future of civilization were tropes that civilians generally identified with, since the nature of the war seemed to confirm them. For the United States and the Soviet Union the fact of enemy aggression also helped to cement a sufficiently enduring consensus in support of the war effort. The second factor was the capacity of the states to supply the essentials of rationed food, welfare, and medical care, all of which were better managed in the Second World War than in the First. Indeed, understanding civilian needs and balancing those against the demands of the military was for most combatants a high priority. Finally, all governments carefully monitored popular opinion, imposed regimes of censorship, penalized rumour-mongers and dissenters, or, in the case of the dictatorships, or British imperial rule in India, insisted on harsh police terror against any open manifestation of anti-war sentiment or activity. The exception was Italy before September 1943, where the Fascist state failed in all three of these cases: it proved difficult to persuade the majority of the Italian people that the war really was a struggle for national survival; the supply of food and consumer resources was poorly managed (by 1943 agricultural output was only 74 per cent of the level in 1938 and average per capita food consumption down by more than a fifth); and the capacity of the state to stifle all dissent broke down under the influence of a string of military disasters and the onset of heavy bombing.

The experience of civilians in the wartime occupied territories was very different. The populations under German or Italian or Japanese rule faced extreme choices as a result of conquest, which most of them experienced for years on end. The options were stark, since the occupiers had no hesitation in applying a level of terror in the zones of occupation quite distinct from the efforts to quell any signs of domestic dissent. There has long been a tendency to divide the occupied populations into two opposing camps, those who collaborated and those who resisted. The reality was far more complex. Millions of those brought under alien rule tried to cope with the fact by focusing on their own survival and doing as little as possible either to assist or to obstruct the new authorities. Those who inhabited the grey zone between the two extremes sometimes engaged in small acts of concealment or disobedience and sometimes found themselves compelled to collaborate, not necessarily from any sense of sympathy but as a means to earn a living or to avoid penalty. Local officials everywhere found themselves caught between the occupiers, who insisted on compliance, and the local population, who resented the terms of occupation. A minority collaborated freely, whether Chinese warlords hoping for advancement under Japanese tutelage, or philo-Fascists who hoped to profit politically or financially from their collaboration, or tens of thousands of women who crossed the permeable lines between occupied and occupier. Almost all of these groups paid a penalty, often with their lives, when the occupation was over.

If the pattern of collaboration or passive acceptance was complex, so too was the pattern of active resistance—a mosaic of differing groups and sentiments, united by hostility to occupation, but certainly not united in any other sense. After the war, it was not uncommon for people to claim that they had always been a resister, since it suited the new post-war political realities. But the range of resistance activities was very wide, from fighting in regular paramilitary units to hiding Jewish refugees or faking papers, and the pattern of resistance changed over time, becoming more widespread and effective as the prospects for liberation became brighter. Resistance was also crucially dependent on the capacity of the Allied powers to provide support, in the form of money or guns or equipment, so that the wider military contest became blurred with the campaigns fought by civilians for their own liberation, a situation that generated its own problems as the Allies brought their political priorities to bear on the relationship with the resisters. The pattern of resistance in Yugoslavia, for example, or in France, was shaped to a considerable extent by the decision in the West to support Tito rather than the *chetnik* leader, Draža Mihailović, and Charles de Gaulle rather than General Henri Giraud. In Poland, armed resistance was stamped out by the Germans during the Warsaw Uprising in autumn 1944 because the Soviet Union preferred the Communist Poles based in Moscow to the nationalists in the *Armia Krajowa* (Polish Home Army), and failed to assist the rebellion.

The most conspicuous resistance movements were those that actually fought the occupying power in pitched battle. These included the partisan brigades in the Soviet Union operating behind German lines, the Polish Home Army which organized in 1944 for a military showdown with the German occupation, and the rival partisan movements in Yugoslavia, one nationalist-monarchist, one Communist. Each of these movements included an important number of former soldiers or, in the Soviet case, large pockets of stragglers or deserters who ended up on the wrong side of the front line. But many of the partisan fighters were civilians, including contingents of women and children, who joined the fight rather than face forced labour or starvation in the occupied zones as a result of German policies. The Soviet partisans were made up of isolated groups, poorly armed and equipped at first, many of them living a bandit-like existence as they tried to steal food from the local peasantry to survive, avoiding if they could confrontations with the ruthless German anti-partisan movement, organized by the SS General Erich von dem Bach-Zelewski. Once Soviet resistance stiffened, the Soviet government began to organize the partisans as effective military units under a Central Staff for Partisan Warfare, headed by the Belorussian Communist Party secretary, Panteleymon Ponomarenko. Red Army officers, security agents, and Party commissars were infiltrated into the German rear areas to try to impose some kind of order on the partisans. Numbers grew rapidly as German atrocities stoked up anti-German hatred; scorched earth policies and the murder of the Jews brought Jewish recruits and a

Children were mobilized for the Soviet partisan effort behind German lines. Here an 11-year-old boy delivers hay to local guerrilla fighters.

rootless peasantry, many now cut off from their land. The partisan resisters faced a dangerous environment. They were regularly betrayed by local people anxious to avoid accusations of collaboration with terrorism; they were short of weapons and medical equipment; they were tortured and murdered if caught; and they had to be aware all the time that their activity was watched carefully from Moscow. Their exact number may never be known, but by 1943 it was claimed that there were 300,000 partisans, a mix of military experts, Party organizers, and civilian militia that remained a permanent thorn in the German side.

The Polish Home Army was an organization of a different kind, an underworld movement that gave priority to recruiting loyal cells of resisters, supplying them with equipment and avoiding skirmishes with the German security forces as far as possible. In February 1942 the main resistance movement chose the title of the Home Army, under the command of General Stefan Rowecki. He was betrayed to the Gestapo in June 1943 and his place taken by General Tadeusz Bór-Komorowski. Throughout the middle years of the war the Home Army waged a sullen, twilight contest against rival partisan groups with a different agenda. Polish Nationalists, the Polish People's Army, the National Radical Camp, and a number of other Polish organizations sometimes worked alongside the Home Army, sometimes not, but Soviet and Ukrainian partisans were generally hostile. The Home Army was a mix of former soldiers and predominantly young Polish men and women civilians. It was led by Polish partisans trained in Britain and parachuted onto Polish soil, a total of a little more than 300 in all. The Home Army leaders prepared for a final uprising and so rationed their anti-German activities, until in January 1944 they launched Operation Burza to support the approaching Red Army. But when the Russians arrived in eastern Poland, the Polish partisan units there were broken up and their members arrested, because they were deemed to be a threat to a future Communist Poland. Those that remained in western Poland now looked for an opportunity to liberate the rest of the country before the Red Army could arrive. German resistance appeared to be crumbling, and despite arguments among the Polish leaders, Bór-Komorowski fixed the date for an armed uprising in Warsaw of 1 August 1944. There were some 50,000 Home Army fighters in Warsaw, but probably no more than 8,000 of them were adequately armed. The uprising was supported by civilians in the city who built barricades, commandeered vehicles, dug trenches, and appointed civilian guards. The outcome was a long and ferocious battle for the capital in which up to 200,000 civilians lost their lives in one of the grimmest bloodbaths of the war. On 2 October the battle was over and 16,300 of the surviving resisters surrendered to Bach-Zelewski, among them 3,000 women. Around 17,000 were killed or presumed dead.

The defeat and destruction of the Home Army illustrates the extent to which successful resistance depended on the course of the war and the policy of the Allies. In western and southern Europe resistance was organized on a smaller scale and with less of the trappings of military organization, but the resistance communities understood that they were working towards liberation at some point alongside the Western Allies. In Denmark and Norway, resistance was confined to small cells of activists who engaged in terrorist activities against German installations and communications, but

A group of wounded Polish resistance fighters from the Polish Home Army after the abortive Warsaw uprising against the German army and SS. Unusually, they were allowed POW status, but hundreds of thousands of Polish civilians perished in the rising.

were never intended to engage the German army in open battle. In France resistance was eventually widespread, but in the early years of occupation it was divided both regionally and ideologically and small in scale. Between June 1940 and November 1942 only the northern and western half of France was occupied (though the nominally independent rump Vichy state collaborated with the Germans in combating resistance groups based on its territory). Following German occupation of the whole of France the resistance network became more genuinely national. French resistance had begun at once in 1940, but it relied on the initiative of isolated civilian groups who had no common organization and diverse visions of what a post-war France might look like. There was nothing to match the quasi-military organization in Poland or the Soviet Union. Most of the civilian population accepted the reality of their sudden powerlessness. 'All they can think about', complained a French teacher and *résistant* in 1944, 'is "getting through" without coming to harm.'

The early movements, Combat, Libération-Sud, and Francs-Tireurs et Partisans, were based in the south and focused their activity around the publication and dissemination of newspapers. In the north Défense de la France and Libération-Nord were more limited in what they could achieve and eschewed violent confrontation. Only the French Communists from summer 1941, following orders from Moscow, engaged in acts of sabotage against the Germans and acts of terror against collaborators and *vichyistes*, but they were distrusted by other resistance groups. Not until October

French resistance fighters fire at German snipers in Paris in August 1944 shortly before the liberation of the capital by Allied forces. For the French it was important that they were seen to liberate their cities through their own efforts.

1942, following the decision by the exiled Free French leader, General Charles de Gaulle, to set up a consolidated Armée Secrète, did the numerous non-Communist resistance groups begin to forge a common identity, helped by the realization that liberation was no longer just a distant dream. In June 1943, the resistance leader Jean Moulin brought these groups together in the National Council for Resistance, with close links to the Free French in London. Acts of anti-German violence increased across France, and during the course of the year armed groups, the Maquis, formed in the remote rural and mountainous areas of France, a mixture of Communist and nationalist units. They were made up of young men fleeing from the STO, or refugees from German persecution, and it took time before they assumed a more distinctly military character. For many it was more a means to hide away from the German and Vichy authorities. An estimated 11 per cent of all resisters were women. From late 1943 until liberation in summer 1944 the resistance coalesced into a broader-based movement to obstruct German military preparations and help the expected Allied landing, though divisions remained between Communists and non-Communists, and between those happy to accept de Gaulle's leadership and those not. Resistance paid a high cost. Some 90,000

Italian partisan fighters dressed in winter camouflage battle alongside the US 5th Army against the German occupiers in the mountains of central Italy.

resisters were killed or deported, and thousands were subjected to routine torture, women as well as men, most of them civilians.

The resistance movement in Italy was, if anything, even more complex. Anti-Fascist movements had already begun to organize in the spring of 1943 for the moment when Mussolini might be overthrown, so that the structure for a future resistance movement was already in place. The fall of Mussolini in July 1943, and the subsequent Italian surrender and occupation by German forces in September, created the conditions almost immediately for an armed resistance movement. Thousands of Italian soldiers escaped to the mountains to avoid deportation to Germany, where they were joined by political activists of the left and thousands more young Italians who refused to be drafted to fight for the Germans and the Italian Social Republic, the puppet regime set up under Mussolini in the area under German control. By spring 1944 two-thirds of those who were supposed to be conscripted evaded the draft; not all became partisans, but for many there was nowhere else to go. The resistance movements mirrored the revival of organized political parties set up to oppose what was left of Fascism in northern Italy. The Action Party 'Justice and Freedom' brigades fought for a radical democratic Italy; the Italian Communist Party's 'Garibaldi Brigades' fought to overthrow Fascism, but were divided in their political strategy between combining partisan activity with a genuine social revolution, or collaborating with more centrist allies; the Socialist Party disliked collaboration with the Communists and organized its own socialist brigades. In September 1943 the parties united in the National Committee for Liberation (CLN) in their struggle against Fascism and the German occupation, but there remained significant political differences dividing sections of the partisan movement. Resistance could also be quite spontaneous. In late September the civilian population of Naples threw up rough barricades, seized guns, and fought a brief and successful four-day campaign—the 'Quattro Giornate'—against the German garrison.

At its peak it has been estimated that there were 150,000 armed partisans in Italy, a fifth made up of 'Justice and Freedom' units, more than half composed of the Communist 'Garibaldi' brigades. They fought pitched battles with Fascist blackshirt militia and the German army, and engaged in regular acts of sabotage and assassination. Much of their activity was directed against other Italians, which gave the conflict, as it did in France against *vichyistes* collaborators, a civil war character. One of the problems facing resistance movements everywhere was the opposition experienced not just from the occupying enemy but from local communities or institutions which did not share the ideological aims of the resisters or who disliked their use of banditry and terror as instruments of resistance. Denunciation, the use of informers or *agents provocateurs*, bounties paid by the Germans for each dead partisan, and the uncertain assistance of the approaching Allies, all made resistance a risky venture. The regular use of mass collective reprisals by the Germans and their collaborators, including the mass murder of thousands of innocent villagers and townsmen, the killing of civilian hostages, the burning down of villages and farmsteads, had contrary effects. On the one hand atrocity encouraged survivors to join the partisans out of revenge; on the other, local communities often deplored the presence of partisans, or betrayed their whereabouts from fear that they might otherwise be the target of reprisals. Civilian resistance prompted all occupying armies, whether in the Soviet Union or Italy or China, to kill resisters out of hand and to terrorize other civilians into compliance.

With so much at stake, it was important for resistance groups to be able to demonstrate that they were capable of achieving something. This explains the failed effort to seize control of Warsaw, and it also explains the successful takeover of Paris by the Resistance a day or so before the Allied armies reached it in August 1944 and the determination of the Italian partisans to liberate the major cities of northern Italy—Genoa, Milan, Turin, Bologna—before the Allied armies in April 1945. 'We cannot and must not await our freedom from the Allies,' wrote the Italian Communist, Pietro Secchia. The partisans, he continued, could demonstrate that the civilian population 'fought to conquer their own independence and freedom'. It was almost entirely due to Tito's Yugoslav partisan army that large areas of Yugoslavia were liberated from German and Italian rule, while the partisan war in the Soviet Union contributed in a significant way to the defeat of German armies in Belorussia and Ukraine in 1944.

A Soviet woman partisan fighter. Thousands of women joined the guerrilla movement where they not only performed tasks routinely assigned to women, but also fought side-by-side with the men.

Conclusion

The civilian in the Second World War was never very far from a front line imposed by the total character of the conflict. 'There can be little doubt', wrote the British poet and civil defence volunteer, Stephen Spender, after the war, 'that in the minds of Governments as well as peoples the Second World War was labelled the "War of Civilians"'. Whether facing the threat of bombing or coping with the dilemmas of occupation or trying to survive under a weight of wartime regulations and shortages, civilians were faced on a daily basis with the reality of war. Pre-war expectations about total war prepared civilian populations for what they might face, and encouraged mass participation in their own protection and welfare. These expectations also made it easier for states engaged in war to win the co-operation of their populations for accepting sacrifices and running the risks, through civil defence in particular, that total war required of them. The involvement of civilians much more fully in the war effort made it easier to control dissent and enforce compliance, and gave civilians a greater sense that they were contributing as much to a future victory as the armed forces.

In the areas under occupation the role of civilians was very different. Here the existing state structures had failed or been replaced, giving civilians even more responsibility for ensuring their own future either by overturning the occupation, or by throwing in their lot with the occupying power in the hope of benefits from collaboration. Millions abdicated in the face of the dangers posed by the extremes of collaboration and resistance, and simply tried to survive in an increasingly chaotic and menacing world. In its sharpest form the tension between those who opposed and those who collaborated resulted in forms of violent civil war, linked with but distinct from the wider military conflict. By the end of the war there was nothing remarkable in seeing a young civilian man or woman in concocted battledress, carrying a rifle and cartridge belt, willing and able to kill both the enemy and local collaborators, whether in China, Yugoslavia, or Italy. The emergence of 'civilian wars' alongside the formal military conflict changed the character of modern warfare, encouraging greater savagery and intransigence wherever they surfaced.

11 Unnatural Deaths

RICHARD BESSEL

There were corpses on the road. A girl no more than seventeen, slim and pretty, lay on the damp earth, her lips blue with death: her eyes were open, and the rain fell on them. People chipped at bark, pounded it by the roadside for food; vendors sold leaves at a dollar a bundle. A dog digging at a mound was exposing a human body. Ghostlike men were skimming the stagnant pools to eat the green slime of the waters.

(Theodore H. White and Analee Jacoby,
Thunder out of China (New York, 1980), 169.)

This young woman had not met her death at the hands of a soldier; she had not died in a camp; her life did not end in the killing fields of eastern Europe. She starved in the great famine of 1943 in Honan, in north-central China—one of between 2 and 3 million people who perished there at the time. Of the 15–20 million Chinese who died of war-related causes in the Sino-Japanese war between 1937 and 1945, the vast majority were non-combatants: victims of starvation, lack of medicine, increased incidence of infectious diseases, forced labour. When thinking of those who died during the Second World War, we do not often remember people such as that young woman in Honan. Yet she too was a casualty of the Second World War.

The Toll of Military Campaigns

The Second World War led to more deaths than any other human-made event in recorded history. The crude calculus of military losses is well known, even if the numbers necessarily remain inexact. Estimates vary, but altogether (in Europe and Asia) something in the region of 22 million soldiers were either killed in action or died subsequently as a consequence of their injuries. However, the focus of this chapter is not on the casualties that resulted directly from military combat, but on the huge numbers of unnatural deaths that occurred outside the sphere of battle. In a recent consideration of deaths in military combat, Bethany Lacina and Nils Petter Gleditsch have observed:

The number of battle deaths…does not provide a remotely adequate account of the true human costs of conflict. War kills people in less direct (but highly predictable) ways, especially when it causes the collapse of a society's economy, infrastructure of health and human services, and public safety systems…. the toll of war is comprised of not only battle deaths

A victim of the famine in Honan, central China, in 1942.

but deaths due to upsurges in one-sided-violence (e.g. the execution of prisoners of war or a genocidal campaign such as the Holocaust or the Armenian genocide); increases in criminal violence (e.g. an upsurge in crime following the collapse of local policing); increases in unorganized violence (e.g. deadly food riots); and increases in non-violent causes of mortality such as disease and starvation.

As Lacina and Gleditsch note, 'tallying the cost of war quickly defies straightforward accounting'. This is a consequence not simply of the scale of death in war or of its complex and varied nature, but also of the difficulty of attributing some deaths to single, clear-cut causes. Where the extent of 'natural deaths' ends and that of 'unnat-ural deaths' in wartime begins cannot be determined with precision. The best one can hope for is an approximation, a general picture of the deadly consequences of the greatest bloodletting that the world has ever seen: the Second World War.

In contrast to what had happened during the First World War, when civilians comprised at most just over one-third of the dead, during the Second World War at least two-thirds of the victims were civilians. The ratio of civilian to military deaths during the Second World War reflects the wartime campaigns of mass murder committed by warring states, the wanton slaughter of civilians from Serbia and the Soviet Union to China and the Philippines that so disfigured the history of the twentieth century. It also reflects the fact that, unlike in previous wars, death and destruction could be delivered on a massive scale far from the front, for example by bombing, which claimed roughly 600,000 lives in Europe alone during the Second

World War. In Japan, more than 240,000 people were killed and another 313,000 injured as a consequence of American bombing in 1945 even before the atomic bombs were dropped on Hiroshima and Nagasaki. Yet the toll of human life caused by the Second World War extends well beyond those killed deliberately.

The millions of non-combatants who met their deaths in the course of the Second World War succumbed in many different ways, and the campaigns of mass murder carried out in German-occupied Europe in particular form only part of the dreadful catalogue of unnatural deaths during the conflict. It also included huge numbers of people who perished as a result of revenge killings, the forced removal of millions of people, disease, and malnutrition and famine. Of course, these causes of death were not new; they were hardly unique to the Second World War. There had been famine in war before the Second World War and civilians had been slaughtered during earlier conflicts; disease had been a constant companion of soldiers in war; and while the term 'genocide' is new, the phenomenon is not. What made the history of unnatural deaths during the Second World War unique was the combination of the intensity and the extensive nature of the violence that caused them, and the degree to which the deaths were brought about by the actions of states and regimes. Not least, the nature of the war, in particular the extreme levels of violence in the 'war of annihilation' fought on the European Eastern Front and the uncompromising nature of the Japanese conduct of their war, fuelled the disregard for civilized values that led to the deaths of tens of millions of people beyond the direct casualties of battle.

While the total numbers of people who died as a result of the Second World War are vast, the rhythms of death and destruction were far from uniform across time and place. Denmark lost just over 3,000 people during the Second World War, while Lithuania (whose population had been less than two-thirds that of Denmark before the war) lost some 380,000 (including 135,000 Jews). During the first two years of war military casualties in Europe were relatively light (relative, at least, to what came afterwards), the worst of the bombing campaigns still lay in the future, and the systematic mass murder of Europe's Jewish population had only begun. In fact, between September 1939 and December 1941, Europe's population actually increased. In Asia, however, war had been raging between China and Japan since 1937 and had claimed the lives of huge numbers of Chinese civilians, but it was not until the last year of the war that the Japanese civilian population faced death on a massive scale as a result of the American saturation bombing.

When it came, that bombing took a terrible toll. Hundreds of thousands of people were burned to death, crushed in collapsing buildings, or asphyxiated as a consequence. We remain acutely aware of the devastation caused by the atomic bombs dropped on Hiroshima and Nagasaki in August 1945. Yet the loss of life from the conventional attack on Tokyo on the night of 9–10 March 1945 was far greater than that resulting from the atomic bomb in Nagasaki and roughly three times as great as that caused by the fire-bombing of Hamburg in July 1943. American aircraft dropped incendiary bombs on the Japanese capital (where houses were made predominantly of wood) and destroyed 16 square miles of the city, killed between 80,000 and 100,000 people, and made over a million homeless; the victims were, in the words of Major General Curtis LeMay, who masterminded the attack, 'scorched and boiled and baked to death' in what John Dower has described as 'the largest urban conflagration in recorded history'. Altogether, perhaps as many 400,000 people were killed in Japan as a result of bombing by the US army air force.

The death toll from the Allied bombing in Germany probably nearly matched that in Japan, although the campaign had extended over a longer period (while the American bombing of Japan did not begin in earnest until the autumn of 1944). Altogether more than 350,000 people were killed in Germany and Austria as a result. The bombing left mutilated bodies, body parts, burnt and shredded human remains. Disposal of the remains became an increasingly difficult problem, and in the most extreme cases was achieved by burning the masses of bodies—as in Dresden in February 1945, where corpses were stacked on a metal grate in the Altmarkt in the old city, petrol was poured over them and set alight, and the resulting ashes were buried in a communal grave. Yet while the Allied bombing campaigns against Germany and Japan dwarfed air attacks elsewhere, these were far from the only countries

An aerial view of the devastation after repeated incendiary bomb attacks on the city of Tokyo by American B-29 bombers.

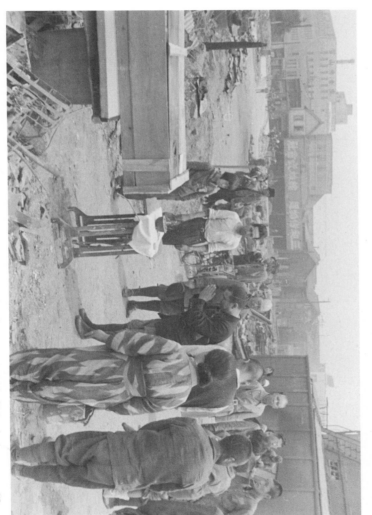

An outdoor funeral ceremony in Shitamachi section of Tokyo after the great air raid of March 9–10 1945. Note that the coffin is made of scraps of wood.

Street scene in Tokyo after the fire bombing of the city in March 1945.

to suffer substantial numbers of civilian deaths due to aerial attack. Already in September 1939 the Luftwaffe bombed Warsaw; in May 1940 German bombers attacked Rotterdam; and in April 1941 the Luftwaffe bombed Belgrade with severe loss of life. Roughly 60,000 people were killed in Britain altogether in waves of German aerial attacks: during the late summer and autumn of 1940 numerous British cities were bombed (London was bombed repeatedly); between April and June 1942 German aircraft attacked a number of English cathedral cities (the so-called 'Baedecker Raids', in retaliation for the British bombing of Lübeck); and during the second half of 1944 and the early months of 1945 the Germans launched their V1 flying bombs and V2 rockets against Britain. Both Italy and France suffered heavy bombing by Allied air forces, leading to over 54,000 civilian dead in France and an estimated 80,000 dead in Italy. In Asia, the Japanese air force attacked Nationalist-held Chinese cities—most notably Chongqing, which was bombed 268 times between 1939 and 1941, leading to the deaths of many thousands of people.

The victims of a stampede caused by a panic during a Japanese air raid lie on a flight of stairs in Chongqing, 5 June 1941.

Mass Murder

Even more so than the bombing of civilians, the campaigns of genocide during the early 1940s occupy a prominent place in the catalogue of death during the Second World War. The assault on the Jewish population of Europe constituted neither the first time nor the last that an attempt has been made to wipe a group of people from the face of the earth; however, the dimensions, the intensity, and the systematic nature of the crime, the use of 'modern' means of mass murder, and the obsessive determination to finish the job set it apart. Contrary to the generally accepted image of the murder of the Jews in German-occupied Europe, probably fewer than half of the Jewish victims met their deaths in concentration and extermination camps. In fact, almost two-fifths of those murdered died in mass shootings—murdered by mobile killing squads and police units charged with exterminating the Jewish population of countless towns and villages across Eastern Europe; yet more perished as a consequence of disease and maltreatment in ghettos and forced-labour camps, or while on the death marches that took place as the concentration-camp empire crumbled during the last months of the war. (In January 1945 the Nazi concentration camps held 714,211 prisoners, of whom about 200,000 were Jews; of that total, between 200,000 and 350,000 died during the winter and early spring of 1945.)

A death march of concentration-camp prisoners near Landsberg in Bavaria, heading for Dachau, in late April 1945.

Mass killing began soon after the outbreak of war. Within weeks of the German attack on Poland, SS units were carrying out massacres of the civilian population. (The first complete extermination of a Jewish community occurred in Ostrów Mazowiecka, a Polish district town north-east of Warsaw, where on 11 November 1939 German police killed 364 people—156 men and 208 women and children.) While the numbers were still relatively small compared with what came later, the launch of the Second World War provided the catalyst for mass murder. After the military campaign in Poland ended with German victory, Jews who attempted to cross the demarcation line with Soviet-occupied Poland were shot; German 'self-defence' (*Selbstschutz*) organizations, under the command of police *Einsatzgruppen*, murdered between 20,000 and 30,000 Poles during the autumn of 1939, and (as the German army commander in Posen noted in November) public shootings were carried out by SS formations 'in almost all larger towns'.

Although there is not space to examine in detail the murder of Europe's Jewish population, the deportation of German Jews from Württemberg, in south-western Germany, at the beginning of December 1941 offers a glimpse into the fate of the millions of Jews who died or were killed during the conflict. While Jews in neighbouring Baden had been deported to a camp at Gurs, at the western edge of the Pyrenees, in October 1940, in Württemberg they were initially allowed to remain in their homes. That lasted until the second half of November 1941, when the Gestapo Office in Stuttgart informed police and local-government authorities in the surrounding region of the forthcoming 'Removal of Jews to the Reichskommissariat Ostland', and Jewish communities throughout the region were then told of their imminent 'evacuation'. Jews from 60 different towns and villages were gathered in late November at a 'collection point' on the site of the 1939 Reich Garden Exhibition in Stuttgart; then, on 1 December 1941, a train with 1,013 Jews from Württemberg left Stuttgart for Riga. There it arrived three days later at a goods railway station, from which the human cargo was marched to an improvised camp just set up on a former farm along the Daugava River, a few kilometres outside the Latvian capital. By the time the camp was dismantled at the end of March 1942, the Jews from that transport were dead: perhaps a quarter succumbed to maltreatment, hunger, cold, and disease in the camp; the remainder who were still alive were taken at the end of March to the Bikernieki Forest on the eastern edge of Riga, where they were shot and dumped in mass graves.

These killings in Riga coincided with the great wave of mass murder that claimed the lives of the vast majority of Europe's Jewish population. In the wake of the German invasion of the Soviet Union in June 1941, sporadic outbursts of murder came to be replaced by systematic killing—the deliberate, organized campaign to exterminate the entire European Jewish population. In an oft-quoted observation, Christopher Browning has noted: 'In mid-March 1942 some 75 to 80 percent of all victims of the Holocaust were still alive, while 20 to 25 percent had perished. A mere eleven months later, in mid-February 1943, the percentages were exactly the reverse.' The shooting campaigns of the *Einsatzgruppen* of the Security Police and Security Service in the USSR, the killings committed by police battalions and their auxiliaries in

German Jews from various towns in Württemberg, assembled in an exhibition hall on the Killesberg in Stuttgart in November 1941, just before they were transported to their deaths in Riga in Latvia.

occupied Poland and elsewhere, the deadly conditions in the ghettos created by the German occupiers in Eastern Europe, and the gas chambers of the extermination camps comprised a campaign of racially-inspired mass murder on a scale that hitherto could scarcely have been imagined and that claimed nearly 6 million victims.

The outbreak of war also provided the catalyst for the Nazis' 'euthanasia' campaign—the destruction of 'life unworthy of life'. Soon after German forces invaded Poland the systematic killing of people in psychiatric institutions began in the *Reichsgaue* of 'Wartheland' and Danzig-West Prussia: between September 1939 and the spring of 1940 more than 10,000 mentally handicapped people—including many who had been shipped into occupied Poland from institutions in Pomerania—were murdered. Within Germany constraints to murder were also lifted: a few weeks after the outbreak of war, Hitler's enabling letter—backdated to 1 September, the day on which war had been declared—launched the 'T4-Action' (after the street address of the office involved: Tiergartenstraße 4 in Berlin); as a result, roughly 70,000 patients in psychiatric institutions were murdered over the next two years. (Although Hitler called an official end to the campaign on 24 August 1941, following protests from the Catholic Church, the killing continued. Altogether over 100,000 psychiatric patients, mentally and physically handicapped people were killed.)

The assault on the Jewish population of Europe and the campaign to rid Germany of 'life unworthy of life' form only a part of the history of the mass murder of civilian populations during the Second World War. Tens of thousands of Sinti and Roma (Gypsies) were also killed. Of the roughly 38,000 Sinti and Roma who had been in Germany and Austria, 20,000 were sent to Auschwitz, where they met their deaths, and another 5,000 deported to Łódź and then murdered in mobile gas vans at Chelmno; only about 13,000–14,000 survived the war. In German-occupied Europe possibly more than 100,000 Roma were killed, primarily in eastern and southern Europe—some in mass shootings, some in Nazi concentration camps. Huge numbers of civilians also met their deaths across Nazi-occupied regions of the Soviet Union in the course of campaigns against (and by) partisans, as a result of punitive policies towards civilian populations, and due to the catastrophic effects of the war and occupation on food supplies. Perhaps most extreme was what occurred in Belarus, described by an American journalist in 1946 as 'the most devastated territory in the world'. There, according to calculations by Christian Gerlach, between 1.6 and 1.7 million people were murdered once the territory fell under German rule—roughly 700,000 prisoners of war, something over half a million Jews, 345,000 people killed in the course of the campaigns against partisans, and about 100,000 others—almost one-fifth of the 9 million people who had been in the territory when German forces arrived in 1941. German occupation in Ukraine also led to massacres, deportations, and brutal campaigns against partisans, and left mountains of corpses in its wake. Nor did the killing occur exclusively in Eastern Europe. During the last two years of the war, after the overthrow of Mussolini in July 1943, the German forces that occupied the northern half of the country committed numerous massacres, resulting in the deaths of more than 9,000 Italian civilians. (More than 11,000 Italian service personnel inside and outside Italy also were killed by the Germans.) And in occupied Greece, reprisals and 'mopping-up operations' in the fighting against partisans led to over 20,000 civilians being shot, hanged, beaten, or burned by Wehrmacht troops in 1943 and 1944. What this meant on the ground was described years later by Alexandros Mallios, a survivor from Komeno, a village in western Greece, where 317 inhabitants died when the Wehrmacht raided it in August 1943:

I was probably the first person to enter the village when the Germans left. All the houses that I passed were burnt. I heard the crackling of the corn burning and thought at first the Germans were still shooting. I did not realise at first what it was. I took another path through the village, but everywhere I looked the houses had been burnt. I saw no one alive. There were many bodies in the street; men, women and children, and most of the bodies appeared to be burnt. I saw one old woman, who apparently burnt to death in a sitting position. The houses were burning as I walked through.

(Quoted in Mark Mazower, *Inside Hitler's Greece*, 195.)

Mallios then continued to his own house, where he found the bodies of his family lying on the road outside.

By no means all the atrocities were committed by Germans. Across war-torn Europe people of various ethnic origins took part in the explosion of deadly violence. In Croatia the Ustaša and its supporters began the killing of thousands of Serbs, Jews, and Roma in ethnically-mixed towns and regions within weeks of the proclamation of their Independent State of Croatia in April 1941, killings that continued in the concentration camps of the Ustaša state. Altogether it has been estimated that 'ethnic cleansing', resistance, and resulting civil war led to the violent deaths of more than 500,000 people in the territory of the Independent State of Croatia between 1941 and 1945. The campaigns of the Ustaša to 'cleanse' their state of Serbs, Muslims, and Jews were described by one Wehrmacht officer as being 'in defiance of all the laws of civilization. The Ustaša murder, without exception, men, women, and children.' In France, when the SS Division 'Das Reich' murdered over 600 inhabitants of the village of Oradour-sur-Glane in the Limousin in June 1944, a substantial proportion—roughly one-third—of the perpetrators were Alsatian. In the occupied Soviet Union, partisans were scarcely less brutal in their treatment of the civilian population than were the occupation forces they opposed, and the Soviet state and Red Army vigorously pursued deserters and enemies, real or imagined, behind the lines.

In Asia too the massacre of civilians was a feature of war. From their invasion of China in 1937, Japanese troops habitually slaughtered Chinese civilians. Perhaps the best-known instance, which assumed iconic status in China, is the massacre that took place in Nanjing (often referred to as 'The Rape of Nanking') during the six weeks after the city fell to Japanese forces on 12 December 1937. Although there is controversy about the total number of victims and although the official Chinese estimate of 300,000 killed is an overestimate, what actually happened after the Japanese arrived was awful enough; tens of thousands of Chinese men were killed and countless women raped and then murdered. (Jean-Louis Margolin has offered more sober estimates, of between 20,000 and 30,000 civilians and between 50,000 and 90,000 military personnel killed.) Nanjing was exceptional not so much for the behaviour of Japanese forces as for the notoriety that the massacre achieved. In their attempt to combat Communist-led partisan warfare in northern China, Japanese forces embarked on a programme of 'rural pacification', a campaign that (in the words of John Dower) 'amounted to indiscriminate terror against the peasantry' and that by 1941–2 had hardened to become the 'three-all' policy: 'kill all, burn all, destroy all' (a policy that paralleled what German occupation forces were doing in Belarus). The precise number of the people who fell victim to the Japanese 'pacification' campaign will never be known, but it has been estimated that in the areas of northern China where Communist forces were active the population fell from 44 million to 25 million, as a result of flight and death.

Such conduct on the part of the Japanese was not limited to China. In the wake of the British surrender in Singapore in February 1942, the Japanese summarily executed at least 5,000 overseas Chinese in the island city—beheading them, drowning them,

A few of the roughly 70,000 American and Filipino soldiers captured by the Japanese at Bataan in April 1942 and forced to march from the southern tip of the Bataan Peninsula on Manila Bay to a prison camp at San Fernando. Over 2,500, the vast majority Filipino, did not survive the six-day march.

machine-gunning or bayoneting them; hundreds of American and Filipino prisoners were bayoneted by their Japanese captors on the infamous Bataan Death March in April 1942; and about 100 Dutch civilians were killed in early 1942 in reprisal for the destruction of oil fields. The sacking of Manila, where probably more than 100,000 people were killed in the final days of Japanese occupation as the American were poised to take the city in February 1945, claimed more lives than did the 'The Rape of Nanking' (see Chapter 2).

Workers, Prisoners, and Civilians

In addition to those who died as a result of deliberate campaigns to kill, huge numbers of people fell victim to what might be termed the collateral damage of callous treatment and denial of considerations that might have preserved life. A prime example is the high mortality among those forced to work in Nazi Germany particularly during the last two years of the war—a consequence of harsh treatment, poor housing, and poor working conditions. It has been estimated that mortality rates among civilian labourers from Eastern Europe and among Italian prisoners of war were between six and seven times those of German workers. Altogether, nearly half a million civilian foreign labourers died while working in the Nazi war economy between 1939 and 1945. When prisoners of war and concentration-camp inmates (including Jews) compelled to work are included in the figures, of the roughly 13.5 million foreigners who worked in the German economy (within the borders of the 'Greater German Reich', i.e. within the German borders of 1942) approximately 2.5 million did not survive the war. No doubt some of them would have died anyway even had the environment in which they lived been decent, but the majority of the deaths were clearly due to the conditions that prisoners and labourers had to endure. However, the precise number of deaths attributable to malnourishment and disease, both of which vastly increased directly or indirectly as a result of the war, is impossible to determine.

In the Far East, while the total numbers were not so large, many tens of thousands of foreign labourers working for the Japanese also died. An estimated 60,000 of the nearly 670,000 Korean workers brought to Japan between 1939 and 1945 to labour in often harsh conditions did not survive the war; roughly 10,000 of the nearly 42,000 Chinese men assembled to work in Japan between 1943 and 1945 perished, many before leaving China or on the boats carrying them to Japan; of the 300,000 foreign labourers drafted to build the Burma–Siam railway in jungle conditions between October 1942 and November 1943, roughly 60,000 did not survive; and the Japanese also scoured Indonesian villages for labourers, tens of thousands of whom died.

Even worse than the fate of foreign labourers during the Second World War was that of prisoners of war, huge numbers of whom did not survive their captivity. Of course, some POWs probably would have died in any event of natural causes during the time they were imprisoned; and during the First World War many prisoners died in captivity due to ill health and poor conditions. However, the high mortality rates among some groups of prisoners and the numbers involved were something quantitatively and qualitatively new. Dreadful conditions in prisoner-of-war camps, and deliberate policies of neglect and worse, led to the deaths of hundreds of thousands. The largest single group of prisoners to die in captivity were Soviet soldiers who fell into German hands. Altogether, of the 5.7 million Soviet prisoners taken by the Germans during the war, 3.3 million died (roughly 2.8 million of whom died between the beginning of the German onslaught in June 1941 and January 1942), as a consequence of exposure, disease, starvation, and execution; as one German corporal, who served in a prisoner-of-war camp, observed in November 1941, what occurred there was 'more murder than war'.

Soviet prisoners were not the only group of captured soldiers who died in German hands. Between 1,500 and 3,000 African soldiers in French service were murdered after they had been taken prisoner during the 1940 campaign in France. After the collapse of Mussolini's regime and after the government of Pietro Badoglio declared war on Germany in October 1943, Italian prisoners in German captivity suffered high death rates. Soldiers surrendering to the Allies could not necessarily be assured of good treatment either, and some were shot rather than taken prisoner. In his memoir *Doing Battle*, Paul Fussell described how his US Army platoon dealt with surrendering German soldiers after a particularly terrible bout of combat:

Most of them now wanted to surrender, and as we shouted, 'Kommen Sie heraus, Hände hoch!' they dragged themselves out, weeping and hoping not to be killed in anger. Many were. Now and then one of our men, annoyed at too much German delay in vacating a position, would throw in a live grenade, saying things like 'Here. Divide that among you.'

(Paul Fussell, *Doing Battle: The Making of a Sceptic* (Boston, 1996), 7.)

However, the overwhelming majority of the approximately 460,000 German soldiers who died in captivity, roughly 360,000, were among the 3.3 million who had been taken prisoner by Soviet forces (most of them at the end of the war) and sent to labour camps.

In the Far East the record was not much better. In their campaigns in China, the Japanese did not necessarily take prisoners. However, the fate of Western soldiers who fell into Japanese hands is well documented: of the soldiers from Western countries captured by the Japanese (including some 50,000 British, 37,000 Dutch, 22,000 Australians and about the same number of Americans, 1,700 Canadians, and a few hundred New Zealanders), nearly 36,000 did not survive their captivity; mortality rates were 34 per cent among the Australians, 25 per cent among the British, and 23 per cent among the Dutch.

It no doubt was inevitable that the violence, cruelty, wanton destruction, and murder that characterized combat and occupation during the Second World War would give rise to deadly acts of revenge when the opportunity presented itself. Perhaps most notorious was the violence committed by Soviet troops against civilians once they crossed onto German territory in late 1944 and 1945. When Soviet soldiers first arrived in the Reich, in East Prussia in October 1944, their commander reminded them of their 'holy oath to avenge themselves against the enemy for all the atrocities committed on Soviet soil'. And 'avenge themselves' they did. The Red Army's final assault on Nazi Germany was accompanied by an orgy of arson, rape, and murder. As a Catholic priest in Görlitz mused after Soviet troops arrived in that city in May 1945, 'Now it's our turn to pay the bill.' It was not only Soviet soldiers who took the opportunity for revenge. Labourers who had been compelled to work in Germany and were free in 1945 often turned on their erstwhile masters; liberated concentration-camp inmates murdered their former guards, sometimes with the assistance of the Allied troops who had freed them; Poles and Czechs took their revenge on Germans in what had been eastern Germany and the Sudetenland. For millions of people the Second World War did not end abruptly with the surrender of the Axis powers, and violence stemming from that war rumbled on long after the formal end of hostilities.

This was particularly true for the huge numbers of people uprooted at the end of the war, the largest group of whom were Germans who fled or were expelled from the east. Altogether, something approaching 12 million Germans were displaced from what had been their homes in the former Prussian provinces east of the new Oder–Neiße border, from Czechoslovakia (primarily from the 'Sudetenland'), from pre-1939 Poland, Hungary, Yugoslavia, Romania, and the Baltic. This comprised perhaps the largest forced removal of human beings in history. Although in their eagerness to emphasize the suffering of the German people the West German government in the 1950s overestimated the numbers of deaths that resulted, the actual losses of about 500,000 were substantial enough: people who froze to death while attempting to flee in the winter of 1945, who died in camps established by Soviet forces and Polish authorities, or who succumbed to malnutrition and disease in regions being cleared of the German population. One doctor estimated that of the roughly 100,000 people remaining in the East Prussian capital of Königsberg when German forces capitulated there in April 1945, nearly three-quarters had died as a result of disease and malnutrition by the spring of 1947. The removal of Germans was only part of the story—and followed on from the brutal campaigns of forced removal that had been undertaken by German occupation forces during the war. Other groups of people, who had the misfortune to find themselves on the wrong side of new borders, also faced brutal expulsion in the wake of the war—most notably the 2.1 million Poles transferred from what had been eastern Poland (and from places of deportation in Siberia and central Asia) to settle in the ruins of what had been eastern Germany.

Hunger, Disease, and Suicide

The hunger suffered by Germans in the east is but one aspect of a larger theme of death by starvation in the Second World War. As the scene described at the beginning of this chapter suggests, famine affected many people during the war. Of course, famine was hardly a new phenomenon. However, during the early 1940s the conditions of war and problems caused by war—disruption to transport links, markets, and world trade, rapidly rising food prices, lack of fertilizer, and the diversion of food resources from the civilian population to the military—exacerbated natural disasters and led to food emergencies in various corners of the world that cost millions of people their lives. Famine was not just some fortuitous event; in some instances it was deliberately brought about—'war by another means', deliberately employed to kill large numbers of people.

Perhaps the most terrible example of man-made famine was that caused by the German blockade of Leningrad, one of the longest and almost certainly the most deadly siege in recorded history. From 8 September 1941 until 27 January 1944, the city was largely cut off from supply—a modern-day siege that lasted 871 days. Cannibalism became rife as the city's population faced starvation (in addition to the effects of constant shelling and bombing). Social norms disintegrated as Leningraders were confronted with terrible choices—such as that faced by a mother who in November 1941 suffocated her infant daughter in order to feed her other children. Altogether, at least 700,000 people (many estimate the figure at one million) perished during the siege of Leningrad—653,000 during the first eleven months. By the time the siege was lifted completely in January 1944, only 557,000 of the 2,489,000 inhabitants registered in the city in September 1941 were left. (Some three-quarters of a million had been evacuated, though many of these also died.) Leningrad was not the

A woman pulls the corpse of a child on a sledge during the siege of Leningrad. During the siege this became a common means of carrying the dead to places where they could be buried.

only city in the German-occupied territories of the Soviet Union that became the object of a deliberate policy of starvation; the Ukrainian capital of Kiev too suffered famine engineered by the German occupiers, leading to many thousands of deaths. (Although they did not engage in anything comparable to the horrific German actions in Eastern Europe, the Allies were not completely innocent of such calculations: when, beginning in late March 1945, the US army air force mounted a massive aerial campaign to place mines in Japan's ports and water routes, it was given the code-name 'Operation Starvation'.)

More generally, the early 1940s were a time of famine in numerous corners of the world—in Greece between 1941 and 1943 (where, according to Red Cross estimates, roughly 250,000 people died either directly or indirectly as a consequence of the famine), in the Netherlands during the Dutch 'hunger winter' of 1944–5, in East Africa, in Vietnam (Tonkin), in China (Honan), and, perhaps worst of all, in Bengal, in British India, in 1943. It has been estimated that 7.5 million people died of starvation and related diseases in China, India, and Vietnam during the second half of the Second World War. The excess mortality due to the famine in Bengal alone was probably more than 3 million, a famine described by Archibald Wavell, who was appointed Governor General and Viceroy of India in 1943, as 'one of the greatest

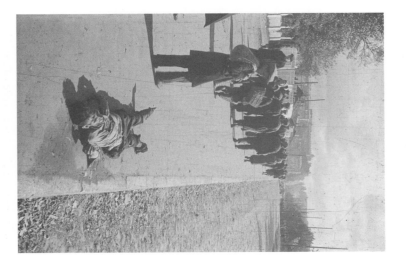

Jews marching on their way out of the city of Kiev to the Babi Yar ravine to be murdered pass corpses lying on the street.

disasters that has befallen any people under British rule'. While there had been earlier harvest failures in Bengal, in 1939 and 1941, these had not resulted in famine; however, wartime priorities of the British colonial administration disrupted food markets, delayed a public proclamation of famine, and effectively deprived millions of the food they needed to survive. This disaster was man-made; as Cormac Ó Gráda has observed, 'Mars played a much bigger role than Malthus.'

Those who died in the famines of the 1940s were victims not just of the misguided, incompetent, or wilful policies of regimes concerned more with fighting a war than with safeguarding the welfare of civilians; they were also victims of economic conditions caused by war, in particular inflation (in the case of China in 1943, hyperinflation) leading to soaring grain prices that put basic foodstuffs beyond the reach of vulnerable social groups. These famines may not all have been direct consequence of deliberate policy or military action, but they were hardly unrelated to the conditions created by war. The Second World War indirectly (through the economic imbalances) as well as directly (through deliberate state policies) led to the deaths of millions of people through starvation.

Death from hunger is, obviously, closely related to death from disease, not least because the widespread malnutrition that accompanied the Second World War in both Europe and Asia left those affected more susceptible to illness. In early 1941

Clara Councell, a Junior Statistician with the United States Public Health Service, observed:

The waging of war has always been attended by increases in the prevalence of disease. The rapid and extensive spread of infection is to be expected under the conditions brought about by the struggles between nations. The concentration and movement of large bodies of men from various parts of the world; the limitless hardships, with fatigue, general malnutrition, famine and exposure; and the lack of medical care, sanitation, and personal hygiene often experienced by civilians and soldiers alike provide the fuses for the explosion of wide-spread epidemics. Refugees and captured and returning prisoners are important instruments in the transmission of disease from enemy to enemy and to all civilian groups.

She went on to note that, 'while certain types of sickness have accompanied armies throughout the centuries, there have nevertheless been some notable changes in the prevalence and severity of wartime infections. It is only in comparatively recent wars that more men have been lost from military action than from disease.'

This last observation—made during the early stages of the Second World War— no doubt reflects both the deadly nature of modern military combat on the one hand and improved medical care on the other. Nevertheless, the numbers of deaths due to disease during the Second World War were considerable. Of the nearly 160,000 Germans who died in the battle for Stalingrad between November 1942 and February 1943, an estimated 110,000 fell victim not to military action directly but to disease (in particular, typhus) and to hunger. War was accompanied by epidemics: in the winter of 1941–2, there were catastrophic outbreaks of typhus in Russia and Poland (and there were some cases in Germany as well); between November 1943 and March 1944 Naples witnessed a dramatic typhus epidemic (brought into the city by soldiers coming back from Tunisia and Ukraine); and typhus became rampant in German concentration camps during the last months of the conflict (when conditions deteriorated calamitously as provisioning broke down while the numbers of prisoners greatly increased—most notably in Bergen-Belsen, where some 17,000 prisoners, among them Anne Frank, succumbed to the disease in March 1945), and erupted outside the camps at the end of the war in various places in Germany (where before the war it had been virtually extinct). In Asia large numbers of Japanese soldiers were suffering from illness or injury at the end of the war, and more than 81,000 of them died before they could be returned to Japan.

Death as a consequence of disease was not just the unfortunate collateral damage of war. It also arose from deliberate attempts to infect people, whether through medical experiments or as a weapon of war. In the 1930s both Germans and Japanese explored possibilities for biological warfare (as, in fact, did the British and the French). During the war, the Japanese engaged in experiments with biological and chemical warfare in China, experiments that led to many deaths: prisoners were injected with lethal infectious diseases and poisons; rats carrying plague-infested

German women prison guards move bodies into a mass grave at Bergen-Belsen concentration camp under the watch of British troops who had just liberated the camp, mid-April 1945. The bodies were removed to mass graves in an effort to stem a typhus epidemic that had swept the camp during the months before its liberation.

fleas were released into fields; plague-infested materials were dropped by air over Chinese communities; flasks filled with plague bacteria were lowered into wells and reservoirs, plague-infested fleas were spread in rice and wheat fields. The results were predictable: deadly outbreaks of plague. The Japanese also spread anthrax and typhoid, and contaminated water sources in Chekiang province, leading to the deaths of many thousands of Chinese as epidemics took their toll in the region in 1942 and 1943.

While the Japanese in China engaged in extensive use of biological and chemical warfare, it was in Europe that the most concerted exercise in biological warfare occurred: the attempt by German forces to precipitate a malaria epidemic in Italy. The attempt to halt the Allied advance up the Italian peninsula in the autumn of 1943 by flooding the marshes to the south of Rome and then introducing the larvae of malaria-producing mosquitoes did not much affect American or British soldiers (who had been given anti-malarial drugs), but it did affect the Italian civilian population, thousands of whom contracted malaria in 1944 as a result.

Finally, a category of unnatural deaths during the Second World War that should not be overlooked is suicide. Suicide is, of course, also not exclusive to wartime.

Nevertheless, the extent of the suicide that accompanied the closing phases of the war in Europe and in Asia is remarkable, and related to the cultures of wartime Germany and Japan. In both cases the military collapse in 1945 was accompanied by a striking number of people choosing to take their own lives (and often the lives of family members as well) rather than face life after defeat.

In Germany, the wave of suicides as the Nazi regime collapsed was not limited to the erstwhile political leadership, military commanders, and functionaries—altogether eight of 41 *Gauleiter*, seven of 47 Higher SS and Police Leaders, 53 of 554 army generals, 14 of 98 Luftwaffe generals, and 11 of 53 admirals killed themselves—it also extended to thousands of less prominent people who killed themselves as Allied forces arrived. In its final report about popular morale in early 1945, the German Security Service observed: 'Many are getting used to the idea of making an end of it all. Everywhere there is great demand for poison, for a pistol and other means for ending one's life. Suicides due to genuine depression about the catastrophe which certainly is expected are an everyday occurrence.' As German military strength crumbled, in some areas suicide became almost a mass phenomenon. In Berlin 3,881 people were recorded as having killed themselves in April 1945 and another 977 in May; in the Pomeranian district town of Demmin roughly 5 per cent of the entire population killed themselves in 1945; and in the Sudetenland, where Germans were now subjected to extreme violence and expulsion, 'whole families would dress up in their Sunday best, surrounded by flowers, crosses, and family albums, and then kill themselves by hanging or poison'.

In the Pacific, the drive to suicide was even greater. Schooled in a culture that did not recognize surrender, Japanese civilians and soldiers alike were instructed to end their lives rather than capitulate to the enemy. As American forces moved towards Japan island by island across the Pacific during 1944 and 1945, Japanese civilians took their own lives and those of their families, sometimes by using hand grenades distributed for the purpose by the Japanese military. Probably the most terrible wave of suicides was what took place on the island of Okinawa as the Americans invaded: Japanese military commanders ordered the civilian population to kill themselves rather than submit to the enemy, and by the time the battle for Okinawa was over, some 95,000 Japanese civilians were dead—some from enemy fire, some killed by Japanese soldiers, friends, and family members, and some by their own hand.

Conclusion

Altogether, the number of unnatural deaths that occurred outside the direct sphere of military combat during and immediately after the Second World War exceeded the number of deaths of soldiers in battle. These deaths continue to shape the memory and understanding of that war, and are central to its history. While civilians have comprised the majority of the casualties of most wars, the scale of the unnatural deaths that occurred during the Second World War set that conflict apart. The history of the Second World War and the memory of that conflict are framed not just by military campaigns and battles, but equally by iconic locations of the mass death of civilians: Dresden, Hiroshima, Auschwitz. However, the extent of unnatural death in the Second World War goes much further, to the villages of Bengal and Greece, to the streets of Manila, to thousands of places where civilians died as a consequence of the Second World War and where no monument stands to remind us of how they met their end.

How can one explain the grisly catalogue of brutality, callousness, inhumanity, and murder that comprises the history of unnatural death during the Second World War? Clearly the conflict provided the catalyst and context for unnatural deaths on a scale unprecedented in recorded history. The preponderance of civilian over military casualties during the Second World War may be seen as a reversion to the normal patterns of death in war. Thus it is not the Second World War that was the exception, but the First (particularly the First World War on the Western Front), in that the overwhelming majority of the casualties during the 1914–18 conflict were soldiers. In most wars, whether we are speaking of the Thirty Years War or the Vietnam War, it has been non-combatants who comprised the majority of those who died. However, many aspects of the deadly violence during the Second World War were new. The first was the sheer scale of what happened. Unnatural death during the Second World War destroyed the lives of millions of people over a substantial portion of the globe, from Italy to the Philippines, from Poland and Ukraine to India and China. Extensive war among industrialized nations combined with incursions into lands regarded as colonial spaces, where the inhabitants were viewed at best as second-class human beings, to produce death on a scale that previously could hardly have been imagined. The second novel aspect was the involvement of the state in killing, not just in a scattered, partial, or exemplary manner, but in organized campaigns of mass murder. Unnatural death was not just a matter of accident or collateral damage, but often of deliberate policy—not just a side effect of war or even a means to a political or economic end, but often a goal in itself. The third was that to a massive extent the war damaged economies, disrupted food production and distribution, and caused the spread of disease, leading indirectly to unnatural death on a huge scale. The fourth was the use of modern technologies that vastly increased the possibilities for killing large numbers of people, whether through bombing, gassing, deliberate starvation, or biological warfare. The fifth, and ultimately perhaps the most important, was the ubiquitous context of violence, an environment where war dissolved normative constraints on behaviour that had taken decades if not centuries to coalesce. The First World War may have been the 'seminal catastrophe' (George Kennan) that caused Europe and the world to descend into the maelstrom of violence that so disfigured the first half of the twentieth century. But it was the Second World War, with its worldwide waves of unnatural death, that comprised the lowest point of that descent.

Unnatural death in the Second World War was a defining feature of the twentieth century. It is framed in memory through the 'Rape of Nanking', the fire-bombing of Hamburg and Tokyo, the death marches across Germany in early 1945, the dropping of atomic bombs on Hiroshima and Nagasaki, and Auschwitz. Yet it also destroyed millions of lives in ways and in places that left little trace—that of the young woman who starved in Honan, of the old woman burnt in Komeno in Greece—the countless individual tragedies that together comprised the enormous human cost of the Second World War.

12 Brains at War

Invention and Experts

DAVID EDGERTON

THE role of experts and of invention in the Second World War is a topic about which we know little but assume a great deal. We assert that war is 'good' for invention, that this or that invention won the war, that it was a 'physicists' war', that 'free science' in free nations triumphed over controlled science in totalitarian nations, and so on. While many of these assumptions might be understandable, they are, as we shall see, often far from valid. A second major area of confusion when talking about invention and experts in the Second World is presented by those two very slippery words, 'science' and 'technology'. In fact, it is probably best to avoid these words altogether. For one thing, such terms can evoke unhelpful ideas of magical powers and encourage misleading meditations on good and evil. For another, 'science' and 'technology' are typically taken to be represented by selected, often atypical, radical innovations, and not by accounts that cover all invention and innovation, or which consider fully the existing body of knowledge and existing inventions. A rather special part tends to stand for the whole. Finally, we need to remember that in the Second World War the term *technology* barely existed in the English language in anything like its modern sense, and the word *science* was typically understood much more broadly than it is today. At the time, people would use terms like machine, engine, technique, device or apparatus where we might use *technology*. They would also have regarded aeroplanes and the radio and radar as 'wonders of science' or 'scientific inventions', whereas today they are firmly in the *technology* camp. A distinction between a narrow conception of *science* and the new concept of *technology* was invented after the war, not least to distinguish science from its role in war.

This chapter concerns itself with the role of experts of many kinds, and (separately) with the inventions, and the developments of inventions, they undertook during the war. It discusses this in relation to the nature of the wars fought by the different belligerents. In focus, treatment, and argument, it differs from most existing treatments of 'science and technology' in the Second World War, which deal only with the greatest powers and with only a handful of innovations closely connected to academic scientific research, particularly in physics: radar, the atomic bomb, rockets. It rejects the overemphasis, seen for example in the American case, on the role of academic physicists, the Office of Scientific Research and Development, and elements of the atomic bomb project, to the detriment of industry, the armed forces, chemists, and engineers. It also avoids the extraordinary invention chauvinism of the post-war years, where, for example, British analysts went to considerable lengths to insist that they, and by implication no one else, had invented the jet, radar, the cavity magnetron, etc., and had indeed made a decisive contribution to the atomic bomb. It discounts, too, the idea of a radical step-change in the overall pace of invention during the war, and also the self-serving argument of many scientists that the war saw a new and dangerous compact between knowledge and power. States and armed services had long used experts, and these technical complexes were the sources of most of the important inventions of the war years.

Experts in Government

The most obvious type of expert to find themselves in positions of power in wartime are serving officers. Despite this, there were no fully military belligerent governments in the Second World War. The Japanese case comes closest: Hideki Tōjō, a career soldier, was Japanese Prime Minister for most of the war. Marshal Pietro Badoglio led Italy on the Allied side in 1943–4. Chiang Kai-shek, another soldier, was 'Generalissimo' of Nationalist China, but he had long been a politician. Stalin gave himself the military rank of Marshal in 1943; Lavrenti Beria got his in 1945; the same year Stalin became a Generalissimo. Winston Churchill had started life as a professional soldier, but that certainly did not define him. All the important war leaders imposed their authority on their armed services. For example, Stalin, Hitler, and Churchill were all critical in strategic decision-making about their armed forces, and in many lower-level matters too. Furthermore, all three were personally concerned with and informed about weapons, raw materials, and industry—the sinews of modern war.

At high ministerial level all governments had key officials with particular technical expertise and interests in charge of production and research. United States Vice-President Henry A. Wallace was a noted agricultural scientist and entrepreneur, who from 1940 to 1943 served as chairman of the Board of Economic Warfare and was chairman of the Supplies, Priorities and Allocations Board, a predecessor of the War Production Board. This was chaired by Donald M. Nelson, a chemical engineer from Sears, Roebuck, the gigantic manufacturer and mail order firm, for the remainder of the war. In the case of the United Kingdom, external experts were brought in to run, at various times, the supply ministries. The Minister of Production was a businessman (Oliver Lyttelton), as was the Minister of Food (Frederick Marquis, Lord Woolton, who had a scientific background). Churchill's personal economic and scientific advisor, the physicist Frederick Lindemann, was given a seat in the cabinet. The wartime German government was full of men with a technical background. The engineer, National Socialist ideologist, and racial theorist Alfred Rosenberg was Reich Minister for the Occupied Eastern Territories. The self-styled agronomist Heinrich Himmler was leader of the SS (and from 1943 Minister of the Interior), controlling a vast military, industrial, and police organization. The railway

A technocrat at table. Donald Nelson (centre), of the US War Production Board, eating dehydrated food.

engineer Julius Dorpmüller was both Minister of Transport and general manager of the German railways, in which capacity he was kept on by the Allies (although he soon died). The animal breeder Richard Darré was Minister of Food and Agriculture from 1933 onwards, replaced in 1942 by his deputy, the agricultural scientist Herbert Backe. The engineer Fritz Todt was Minister of Munitions from 1940 to 1942. The architect Albert Speer succeeded him in 1942. His deputy was an engineer and another long-standing Party supporter, Karl-Otto Saur. In Japan, it may be noted, the Emperor was a biologist, but the key industry minister was Nobusuke Kishi, a career administrator and Minister of Commerce and Industry (later subsumed within Munitions): post-war he became Prime Minister. Kishi effectively ran the Ministry of Munitions after 1943, although the Prime Minister was nominally the minister in charge. In Vichy France, the Minster of Industrial Production from 1942 was the young engineer, Jean Bichelonne.

In the Soviet Union, within the all-powerful State Defence Committee (the GKO), two figures ran procurement: Lavrenti Beria—head of the NKVD including the GULag system, who had studied at the Baku Polytechnicum—and Giorgi Malenkov (a graduate of Moscow's 'Highest Technical School', of which Alfred Rosenberg was also a graduate). The two main ministers under them were young engineers, workers or peasants by origin, who had become Party members and activists early in their lives and were sent to elite educational institutions. The Minister for the Defence Industry (concerned mainly with land armaments) between 1939 and 1941 was Boris

L. Vannikov, Party member from 1919 and graduate of Moscow's Highest Technical School. After the war he was in charge of the Soviet atomic bomb project under Beria. He was succeeded by D. F. Ustinov in 1941, only 33 years old, trained at the Leningrad Military-Technical Institute (the old military engineering school of the Tsarist Empire); he was to be a key figure in the Soviet state into the post-war years, alongside better-known working-class figures who rose through technical education and the war like Khrushchev, Brezhnev, and Kosygin. The Ministry of Aviation was run during the war by Aleksei Ivanovich Shakhurin, in his late thirties, and a graduate of the Moscow Engineering-Economics Institute who had previously worked in the

Yak fighters, designed by Alexander Yakovlev (1906–89), being assembled in the USSR, March 1942.

aircraft industry. Alexander Yakoklev (1906–89), the designer of the Yak fighters, was Vice-Minister of the Aviation Industry (1940–6).

It is erroneous to think of expertise independently of politics. The technical experts at the head of the Soviet system were committed Communists; those of the Third Reich were typically National Socialists. British experts like Lyttelton and Lindemann were in office as Conservatives, indeed personal associates of the Prime Minister. Henry Wallace was a committed New Dealer. Yet the idea of the non-political expert has had a certain resonance, especially in relation to Germany. After the war, Albert Speer and various generals presented themselves as such, and argued indeed that this is why they were successful, and that Germany would have been more successful in war had it not been run by ideological National Socialists. However, in recent years it has become very clear that a huge mass of German experts and technocrats were active planners and perpetrators of policies closely associated with National Social-ism—Nazism was not a wild throwback from modernity into an anti-expert culture but an incarnation of it. For example, on the eve of the invasion of the USSR Darré and Backe prepared a plan which made brutally clear the policy to be pursued: to feed the German armies, and to feed Germany better, they would have to take the surplus of agricultural production from the Ukraine and other productive conquered areas. The remaining population, principally in the cities of the USSR, would have to starve. Albert Speer himself, in spite of his later claims, was without question a committed National Socialist. A close confidant of Hitler, he oversaw a huge expansion in the use of slave labour (a central part of the production surge late in the war) and worked closely with the SS. The SS also had its own technocrats, including the engineer Dr Hans Kammler. Responsible for the construction of concentration and extermination camps, he was put in charge of underground factories and the entire V2 programme, as well as the production of jet aircraft.

It would also be a mistake to see the Second World War as somehow representing a 'perversion' of science. To be sure many experts, including doctors and scientists, did some very terrible things, but they did so in contexts where terrible things were the order of the day. They were no more perverted than anyone else. There was in any case no novelty in learned individuals applying their imagination to killing; scientific research had been central to the war-making capacity of states for decades at least. Yet the defence of science from association with war led to the odd but influential claim that engagement in offensive war was a problem of conscience for scientists especially. It was not, but the idea that it was or should have been permeates much older literature, particularly on the development of atomic weapons. This is true not only in the case of Germany and Japan, but in the case of the United States as well. In the post-war literature there were attempts to count experts on the side of good, and the old fashioned military and politicians on the side not of evil, but of indifference to suffering. In Britain some scientists sought to portray strategic bombing as something scientists had advised against, ignoring the fact that many scientists were for it, and that to many it represented the acme of a scientific way of war. After the war, there were many stories of US atomic scientists being struck with conscience attacks on the eve of the atomic bombings, and indeed afterwards. These were hogwash, but ideologically significant. Robert Oppenheimer, a senior Manhattan Project scientist, was in favour of the bombing, and when he intoned 'I am becoming death' (if indeed he did it at the time at all), he surely knew that he was alluding to a famous scene in the Bhagavad Gita where the world is purged of sin in an orgy of destruction analogous to the Flood. Like so many other scientists, Oppenheimer did his duty, with skill and with commitment. All in all, there was a distinct lack of frankness from scientists on both sides regarding their attitudes to the war. For instance, German physicists claimed—falsely—that they actively prevented Germany from getting a bomb—whereas in fact they were working to make one. The key Japanese physicist involved in the Japanese bomb project was, likewise, less than frank about what his team was trying to do. Allied nuclear scientists too were hardly candid, implying that many had been or became hostile to atomic bomb development when in fact there were hardly any dissenters. Although problems of conscience loomed large in the *post-war* literature on science and war, this should not be taken as a reflection of attitudes during the war itself.

We also need to be wary of the claim that expert communities somehow mobilized themselves to fight war in their own ways. Experts in some places like Britain would tell the story of their contribution to war in this way, to claim credit for developing new war-winning devices on their own. In fact, however, the great majority fitted into existing structures and worked on existing projects. In the case of Germany, experts later proclaimed that they were dragged into war work; to counter this, historians have pointed to the 'self-mobilization' of experts in order to benefit from war. Having said this, we do need to recognize that experts were not free men, either in the Allied or the Axis countries. They too were conscripted, and their contributions were similar to all those other people who were conscripted into the war effort. In the case of experts in occupied countries we may note that their fate and their response to it were no different from that of anyone else in their countries' elites. In the West there was a fine line between collaborating and carrying on. In Eastern Europe experts, as part of the elite, were in particular danger. There was a very great difference in being, say, a plant breeder in German-occupied Ukraine and a plant breeder in German-occupied Norway or France.

Experts

All the nations at war relied on experts in peacetime, but war required experts in new places, new sorts of experts, and perhaps more experts overall. War required medics, engineers, scientists, managers, and some linguists and anthropologists; it needed few clergy, lawyers, classicists, or historians. Engineers were needed as builders and destroyers of fortifications, of roads, bridges, railways, airfields, and ports, for modern armies relied on new physical infrastructures. New airfields were built in their hundreds, and thousands of miles of oil-pipeline were laid. Two hundred miles of a new Thailand–Burma Railway were built by the Japanese with the labour of locals

The German army marched into Poland with large numbers of horses, which, like soldiers, required expert medical attention.

Über eine Notbrücke dem Feinde entgegen

and prisoners of war. The Ledo/Stillwell Road from India into Burma was built between 1942 and 1945 by US engineers and local and US labour (much of it African-American). The US Army Corps of Engineers became the home of the Manhattan Engineer District, which ran the atomic bomb project. All armies required medical officers right up close to the front line, men who would have been in the main civilian doctors in peacetime. On some fronts veterinarians were needed, as on the Eastern Front where horses were used extensively by the competing armies. In the British case there was a sudden and unexpected demand for vets during the Italian campaign of 1943–5 thanks to the extensive use of mules for transport in the mountainous terrain.

While no army had a core of scientists alongside its formations of engineers and doctors, the chemical warfare and signal services had high concentrations of chemists and physicists. All the belligerents had chemical warfare services, and programmes to make and use them, to develop new ones and new methods of use. All deployed vast arsenals of chemical shells, rockets and bombs, filled with lewisite, mustard, phosgene, and, in the case of the German forces, nerve agents too. The US Chemical Warfare Service was active in the creation and deployment of incendiary weapons, not least for dropping from the air. Chemical weapons in the sense of poisonous gases

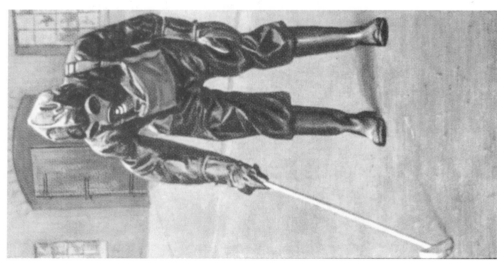

A card issued by British cigarette maker W.D. & H.O. Wills in 1938 illustrating a method for detecting mustard gas, a standard chemical warfare agent.

were generally not used, though they were employed on a limited scale by the Japanese against the Chinese from the late 1930s into the 1940s and had been used by the Italians in Ethiopia. The formations concerned with signals expanded or multiplied with the deployment of many varieties of new radio equipment, including radar.

One particularly notable feature of the Second World War was the mobilization of experts in non-uniformed roles. Research and development was generally carried out by civilians within or under contract to military structures. Cryptography was generally done by civilians. Civilian parts of government were also directly concerned with prosecuting the war effort—thus the British Ministry of Economic Warfare recruited economists who were also involved in bombing policy. Agronomists, veterinarians, and doctors were all recruited to promote the capacities of the civil economy and society in wartime. In many places there were novel efforts to increase output and

Gas masks were standard for soldiers everywhere, including the Chinese troops shown here, the only ones to need them.

productivity. For example, British agricultural experts were sent to the Middle East to help increase local food production in the face of low food and fertilizer imports. In war industries too more experts were needed—engineers, scientists, management experts—to help build up and organize the massively increased production of tanks, guns, aircraft, and the rest.

Trials, Investigations, and Surveys

Experts were needed to assess how well things worked, and how their working might be improved. Weapons needed to be compared with each other, defences probed, and so on. There were systematic mathematical and statistical analyses of actual operations using data collected in many forms, including photographic analysis ('operations research' in British parlance), which led to new operational guidelines. New aeroplanes had to be flown again and again by test pilots. New guns needed tables of trajectories prepared empirically and mathematically. The US army's Aberdeen Proving Ground in Maryland had over 20,000 personnel in wartime. At the Dugway Proving Ground in Utah (where chemical and biological weapons were tested) incendiary bombs were tested on full-scale model reproductions of German and Japanese housing and industrial units. Émigré German architects, including the famous modernist Eric Mendelsohn, designed the German buildings; Antonin Raymond, a Czech architect who had worked in Japan, the Japanese. Systematic large-scale testing was crucial to choosing between essentially simple new weapons such as incendiary bombs. The M-69 'cluster bomb' of napalm incendiaries, for instance, came out the winner of tests in the summer of 1943. Napalm was a jellied petrol devised by the chemist Louis Fieser at Harvard and the Standard Oil company, which later produced it. A second new incendiary based on magnesium powder and napalm called 'goop' (made by Henry Kaiser's Permanente Metals Corporation) was used somewhat later in M-74 incendiary bombs. These simple incendiaries, millions of them, and especially simple napalm, killed more Japanese civilians than the two atomic bombs.

The British, with the Canadians and Australians, conducted chemical warfare trials with volunteers in Britain, and also in Alberta and Queensland. Tests were conducted by British and Australian doctors on treatments for and prophylaxis against malaria, which resulted in new drug regimes based on mepacrine/atabrine. In the USA and elsewhere new and old insecticides were tested for efficacy and effectiveness in the field, leading for example to the widespread use of DDT in the final years of the war. The Japanese and German military-medical authorities used prisoners for very wide-ranging testing, sometimes to the death, testing, for example, resistance to extreme cold, chemical and biological weapons, vaccines, methods of sterilization, and in some cases experiments not directly related to war at all. Unit 731, a large site where much research was done on chemical and biological warfare by the Japanese in Manchuria,

German jet pilot Hannah Reitsch receives the Iron Cross

The 'German village' in the Incendiary Test Area, Dugway Proving Ground, Utah, photographed in 1994.

brought about the deaths of 3,000 people in ten years. It was not the only site of experimentation or research, but its huge scale is testimony to the size of the Japanese chemical and biological warfare effort. After the war the United States tried 23 German doctors for participating in such trials; seven were executed. It did not put the Japanese doctors on trial, though the Soviet Union did, but both powers learnt from what the Japanese did in biological warfare, as well as from the Germans.

Invention

Invention in wartime was less important to the outcome of the war than is sometimes implied. After all, it generally takes years for novel techniques to be developed and deployed, and thus to have military significance. We would expect therefore most of the weapons used during the war to have been invented, or designed, either before or during the early stages of the war. And that was indeed the case. In fact, all the belligerents had new weapons ready for war by the late 1930s as a result of a major arms race from the early 1930s, and lots of weapons in preparation which would be ready later in the war. Much of this was shared: there was important international traffic in aviation and in arms, with the Soviet Union in particular essentially buying, copying, and developing foreign machines—the DC-3 transport, for example, and

The Anderson shelter, specially designed before the war to provide cheap protection from bombing to poor British people with gardens.

aero engines from Bristol, Gnome-Rhone, Hispano-Suiza, and Curtiss-Wright. The T-26 tank derived from the Vickers 6-ton. The BT-5 and BT-7, made in huge numbers in the late 1930s, and the T-34, used an American (Christie) suspension system. The British acquired rights to the Christies in the late 1930s, and the Christie suspension was a feature of their main cruiser tanks. Similarly, the extraction of petrol from coal and techniques for making synthetic rubber were known around the world, though used to differing extents.

Those with experience of weapons development knew that even a long war was unlikely to be long enough to allow for completely new weapons to emerge during it. Indeed, some senior British scientific advisors assumed in 1939 that the research effort would actually *decrease*; some involved in operational research argued in 1941 and subsequently that R&D staff should be transferred to learning how to use weapons, rather than develop new ones. In Germany aeronautical research staff were released at the beginning of the war to go to the forces and into industry, while the Germans stopped their atomic bomb programme in 1942 because they calculated that it was unlikely to be made operational before the end of the war. Similarly, the order went out in Germany in June 1944 to cut back radically even on modifications to weapons. It is not entirely clear exactly what these orders entailed, but new projects were continued, and some were even started, in spite of them, including much of the jet engine programme and the *Volksjaeger* (people's fighter) project (which started in September 1944).

Nevertheless, at least in the most important powers, investment in research and development appears to have increased overall as the war progressed. There were very good reasons and pressures for expanding such work. Novel dangers emerged which needed to be countered. Potential dangers needed to be countered too. As a result, developing, improving, and adapting weapons, and doing so quickly, became a central part of war fighting. Furthermore, the widespread belief in the importance of novel weapons overrode realistic expectations of when they might be ready for deployment, and sometimes of their effectiveness too. Indeed many of the most famous (though not all) of the inventions of the Second World War were expensive follies in retrospect, for they did not affect the outcome of the war. The atomic bomb, the V2 programme, the various jet engine projects cost more than they benefited their creators. Nor were these the only examples. For instance, the Germans put massive resources into the development of the first true submarine, the Type XXI (the first submarine designed to operate primarily submerged, rather than essentially as a surface ship that *could* submerge if necessary). The Type XXI was roughly twice as large as the standard Type VII U-boat, but only two ever went into service, and this at the very end of the war.

But where did inventions come from? In the Anglo-American world especially (but by no means exclusively), modern war was seen as something transformed by the products developed from civilian industry and science. A typical trio would be the internal combustion engine (and aviation in particular), radio, and chemicals. Yet even in these three fields the story is not so simple. Aeroplanes and tanks had long been specialist areas dominated by the military and military industries. Radio had, in many ways, a military origin—before the Great War the most important user was the Royal Navy. Important radio (and radar) developments came from military and related laboratories. In the case of chemicals the case for the civilian origins of military innovations is stronger, but here too we need to note the very long-standing specialized institutions for the development of propellants, explosives, and chemical weapons. In fact, military-technical innovation was everywhere principally the product of powerful military-scientific complexes focused on government and industrial laboratories, test ranges, workshops, and design offices. Having said this, amidst this world of military research organizations, great firms, and to a much lesser extent universities, we should still not forget the role of individual inventors, often members of the armed services, such as the RAF officer Sir Humphrey de Vere Leigh who invented a spotlight for aircraft to illuminate submarines on the surface of the sea.

In the United States there was an enormous build-up of existing military and industrial facilities, such as the Naval Research Laboratory, or the great aircraft and aero-engine firms, as well as great commercial enterprises like Du Pont and Bell Telephone. A new organization was established, reporting to the President, the Office of Scientific Research and Development (OSRD), which supplemented the research and development efforts of the army and navy. It gave contracts to elite universities, which created great new organizations such as the MIT Radiation Laboratory, which was the main centre for radar research and development in the USA. However, it is important to get these various organizations into perspective. For instance, the OSRD, while important, is rather over-represented in many accounts; in terms of R&D expenditure it actually came third after the army (and its gigantic air force) and the navy. Similarly, the research and development part of the Manhattan Project is routinely overestimated because of the tendency to picture the whole project as a research and development effort. Most of the $2 billion the whole project cost went to build two nuclear factories at Oak Ridge and Hanford, an effort undertaken by large corporations, including DuPont; the research and development part of the project came to a mere $70 million. It represented only a small fraction of overall war-related R&D expenditure in the United States: in the fiscal year 1945 the Office of Scientific Research and Development spent around $100 million, while the US army and navy spent $700 million on research and development alone.

The uranium bomb 'Little Boy' being loaded into the bomb bay of the *Enola Gay*, which released it over Hiroshima in August 1945.

In Germany the great centres of research and development were divided between government laboratories and private industry. The Peenemünde Army Research Centre (*Heeresversuchsanstalt Peenemünde*) on Germany's Baltic coast, which developed the A4 (later known as the V2) rocket, would be an example of a state institution. And IG Farben on the other hand, the great German chemical combine, would be an example of private-funded research. In Japan, the army and navy maintained separate organizations for research and development, with a number of smaller supplementary agencies developed after 1942. The Soviet Union, with its planned economy, was also planning and militarizing research from the 1930s, including many institutes of its Academy of Sciences. These and other institutes were supplemented by a distinct Soviet institution, the *Sharashka*—research, design, and development centres staffed by political prisoners held by the NKVD. One such centre based in Moscow produced the Petlyakov Pe-2 bomber and the Tupolev Tu-2 bomber, two very important Soviet wartime aircraft.

Aero-Engines and Fuels

Pre-war and wartime military technological development is well illustrated by the central case of the aero-engine and related sectors. Aero-engines were much more complex and expensive to develop than air frames, and for this reason alone far fewer were developed. Right through the war there was a search for new, more powerful and more fuel-efficient engines in all the main belligerent countries, and the development also of new types of engine. The engines available at the end of the war to Britain and the USA were much more powerful than those of 1939, and were to power bombers and civil airliners for years to come.

Very few companies made powerful aero-engines and they came in relatively few types, with different firms often specializing in different types of engine. In Germany, for instance, BMW made radial engines (from the 1930s), while Junkers (JUMO) and Daimler Benz made inline engines; in Britain Rolls-Royce made inline engines and Bristol made radials; in Japan Mitsubishi and Nakajima made radials. (In a radial engine the cylinders 'radiate' outward from a central crankcase like the spokes of a wheel; an inline engine has banks of cylinders in line with each other, usually one behind the other.) The US industry was dominated by two radial firms, Pratt & Whitney and Curtiss-Wright, the French by the radial firm Gnome et Rhône and the inline Hispano-Suiza. The Soviet design bureaux were similarly specialized, developing versions of engines from other countries. Mikulin (BMW) and Klimov (Hispano-Suiza) made inline engines and Shvetsov (Wright) and Tumansky (Gnome et Rhône) made radials.

All the major engines of the war—and there were a handful for each belligerent power—were of pre-war design. The most produced engine of the war was the Pratt & Whitney Twin Wasp designed in the 1930s, 173,618 of which were produced. It was a 30-litre engine of around 1,000 horse power, typical of the most powerful engines of the beginning of the war, like the Rolls-Royce Merlin (famously used on the

HOCHGESCHWINDIGKEITSKANAL.
Bauerschwindigkeit (1900 km/Std.   Meßstrecke 2,7 m Durchmesser.

Two technicians working in the 'Hermann Goering' wind tunnel in Braunschweig, Germany, 1940.

Spitfire). Enormous effort was made in improving these engines, such as the Merlin, which went through many versions, and which powered aircraft before, during, and indeed well after the war. Yet designers were already looking to produce engines of two or three times that power, and after much trial and tribulation some went into production during the war: the Bristol Centaurus (18 cylinder, 2,500+ horsepower), the Wright Duplex Cyclone R-3350 (18 cylinder, 54 litre, 2,500+ horsepower) which powered the B-29 Superfortress bomber, and the inline Napier Sabre (24 cylinder, 36 litre, 2,500–3,500 horsepower); of these, the Duplex Cyclone was the most used during the war, the other two were only of minor significance. The most powerful engine to emerge from the war was the Pratt & Whitney Wasp Major (28 cylinder, 70 litre, 3,000+ horsepower)—it was to power a post-war version of the B-29, the Boeing

A priest leading the prayers of a B-17 Flying Fortress bomber crew at an airfield in southern England, 1944.

Stratocruiser airliner, and the first intercontinental nuclear bomber, the B-36 of the 1950s. No other nation had anything like it. The Japanese and the Soviets were not in this competition during the war. For its copy of the B-29, the Tu-4, the Soviet Union only got an equivalent to the Duplex Cyclone in 1947, developed in various stages from a Soviet derivative of the Cyclone. The Soviet Union started developing a Wasp major equivalent in the late 1940s, but it was cancelled in the 1950s. Germany tried and failed to produce large engines like the radial BMW 802 and 803, and the inline Jumo 222. Only Britain was in the race, but it was behind the USA, and it too had its failures.

Aero-engines required specialized fuels. While in the early days aviation spirit was essentially a particular grade of motor spirit, by the Second World War it was essentially highly refined motor spirit with large additions of manufactured hydrocarbons (iso-octane and others) and quantities of tetraethyl lead. While the base could be made from refining, or the hydrogenation of coal, the remainder required particular chemical processing. The international oil industry, working in collaboration in some cases, came up with important new means of doing this. A major step came with the development of Houdry catalytic cracking in the late 1930s, which increased the proportion of petroleum that could be turned into petrol, and also produced by-products which were used to make iso-octane fuel; the second great innovation was the alkylation process, which was to be used on a vast scale in US and British-owned plants, also to make iso-octane. These novel techniques were very rapidly introduced, and at great cost. The Germans made very limited use of cracking and of alkylation. They were not able to use most of the butane and propane (by-products of hydrogenation) for iso-octane as they needed it for bottled gas, on which they relied. Germany had much less aviation spirit than the Allies and it was typically of a lower octane rating.

But the US aero-engine industry, in spite of its prowess, was not the harbinger of the future. The jet engine was a project with pre-war origins, based on research conducted in many countries. These developments yielded weapons of marginal impact on the war. In 1940 the Italians flew an aircraft powered by jet combustion, with air compressed by a conventional aero-engine. Such arrangements were to be used by the Japanese and the Soviets on a small scale at the end of the war. In Germany a centrifugal compressor engine first powered a jet aircraft in 1939, followed by a British one in 1941. Both countries were also already developing axial engines (a very compact, cylindrical type of engine in which the pistons are arranged around an output shaft, with their axes parallel to the shaft). In 1945 the Japanese built a small number of turbojets and aircraft powered by them, partially based, it seems, on

The ME262, the most produced jet aircraft of the war. Powered by engines which were cheap to make and fuel, it nevertheless had negligible impact.

German models. During the war, Britain went on to produce a small number of centrifugal jet engines which powered the Meteor fighters in action during the last year of the war; the Germans produced very much larger numbers of axial engines, many built by slave labourers alongside the V2 rockets in underground factories in the Harz mountains. The jet was for the Germans an engine of desperation, produced quickly, cheaper in terms of manpower and materials than conventional aero-engines. Jet aircraft used cheaper fuel, and achieved high speeds, but they proved to be extremely dangerous for their pilots and had only a minimal effect on the air war. By the end of the war Britain had many better jet engines ready for production than Germany—it could afford to continue development on a grander scale. After the war, the Soviets started building German Jumo 004s and BMW 003s, but these were superseded by copies of British engines—the wartime Rolls-Royce Derwent, and the immediately post-war Nene. The US programme was largely derived from the British, and led by the end of the war to the output of a small number of jet-powered aircraft.

New airframes were easier and faster to develop and some important ones did come into use during the war. But to put this in context it is worth noting the extent to which developments of 1930s airframes were in use right to the end of the war. Germany continued to produce old aircraft, indeed on an increasing scale, notably the pre-war fighter, the Bf109, which was by then very cheap to produce; but the Germans proved unable to bring a new generation of higher-performance engines or aircraft into use. The Japanese introduced new aircraft throughout the war years, including the Kawanishi N1K-J *Shiden* in 1943 and the Nakajima Ki-84 in 1945 (both fighters). Italy was not able to bring new fighters into production, but they were developing them. In the case of the Soviet Union there were also important new aircraft—the twin-engine bomber Tupolev Tu-2 went into service in 1942, as did the Lavochkin La-5 fighter, and the Lavochkin La-7 in 1944. The Yakovlev series of fighter aircraft, including the famous Yak-9 introduced in 1942, were eventually made in vast numbers.

In the case of tanks the turnover of models was considerably faster—the tanks in the field in 1940 were gone by 1943, at least for the major powers. By the end of the war, wartime designs were fully in use. The Germans started design work on the Panther and Tiger I tanks after June 1941; both were in use in early 1943. The Tiger II was designed in 1943, and saw service in 1944. The British tanks of 1944 were designed in 1940/41, and impressive new tanks appeared in 1945. All these tanks of 1945 were much more powerful than the tanks on the battlefield in 1939 or 1941.

Perhaps the most important wartime development was radar, which saw very significant refinements and extensions during the war. The resonant cavity magnetron (a very notable improvement on the long-known magnetron, achieved by the British and the Japanese) was developed in 1940, and was soon in widespread use; another was the SCR-584 (short for Signal Corps Radio number 584) radar designed by MIT in the USA from 1940. Together with the Bell Telephone M-9 electrical anti-aircraft gun director and the proximity fuse, it transformed anti-aircraft fire into a highly effective weapon. Neither the German nor Japanese air defences, weak for other reasons too, had anything like them. In 1940 all the powers were comparable in their ability to bomb and to defend against bombers, but by the end of the war the story was very different. Germany could not bomb Britain in the way Britain bombed Germany; it did not have the large bombers, nor did it have the air defence equipment Britain did. Most British bombers got through the German radar, anti-aircraft gun, and fighter defences, but British air defence may well have been more effective, as indicated by the destruction of the V1 flying bombs using fighters and radar-guided anti-aircraft fire with proximity-fused shells. Japan clearly did not have the kind of bombing air force the USA did, nor was it able to resist attacks, though it did have, as Germany did, air defence radar and effective fighters. There is no doubt that the density of development of radar was greatest in the USA, Britain, and Germany, but something was happening nearly everywhere.

Sharing

Radar provides a nice example of a novel technique arising at much the same time everywhere, and used by every major belligerent. Although one could be forgiven in Britain for believing that it was a British invention, in actual fact every power had demonstrated radar before the war, and everyone went into war with some radar equipment. There was also a good deal of transfer of radar equipment by various means—thus the Japanese quickly copied British and US radars captured in 1942; the

Nearly all belligerents used radar. The first US army radar, SCR-268, of pre-war design, assisting anti-aircraft guns near the Anzio beachhead, Italy, 1944.

Soviet Union copied British radars, as well as getting large numbers through Lend Lease from Britain and Canada; Germany copied a captured British resonant cavity magnetron, although only towards the end of the war. In 1943 the Germans developed 10cm radar following the capture of a British set. The lack of transfer between the Axis powers is also notable—the Japanese did not share their cavity magnetron with the Germans, and while the Germans did share their air defence radars with the Japanese, they were copied only slowly. Anglo-American sharing, on the other hand, was remarkable (at least from 1940 onwards), covering most but not all developments, but certainly including the British resonant cavity magnetron, the proximity fuse, the jet engine, the early development of the atomic bomb, and much else besides.

All the major belligerents had expert researchers who believed an atomic bomb was a possibility and worked on it. Most believed that it could not be done (by anyone) before the war ended, and for this reason did not invest heavily in it. In Germany a project was under way under the supervision of Army Ordnance between 1939 and 1941; it was then transferred to civil control because it was not immediately needed, but continued to be supported on a similar scale. The Germans decided against building a bomb because they estimated it would be made too late to affect the war, not because, as some later suggested, German scientists did not want to, or were not able to. The Japanese army and navy were supporting very small scale work from 1940, which got a boost in 1943, but achieved very little. A Soviet bomb project got the go-ahead in 1943. On the largest scale at the beginning of the war and well into 1941 was the British project, launched in 1939. Only the USA launched a full-scale project before it entered the war, but it was still too late to be used against the initial intended target, Germany.

Themes

There were some important differences in the approach to weapons development between the various belligerent powers. For example, in both Japan and Germany there was a certain tendency towards gigantism. At the time of the Pearl Harbor attack, Japan had a strong and well equipped navy, and had three ships, the battleships *Yamato* and *Musashi*, and the aircraft carrier *Shinano*, which were the largest and in many respects the most powerful warships in the world. *Yamato* and *Musashi* had standard displacement of 63,000 tons each (when fully loaded, 73,000 tons) and a maximum range of 45,000 yards; these were the largest naval guns in the world. During 1944 the Japanese brought out the *I-400* class, three huge submarines whose primary mission was bombing the Panama Canal and cities of the United States. They had a displacement of 5,550 tons each and a length of 400 feet, making them considerably larger than any other submarine until the 1960s. Remarkably, each submarine carried three bomber aircraft, carrying either bombs or a torpedo. German gigantism is well exemplified in their tank programme, with the King Tiger coming in at nearly 70 tons, and with two prototypes of a gigantic 188-ton Panzer VIII (the

'Maus'); the British and Americans built prototypes of tanks of the same scale, but did not go as far as the Germans did. In artillery the Germans also went big, building and deploying two gigantic 800mm railway guns; only one was ever used. They had even bigger guns in development. In addition, the Germans had around 25 K-5 280mm railway guns (similar calibre to a naval gun, but with a much longer range). Perhaps the clearest example of British gigantism was a project discussed at high level but never put into practice: the Habbakuk, a gigantic aircraft carrier made of ice, with a projected displacement 50 times that of conventional carriers.

At the other end of the scale, both Germany and Japan were to develop many small improvised and relatively cheap weapons as well. In addition to jet engines, Germany aimed to produce a cheap fighter aeroplane, the *Volksjaeger*. Towards the end of the war the Japanese developed a Kamikaze aircraft bomb, the rocket-powered and human-controlled Baka bomb, as well as the Shinyo, a small special attack boat to be manned by middle-school boys of 15 and 16 years of age, and the Kaiten midget suicide submarines. The Fukuru were equipped to walk underwater and ram an explosive bomb against the hull of an enemy landing craft. At the war's end, there were 4,000 Fukurus stationed at the Yokosuka naval base, of whom 1,200 were fully trained. Given their lack of shipping the Japanese had a plan to make use of sea currents to drift floating barrels of goods to Japan, locatable by radio.

One obvious and important effect of war was that it cut off belligerents from one another, and led to the imposition of powerful controls on trade. In essence belligerents could obtain resources only from areas under their control. This represented a very major change from peacetime, and particularly affected the Axis powers. The Allies had access to all the materials they needed, with only a few exceptions, the most important of which were rubber, pyrethrum (an insecticide made from the dried flower heads of plants from the chrysanthemum family), and quinine. Germany and Japan were in much weaker positions. In the case of Germany high expenditure on research was to a considerable extent the result of efforts to produce synthetic petrol, rubber, textiles, and so on, without relying on supplies from overseas. By the Second World War Germany had many plants for hydrogenating coal and coal products to make oil; and plants to make synthetic rubber from coal. Practically all of Germany's aviation spirit came from synthetic plants, and accounted for half their output. These projects continued to consume research and production capacity. Germany had over ten of these massive hydrogenation plants—larger than any other sort of chemical plant—whereas Britain had two. But Britain got its oil from massive refineries across the seas.

Japan also looked to domestic supplies, particularly of fuel. Shale oil reserves were exploited in Manchuria and a plant for synthetic oil was built. In Japan late in the war the navy and to a lesser extent the army started a research programme to get aviation spirit by the distillation and processing of pine root oil; new small-scale techniques were designed, to avoid the danger from bombing, and there was a plan, largely realized by the end of the war, to operate 36,000 retorts and produce 360,000 kilolitres of aviation spirit per annum. In Allied China, the Nationalists distilled pine root and other materials to make gasoline. There was a lot of small-scale innovation across Allied China, far from the major centres for research, which were now in many cases occupied by the Japanese.

In a few cases the Allies had to resort to synthetic substitutes based on German techniques because of the Japanese conquest of resources in South-East Asia. A drug originally developed in Germany was made to replace quinine; and German synthetic rubber processes were developed in the USA. Standard Oil started a pilot for synthetic BUNA-S rubber in 1939 on the basis of IG Farben patents it controlled; in 1942 it was forced to hand these over to the US government, which resulted in a collaborative research and development programme between all the main firms involved in rubber production. Although the decision to use petroleum as the feedstock rather than grain alcohol was initially controversial, nevertheless, within two years more synthetic rubber was being made in the USA than had been available from pre-war imports, amounting to some seven times the level of German production. Most of this was styrene, otherwise known as GR-S (Government Rubber), the American name for BUNA-S rubber.

Autarky. a Butadiene plant in the United States, built for the US synthetic rubber programme, which made the world's largest importer self-sufficient.

Drugs and Insecticides

The Second World War was in part an enhanced war against insects and germs. The Swiss company Ciba-Geigy of Basel had been working on new insecticides from the 1930s, and had discovered the powerful insecticidal effect of DDT, which it launched in 1940. It was taken up on a small scale by the Germans, but most effectively by the Americans and the British. Field trials were undertaken in Tunisia in June 1943, and in the winter of that year it was used with pyrethrum to de-louse the population of Naples, averting a typhus epidemic. Lice were controlled in continental Europe by a long-established method of fumigation of clothes and buildings with Zyklon B. This was a staple insecticide used in de-lousing across the Reich, including in concentration camps where the risk of lice infestation and typhus was great. In two extermination camps it was infamously used to kill human beings, but by far its most widespread use was for de-lousing. In spite of its terrible reputation as a method of extermination, in terms of numbers killed Zyklon B was actually a less significant weapon of genocide than the carbon monoxide gas used in the other German extermination camps.

The Zyklon B formulation of hydrogen cyanide, long used for killing lice, and used against people in some German extermination camps.

DDT was also used against mosquitoes, in North Africa and in Italy; in 1944 it began to be used on a mass scale in the Pacific, with air drops of DDT to kill mosquitoes on Pacific islands in advance of the landing of US troops. British troops went into northern France with DDT-impregnated battle dress to ward off lice. The effects of DDT were astounding—it was much more powerful and effective than any other insecticide. The British also came up with gammexane, only used after the war, but also an astonishingly powerful killer of insects. DDT was far from being the only insecticide in use. Pyrethrum, which had to be planted in Africa, as supplies from the east were lost to the Allies, was widely used against lice and mosquitoes. German insecticide research of the 1930s at IG Farben produced organo-phosphates which were developed and manufactured as nerve gases for use against humans—Tabun, Sarin, and Soman. Britain also experimented with an organo-phosphate nerve agent during the war. Only after the war were organo-phosphates used as insecticides.

The killing of germs inside the human body was revolutionized in the later 1930s by a new drug invented by IG Farben called prontosil, the first of the sulphonamide

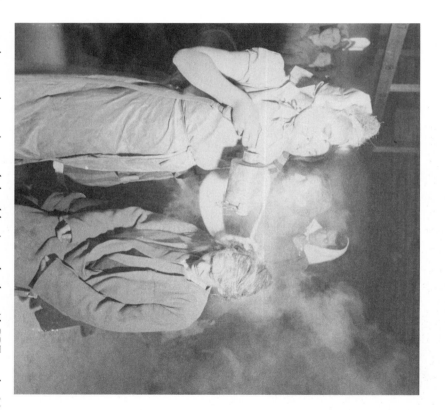

group of antimicrobial compounds. Developed by French and British companies into a range of drugs with wide-ranging anti-bacterial properties, they were manufactured on a vast scale during the war until they were replaced in many applications by penicillin. This became available by the end of the war and overshadowed the reputation of the earlier sulphonamides as miracle drugs. Penicillin came onto the agenda in 1940, and was in serious use by 1944, hugely improving treatment of bacterial infection. Following clinical trials, an earlier IG Farben product, the anti-malarial atebrine or mepacrine, became not only a method of treatment (in light of a lack of quinine in Allied hands), but also a new and effective prophylactic, based on regimes worked out on volunteers in Queensland, Australia. A new British anti-malarial, paludrine, came in too late for the war effort, as did chloroquine, whose usefulness was established in the USA.

Making the originally German anti-malarial drug mepacrine in Britain.

Assessment

There are many claims for this or that new machine during the war—it won the war, shortened the war, was decisive, fundamental, and so on. Yet working out the impact of a new machine or invention is in fact extremely difficult. The United States Strategic Bombing Survey undertook perhaps the most complete assessment ever of the effects of bombing in Europe and the Pacific, and that subject is still highly controversial.

How are we to assess? The first point is that we need to compare the effects of a particular weapon or technique with the best available alternative at the time. To take one example, the atomic bomb was impressively destructive, but much less so when compared with a conventional raid. The detonation of one uranium and one pluto-nium bomb over Japanese cities in August 1945 marked rather than brought about the end of the war. They brought much less destruction to Japan than the raids with high explosives and incendiaries. One also needs to look at both sides of the military equation. Take the case of code-breaking. Assessment of its impact on the course of the war cannot be based simply on analysis of the positive effects on one side; it must also include analysis of the damage done by the enemy's code-breaking to the other. Furthermore, single machines are very rarely used in isolation: the Battle of Britain was won by much more than radar; the Battle of the Atlantic involved not only submarines, depth charges, and sonar, but also direction finding, radar, and cryptog-raphy. Furthermore, we need to differentiate very clearly between the effect these innovations had on the *nature* of war on the one hand and their effect on the actual *outcome* of the war on the other.

In this context, it is clear that the impact of some of the most famous military novelties produced during the war has been exaggerated. Indeed, many of the most famous wartime inventions consumed inventive resources during the war and had no pay-off during it. The atomic bomb would have been regarded as a scandalously expensive way to destroy two cities had war been abolished in 1945. The V2 rocket cost more lives among the slave workers who built it than it did among the attacked populations. It was so unlikely to cause more damage than it cost to produce that British intelligence had difficulty in believing that it was being developed. Similarly, many of the most famous British inventions were poor investments—the bouncing bomb, the Mulberry Harbour, and the PLUTO pipeline all had limited impact and high costs. The power of Germany did not rest on the V2, or that of the USA on atomic bombs, or that of Britain on bouncing bombs. It rested instead on a mass of less well known and more mundane machines, and on expertise in their deployment and production—as well as on a host of other factors, such as economic resources, which lay outside the realm of invention and innovation.

Such complexity makes the overall story difficult to summarize. But we may do so as follows: the most striking feature in terms of the deployment of new machines, operated by new experts and new procedures, is that the power of the United States and the United Kingdom stands out. Rich enough and with access to resources on a global scale, they were able to fight a war of often new machines, and fight their way

The famous but unnecessary PLUTO petrol pipeline being laid across the English Channel after D-Day.

to victory with much lower casualties than their enemies, or their ally, the Soviet Union. It was a question of both quantity and quality. Neither Germany nor Japan had anything like, for example, the vast fleets of four-engine bombers that devastated their cities in 1944/45. The sheer quantity of tanks and artillery deployed by the USA, the USSR, and Britain overwhelmed the German and Japanese forces and rendered redundant any small technical lead they might have had in particular areas. The United Nations, as the Allies styled themselves from 1942, also deployed an ideology suggesting that new powerful weapons were, in the hands of a righteous world organization, transforming the world for the better, an argument that was later associated with calls for the international control of atomic weapons.

It would be a mistake, however, to characterize the whole of the Second World War as a new kind of war determined by new machines, as much general writing used to do. Most of the war was fought with weapons and at speeds familiar from the Great War. In many places on the Eastern Front in Europe and in Asia it was fought in ways which might have seemed backward by the standards of the Western Front in the Great War. Much of the war consisted of brutal operations on a vast scale against partisans and guerrillas, which called for experts in terror and interrogation and torture.

If the outcome of the war had been decided by the capacity to innovate in military machines in the late 1930s then the war would have been won by a European power, Germany or Britain. This is true whether we are discussing military aviation, or novel techniques like radar, atomic bombs, or jet engines. What differed across countries was rarely the basic knowledge, or the idea, but the capacity to develop and make weapons, both old and new. The degree of dissemination of the basic ideas, even with regard to nuclear bombs and radar, is an indication of this. Though the two great powers that emerged, the USA and the USSR, were not in the lead in innovation in the 1930s, by the end of the war the USA was clearly without question the leader in many fields, though not in every one. It had copied and built on European work with astonishing speed. It emerged as easily the most inventive power on earth. By contrast the Soviet Union still had a lot of catching up to do, and was able to do so in some areas after the war with remarkable speed, if at very high cost. But clearly innovation and expertise were not everything. Indeed, in the opinion of many, the war was won by cultures in which experts were not especially valued; this was a war of Romans, not of Greeks.

It is telling all the same that the experts of defeated nations were sometimes, and by various means, taken to work for the victors after 1945. Rocket engineers from Germany went to the USA, USSR, and France; experts in uranium chemistry and nuclear physics to the Soviet Union, aerodynamicists everywhere. Japanese biological warfare experts worked for the USA. Secret policemen were recruited to secret services they once opposed. Even where people were not transferred, large quantities of documentation and materials went from Germany to the victorious Allies—covering a vast range of military equipment and industrial processes. German nerve gases and rockets, for example, were to equip all the major post-war armed services.

It is commonly suggested that the war stimulated inventive activity, and that this had important consequences in the peace which followed. In fact it is difficult to say whether this is the case, but we can be reasonably certain that military invention was stimulated by the war, as was invention to meet the particular needs of war in other ways. By the same token, it is likely that all other kinds of inventive activity actually declined during the war. The extent to which swords were later turned into plough-shares is the key issue, and on this topic we have little systematic knowledge. We know however that wartime military development preceded an unprecedented technological arms race which continued to dominate research and development budgets for dec-ades to come. And wartime developments which did nothing for their producers during the war, notably rockets, nuclear weapons, nerve gases, and biological weap-ons, all became central to post-war arms development. Mercifully they were little used. Though many millions would die in wars after 1945, they generally fell victim to machines and equipment already very familiar to the belligerents during the Second World War.

13 The Culture of War

Ideas, Arts, and Propaganda

DAVID WELCH

Introduction

ONE of the most significant lessons to be learnt from the experience of war in the twentieth century was that public opinion could no longer be ignored as a determining factor in the formulation of government policies. Unlike wars in previous centuries, 'total war' meant that whole nations and not just professional armies were locked together in mortal combat. 'Total war' can be defined as warfare in which vast human, material, and emotional resources were marshalled to support military effort. The Second World War served to increase the level of popular interest and participation in the affairs of state. The gap between the soldier at the front and civilian at home was narrowed substantially in that the entire resources of the state, military, economic, cultural, and psychological, had to be mobilized to the full in a fight to the finish. The 'ordeal' of total war required that civilians must also 'fall-in' and participate (and possibly suffer) in the war effort. In such a struggle, morale came to be recognized as a significant military factor and propaganda emerged as the principal instrument of control over public opinion and an essential weapon in the national arsenal.

The legacy of the First World War was very important because it would largely determine how the belligerents viewed propaganda at the outbreak of hostilities in 1939. In the democracies, especially, the very idea of propaganda was regarded with suspicion and distaste. The British government regarded propaganda as politically dangerous and even morally unacceptable in peacetime. It was, as one official wrote in the 1920s, 'a good word gone wrong—debauched by the late Lord Northcliffe'. During the inter-war period, propaganda was often used in a pejorative sense. Writing in 1936, the American social scientist Leonard Doob observed that 'the word propaganda has had a bad odor. It is associated with the war and other evil practices.' The totalitarian dictatorships on the other hand took very different lessons from the experience of the Great War and, when they came to power in the inter-war years, immediately introduced propaganda agencies into the formal structure of state. In Britain, however, the impact of propaganda on political behaviour was so profound that during the Second World War, when the government attempted to 'educate' the populace regarding the existence of Nazi extermination camps, it was not immediately believed since the information was suspected of being more 'propaganda'.

Thus, for all the negative connotations that have been attached to it, most governments were alert to the desirability in total war of utilizing propaganda to present their case to publics both at home and abroad. In modern warfare, propaganda is required to (1) mobilize hatred against the enemy; (2) convince the population of the justness of one's own cause; (3) enlist the active support and co-operation of neutral countries; and (4) strengthen the support of one's allies. Having sought to pin war guilt on the enemy, the next step is to make the enemy appear savage, barbaric, and inhumane.

Philip M. Taylor has observed that 'the Second World War witnessed the greatest propaganda battle in the history of warfare'. For six years, the belligerent states employed propaganda on a scale that dwarfed that of all other conflicts, including the First World War. The Second World War was a battle between two new types of regime struggling for supremacy with one another in a battle for the future. Modern democracy and totalitarian dictatorship had both emerged from the First World War, and the outbreak of hostilities in 1939 was a testimony to their mutual incompatibility. There followed a struggle between mass societies, a war of political ideologies in which propaganda was a significant weapon.

During the Second World War all forms of communication—including that of art and culture—were appropriated and controlled by means of strict censorship regulations, in order to play a part in the propaganda process. In the totalitarian police states such as Italy, Germany, Japan, and the Soviet Union this posed few problems as the media—indeed art in general—had become part of the apparatus of state. In the liberal democracies, on the other hand, this proved more problematic. Nevertheless, on the propaganda front, Britain appeared to be much better prepared than in the First World War. A Ministry of Information (which had been ignobly dismantled in 1918) had been mooted and planned for some time, and came into being within a matter of days after the declaration of war in 1939. Britain's principal propaganda structures were the Ministry of Information (MoI) for home, Allied, and neutral territory, and the Political Warfare Executive (PWE) for enemy territory. The programmes of the British Broadcasting Corporation (BBC) earned Britain a powerful reputation for credibility that proved an asset long after the war had ended. When Sir John Reith, the former Director General of the BBC, was appointed Minister for Information in 1940, he laid down two fundamental axioms, that 'news is the shock troops of propaganda' and that propaganda should tell 'the truth, nothing but the truth and, as near as possible, the whole truth'.

War is one of the most intense emotional experiences in which human beings as members of a community can be involved. One of the features of modern warfare is that it puts nations to the test. As such, war can be an instrument of social, political, and cultural change; the more 'total' the war, the greater the test of a nation's resources. War is, in its very essence, negative and destructive; it cannot of itself create anything new. Therefore a key question in this chapter is to what extent the war experience brought about change in ideas and the arts and how important was propaganda in the battle for 'hearts and minds'. Or did war merely act as an accelerator of changes that were already taking place? For example, was the Second World War a continuation of the First World War? Is the literature and art of the Second World War inferior to that of the First? Certainly the Second World War was different; less static trench war, more truly a world war, more a 'People's War' and more a 'Total War' presenting an ideological and even a racial conflict. It was also arguably, from the Allied point of view, a morally justified war, thus invalidating humanitarian 'protest' literature and art.

When analysing the impact of war there is also the problem of an arbitrary or misleading 'periodization'. Not all 'war literature', for example, is published during the conflict, but may emerge long after. Evelyn Waugh's *Sword of Honour* trilogy (1952–61) is a case in point, as indeed are Heinrich Böll's novels and short stories, such as *The Train Was on Time* (*Der Zug war pünktlich*, 1949), which attempted to come to terms, from a German perspective, with the memory of Nazism, the war, and the Holocaust. In countries under Nazi occupation, the test of intellectual survival during the war became one of identification with resistance movements. Jean-Paul Sartre's novel sequence, *Roads to Freedom* (1945–9), acquired popularity in intellectual circles after the war for its existential philosophy and the manner in which it explored the morality in a commitment to resistance. Sartre's 'resistance' suggested that only out of personal commitment and action could sense be made of a human predicament which was otherwise mystifying. On the other hand, some artists may react by consciously ignoring war and deliberately creating an alternative experience. T. S. Eliot's *Four Quartets* (1944) might seem the literary equivalent of Barbara Hepworth's sculptures.

Britain Can Take It

In Britain at least, the start of the Second World War did coincide with a number of important shifts in the literary scene. W. B. Yeats, Virginia Woolf, and James Joyce all died at the beginning of the conflict, and in 1939 W. H. Auden emigrated to the USA. With Ezra Pound, of the leading post-1918 writers, isolated in Italy, only Eliot and E. M. Forster actively survived. At the same time three new periodicals were founded: Cyril Connolly's *Horizon* (1939), Tambimuttu's *Poetry London* (1939), and John Lehmann's *Penguin New Writing* (1940). Writing in *Horizon*, Connolly lamented that the outbreak of war and Auden's abandonment of 'the sinking ship of European democracy' marked a decisive break with the 'social realism' of the Thirties: 'the war is separating culture from life and driving it back on itself . . . Our standards are aesthetic, and our politics in abeyance . . . It is a war which awakens neither Pity nor Hope . . . '.

Angus Calder has suggested that writers of the Second World War characteristically exhibited a 'sceptical confusion'. This may be due to the fact that, unlike in the First World War, many writers who were now employed in the service of the state for propaganda purposes did not experience at first hand the trauma of fighting at the front. War literature may therefore also be a vicarious experience for those who did

Evelyn Dunbar, *The Queue at the Fish Shop*, 1944.

376 *David Welch*

not encounter the real thing. Secondly, artists largely agreed that Nazism represented a monstrous evil, such a consensus left little scope for anti-war views. This, in turn, led to a restrained, sceptical, low-keyed, and empiricist tone that tended to work against romanticism. Poetry and literature of the Second World War contained a purposeful realism: we see this in the stark brutality of Keith Douglas's poems, such 'Simplify Me when I'm Dead' or 'Desert Flowers' ('the shell and the hawk every hour | are slaying men and jerboas, slaying | the mind . . . '), and in Frank Thompson's finest work, 'An Epitaph for My Friends', when he describes young men leaving 'our books and flowers' to go to war. Although rarely apathetic, poetry and literature did not exhibit the more sentimental and heroic rhetoric (the emotional anti-war or 'pity' of war) that characterized the works of many of the war poets of the 1914–18 conflict.

Nevertheless, the Second World War had some surprisingly positive side effects, for Britain at least. The National Monuments Records began life during the war, prompted by the urgent need to photograph historic buildings imperilled by the Blitz. In the visual arts one of the most valuable wartime initiatives was the Official War Artists scheme (funded by the Pilgrim Trust) which ran from 1939 to 1943 and commissioned paintings (largely watercolours) of cherished buildings and landscapes perceived to be under threat. It prompted not only the famous bomb-damaged ruins captured by John Piper, but also evocative painting by Eric Ravilious and Evelyn Dunbar evoking the alien world of submarines and the rural heroism of land girls and ordinary citizens queuing stoically for rationed food.

A. J. P. Taylor claimed that in Britain the integration of artists and intellectuals into the war effort was much more successful than in the First World War. Partly this was due to the fact that the range of activities open to intellectuals increased not only in the administrative and economic fields of government but in propaganda broadcasting and liaison with resistance movements (J. B. Priestley's BBC radio broadcasts, Sefton Delmer's black propaganda to Europe). William Beveridge, Director of the London School of Economics, advised in the reconstruction of the social security system; Kenneth Clark, Director of the National Gallery, was responsible for commissioning official war artists; and John Maynard Keynes chaired the Council for the Encouragement of Music and the Arts (CEMA).

Perhaps the most illustrative example was the role played by Kenneth Clark in establishing a War Artists Advisory Committee (WAAC) within the Ministry of Information that was ready to commission artists when war broke out in 1939. The scheme's intention was to create a historical and artistic record of Britain's involvement in war and to bolster morale through exhibitions and publications. Emphasis was placed on art that would embody a message about liberal cultural values—the antithesis of the controlled and centralized aesthetic of the Nazis (and the Soviets). Clark emphasized the unique role of art and the insight and vision that artists could bring to an understanding of war. The WAAC programme exploited a growing interest in the visual arts that can be traced back to the First World War, and it served to transform British visual culture. By 1946, the programme had employed over 400 artists (2,000 had applied) and acquired over 6,000 works. Artists employed a variety of styles, from traditional to more modern (although it is probably fair to say that the majority of the compositions adhered to the representational)—from Stanley Spencer's teeming shipyards on the Clyde to Graham Sutherland's animated city and landscapes, and from Paul Nash's powerful imagery of British power and resistance to Edward Ardizzone's intimate scenes of daily life during the London Blitz. Interestingly, abstract art did not fit into the programme, excluding artists such as Ben Nicholson.

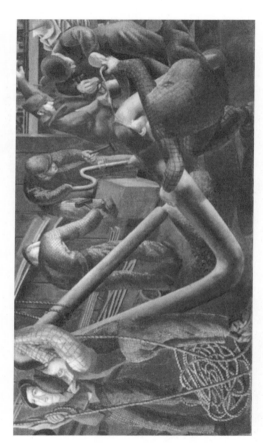

Stanley Spencer, *Plumbers*, 1940.

Edward Ardizzone, *Home Guards at the Local*, 1940.

Graham Sutherland, *Devastation, 1941: An East End Street*, 1941.

In the Second World War, advances in war technology and particularly the emergence of the bomber served to transform the experience of civilians fighting under the new conditions of total war. The home front attracted, not surprisingly, major artists and significant commissions, and arguably the most memorable art of the war was done there, even though remarkable pictures were made of the overseas theatres of operations. As the public wanted to be reassured of the nation's capacity to produce armaments and their effective use, compositions of industrial sites and workers produced a new iconography. Offices and factories are stages for a shifting social order, adjusted and attuned to wartime needs. They also reveal the new roles undertaken by women for the war effort—from performing menial tasks with the Auxiliary Territorial Service to complex work in armaments factories. Many pictures tend to indicate that the war artists had no doubt that a form of class reconciliation and social evolution was taking place. Interestingly, this was most often reflected in the work of female war artists. To highlight the part women factory workers played in Britain's war effort, Laura Knight painted Ruby Loftus at work in Newport. In Elsie Hewland's *A Nursery School for War Workers' Children* (1942) we see hints of the changes not just for the children but for their mothers called into unfamiliar duties. Nursery schools were a new support for women conscripted into full-time employment.

Henry Moore's two wartime series of drawings, of bomb shelters and of coal mining, established his reputation. During the Blitz (1940–2), up to 100,000 people

Laura Knight, *Ruby Loftus Screwing a Breech-Ring*, 1941.

Henry Moore, *Pink and Green Sleepers*, 1941.

regularly sheltered in London's underground. Moore captured the mood of calm defiance in the shelters with his figurative sculptural forms, though contemporary popular reaction was critical of Moore's Modernism. At his own suggestion, Moore was commissioned in 1941 by the WAAC to make drawings at Weldale Colliery where his father had worked. The drawings continued the underground themes of his shelter drawings but the humans' reaction to their environment is very different. Whereas the shelterers sought sleep and waited passively for the German bombers to pass over, the miners, unconstrained, fight against the coalface.

In 1940, Paul Nash was made an Official War Artist to the Royal Air Force and produced some of the finest paintings of the war. His *Battle of Britain* (1941) captured the RAF's great aerial victory over the advancing Luftwaffe. In his highly symbolic *Totes Meer* (Dead Sea, 1940–1), Nash depicts a shoreline holding back waves composed of German aircraft wings and fuselage. It is a dead sea made up of broken aeroplanes that are 'static and dead'. His *Battle of Germany* (1944) combines the abstraction of *Totes Meer* with the drama of *Battle of Britain*. The coastline, as seen from a bomber, is evaporating in multi-coloured smoke.

Kenneth Clark's vision shaped what emerged. Britain's Second World War art programme went out of its way to encourage the painting of non-violent, sentimental, and rather parochial scenes of Britons 'doing their bit', intended to inspire people to protect their countryside and ways of life. As most artists supported the war aims they tended to shy away from the confrontational.

What we have in all these pictures is not a form of crude propaganda based on idealized images entirely dissociated from reality, but a far more subtle one, founded on implicit assumptions about the British national character. There were, however,

Doris Zinkeisen, *Belsen*, 1945.

exceptions towards the end of the war. Doris Zinkeisen worked for the Red Cross in Europe and her painting *Belsen* (1945) records her visit to the extermination camp within days of it being liberated. Edward Burra produced a striking watercolour, *Skull in a Landscape* (1946), that exposed the cruelty of war as a descent into barbarism.

Similarly, Leslie Cole captured the horror and brutality of imprisonment in the war in the Far East. Cole's painting has a haunting sense of redemption from the dark, restrictive act of internment, as skeletal, malnourished mothers and children undertake the everyday act of cleansing and washing.

It seems clear that during the war the arts came to represent in a very real sense something that the British felt they were defending against Nazi tyranny and obscurantism: thus we have the founding in 1939 of the Council for the Encouragement of Music and the Arts (CEMA), which was given official government recognition and a subsidy of £50,000 (not without its critics at the time) to sponsor concerts and theatrical productions that toured the country and raised morale. Strenuous efforts were also made to ensure that the British cinema industry should not suffer the knock-out blow dealt in 1914–18. Protection was maintained and film-makers were encouraged to stay at work. If many of the feature films produced were mawkish in their patriotic message, for the first time a genuine British style with real roots in British experience was discernible. A new school of directors, including Sidney Gilliat, David

Lean, and Carol Reed, established itself and important films such as *The Way Ahead* (1944) and *Brief Encounter* (1945) were produced.

By the outbreak of war, film had become *the* mass-medium of the first half of the twentieth century. In wartime, going to the movies remained what it had become in the 1930s, a normal part of everyday life, by far the most popular form of entertainment, particularly for the working class. The cinema then was the most important medium for both entertainment and propaganda and was extensively used by governments of all the combatants during the Second World War. In Britain, for example, 19 million people went to the cinema every week and by 1945 the figure had risen to 30 million—two-thirds the population. Although the long-established Hollywood dominance was never seriously challenged by the British film industry during the war, British cinema none the less enjoyed something of a golden age between 1939 and 1945, both in terms of popularity and critical acclaim.

One of the reasons for this was that British films were now portraying ordinary working people in a serious light rather than as caricature figures of fun. The People's War demanded that the strict censorship of the pre-war years, as exercised by the British Board of Film Censors (BBFC), be more relaxed in its treatment of social issues. Walter Greenwood's novel *Love on the Dole*, for example, banned by the BBFC, was produced in 1940. Much of this was due to the influence of the documentary film-makers who had made major contributions to British cinema in the 1930s. The Ministry of Information had initially ignored the commercial film industry at the

Leslie Cole, *British Women and Children Interned in a Japanese Prison Camp, Syme Road, Singapore*, 1945.

outbreak of war because of the emphasis placed by the government on newsreel propaganda, but after 1940 the MoI eagerly recruited them to make films that portrayed the British at war for the purposes of morale, not least because the audiences now demanded them. The poet-director Humphrey Jennings produced an exceptional body of work, notably *Listen to Britain* (1941), *Fires Were Started* (1943), and *A Diary for Timothy* (1945). Like the newsreels, the official documentary films presented not reality as such but an illusion of reality. Nevertheless, these films remain a moving, if somewhat sentimental, record of the British people at war.

Most people went to the cinema to see the main feature and to escape from the realities of war. Romantic melodramas and films such as *The Wicked Lady* (1945), starring James Mason and Margaret Lockwood, were what the public longed to see, and studios such as Gainsborough duly obliged. The MoI recognized that 'for the film to be good propaganda, it must be good entertainment', and between 1939 and 1945 a number of classic propaganda films were produced. The films of Powell and Pressburger—*Contraband* (1940), *49th Parallel* (1940), *One of Our Aircraft is Missing* (1942), *The Life and Death of Colonel Blimp* (1943), *A Canterbury Tale* (1944), and *A Matter of Life and Death* (1946)—made notable cinematic contributions, as did those of Anthony Asquith, Carol Reed, and Charles Frend. These film directors recognized that propaganda, if skilfully handled, could most effectively be insinuated while the audience was relaxed and off its guard. Such films also bear witness to the way the war acted as a creative catalyst for the British film industry.

The arts, alongside social welfare and economic democracy, came to symbolize the antithesis of Hitlerism. Altogether the cultural gains of the war were very real ones: the founding of CEMA (renamed the Arts Council at the end of the war) as an agent of state patronage to the arts was an event of major significance. Writing in the *Music Review* in 1947, R. J. Manning declared that 'despite the blackout and general war-weariness, music has had in this country an extraordinary flowering'. The wartime National Gallery concerts organized by Dame Myra Hess (and captured so memorably in Humphrey Jennings's documentary film, *London Can Take It*) were intended to raise the morale of Londoners. Bomb damage had closed Sadler's Wells Opera in 1941, forcing the company to tour the provinces for four years. The reopening of the Sadler's Wells Theatre in the summer of 1945 was celebrated with the first performance of Benjamin Britten's *Peter Grimes*—one of the true operatic masterpieces of the twentieth century (exploring the struggle of the individual against the masses). Britain's musical renaissance continued. By taking over the running of the Henry Wood Promenade Concerts, the BBC made them available to a much wider public. In 1946 the Third Programme was established to provide a vehicle for classical music—although from the outset it was the preserve of a very limited audience and thus served to emphasize the exclusiveness of minority culture. In 1947 the Edinburgh Festival of Music and Drama was inaugurated.

Appreciation of painting appeared to be growing. Art sales did well, and the great Van Gogh Exhibition of 1947 attracted 12,000 visitors per day to the Tate Gallery. The best of British painting was essentially individualistic and unaffected by conformity to any prevailing movement or style. It ranged through the flat, patterned landscapes of Ivon Hitchens, the intense romanticism of John Piper, to the bustling humanity of L. S. Lowry's Lancashire scenes of everyday life. In his autobiography, *Indigo Days*, Julian Trevelyan commented: 'Wartime feeling amongst painters accounts for the more tolerant and catholic acceptance of various styles that has come about since.'

While the arts, as well as social welfare and economic democracy, came to symbolize the antithesis of Hitlerism, Britain was actually slow to specify its war aims and did so only when pressed by US President Franklin Roosevelt. Roosevelt's attempts to tie Britain to concrete war aims and Churchill's desperation to bind the US to the war effort helped provide motivations for the meeting which produced the Atlantic Charter in August 1941, which prepared the way for the post-war United Nations. The Charter played its part in convincing the American people that the war was a noble cause and not just a bid to save the British Empire. At home the propaganda apparatus during the war perpetuated the notion of a 'people's war' and emphasized the possibility of post-war social change. The renewed emphasis on central planning in Britain during the war was endorsed by the government and given maximum scope because Churchill left so much of the 'home front' to Labour ministers like Ernest Bevin at the Ministry of Labour, Herbert Morrison at the Home Office, and later Hugh Dalton at the Board of Trade. The government moved in a corporatist direction and Britain's wartime controlled and planned economy was perceived by contemporaries as a success; it has been argued that this perception of the success of a state-controlled economy did much to ensure the Labour Party's victory in the 1945 general election. The war became a key point of reference in post-war British politics, and allusions to Britain's war experience continue to this day to figure in a number of political campaigns.

National Socialist Germany: A People's Community

The strict regulation of the art world under various totalitarian regimes was unprecedented in the annals of art history and represented the high point of the appropriation of art as propaganda. For the totalitarian dictatorships of Germany, Italy, Japan, and the Soviet Union, war did not really change policy radically. Art had for some years served the political purposes of totalitarian masters: in such regimes, art and culture had been mobilized from the outset in the service of the state—to different degrees and for different purposes. So, the main difference between the war art of the totalitarian and democratic countries is, arguably, one of function. The least significant work emanated from Germany, where there had been a mass exodus of the most distinguished figures in all spheres of culture following the National Socialist election victory in March 1933. After the war, following its defeat, Germany would ultimately be humiliated, divided, and partitioned.

Our emotional response to German art under the Nazis is overshadowed by history; this makes it impossible to divorce aesthetics from their political and ideological context. In Germany, culture had been co-ordinated since the Nazi take-over in 1933 and art had to serve the political purposes of its Nazi masters. One of the first government ministries to be set up when the Nazis came to power in 1933 was the Reich Ministry for Popular Enlightenment and Propaganda (RMVP). Its Minister, Joseph Goebbels, believed that the function of the new Propaganda Ministry was to co-ordinate the political will of the nation with the aims of the Nazi state. To this end a Reich Chamber of Culture consisting of seven separate chambers covering all aspects of cultural life was set up under the control of the Propaganda Ministry. The Nazis quickly set about monopolizing the means of communication by a process known as *Gleichschaltung* (co-ordination), which referred to the obligatory assimilation within the Nazi state of all political, economic, and cultural activities. *Kulturpolitik* (cultural policy) was an important element in German life, but the Nazis were the first party systematically to organize the entire cultural life of a nation. In February 1933 two members of the Prussian Academy of Arts, Käthe Kollwitz and Heinrich Mannn, who were critical of the Nazis, were forced to resign. Thirteen other members resigned in protest, including Thomas Mann and Alfred Döblin. A few months later 20,000 works of 'undesirable and pernicious' writers were burnt in staged ceremonies throughout Germany. The RMVP ominously proclaimed, when it announced the Theatre Law of 15 May 1934: 'The arts are for the National Socialist State a public exercise; they are not only aesthetic but also moral in nature and the public interest demands not only police supervision but also guidance.' Under the Nazis, art was seen as an expression of race and would underpin the political renaissance that was taking place. Whereas Modernism was associated with 'decadent' Jewish–Liberal culture, art under National Socialism would be rooted in the people as a true expression of the spirit of the People's Community (*Volksgemeinschaft*). This 'national realism' created a new form of iconography for National Socialist art, which, although limited, was generally of a high technical quality. In contrast, Fascist Italy saw some crossover between official art and Modernism and Futurism. Italian art and culture were allowed to flourish without too many dogmatic rules, but Mussolini's theme of 'modernization' informed his totalitarian state; 'art was to reflect modern life'.

The tenets of officially approved 'German Art' were displayed at the House of German Art in Munich which Hitler opened in 1937. A favoured theme for Third Reich artists was portraits of the Führer. These became so numerous that Hitler finally decreed that only one would be displayed 'officially' at each annual Greater German Art Exhibition. The portrait chosen for the grand opening in 1937 was Heinrich Knirr's 'Adolf Hitler, der Schöpfer des Dritten Reiches und Erneuerer der deutschen Kunst' (Hitler, the Creator of the Third Reich and Renewer of German Art). Apart from portraits of Hitler, the permanent collection consisted largely of the depiction of idyllic rural scenes and heroic individuals in monumental poses. Portrayals of the workers themselves were generally subordinated to displays of heavy industry, and unemployment was never shown. The war absorbed much of the energy of the country, but it never extinguished the National Socialists' preoccupation with the arts. The Greater German Art Exhibitions were widely used as a morale booster.

Opening the fourth exhibition, in the first year of the war, Goebbels stressed the role of art as the best way of uplifting people in times of sorrow and deprivation. In fact, 751 artists displayed 1,397 works. The war became the new inspiration for the artist and many rooms in the House of German Art were devoted to war art. The Director of the National Museum in Berlin boasted that, while the British Museum and the Louvre had begun fearfully to evacuate their treasures, the German museums had not been silenced like those of the enemy: 'The German museums do their duty by serving the people and waiting for victory.'

In all the Greater German Art Exhibitions, landscape painting dominated. It was seen as the genre in which the National Socialist spirit could best be expressed. The new landscape painting followed closely the tradition of the Romantic painters, especially Caspar David Friedrich and Philipp Otto Runge. Closely linked with the idea of peasant life was the idea of the family. The family was more than just individual children and parents. The German people as a whole was seen as an interlacing of all German families of the same race. Here too art became a prime spokesman of National Socialist philosophy and policy. Art, as an arm of propaganda, was intended to advertise the achievements of the regime. The major national exhibitions were complemented by many local ones. In 1941, a thousand art exhibitions were held. The new war art was exhibited in galleries, museums, and factories for the war workers. Art exhibitions were also held in the occupied territories. Many artists were selected to become official war artists and worked within the Division of Visual Arts (*Staffel der Bildenden Künste*). At the start of the war forty-five were appointed and this eventually increased to eighty. The quantity produced was extraordinary and it was used for special exhibitions that toured the country.

The technical mobilization of German radio as the 'voice of the nation' is a history of remarkable achievement and it was the role of artists and poster designers to record such achievements. To increase the number of listeners, the Nazis persuaded manufacturers to produce one of the cheapest wireless sets in Europe, the VE 301D1 or *Volksempfänger* (people's receiver). A poster issued by the RMVP advertising the 'people's radio' showed one of these uniform radio sets surrounded by thousands of people with the caption: 'All Germany listens to the Führer with the People's Radio.' Community and family gatherings around the radio to listen to Hitler were a popular subject for artists as well. By the beginning of the war over 70 per cent of all households owned a wireless set—the highest percentage anywhere in the world.

The war was seen as a battle for the salvation of German culture and served also to heighten the major propaganda themes of the regime. In striking contrast to what happened during the First World War, during the 1939–45 conflict millions of Germans encountered deadly and destructive violence *within* Germany. Revealingly, the suffering of war is almost totally absent from art; artists were discouraged from recording how civilians coped with the pressure of Allied bombing raids on their cities. Such fortitude was not considered sufficiently 'heroic'; instead, art was used to bolster the lie of a victorious Germany. Moreover, unlike in Britain, where women had been conscripted both into the fighting front and the home front, in National

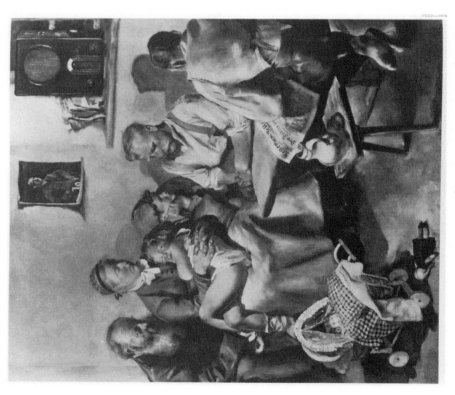

Paul Matthias Padua, *The Leader Speaks*, 1939. A rural family listens to a Hitler speech on their *Volksempfänger*.

Socialist Germany Hitler resisted demands that women should be mobilized. German artists continued, therefore, to depict women either working on the land or as mothers and homemakers. Sculpture continued to depict the ideal Aryan body in grandiose classical Greek poses, and the Aryan heroic soldier-worker was eulogized, whilst National Socialist architecture too remained mostly an instrument of self-glorification. By contrast, the Jewish 'enemy from within' was lampooned in obscene propaganda caricatures. Painters like Elk Eber, Fritz Erler, Wihlem Sauter, and Franz Eichhorst specialized in glorifying soldiers and victorious battles, as Nazi propaganda regularly suggested a continuity between the First World War and the Second. In Wilhelm Sauter's *The Eternal Soldier* (1940) the two are juxtaposed, suggesting that they are both part of the same struggle. In Hans Schmitz-Wiedenbrück's *Workers, Farmers and Soldiers* (1941), all three pillars of the state are elevated to iconic status, conveying the National Socialist message of Aryan solidarity and heroic sacrifice.

Hans Schmitz-Wiedenbrück, *Workers, Farmers and Soldiers*, 1941.

While the Nazis admired Greek art, their tightly proscribed cultural policy created bland, arrogant, bombastic works that now look like the stuff of kitsch cartoon fantasy comics—but totally drained of humour and irony.

Before the outbreak of the Second World War, Germany was already experiencing many of the developments which in Britain only came with the actual advent of the war. Germany had been 'co-ordinated' and that entailed the mobilization of society and the economy. The transition from peace to war was therefore not a sharp one. Secondly, it was not so much the war that had such a lasting and profound change on post-war Germany as the influence and needs of the occupying powers once Nazism was defeated. The Soviet Union totally reorganized society and economy in East Germany, while West Germany was essentially re-created in the image of the occupying Western liberal democracies. Total war therefore was not an independent cause of social change. Its influence was shaped decisively by the nature of the regime which waged it and that of the regimes which followed it.

The Soviet Union and the Great Patriotic War

The Second World War was known in Russia as the 'Great Patriotic War', and propaganda played a central role in rallying the Soviet population to resist the Nazi invasion. The German attack on the Soviet Union (Operation Barbarossa) found the regime of Joseph Stalin ill prepared for battle. After the initial shock, the formidable Soviet propaganda machine hit its stride almost immediately. Soviet propaganda was supervised by the Directorate of Propaganda and Agitation of the Central Committee under A. S. Shcherbakov and administered by the newly established Soviet Information Bureau. Within two days of the invasion Vyacheslav Molotov, the commissar for foreign affairs, addressed the nation by radio in defiant tone. Newsreels captured the grim-faced determination of Soviet citizens while listening to his speech, images that were on Soviet screens within a week. Stalin was able to launch his call to arms at the start of July. He addressed his audience as 'brothers and sisters' (not comrades) and called for a defence of the *rodina* (motherland).

Indeed, following the Nazi invasion, the Soviet media and art and culture in general were mobilized to support the struggle against Germany. The 'Great Patriotic War' was depicted as a clash of two ideologies, with the Russian people united in a struggle for a no-compromise victory. Because of the way in which culture had been politicized in Soviet Russia, the impact of the war on art and propaganda shifted according to different phases of the conflict. Between 1941 and 1945 artists completely focused on the war. In the middle stages of the war, artists had more freedom than usual and were able to draw on reserves of Russian historical traditions. But as the war came to an end, official control returned. Art and culture became as debased as in Nazi Germany, being almost entirely confined to celebrating the glories of Stalin. The official portrait, the historical painting, and the battle piece constituted the core of Soviet official art during the latter period of the war—as was the case in Nazi Germany and Fascist Italy.

Prior to the war, artists in Russia had been forced to adjust to the ideological demands of the regime. The death of Gorky had removed the intellectuals' only powerful protector, and the last link with the earlier tradition of the relative freedom of revolutionary art. Then war broke out and the picture altered again. Everything was mobilized for war. The best war poems of Boris Pasternak and Anna Akhmatova

Alexander Laktionov, *Joseph Stalin Speaking on 7 November 1941*, 1942.

sprang from the most profound feeling, but were too pure artistically to be considered as possessing adequate direct propaganda value, and were consequently frowned upon by the literary mandarins of the Communist Party. On the other hand, the great film director Sergei Eisenstein was able to exploit Stalin's admiration for historic Russian figures such Alexander Nevsky and Ivan the Terrible to make rousing propaganda films that suited the wartime propaganda objectives of the regime. In the case of *Alexander Nevsky* (1938, subsequently re-released after the German invasion), the Russian victory over the Teutonic Knights in the thirteenth century was considerably heightened by the rousing patriotic score of Sergei Prokofiev. In such desperate moments the Soviet government had to rely on the support of the people. To increase popular enthusiasm for the war, Stalin reshaped his domestic policies to heighten the patriotic spirit. Nationalistic slogans replaced much of the Communist rhetoric in official pronouncements and the mass media. The cities of Leningrad and Stalingrad became physical embodiments of—and thus propaganda gifts to—the Soviet Union's moral right to victory. In August 1942, for example, the besieged city of Leningrad heard Dmitri Shostakovich's Seventh Symphony for the first time and wept. The night before the Russians had shelled the surrounding Germans into silence. Now they pointed radio loudspeakers at them and played Shostakovich's melodic response to war (a copy of the completed score had been dropped into the besieged city from a light aircraft). Both Shostakovich and Prokofiev had, prior to war, been criticized for their 'formalism' and 'bourgeois decadence'. While neither composer would be fully accepted by purists within the Party, the regime recognized that their stirring music suited the exigencies of total war.

The dynamic tradition of Russian modernist, revolutionary art gave way in the war years to a dreary academic style glorifying the Party, the state, or workers. Art had to adjust to the new demands of war; instead of being used to 'educate' the masses to the economic achievement of the regime and the successes of the 'planned' political economy, art now served to inspire the people to resist Nazism and to participate in ultimate victory. Only political posters remained a vibrant and modern aesthetic medium—and arguably the most effective means of conveying propaganda to the less literate. The tradition of Mayakovsky and the Civil War was revived by some of the best-known artists, such as Sokolov-Skaya, Denisovsky, and Lebedev. The posters often took the form of caricatures of the Nazi leaders; in particular Goebbels, who was depicted by Efimov in the satirical magazine *Krokodil* as Mickey Mouse with a swastika tail, and by Vladimir Lebedev as a braying donkey. Russian posters celebrated the Russian army and people as unfailingly displaying great fortitude and patriotic fervour. In B. A. Mukin's 1941 poster 'We will defend our mother Moscow', the artist shows soldiers and armed civilians before the Kremlin. The poster was printed at a time when German forces were within striking distance of the capital and the Russian government had moved to Volga. A month later the Russian counter-offensive began and Hitler's plan for the rapid conquest of European Russia had failed. When victory was close at hand, artists lost no time in proclaiming the strength of the Red Army. The drama of defence was replaced in Soviet art by the exultation of liberation.

Kukriniksi, 'The East Front General seeks orders while Hitler deliberates', 1944. (Kukriniksi was the collective pseudonym of three painters, Mikhail Kupriianov, Porfiri Krylov, and Nikolai Sokolov.)

The evolution of so much Soviet art and culture of the 1930s which represented a self-contained artistic process was cut short by the war and prevented from realizing much of its potential. In architecture, for example, the impact of the war led to some inflated designs, mainly due in the aftermath of war to the understandable desire to restore devastated cities. The search for new visual forms appropriate for a situation of national tragedy was particularly difficult, since these were supposed to evoke a wide range of historical associations. A 'great patriotic war' it may have been, but at the front, martial resolve was stiffened by the most terrifying discipline. Memory and heroism, grief and fortitude—these different modulations of the theme of Victory found expression through architectural elements deliberately chosen to convey a timeless quality. After the victory over Nazi Germany, the country fell into a sort of euphoria with spectacular parades, elaborate buildings, and a general atmosphere of triumph and celebration. This outpouring affected all branches of art including film, music, visual arts and, as mentioned above, architecture. Victory contributed to the

B. A. Mukin, 'We will defend our mother Moscow', 1941.

growing conservatism and celebration of Soviet nationalism. The nation was transformed into an enormous theatre with sets on a grand scale—but all rather one-dimensional and concentrated. Yet such was the grip of the Soviet regime by the late 1930s that war produced few significant changes in the structure or political culture of Soviet society. Russia's relationships with the outside world in the 1940s, together with Stalin's paranoid fear of contamination from Western influences and ideas, imposed profound constraints on social change.

The end of the Second World War saw the Soviet Union emerge as one of the world's two greatest military powers. Its forces occupied most of Eastern Europe. These achievements came at a high cost, including the deaths of an estimated 27 million Soviet soldiers and civilians. The loss itself was fruitful propaganda material during the war and for decades thereafter. The dramatic events of the war years left a deep impact on Soviet literature, which was soon utilized in a propagandizing capacity. A genre of patriotic essays blossomed, including *Volga-Stalingrad* (1942) by Vassilii Grossman, who declared: 'Here it is, the Russian character at large! A person might seem so ordinary, but as disaster strikes, no matter whether big or small, out comes a great strength—personal beauty.' In *A Man's Life Story* (1942) Mikhail Sholokov wrote: 'I hope that this man, a Russian man of iron will, will survive and raise a son strong enough to cope with any difficulties, overcome all kinds of hardship.' Soviet literature of the period, like all Russian popular culture, urged the population to take action and stressed their moral superiority. The horror stories unearthed by Soviet camera teams as the Red Army moved west only underscored this moral certainty. The victory celebrations in Red Square in the summer of 1945 ushered in a new period of conviction—repeated each year in the poignant celebrations on 'Victory Day' (9 May).

The USA: 'Artists for Victory'

American propaganda during the Second World War can be divided into two phases: a period of neutrality from September 1939 to December 1941, during which debate raged among the population at large, and the period of US involvement in the war, when the government mobilized a major propaganda effort through the Office of War Information (OWI). Both phases witnessed a key role being played by the commercial media. The widespread feeling that the US involvement in the First World War had been a mistake cooled American reactions to the outbreak of war. The great neutrality debate began in earnest following the fall of France in June 1940. The pro-Allies lobby consisted of the moderate Committee to Defend America by Aiding the Allies and an actively interventionist Century Group (later known as the Fight for Freedom Committee). The pro-neutrality position was represented by the America First Committee. The isolationist camp included newspapers—especially those owned by William Randolph Hearst, and the influential *Chicago Tribune*—and such well-known individuals as Charles Lindbergh. Both sides used rallies, petitions, and demonstrations to advance their causes. In Hollywood, Warner Bros. released a number of films with a political message, including *Foreign Correspondent* (1940) and *Confessions of a Nazi Spy* (1939). Isolationists in the Senate denounced such ventures as propaganda on behalf of Jewish and pro-British vested interests.

President Roosevelt initially took a back seat in the debate because of the impending presidential election. In December 1940 he demonstrated more active leadership by advancing his 'Lend Lease' aid policy through a 'fireside chat' over the radio. The Lend Lease Act, promising 'all aid short of war', passed Congress on 15 March 1941. As part of its policy of rearmament, the Roosevelt administration established a number of propaganda and information organizations, including the Rockefeller Bureau to rally opinion in Latin America (1940); the Office of Government Reports (1939) and Office of Facts and Figures (1940) to present information at home; and the Office of the Coordinator of Information, a new covert intelligence agency that included a propaganda branch. In August 1941 Roosevelt and Churchill signed the Atlantic Charter, which set goals for the post-war world and called for a United Nations to promote international co-operation. By the time of the Japanese attack on

394 *David Welch*

Pearl Harbor, 7 December 1941, the debate over US foreign policy had been all but settled.

In the summer of 1942 the US government regrouped its various propaganda agencies into a single Office of War Information (OWI), although some psychological operations remained under the new Office of Strategic Services (OSS). At home, campaigns conceived in collaboration with the commercial media included an effort to engage women in heavy-duty war work. During this campaign the *Saturday Evening Post* artist Norman Rockwell created the character of 'Rosie the Riveter', whose iconic image become the personification of the emancipated American working woman in wartime. In Rockwell's poster, Rosie has big muscular arms; her penny loafers are atop a copy of Hitler's *Mein Kampf*. According to the *Encyclopedia of American Economic History*, Rosie the Riveter inspired a social movement that increased the number of working American women from 12 million to 20 million by 1944, a 57 per cent increase from 1940.

Some of the most important ideological initiatives came from outside the OWI. In January 1941 Henry Luce, the editor of *Time*, wrote an editorial proclaiming the 'American Century'. The idea that the time had come for American global leadership gained wide acceptance during the war. Internationalism received a boost from lawyer and Republican presidential candidate Wendell Willkie and his book *One World* (1943). Roosevelt also contributed to the nation's morale, especially in his definition of Allied war aims. The notion of the Four Freedoms, dating from January 1941 (freedom of speech and of worship, freedom from fear and from want), proved

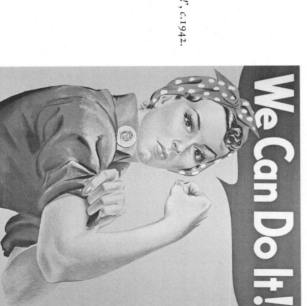

J. Howard Miller's poster *'We Can Do It!'*, c.1942.

particularly potent both in the United States and around the world. For a highly successful war bond drive Rockwell produced a series of paintings illustrating each of these freedoms.

By the time America had entered the war, the federal sponsorship of public art following the Depression had already fostered the notion that artists had a role to play in times of crisis. In 1941 *Life* magazine commissioned artists including Tom Lea, Paul Sample, and Byron Thomas to produce works for a nation preparing for war. In 1941, Griffith Baily Coale, anticipating that a war was imminent, had persuaded the navy that it should send competent artists into the field to capture all phases of the war and all the major naval operations. This became the Navy Combat Art Programme, which eventually included eighty-five artists. In November 1941, the army compiled a similar list. The programme was under the umbrella of the War Department Art Advisory Committee (WDAAC), which included established artists such as George Biddle, who was appointed chairman, and the writer John Steinbeck. WDAAC commissioned twenty-three serving artists and nineteen civilians, all of whom served in a number of theatres of war until Congress cut funding in 1943—by which time 2,000 works had portrayed wartime experience from an American perspective. In a letter of instruction, Biddle encouraged artists, carrying on the New Deal tradition of art depicting the common man and woman, to 'capture the essence and spirit of war'.

Life took on the cancelled programme and, working closely with the army, which provided transportation and accommodation, continued to commission artists such

Fred Vidar, *Dead Japanese*, 1943.

A stamp by Tony Palazzo of Artists for Victory, 'Keep the Goose Step Out of America!', 1942. It is from a set of 50 issued to show the work of the winners of the 1942 National War Poster Competition.

as Biddle, Edward Reep, Sidney Simon, and Frede Vidar. In February 1942, the Office of Emergency Management opened an exhibition of war art at the National Gallery in Washington, DC. Over 1,000 artists submitted 2,582 pieces of art. In the following year *Life* held its own exhibition consisting of its commissioned paintings at the Metropolitan Museum of Art. This inspired a competition entitled 'America at War' organized by Artists for Victory, with the winning entries touring American cities in the autumn of 1943. Most of the entries focused on patriotic themes intended to remind Americans why they were fighting. One of the winners, Jacob Lawrence, depicted a tightly knit black community going about their leisurely pursuits at a time when black Americans were making a major contribution to the war effort yet received little visibility. The United States used official propaganda to orient troops and to motivate its civilian population, most famously in the US Army Signal Corps film series *Why We Fight* directed by Frank Capra. Hollywood, however, was quick to mobilize and enlist in the war cause. Many of the films produced during the war were patriotic rallying cries that affirmed a sense of national purpose. Combat films of the war years emphasized patriotism, group effort, and the value of individual sacrifices for a larger cause. Films like *Air Force*, *Destination Tokyo*, *Flying Tigers*, *Guadalcanal Diary*, *Objective, Burma!*, *Thirty Seconds Over Tokyo*, and *Wake*

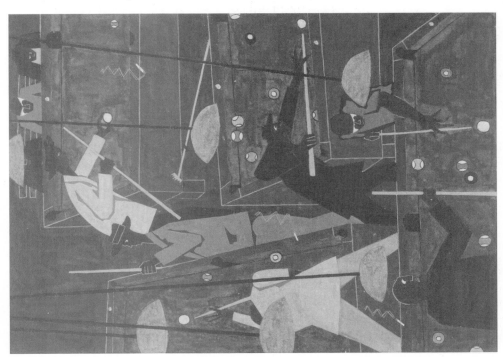

Jacob Lawrence, *Pool Parlor*, 1942.

Island gave viewers on the home front a vicarious sense of participating in the war. They portrayed the Second World War as a people's war, typically featuring a group of men from diverse ethnic backgrounds who are thrown together, tested on the battlefield, and moulded into a dedicated fighting unit. Many wartime films featured women characters playing an active role in the war by serving as combat nurses, riveters, welders, and long-suffering mothers who kept the home fires burning. Even cartoons, such as Donald Duck, *Der Fuehrer's Face*, Bugs Bunny, *Nips the Nips*, and Tom and Jerry, *The Yankee Doodle Mouse*, contributed to morale by juxtaposing crude stereotypes of the enemy with American 'democracy in action'.

During the war the US government carefully controlled its use of atrocity stories, a tactic that had been much discredited following the First World War. The American public seemed reluctant to believe the first news of Nazi genocide (which came from Jewish and Polish sources), and the US government made little attempt to further

publicize the story. The government often released news of Japanese atrocities in a very controlled way—often several months after the events became known—though not in the case of the notorious Bataan Death March, in which thousands of Allied soldiers died on their way to Japanese prisoner-of-war camps.

The approach varied between the European and Pacific theatres. Whereas in Europe the United States depicted the enemy as an evil regime, in Asia the enemy was depicted as an entire race. US war bond posters variously pictured the Japanese as rat-like or simian monsters. US newspaper cartoons took up the theme without official prompting, with the result that the fanatical Japanese soldier became a familiar and enduring stereotype. Parallel Japanese ideas about their sense of superiority to the West led to a war of mutual extermination on the island battlefields of the Pacific. Such crude, racially based propaganda laid the foundation for US use of the atomic bomb against Japan in August 1945.

The extraordinary level of government and commercial propaganda in the United States during the war created a number of myths that crumbled in the post-war period. Joseph Stalin proved to be something less than the avuncular nationalist of US

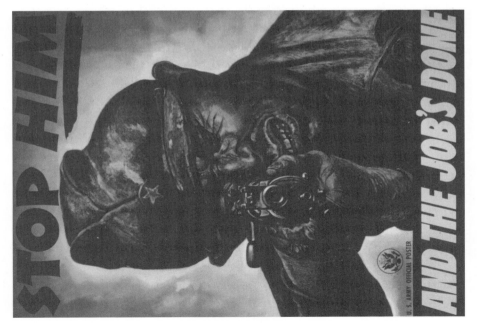

'Stop him...and the Job's Done', US anti-Japanese poster, 1942.

wartime propaganda, nor did Chiang Kai-shek in China live up to his image as the democratic strongman of Asia. In Republican propaganda the apologies for Stalin were seen as evidence of left-wing domination of the Roosevelt administration, and the 'loss' of China became evidence that Chiang had been betrayed by an American enemy within. Such claims set the stage for McCarthyism. The apparatus of US wartime propaganda, such as the Voice of America (VOA) radio station, survived the war to become the core of the US propaganda effort in the Cold War. On the battlefield General Dwight D. Eisenhower became convinced of the power of the 'P' (psychological factor) in warfare and championed the use of propaganda during his presidency.

Conclusion

The characteristic features of Modernism were apparent before 1914, but it is widely accepted that the First World War did have a profound effect on the subject matter, beliefs, and modes of expression of artists and thinkers. The Second World War came to a much less naïve world, and therefore did not have the same effect in transforming modes of thought and expression. It was, nonetheless, an experience of enormous intensity, and resulted in the production of a considerable body of work related directly to that experience. The horrific, powerful, and sometimes uplifting experiences of the Second World War were deeply etched into cultural artefacts at all levels, but there was no significant general shift in direction, such as is possible to associate with the First World War.

It could be argued that while the trauma of the First World War turned intellectuals in on themselves and towards the esoteric modes of Modernism, the Second World War, as a war of peoples and partisans, induced a turning back to realism. Such 'realism', however, was shaped less by the exigencies of war, and rather more by the ideological straitjackets of both the right and left, that defined the different regimes engaged in the conflict. Art therefore had an important educational and propagandistic role in that it was employed to teach, inform, and inculcate the state's value systems. After six years of war and a generation of totalitarianism, 'culture', to use Neal Ascherson's phrase, 'had been taken to the bath-house, to be shaved, deloused and scrubbed'. Thus, the Second World War was more clearly ideological in its motives and in the manner in which belligerents justified their war aims and were prepared to use art to reinforce the power of political rulers. Combatants were clearly designated by widely contrasting ideological beliefs, and, for the Western democracies at least, people knew what they were fighting for and against, in contrast to the more oblique war aims of the First World War. The war changed very little and was simply a continuation by other means. There were no 'big ideas' to justify war aims that accompanied the outbreak of war in 1914. All hope of returning to the European status quo of 1914 had been shattered. The fate of the historic states of Europe which had dominated the world in the late nineteenth century now depended on two great 'superpowers' that had come together late in the war to form an unlikely alliance against Fascism.

Propaganda came of age in the twentieth century. The developing mass and multimedia offered a fertile ground for propaganda, and global conflict provided the impetus needed for its growth. The far-reaching impact of the Second World War led to new political and sociological theories on the nature of man and modern society—particularly in the light of the rise of totalitarian police states. Some writers, such as the American sociologist Daniel Bell, talked about an 'end of ideology'. Individuals were viewed as undifferentiated and malleable while an apocalyptic vision of mass society emphasized the alienation of work, the collapse of religion and family ties, and a general decline in moral values. Culture, it was suggested, had been reduced to the lowest common denominator for mass consumption and the masses were generally seen as politically apathetic yet prone to ideological fanaticism, vulnerable to manipulation through the media—particularly the new medium of television—and viewed as a 'magic bullet' or 'hypodermic needle' by means of which opinions and behaviour could be controlled. The propaganda battle to 'win hearts and minds' that had been waged so fiercely in the Second World War continued during the period of economic and political hostility between Communist and capitalist countries known as the Cold War. Propagandists on all sides utilized their own interpretations of the truth in order to sell an ideological point of view to their citizens and to the world at large.

Plus ça change, plus c'est la même chose.

14 From World War to Cold War

GEOFFREY ROBERTS

As the Second World War drew to a close the leaders of the victorious Allied coalition proclaimed their commitment to a peacetime grand alliance that would guarantee peace and security for all states. 'Only with the continuing and growing cooperation and understanding among our three countries,' declared Stalin, Churchill, and Roosevelt at the Yalta summit in February 1945, 'can the highest aspiration of humanity be realized—a secure and lasting peace.'

Roosevelt, the pivotal figure in the triangular relationship of the Big Three, died in April and there were fears the grand alliance would fall apart. His successor as President of the United States was Harry S. Truman and when a couple of weeks later he met Vyacheslav Molotov, the Soviet foreign minister, there was some tough talking between the two men. At issue was the political composition of the Polish government. Poland had been liberated from German occupation by the Red Army and Stalin used Soviet military power to ensure a Polish government friendly to the USSR. Britain and the United States wanted a broader-based government, a stance that Truman pressed on Molotov. In his memoirs Truman claimed Molotov had been so shocked by the tone of their conversation that he complained he had never before in his life been talked to like that. Truman's reply was to assert that if the Soviet Union stuck to its agreements he wouldn't be. This closing exchange, unrecorded in either the American or the Soviet official reports of the meeting, was a figment of Truman's imagination. But the spat about Poland was very real and was a harbinger of future tensions in Soviet–Western relations. In the short term, however, the dispute was resolved by a compromise agreement resulting in a more diverse Polish government, albeit one remaining under Soviet control. By the time of the Potsdam Conference in July–August 1945 harmony in Soviet–American relations had been restored. At the close of the conference Stalin, Truman, and Clement Attlee (Churchill's successor as British Prime Minister) proclaimed they had 'strengthened the ties . . . and extended the scope of their collaboration and understanding' and had renewed their confidence in their ability to deliver 'a just and enduring peace'.

Within two years of this grand declaration the coalition which had defeated Hitler was in disarray and a 'Cold War' was developing between the Soviet Union and its erstwhile British and American allies. By the end of the 1940s Europe had split into competing political, ideological, and military blocs and the spectre of a new world war loomed as the Soviet Union and the United States confronted each other across what Churchill called the 'iron curtain'. Post-war demobilization of armed forces had been halted and powers both sides of the Iron Curtain divide were feverishly rearming. Fuelling this heated atmosphere was American and Soviet possession of atomic weapons, beginning the nuclear arms race. In 1950 these Cold War tensions spilled over into a proxy US/USSR war in Korea—a three-year conflict that claimed more than a million lives.

Peacemaking

One early public sign that the grand alliance could be in trouble came at the first meeting of the Council of Foreign Ministers (CFM) in London in September 1945. The CFM had been established by the Potsdam Conference to draw up peace treaties to be signed by defeated enemy states. The council's main task was to compose a peace treaty for Germany but it agreed to deal first with the minor Axis states—Bulgaria, Hungary, Italy, and Romania—and with Finland, a German ally in the war against the Soviet Union which was not a formal member of the Axis alliance. These treaties, it was expected, would be sorted out quite quickly. However, Bulgaria and Romania had pro-Soviet governments which Britain and the United States refused to recognize until elections had been held. It would not be possible for peace treaties to be signed with those states without such diplomatic recognition.

Bulgaria, Poland, and Romania, together with Hungary, Czechoslovakia, and Yugoslavia, were included in the Soviet sphere of influence in Eastern Europe—a region Stalin designated as vital to the USSR's post-war security. At a minimum this meant maintaining friendly governments and allotting a significant role to the Soviets' local Communist allies. Since the Red Army had conquered most of Eastern Europe on its victorious march to Berlin, Stalin was in a strong position to demand what he wanted. The Soviet position was bolstered by growing popular support for the Communist parties of Eastern Europe. Admittedly only in Czechoslovakia and Yugoslavia did this support approach a popular majority, but it was significant elsewhere too. Domestic opposition to East European Communism was discredited by its connections to the old authoritarian regimes of the region, many of which had been allied to Germany during the war. With Soviet support the East European Communists were a formidable force. A similar post-war upsurge in support for Communism took place in Western Europe, most notably in France and Italy where Communists had played a significant role in anti-Nazi and anti-Fascist resistance. In both countries the Communist parties were hugely popular and leading participants in the ruling coalition governments.

While the British and Americans accepted that the Soviets had legitimate security interests in Eastern Europe they were determined to oppose Soviet domination, especially where it meant the exclusion of their own influence. They based their stance on the commitment in both the Atlantic Charter and the Yalta Declaration on Liberated Europe to give the peoples of Eastern Europe the freedom to choose their own governments.

The scene was set for the logjam at the London CFM meeting at which Western refusal to recognize the Bulgarian and Romanian governments was countered by Soviet obstruction of other peace treaties, especially for Italy, which lay in the Anglo-American sphere of influence.

Stalin's annoyance at the lack of Western restraint in relation to the USSR's sphere of influence in Eastern Europe was compounded by the Soviet Union's exclusion from any effective say in the detail of the post-war occupation of Japan. The USSR had entered the Far Eastern war in August 1945 in return for a number of territorial concessions in relation to China and Japan. But Stalin also expected that Japan, like Germany, would be jointly occupied by the Allies and divided into zones of military jurisdiction. Indeed, the Soviets had planned to invade and occupy the Japanese home island of Hokkaido but were thwarted by the sudden end to the war brought about by the shock and awe of the American atomic bombing of Hiroshima and Nagasaki and by the Red Army's massive invasion of Japanese-occupied Manchuria.

After a month of fruitless discussions the London CFM closed without any agreements being reached. The ostensible reason for failure was a procedural dispute about the participation of France and China in the council's deliberations: the Soviets wanted to restrict their participation in discussion to issues that directly concerned them, while the British and Americans wanted the French and Chinese involved in all proceedings. The Soviets did not relish the prospect of being a minority of one in a five-sided discussion. But the substantive reason for the CFM's failure was the dispute about Bulgaria and Romania. Both sides attempted to put a brave face on what happened but it was clear the grand alliance had flunked its first post-war test.

Some historians define the clash over Bulgaria and Romania at the London CFM as the beginning of the Cold War. However, three months later, in December 1945, tripartite negotiations were resumed at a conference of the American, British, and Soviet foreign ministers in Moscow (the French and Chinese were not invited to this gathering). This meeting successfully brokered a deal to broaden the political basis of the Bulgarian and Romanian governments in exchange for Western diplomatic recognition. Agreement was also reached on strengthening the Soviets' advisory role in the occupation of Japan.

These successes paved the way for CFM discussions on the peace treaties for the minor Axis states to resume. Those proved to be prolonged, tedious, often rancorous, but occasionally leavened by a little humour. The talks took place between Molotov, Ernest Bevin, the British Foreign Secretary, and James F. Byrnes, the US Secretary of State.

Molotov had been Stalin's right-hand man since the 1920s. In the 1930s he served as Soviet Prime Minister and presided over a maelstrom of mass violence and political terror resulting in the deaths of several million citizens. In 1939 he became Soviet foreign minister and was involved in negotiations with the British and French for a triple alliance against Germany. When on the eve of the Second World War these negotiations failed, he and Stalin turned instead to a deal with Hitler, signing the German–Soviet non-aggression pact. During the war Molotov became a central figure in the diplomacy of the grand alliance, acclaimed often in the Western press as a skilful diplomat and politician. He had a well-deserved reputation as a tough and astute negotiator who could be annoyingly persistent in pursuit of Soviet policy goals. During the post-war CFM negotiations he became known as Mr Nyet—the man who liked to say no to Western proposals. However, subsequent research has revealed that Molotov was more inclined than Stalin to compromise with the West. Indeed, towards the end of his life Stalin denounced Molotov as an appeaser of Western capitalism. Molotov's greatest claim to fame was the improvised incendiary device named after him. This dated from the Soviet–Finnish war of 1939–40 when the Finns had taken to attacking pockets of surrounded Soviet troops by throwing lit glass bottles filled with petrol, known derisively as 'Molotov cocktails'.

As a tough negotiator Molotov met his match in Bevin. Before the war Bevin had been leader of Britain's biggest trade union and had often clashed with British Communist trade unionists about policy and control of the union. During the war he had served as Minister of Labour and National Service in Churchill's coalition government

Vyacheslav Molotov, the Soviet Union's People's Commissar for Foreign Affairs and Foreign Minister, 1939–49 and 1953–6. Molotov was, in effect, Stalin's deputy. He favoured a more conciliatory line in negotiations with the West, a position that led to a falling out with Stalin a few months before the dictator's death in March 1953.

British Foreign Secretary, Ernest Bevin, and Labour Prime Minister, Clement Attlee. As a former trade union leader Bevin had often clashed with Communist activists. This experience served him well when dealing with Molotov during the post-war peace negotiations, as did his skill as a trade union negotiator.

and became Foreign Secretary when the Labour Party won the 1945 General Election. Molotov may have been a Bolshevik but it was Bevin who came from a working-class background. Bevin could be abrasive and he did not get on with Molotov personally or politically. The two men often clashed sharply in the CFM negotiations.

James F. Byrnes was an experienced, skilful, and sophisticated American politician from South Carolina. He was more inclined than was Bevin to negotiate a peace settlement reflecting the post-war reality of Soviet and Western spheres of influence in Europe, provoking Truman to accuse him of 'babying the Soviets'. During the CFM negotiations Byrnes offered to sign a 25-year pact on disarmament and demilitarization of Germany. Molotov was interested in negotiating such a treaty but was overruled by Stalin, who suspected the West's aspiration was to dislodge the Soviet Union from occupied Germany while at the same time entrenching the United States' position in post-war Europe. Byrnes's patience in the prolonged CFM negotiations was instrumental in securing at least some successes.

A particular feature of the CFM negotiations was their open character—arguments were thrashed out in the press as well as behind closed doors. However, such publicity further polarized opinion between the Soviet Union and the Western states and facilitated lobbying by interested parties. Communist Yugoslavia, for instance, was active in procuring Soviet support for its claim to the Italian city of Trieste—a dispute that was resolved by the decision to internationalize the city until it was reunited with Italy in 1954.

James F. Byrnes, President Truman's Secretary of State, 1945–7. Byrnes left office in January 1947 when negotiations about the post-war peace treaties with the minor Axis states were complete. He was replaced by George C. Marshall, who had been Chief of Staff of the US Army during the Second World War. In June 1947 he put forward the idea of the 'Marshall Plan'—an economic aid programme to help post-war European recovery.

During these CFM negotiations a Western proposal for the final terms of the peace treaties to be agreed by a broader peace conference involving other Allied nations as well as the great powers became a major procedural issue. The Soviets refused to accept the plan, fearing they would be outvoted at such a conference. Throughout the CFM negotiations Molotov continued to insist on tripartism, on co-decision-making with unanimity between Britain, the Soviet Union, and the United States. Molotov did, however, agree to a peace conference being convened in Paris in summer 1946.

The model for the conference was the Versailles conference of 1919–20 which led to the peace treaty with Germany after the First World War. But there were a number of differences between the two conferences.

First, there were fewer states represented at the Paris conference (21 as opposed to 27). This was because the criterion for representation was that a state had to have waged war against the Axis with substantial military force, whereas Versailles could be attended by any state that had declared war or broken diplomatic relations with the defeated powers. Secondly, the Versailles treaty was drafted and agreed at the conference itself. In 1946 the delegates were presented with detailed drafts prepared by the CFM and it was this body that ultimately decided the peace treaties. At Versailles the great powers had protected their position by a weighted voting system in which they each got five votes. In 1946 all states were equal in voting terms, but since the conference was consultative rather than decision-taking the democracy was a bit of a façade. Thirdly, the defeated powers were excluded from the Versailles discussions, attending only to sign peace treaties whose terms were dictated by the victor states; in

1946 the five states whose peace treaties were being considered were invited to present their views on what was being proposed. Germany was not invited to attend: a German peace treaty was not discussed in Paris in 1946 and, in any event, there was no central German administration to invite because the country was divided and occupied. Fourthly, the proceedings leading to the Versailles treaty were conducted mostly in secret, in contrast to the 1946 conference, which was an exercise in public diplomacy. The public staging of the Paris conference accentuated differences of opinion, particularly between Britain and the United States, on the one hand, and the Soviet Union, on the other. Finally, while both conferences were dominated and controlled by the great powers—Britain, France, and the United States in 1919–20, Britain, the United States, and the Soviet Union in 1946—the differences and divisions within these groups of states were far greater after the Second World War. The dominant powers at Versailles were liberal capitalist democracies who shared a common identity and many goals and interests. The Anglo-American-Soviet

The Paris Peace Conference of 1946 was the post-Second World War version of the Versailles peace conference but it was a pale imitation of its illustrious First World War predecessor. All the important negotiations took place before and after the conference and it did not consider the most important post-war question—the future of Germany.

President Harry Truman shaking hands with American diplomat, Edward Stettinius, at the founding conference of the United Nations, June 1945. The UN was the brainchild of Truman's predecessor President Franklin Delano Roosevelt. In its early years the UN was heavily dominated by the great powers.

partnership after the Second World War was complicated by the Communist–capitalist division as well as by a long history of antagonism that dated back to the Bolshevik seizure of power in Russia in 1917.

The Paris peace conference was held in the Palace of Luxembourg in Paris and lasted for more than two months (29 July–15 October 1946). It agreed a series of recommendations which were then considered by the CFM. After a final round of wrangling at a meeting of the CFM in New York, agreement was reached—much to the relief of Bevin, Byrnes, and Molotov, who had devoted so much time to the negotiations. In the circumstances, concluding peace treaties with Bulgaria, Finland, Hungary, Italy, and Romania in February 1947 was a significant achievement, proving that though the grand alliance might be tottering, it had not yet collapsed.

The grand alliance had other successes in this period too, most notably founding the United Nations in San Francisco in June 1945. Heading the successor to the

British cartoonist David Low's representation of the trial of Nazi war criminals at Nuremburg in October 1946. The Nazi leaders were charged with waging aggressive war and crimes against humanity. Twelve of the accused were sentenced to death, seven received prison sentences, and three were acquitted.

VERDICT

(Copyright in All Countries)

TUESDAY, OCTOBER 1, 1946

League of Nations was a Security Council on which sat Britain, China, France, the Soviet Union, and the United States as permanent and veto vote-wielding members. The veto was a wartime invention designed to meet Soviet demands made at Yalta for the future Security Council's actions to be based on unanimity. As Stalin had argued, great power unity was essential if the UN was to be an organization capable of securing peace for the next fifty years.

The Nuremberg trial of major Nazi war criminals in 1945–6 was another important success for the grand alliance. Some commentators called it 'victors' justice', but the trial, conviction, and execution of many leaders of the Third Reich on charges of human rights violations and conspiracy to wage aggressive war was a political and diplomatic success that helped to draw a line under the conflicts of the Second World War.

There was a similar trial of major Japanese war criminals in Tokyo in 1946–7, which resulted in the execution of seven defendants, including General Hideki Togo, Japan's Prime Minister during the war. This trial proved to be even more controversial than Nuremberg, at least in retrospect, with many arguing that Japan had not conspired to wage an aggressive war to the same extent as Germany.

Efforts to bring to court major Italian war criminals faltered in the face of the outbreak of the Cold War. In 1948 Marshal Rodolfo Graziani—the only Fascist general to remain loyal to Mussolini after the dictator was deposed in July 1943—was convicted of war crimes and sentenced to 19 years in gaol by an Italian military tribunal but he was released after a few months.

The German Question

What to do with Germany was the greatest challenge facing the grand alliance. The Big Three had agreed during the war that a defeated Germany would be jointly occupied by the Allies, to be denazified, demilitarized, and democratized. To this end Germany was to be divided into Soviet and Western zones of military occupation (France was later given a small zone in southern Germany). The city of Berlin was also to be so divided, despite its location deep within the designated Soviet zone of occupation in eastern Germany. Each country would control its own occupation zone and there was to be an Allied Control Council to co-ordinate the implementation of agreed policies. At Tehran, Yalta, and other summit meetings there had been talk about dismembering Germany—breaking it into a number of smaller states—but by the end of the war both the Soviets and their Western allies found it convenient to drop this idea. Instead, Germany would be reunited after the war, the political basis for which needed to be the subject of further inter-Allied negotiations.

Negotiations on a peace treaty for Germany began at the Moscow CFM conference in March–April 1947. Yet by the time these discussions began the supposedly temporary occupation zones were already solidifying into more permanent divisions. An ongoing process of capitalist economic integration in the western zones disconnected them from the Soviet occupation zone, while in eastern Germany the Communists were, with Moscow's help, consolidating their position and pushing for socialist development.

At the Moscow CFM the Soviets argued for a unified German administration whose purpose would be to work towards political and economic integration of all Allied zones of occupation. The Western powers favoured a looser political structure—to protect their position in West Germany—and insisted on prior resolution of various economic questions, above all the issue of reparations. At Yalta it had been agreed Germany would pay $20 billion in reparations, half of which would go to the Soviets and would be paid not in money (as had happened after the First World War) but in machinery and deliveries from current production. Crucially, these reparations were to be produced from Western occupation zones as well as from the Soviet zone. The Western point of view held that reparations threatened post-war economic recovery not only in Germany but also in Europe as a whole. The British and Americans were concerned, too, that if reparations crippled West German economic recovery they would have to provide aid and would, in effect, end up paying the reparations bill as had happened after the First World War.

The Moscow CFM was not as divisive as the failed London session of September 1945 but it too closed without reaching agreement. German peace treaty discussions continued at future CFM meetings but the looming hostilities of the Cold War increasingly influenced proceedings. Soviet–Western negotiations about reuniting Germany were destined to fail. Indeed, by October 1949 two separate states had been established in West Germany and East Germany.

The Soviets were desperate to avert the post-war division of Germany because they feared a revived West Germany—the biggest, most populous, and heavily-industrialized portion of the country—would join an anti-Soviet Western bloc. In June 1948 they used the pretext of currency reform in Western zones of occupation—which they said would destabilize the economy of the Soviet zones—to blockade land routes into West Berlin. Faced with the prospect of 2.5 million West Berliners starving from lack of supplies, the Western powers staged an airlift to provide for their zones in the German capital. In the course of the next year some 700 Western planes flew a quarter of million flights in and out of Berlin.

Civilians in Berlin watch an American C-54 cargo plane air-lifting supplies to the blockaded western sectors of the city in 1948. The blockade and the airlift lasted from June 1948 to May 1949. Historians disagree as to whether Stalin was trying to force the Western powers to relinquish control of West Berlin or force them to negotiate about the future of Germany as a whole.

The Berlin airlift was the first great crisis of the Cold War, seen in the West as an attempt by the Soviets to force the Americans, British, and French to abandon their occupation zones in West Berlin. In fact, the Soviet aim was rather more modest: to force the Western states to return to negotiations on the German question. Indeed, the Soviet blockade was lifted in May 1949 when agreement was reached on convening a CFM meeting in Paris. The meeting took place a month later but, again, no agreement was reached. The *de facto* resolution of the German question became division of the country into a pro-Soviet German Democratic Republic and a pro-Western Federal Republic of Germany. While the Soviets feared a German revival, the West was preoccupied by the perceived threat to its interests from the USSR and its Communist allies.

The Iron Curtain

Winston Churchill's so-called 'Iron Curtain' speech in Fulton, Missouri in March 1946 was a clear, early sign of why the post-war grand alliance was in danger of disintegrating. Although Churchill was no longer British Prime Minister when he went to Westminster College to receive an honorary degree and give a speech, President Truman was on the platform (Missouri was Truman's home state).

Churchill's lecture entitled 'The Sinews of Peace' proposed extending from 20 years to 50 years the term of the 1942 Anglo-Soviet treaty of alliance. 'We aim at nothing but mutual assistance and collaboration with Russia', said Churchill, who expressed 'strong admiration and regard for the valiant Russian people and for my wartime comrade, Marshal Stalin'. The sting came in the tail of this section of the speech:

From Stettin in the Baltic to Trieste in the Adriatic an *iron curtain* has descended across the Continent. Behind that line lie all the capitals of the ancient states of Central and Eastern Europe. Warsaw, Berlin, Prague, Vienna, Budapest, Belgrade, Bucharest and Sofia, all these famous cities . . . lie in what I must call the Soviet sphere, and all are subject in one form or another, not only to Soviet influence, but to a very high and, in some cases, increasing measure of control from Moscow . . . The Communist parties . . . have been raised to pre-eminence and power far beyond their numbers and are seeking everywhere to obtain totalitarian control.

Churchill's moral was that the Western democracies had to stick together and take a strong stand in defence of their principles. The Russians had no respect for weakness, Churchill told his audience, and he drew a parallel with the appeasement policies that had allowed Hitler to unleash war. To prevent similar events happening again 'a good understanding' had to be reached with the Soviet Union.

Stalin responded to Churchill's speech in an interview with *Pravda* on 14 March. According to Stalin, Churchill was trying to provoke a new war and was an advocate of English-speaking domination of the world. Stalin did not mention the 'Iron Curtain' but he frankly asserted the USSR's right to friendly regimes in Eastern Europe, given that these states had provided a platform for German aggression against the Soviet Union. In conclusion Stalin alluded to Churchill's role in the anti-Bolshevik coalition that had intervened in the Russian civil war and promised that if 'Churchill

Former British prime minister Winston Churchill speaking in Fulton, Missouri on 5 March 1946. Churchill spoke of an 'iron curtain' descending across central and eastern Europe, behind which was a Soviet sphere of influence and control. Missouri was President Truman's home state and his presence on the stage behind Churchill added to the speech's authority as a statement of Western policy.

and his friends' succeeded in organizing a 'new march against Eastern Europe' they 'will be beaten again as they were beaten in the past'. On one point Stalin agreed with Churchill: Communists had increased their influence in Eastern Europe because, according to the Soviet dictator, they had been the most fearless fighters against Fascism. Stalin pointed out, too, that support for Communists was also growing in Western Europe.

Churchill's speech was interpreted by the Soviets as evidence of a Western policy tendency to break with the grand alliance and to end post-war collaboration with the Soviet Union. In a speech of November 1946 Stalin's ideology chief, Andrei Zhdanov, identified two tendencies in the post-war world: the peaceful tendency represented by the Soviet Union and the tendency represented by the forces of expansionism and aggression. Zhdanov also lamented changing Western attitudes towards their former wartime ally:

One reads and wonders how quickly the Russians have changed. When our blood streamed in the battlefields they admired our courage, bravery, high morale and boundless patriotism. And now that we wish, in cooperation with other nations, to make use of our equal rights to participate in international affairs, they begin to shower us with abuse and slander, to vilify and abuse us, saying at the same time that we possess an unbearable and suspicious character.

In March 1947 it was Truman's turn to make statements indicating the coming Cold War. In a dramatic speech to the US Congress he called upon the United States to act in defence of the 'free world'. Truman did not mention the Soviets or the Communists but it was clear who the target was:

The peoples of a number of countries...have recently had totalitarian regimes forced upon them against their will. The Government of the United States has made frequent protests against coercion and intimidation...in Poland, Romania and Bulgaria...At the present moment in world history nearly every nation in the world must choose between alternative ways of life...One way of life is based on the will of the majority...The second way of life is based upon the will of the minority forcibly imposed upon the majority...I believe it must be the policy of the United States to support free peoples who resist attempted subjugation by armed minorities or by outside pressures.

Truman's speech came to be known as the Truman Doctrine and was closely associated with the policy of containment advocated by George Kennan, the American chargé d'affaires in Moscow. In 1946 Kennan's dispatches to Washington had an important influence on American perceptions of post-war Soviet policy. Then in July 1947 Kennan published an anonymous article, attributed to author X, in the influential US journal *Foreign Affairs* called 'The Sources of Soviet Conduct'. In this article Kennan described a messianic, expansionist state that could not be negotiated with but could be contained by the adroit deployment of countervailing power.

Kennan's article did not use the term 'Cold War' but American journalist Walter Lippmann wrote a series of newspaper pieces in response to him, later published as a

George F. Kennan, an American diplomat in Moscow, 1944–7. He was widely regarded as the architect of the US doctrine of containment—opposing Communism and the Soviet Union by the deployment of countervailing power—a doctrine that he later repudiated.

booklet entitled *The Cold War*. This popularized the concept of the Cold War as shorthand for the growing tensions in Soviet–Western relations. But Lippmann did not share Kennan's view that Soviet expansionism was the ineluctable result of a messianic Communist ideology. Rather, the tensions were the result of the outcome of the war and the consequent expansion of Soviet military power, and could best be dealt with by negotiation and agreement.

The Arc of Crisis

The practical purpose of Truman's speech was to persuade Congress to vote financial aid for Greece and Turkey. Problems with these two countries were part of a southern arc of crisis in early post-war Soviet–Western relations that also encompassed Iran and North Africa.

Soviet support for a Communist-led insurgency against its pro-Western government was the source of tension in relation to Greece. During the war Soviet support for the Greek partisans had been constrained by the Stalin–Churchill percentages agreement of October 1944 which had allocated the country to Britain's sphere of influence in exchange for recognition of Soviet predominance in Bulgaria, Hungary, and Romania. When the war ended Soviet policy changed and Moscow began to criticize the 'reign of terror' in Greece unleashed by the conservative Royalist government with British support. At the London CFM the Soviets attempted to trade reticence on the Greek question in exchange for Western recognition of the Bulgarian and Romanian governments, but the equivalence was not accepted by Bevin and Byrnes. At the Moscow foreign ministers' conference of December 1945 the Soviets demanded withdrawal of British forces from Greece. This demand was part of a substantial Soviet campaign in 1946 for a general withdrawal of Western armed forces from foreign countries. But Soviet support for the Greek insurgents remained more rhetorical than real. Stalin did not agree with the militant tactics of the Greek Communists and not until 1947–8 did the Soviets begin to offer substantial material aid to the Communist side of the civil war. However, from the outset Greek partisans were supported by Communist Yugoslavia, Bulgaria, and Albania, and the West perceived Moscow as being responsible for this aid.

The crisis in Soviet–Western relations over Iran resulted from a dispute over post-war troop withdrawals from the country. In August 1941 British and Soviet forces had entered Iran to overthrow German influence in the country, protect oil supplies, and secure allied supply routes to the USSR. Soviet troops occupied north Iran, with the British in the south, and the Iranians remaining nominally in control of the central region. Under a January 1942 Treaty of Alliance with Iran the British and the Soviets both pledged to withdraw their forces six months after the end of the war.

The Soviets had long coveted an Iranian oil concession and took advantage of the occupation to further their interests. But negotiations failed when the Iranians decided not to grant any more oil concessions until Allied troops were withdrawn after the war. To put pressure on the Iranians the Soviets supported an independence

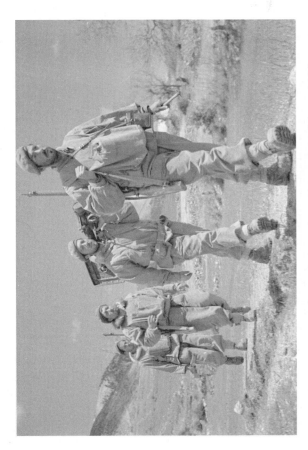

1948: a band of Greek Army commandos on the move during the Greek Civil War, which began in 1946 when Communist-led partisans launched a violent struggle to overthrow the conservative government which, with the aid of the British, had come to power in Greece after the war. The Communist military campaign lasted until 1949 when it was called off on Stalin's advice.

movement in southern Azerbaijan that demanded political–cultural autonomy and closer links with Soviet (i.e. northern) Azerbaijan. The Soviets used violent clashes between the Iranian authorities and the Azerbaijan independence movement as an excuse to delay troop withdrawal after the war. The Iranian response was to raise the issue at the United Nations so the Soviets came under international pressure to withdraw their troops. A compromise on a possible oil deal with Iran led eventually to the withdrawal of Soviet troops in May 1946. Subsequently, the Azerbaijan independence movement was crushed by Tehran and its leaders forced to flee to the Soviet Union. In a letter to one of these refugee Azeri leaders Stalin justified the Soviet troop withdrawal in these terms:

The presence of Soviet troops in Iran undercut the foundations of our liberationist policies in Europe and Asia. The British and Americans said to us that if Soviet troops could stay in Iran, then why could not British troops stay in Egypt, Syria, Indonesia, Greece, and also American troops—in China, Iceland, in Denmark. Therefore we decided to withdraw troops from Iran and China, in order to seize this tool from the hands of the British and Americans, to unleash the liberation movement in the colonies and thereby to render our liberationist policy more justified and efficient.

The Soviet–Western clash over Turkey came as a result of Stalin's efforts to control access from the Mediterranean to the Black Sea. The Black Sea Straits were controlled by Ankara under the terms of the 1936 Montreux Convention. Although the USSR was a signatory to the agreement Stalin was dissatisfied and complained bitterly to the

British and Americans during the war, asking how they would feel with no control over the Suez or Panama canals.

In March 1945 Molotov told the Turks the USSR would not renew the 20-year 1925 Soviet–Turkish Treaty of Friendship and Neutrality. The Soviets wanted a new treaty to establish joint Soviet–Turkish control over access to the Black Sea and to allow Soviet military bases to be established on the Straits. This was not the first time Molotov had demanded control of the Straits. When he visited Hitler in Berlin in November 1941 it had been a key Soviet proposal as part of a deal to revive the faltering Nazi–Soviet pact, a demand rejected by Hitler, who by this time was intent on war with the USSR. When Molotov revived this idea at the end of the Second World War he also raised the stakes by making some Soviet territorial demands in relation to Armenian and Georgian lands previously ceded by the USSR to Turkey in the 1920s.

The Turks stalled, saying that changing the regime governing the Straits was a matter for multilateral negotiations, and they were supported in this by the Western powers. The disappointed Soviets pointed out to the British that during the First World War London had been prepared to concede Constantinople to Tsarist Russia. At the same time Stalin rejected military speculation about a possible Soviet–Turkish war over the Straits while ordering military manoeuvres along the Soviet borders with Turkey.

When in August 1946 Moscow sent Ankara a diplomatic note on the revision of the Montreux Convention, the Soviet–Turkish crisis over the Straits came to a head. The Soviet note demanded, in effect, joint control of the Straits with Turkey. But, when confronted with Turkish and Western resistance to his demands, Stalin backed away from a confrontation over the Straits, notwithstanding advice from the Soviet ambassador in Ankara that the USSR should ratchet up the 'war of nerves' with Turkey.

Often seen as the most brazen example of attempted Soviet expansionism after the war was Moscow's demand for trusteeship over the Italian colony of Tripolitania (Western Libya). The issue arose in the context of discussions to replace League of Nations' mandate territories with a system of international trusteeship to govern former colonies until they became fully independent. Crucially, this new system would also apply to the ex-colonies of the defeated Axis states. At the London CFM in September 1945 the Soviets requested that Tripolitania should become a trust territory under their control. Molotov's rationalization of this demand is worth quoting for the light it throws on the post-war aspirations and pretensions of the USSR:

The Soviet Government considered the future of Tripolitania as of primary importance to the Soviet people and they must press their request to assume the trusteeship of that territory. The Soviet Government claimed the right to active participation in the disposal of the Italian Colonies because Italy had attacked, and had inflicted enormous damage upon, the Soviet Union.... The territory of the Soviet Union was vast, stretching from the extreme east far into the west. It had a sea outlet in the north: it must also have use of ports in the south, especially since it now had the right to use Dairen and Port Arthur in the Far East. The Soviet Government had no intention of restricting in any way the facilities available to the British Commonwealth for maintaining communications with all parts of the world. But Britain should not hold a monopoly of communications in the Mediterranean. Russia was anxious to have bases in the Mediterranean for her merchant fleet. World trade would develop and the Soviet Union wished to take her share in it. Further … the Soviet Government possessed wide experience in establishing friendly relations between various nationalities and was anxious to use that experience in Tripolitania. They would not propose to introduce the Soviet system into Tripolitania. They would take steps to promote a system of democratic government.

Molotov pressed this argument in private meetings with Bevin and Byrnes but made no headway. To the chagrin of both Molotov and Stalin, the West made no concessions on the trusteeship issue and Soviet ambitions in the eastern Mediterranean remained unfulfilled, although the USSR did acquire a naval base in Syria in 1971.

From Moscow's point of view it had acted with restraint in relation to Greece and saw its demands in relation to Iran, Turkey, and Tripolitania as reasonable and a just reward for the USSR's role and sacrifices in winning the war. From the British and American point of view, however, Stalin's actions represented a pattern of aggression and expansion that threatened their core interests. The disputes also raised in Western minds the question of what the Soviets might have in mind for Western Europe should they be given the chance to extend their power and influence in that direction.

The Marshall Plan

By the time of Truman's March 1947 speech the Western powers had begun to adopt a Cold War stance in relation to the USSR—they no longer believed it was possible to negotiate with the Soviets, were concerned about the consolidation of the Communist grip on Eastern Europe, and felt threatened by the strength of the Communists and their allies in Western Europe. The emergent Western policy was one of containment—deploying countervailing power to stop Soviet expansionism combined with an increasingly militant response to the Communist political and ideological challenge.

The Soviet response to Truman's speech was somewhat subdued compared with their reaction to Churchill's Iron Curtain rhetoric, perhaps because they did not want to spoil the Moscow CFM which took place around the same time. Also the Soviets—unlike their Western counterparts—had not given up completely on continuing the grand alliance and hoped a workable collaboration with the West was still possible. But the next crisis in Soviet–Western relations would propel them into a full-blown Cold War position, too.

In June 1947 Byrnes's successor as US Secretary of State, George C. Marshall, spoke at Harvard University on the need for a large-scale programme of American financial support to aid European economic recovery. Behind Marshall's proposal lay American fears of a Communist takeover in a Western Europe that remained war-ravaged and impoverished. In sponsoring a European economic recovery to contribute to political stability, Marshall aimed to undermine support for the Communist left, especially in key countries such as France and Italy.

Although the Americans were thinking mainly in terms of Western Europe, the Soviet Union and Eastern Europe were not excluded from the proposed aid programme. Indeed the British and French governments responded to Marshall's speech by inviting the Soviets to a conference in Paris to discuss a pan-European response to the plan.

The Soviet response to the Marshall Plan was mixed. On the one hand, Moscow welcomed the possibility of American loans and grants, for themselves and their East European allies. Soviet economists advised the Marshall Plan was a response to America's post-war economic problems, particularly a lack of demand for its exports in Europe. The plan's purpose was to provide dollars to Europeans so that they could buy American goods and services. On the other hand, the Soviets feared the Marshall Plan as an economic counterpart of Truman's speech—a means of using American financial muscle to build an anti-Soviet alliance in Europe.

Stalin decided to find out if the Marshall Plan was a political threat or an economic opportunity. At the end of June Molotov was sent to Paris to negotiate with Bevin and Georges Bidault, the French foreign minister. In Paris Molotov's worst fears were confirmed when the British and French insisted (in accordance with Marshall's express wishes) on a co-ordinated and pan-European economic aid plan. This was seen by the Soviets as a Western device to interfere in the economic and political life of Communist-controlled East Europe. In the worst-case scenario they feared their sphere of influence in Eastern Europe would unravel.

The Soviet Union withdrew from the Marshall Plan talks and insisted that their East European allies should not participate either. Moscow then launched a diplomatic and political campaign against the Marshall Plan. In a speech to the UN in September 1947 Soviet deputy foreign minister Andrei Vyshinsky denounced the plan thus:

The Marshall Plan constitutes in essence merely a variant of the Truman Doctrine…the implementation of the Marshall Plan will mean placing European countries under the economic and political control of the United States and direct interference in the internal affairs of those countries…this plan is an attempt to split Europe into two camps…to complete the formation of a bloc of several European countries hostile to the interests of the democratic countries of Eastern Europe and most particularly to the interests of the Soviet Union.

The Cominform

That same month the Soviets launched the Communist Information Bureau (Cominform) at a conference in Poland. This was an organization of the ruling European Communist parties plus the French and Italian Communists, who had recently been ousted from their respective coalition governments. Zhdanov gave the keynote speech, using the Marshall Plan to illustrate his argument about how the post-war split between two trends, which he had identified a year earlier, was now solidified in the formation of two blocs or camps:

The further we are removed from the end of the war, the more clearly do the two basic orientations in postwar international politics stand out, corresponding to the division…into two basic camps: the imperialist and anti-democratic camp…and the anti-imperialist and democratic camp… The principal leading force in the imperialist camp is the USA… The fundamental aim of the imperialist camp is to strengthen imperialism, prepare a new imperialist war, fight against socialism and democracy, and give all-round support to reactionary and anti-democratic, pro-fascist regimes and movements. For the performance of these tasks the imperialist camp is ready to rely on reactionary and anti-democratic elements in all countries and to back former war-enemies against its own wartime allies. The anti-imperialist and anti-fascist forces constitute the other camp with, as their mainstay, the USSR and the countries of new democracy… The aim of this camp is to fight against the threat of new wars and imperialist expansion, to consolidate democracy and to uproot what remains of fascism.

Zhdanov's two-camps speech, as it came to be known, was the Soviet riposte to the Truman Doctrine and the Marshall Plan, in effect a counter-declaration of the Cold War. It signalled an acceleration of the Communization, Sovietization, and Stalinization of Eastern Europe. *Communization* entailed the establishment of single-party Communist control, instead of the left-wing coalitions that had hitherto prevailed. This meant Communist control of the state and state control of the press; the dissolution and repression of opposition parties and an end to independent left-wing parties by forced socialist–Communist party mergers; and totalitarian political control of social and private life. *Sovietization* meant the imposition of the Soviet model of socialism: state-owned and controlled economies, centralized state planning, and collectivized agriculture. *Stalinization* meant the introduction, albeit on a smaller scale, of the personality cult and political terrorism—purges, arrests, show trials, and executions—that characterized Stalin's rule in the Soviet Union.

Contrary to Western perceptions, the Communization, Sovietization, and Stalinization of Eastern Europe did not take place all at once or according to a single timetable or pattern. Even before the Cominform conference the process of transforming what was called people's or new democracy into full-blown Communist regimes on the Soviet model was far advanced in several countries (Bulgaria, Romania, and Yugoslavia), while in others (Hungary and Poland) there appeared to be distinct tendencies in that direction. The trend was least marked in Czechoslovakia, a country with an established tradition of parliamentary democracy (the pre-war politics of the other East European states was more authoritarian than democratic) and where the Communists and their socialist allies had won a majority in the 1946 elections. However, a government crisis in Prague in February 1948 resulted in the liberal and centre parties being ousted from power and an end to the Czechoslovak experiment in coalitionist people's democracy. The events in Prague were seen as a Communist coup by the West, crushing the last vestige of democracy in Eastern Europe. Western public opinion was also shocked by the death shortly after these events of Jan Masaryk, the Czechoslovak foreign minister. Masaryk was found dead from a fall from his office building. The official explanation was that he had committed suicide but many suspected that he had been murdered by defenestration.

Mass rally of Communists during the Prague coup in Czechoslovakia in February 1948 that ousted non-Communist members from the coalition government. Czechoslovakia was the one country in central and eastern Europe where the Communists and the socialist allies had a democratic majority. But even in Czechoslovakia the Communists felt compelled to seize all power for themselves.

A crack did appear in the Communist bloc in June 1948 when Yugoslavia was expelled from the Cominform. But what happened next confirmed Western perceptions about Communist Eastern Europe being a dark, alien, and threatening place. A dispute over foreign policy had created the split between Stalin and Josip Broz Tito, the Yugoslav Communist leader. Tito wanted to pursue a relatively independent foreign policy, especially in relation to Balkan affairs, and tried to form a federation with Communist Bulgaria without Stalin's consent. He rebelled when the Soviet dictator insisted he fall into line with Soviet policy. The Soviets responded by accusing Yugoslavia of nationalism, opportunism, and anti-Sovietism. Parallels were drawn between Tito and Trotsky, Stalin's arch-rival of the 1920s, who had been expelled from the USSR and assassinated by a Soviet agent in Mexico in 1940. The dispute escalated as the 'Titoites' were accused of being imperialist agents trying to restore capitalism in Yugoslavia. A hunt for Titoite heretics was launched throughout Eastern Europe, leading to a number of 'nationalists', 'spies', and 'right-wing deviationists'

Rudolf Slansky, former leader of the Czechoslovak Communist Party on trial for treason in Prague in 1952. Slansky was a one of a number of party leaders, many of them Jewish, arrested as part of a purge that swept through the Communist parties of Eastern Europe in 1949–52.

being unmasked, arrested, imprisoned, and executed. In Czechoslovakia in 1952, fourteen former Communist party leaders, many of them Jewish, were the victims of a political show trial and summary execution for anti-Communist treachery. That same year a so-called 'Doctors' Plot' to assassinate Soviet leaders was unmasked in the USSR. Again, many of the accused were Jewish (all were later rehabilitated and deemed innocent). In 1948 the Soviet Union had supported the creation of an independent state of Israel, but backed away from this stance when Israel began to align itself with the West in the Cold War. In 1953 the USSR ended diplomatic relations with Israel, but these were restored a few months later, not long after Stalin's death.

NATO

Western perceptions of Stalin's foreign policy as aggressive and expansionist were confirmed by the Soviet and Communist takeover in Eastern Europe, in which the Soviets welded what had been a sphere of influence into a tightly controlled bloc. In

April 1949 this prompted Britain, Canada, the United States, France, and other West European countries to establish the North Atlantic Treaty Organization (NATO)—a military and political defence organization directed against the perceived Soviet threat. While the NATO powers did not fear an immediate Soviet attack, they did not rule one out in the medium to long term. The organization was also concerned to deter the Soviet Union's use of military blackmail to extract political concessions.

According to Lord Ismay, NATO's first Secretary General, the threefold purpose of the organization was to 'keep the Russians out, the Americans in [Europe] and the Germans down'. As the Cold War warmed up the first purpose became the priority and, by 1950, the Western states had decided to rearm West Germany and incorporate its armed forces into a European army. To the Soviets, however, NATO was not a defence organization but an aggressive bloc directed against them, compounding the threat of impending German rearmament as it became more acute with the dawn of the nuclear age.

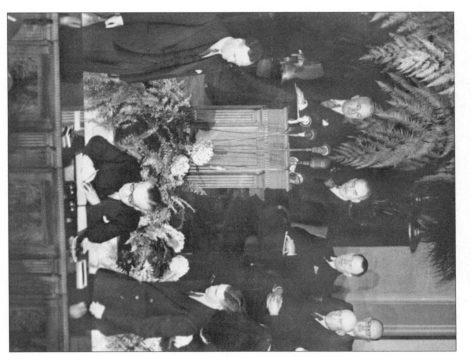

British foreign affairs minister, Ernest Bevin, signs the North Atlantic Treaty in April 1949. The formation of NATO was followed by the rearmament of West Germany and its integration into the Western military-political bloc. The Soviets responded by signing a defence pact with their Communist allies in Eastern Europe in Warsaw in May 1955.

During the war the Americans had created a massive programme—the Manhattan Project—to develop an atomic bomb, initially with deployment against Germany in mind. Their first atom bomb test took place in July 1945. Famously, Truman told Stalin about the bomb at the Potsdam Conference. Stalin was already well informed about the progress of the American bomb project, thanks to Soviet spies, and showed little interest in Truman's news. However, after the use of atomic bombs in Japan Stalin authorized a priority project to develop a Soviet bomb. Four years later, in August 1949, the Soviets conducted their own atomic bomb test.

While the USA had an atomic weapons monopoly the Americans tried to turn this to political advantage. Some historians claim the bombing of Hiroshima and Nagasaki was a political, not a military, act constituting the first event of the Cold War. But

The first Soviet atomic bomb test, 29 August 1949. The West was shocked at how quickly the Soviets built their bomb, which was aided by atomic espionage. In August 1953 the Soviet Union conducted its first thermonuclear (hydrogen bomb) test, less than a year after the United States had tested its first H-bomb. Thermonuclear weapons were hundreds of times more powerful than the atom bombs dropped on Hiroshima and Nagasaki by the United States in August 1945.

Stalin paid little heed to the Americans' efforts at atomic diplomacy. At the London CFM Molotov joked that maybe Byrnes had an atomic bomb in his pocket. In the 1940s atomic weapons were not the awesome instrument they later became when hydrogen bombs a thousand times more powerful than those dropped on Japan were developed. As Stalin told Władysław Gomułka, the Polish Communist leader, in November 1945, 'not atomic bombs but armies decide wars'. Soviet deployment of conventional forces in Europe more than counterbalanced the atomic bomb, even though between 1945 and 1948 troop numbers were reduced from 11 million to 3 million. Even in 1952, when the United States possessed a substantial nuclear armoury, Stalin was convinced the Americans were incapable of fighting a large-scale war: 'they are pinning their hopes on the atom bomb and air power. But one cannot win a war with that. One needs infantry, and they don't have infantry; the infantry they do have is weak.'

At the United Nations a series of discussions took place on establishing international controls over atomic energy. Under the Americans' Baruch Plan, the United States would retain its monopoly of atomic weapons until a foolproof system of international inspection and control could be put in place. The Soviet alternative proposed an immediate prohibition on all nuclear weapons, which would have meant the Americans also giving up theirs. Neither position prevailed. Instead the Soviets pressed ahead with their project and the British started one too, following the US decision to deny them access to nuclear technology despite the fact that British scientists had been instrumental in launching what later became the successful Manhattan Project.

A series of spy scandals in 1945–6 concerning Soviet atomic espionage further soured Soviet–American relations. The revelations about Soviet spying convinced Truman that Moscow could not be trusted on nuclear technologies and that co-operation with Stalin on atomic issues would be domestically and politically too complicated. The Soviets also had spies among the British, notably Donald Maclean, who worked in the British embassy in Washington and had access to Anglo-American information on atomic developments, although this did not become known until Maclean defected to the Soviet Union in 1951.

While the atomic arms race of the 1940s was a complicating factor in Soviet–Western relations it was not a primary cause of the Cold War. However, as the Cold War developed the nuclear factor grew in importance. Above all, nuclear knowledge made the Cold War more dangerous. The effect of this on the Soviets was paradoxical. Fearing nuclear war, the Soviets sponsored a massive international peace movement alongside their building of atomic bombs. The peace movement's central demand was prohibition of nuclear weapons and in 1950 the movement launched the Stockholm Appeal, an anti-nuclear petition which successfully gathered a half a billion signatures—equivalent to a quarter of the world's population at that time. Many of the signatures came from within the Communist bloc but tens of millions did not. Spurred by the nuclear danger there developed a significant opposition to the cold war in the late 1940s, by no means all of it pro-Communist. This movement's success

Donald Maclean, Soviet spy and a member of the Cambridge ring which included Kim Philby and Guy Burgess. Maclean passed atomic secrets to the Soviets in the late 1940s and early 1950s. Together with Burgess he defected to the USSR in 1951. The most ideological of the Cambridge spies, Maclean believed that the United States was preparing to launch a political and military crusade against the Soviet bloc. He remained a Communist but in later life he became an advocate of the democratic reform of the Soviet political system.

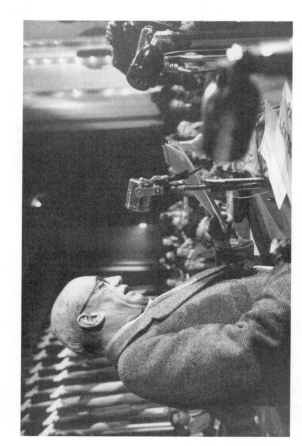

The artist Pablo Picasso speaking at the Communist-inspired Paris Peace Congress in April 1949. Many prominent western artists, scientists, and writers supported Communist-led peace campaigns in the late 1940s and 1950s when the Soviet Union's prestige as result of its role in defeating Hitler was still very high and when there were intense fears about the danger of a new world war.

contributed to a temporary respite in the Cold War after Stalin's death in 1953 when, for a time, Soviet–Western negotiations about the shape of the post-war world resumed.

The Korean War

In Europe the Cold War began in the mid to late 1940s and Europe remained its epicentre until it ended forty years later. But during the 1950s it developed into a global struggle. The outbreak of the Korean War in June 1950, a precipitating event in this globalization of the Cold War, also intensified and militarized the East–West confrontation in Europe.

Until 1945 Korea was a Japanese colony. When Japan surrendered, the country was divided along the 38th parallel into Soviet and American zones of occupation. The intention was to reunite the country following national elections but, as happened in Germany, the two occupation regimes hardened into competing states: an authoritarian Communist regime in the North headed by Kim Il-sung and an authoritarian capitalist regime in the South headed by Syngman Rhee. In 1949 Soviet and American troops withdrew, and the scene was set for a clash between Kim and Ree, each of whom aspired to reunite Korea under their leadership.

In October 1949 Mao Zedong's Chinese Communists came to power in Beijing and proclaimed the People's Republic of China. At the end of 1949 Mao travelled to Moscow to meet Stalin and to sign the Sino-Soviet Treaty of Friendship, Alliance and Mutual Assistance. The most populous country in the world was now allied to the biggest country in the world and both were ruled by the Communists.

Mao's triumph convinced Stalin that a revolutionary wave was rising in the Far East, making him more susceptible to Kim Il-sung's claim that if he was allowed to invade South Korea the invasion would be met by a revolutionary upsurge and the war would be quickly won. Stalin did, however, remain cautious, particularly in his concerns about how the Americans would respond. But by early 1950 there seemed to be indications that the Americans considered occupied Japan to be within their sphere of interest, while excluding Korea. In those circumstances Stalin gave permission for the North Korean invasion of South Korea in June 1950.

All went well for Kim Il-sung at first and, by the end of the summer, most of the country was in Communist hands. The South Korean capital of Seoul was captured and Ree's forces were driven into the country's south-east corner around the port of Pusan where they managed to hold out. This gave the United States time to mobilize and intervene in support of South Korea. It did so under the banner of the United Nations—made possible by the Soviet Union's absence from the Security Council in protest at the West's refusal to give China's seat on the council to Mao's People's Republic.

In September 1950 General Douglas MacArthur mounted an amphibious operation at Inchon, outflanking the North Koreans, who were forced back across the 38th parallel border. MacArthur then advanced and captured Pyongyang, the North

Korean capital. By November the American-led UN forces were approaching the Korean–Chinese border and it was only the intervention of large numbers of Chinese Communist 'volunteers' that saved Kim Il-sung from defeat. Thereafter the war stalemated along the 38th parallel and came to an end when a ceasefire was signed in July 1953. During the war there were reports that nuclear weapons might be used to break the deadlock but the conflict remained limited.

Kim Il-sung was the main instigator of the Korean conflict and his role illustrated the critical impact secondary actors could have on the course of the Cold War. In the West, however, the North Korean attack was perceived as an expansionary Soviet move being directed from Moscow, prompting a significant acceleration of Western rearmament programmes. Between 1950 and 1952 the US defence budget increased from US$13 billion to US$57 billion. At the Lisbon NATO conference in 1952 the

American marines headed towards the beaches on Inchon in Korea, during an operation that turned back the North Korean Communist invasion of South Korea. In charge of the landings was General Douglas McArthur. Truman removed him as commander of UN and US forces in Korea in April 1951 because McArthur wanted to pursue a more aggressive military strategy.

China's Communist leader Mao Zedong with Kim Il Sung, the North Korean leader who attacked South Korea in June 1950. Only an American military intervention saved the south from a Communist takeover, Kim Il-sung was supported by both China and the Soviet Union during the Korean War, 1950–3.

decision was made to deploy nearly 100 divisions to counter the threat of a Soviet attack on Western Europe. The Soviets responded in kind. By 1953 the armies of the USSR's East European allies numbered more than a million while Soviet armed forces had increased to over 5 million. In May 1955 the Soviet–East European bloc signed up to the Warsaw Pact as a direct counter to NATO. This completed the process of forming two Cold War blocs in Europe. The wartime grand alliance was well and truly dead.

Historians and the Cold War

Arguments about who was responsible for the break-up of the grand alliance and the onset of the Cold War were an integral part of the ideological struggle between East and West. In the West, the predominant view has been that the Cold War was caused by Soviet and Communist expansion into Eastern Europe. But others have argued that the British and Americans over-reacted to moves the Soviets had intended as defensive. The compromise view is that both sides were to blame and the Cold War erupted as the result of a series of mutual misunderstandings and miscalculations. So, although the Cold War was not inevitable, deep political and ideological differences in the post-war period were highly likely to emerge and be given expression given the previous antagonisms in Soviet–Western relations dating back to the 1917 revolution that had brought the Communists to power. In retrospect the Cold War does have an air of inevitability about it. But that was not how the Allied leaders saw the world in 1945.

They believed then that any difficulties within the grand alliance could be overcome, just as they had been during the war. Even as the grand alliance disintegrated in 1945–7 the key participants could not quite believe what was happening. As one American official, W. W. Rostow, put it, the Cold War crystallized as 'the result of an incremental, interacting process rather than as a purposeful clash of wills and lucid strategies'.

The Cold War in Perspective

Viewed in a broader historical perspective, the outbreak of the Cold War in the mid-1940s was but a phase in the struggle between Soviet Communism and Western capitalism that had commenced in 1917 when the Bolsheviks seized power in Russia. The Bolsheviks aimed to spread socialism globally as well as to construct a socialist society in Russia. This global revolutionary impulse created tensions in Soviet–Western relations that became even more intense after the Second World War when the USSR emerged as a global superpower at the head of a Communist bloc.

The other superpower to emerge as a result of the war was the United States, and with the failure of the grand alliance the geopolitical and ideological struggle that was the Cold War took the form of an American–Soviet confrontation in the centre of Europe. One consequence of this confrontation was the resolution of what had hitherto been the dominating issue of European international politics—the German question—which was dealt with by the post-war division of the country and the integration of the two German states into their respective blocs.

The Second World War also undermined the position of Britain and France as world powers and hastened the disintegration of the European colonial empires. This created a new terrain on which to wage the Cold War as the United States and the Soviet Union vied with each other for power and influence in the so-called Third World that lay outside the capitalist and Communist blocs.

Another major beneficiary of the war was the Chinese Communist Party. It was during the national-patriotic war against Japan that Mao's Communists built their political base and military power. The Chinese Communist regime proved to be as brutal and effective as the Soviet Union. Under Communist tutelage China rose to pre-eminence in global politics, initially in the context of the Sino-Soviet alliance and then as a result of the Sino–Soviet split which created a series of triangular relationships and rivalries of Washington, Moscow, and Beijing.

The outcome of the Second World War was determined by the resources, battles, and strategies of the greatest powers. They dominated the Cold War too, but the role of secondary players was not negligible. Britain played a central role in the formation and consolidation of NATO, as did France. Politicians in both German states man-oeuvred successfully to entrench their respective regimes and to preclude reunification on anything other than their own terms, while Kim Il-sung manipulated Stalin into authorizing a futile war in Korea.

In the *longue durée* of the Cold War the greatest legacy of the Second World War was nuclear weapons. Without the war the atomic bomb would not have been developed so quickly, if at all. Without the Cold War there would not have been a nuclear arms race and international control of nuclear energy would have been a more realistic possibility.

There were many reasons why the Cold War remained cold and did not develop into a new world war. Neither side wanted a major war. An ideology of peace prevailed on both sides of the Iron Curtain, within elites and among the general population. By the early 1960s the Cold War in Europe was a tense but stable confrontation between rival blocs that took care not to threaten each other's vital interests. But the main reason a general peace prevailed in Europe during four decades of Cold War was the existential threat to humanity posed by nuclear weapons.

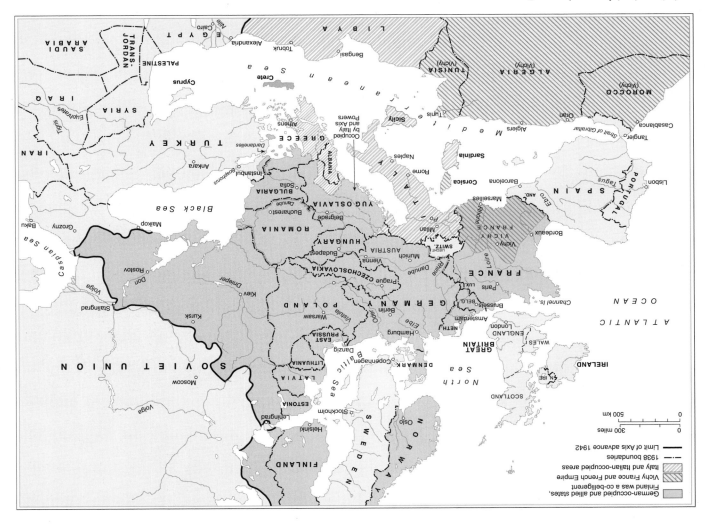

1. Axis territorial expansion 1938–42

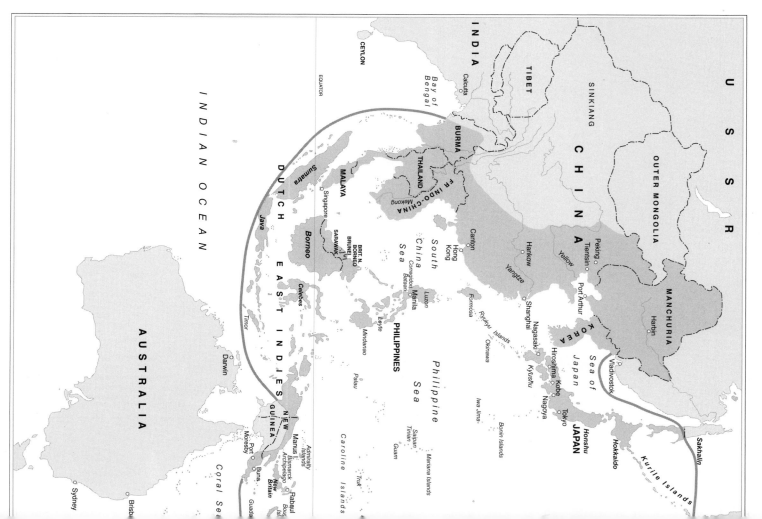

2. Japanese territorial expansion 1931–42

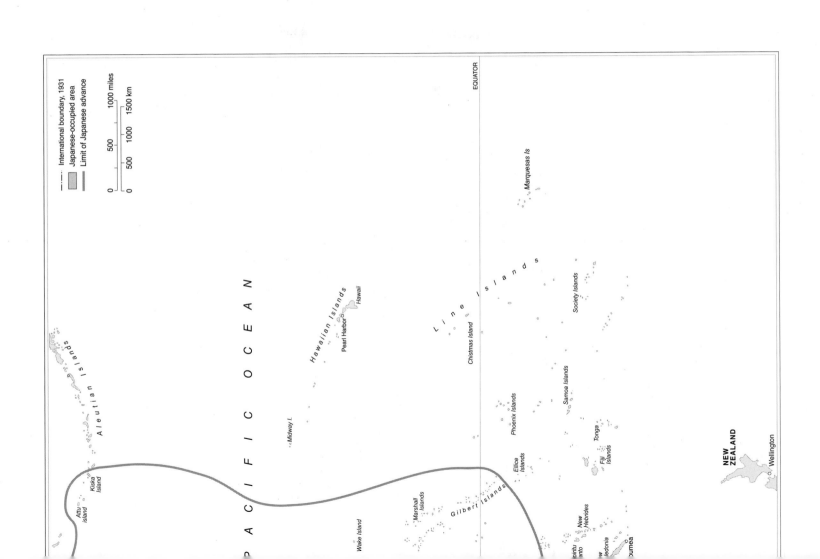

International boundary, 1931
Japanese-occupied area
Limit of Japanese advance

0   500   1000 miles
0   500   1000   1500 km

EQUATOR

P A C I F I C   O C E A N

Aleutian Islands

Attu Island
Kiska Island

Midway I.

Wake Island

Marshall Islands

Gilbert Islands

Hawaiian Islands
Pearl Harbor
Hawaii

Line Islands

Christmas Island

Phoenix Islands

Samoa Islands

Society Islands

Marquesas Is

Ellice Islands

Fiji Islands

Tonga

New Hebrides

Espiritu Santo

New Caledonia

Noumea

NEW ZEALAND
Wellington

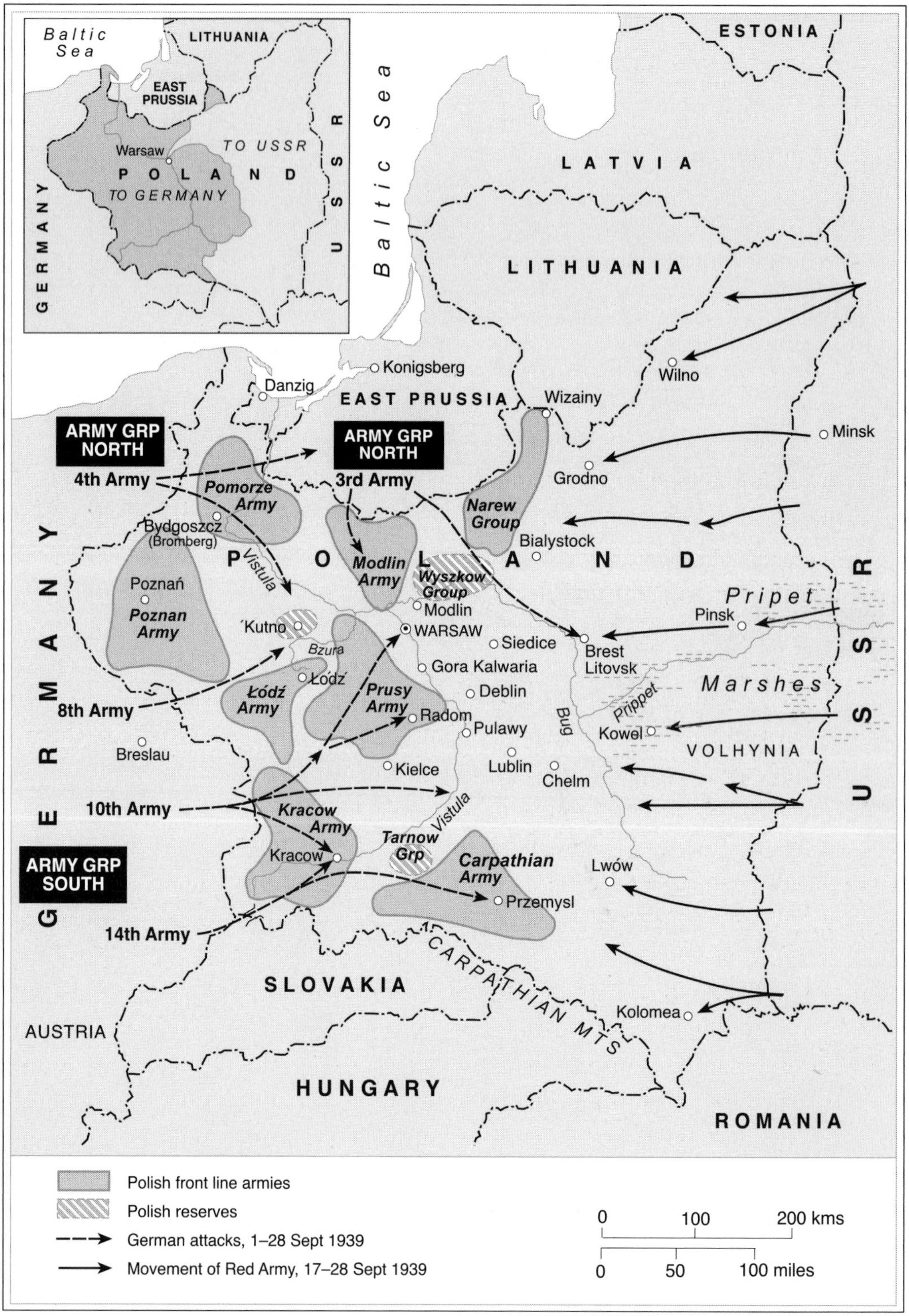
Baltic Sea
LITHUANIA
EAST PRUSSIA
Warsaw
TO USSR
POLAND
TO GERMANY
GERMANY
USSR
Baltic Sea
ESTONIA
LATVIA
LITHUANIA
Wilno
Konigsberg
Danzig
EAST PRUSSIA
Wizainy
Minsk
ARMY GRP NORTH
4th Army
ARMY GRP NORTH
3rd Army
Grodno
Pomorze Army
Narew Group
Bydgoszcz (Bromberg)
Bialystock
POLAND
Vistula
Modlin Army
Wyszkow Group
Modlin
Poznań
Poznan Army
Pripet
Pinsk
Kutno
WARSAW
Siedice
Brest Litovsk
Bzura
Gora Kalwaria
Łódź
Łódź Army
Prusy Army
Marshes
Deblin
8th Army
Radom
Pulawy
Bug
Pripet
Kowel
Breslau
VOLHYNIA
Kielce
Lublin
Chelm
GERMANY
10th Army
Kracow Army
Vistula
Tarnow Grp
Kracow
Carpathian Army
Lwów
ARMY GRP SOUTH
Przemysl
14th Army
CARPATHIAN MTS
SLOVAKIA
Kolomea
AUSTRIA
HUNGARY
ROMANIA
Polish front line armies
Polish reserves
German attacks, 1–28 Sept 1939
Movement of Red Army, 17–28 Sept 1939
0 100 200 kms
0 50 100 miles
3. The German campaign in Poland, September 1939

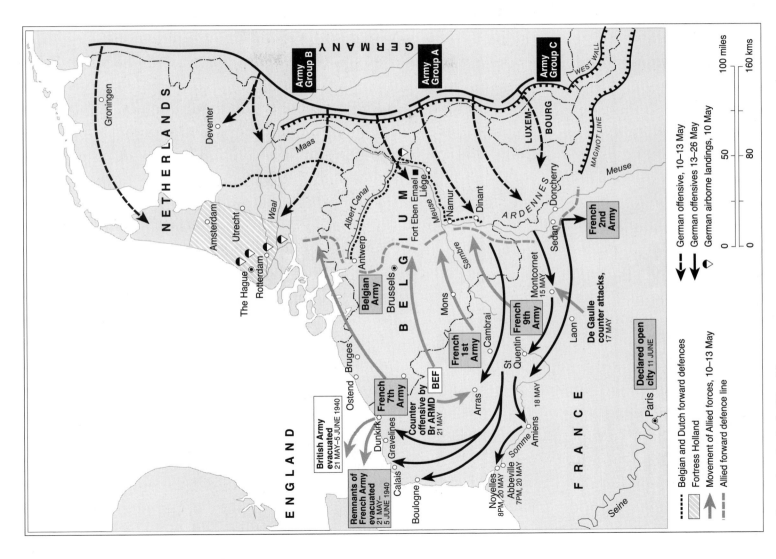

NETHERLANDS

Groningen

Deventer

GERMANY

Army
Group B

Army
Group A

Army
Group C

WEST WALL

Maas

Amsterdam

Utrecht

Waal

The Hague
Rotterdam

BELGIUM

Antwerp

Albert Canal

Fort Eben Emael
Liége

Meuse

Namur

Dinant

ARDENNES

LUXEM-
BOURG

Sedan

Doncherry

Meuse

MAGINOT LINE

French 2nd
Army

Belgian
Army

Brussels

Mons

Sambre

Montcornet
15 MAY

French 9th
Army

De Gaulle
counter attacks,
17 MAY

Cambrai

Laon

French
1st
Army

St
Quentin

Bruges

Ostend

BEF

French
7th
Army

Arras

18 MAY

Amiens

Counter
offensive by
Br ARMD
21 MAY

Somme

ENGLAND

British Army
evacuated
21 MAY–5 JUNE 1940

Dunkirk
Gravelines

Novelles
8PM, 20 MAY

Abbeville
7PM, 20 MAY

Remnants of
French Army
evacuated
21 MAY–
5 JUNE 1940

Calais

Boulogne

FRANCE

Paris

Declared open
city 11 JUNE

Seine

100 miles

160 kms

0   50   80

German offensive, 10–13 May

German offensives 13–26 May

German airborne landings, 10 May

Belgian and Dutch forward defences

Fortress Holland

Movement of Allied forces, 10–13 May

Allied forward defence line

4. German invasion in the West, May 1940

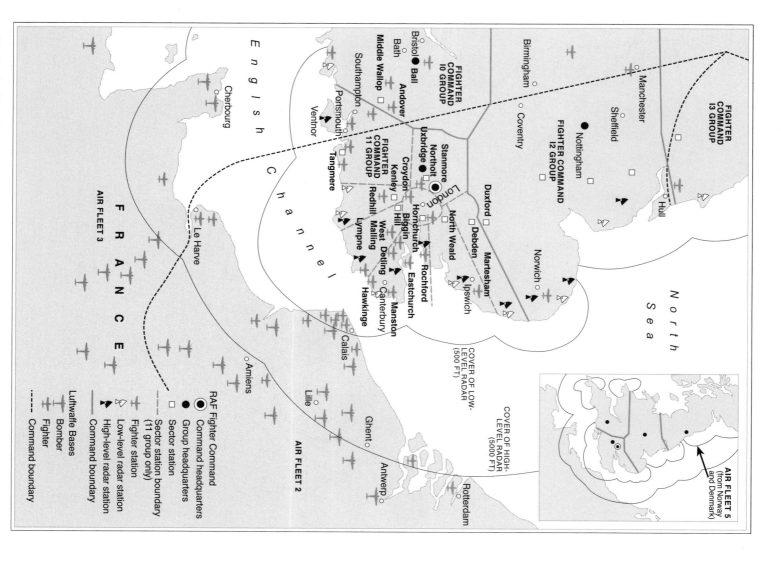

FIGHTER COMMAND 10 GROUP

FIGHTER COMMAND 11 GROUP

FIGHTER COMMAND 12 GROUP

FIGHTER COMMAND 13 GROUP

English Channel

North Sea

F R A N C E

AIR FLEET 3

AIR FLEET 2

Cherbourg

Le Have

Amiens

Lille

Calais

Ghent

Antwerp

Rotterdam

Bristol ● Ball
Bath
Middle Wallop
Andover
Southampton
Portsmouth
Ventnor
Tangmere
Uxbridge
Croydon
Kenley
Redhill
West Malling
Biggin Hill
Lympne
Hawkinge
Manston
Canterbury
Eastchurch
Rochford
Hornchurch
North Weald
Debden
Martlesham
Ipswich
Norwich
Duxford
Stanmore
Northolt
London
Birmingham
Coventry
Nottingham ●
Sheffield
Manchester
Hull

Command boundary

Luftwaffe Bases
Bomber
Fighter
Command boundary

◎ Command headquarters
● Group headquarters
□ Sector station
Sector station boundary (11 group only)
Fighter station
Low-level radar station
High-level radar station
Command boundary

RAF Fighter Command

COVER OF LOW-LEVEL RADAR (500 FT)

COVER OF HIGH-LEVEL RADAR (5000 FT)

AIR FLEET 5 (from Norway and Denmark)

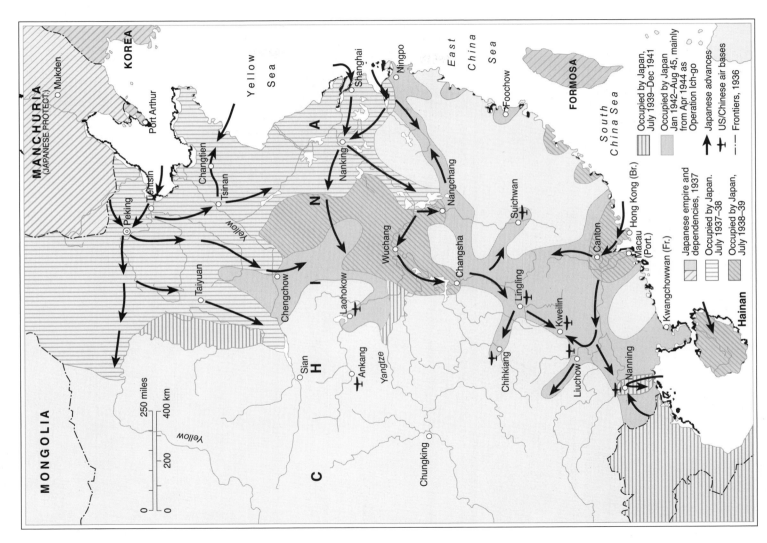

6. Japan's campaigns in China 1937–45

Map labels:

MANCHURIA (JAPANESE PROTECT.)

KOREA

MONGOLIA

CHINA

FORMOSA

Hainan

Yellow Sea

East China Sea

South China Sea

Mukden
Port Arthur
Peking
Tientsin
Changtien
Tsinan
Taiyuan
Yellow
Chengchow
Sian
Ankang
Laohokow
Yangtze
Chungking
Yellow
Wuchang
Nanking
Shanghai
Ningpo
Foochow
Nanchang
Changsha
Lingling
Suichwan
Chihkiang
Kweilin
Liuchow
Nanning
Canton
Hong Kong (Br.)
Macau (Port.)
Kwangchowwan (Fr.)

Scale:
0   250 miles
0   200   400 km

Legend:
Occupied by Japan, July 1939–Dec 1941
Occupied by Japan Jan 1942–Aug 45, mainly from Apr 1944 as Operation Ich-go
Japanese advances
US/Chinese air bases
Frontiers, 1936
Japanese empire and dependencies, 1937
Occupied by Japan, July 1937–38
Occupied by Japan, July 1938–39

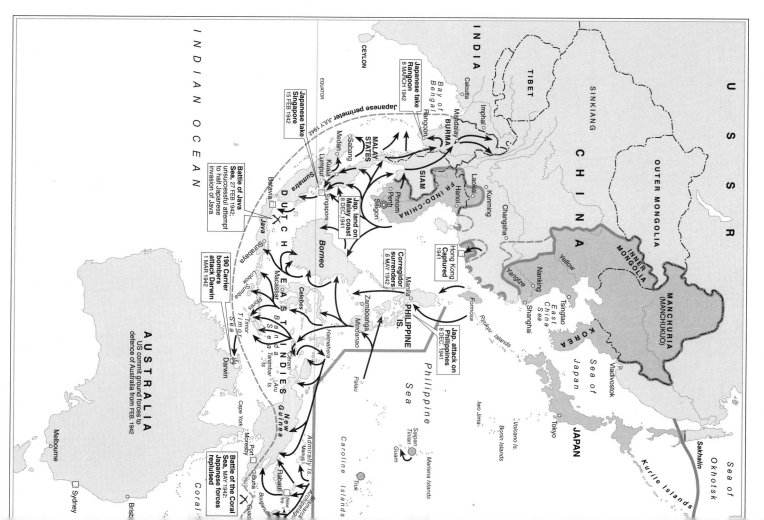

7. Japan's advance in the Pacific War 1941–2

Japanese take Rangoon 8 MARCH 1942

Japanese take Singapore 15 FEB 1942

Battle of Java Sea, 27 FEB 1942; unsuccessful attempt to halt Japanese invasion of Java

190 Carrier bombers attack Darwin 1 MAR 1942

Jap. land on Malay coast 8 DEC. 1941

Corregidor surrenders 6 MAY 1942

Hong Kong Captured 1941

Jap. attack on Philippines 8 DEC. 1941

Battle of the Coral Sea, MAY 1942; Japanese forces repulsed

AUSTRALIA
US commit ground forces to defence of Australia from FEB. 1942

EQUATOR

Japanese perimeter JULY 1942

INDIAN OCEAN

Bay of Bengal

CEYLON

INDIA

TIBET

SINKIANG

C H I N A

OUTER MONGOLIA

U S S R

INNER MONGOLIA

MANCHURIA (MANCHUKUO)

KOREA

JAPAN

Sea of Japan

Sea of Okhotsk

Sakhalin

Kurile Islands

Vladivostok

Tokyo

Iwo Jima

Bonin Islands

Volcano Is.

Ryukyu Islands

Formosa

Shanghai

Nanking

Tsingtao

Yellow Sea

East China Sea

Yangtze

Changsha

Kunming

Lao kai

Hanoi

FR. INDO-CHINA

Phnom Penh

Saigon

SIAM

BURMA

Mandalay

Rangoon

Imphal

Calcutta

MALAY STATES

Sabang

Medan

Kuala Lumpur

Singapore

Sumatra

Batavia

D U T C H   E A S T   I N D I E S

Java

Surabaya

Borneo

Macassar

Celebes

Lombok

Flores

Sumba

Timor

Bali

Timor Sea

Arafura Sea

Banda Sea

Tanimbar Is.

Aru Is.

Ceram

Halmahera

Zamboanga

Mindanao

PHILIPPINE IS.

Manila

Palau

Philippine Sea

Caroline Islands

Mariana Islands

Saipan
Tinian
Guam

Truk

New Guinea

Port Moresby

Buna

Cape York

Admiralty Is.

Manus

Bismarck Archipelago

New Britain

Rabaul

Bougainville

Guadalcanal

Coral Sea

AUSTRALIA

Melbourne

Sydney

Brisbane

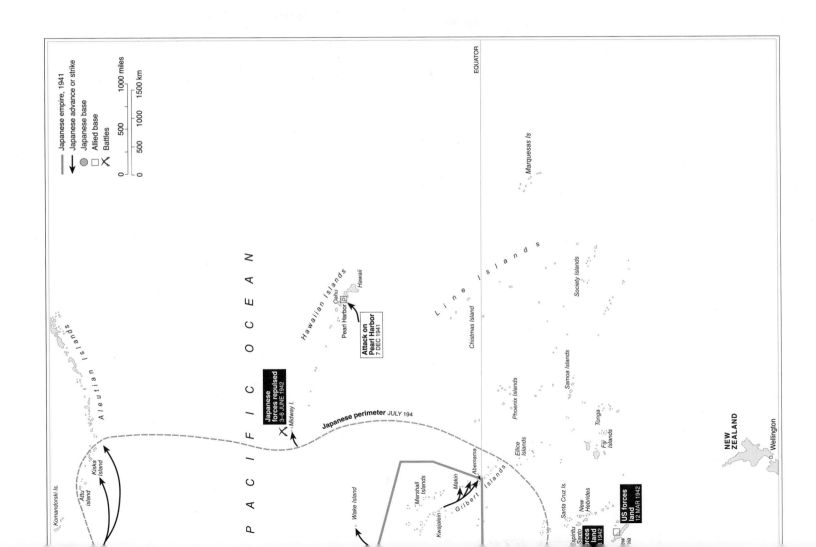

PACIFIC OCEAN

Japanese empire, 1941
Japanese advance or strike
Japanese base
Allied base
Battles

0   500   1000 miles
0   500   1000   1500 km

EQUATOR

Komandorski Is.

Attu Island
Kiska Island
Aleutian Islands

Wake Island

Kwajalein
Marshall Islands
Makin
Abemama
Gilbert Islands

Midway I.

Japanese forces repulsed 3–6 JUNE 1942

Japanese perimeter JULY 194

Hawaiian Islands
Oahu
Pearl Harbor
Hawaii

Attack on Pearl Harbor 7 DEC 1941

Line Islands

Chistmas Island

Marquesas Is

Phoenix Islands

Samoa Islands

Society Islands

Ellice Islands

Tonga

Fiji Islands

Santa Cruz Is.
New Hebrides

Espiritu Santo

US forces land 12 MAR 1942

NEW ZEALAND
Wellington

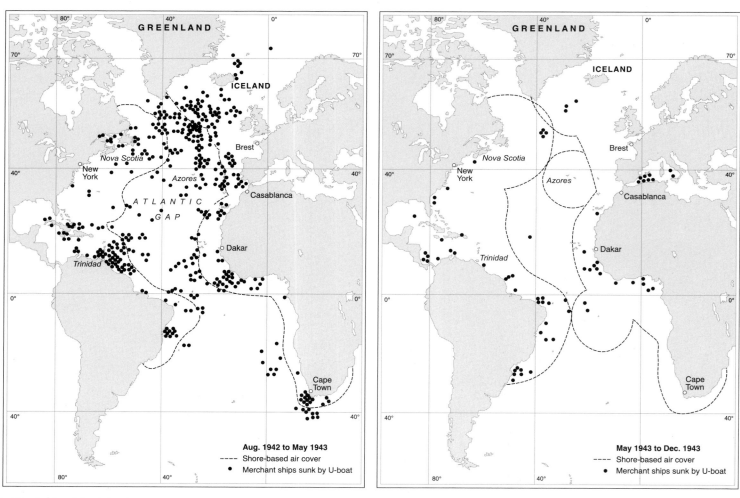

Aug. 1942 to May 1943
- - - - Shore-based air cover
● Merchant ships sunk by U-boat

May 1943 to Dec. 1943
- - - - Shore-based air cover
● Merchant ships sunk by U-boat

8. The Battle of the Atlantic 1943

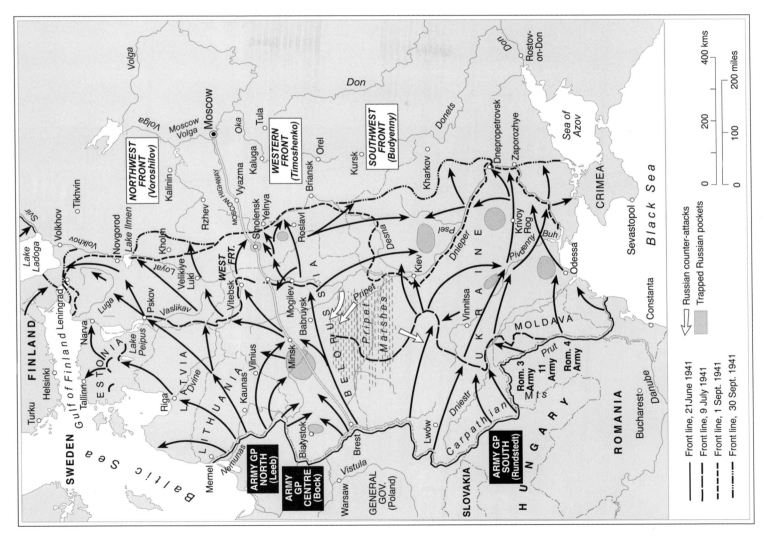

9. Operation Barbarossa 1941

Map labels:

SWEDEN

FINLAND

Turku · Helsinki

Volga

Volga

Moscow
Volga

MOSCOW

NORTHWEST
FRONT
(Voroshilov)

Tikhvin

Volkhov
Svir

Lake
Ladoga

Lake Ilmen

Novgorod

Kalinin

Rzhev

Vyazma

Oka

Kaluga

Tula

WESTERN
FRONT
(Timoshenko)

Orel

Kursk

SOUTHWEST
FRONT
(Budyenny)

Kharkov

Donets

Don

Rostov-
on-Don

Sea
of
Azov

CRIMEA

Sevastopol

Black Sea

Dnepropetrovsk

Zaporozhye

Krivoy
Rog

Buh

Pivdenny

Odessa

Constanta

ROMANIA

Bucharest
Danube

HUNGARY

SLOVAKIA

Rom. 3
Army

11
Army

Rom. 4
Army

Mts

Carpathian

Lwów

Dniestr

Prut

MOLDAVA

Vinnitsa

UKRAINE

Kiev

Psel

Dnieper

Desna

Roslavl

Yelnya

Smolensk

MOSCOW HIGHWAY

WEST
FRT.

Mogilev

Babruysk

BELORUSSIA

Pripet

Pripet
Marshes

Minsk

Białystok

Brest

Vistula

Warsaw

GENERAL
GOV.
(Poland)

Vilnius

Kaunas

LITHUANIA

Memel
Nemunas

Velikiye
Luki

Kholm

Loval

Vitebsk

Vaslikav

Pskov

Luga

Dvine

Dvina

LATVIA

Riga

Lake
Peipus

ESTONIA

Tallinn

Narva

Gulf of Finland

Leningrad

Volkhov

Baltic Sea

Legend:

Army GP NORTH (Leeb)

ARMY GP CENTRE (Bock)

ARMY GP SOUTH (Rundstedt)

Russian counter-attacks

Trapped Russian pockets

Front line, 21 June 1941

Front line, 9 July 1941

Front line, 1 Sept. 1941

Front line, 30 Sept. 1941

400 kms

200 miles

200

100

0

0

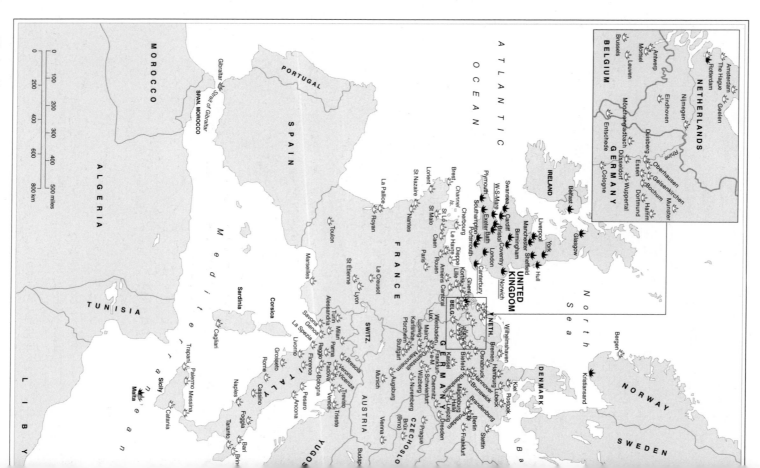

10. The bombing campaigns in Europe 1940–5

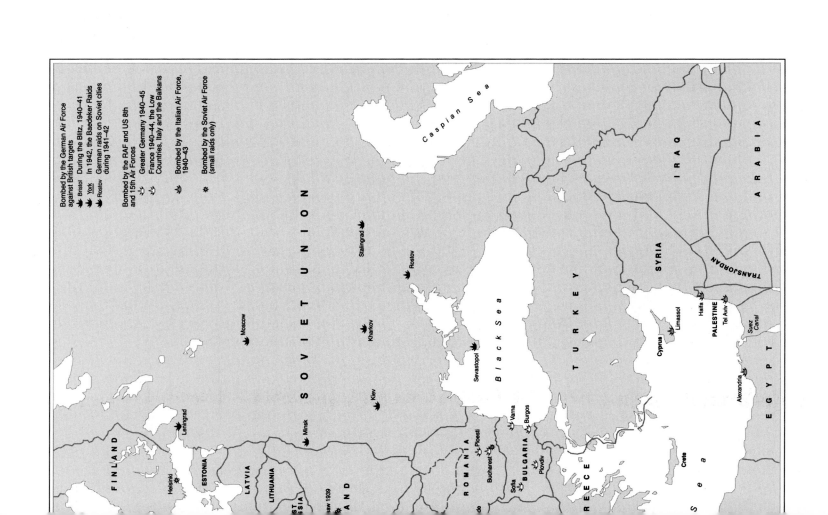

Bombed by the German Air Force
against British targets

➤ Bristol   During the Blitz, 1940–41

➤ York   In 1942, the Baedeker Raids

➤ Rostov   German raids on Soviet cities
           during 1941–42

Bombed by the RAF and US 8th
and 15th Air Forces

✈ Greater Germany 1940–45
  France 1940–44, the Low
  Countries, Italy and the Balkans

✈ Bombed by the Italian Air Force,
  1940–43

✻ Bombed by the Soviet Air Force
  (small raids only)

FINLAND

Helsinki

ESTONIA

LATVIA

LITHUANIA

EAST PRUSSIA

POLAND

Warsaw 1939

Leningrad

Minsk

Kiev

Moscow

SOVIET UNION

Kharkov

Stalingrad

Rostov

ROMANIA

Ploesti

Bucharest

BULGARIA

Sofia

Plovdiv

Varna

Burgos

Sevastopol

Black Sea

Crete

GREECE

Sea

TURKEY

Cyprus

Limassol

SYRIA

IRAQ

TRANSJORDAN

Haifa

Tel Aviv

PALESTINE

Suez
Canal

Alexandria

EGYPT

ARABIA

Caspian Sea

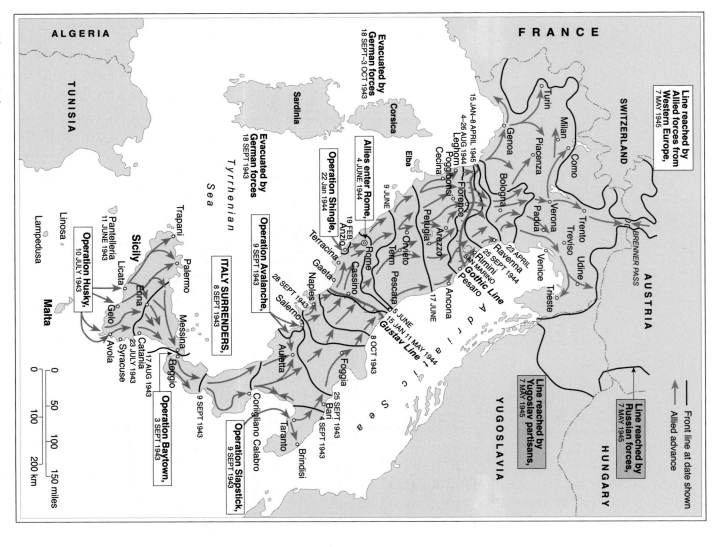

11. The war in Italy 1943–5

ALGERIA

TUNISIA

Sardinia

Corsica

Tyrrhenian Sea

Evacuated by German forces
18 SEPT–3 OCT 1943

Evacuated by German forces
18 SEPT 1943

Linosa

Lampedusa

Malta

Operation Husky,
10 JULY 1943

Pantelleria
11 JUNE 1943

Trapani

Palermo

Sicily

Licata

Gelo

Etna

Catania
23 JULY 1943

Syracuse

Avola

Messina

ITALY SURRENDERS,
8 SEPT 1943

Operation Avalanche,
9 SEPT 1943

Operation Shingle,
22 Jan 1944

Allies enter Rome,
4 JUNE 1944

17 AUG 1943

Reggio

Operation Baytown,
3 SEPT 1943

9 SEPT 1943

Corigliano Calabro

Taranto

Brindisi

Operation Slapstick,
9 SEPT 1943

Auletta

Salerno
28 SEPT 1943

Naples

Gaeta

Terracina

Cassino

Rome

Anzio
19 FEB

Ontieto

Terni

9 JUNE

Pescara

17 JUNE

8 OCT 1943

Foggia
25 SEPT 1943

Bari
4 SEPT 1943

Ancona

5 JUNE
15 JAN 11 MAY 1944
Gustav Line

Perugia

Arezzo

Cecina
Poggibonsi
Leghorn

Elba

Florence

Bologna

15 JAN–8 APRIL 1945
4–26 AUG 1944

Genoa

Turin

Milan

Piacenza

Como

Padda

Verona

Trento

Treviso

Udine

Venice

Trieste

23 APRIL

Ravenna
25 SEPT 1944
Rimini
SAN MARINO
Gothic Line
Pesaro

FRANCE

SWITZERLAND

BRENNER PASS

AUSTRIA

HUNGARY

YUGOSLAVIA

Line reached by Allied forces from Western Europe,
7 MAY 1945

Line reached by Russian forces,
7 MAY 1945

Line reached by Yugoslav partisans,
7 MAY 1945

—— Front line at date shown
→ Allied advance

0   50   100   200 km
0   50   100   150 miles

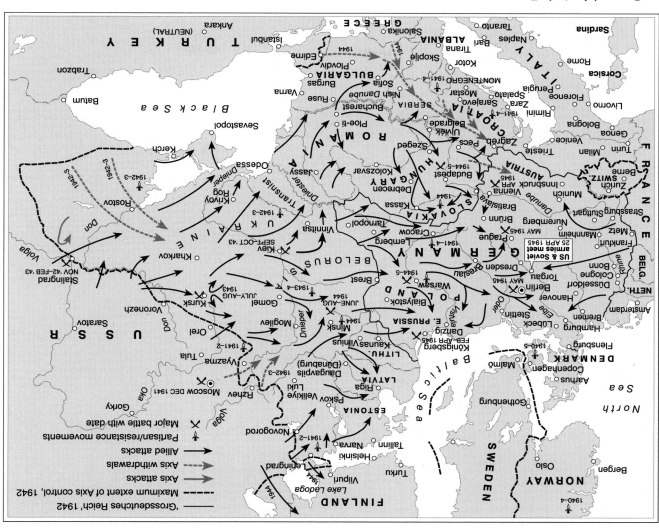

12. German defeat in the East 1943–5

Maximum extent of Axis control in Eastern Europe, 1942

1000 Pre-war Jewish population, except Czechoslovakia, Romania and Hungary which are 1940 figures

1000 Numbers of Jewish people who died or were killed during the war

● Main concentration camp, with date of foundation

● Extermination camps from 1942

North Sea

Baltic Sea

FINLAND
1618
8

NORWAY
1800
758

SWEDEN
8000

ESTONIA
4500
1000

LATVIA
95 000
77 000

Riga

Moscow

Volga

Oka

USSR
3 028 538
1 050 000

DENMARK
6500
116

LITHUANIA
145 000 *135 000*
Ninth Fort (Kaunas)
1941

GREAT BRITAIN
330 000

Neuengamme 1940

EAST PRUSSIA

Ravensbrück ● 1936
Danzig
1000
Stutthof 1939

GERMANY
499 682 *150 000*
Sachsenhausen
1936

Esterwegen 1943
NETH. 140 000 *102 000*
'S Hertogenbosh 1943

Mittelbau-Dora
1943

Berlin

Oder

Vistula

Chetmno
1941

Treblinka
1942

Maly Trostinets
1942

WHITE RUSSIA (BYELORUSSIA)

Dnieper

Don

Volga

BELG.
90 000
23 484

Sachsenburg
1933

Buchenwald
1937

Gross-Rosen 1941

Warsaw 1943

POLAND
3 350 000
2 890 000

Sobibor 1942
Majdanek 1943

UKRAINE

Dnieper

LUX.
3144
720

Paris

Theresienstadt 1941

Flossenbürg
1938

Plaszow M.
1943

Belzec
1942

Bar
1941

Rhine

Natzweiler 1941

FRANCE
270 000
76 134

Elbe

Danube

CZECHOSLOVAKIA
207 261 *143 297*

Auschwitz 1940

Balanovka
1942

Dachau
1933

Mauthausen 1941

SWIT.
18 000

AUSTRIA
191 481 *48 767*

HUNGARY
825 000
400 000

Danica 1941

Edinet
1941

Dniester

ROMANIA
564 097
120 919

Loborgrad 1941

Jasenovac 1941
Stara Gradiska 1941

Djakovo 1941

Zemun 1941

Black Sea

Jadovno 1941
Kruscia 1941

CROATIA

Tasmajden 1941

Sajmitste 1941

Danube

ITALY
46 656
6513

YUGOSLAVIA
82 242
67 288

SERBIA

MONTE

Adriatic Sea

Corsica

Rome

ALBANIA
204
591

BULGARIA
48 398

TURKEY
55 000

Sardina

GREECE
74 000 *59 185*

13. The Holocaust in Europe 1941–5

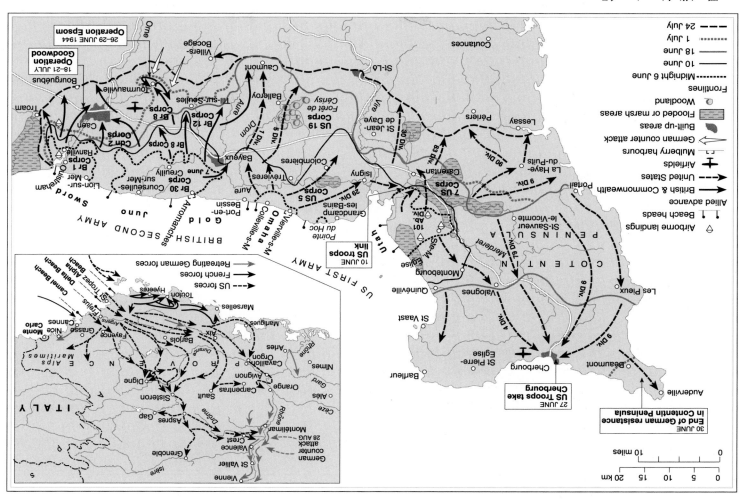

14. The Allied invasion of France

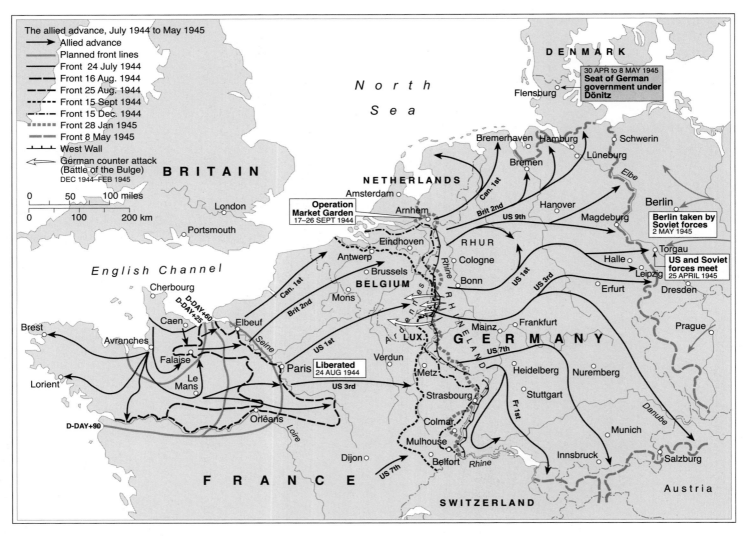

The allied advance, July 1944 to May 1945

→ Allied advance
Planned front lines
—— Front 24 July 1944
–·– Front 16 Aug. 1944
– – Front 25 Aug. 1944
····· Front 15 Sept 1944
–·– Front 15 Dec. 1944
····· Front 28 Jan 1945
– – Front 8 May 1945
—+— West Wall
← German counter attack
(Battle of the Bulge)
DEC 1944–FEB 1945

0   50   100 miles
0   100   200 km

DENMARK

Flensburg

30 APR to 8 MAY 1945
Seat of German government under Dönitz

North Sea

BRITAIN

London

Portsmouth

English Channel

Cherbourg
Caen
D-DAY+60
D-DAY+25
Brest
Avranches
Falaise
Le Mans
Lorient
D-DAY+90
Orléans

Elbeuf
Seine
Paris
Liberated 24 AUG 1944
US 3rd
Loire

Dijon

FRANCE

NETHERLANDS
Amsterdam
Operation Market Garden 17–26 SEPT 1944
Arnhem
Eindhoven
Antwerp
Brussels
BELGIUM
Mons
Can. 1st
Brit 2nd
US 1st
LUX.
Verdun
Metz
Strasbourg
Colmar
Mulhouse
Belfort
US 7th
Rhine

SWITZERLAND

Bremerhaven
Bremen
Hamburg
Schwerin
Lüneburg
Hanover
Can. 1st
Brit 2nd
US 9th
RHUR
Cologne
Bonn
US 1st
US 3rd
Mainz
Frankfurt
GERMANY
Heidelberg
Nuremberg
US 7th
Fr 1st
Stuttgart
Rhine
Innsbruck
Munich

Elbe
Berlin
Berlin taken by Soviet forces 2 MAY 1945
Magdeburg
Halle
Torgau
US and Soviet forces meet 25 APRIL 1945
Leipzig
Erfurt
Dresden
Prague
Danube
Salzburg
Austria

15. The defeat of Germany in the West

16. The defeat of Japan in the Pacific War

Sea of Okhotsk

Kamchatka

Sakhalin

17 AUG 1945

spuelsi llinu

10 OCT 1943

Khabarovsk

Sea of Japan

Hokkaido

JAPAN

Tokyo

Hiroshima
6 AUG 1945

**MANCHURIA
(MANCHUKUO)**

**Soviet army
attacks**
9 AUG 1945

Peking
Tientsin

Dairen

Seoul

KOREA

Pusan

Nagasaki
9 AUG 1945

Shanghai

**Bombing
raids**
from JUNE
1944

Nanking

**Jap.
Ichi-Go
offen-
sive**

Amoy

Formosa

**Chinese
counter
offensive
APR–JUNE
1945**

Kunming

Lashio

Canton

Hong
Kong

Hainan

**Chinese advance into
Burma after OCT 1943**

HANOI

FR. INDO-CHINA

Mandalay

BURMA

**British offensive into
Burma after NOV 1944
Rangoon retaken
MAY 1945**

**Japanese offensive into
N.E. India FEB–JUNE 1944**

Rangoon

Calcutta

Bay of
Bengal

SIAM

Bangkok

Phnom
Penh

Saigon

Gulf
of
Siam

MALAY
STATES

Medan

Kuala
Lumpur

Singapore

Sumatra

Batavia

Surabaya

Java

Bandjarmasin

Borneo

Sarawak

Brunei

Tarakan
JULY 1945

Macassar

Lobok

Celebes

DUTCH EAST INDIES

Amboina
Ceram
Sorong

Flores

Timor

Sumba

Banda
Sea

Aru
Is

Tanimbar
Is

Halmahera

Zamboanga

Sulu
Sea

Manila

PHILIPPINE IS.

JAN 1945

Battle of
Leyte Gulf.
Heavy Jap.
navy loss
25 OCT 1944

20 OCT
1944

MAY 1945

MAY 1945

**Direct air attack on
Japan from Okinawa
from MAY 1945**

**Battle of
Philippine Sea.
Japanese carrier
aviation destroyed
JUNE 1944**

Okinawa

SEPT 1944

JULY 1944

JULY 1944

SEPT 1944

Mariana Islands

Saipan
Tinian

SEPT 1944

Caroline Islands

Truk

**20th Air Force begins
direct attack on Japan
from 24 NOV 1944–14 AUG 1945**

Iwo Jima FEB–MAR 1945

**Fighters
sweep
over Japan
from MAY 1945**

Volcano Is.

Bonin Islands

Admiralty
Is

Manus I.
FEB 1944

Bismarck
Archipelago

Rabaul

New
Br.

Bougainville

Solomon
Is

NOV
1943

Guadalcanal
7 AUG 1942–
9 FEB 1943

Coral Sea

**Japanese
ground
forces
repulsed
17–25 SEPT
1942**

Cape York

Port
Moresby

Buna

Wewak

Hollandia

NEW GUINEA

MAY 1944

JULY 1944

SEPT 1944

Darwin

AUSTRALIA

Brisbane

Sydney

Melbourne

INDIAN OCEAN

EQUATOR

CEYLON

INDIA

TIBET

OUTER MONGOLIA

CHINA

U S S R

East
China
Sea

Yellow
Sea

Gulf of Tonking

Shikoku

Kyushu

Shanghai

Sea of
Japan

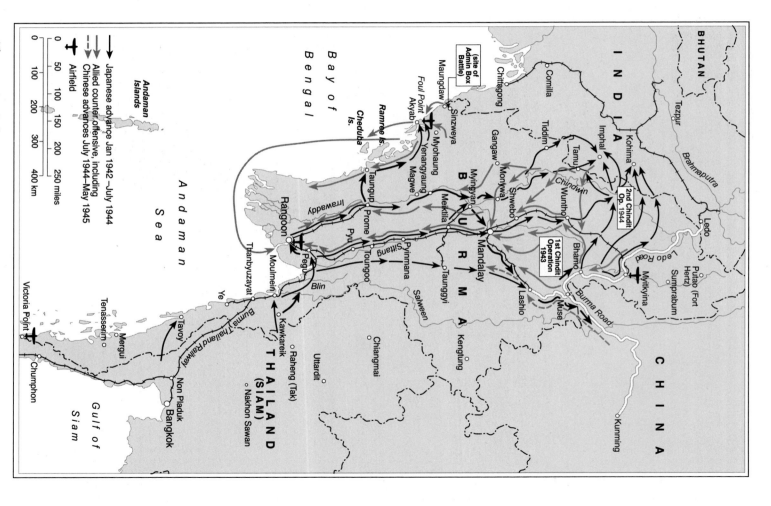

17. The campaigns in Burma 1942–45

BHUTAN

INDIA

CHINA

BURMA

THAILAND (SIAM)

Bay of Bengal

Andaman Sea

Gulf of Siam

Andaman Islands

Airfield

Japanese advance Jan 1942–July 1944

Allied counter-offensive, including
Chinese advances July 1944–May 1945

| 0 | 50 | 100 | 150 | 200 | 250 miles |

| 0 | 100 | 200 | 300 | 400 km |

(site of Admin Box Battle)

Ramree Is.

Cheduba Is.

Foul Point

Akyab

Sinzweya

Maungdaw

Myohaung

Yenangyaung

Magwe

Irrawaddy

Taungup

Rangoon

Pegu

Blin

Moulmein

Thanbyuzayat

Ye

Burma Thailand Railway

Kawkareik

Raheng (Tak)

Uttaradit

Chiangmai

Non Pladuk

Bangkok

Nakhon Sawan

Chumphon

Victoria Point

Tenasserim

Mergui

Tavoy

Prome

Pyu

Siltang

Toungoo

Pyinmana

Taunggyi

Salween

Kengtung

Kunming

Meiktila

Mandalay

Lashio

Muse

Bhamo

1st Chindit Operation 1943

Burma Road

Ledo Road

Myitkyina

Sumprabum

Putao (Fort Hertz)

Ledo

Tamu

Imphal

Kohima

Tezpur

Brahmaputra

Tiddim

Gangaw

Monywa

Myingyan

Shwebo

Wuntho

Chindwin

2nd Chindit Op. 1944

Comilla

Chittagong

NATO (founded 1949)
Year shown for later membership

Warsaw Pact (founded 1955)
Albania withdrew 1968

Yugoslavia, communist but non-aligned

0   300 miles
0   500 km

SAUDI ARABIA
JORDAN
ISRAEL
LEBANON
Cairo
Nile
EGYPT
LIBYA
IRAQ
SYRIA
Euphrates
Tigris
IRAN
Cyprus
Crete
TUNISIA
ALGERIA
MOROCCO
Gibraltar (Br.)
M e d i t e r r a n e a n   S e a
TURKEY (1952)
GREECE (1952)
Aegean Sea
Athens
Ankara
Istanbul
Dardanelles
Bosphorus
Sicily
Malta
Sardinia
Naples
Rome
Corsica
Barcelona
SPAIN (1982)
PORTUGAL
Madrid
Lisbon
Tagus
Ebro
AND.
ALBANIA
Tirana
BULGARIA
Sofia
YUGOSLAVIA
Belgrade
Danube
Bucharest
ROMANIA
Black Sea
Sea of Azov
Caspian Sea
Volga
Don
Dnieper
Kiev
Adriatic Sea
Trieste
Po
ITALY
Rhône
FRANCE
Geneva
SWITZ.
Rhine
AUSTRIA
Vienna
HUNGARY
Budapest
CZECHOSLOVAKIA
Prague
POLAND
Warsaw
Vistula
Oder
Elbe
Berlin
EAST GERMANY
WEST GERMANY
Loire
Paris
LUX.
BELG.
Brussels
NETH.
Danube
Minsk
Kaliningrad
USSR
Moscow
Leningrad
Lake Ladoga
Lake Onega
Helsinki
FINLAND
Gulf of Bothnia
SWEDEN
Stockholm
Baltic Sea
DENMARK
Skagerrak
North Sea
NORWAY
Oslo
English Channel
London
UNITED KINGDOM
Dublin
Irish Sea
IRELAND
ATLANTIC OCEAN

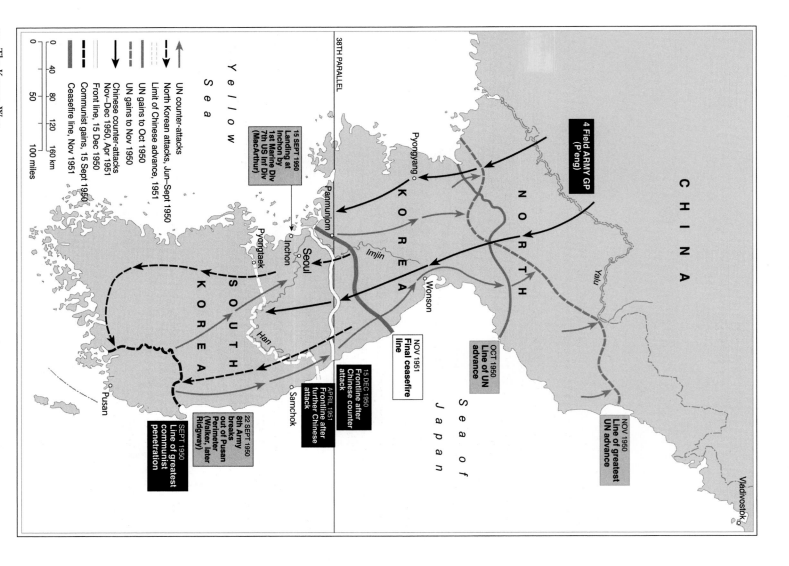

19. The Korean War

CHINA

NORTH KOREA

SOUTH KOREA

Yellow Sea

Sea of Japan

38TH PARALLEL

4 Field ARMY GP (P'eng)

Pyongyang

Panmunjom

Imjin

Wonson

Han

Pyongtaek

Inchon

Seoul

Samchok

Pusan

Yalu

Vladivostok

15 SEPT 1950 Landing at Inchon by 1st Marine Div 7th US Inf Div (MacArthur)

NOV 1950 Line of greatest UN advance

OCT 1950 Line of UN advance

NOV 1951 Final ceasefire line

15 DEC 1950 Frontline after Chinese counter attack

APRIL 1951 Frontline after further Chinese attack

22 SEPT 1950 8th Army breaks out of Pusan Perimeter (Walker, later Ridgway)

SEPT 1950 Line of greatest communist penetration

UN counter-attacks
North Korean attacks, Jun–Sept 1950
Limit of Chinese advance, 1951
UN gains to Oct 1950
UN gains to Nov 1950
Chinese counter-attacks Nov–Dec 1950, Apr 1951
Front line, 15 Dec 1950
Communist gains, 15 Sept 1950
Ceasefire line, Nov 1951

0   40   80   120   160 km
0   50   100 miles

FURTHER READING

1. THE GENESIS OF WORLD WAR

LEGACIES OF THE FIRST WORLD WAR

Carole Fink, *The Genoa Conference: European Diplomacy, 1921–22* (Chapel Hill, 1984).

Robert Gerwarth and John Horne (eds.), *War in Peace: Paramilitary Violence after the Great War* (Oxford, 2012).

Margaret MacMillan, *Paris 1919: Six Months that Changed the World* (New York, 2001).

Erez Manela, *The Wilsonian Moment: Self-Determination and the International Origins of Anticolonial Nationalism* (Oxford, 2007).

Panikos Panayi and Pippa Verdee, *Refugees and the End of Empire: Imperial Collapse and Forced Migration in the Twentieth Century* (London, 2011).

Eric Weitz, 'From the Vienna to the Paris System: International Politics and the Entangled Histories of Human Rights, Forced Deportations and Civilizing Missions', *American Historical Review*, 113/5 (2008), 1313–43.

THE LEAGUE OF NATIONS

Thomas W. Burkman, *Japan and the League of Nations: Empire and World Order, 1914–1938* (Honolulu, 2008).

Patricia Clavin, *Securing the World Economy: The Reinvention of the League of Nations, 1920–1946* (Oxford, 2013).

Thomas R. Davies, *The Possibilities of Transnational Activism: The Campaign for Disarmament between the Two World Wars* (Leiden, 2007).

Michael Kennedy, *Ireland and the League of Nations, 1919–1939* (Blackrock, 1996).

Daniel Lacqua (ed.), *Internationalism Reconfigured: Transnational Ideas and Movements Between the Wars* (London, 2011).

Eddy Lee, Lee Swepston, and Jasmien van Daele, *The ILO and the Quest for Social Justice, 1919–2009* (Geneva, 2009).

Helen McCarthy, *The British People and the League of Nations: Democracy, Citizenship and Internationalism, c. 1918–1945* (Manchester, 2011).

Dominique Marshall, 'The Formation of Childhood as an Object of International Relations: The Child Welfare Committee and the Declaration of Children's Rights of the League of Nations', *International Journal of Children's Rights*, 7/2 (1999).

Susan Pedersen, 'Back to the League of Nations', *American Historical Review*, 112/4 (2007), 1091–117.

Susan Pedersen, 'Getting out of Iraq—in 1932', *American Historical Review*,115/4 (2010), 975–1000.

Sarah D. Shields, *Fezzes in the River: Identity Politics and European Diplomacy in the Middle East on the Eve of World War II* (Oxford, 2011).

Glenda Sluga, *Internationalism in the Age of Nationalism* (Philadelphia, 2013).

Peter Yearwood, *Guarantee of Peace: The League of Nations and British Policy* (Oxford, 2005).

ECONOMIC CRISIS

Liaquat Ahamed, *Lords of Finance, 1929: The Great Depression—and the Bankers Who Broke the World* (London, 2010).

Peter J. Cain and A. G. Hopkins, *British Imperialism: Crisis and Deconstruction, 1914–1990* (London, 1993).

Patricia Clavin, *The Great Depression in Europe, 1919–1939* (London, 2000).

Barry Eichengreen, *Golden Fetters: The Gold Standard and the Great Depression, 1919–1939* (Oxford, 1992).

FOREIGN POLICY

Robert W. D. Boyce and Joseph A. Maiolo, *The Origins of World War Two: The Debate Continues* (London, 2003).

Robert Dallek, *Franklin D. Roosevelt and American Foreign Policy, 1917–1941* (New York, 1979).

John Darwin, *The Empire Project: The Rise and Fall of the British World-System, 1830–1970* (Cambridge, 2009).

Barbara Farnham, *Roosevelt and the Munich Crisis: A Study in Political Decision-Making* (Princeton, 1997).

Patrick Finney (ed.), *The Origins of the Second World War* (London, 1997).

Talbot C. Imlay, *Facing the Second World War: Strategy, Politics and Economics in Britain and France, 1938–1940* (Oxford, 2003).

Akira Iriye, *The Origins of the Second World War in Asia and the Pacific* (2nd edn, London, 2003).

Peter Jackson, *France and the Nazi Menace: Intelligence and Policy-Making, 1933–1939* (Oxford, 2000).

Roch Legault and B. J. C. McKercher, *Military Planning and the Origins of the Second World War in Europe* (Westport, Conn., 2001).

Robert Mallett, *Mussolini and the Origins of the Second World War, 1933–1940* (Basingstoke, 2003).

Sally Marks, *The Illusion of Peace: International Relations in Europe, 1918–1933* (Basingstoke, 2003).

Keith Neilsen, *Britain, Soviet Russia and the Collapse of the Versailles Order, 1919–1939* (Cambridge, 2006).

R. A. C. Parker, *Chamberlain and Appeasement* (London, 1993).

Anita Prazmowska, *Eastern Europe and the Origins of the Second World War* (London, 2000).

Geoffrey K. Roberts, *The Soviet Union and the Origins of the Second World War: Russo-German Relations and the Road to War, 1933–1941* (London, 1995).

Reynolds M. Salerno, *Vital Crossroads: Mediterranean Origins of the Second World War, 1935–1940* (Ithaca, 2002).

Zara Steiner, *The Lights that Failed: European International History, 1919–1933* (Oxford, 2007).

Zara Steiner, *Triumph of the Dark: European International History, 1933–1940* (Oxford, 2011).

Martin Thomas, *Britain, France and Appeasement: Anglo-French Relations in the Popular Front Era* (Oxford, 1996).

Adam Tooze, *The Wages of Destruction: The Making and Breaking of the Nazi Economy* (London, 2006).

Donald Cameron Watt, *How War Came: The Immediate Origins of the Second World War, 1938–1939* (London, 1989).

2. THE JAPANESE EMPIRE AT WAR, 1931–1945

Michael A. Barnhart, *Japan Prepares for Total War: The Search for Economic Security, 1919–1941* (Ithaca, 1987).

Christopher Alan Bayly and Timothy Norman Harper, *Forgotten Armies: The Fall of British Asia, 1941–1945* (London, 2005).

Anthony Beevor, *The Second World War* (New York, 2012).

Sugata Bose, 'Starvation amidst Plenty: The Making of Famine in Bengal, Honan, and Tonkin, 1942–1945', *Modern Asian Studies*, 24 (October 1990), 699–727.

Paul Burtness and Warren Ober, 'President Roosevelt, Admiral Stark, and the Unsent Warning to Pearl Harbor: A Research Note', *Australian Journal of Politics and History*, 57 (2011), 580–8.

Parks Cable, *Facing Japan: Chinese Politics and Japanese Imperialism, 1931–1937* (Cambridge, Mass., 1991).

Richard Connaughton, John Pimlott, and Duncan Anderson, *The Battle For Manila* (London, 1995).

John Costello, *The Pacific War, 1941–1945* (New York, 1982).

James B. Crowley, *Japan's Quest for Autonomy: National Security and Foreign Policy, 1930–1938* (Princeton, 1966).

Frederick R. Dickinson, *War and National Reinvention: Japan in the Great War, 1914–1919* (Cambridge, Mass., 1999).

Walter Dingman, *Power in the Pacific: The Origins of Naval Arms Limitation, 1914–22* (Chicago, 1977).

John Dower, *War Without Mercy: Race and Power in the Pacific War* (New York, 1986).

Edward J. Drea, *Japan's Imperial Army: Its Rise and Fall, 1853–1945* (Lawrence, Kan., 2009).

Bui Minh Dung, 'Japan's Role in the Vietnamese Starvation of 1944–1945', *Modern Asian Studies*, 29 (July 1990), 573–618.

Richard Frank, 'Ketsu Go: Japanese Political and Military Strategy', in Tsuyoshi Hasegawa (ed.), *The End of the Pacific War: Reappraisals* (Stanford, 2007), 65–94.

Erik Goldstein and John Maurer (eds.), *The Washington Conference, 1921–22: Naval Rivalry, East Asian Stability and the Road to Pearl Harbor* (London, 1994).

Ian Gow, *Military Intervention in Pre-War Japanese Politics: Admiral Kato Kanji and the 'Washington System'* (London, 2004).

Sheldon H. Harris, *Factories of Death: Japanese Biological Warfare, 1932–1945, and the American Cover-Up* (New York, 1995).

Tsuyoshi Hasegawa, *Racing the Enemy: Stalin, Truman, and the Surrender of Japan* (Cambridge, Mass., 2005).

Tsuyoshi Hasegawa, 'The Atomic Bombs and the Soviet Invasion: Which Was More Important in Japan's Decision to Surrender?', in Tsuyoshi Hasegawa (ed.), *The End of the Pacific War: Reappraisals* (Stanford, 2007), 113–45.

Max Hastings, *All Hell Let Loose: The World at War 1939–1945* (London, 2011).

Ikuhiku Hata, 'The Marco Polo Bridge Incident, 1937', in James William Morley (ed.), *The China Quagmire: Japanese Expansion on the Asian Continent 1933–1941* (New York, 1983).

Satoshi Hattori with Edward J. Drea, 'Japanese Operations from July to December 1937', in Mark Peattie, Edward J. Drea, and Hans van de Ven (eds.), *The Battle for China: Essays on the Military History of the Sino-Japanese War of 1937–1945* (Stanford, 2011).

George Hicks, *The Comfort Women: Japan's Brutal Regime of Enforced Prostitution in the Second World War* (New York, 1995).

Leonard Humphreys, *The Way of the Heavenly Sword: The Japanese Army in the 1920s* (Stanford, 1995).

Chang-tai Hung, *War and Popular Culture: Resistance in Modern China, 1937–1945* (Berkeley, 1994).

Michael Hunt and Steven Levine, *Arc of Empire: America's Wars in Asia from the Philippines to Vietnam* (Chapel Hill, 2012).

Nobutaka Ike (ed.), *Japan's Decision for War: Records of the 1941 Policy Conferences* (Stanford, 1967).

Akira Iriye, *The Origins of the Second World War in Asia and the Pacific* (New York, 1987).

Chalmers A. Johnson, *Peasant Nationalism and Communist Power: The Emergence of Revolutionary China 1937–1945* (Stanford, 1962).

Donald A. Jordan, *China's Trial By Fire: The Shanghai War of 1932* (Ann Arbor, 2004).

Zhifen Ju, 'Labour Conscription in North China: 1941–1945', in Stephen R. MacKinnon, Diana Lary, and Ezra Vogel (eds.), *China at War: Regions of China, 1937–1945* (Stanford, 2007), 207–26.

Gregory J. Kasza, 'Fascism From Above? Japan's Kakushin Right in Comparative Perspective', in Stein Ugelvik Larsen (ed.), *Fascism Outside Europe: The European Impulse against Domestic Conditions in the Diffusion of Global Fascism* (Boulder, Colo., 2001).

Ken C. Kawashima, *The Proletarian Gamble: Korean Workers in Interwar Japan* (Durham, NC, 2009).

Walter LaFeber, *The Clash: U.S.–Japanese Relations Throughout History* (New York, 1997).

Diana Lary, 'Drowned Earth: The Strategic Breaching of the Yellow River Dyke, 1938', *War in History*, 8 (2001), 191–207.

Diana Lary, *The Chinese People at War: Human Suffering and Social Transformation, 1937–1945* (Cambridge, 2010).

Diana Lary and Stephen MacKinnon (eds.), *Scars of War: The Impact of Warfare on Modern China* (Vancouver, 2002).

David J. Lu, *Japan: A Documentary History. The Late Tokugawa Period to the Present* (New York, 1997).

Stephen MacKinnon, *Wuhan, 1938: War, Refugees and the Making of Modern China* (Berkeley, 2008).

James L. McClain, *Japan: A Modern History* (New York, 2002).

David Marr, *Vietnam 1945: The Quest for Power* (Stanford, 1995).

Jonathan Marshall, *To Have and Have Not: Southeast Asian Raw Materials and the Origins of the Pacific War* (Berkeley, 1995).

Rana Mitter, *Forgotten Ally: China's World War II, 1937–1945* (London, 2013).

Ian Nish, *The Anglo-Japanese Alliance: The Diplomacy of Two Island Empires 1894–1907* (London, 1966).

Ian Nish, *Alliance in Decline: A Study in Anglo-Japanese Relations 1908–23* (London, 1972).

Philipps O'Brien, *The Anglo-Japanese Alliance, 1902–1922*, (London, 2004).

S. C. M. Paine, *The Wars for Asia, 1911–1949* (Cambridge, 2012).

Brandon Palmer, *Fighting for the Enemy: Koreans in Japan's War, 1937–1945* (Seattle, 2013).

Mark Peattie, Edward J. Drea, and Hans van de Ven (eds.), *The Battle for China: Essays on the Military History of the Sino-Japanese War of 1937–1945* (Stanford, 2011).

R. Keith Schoppa, *Revolution and its Past: Identities and Change in Modern Chinese History* (New Jersey, 2002).

C. Sarah Soh, *The Comfort Women: Sexual Violence and Postcolonial Memory in Korea and Japan* (Chicago, 2008).

Jonathan Spence, *The Search for Modern China* (New York, 1990).

David Joel Steinberg, *In Search of Southeast Asia: A Modern History* (Honolulu, 1971).

Jay Taylor, *The Generalissimo: Chiang Kai-shek and the Struggle for Modern China* (Cambridge, Mass., 2009).

Michael Weiner, *Race and Migration in Imperial Japan* (London, 1994).

Alex Woodside, *Community and Revolution in Modern Vietnam* (Boston, 1976).

Odoric Y. K. Wou, *Mobilizing the Masses: Building Revolution in Henan* (Stanford, 1994).

Louise Young, *Japan's Total Empire: Manchuria and the Culture of Wartime Imperialism* (Berkeley, 1998).

3. THE ITALIAN WARS

H. James Burgwyn, *Mussolini Warlord: Failed Dreams of Empire, 1940–1943* (New York, 2012).

John Gooch, *Mussolini and his Generals: The Armed Forces and Fascist Foreign Policy, 1922–1940* (Cambridge, 2007).

Andrew Knapp and Claudia Baldoli, *Forgotten Blitzes: France and Italy under Allied Air Attack, 1940–1945* (London, 2012).

MacGregor Knox, *Common Destiny: Dictatorship, Foreign Policy, and War in Fascist Italy and Nazi Germany* (Cambridge, 2000).

MacGregor Knox, *Hitler's Italian Allies: Royal Armed Forces, Fascist Regime, and the War of 1940–43* (Cambridge, 2000).

Nicola Labanca, *Oltremare. Storia dell'espansione coloniale italiana* (Bologna, 2002; 2nd edn 2007).

Nicola Labanca (ed.), *I bombardamenti aerei sull'Italia. Politica, Stato, società (1939–1945)* (Bologna, 2012).

Claudio Pavone, *Una guerra civile. Saggio storico sulla moralità nella Resistenza* (Turin, 1991).

Piero Piero and Giorgio Rochat, *Pietro Badoglio* (Turin, 1974).

Giorgio Rochat, *Le guerre italiane 1935–1943* (Turin, 2005).

4. THE GERMAN WARS

Omar Bartov, *Hitler's Army: Soldiers, Nazis and War in the Third Reich* (Oxford, 1991).

Richard Bessel, *Nazism and War* (London, 2004).

Horst Boog et al., *Germany and the Second World War. Volume IV: The Attack on the Soviet Union* (Oxford, 1999).

Richard Evans, *The Third Reich at War* (London, 2008).

Christian Hartmann, *Operation Barbarossa: Nazi Germany's War in the East* (Oxford, 2013).

Ulrich Herbert (ed.), *National Socialist Extermination Policies: Contemporary German Perspectives and Controversies* (Oxford, 2000).

Ian Kershaw, *Fateful Choices: Ten Decisions that Changed the World, 1940–41* (London, 2007).

Evan Mawdsley, *Thunder in the East: The Nazi-Soviet War 1941–1945* (London, 2005).

Ernest May, *Strange Victory: Hitler's Conquest of France* (London, 2009).

Geoffrey Megargee, *Inside Hitler's High Command* (Lawrence, Kan., 2000).

Richard Overy, *The Bombing War: Europe 1939–1945* (London, 2013).

John Ray, *The Night Blitz, 1940–1941* (London, 1996).

Richard Rhodes, *Masters of Death: The SS-Einsatzgruppen and the Invention of the Holocaust* (New York, 2003).

Timothy Snyder, *Bloodlands: Europe between Hitler and Stalin* (London, 2010).

David Stafford, *Endgame 1945: Victory, Retribution, Liberation* (London, 2007).

David Stahel, *Operation Barbarossa and Germany's Defeat in the East* (Cambridge, 2009).

Jill Stephenson, *Hitler's Home Front: Württemberg under the Nazis* (London, 2006).

5. THE WEST AND THE WAR AT SEA

C. B. A. Behrens, *Merchant Shipping and the Demands of War* (London, 1955).

David Brown, *Atlantic Escorts: Allied Anti-Submarine Vessels 1939–1945* (London, 2006).

Worrall Carter, *Beans, Bullets and Black Oil: The Story of Fleet Logistics Afloat in the Pacific During World War Two* (Washington, DC, 1953).

Anthony Cumming, *The Royal Navy and the Battle of Britain* (London and Annapolis, Md., 2010).

David Edgerton, *Britain's War Machine* (London, 2012).

George Franklin, *Britain's Anti-Submarine Capability 1919–39* (Abingdon, 2003).

Jack Greene and Alessandro Massignani, *Naval War in the Mediterranean 1940–43* (Barnsley, 2011).

Eric Grove, *Sea Battles in Close Up: World War II*, Vol. 2 (Shepperton and Annapolis, Md., 1993).

Eric Grove, *The Price of Disobedience: The Battle of the River Plate Reconsidered* (Stroud and Annapolis, Md., 2000).

Eric Grove and Martin Stephen, *Sea Battles in Close Up: World War II*, Vol. 1 (Shepperton and Annapolis, Md., 1988).

Arnold Hague, *The Allied Convoy System 1939–1945: Its Organisation, Defence and Operation* (London, 2003).

David Hobbs, *The British Pacific Fleet: The Royal Navy's Most Powerful Striking Force* (Barnsley 2011).

Marc Milner, *Battle of the Atlantic* (Stroud, 2011).

Samuel Elliot Morison, *The Two Ocean War* (New York, 1997).

Samuel Elliot Morison, *History of US Naval Operations in World War II*, 14 volumes (Annapolis, Md., 2010–12).

Mark Parillo, *The Japanese Merchant Fleet of World War II* (Annapolis, Md., 1993).

Jonathan Parshall and Anthony Tully, *Shattered Sword: The Untold Story of the Battle of Midway* (Dulles, Va., 2008).

Stephan Roskill, *The War at Sea*, Vols. I, II, III Part 1, and III Part 2 (Uckfield, 2004).

Kevin Smith, *Conflict over Convoys: American Logistics Diplomacy in the Second World War* (Cambridge, 2002).

Adam Tooze, *The Wages of Destruction: The Making and Breaking of the Nazi Economy* (London, 2007).

Martin Van Creveld, *Supplying War: Logistics from Wallenstein to Patton* (Cambridge, 2004).

Albert Weeks, *Russia's Life Saver: Lend Lease Aid to the USSR in World War II* (Lanham, NY, Toronto, and Plymouth, 2004).

H. P. Willmott, *The Last Century of Sea Power. Volume 2: From Washington to Tokyo* (Bloomington, Ind., 2010).

David Wragg, *Plan Z: The Nazi Bid for Naval Dominance* (Barnsley, 2008).

Alan Zimm, *Attack on Pearl Harbor: Strategy, Combat, Myths, Deceptions* (Oxford, 2013).

6. THE ALLIES FROM DEFEAT TO VICTORY

GENERAL SURVEYS

John Ellis, *Brute Force: Allied Strategy and Tactics in the Second World War* (London, 1990).

Evan Mawdsley, *World War II: A New History* (Cambridge, 2009).

Richard Overy, *Why the Allies Won* (2nd rev. edn, London, 2006).

Gerhard Weinberg, *A World at Arms: A Global History of the World War II* (rev. edn, Cambridge, 2005).

BRITISH EMPIRE

David Edgerton, *Britain's War Machine: Weapons, Resources, and Experts in the Second World War* (Oxford, 2011).

David French, *Raising Churchill's Army: The British Army and the War against Germany, 1919–1945* (Oxford, 2000).

Grand Strategy, 7 vols. (London, 1956–76), the British official history, under several editors, including J. Butler, J. Ehrman, and M. Howard.

Talbot Imlay, *Facing the Second World War: Strategy, Politics, and Economics in Britain and France, 1938–1940* (Oxford, 2003).

SOVIET RUSSIA

G. Krivosheev (ed.), *Soviet Casualties and Combat Losses in the Twentieth Century* (London, 1997).

Evan Mawdsley, *Thunder in the East: The Nazi-Soviet War 1941–1945* (London, 2005).

Geoffrey Roberts, *Stalin's Wars: From World War to Cold War, 1939–1953* (New Haven, 2006).

UNITED STATES

Maurice Matloff, *Strategic Planning for Coalition Warfare*, 2 vols. (Washington, 1980/1959), official US Army 'green book'; volumes cover 1941–2 (with E. Snell) and 1943–4. http://www.history.army. mil/html/bookshelves/collect/usaww2.html

Forrest Pogue, *The Supreme Command* [The European Theater of Operations] (Washington, 1954/ 1989), official US Army 'green book'. http://www.history.army.mil/html/bookshelves/collect/ usaww2.html

Mark Stoler, *Allies and Adversaries: The Joint Chiefs of Staff, the Grand Alliance, and U.S. Strategy in World War II* (Chapel Hill, 2000).

STRATEGIC BOMBING

Tami Davis Biddle, *Rhetoric and Reality in Air Warfare: The Evolution of British and American Ideas about Strategic Bombing, 1914–1945* (Princeton, 2002).

Richard Overy, *The Bombing War: Europe 1939–1945* (London, 2013).

Charles Webster and Noble Frankland, *The Strategic Air Offensive Against Germany*, 4 vols. (London, 1961).

GERMAN PERSPECTIVES

Germany and the Second World War, 9 vols. (Oxford, 1990–). Although this 'official' history is told from the German point of view it includes chapters which are essential reading on the effects of Allied strategy. The final volumes have not yet been translated.

Rüdiger Overmans, *Deutsche militärische Verluste im Zweiten Weltkrieg* (Munich, 1999).

Adam Tooze, *The Wages of Destruction: The Making and Breaking of the Nazi Economy* (London, 2006).

7. FIGHTING POWER: WAR-MAKING AND MILITARY INNOVATION

Paul Addison and Angus Calder (eds.), *Time to Kill: The Soldiers' Experience of War in the West, 1939–1945* (London, 1997).

Louis Allen, *Burma: The Longest War 1941–45* (London, 1984).

Omer Bartov, *Hitler's Army: Soldiers, Nazis and War in the Third Reich* (Oxford, 1991).

Omer Bartov, *The Eastern Front, 1941–1945: German Troops and the Barbarization of Warfare* (London, 2nd edn 2001).

Anthony Beevor, *Stalingrad* (London, 1998).

Tami Davis Biddle, *Rhetoric and Reality in Air Warfare: The Evolution of British and American Ideas about Strategic Bombing, 1914–1945* (Princeton, 2002).

Brian Bond and Kyoichi Tachikawa (eds.), *British and Japanese Military Leadership in the Far Eastern War 1941–1945* (London, 2004).

Joanna Bourke, *An Intimate History of Killing: Face to Face Killing in Twentieth-Century Warfare* (London, 1999).

Craig Cameron, *American Samurai: Myth, Imagination and the Conduct of Battle in the First Marine Division, 1941–1951* (Cambridge, 1994).

Eliot Cohen and John Gooch, *Military Misfortunes: The Anatomy of Failure in War* (New York, 1991).

Martin Van Creveld, *Fighting Power: German and US Army Performance, 1939–1945* (London, 1983).

Michael Doubler, *Closing with the Enemy: How GIs Fought the War in Europe, 1944–45* (Lawrence, Kan., 1994).

John Ellis, *The Sharp End of War: The Fighting Man in World War Two* (London, 1982).

John Ellis, *Brute Force: Allied Strategy and Tactics in the Second World War* (London, 1990).

Jürgen Förster, 'Evolution and Development of German Doctrine 1914–45', in J. Gooch (ed.), *The Origins of Contemporary Doctrine* (London, 1997), 18–31.

David French, *Raising Churchill's Army: The British Army and the War Against Germany, 1919–1945* (Oxford, 2000).

Stephen Fritz, *Frontsoldaten: The German Soldier in World War Two* (Lexington, Ky., 1995).

Ian Gooderson, *Air Power at the Battlefront: Allied Close Air Support in Europe 1943–1945* (London, 1998).

Mark Harrison (ed.), *The Economics of World War Two: Six Great Powers in International Competition* (Cambridge, 1998).

Mark Harrison, *Medicine and Victory: British Military Medicine in the Second World War* (Oxford, 2004).

Paul Kennedy, *Engineers of Victory: The Problem Solvers who Turned the Tide in the Second World War* (London, 2013).

MacGregor Knox, *Hitler's Italian Allies: Royal Armed Forces, Fascist Regime, and the War of 1940–1943* (Cambridge, 2000).

John McManus, *The Deadly Brotherhood: The American Combat Soldier in World War II* (Novato, Calif., 1998).

David Marston, *Phoenix from the Ashes: The Indian Army in the Burma Campaign* (Westport, Conn., 2003).

Catherine Merridale, *Ivan's War: The Red Army 1939–45* (London, 2005).

Alan Millett and Williamson Murray (eds.), *Military Effectiveness. Vol. 3: The Second World War* (London, 1988).

Marc Milner, *Battle of the Atlantic* (Stroud, 2005).

Williamson Murray and Alan Millett (eds.), *Military Innovation in the Interwar Period* (Cambridge, 1996).

Richard Overy, *Why the Allies Won* (London, 1995).

Richard Overy, *Russia's War* (London, 1997).

Richard Overy, *The Bombing War: Europe 1939–1945* (London, 2013).

Ben Shephard, *A War of Nerves: Soldiers and Psychiatrists, 1914–1994* (London, 2000).

Russell Weigley, *Eisenhower's Lieutenants: The Campaign of France and Germany, 1944–1945* (Bloomington, Ind., 1999).

8. ECONOMIES IN TOTAL WAR

Lizzie Collingham, *The Taste of War: World War Two and the Battle for Food* (London, 2011).

Geoffrey Field, *Blood, Sweat, and Toil: Remaking the British Working Class, 1939–1945* (Oxford, 2011).

Mark Harrison (ed.), *The Economics of World War II: Six Great Powers in International Comparison* (Cambridge, 1998).

Warren Kimball, David Reynolds, and Alexander Chubarian (eds.), *Allies at War: The Soviet, American and British Experience 1939–1945* (New York, 1994).

Hein Klemann and Sergei Kudryashov, *Occupied Economies: An Economic History of Nazi-Occupied Europe, 1939–1945* (London, 2012).

Alfred Mierzejewski, *The Collapse of the German War Economy: Allied Air Power and the German National Railway* (Chapel Hill, 1988).

Alan Milward, *War, Economy and Society 1939–1945* (London, 1987).

W. Moskoff, *The Bread of Affliction: The Food Supply in the USSR during World War II* (Cambridge, 1990).

Richard Overy, *War and Economy in the Third Reich* (Oxford, 1994).

Richard Overy, *Why the Allies Won* (London, 2006).

Lennart Samuelson, *Tankograd: The Formation of a Soviet Company Town: Cheliabinsk 1900–1950s* (Basingstoke, 2011).

Adam Tooze, *The Wages of Destruction: The Making and Breaking of the Nazi Economy* (London, 2006).

Harold Vatter, *The US Economy in World War II* (New York, 1985).

9. FRONT LINE 1: ARMED FORCES AT WAR

Paul Addison and Angus Calder (eds.), *Time To Kill: The Soldier's Experience of War in the West 1939–1945* (London, 1997).

Michael Burleigh, *Moral Combat: A History of World War II* (London, 2010).

Edward Drea, *Japan's Imperial Army: Its Rise and Fall, 1853–1945* (Lawrence, Kan., 2009).

David French, *Raising Churchill's Army: The British Army and the War Against Germany 1919–1945* (Oxford, 2001).

Stephen Fritz, *Frontsoldaten: The German Soldier in World War II* (Lexington, Ky., 1997).

Lee Kennett, G.I. *The American Soldier in World War II* (Norman, Okla., 1997).

David Killingray and Martin Plaut, *Fighting For Britain: African Soldiers in the Second World War* (Woodbridge, 2010).

Catherine Merridale, *Ivan's War: The Red Army 1939–1945* (London, 2005).

Alan Millett and Williamson Murray (eds.), *Military Effectiveness*, Vol. 2: *The Interwar Period*, and *Military Effectiveness*, Vol. 3: *The Second World War* (Cambridge, new edn, 2010).

Mark Peattie, Edward Drea, and Hans Van de Ven (eds.), *The Battle for China: Essays on the Military History of the Sino-Japanese War of 1937–1945* (Stanford, 2011).

Ronald Spector, *At War at Sea: Sailors and Naval Combat in the Twentieth Century* (London, 2001).

10. FRONT LINE II: CIVILIANS AT WAR

Claudia Baldoli and Andrew Knapp, *Forgotten Blitzes: France and Italy under Allied Air Attack, 1940–1945* (London and New York, 2012).

Claudia Baldoli, Andrew Knapp, and Richard Overy (eds.), *Bombing, States and Peoples in Western Europe, 1940–1945* (London, 2011).

John Barber and Mark Harrison, *The Soviet Home Front, 1941–1945: A Social and Economic History of the USSR in World War II* (London, 1991).

Tom Behan, *The Italian Resistance: Fascists, Guerrillas and the Allies* (London, 2009).

Ralf Blank and Jörg Echternkamp, *Germany and the Second World War.* Vol. 9, Part 1: *German Wartime Society 1939–1945* (Oxford, 2008).

Philippe Burrin, *France under the Germans: Collaboration and Compromise* (New York, 1996).

Roger Chickering, Stig Förster, and Bernd Greiner (eds.), *A World at Total War: Global Conflict and the Politics of Destruction, 1937–1945* (Cambridge, 2005).

Lizzie Collingham, *The Taste of War: World War Two and the Battle for Food* (London, 2011).

Gerald Feldman and Wolfgang Seibel (eds.), *Networks of Nazi Persecution: Bureaucracy, Business and the Organization of the Holocaust* (New York, 2005).

Geoffrey Field, *Blood, Sweat and Toil: Remaking the British Working Class, 1939–1945* (Oxford, 2011).

Shannon Fogg, *The Politics of Everyday Life in Vichy France: Foreigners, Undesirables, and Strangers* (Cambridge, 2009).

Susan Grayzel, *At Home and Under Fire: Air Raids and Culture in Britain from the Great War to the Blitz* (Cambridge, 2012).

Leonid Grenkevich, *The Soviet Partisan Movement 1941–1944* (London, 1999).

Ulrich Herbert, *Hitler's Foreign Workers* (Cambridge, 1996).

Julian Jackson, *France: The Dark Years, 1940–1944* (Oxford, 2001).

Pat Jalland, *Death in War and Peace: A History of Loss and Grief in England, 1914–1970* (Oxford, 2010).

Helen Jones, *British Civilians in the Front Line: Air Raids, Productivity and Wartime Culture, 1939–1945* (Manchester, 2006).

Hein Klemann and Sergei Kudryashov, *Occupied Economies: An Economic History of Nazi-Occupied Europe, 1939–1945* (London, 2012).

Halik Kochanski, *The Eagle Unbowed: Poland and the Poles in the Second World War* (London, 2012).

Anna Krylova, *Soviet Women in Combat: A History of Violence on the Eastern Front* (Cambridge, 2010).

Olga Kucherenko, *Little Soldiers: How Soviet Children Went to War, 1941–1945* (Oxford, 2011).

Mark Mazower, *Hitler's Empire: Nazi Rule in Occupied Europe* (London, 2008).

Alan Milward, *War, Economy and Society 1939–1945* (London, 1977).

William Moskoff, *The Bread of Affliction: The Food Supply in the USSR during World War II* (Cambridge, 1990).

Richard Overy, *Russia's War* (London, 1998).

Richard Overy, *The Bombing War: Europe 1939–1945* (London, 2013).

Anna Reid, *Leningrad: Tragedy of a City under Siege, 1941–44* (London, 2011).

David Reynolds, Warren Kimball, and Alexander Chubarian (eds.), *Allies at War: The Soviet, American and British Experience, 1939–1945* (New York, 1994).

Sonya Rose, *Which People's War? National Identity and Citizenship in Wartime Britain, 1939–1945* (Oxford, 2003).

Timothy Snyder, *Bloodlands: Europe between Hitler and Stalin* (London, 2010).

Stephen Spender, *Citizens in War—And After* (London, 1945).

Jill Stephenson, *Hitler's Home Front: Württemberg under the Nazis* (London, 2006).

Dietmar Süss, *Death from the Skies: How the British and Germans Survived Bombing in World War II* (Oxford, 2014).

Keith Sword, *Deportation and Exile: Poles in the Soviet Union, 1939–1948* (Basingstoke, 1996).

Julia Torrie, *For Their Own Good: Civilian Evacuations in Germany and France, 1939–1945* (New York, 2010).

Olivier Wieviorka, *Une certaine idée de la Résistance: Défense de la France 1940–1949* (Paris, 1995).

11. UNNATURAL DEATHS

Claudia Baldoli and Andrew Knapp, *Forgotten Blitzes: France and Italy under Allied Air Attack 1940–1945* (London and New York, 2012).

John Barber (ed.), *Life and Death in Besieged Leningrad, 1941–44* (Basingstoke, 2005).

Karel C. Berghoff, *Harvest of Despair: Life and Death in Ukraine under Nazi Rule* (Cambridge, Mass., 2004).

Richard Bessel, *Nazism and War* (London and New York, 2004).

Richard Bessel, *Germany 1945: From War to Peace* (London and New York, 2009).

Sugata Bose, 'Starvation amidst Plenty: The Making of Famine in Bengal, Honan and Tonkin, 1942–45', *Modern Asian Studies*, 24/4 (October 1990).

Clara E. Councell, 'War and Infectious Disease', *Public Health Reports* (1896–1970), vol. 56, no. 12 (21 March 1941), 547–73.

John Dower, *War without Mercy: Race and Power in the Pacific War* (London and Boston, 1986).

Christian Gerlach, *Kalkulierte Morde. Die deutsche Wirtschafts- und Vernichtungspolitik in Weißrußland 1941 bis 1944* (Hamburg, 1999).

Christian Goeschel, *Suicide in Nazi Germany* (Oxford, 2009).

Paul Greenough, *Prosperity and Misery in Modern Bengal: The Famine of 1943–1944* (New York and Oxford, 1982).

Sheldon H. Harris, *Factories of Death: Japanese Biological Warfare 1932–45 and the American Cover-Up* (London and New York, 1994).

Violetta Hionidou, *Famine and Death in Occupied Greece, 1914–1944* (Cambridge, 2006).

Bethany Lacina and Nils Gleditsch, 'Monitoring Trends in Global Combat: A New Dataset of Battle Deaths', *European Journal of Population*, vol. 51 (2005), 145–66.

Diana Lary and Stephen MacKinnon (eds.), *Scars of War: The Impact of Warfare on Modern China* (Toronto, 2001).

Peter Longerich, *Holocaust: The Nazi Persecution and Murder of the Jews* (Oxford, 2010).

Keith Lowe, *Savage Continent: Europe in the Aftermath of World War II* (New York, 2012).

Jean-Louis Margolin, *L'armée de l'empereur. Violence et crimes du Japon en guerre, 1937–1945* (Paris, 2007).

Mark Mazower, *Inside Hitler's Greece: The Experience of Occupation, 1941–44* (New Haven and London, 1993).

Norman M. Naimark, *Fires of Hatred: Ethnic Cleansing in Twentieth-Century Europe* (Cambridge, Mass. and London, 2001).

Cormac Ó Gráda, *Famine: A Short History* (Princeton, 2009).

Rüdiger Overmans, *Deutsche militärische Verluste im Zweiten Weltkrieg* (Oldenbourg, 1999).

Richard Overy, *Russia's War* (London, 2010).

Richard Overy (ed.), *Bombing, States and Peoples in Western Europe 1940–1945* (London and New York, 2011).

Richard Overy, *The Bombing War: Europe 1939–1945* (London, 2013).

Amartya Sen, *Poverty and Famines: An Essay on Entitlement and Deprivation* (Oxford, 1981).

Mark Spoerer and Jochen Fleischhacker, 'Forced Laborers in Nazi Germany: Categories, Numbers, and Survivors', *The Journal of Interdisciplinary History*, 33/2 (2002).

Dietmar Süss, *Death from the Skies: How the British and Germans Survived Bombing in World War II* (Oxford, 2014).

Jozo Tomasevich, *War and Revolution in Yugoslavia, 1941–1945: Occupation and Collaboration* (Stanford, 2001).

Paul Julian Weindling, *Epidemics and Genocide in Eastern Europe 1890–1945* (Oxford, 2000).

Michael Zimmermann, *Rassenutopie und Genozid. Die nationalsozialistische 'Lösung der Zigeuner-frage'* (Hamburg, 1996).

12. BRAINS AT WAR: INVENTION AND EXPERTS

Michael Thad Allen, *The Business of Genocide: The SS, Slave Labor and the Concentration Camps* (Chapel Hill, 2002).

Götz Aly and Susanne Heim, *Architects of Annihilation* (London, 2002).

Donald H. Avery, *The Science of War: Canadian Scientists and Allied Military Technology during the Second World War* (Toronto, 2004).

Louis Brown, *A Radar History of World War II: Technical and Military Imperatives* (Bristol, 1999).

Ute Deichmann, *Biologists under Hitler* (Cambridge, Mass., 1996).

David Edgerton, 'British Scientific Intellectuals and the Relations of Science, Technology and War', in Paul Forman and José Manuel Sánchez Ron (eds.), *National Military Establishments and the Advancement of Science: Studies in 20th Century History* (Dordrecht, 1996).

David Edgerton, *Britain's War Machine: Weapons, Resources and Experts in the Second World War* (London, 2011).

Hermione Giffard, 'Engines of Desperation: Jet Engines, Production and New Weapons in the Third Reich', *Journal of Contemporary History*, 48/4 (October 2013), 821–44.

John Gimpel, *Science, Technology, and Reparations: Exploitation and Plunder in Postwar Germany* (Stanford, 1990).

Margaret Gowing, *Britain and Atomic Energy* (London, 1964).

Walter Grunden, *Secret Weapons and World War II: Japan in the Shadow of Big Science* (Lawrence, Kan., 2005).

Guy Hartcup, *Effect of Science on the Second World War* (London, 2000).

Historia Scientiarum, Vol. 14, No. 3 (March 2005), Special Issue: Comparative History of Nuclear Weapons Projects in Japan, Germany, and Russia in the 1940s.

Historia Scientiarum, Vol. 15, No. 3 (March 2006), Special Issue: Science, War, and Colonization in East Asia.

Alexei B. Kojevnikov, *Stalin's Great Science: The Times and Adventures of Soviet Physicists* (London, 2002).

Nikolai Krementsov, *Stalinist Science* (Princeton, 1997).

Robert J. Lifton, *The Nazi Doctors: Medical Killing and the Psychology of Genocide* (New York, 1986).

Ad Maas and Hans Hooijmaijers, *Scientific Research In World War II: What Scientists did in the War* (London, 2008).

Peter Mandler, *Return from the Natives: How Margaret Mead Won the Second World War and Lost the Cold War* (London, 2013).

David A. Mindell, *Between Human and Machine: Feedback, Control, and Computing Before Cybernetics* (Baltimore, 2002).

Pap A. Ndiaye, *Nylon and Bombs: DuPont and the March of Modern America* (Baltimore, 2007).

Robert Neer, *Napalm: An American Biography* (Cambridge, Mass., 2013).

M. J. Neufeld, *The Rocket and the Reich: Peenemünde and the Coming of the Ballistic Missile Era* (Washington, DC, 1995).

Osiris, 2nd Series, Vol. 20, Politics and Science in Wartime: Comparative International Perspectives on the Kaiser Wilhelm Institute (2005), 263–88.

Rebecca A. Ratcliff, *Delusions of Intelligence: Enigma, Ultra, and the End of Secure Ciphers* (Cambridge, 2006).

James Reardon-Anderson, *The Study of Change: Chemistry in China, 1840–1949* (Cambridge, 2003).

R. Rhodes, *The Making of the Atomic Bomb* (New York, 1986).

Margit Szöllösi-Janze (ed.), *Science in the Third Reich, German Historical Perspectives* (Oxford, 2001).

William Thomas, *Rational Action: The Sciences of Policy in Britain and America, 1940–1960* (Cambridge, Mass., forthcoming).

Mark Walker, *German National Socialism and the Quest for Nuclear Power* (Cambridge, 1989).

Raymond C. Watson, Jr., *Radar Origins Worldwide: History of its Evolution in 13 Nations through World War II* (Bloomington, Ind., 2009).

Waqar Zaidi, "Aviation Will Either Destroy or Save our Civilization": Proposals for the International Control of Aviation, 1920–1945', *Journal of Contemporary History*, 46 (2011), 150–78.

Waqar Zaidi, 'A Blessing in Disguise: Reconstructing International Relations through Atomic Energy, 1945–1948', *Past and Present* Supplement 6 (2011), 309–31.

13. THE CULTURE OF WAR: IDEAS, ARTS, AND PROPAGANDA

Art and Power: Europe under the Dictators 1930–45, Hayward Gallery, London, 1996.

Art from the Second World War, London. Imperial War Museum, London, 2007.

Jan Bank, *Religion in Europe During World War II* (London, 2012).

Laura Brandon, *Art and War* (London, 2009).

Nicholas J. Cull, David Culbert, and David Welch, *Propaganda and Mass Persuasion: A Historical Encyclopedia, 1500 to the Present* (Santa Barbara and Oxford, 2003).

Igor Golomstock, *Totalitarian Art* (London, 1990).

Barbara McCloskey, *Artists in World War II* (Westport, Conn., 2005).

Peter Paret, Beth Irwin Lewis, and Paul Paret, *Persuasive Images: Posters of War and Revolution* (Princeton, 1992).

Philip M. Taylor, *The Munitions of the Mind: A History of Propaganda from the Ancient World to the Present* (Manchester, 1995).

Martin Van Creveld, *The Culture of War* (New York, 2008).

David Welch, *Propaganda Power and Persuasion* (London, 2013).

GREAT BRITAIN

Anthony Aldgate and Jeffrey Richards, *Britain Can Take It: The British Cinema in the Second World War* (Edinburgh, 1994).

James Chapman, *The British at War: Cinema, State and Propaganda, 1939–1945* (London, 1998).

Charles Cruickshank, *The Fourth Arm: Psychological Warfare, 1938–1945* (Oxford, 1981).

Nicholas J. Cull, *Selling War: British Propaganda and American 'Neutrality' in World War Two* (New York, 1995).

Ian McLaine, *Ministry of Morale: Home Front Morale and the Ministry of Information in World War II* (London, 1979).

Arthur Marwick, *Britain in the Century of Total War* (Harmondsworth, 1970).

Philip M. Taylor, *British Propaganda in the Twentieth Century: Selling Democracy* (Edinburgh, 1999).

GERMANY

Peter Adam, *The Arts of the Third Reich* (London, 1992).

Robert Herzstein, *The War That Hitler Won: The Most Infamous Propaganda Campaign in History* (London, 1979).

David Welch, *Propaganda and the German Cinema 1933–4* (Oxford, 1983; rev. edn London, 2001).

David Welch, *The Third Reich: Politics and Propaganda*. London, 2002).

SOVIET UNION

Victoria A. Bonnel, *Iconography of Power: Soviet Official Posters under Lenin and Stalin* (Berkeley, 1997).

Martin Eben, *The Soviet Propaganda Machine* (New York, 1987).

Geoffrey Hosking, *A History of the Soviet Union* (London, 1992).

Peter Kenez, *The Birth of the Propaganda State: Soviet Methods of Mass Mobilization, 1917–1929* (Cambridge, 1985).

Richard Pipes, *Russia under the Bolshevik Regime* (London, 1994).

Graham Roberts, *Forward Soviet! History and Non-Fiction Film in the USSR* (London, 1999).

Richard Taylor, *Film Propaganda: Soviet Russia and Nazi Germany* (London, 1998).

USA

John M. Blum, *V Was for Victory: Politics and American Culture during World War II* (New York, 1976).

Steven Casey. *Cautious Crusade: Franklin D. Roosevelt, American Public Opinion and the War against Nazi Germany* (New York, 2001).

John Dower, *War without Mercy: Race and Power in the Pacific War* (New York, 1986).

Robert Henkes, *World War II in American Art* (Jefferson, NC, 2001).

George H. Roeder, *The Censored War: American Visual Experience during World War Two* (New Haven, 1993).

Richard W. Steele, *Propaganda in an Open Society: The Roosevelt Administration and the Media, 1933–1941* (Westport, Conn., 1985).

Allan M. Winkler, *The Politics of Propaganda: The Office of War Information, 1942–1945* (New Haven, 1978).

JAPAN

John Dower, *War without Mercy: Race and Power in the Pacific War* (New York, 1986).

John Dower, *Embracing Defeat: Japan in the Wake of World War II* (New York, 1999).

Theodore Friend, *The Blue-Eyed Enemy: Japan Against the West in Java and Luzon, 1942–1945* (Princeton, 1988).

Sheldon Garon, *Molding Japanese Minds: The State in Everyday Life* (Princeton, 1997).

Saburo Ienaga, *The Pacific War, 1931–1945* (New York, 1978).

L. D. Meo, *Japan's Radio War on Australia* (Melbourne, 1968).

Masaharu Sato and Kushner Barak, 'Negro Propaganda Operations: Japan's Short-Wave Radio Broadcasts for World War II Black Americans', *Historical Journal of Film, Radio and Television, 19/1* (1999), 5–26.

Ben-Ami Shillony, *Politics and Culture in Wartime Japan* (New York, 1981).

Louise Young, *Japan's Total Empire, Manchuria and the Culture of Wartime Imperialism* (Berkeley, 1998).

14. FROM WORLD WAR TO COLD WAR

MEMOIRS AND BIOGRAPHY

Alan Bullock, *The Life and Times of Ernest Bevin, Foreign Secretary 1945–51* (London, 1983).

James F. Byrnes, *Speaking Frankly* (New York, 1947).

468 *Further Reading*

Winston S. Churchill, *The Second World War*, 6 volumes (London, 1948).

George F. Kennan, *Memoirs*, Vol. 1 (London, 1968).

Geoffrey Roberts, *Molotov: Stalin's Cold Warrior* (Washington, DC, 2012).

THE GRAND ALLIANCE

Diane S. Clemens, *Yalta* (Oxford, 1970).

Michael Dobbs, *Six Months in 1945: FDR, Stalin, Churchill, and Truman—From World War to Cold War* (London, 2012).

Robin Edmonds, *The Big Three* (London, 1991).

Jonathan Fenby, *Alliance: The Inside Story of How Roosevelt, Stalin and Churchill Won One War and Began Another* (London, 2008).

Martin H. Folly, *Churchill, Whitehall and the Soviet Union* (London, 2000).

William H. McNeill, *America, Britain and Russia: Their Conflict and Co-Operation and Conflict, 1941–1946* (London, 1953).

Vojtech Mastny, *Russia's Road to the Cold War* (New York, 1979).

Serhii M. Plokhy, *Yalta: The Price of Peace* (London, 2011).

David Reynolds, *From World War to Cold War: Churchill, Roosevelt, and the International History of the 1940s* (Oxford, 2006).

Geoffrey Roberts, *Stalin's Wars: From World War to Cold War, 1939–1953* (London, 2006).

Martin J. Sherwin, *A World Destroyed: The Atomic Bomb and the Grand Alliance* (New York, 1975).

THE COLD WAR

Campbell Craig and Sergey Radchenko, *The Atomic Bomb and the Origins of the Cold War* (London, 2008).

Lynn E. Davis, *The Cold War Begins* (Princeton, 1974).

Anne Deighton, *The Impossible Peace: Britain, the Division of Germany, and the Origins of the Cold War* (Oxford, 1993).

Denna F. Fleming, *The Cold War and its Origins*, 2 volumes (New York, 1961).

Fraser J. Harbutt, *Iron Curtain: Churchill, America, and the Origins of the Cold War* (Oxford, 1986).

John Lewis Gaddis, *The United States and the Origins of the Cold War, 1941–1947* (New York, 1972).

James L. Gormly, *The Collapse of the Grand Alliance, 1945–48* (Baton Rouge, La., 1987).

Caroline Kennedy-Pipe, *Stalin's Cold War* (Manchester, 1995).

Robert L. Messer, *The End of an Alliance: James F. Byrnes, Roosevelt, Truman, and the Origins of the Cold War* (Chapel Hill, 1982).

Patricia Dawson Ward, *The Threat of Peace: James F. Byrnes and the Council of Foreign Ministers, 1945–1946* (Kent, Ohio, 1979).

John Wheeler-Bennett, *The Semblance of Peace: The Political Settlement after the Second World War* (London, 1972).

Daniel Yergin, *Shattered Peace: The Origins of the Cold War* (Boston, 1978).

PICTURE ACKNOWLEDGEMENTS

Pg No:	Credit line
8	Courtesy of Hoover Institution Library & Archives, Stanford University, Political Poster Collection, DK3 pt 1 and pt 2
9	Courtesy of Hoover Institution Library & Archives, Stanford University, Political Poster Collection, IT 365
10	UNOG Library, League of Nations Archives
12	Periodicals Department of the Enoch Pratt Free Library
14	Courtesy of Hoover Institution Library & Archives, Stanford University, Political Poster Collection, IT 96
16	UNOG Library, League of Nations Archives
19	UNOG Library, League of Nations Archives
20	University of Kent, www.cartoons.ac.uk; David Low 'The Won't Waits' from 'The Daily News' 20th December 1920
21	© RIA Novosti / TopFoto
23	Courtesy of Hoover Institution Library & Archives, Stanford University, Political Poster Collection, HU11 and HU 13
25	UNOG Library, League of Nations Archives
27	UNOG Library, League of Nations Archives
28	© Roger-Viollet / TopFoto
29	UNOG Library, League of Nations Archives
30	UNOG Library, League of Nations Archives
32	© akg-images
33	© Roger-Viollet / TopFoto
36	© AP/Press Association Images
39	© IWM, E26535
41	© Gamma-Keystone via Getty Images
42	© Advertising Museum Tokyo
44	© ullsteinbild / TopFoto
45	Steve Lee
49	Steve Lee
54	Steve Lee
56	© University of Shiga Prefecture Library
57	© University of Shiga Prefecture Library
58	Courtesy of Hoover Institution Library & Archives, Stanford University, Political Poster Collection, US3484
58	Photo by The Mainichi Newspapers/AFLO
59	© IWM, JAR1240
63	© IWM, SE4523
65	Library of Congress, Washington DC: USZ62-114392
67	© IWM, SE3891
69	© IWM, IB4152C
70	Glenn Eve, www.pacificwarphotos.com
71	Library of Congress, Washington DC: USZ62-111427
75	© ullsteinbild / TopFoto

470   *Picture Acknowledgements*

79   Courtesy of Fototeca dell'Archivio dell'Ufficio storico dello stato maggiore dell'esercito, Rome
80   © 2006 Alinari / TopFoto
82   © 2006 Alinari / TopFoto
83   Courtesy of Fototeca dell'Archivio dell'Ufficio storico dello stato maggiore dell'esercito, Rome
86   Courtesy of Fototeca dell'Archivio dell'Ufficio storico dello stato maggiore dell'esercito, Rome
88   Scherl / Sueddeutsche Zeitung Photo
88   Courtesy of Fototeca dell'Archivio dell'Ufficio storico dello stato maggiore dell'esercito, Rome
89   Courtesy of Fototeca dell'Archivio dell'Ufficio storico dello stato maggiore dell'esercito, Rome
91   Courtesy of Fototeca dell'Archivio dell'Ufficio storico dello stato maggiore dell'esercito, Rome
93   Scherl / Sueddeutsche Zeitung Photo
96   © AP / TopFoto
97   Courtesy of Fototeca dell'Archivio dell'Ufficio storico dello stato maggiore dell'esercito, Rome
98   Courtesy of Fototeca dell'Archivio dell'Ufficio storico dello stato maggiore dell'esercito, Rome
99   Courtesy of Fototeca dell'Archivio dell'Ufficio storico dello stato maggiore dell'esercito, Rome
101   Courtesy of Fototeca dell'Archivio dell'Ufficio storico dello stato maggiore dell'esercito, Rome
102   © bpk
106   Courtesy of Fototeca dell'Archivio dell'Ufficio storico dello stato maggiore dell'esercito, Rome
112   © IWM, HU106374
113   © IWM, HU81210
114   © IWM, MH13110
115   © IWM, MH13369
116   © IWM, RML342
117   © IWM, MH10935
118   © IWM, HU75995
119   © IWM, MH13382
120   © IWM, H6318
121   © IWM, MH11546
121   © IWM, HU39455
122   © IWM, HU39517
122   © IWM, HU52264
123   © IWM, CM1309
125   © IWM, HU86369
127   © Bettmann/CORBIS
130   © IWM, CH15670
130   © IWM, HU5175
132   © IWM, C2644
137   © IWM, Q18547
141   © IWM, A6793
145   National Archives, Washington DC: RG 80-G 41615
146   © IWM, NY7568
147   © IWM, A8812
148   © IWM, A30337
149   © IWM, H42406
150   © IWM, A27518
152   © IWM, A12090
153   © IWM, A25750
157   © IWM, A25750
158   © IWM, A25750

159 © ullsteinbild / TopFoto
160 © IWM, A24012
162 National Archives, Washington DC: RG 80-G 47042
163 © IWM, CL2749
164 © IWM, A26564
166 National Archives, Washington DC: RG 80-G 496172
170 © IWM, F4353
172 UIG via Getty Images
173 © Punch Limited
175 Getty Images
177 Bundesarchiv, photo 169-0423, photo by O.Ang
180 Supplied by Llyfrgell Genedlaethol Cymru/The National Library of Wales/Solo Syndication / Associated Newspapers Ltd.
181 National Museum of the U.S. Air Force (R)
182 Courtesy of Hoover Institution Library & Archives, Stanford University, Political Poster Collection, US7151
182 Supplied by Llyfrgell Genedlaethol Cymru/The National Library of Wales/Solo Syndication / Associated Newspapers Ltd.
183 © IWM, A12022
184 Supplied by Llyfrgell Genedlaethol Cymru/The National Library of Wales/Solo Syndication / Associated Newspapers Ltd.
185 Bundesarchiv, photo 183-E0406-0022-010, photo by O.Ang
188 © IWM, ART 15548; Estate of W J Philpin-Jones
191 © IWM, CM5480
193 © IWM, EA26941
194 UIG via Getty Images
197 © IWM, BU2336
198 Vaughn Shoemaker
203 © Robert Hunt Library/Mary Evans
203 © Robert Hunt Library/Mary Evans
205 © IWM, E1579
207 National Archives, Washington, DC: RG-80G 480034
208 Mary Evans / SZ Photo / Scherl
208 © IWM, MH29427
210 © IWM, CL2537
212 Mary Evans/Interfoto
216 Mary Evans/Interfoto
220 National Archives, Washington DC: 80-G-414423
221 © IWM, B5130
223 © IWM, CF145
224 © IWM, IND3469
226 National Archives, Washington, DC: U-210 RG38 UD 38 Bx 11
227 © IWM, E(MOS)1436
229 © IWM, EA16611
230 © IWM, NYP69366
233 Library of Congress, Washington DC: LC-USE6-D-003541
235 © IWM, D1497
236 © IWM, D12619

472 *Picture Acknowledgements*

238 © IWM, HU8799
239 Library of Congress, Washington DC: LC-USZ62-92190
240 © IWM, H18068
241 © IWM, D4321
242 Getty Images
245 UIG via Getty Images
246 © IWM, EA22916
247 © Eisenbahnstiftung/dpa/Corbis
248 © IWM, P177
249 © IWM, HU31755
250 © IWM, D2839
252 © IWM, P1944
252 Time & Life Pictures/Getty Images
254 Library of Congress, Washington DC: LC-USZ62-104726
256 © IWM, HU50593
259 © IWM, E53
260 © IWM, NYF45290
263 © IWM, A2206
264 © IWM, HU5131
268 © IWM, CH1442
269 © IWM, HU64140
271 © IWM, BU9302
272 © IWM, IB2789C
274 © IWM, HU55566
277 © IWM, (MOI)FLM1477
277 © IWM, HU40239
279 © IWM, NYP69993
280 © IWM, E4175
281 © IWM, HU109708
284 © IWM, EA41430
285 © IWM, B1010
289 © IWM, B6009
291 © IWM, EA69243
294 AP/Press Association Images
295 © IWM, MISC60739
296 © IWM, HU103753
298 © Bettmann/CORBIS
299 © IWM, KF112
300 © Bettmann/CORBIS
301 © IWM, D1606
304 © Kirn Vintage Stock/Corbis
305 © akg-images / ullstein bild / Harald Lechenperg
306 © Berliner Verlag/Archiv/dpa/Corbis
308 © Popperfoto/Getty Images
310 © CORBIS
311 © Bettmann/CORBIS
315 © UIG via Getty Images
316 © Hulton-Deutsch Collection/CORBIS
317 © Bettmann/CORBIS
318 © IWM, NA21669

320 © akg-images / Universal Images Group / Sovfoto
323 From the American Geographical Society Library, University of Wisconsin-Milwaukee Libraries
325 Time & Life Pictures/Getty Images
326 Koyo Ishikawa
326 Tohosha Archive, The Center of the Tokyo Raids and War Damage
327 © AP/Press Association Images
328 © Archive Manfred Deiler, 2014
330 © Stadtarchiv Stuttgart
333 National Archives, Washington DC: 127-G-11454I
337 © Getty Images
338 Archiv des Hamburger Instituts fuer Sozialforschung / Archives of the Hamburg Institute for Social Research
340 © Time & Life Pictures/Getty Images
346 Library of Congress, Washington DC: LC-USE6_D_010097
347 Library of Congress, Washington DC:LC-USZ62-15745
350 UIG History/Science & Society Picture Librar
351 UIG History/Science & Society Picture Library
352 © IWM, IB4336
353 Library of Congress, Washington DC:LC-USZ62-96548
354 Library of Congress, Washington DC:HAER UTAH,23-DUG,2A-6
355 Royal Photographic Society/National Media Museum/ Science & Society Picture Library
357 © Getty Images
359 Library of Congress, Washington DC: LC-USZ62-68396
360 © Galerie Bilderwelt / Contributor / Getty Images
361 © IWM, MH24073
363 Library of Congress, Washington DC: LC-USZ62-80651
366 Library of Congress, Washington DC:LC-USW33-028393-C
367 © IWM, RR2206
368 © IWM, BU5467
369 © IWM, D3841
371 © IWM, T30
376 © IWM, LD3987
377 © IWM, detail of ART 5000
378 Graham Sutherland *Devastation, 1941: An East End Street, 1941* Tate © Tate London 2014
378 © IWM, LD1345
379 © IWM, LD2850
380 Henry Moore *Pink and Green Sleepers, 1941,* Tate © Tate London 2014
381 © IWM, LD5467
382 © IWM, ART LD5620
387 © bpk
388 © akg-images
389 Sebastopol Art Museum, Sebastopol, Ukraine / Bridgeman Images
391 Private Collection / Peter Newark Historical Pictures / Bridgeman Images
392 Courtesy of Hoover Institution Library & Archives, Stanford University, Political Poster Collection, RU/SU 1922.5
394 Private Collection / Peter Newark American Pictures / Bridgeman Images
395 'Dead Jap' from the German Art Collection, 1889-1980, Southwest Collection/Special Collections Library, Texas Tech University, Lubbock, Texas

474   *Picture Acknowledgements*

396 'Sticker, Slave World or Free World: Keep the Goose Step Out of America from Artists for Victory Exhibit in Miniature, 1943 Tony Palazzo (American, 1905–1970), designer Artists for Victory Inc., New York City, publisher Ever Ready Label Corp, New York City, printer 2 ¾ x 1 ¾ inches (7.0 x 4.4 centimeters) The Wolfsonian–Florida International University, Miami Beach, Florida, The Mitchell Wolfson, Jr. Collection 87.19.4 Photo: Lynton Gardiner "Published with the permission of The Wolfsonian – Florida International University (Miami, Florida)"

397 © ARS, NY and DACS, London 2014, The Metropolitan Museum of Art, 2014 © Photo SCALA, Florence

398 © Walt Disney Pictures/Kobal Collection

399 Courtesy of Hoover Institution Library & Archives, Stanford University, Political Poster Collection, US7153

405 Time & Life Pictures/Getty Images
406 Getty Images
407 Time & Life Pictures/Getty Images
408 Time & Life Pictures/Getty Images
409 Time & Life Pictures/Getty Images
410 By permission of Solo Syndication / Associated Newspapers Ltd : British Cartoon Archive,
412 Time & Life Pictures/Getty Images
414 Time & Life Pictures/Getty Images
415 Getty Images
417 Getty Images
422 © akg-images
423 © CTK / Alamy
424 AFP/Getty Images
425 UIG via Getty Images
427 © 1999 AP/Topham
427 Time & Life Pictures/Getty Images
429 Time & Life Pictures/Getty Images
430 ChinaFotoPress/Getty Images

Plate 1   Courtesy of Hoover Institution Library & Archives, Stanford University, Political Poster Collection, FR 477
Plate 2   Courtesy of Hoover Institution Library & Archives, Stanford University, Political Poster Collection, HU 1
Plate 3   Steve Lee
Plate 4   Steve Lee
Plate 5   © IWM, LD4963
Plate 6   UniversalImagesGroup / Contributor/ Getty Images
Plate 7   © IWM, COL115
Plate 8   © IWM, COL176
Plate 9   © IWM, TR1144
Plate 10   U.S. Naval Institute
Plate 11   © IWM, PST8359
Plate 12   University of North Texas; http://digital.library.unt.edu/ark:/67531/metadc414/
Plate 13   Mary Evans/Epic/Tallandier
Plate 14   Getty Images/Science Faction
Plate 15   © IWM, PST6138
Plate 16   © IWM, TR2130
Plate 17   © IWM, ART LD 5254

Picture Acknowledgements 475

Plate 18   Courtesy of Hoover Institution Library & Archives, Stanford University, Political Poster
           Collection, UK2788
Plate 19   © IWM, PST13880
Plate 20   © Minnesota Historical Society/CORBIS
Plate 21   © akg-images
Plate 22   Time & Life Pictures/Getty Images
Plate 23   Library of Congress, Washington DC: ra35357u
Plate 24   © Bettmann/CORBIS
Plate 25   © IWM, LD4526
Plate 26   Private Collection / Bridgeman Images
Plate 27   Print Collector/Getty Images
Plate 28   National Archives, Washington DC: CETO 1860 OSC

INDEX

Page numbers in *italics* refer to illustrations

ABC-1 strategy 178, 179
Abyssinia 290
Acheson, Dean 53
active resistance, civilian 314–17
Admiral Graf Spee 138
Admiral Scheer 140
Adowa 27
Afghanistan 223
Afrika Corps 131
Agedabia 89
Aghelia 89
agricultural production 22, 24, 352
aircraft 230, 243t, 262, 347
  aero-engines 358–60
  airframes 362
  civilian casualties 92, 93, 104
  daylight raids 226, 227, 229
  defence system 225
  development 209, 247
  German advantage 202
  Italian-Ethiopian war 27
  importance of 200–1
  jet aircraft 361–2
  production 243
  strategic bombing 200
  support role 219
aircraft carriers 220, 221
air-raid shelters 295, 301–2
Aisne, River 275
Akhmatova, Anna 389
Alam El Halfa 89, 131
Alamein 87, 88, 89, 131, 132, 154, 183, 276
Alaric, Operation (later Operation Axis) 93, 94, 95
Albania 34, 81, 84, 85
'Alexander communiqué' 101
Alexander Nevsky (film) 390
Algeria 154, 184
alkylation process 361
Allied Control Council 411
Alsace-Lorraine 13
'Amau Doctrine' 26
American Red Cross 281
Amiens 287
amphibious operations 157, 221–2
  diverted to Mediterranean 158
  Japan 165
  Korea 428
  Mariana Islands 159

Operation Torch 184
Saipan 160
Andaman Islands 158
Anderson, Sir John 245
Anderson shelters 302, 355
Anglo-French Alliance (1939) 168, 169–70
Anglo-German Naval Agreement (1935) 29, 135, 136
Anglo-Japanese Alliance (1902) 37
Anglo-Soviet treaty (1942) 413
Annapolis 266
Anschluss 29, 111
anthrax 340
Anti-Comintern Pacts (1936/1937) 28, 43
anti-Communism 35, 48, 49, 111, 423
anti-Fascist movements
  Balkans 85
  Italian 76, 92–102, 104, 106, 319
Anti-Fascist Organization (later Anti-Fascist People's Freedom League) 55
anti-Semitism 28, 78, 127, 128, 260
  see also Jews
Antwerp 164
Anzio 157, 191, 193
Arab-Israeli War (1948) 5
Arakan campaign 223
Archangel 126
Ardennes 195, 196
Ardizzone, Edward 378
Arizona 54, 146
Armée Secrète 318
Armia Krajowa (Polish Home Army) 314, 315, 316
Arnim, Hans-Jürgen von 184
Artists for Victory 396
arts, and propaganda 373–5
  in Britain 375–84
  Nationalist Socialist Germany 384–8
  Soviet Union 388–93
  USA 393–9
Aryan race 21, 28, 267, 387
Asquith, Anthony 383
Assinboine 226
Astrakhan 126, 131
atebrine 369
Athenia 137

Atlantic, Battle of the 141, 144–8, 151, 155, 276
Atlantic Charter (1941) 54, 128, 142, 384, 393, 404
Atlee, Clement 402, 406
atomic bomb 208
  assessment of 370
  civilian casualties 293, 324
  development 211, 214, 364
  and Japanese surrender 72, 73
  scientists 348, 349, 350
  USSR plan 425–6
atrocities 328–36
  Allied 99, 291, 292
  German 76, 95, 104, 108, 126, 127–8, 290
  Italian 290
  Japanese 50, 59, 70, 289, 290, 332
  against resistance 319, 320
  Soviet 290, 291
ATS (Auxiliary Territorial Service) 270–1
Auden, W. H. 375
Aung San 56
Auschwitz 331
Australia 33, 60, 213, 259
Austria
  bombing casualties 325
  financial crisis 25
  food security 22
  German claim for *Anschluss* 29
  hyperinflation 24
  losses of territory 13
  unemployment 24
authoritarianism
  Eastern Europe 403, 421
  France 52
  Japan 37, 48, 49–51
  Korea 428
  rise of 22, 25
  youth organizations 274
Auxiliary Territorial Service (ATS) 270–1
Avalanche, Operation 360–1
aviation fuel 360–1
Axis agreement (1936) 28
Azerbaijan 417

Backe, Herbert 346, 348
Baden 329

478 Index

Badoglio, Pietro 80
on armistice 95
on invasion of Greece 84
'Kingdom of the South' 76, 97
leader of government 94, 345
and military leadership 79
'Baedeker Raids' 327
Bagration, Operation 194–5
Balbo, Italo 81
Balkans
anti-Fascist resistance 85
division of 84
Fascism in 84
Italian occupation 81, 84–5
prisoners of war 93
Yugoslav resistance 91, 95
Baltic Sea 163
Bao Dai, Emperor 62
Barbarossa, Operation 124, 125, 126–8, 174–6, 237, 388
Bardia, Libya 205
Bataan 59, 333
Bataan Death March 398
Bay of Bengal 158
BBC (British Broadcasting Corporation) 282, 374, 376, 383
BBFC (British Board of Film Censors) 382
BEF (British Expeditionary Force) 114, 116, 170
Beightler, Robert S. 71
Beijing 44, 45
Belarus 331, 332
Belfast 238
Belgium 115, 116, 170
Belgrade 327
Beria, Lavrenti 34, 345, 346, 347
Bell, Daniel 400
Belorussia 194, 276
Beneš, Edvard 31
Bengal 306, 337, 338
Benghazi 89
Bergen-Belsen 339, 340
Beveridge, William 376
Bevin, Ernest 245, 251, 252, 384, 404, 405, 406, 424
Bichelonne, Jean 346
Biddle, George 395
biological warfare 339, 353, 354
Bismarck 142
Bismarck Islands 160
Black Sea Straits 417, 418

Blitzkrieg 120, 121, 176, 204, 301, 302, 307
Bloch, Ivan 18
Blücher 138
Blue, Operation 131, 177, 178
Bolero, Operation 150, 151, 154
Böll, Heinrich 375
Bologna 105
Bolshevism 20, 30, 126
border security 17–18
Bonnet, Georges-Étienne 29
Bór-Komorowski, Tadeusz 315, 316
Boyd Orr, John 21
Bracken, Brendan 72
Brauchitsch, Walter 124
Breslau 261
Brest 151
Briand, Aristide 24
'Briand Plan' 24
Briansk-Kharkov operation 189
Britain
alien internment 309
Allies 17, 136, 139, 168, 178, 179
appeasement 33
Bengal famine 306
bombing casualties 327
colonialism 52
concessions to Hitler unpopular 31
conscription 251
currency overvaluation 25
and Egypt 86
equipment production 206
Essential Work Order 251
evacuation 307, 308
'Four-Power Pact' 77
German blockade 121
health 303
inflation 24
Labour Party 384
League of Nations 17
military strength 78
National Service Acts 235
opposition to Axis powers 28
opposition to Soviet influence 403, 404
pledge of Polish security 34
pressure from Japan re aid to China 52
pre-war economy 235
propaganda 374, 375–84
religion 286
retreat in Burma 60
review of Japanese strength 222
strikes 251
support troops 209, 210
and threat of Nazism 30
trade 26, 33, 236
wartime economy 236, 245, 247, 248
weapons development 365
women workers 251, 270
Britain, Battle of 120, 171, 278

British air force see Royal Air Force
British and Commonwealth Western Desert Force 202
British army
Auxiliary Territorial Service (ATS) 270–1
class distinction 266
demographic of 211
effect of petrol shortage 210
evacuation from Greece 124
home contact 282
inexperience of mobile warfare 117
lack of strength 171
Normandy landings 159, 193, 195
North Africa 124, 131
specialization of forces 262
training 212, 223
War Office Selection Boards 266
British Board of Film Censors (BBFC) 382
British Broadcasting Corporation (BBC) 282, 374, 376, 383
British Empire
Burma 291
civil defence in 297
gold standard 24
Japan and 148
importance of 171, 172
sea power 135, 136
strengthening of 26
shipbuilding 151
support for French 169, 170
troops from 179, 258, 259, 260, 267
USA and 174
war in Asia 176
British Expeditionary Force (BEF) 114, 116, 170
British navy see Royal Navy
'British Pacific Fleet' (BPF) 165, 166
British-Indian army 223
British-Soviet Alliance 174–5, 176
Britten, Benjamin 383
Brooke, Sir Alan 179
Browning, Christopher 329
Budapest 195
Bulgaria
Axis control 85
CFM 403, 404
food security 22
and USSR 124, 195, 416
Bulge, Battle of the 195, 199
Burma
Allied operation abandoned 154, 158
anti-Fascism 55
European colonial interest 52
fall of 222, 223–4
independence of 5
Japanese invasion 56, 57, 59, 60, 67, 68
jungle training 223, 276
religion of forces 285, 286

Burma Independence Army
(later Burma Defence Army) 57
Burma–Siam railway 334
Burra, Edward 381
Burza, Operation 315
Byrnes, James F. 404, 406, 407

Calcutta 60
Calder, Angus 375
Campo Imperatore 96
Canada
casualties 267
conscientious objection 260
growing importance of 33
internees 309
shipbuilding 152
supplies and loans 236, 240
volunteers and conscripts 259
Canadian navy 142, 151
cannibalism 336
Canton 33
Capo Matapan 87
Capo Spada 87
Capo Teulada 87
Caporetto 94
Capra, Frank 288, 396
Caribbean 148
Caroline Islands 37
Carpathian Mountains 190
Casablanca Conference (1943) 133,
186, 191
Caserta 105
Caucasus 176, 178, 186
Cavagnari, Domenico 81
CCP (Chinese Communist Party)
42–3, 60, 61, 261, 275, 431
Cefalonia 95
CEMA (Council for the
Encouragement of Music and
the Arts) 376, 381, 383
censorship 374
Century Group (later Fight for
Freedom Committee) 393
Ceylon 148, 149
CFM (Council of Foreign
Ministers) 403, 404, 406–7, 409,
411–12
Chamberlain, Neville 26, 31,
32, 34
Changzhou 46
Chelmno 331
chemical warfare 27, 339, 350,
351, 353
Chiang Kai-shek 39
armies weakened 69
breaching of dyke 46, 47
as soldier 345
war with Japan 38, 43, 44, 273
children 298, 299–300, 315

China
access to resources 365, 366
bombing casualties 273
conscription 273
effect of First World War 37
famine 60, 69, 306, 322, 323
forced labour 62, 63, 334
GMD Party 38, 43, 48
impact of war with Japan 26, 35,
50, 52, 68–9
Jiangxi Soviet 43
May Fourth Movement 38
National Revolutionary Army 38,
39, 40
nationalism 38, 48, 60, 61
New Fourth Army Incident 48
'northern expedition' 38
peasantry as politically aware 61
political violence 10
resistance movement 42, 47, 48
'rural pacification' by Japanese 332
'scorched earth' 46
social welfare 47
unification of 5
use of militia 261
War of Resistance 44–8, 52, 68, 72
Warfare Child Welfare
Committee 47
warlords 37
Chinese air force 267
Chinese army 48, 61, 62, 63, 273
China Expeditionary Army 69
Chinese Communist Party (CCP)
42–3, 60, 61, 261, 275, 431
cholera 63
Chongqing 47, 294, 327
Choson dynasty (Korea) 36, 37
Christianity 286–7
Christie suspension system 355
Churchill, Winston 39, 191
Atlantic Charter 54
on Berlin 198
Directorate of Combined
Operations 221
food shipment to Greece 305
on Iron Curtain 413, 414
joint landing NW Africa with
USA 179
on Madagascar 149
open to outside aid 171
Operation Torch 181
and RAF bomber use 179
reaction to Italian invasion
Egypt 143
on Russian success 190
and shipping losses 140, 141
as soldier 345
strategy in Allied debate 179
Tolstoy Conference (Moscow) 197
and war aims 384
Ciano, Galeazzo 118

Ciba-Geigy 367
Cieszyn (Teschen) 31
Cincar-Marković, Aleksandar 122
Citizen's Military Force
(Australia) 259
civil defence 294–302
Australia 298
Britain 295, 297, 298, 299,
300, 302
Children and 298, 299–300
France 297
Germany 295, 296, 297, 299,
300, 302
Hong Kong 297, 299
Italy 297, 302
New Zealand 298
reliance on volunteers 4
sense of community 295
USA 297, 298
USSR 296, 297, 299
women 298
civilian casualties 293, 323–4
Abyssinia 290
Battle of the Ruhr 191
Britain 302
and evacuation 308
genocide 328–33
Germany 129, 228, 300, 302
Italy 92, 104
Japan 68, 229
Jinan 39, 40
Manila 70, 71
members of resistance 319
militia 261
Nanjing 46
Poland 316
Roosevelt on 72
Shanghai 42, 46
Tokyo bombing 72
civilian experts 351, 352
civilians
forced labour Japanese 62, 63
movement of 309
in occupied territories 313
use alongside forces 3, 261
see also home front
Clark, Kenneth 376, 377, 380
Clemenceau, Georges 17
coal supply 234, 237
Coale, Griffith Baily 395
code-breaking 142, 151, 217,
225, 370
Cold War 107–8, 411, 412–13,
415–16, 419–32
atomic arms race 426
Korean war 403, 428–30
Marshall Plan 419–20, 421
and NATO 423, 424–7
propaganda 399, 401
Cole, Leslie 381, 382
collaboration 239, 240–1, 313, 314

480 *Index*

Cologne 179
Combat movement 317
CBO ('Combined Bomber
  Offensive') 191
'comfort women' 64
Cominform 420, 421–3
Comintern 420
Councell, Clara 339
Committee to Defend America by
  Aiding the Allies 393
Commonwealth War Memorial
  Cemetery, Kandy 68
Communism
  Britain 405
  China 43, 46, 48, 50, 69, 261, 332
  Eastern Europe 403, 406, 411, 414,
    419–23
  France 317, 318, 420
  internment 309, 310
  Italy 92, 100, 106, 107, 319, 420
  Poland 314, 316
  revolutions 7, 10
  South East Asia 55, 60
  Soviet as threat to Germany 110,
    118, 124, 126
  USSR 200, 265, 270, 288, 348, 390,
    413, 416
Communist International 43
Communization 421
concentration camps
  conscientious objectors 260
  disease 339, 340, 367
  forced labour 333
  genocide 133, 328
  internment 309, 310
  and public opinion in USA 66
  Roma 331
  Ustaša 332
Connolly, Cyril 375
conscientious objection 260
conscription 274
  Australia 259
  Britain 235, 251, 262
  Germany 29, 288
  Italy 319
  Japan 62, 273
  Korea 62, 267
  USA 172
  USSR 255, 258, 268
Convention on Prisoners of War 103
convoys 137–8, 139, 140–2
  American losses 224
  Arctic 156
  Atlantic 151, 154–5
  defeat of U-boats 225
  Japanese 161
  and loss of shipping 147, 148
  magnetic mines 137
  to Malta 153, 154
  Pacific 156
  US protection 174
  to USSR 156

Coral Sea, Battle of the 60, 150
Corbett, Sir Julian 135
Corfu incident (1923) 77
Corregidor 55
Corsica 81, 83, 84
Councell, Clara 339
Council for the Encouragement of
  Music and the Arts (CEMA) 376,
    381, 383
Council of Foreign Ministers
  (CFM) 403, 404, 406–7, 409,
    411–12
Crete 84, 85, 124, 143
crimes against humanity 290
criminality 289–92
Croatia 81, 84, 85, 332
Crusader, Operation 174
cryptography 351
Czechoslovakia 421, 423
  alliance with France 17
  food security 22
  German claim for union 29, 31
  land appropriation 129
  post war 403
  Prague coup 421, 422, 423

Dairen (Dalian) 37
Daladier, Edouard 31
Dalmatia 84
Dalton, Hugh 384
Danzig (Gdańsk) 13, 32, 34, 112
Danzig crisis (1939) 169
Darré, Richard 346, 348
Darwin, Charles 18
D-Day 158, 193–4, 196
DDT 353, 367, 368
deaths 322–7
  civilian 323–4, 335–6
  disease 338–40
  famine 336–8
  genocide 328–33
  German on Eastern Front 132, 175,
    189, 199
  Manila 71
  military 322
  prisoners of war 333–5
  'Rape of Nanjing' 46
  Soviet 189, 199, 392, 404
  suicides 340, 341
  USA 199
deception operations 155, 194
declaration of war 34
Decoux, Jean 62
'deep operation' 188
Défense de la France movement 317
deferment of service 260
deflation 24, 25
Delmer, Sefton 376
demoralization, and propaganda 4
Denmark 115, 303, 316, 324
deportations 290, 309–12

desertion 212, 275, 282
Deso, Alois 19
Deutsche Volksturm 261
Deutschland (later Lützow) 261
Dieppe 152
disease 210, 338, 339–40
displacement 255, 306, 307–9,
    335, 336
Dnepr River 189, 190
Dnestr River 190
'Doctors' Plot' 423
Döblin, Alfred 385
Dodecanese Islands 77
Doing Battle (Fussell) 334
Dönitz, Karl 121, 131, 140, 151,
    156, 225
Doob, Leonard 373
'Doolittle' air raid 65
Dorpmüller, Julius 346
Douglas, Keith 376
Douhet, Giulio 81, 92
Dower, John 325, 332
Dower, Roger 66, 72
Dragoon, Operation 164, 165
Dresden 325
drugs 367–9
Dunbar, Evelyn 376
Dunkirk 116, 138, 170, 178
Dutch Indies 53

'Eagle Attack' 139
Eagle Day (Adlertag) 120
East Africa 85–6, 337
East Indies 161
East Prussia 197, 199
Eastern Front 91, 124–32
  losses 243, 324
  ideology 268
  militia 261
  non-combatants 269, 324
  Polish troops 281
  reduced German forces 159, 167
  Soviet resources 257
  Soviet threat 118, 121
  transformed Red Army 217–18
  use of horses 350
  'war on civilians' 104
'economic appeasement' 30, 31
Economic Consequences of the Peace,
  The (Keynes) 13
economic security 2, 3, 18, 20–4,
    256, 303
economic warfare 169, 171, 254
economies 232–9
Eden, Anthony 20
Efimov, Boris 390
Egypt 81, 86, 87, 131, 202
Eire (Ireland) 10, 267
Eisenhower, Dwight 95, 193, 195,
    198, 399
Eisenstein, Sergei 390

Eliot, T. S. 375
Empire Air Training Scheme (later the Commonwealth Air Training Plan) 278
Enigma coding machine 216, 217
Enola Gay 293, 357
ENSA (Entertainments National Service Association) 283
entertainment 283, 284
Estonia 34
Eternal Soldier, The (Sauter) (painting) 387
Ethiopia 27, 32, 78, 85, 143
ethno-nationalism 18, 21, 22
European Recovery Program (Marshall Plan) 256, 419–20
evacuation 307–9
exchange controls 26
exemptions, military service 260
experts 345–9, 350–2, 372
extermination camps 328, 330, 367, 374

famine 324, 336–8, 339
  Bengal 154, 306
  China 46, 60–2, 69, 306, 322, 323
  Greece 305, 306
  Japan 68, 166, 309
  USSR 260, 305, 334
  Vietnam 60–2
Fascism
  German 48, 50
  Italian 15, 27–8, 74–94, 96, 100–4, 107–9, 171, 260, 265, 297, 313, 319, 385
  rejection of League of Nations 18
  Zhdanov on 421
  see also Neo-Fascism
Fascist March (1922) 84
Federal Republic of Germany 413
Felix, Operation 123
Feng Yuxiang 43
Fieser, Louis 353
'fifth column' 309, 312
film 381, 382–3, 393, 396–7
Finland 34, 126, 183, 267, 274, 403
First World War
  air-raid precautions 294
  continuity in German ideology 387
  effect of experience in 273
  few civilian casualties 342
  and origins of Second 7, 20
  prisoners of war 334
  propaganda 373
Firth of Forth 139
Fishing, Operation 34
Five Power Naval Limitation Treaty (1922) 144, 145
Florence 100, 105
food supplies 20, 22, 281, 303
forced labour 108, 303, 333–4

Ford Company of America 242
Forster, E. M. 375
Fortitude, Operation 217
Fosdick, Raymond 11
Four Quartets (Eliot) 375
'Four-Power Pact' (1933) 77
Fourteen Points (Wilson) 11, 13, 24
France
  abandonment of Czechoslovakia 31
  African prisoners of war 334
  alliance with Britain 136, 169
  Armée d'Afrique 268
  asks for armistice 116
  bombing casualties 327
  colonialism 52, 53, 61
  concessions to Hitler unpopular 31
  defeat of Vichy government 61
  and defence of Poland 34
  economic weakness 31
  evacuation 307
  food consumption 304, 305
  'Four-Power Pact' 77
  forced labour 312
  foreign policy 31
  Italian invasion of 83, 84, 116
  Jewish internment 309
  liberation of 195
  League of Nations 17
  Little Entente alliances 17, 22
  massacres 332
  military strength 78
  occupation of 84, 116–17, 170, 171, 196
  in opposition to Axis powers 28
  relationship with Japan 52, 61, 62
  religion 286
  resistance 194, 314, 317–18, 319
  Service du Travail Obligatoire (STO) 312
  Spanish volunteers 268
  and threat of Nazism 30
Franco, Francisco 27, 78, 121, 123
Francs-Tireurs et Partisans movement 317
Frank, Anne 339
Free French 286, 318
Freetown, Sierra Leone 137
French air force 117
French army 116, 275
French Expeditionary Corps 291
French navy 154
Frend, Charles 383
Freyberg, Sir Bernard 273
Friedrich, Caspar David 386
Fussell, Paul 334
Futurism 385

Gallipoli 221
Gambier Bay 162
gammexane 368
gas masks 296, 352

Gaulle, Charles de 318
Gdansk (Danzig) 13, 32, 34, 112
General Agreement on Trade and Tariffs (GATT) 256
General Tariff Act, imperialist 26
Genoa 105
genocide 45, 128, 133, 328–33
Gerlach, Christian 331
German air force (Luftwaffe)
  air defence 192
  Battle of Britain 120
  destruction British carriers 143
  'Eagle Attack' 139
  inferiority of 125, 130, 131, 171
  losses 128, 228, 279
  Norwegian route 138
  paratroops 123
  protection for Operation Sea Lion 119
  reduction in 196
  shortage of aircraft 261–2
  shortage of fuel 165
  sinking of convoys 140
  strategic bombing 225, 226
  strength of 170, 202
  training 278
  transfer to Mediterranean and Germany 189
  war with USSR 131
  women recruits 270
German army
  Afrika Corps 210
  decentralized command 204
  defeat on Eastern front 159
  deployment of troops Normandy landings 193
  fuel shortages 144
  Greek campaign 122
  harsh disciplinary system 212
  Hitler as commander-in-chief 131
  invasion of USSR 90, 118–19, 121, 126–8, 131, 152, 183, 209, 267
  lack of support troops 263, 264
  lessons from First World War 204
  logistical problems 209
  losses 128, 175, 176, 177, 178, 183, 187, 189, 190, 195
  as meritocratic 264, 265
  Nazi propaganda 288
  North African campaign 123, 124
  occupation of France 116
  Operation Blue 177, 178
  Panzer divisions 116, 131, 156, 170, 172, 173, 178, 187, 193, 206–7, 219, 243, 364
  prisoners taken 290
  racism in 290
  retreat from Moscow 128
  strength of 133, 170, 202
  support for Axis allies 178
  training 211, 214, 275, 276

German Democratic Republic 413
German navy 142–4
  attacks on shipping 139
  blockade 136
  First World War 276
  inferiority of 135, 137, 138
  losses 138
  in Mediterranean 144
  Norway 138, 156
  scrapping of surface fleet 156
  'Z' plan to extend abandoned 136
  see also submarines
German 'New Order' 310
Germany
  aero-engines 358, 360
  aggression 169
  air-sea blockade on Britain 121
  anti-Communism and
    anti-Semitism 110
  armaments manufacture 129
  arts under National Socialism 384–8
  attack on France 84
  biological warfare 340
  'bloodless victories' 111
  civil defence 129
  colonialism 13, 15, 129
  conscription 29, 288
  declaration of war on USA 144, 147
  defeat at Stalingrad 132
  demilitarization post First World
    War 13
  disarmament 5
  division of 411, 412, 413
  domination of Europe 117, 118
  economy 2, 25, 29, 171, 232–3,
    234, 240, 244, 245, 246–7, 253–5
  effect of Allied blockade 165
  equipment production 206
  evacuation 307, 308, 309
  expansionism 31, 35, 129, 233
  food consumption 303
  forced labour 133, 244
  foreign policy 28–30, 110, 111–13
  'Four-Power Pact' 77
  Gestapo 126
  'have not' power 26
  hyperinflation 24
  imports from occupied
    territories 303
  improvements in weaponry 129
  incendiary bombing by British 72
  increased air defences 179
  inflation 12
  invasion of Czechoslovakia 32
  isolation 113–25, 126
  and Italy 75, 76, 93, 104, 143,
    187, 241
  jet aircraft 361–2
  labour shortages
  League of Nations 15, 40
  losses equipment and men 243
  military preparation 29, 78, 114,
    171, 172, 243
  murder of psychiatric patients 330
  National Socialist Party 17, 110,
    111, 261
  North Africa campaign 87
  Peenemünde Army Research
    Centre 358
  planned invasion of Britain 118–19,
    120, 138–9
  Polish campaign 114
  propaganda 385–7
  rationing 255
  rearmament 32, 237
  religion 287
  re-militarization 111
  reserved occupations 260
  Second Four-Year Plan 111, 233
  Security Service (SD) 126
  suicides at collapse of regime 341
  surprise attack on USSR 174–5
  total Wehrmacht losses 199
  on USA involvement 128, 181
  use of foreign labour 253, 254
  use of militia 261
  weapons development 355, 356,
    358, 364, 365
  women in armed forces 270
  women workers 253, 254
Germany on the Rise 253, 254
  (Godo Takuo) 49
Gibraltar 123
Gilbert Islands 160
Gleditsch, Nils Petter 322, 323
GMD (Guomindang Party) 38, 43, 48,
  60, 61
Gneisenau 138, 140, 142
Godo Takuo 49
Goebbels, Joseph 133, 385, 386
gold standard 25, 26
Gomorrah, Operation 287
Göring, Hermann 111, 119, 123, 133,
  261, 262
Gorky, Maxim 389
Görlitz 335
Gosplan state planning agency 244
Grand Alliance 166, 176–85, 186,
  199, 257
Graziani, Rodolfo 102, 103,
  290, 411
Greater East Asia Co-Prosperity
  Sphere 53, 57
Greece
  British influence agreed 416
  British withdrawal from 143
  civil war 5, 417
  famine 305, 306, 337
  German invasion of 84, 124, 187
  Italian invasion of 81, 84, 123
  partisans supported by
    Communists 416
  US aid 416
Greenwood, Walter 382
Grenzpolitiker (border politicians) 17
Grossman, Vassili 392
Guadalcanal 66
Guam 37
Guandong army 43
Guderian, Heinz 116, 117
Guomindang Party (GMD) 38, 43, 48,
  60, 61
Gurkhas 68, 224
Gurs 329
Gustav Line 190
Gypsies 311, 330

Halder, Franz 124, 126
Halifax, Nova Scotia 137
Halsey, William 66, 70
Hamburg 287, 324
Hanford 357
Harbin 37, 50
Harris, Arthur 179, 191, 227, 228
Hasegawa Tsuyoshi 72, 73
Hashida Kunihiko 36
Hawaii 180
Hearst, William Randolph 393
Henan 60
  see also Honan
Herriot, Édouard 29
Hess, Dame Myra 383
Hewland, Elsie 379
Hideki, General 410
high frequency radio
  direction-finding equipment
  (HFDF or 'Huffduff') 151
Hilfswillige ('voluntary helpers') 267
Himmler, Heinrich 126, 129, 345, 311
Hipper 138, 140
Hirohito, Emperor 50, 72, 73, 230
Hiroshima 72, 208, 214, 293, 324, 425
Hitler, Adolf 75, 115, 118, 121, 122,
  after defeat at Stalingrad 132
  and 'New Order' 310, 311
  assassination attempt 133
  and British Empire as sea
    power 135
  cancellation of Locarno
    Treaties 28, 29
  criticism of Japanese emperor 51
  decision-making 219, 220
  distracted from USSR attack 153
  economic decisions 246
  effect of rise on Italy 77
  foreign policy 30, 110, 111–13
  invasion of Czechoslovakia 32
  on Italian change of policy 94
  on Jewish deaths as revenge 176
  on Jewish people in enemy
    states 133
  Lebensraum 118–19
  portraits of 385

Raumpolitiker
  (spatial politician') 17
scrapping of surface fleet 156
T-4 action 330
trade policy 31
war in Belorussia 194
war in Tunisia 184
on war with USSR 124–5, 126, 127, 131
Zitadelle offensive 155
Hitler Youth 274
HMS Hood 142
Ho Chi Minh 55
Hokkaido 64
home contact 280–2, 292
home front 300, 301–20
  and commitment to war 3–4
  evacuation 306–9
  food shortages 303–6
  forced labour 312
  internment 309–12
  Labour ministers 384
  as subject for painting 379
home front economy 248, 249–55
Home Guard 295
Homma Masaharu 59
Honan (China) 337
Hong Kong 35, 52
Horizon 375
horses 209, 210, 350
Houdry catalytic cracking 361
House of German Art, Munich 385
housing shortage 255
Hull, Cordell 53
Humber River 139
Hundred Regiments Campaign 48
Hungary
  Axis control 85
  CFM 403
  food security 22
  hyperinflation 24
  invasion of USSR 126, 178, 195
  losses of territory post First World War 13
  preferential trade access to Germany 31
  Soviet influence agreed 416
Husky, Operation 187
hyperinflation 24, 338

Iasi-Kishenev operation 195
Ibárruri Gómez, Dolores (*La Pasionaria*) 28
Ichang 52
Ichi-Go (Number One) operation 68–9
identity documentation 18
illiteracy 265, 273
IMIs (Italian Military Internees) 103–4, 105
immigration controls 17, 18

imperial renewal, post First World War 26–7
Imphal 67, 68, 209, 223, 286
incendiary bombing 71, 72, 229, 324, 353
Inchon 428, 429
India
  British army in 222
  effect of Ceylon 148
  importance to Britain 33
  independence 5
  Japanese plan to invade 67
  religion 285, 286
Indian National Army (INA) 60, 67, 259
Indian Ocean 143, 165
Indigo Days (Trevelyan) 384
Indochina 52, 53, 61
Indochinese Communist Party 55
Indonesia 5, 52, 55, 334
inflation 24, 232–3, 238, 338 *see also* home front economy
Inner Mongolia 43
innovations, military 214–15
insecticides 367–9
intelligence 142, 154, 155, 215–17
International Bank for Reconstruction and Development 256
International Committee of the Red Cross 103
International Court of Justice 108
international economy 255–7
international gold standard 24, 25
International Monetary Fund 256
International Red Cross 47
International Settlement Zone 46
internationalism 394
internment 4, 85, 309–12 *see also* Italian Military Internees
invention 344, 345, 354–8, 370
Iran 156, 416–17
Iraq 143
Ireland (Eire) 10, 267
Iron Curtain 403, 413–15, 416
iron ore 138, 143, 156
Islam 286
Ismay, Lord 424
Israel 5, 423
Italian air force 92, 241
Italian army 75, 77–84
  Balkan front 84–5
  after Operation Husky 187
  German occupation 95–100, 102–3
  loss of East Africa 85–6
  losses in Libya and Egypt 202
  Mediterranean 92–4
  North Africa 86–9
  peasant based 265
  USSR 89, 90, 91
Italian Military Internees (IMIs) 103–4, 105

Italian navy 143, 171, 258, 262
Italian-Ethiopian War (1935) 78, 79
Italy
  Action Party 92, 319
  Allied invasion 105, 156, 190
  Allied Military Government of Italy 97
  ally with Nazi Germany 74, 75, 76, 78, 90
  Anglo-American distrust of 95
  Anti-Fascist movement 76, 92, 93, 94, 98, 100–2, 104
  anti-Semitism 28, 78
  arts under Fascism 385
  attack on France 83, 84
  Auxiliary Troops 98
  'black brigades' 103
  bombing casualties 327
  CFM 403
  civilian hardship 313
  as 'co-belligerent' 95
  collaboration with occupying force 102
  collapse of Empire 85–6
  Communism post war 106, 107
  conscription by RSI 78, 103, 319
  currency overvalued 25
  division of 76, 97, 104
  economy and war effort 257
  entry into war 74, 116, 118, 143, 170
  equipment 87, 206
  evacuation 307
  Fascism 74–89, 91–4, 96, 104
  First World War 77
  forces massacred 331
  'Four-Power Pact' 77
  'Garibaldi Brigades' 319
  German 'Gothic Line' 105
  German occupation 76, 95–6, 100, 102–3, 103
  'guerra di rapido corso' ('lightning war') 79
  'have not' power 26
  invasion of Ethiopia 27
  Italian Auxiliary Divisions 76
  'Italian Liberation Corps' 97
  Italian Social Republic (RSI) 97, 100, 102–3, 103
  joins NATO 106
  Kingdom of the South 76, 97–8, 100
  lack of armaments 79
  legacy of war 106–7
  liberation 98–9, 100, 105
  massacres of civilians 331
  merchant fleet 234
  militarism 81, 82
  military deferment 260

484 Index

Italy (cont.)
Military Mission Italian Army
(MMIA) 97, 98
military strength 78, 80, 81–2
militia 82, 265
National Committee for Liberation
(CLN) 319
'National Republican Guard'
(GNR) 103
Neo-Fascism 76, 103
partisans 100–2
press censorship 75
pre-war economy 232, 234
prisoners of Allies 103, 104
prisoners of war 92
rejection of war 113
reliance on imports 234
resistance 318, 319, 320
Socialist Party 319
state control 49
strikes 91
submarine conflict with British 78
unification 77
United Nations 106
war in USSR 89, 90–2, 126, 178
war on Greece declared 123
Iwo Jima 165

Jacoby, Analee 322
Japan 35–73
access to resources 55, 365
army on 'total war' 38
attempted invasion of India 209
biological and chemical warfare 49,
50, 339, 340
bombing casualties 165, 229,
324, 325
and Britain 36, 37, 148
China and South East Asia
offensive 39, 67–71
colonialism 51, 66
conscription 62, 253
declaration of war 144
dependence on imports 32, 33, 53,
144, 161, 165, 166, 234
disarmament 5
Empire 36–9, 40
equipment production 206
evacuation 307, 308, 309
expansionism 37, 40
famine 166, 306
First World War 36
forced labour 62–4, 253, 267
and Germany 37, 48, 49, 52, 66,
136, 241
gold standard 26
'have not' power 26
history of totalitarianism 50
idea of racial purity 51
importance of religion 51
Indochina 145

internment 309
kokutai (national policy) 50
League of Nations 15, 40
Malay peninsula 202, 203
Manchurian war 32, 113
massacre in China 332
Meiji rule 36, 37, 50
merchant fleet 234
militarism 35, 38, 48, 49–51
monarchy 50
nationalism 26
overthrow French colonial
regime 62
Pacific War 64, 65–6, 135
planned invasion South East
Asia 52–3
political parties 50
poor intelligence 215
post war 404
pre-war economy 232, 234
propaganda 66
response to GMD China 38
roots of war against China 36, 37
suicides 341
surrender 72–3
'Tripartite Pact' 52
and USA 37, 38, 52
and USSR 33, 55, 136, 156
wartime economy 240
weapons development 358, 364
women workers 253
Japanese air force
attacks Pearl Harbor 24, 145, 146
Kamikaze 66, 162, 166
Mariana Islands 161
Japanese army (IJA)
Burmese campaign 223
harsh disciplinary system 213
power of 40
reputation incorrect 275, 276
social structure of 265–6
suicide attacks 213
surrender 289
training of pilots 278, 279
use of bicycles in Singapore 205
Japanese navy (IJN)
amphibious landings 221
carriers 160, 161, 220
increase in size and power 144, 145
prestige of 262
shortage of vessels 148
training of pilots 279
Jennings, Humphrey 383
Jericho, Operation 287
Jervis Bay 140
Jews
caricatures in Germany 387

'Doctors' Plot' accused 423
genocide 4, 32, 126, 128, 290, 128,
324, 328–30, 332
internment 309
land appropriation 129
Lithuanian 324
planned extermination of
311, 312
as alleged threat to German
security 30, 127
Jimmu, Emperor 66
Jinan 39, 40
Juin, Alphonse 291
Jungle Book, The (military training
pamphlet) 223
jungle warfare 275, 276

Kaiser, Henry 239
Kamikaze (Divine Wind) 286
Kammler, Hans 348
Kampfgemeinschaft
('battle community') 288
Kandy, Ceylon 68
Kasserine Pass, Battle of 218, 219
Kato Tomosaburo 38
Katsura Taro 37
Kawabe Torashiro 72
Keitel, Wilhelm 115
Kelen, Emery 19
Kellogg–Briand Pact (1928) 32
Kennan, George 342, 415, 416
Kesselring, Albert 102, 265
Ketsu-Go, Operation 72
Keynes, John Maynard 13, 235, 376
Kharkov, Battles of (1942/1943)
177, 187
Khrushchev, Nikita 156, 241
Kiev 126, 337, 338
Kijūrō Shidehara 39
Kim Il Sung 42, 428, 429, 430, 431
King George V 142
Kishi Nobosuke 346
Kleist, Ewald von 116, 131
Knight, Laura 379
Knir, Heinrich 385
Kohima 67, 68, 209, 223, 224
Kollwitz, Käthe 385
Komsomol 299
Konev, Ivan 197, 198, 265
Königsberg 336
Konoe Fumimaro 44, 45, 51, 52, 53,
54, 72
Korea
border disputes 33, 36
division of 428
forced labour 62, 63, 64, 334
Japanese atrocities 50
sex slavery 63, 64
state control 49
Korean War 5, 403, 428–30
Kosovo 85

Kristallnacht 32
Krokodil 390
Kukrinksi 391
Kursk, Battle of 155, 187, 208, 218
Kutuzov, Operation 189
Kyushu 69

Lacina, Bethany 322, 323
Laktionov, Alexander 389
Lampedusa 92
Landing Ships Tanks (LSTs) 157
Landis, James 297
Latvia 34
Lawrence, Jacob 396, 397
League of Nations
  achievements 15, 17
  collapse of 5
  and Danzig 13
  failure to halt Japanese
    aggression 26
  on food security 22
  German exit 40
  Health Organization 21
  Japanese exit 40
  as key to Wilson's plan 11
  lack of racial equality 17
  legitimacy rejected 18
  membership of 15
  and nation-state 17
  post war 418
  rejected by Italy 78
  satirical illustration of 19, 25
Lebedev, Vladimir 390
Lebensraum 30, 118
Leclerc, Philippe 286
Ledo/Stillwell Road 350
Lehmann, John 375
LeMay, Curtis 72, 325
Lend Lease act (USA) 173
  to Britain 157, 165
  to China 273
  importance of 239, 240
  Roosevelt and 174, 393
  shipping safety 140
  to USSR 156, 168, 178, 183,
    189, 218
Leningrad
  evacuation 336
  German army objective 126
  as propaganda 390
  siege of 261, 336, 337
Leyte Gulf, Battle of 70, 161, 162
Libération-Nord movement 317
Libération-Sud movement 317
Libya 77, 78, 87, 174, 202
  lice infestation 367, 368
Lindemann, Frederick 345
Lippmann, Walter 415, 416
Lisbon Conference (1952) 429
literature, war 375–6

Lithuania 324
Little Saturn, Operation 90
Liverpool 137
Lloyd George, David 13
Locarno Treaties (1925) 28, 29
Lodz 114, 331
logistics 209–10, 211
London 235, 301
  Battle of Britain 120
  bombing casualties 327
  economic centre 7
  morale 383
  V1 and V2 bombing 209
London, Treaty of (1915) 15
London Can Take It (film) 383
Love on the Dole (Greenwood) 382
Low, David 20
LSTs (Landing Ships Tanks) 157
Lübeck 327
Luce, Henry 394
Lushun (Port Arthur) 37
Lüth, Wolfgang 288
Lützow 142
Luxembourg 170
Lyttelton, Oliver 345

MacArthur, Douglas 59, 64, 70, 160, 428
Maclean, Donald 426, 427
Madagascar 148, 149
Maginot Line 116, 117, 170
Maikop 131
malaria 47, 63, 340, 353, 368, 369
Malay peninsula 202, 203
Malaya
  European colonial interest 52
  fall of 222
  impact of Second Sino-Japanese
    War 35
  Japanese attack 55, 204
  prisoners of war against British
    colonialism 60
  recapture 165
Malaya, Battle of 59, 60
Malayan Peoples' Anti-Japanese
  Army 55
Malenkov, Giorgi 346
Mallios, Alexandros 331, 332
malnutrition 21, 69, 255, 290, 324,
  336, 338
Malta 87, 131, 144, 153, 154
Manchester 120
Manchukuo 26, 32, 40
Manchuria
  border disputes 33
  Japanese invasion 26, 35, 40–3, 44
  Japanese seizure of Russian
    holdings 37
  Tanaka plan 39–42
Manhattan Project 349, 357, 425, 426
Manila 70, 71, 333
Mann, Heinrich 385

Mann, Thomas 385
Manna, Operation 287
Manning, R. J. 383
Manstein, Erich von 187
Mao Zedong 43, 428, 430
Maquis 318
Marco Polo Bridge 68
Margolin, Jean-Louis 332
Mariana Islands 37, 68, 72, 159,
  160–1, 192, 229
Marquis, Frederick (Lord
  Woolton) 345
Marseilles 164
Marshall, George C. 179, 192, 256,
  271, 419–20
Marshall Islands 37, 160
Marshall Plan (European Recovery
  Program) 419–20, 256
Masaryk, Jan 421
Matsui Iwane 61
Matsuoka Yosuke 52
Mauretania 150
Mayakovsky, Vladimir 390
McCarthyism 399
Mediterranean Sea 87, 143, 153, 156
Meetinghouse, Operation 71
Mein Kampf (Hitler) 51, 119
Melanesia 284
Mendelsohn, Eric 352
mepacrine 369
merchant shipping 143, 154, 164,
  224, 234
Mers-el-Kébir 138
Messe, Giovanni 184
Meuse River 116
micro-weaponry 365
Midway, Battle of 66, 150, 180, 217
Milan 96, 105
military production 242–8
militia 82, 103, 261, 265, 319
Millennium, Operation 179
Miller, Howard 394
Ministry of Information (MoI) 374
Minsk 194
Missouri 54
Modernism 385, 399, 400
Mola, Emilio 309
Mölders, Werner 287
Molotov, Vyacheslav 124, 181, 388,
  402, 404–7, 418–19
'Molotov cocktails' 405
Molotov–Ribbentrop Non-Aggression
  Pact (1939) 112, 113, 136
  monarchy, declining role of 7
Mongolia 35
Monroe Doctrine 26
Monte Cassino 287
Montenegro 81, 85
Montgomery, Sir Bernard
  Alamein 131, 183
  on British soldiers 213, 282

486 Index

Montgomery, Sir Bernard (cont.)
on effect of training on morale 276
experience 273
rejection of plan by
Eisenhower 195
religion 286, 287
Montreux Convention (1936)
417, 418
Moore, Henry 379, 380
morale 211–13
civilian 226
and postal service 280
and rations 281
and training 276
Morgenthau, Henry 255
Morocco 154, 184
Morrison, Herbert 295, 384
Moscow 126, 128, 144, 177
Moscow, Battle of 175, 176, 261
Moscow Conference (Tolstoy
Conference) (1944) 197
Moulin, Jean 318
Mountbatten, Lord Louis 158
Mukin, B. A. 390, 392
Mulberry artificial harbours 159, 194
Munich Agreement (1938) 31
Musashi 162, 364
Mussolini, Benito
after division of Italy 97
and armed forces 79, 80
and arts 385
attack on France 84
collapse of government 187
declaration of
'non-belligerence' 113
declaration of war 28, 74–5,
83, 116
fall of 94, 319
Fascism 77
German rescue 96
head of RSI 103
and Hitler 109
invasion of Albania 34
invasion of Greece 84
loss of confidence in 91
plans for Italian expansionism 81
and political unrest post First World
War 15
rejection of German plan for Libyan
occupation 123
threat to France 34
totalitarian regime established 77
on war with Ethiopia 27
Mutaguchi Renya 68, 223
MVSN (Voluntary Militia for National
Security, Italy) 82, 265

NAAFI (Navy, Army, and Air Force
Institute) 283
Nagas people 68
Nagasaki 72, 214, 324, 425

Nakajima Kesago 59
Nanjing (Nanking) 38, 39, 50, 59,
289 see also 'Rape of Nanjing'
Nanjing Massacre Memorial Hall 45
napalm 72, 353
Naples 95, 319, 367
Narvik 138
Nash, Paul 380
National Monuments Records 376
'national realism' 385
National Socialism (Nazism)
and art 376, 377, 384–8
defeat of 196–9, 201
food rationing 21
importance of experts 348
ideology 66, 260, 267, 284, 287,
288, 290, 330, 348
propaganda 21, 385–8
on role of women 270
USA opposition to 169, 174
National Socialist Party
(NSDAP) 110, 261
National Socialist People's Welfare
(NSV) 299
National Union for Anti-Aircraft
Protection (UNPA) 297
NATO (North Atlantic Treaty
Organization) 106, 423,
424–7, 428
Navy, Army, and Air Force Institute
(NAAFI) 283
Navy Combat Art Programme
(USA) 395
Nazi–Soviet Pact (1939) 34
Nazism see National Socialism
Nelson, Donald 245, 345, 346
Neo-Fascism 76, 96, 100, 103,
106, 107
Neptune, Operation 158
nerve gas 368
Netherlands
colonialism 52
famine 287, 304, 337
farming 303, 304
German occupation 115, 116, 170
return of forced workers 312
Netturno 191
Neuilly, Treaty of 11
neutral countries
effect of war on 1
foreign volunteers 267, 268
Low Countries 170
Norway 170
propaganda and 374
USA 34, 393
USSR 171, 174
New Guinea 55, 64, 160, 180, 259
'New Man' 104
New Mediterranean Order 81, 86
'New Order' 51, 52, 53, 124, 128, 310
New York 7

New Zealand 33
newsreels 40
Nicolson, Harold 13, 15
Nimitz, Chester 64, 160
NKVD (People's Commissariat for
Internal Affairs) 299, 346
Nomura Kichisaburo 53
Normandy, Battle of 158–9, 160,
192–4, 195, 222
North Africa
Allied navies 154
German campaign 87, 131, 153, 183
Italian ambition 76, 86, 87–9, 183
North Atlantic, battle of 224–5
North Atlantic Treaty Organization
(NATO) 106, 423, 424–7, 428
Northern Ireland 260
Norway 115, 156, 170, 221, 316
NSDAP (National Socialist
Party) 110, 261
NSV (National Socialist People's
Welfare) 299
Nuremberg war trials 410
nutritional science 20–1

Ó Gráda, Cormac 338
Oak Ridge 357
O'Connor, Sir Richard 202, 205
Oder River 196
Odessa 126, 290
Office of War Information
(OWI) 393, 394
Official War Artists 376
oil supplies
Axis powers shortage of 82, 176,
206–7
British 151
as essential to warfare 2, 131,
143, 240
and German invasion of USSR 152
OKW (Hitler HQ) 152, 155, 156
Oklahoma 146
Okinawa 36, 65, 165–6, 341
Omaha beach, Normandy 193
One World (Wilkie) 394
Oppenheimer, Robert 349
Oradour-sur-Glane 332
Orel, Operation 189
organo-phosphates 368
Origin of Species, The (Darwin) 18
Orlando, Vittorio Emanuele 15
Osaka 254
Osoaviakhim (Society for Assistance to
Defence) 275, 296
Ostrogorsk-Rossosk 90
Ostrów Mazowiecka 329
Overlord, Operation 157, 158, 192–4,
195, 196

Pacific War 64, 65–6
'Pact of Steel' (1939) 28

Padua, Paul Matthias 387
painting 376–81, 383, 384, 385–7
Pakistan 5
Palau islands 37
Palazzo, Tony 396
Palestine 33
Pantelleria 92
Papua 259
Pariani, Alberto 81
Paris 61, 83, 116, 320
Paris Conference (1946) 407–9
Paris Peace Conference (1919) 11, 13, 15, 17, 22, 29
Paris Peace Treaty (1947) 106
Parit Sulong, Jahore 59
partisans 314–16, 317, 319–20
  deaths 331–2
  Greek 416
  intelligence source 216
  Italian 100–1, 104
  Red Army 261
Pasionaria, La (Dolores Ibárruri Gómez) 28
Pasternak, Boris 389
Patton, George S. 219, 291
Paulus, Friedrich 121, 131, 132, 185
Pearl Harbor 24, 54, 55, 145–6, 213, 394
Penguin, Forces' Bookclub 283
Penguin New Writing 375
penicillin 369
People's Commissariat for Internal Affairs (NKVD) 290, 346
People's Community (Volksgemeinschaft) 263, 264, 385
People's Republic of China 428, 429
Pétain, Philippe 116
Peter Grimes (Britten) 383
Phibun Songkhram 55
Philippine Sea, Battle of the 160–1, 220
Philippines
  American naval attacks 64, 161, 192
  amphibious landings 221
  Japanese offensive 55, 59, 69, 70
  physical punishment 265, 266
Picasso, Pablo 427
Pilgrim Trust 376
Piombino 95
Piper, John 376
plague 340
Plunder-Varsity, Operation 197
PLUTO petrol pipeline 371
Poetry London 375
Poland
  alliance with France 17
  atrocities by Soviet army 290
  borders moved 5
  Britain and France unable to aid 169

deportations 309
displacement 311, 336
exclusion from security negotiations 31
German atrocities in 126, 290
German claim for union 29
German invasion of 169
  hyperinflation 24
land appropriation 129
  post war 402, 403
resistance 314, 315–16
troops in diaspora 280, 281
USSR offensive 34, 196
war desired by Hitler 112
women in armed forces 270
Polish Home Army (Armia Krajowa) 314, 315, 316
political posters 390
Political Warfare Executive (PWE) 374
Pomerania 197, 330
Ponomarenko, Panteleymon 314
Poor People's Refuge, Changsha 69
Port Arthur (Lushun) 37
Port Moresby 60, 149
Porta San Paolo, Rome 95
Potsdam Conference (1945) 402, 403
Powell, Michael 383
POWs see prisoners of war
Prague 34, 421, 422
Pratt & Whitney Twin Wasp engine 358
Pravda 413
Pressburger, Emeric 383
Prien, Günther 141
Priestley, J. B. 376
Prince of Wales 60, 142
Prinz Eugen 142
prisoners of war (POWs) 89, 116
  Convention on Prisoners of War 103
  forced labour 62–3, 129, 254, 333–5, 350
  Italian 94, 97
  Jewish 127
  numbers of 92
  Polish 280
  Red Army 189, 267
  violence and murder of 59, 60, 65, 290–2, 331, 333–5
Prokhorovka 156
Prokofiev, Sergei 390
pronatalism 18
prontosil 368
propaganda 287, 288–9
  civilian morale 4, 302
  importance of 373, 374
  and intellectuals 376
  and post war reality 398, 399
  and financial contribution to war effort 303
  use of stereotypes 397, 398

Prussia 12
Prussian Academy of Arts 385
psychiatric patients, murder of 330
psychological warfare 46
Pu Yi, Emperor 40
Punjabis 68
Punta Stilo 87
PWE (Political Warfare Executive) 374
Pyongyang 428
pyrethrum 368

Qingdao (Tsingdao) 37
Queen Elizabeth 151
Queen Mary 151

Rabe, John 46
racial equality 15, 17
racial segregation, armed forces 260, 261
racism
  German 267, 290
  Italian 78
  Japanese 48, 64, 65
  Western 51, 65, 66, 68, 71
radar 362–4
  advances during course of war 3
convoy escorts 141, 142
  development of 356
US air force and 160
radio broadcasting 282, 283, 356, 386, 388, 389
Ramsay, Bertram 158
Rangoon 68
rape
  Italy 99, 291
  Manila 70
  'Rape of Nanjing' 46, 289, 332
Red Army 290, 291, 335
Rastenburg 96, 127
ration cards 249
rationing 303–5
Ravilious, Eric 376
Raymond, Antonin 352
reciprocal aid 240, 241
recruitment, military 259–63, 264
Reed, Carol 383
refugees 47, 60
Reich Labour Service 274, 283
Reich Ministry for Popular Enlightenment and Propaganda (RMVP) 385
Reichenau, Walter von 290
Reichsluftschutzbund (Reich Air Defence League) 296, 300
Reith, Sir John 374
Reitsch, Hannah 353
religion 284, 285–7
Remagen 197
Repulse 60, 145

488 Index

reserved occupations 260
resistance
  Belgian 115
  Chinese 42, 47, 48
  civilian 312, 313–20
  Communists and 403
  Dutch 115
  French 194
  German atrocities 319, 320
  intellectuals 375, 376
  Italian 76, 85, 95, 98, 100–1, 102–4, 105, 107–8
  South-East Asia 55, 56
  Yugoslav 85, 91, 95
Ribbentrop, Joachim von 32, 113, 169
Riga 195, 329
Risorgimento 97
RMVP (Reich Ministry for Popular Enlightenment and Propaganda) 385
Roads to Freedom (Sartre) 375
Rochat, Giorgio 83, 90
Rockwell, Norman 394, 395
Rodney 142
Roma 331, 332
Romania
  alliance with France 17
  army peasant based 265
  CFM 403, 404
  change of side 171
  collapse of German position 195
  food security 22
  route for Red Army 195
  Soviet influence agreed 416
  support for German army 178
  USSR expansionism 34, 118, 126
Rome 95, 99, 105, 106
Rommel, Erwin 87, 88, 116, 124, 131, 143–4, 190, 273
Roosevelt, Franklin Delano 191
  'Arsenal of Democracy' speech 173, 174
  Atlantic Charter 54
  death of 198, 402
  election 25
  joint landing NW Africa with Britain 179
  on neutrality 34
  propaganda 393, 395
  reaction to Pearl Harbor attack 146
  and South East Asian situation 52–3
  support for British in Middle East 143
  and war aims 384
  on war in China 72
Rosenberg, Alfred 345, 346
Rosie the Riveter 249, 394
Rostov 178
Rostov, Battle of 175, 176
Rostow, W. W. 431

Rotterdam 327
Roundup, Operation 178
Rowecki, Stefan 315
Royal Air Force (RAF)
  Bomber Command 129, 179, 191, 196, 226–7, 228, 267
  bombing offensives 72, 196
  British Empire volunteers 267
  carrier-based 142, 143
  class distinction in 266
  command in Mediterranean 144
  D-Day 158, 193–4, 196
  effect on German morale 125
  incendiary bombing 72
  Pathfinder Force 227
  prestige of 262
  strategic bombing 169, 179
  training 278
  US volunteers 267, 268
Royal Navy
  amphibious landings 221, 222
  blockades 144, 171
  'British Pacific Fleet' 165, 166
  class distinction in 266
  defeat Italian fleet 143
  defence of Crete 143
  Dunkirk 138
  Fleet Air Arm 158
  invasion of Sicily 155
  Kamikaze losses 166
  Normandy landings 158–9
  and Pearl Harbor 146
  prestige of 262
  shipping repairs 140–1
  strength of 136
  superiority of 171
  and US against Japan 165
Royal Oak 141
Ruhr, Battle of the 191
Rumiantsev, Operation 189
Rundstedt, Gerd von 190, 193
Runge, Philipp Otto 386
Russo-Finnish Winter War (1939–40) 217
Russo-Japanese war (1904–5) 37
Ryukyus 64, 65

Saarland 30
Sadler's Wells Theatre 383
Saint-Germain-en-Laye, Treaty of 11
Saipan 160
Sakhalin Island 37
Salerno 187, 193
Salò 96
Salò republic (Italian Socialist Republic) 102
sanitation 210
Sartre, John-Paul 375
Sauckel, Fritz 254
Saur, Karl-Otto 346

Sauter, Wilhelm 387
Scapa Flow 141
Schacht, Hjalmar 110, 111
Scharnhorst 138, 140, 142, 156
Schandvertrag, Der 29
Schleswig Holstein 112
Schlieffen Plan (1914) 114
Schmitz-Wiedenbrück, Hans 387
Schweinfurt 227
science, military 3, 348–9
Schutzstaffel (SS) 126, 155, 213, 329, 332, 348
Sea Lion, Operation 118, 119, 120, 138–9
Secchia, Pietro 320
'Second Front' 181
Second Sino-Japanese War 44–8
  effect of 35, 36
  civilian casualties 293, 322
  Japanese atrocities 289, 290
  preparedness 272–3
  as 'total war' 45
Selassie, Emperor Haile 27
self-determination 11, 13, 15
Seoul 428
Serbia 84, 85, 332
Sevastopol 131
Shakhurin, Aleksei Ivanovich 347
Shanghai 45, 46, 293
Shanghai Anti-Japanese National Salvation Association 42
Shanghai Expeditionary Force 61
Shanghai 'Incident' 42, 43
Shcherbakov, A. S. 388
Shi Liang 47
Shidehara Kijiro 38, 39
Shinano 364
Shintoism 51
shipbuilding 243t
shipping
  Allied losses 151–2, 154–6, 224–5
  Japanese losses 161
  North African campaign 154
  supplies after D-Day 164–5
Sho-Go, Operation 69
Sholokov, Mikhail 393
Shostakovich, Dmitri 390
Sicily 92, 93, 155, 187, 190, 291
Sidi Barrani 87, 89
Siegfried Line 195
signals intelligence 216, 217
Silesia 197

Singapore
British misconception re
 safety 204, 205
British surrender 332
ethnic cleansing 59
European colonial interest 52, 60
fall of 55, 203, 222
Japanese atrocities 59, 332
Japanese surrender 165
Singapore Overseas Chinese Army 55
Sino-Japanese war (1937) 35, 44–8
deaths of non-combatants 322,
 324, 332
Japanese atrocities 289
preparedness 272, 273
Sino-Soviet Treaty of Friendship,
 Alliance and Mutual Assistance
 (1949) 428
Sinti 331
Sirte 89
Slansky, Rudolf 423
Slim, Sir William 223, 224, 231,
 276, 285
Slovakia 84, 85, 26
Social Darwinism 18
social realism 375
Sollum 87, 89
Solomon Islands 150, 160, 180
Somalia 77, 78
Somme, River 275
Song Meiling 47
Sook Chin 59
South Africa 33
Soviet–Finnish war (1939–40) 405
Sovietization 421
Soviet–Turkish Treaty of Friendship
 and Neutrality (1925) 418
Spanish Civil War (1936–39) 27, 32,
 34, 78, 79, 81, 268
Spanish–American War (1898) 37
Special Operations Executive 55
Speer, Albert 162, 247, 346, 348
Spencer, Stanley 377
Spender, Stephen 321
spying 426
SS (Schutzstaffel) 126, 155, 213, 329,
 332, 348
Stalin, Joseph 191
appeasement with Germany 169
on Chiang 43
control of war economy 244
defence of Moscow 131, 176, 177
denounces Molotov 405
expansionism 34
fear of Western ideas 392
foreign policy 422
and German invasion 126, 172
on Greek Communists 416
ignoring of intelligence 215, 216
and invasion South Korea 428, 431
on Iranian crisis 417

on 'Iron Curtain' speech 413, 414
as military leader 188, 196, 345
and nationalist propaganda 390
offensive on Berlin 198
on peace 402
on post war Japan 404
purges of armed forces 217
reaction to Marshall Plan 420
rejection of post-war German
 treaty 406
support for Roosevelt 192
on Turkish crisis 417
on USSR against Japan 193
USSR atomic bomb
 development 425, 426
on 'Volga Germans' 310
Stalin–Churchill percentages
 agreement (1944) 416
Stalingrad 131–2, 152, 178, 390
Stalingrad, Battle of 184, 185, 186,
 212, 218, 339
Stalinization 421
Starvation, Operation 337
steel production 234, 237
Steinbeck, John 395
sterling bloc, creation of 26
Stimson, Henry 54
Stockholm Appeal (1950) 426
strategic bombing 225, 226–30
submarines
 Allied improvements 129, 131
 Japanese gigantism 364
 loss of U-boats 142, 143, 155,
  162, 278
 new type U-boat 162–4, 356
 scientific research on detection 225
 shipping losses 129, 136–7, 138,
  139, 147, 148
 training 276
 U-boat production 121, 140,
  151, 154
 Wolf Packs 121, 140, 142, 224–5
Sudetenland 29, 31
Suez Canal
 British hold on 85–6
 German campaign 123, 131
 Italian ambition 81, 87, 123, 234
suicide 340, 341
suicide attacks 224
sulphonamides 368, 369
Sunflower, Operation 124
Sutherland, Graham 378
Sweden 138
Sword of Honour (Waugh) 375
Syngman Rhee 428
synthetic substitutes 366
Syria 143, 419

'T4-Action' 330
Taiwan 36, 47, 62, 161, 166
Takahashi, Korekiyo 26

Tambimuttu 375
Tanaka Giichi 38, 39
Tanganyika 13
tanks 3, 156, 207, 209, 243t, 362
Taranto 87, 143, 171
tariffs and quotas 24
Tate Gallery 383
Taylor, A. J. P. 376
Taylor, Philip M. 374
Tehran Conference (1943) 191, 192
Terrace, British Columbia 259
Teschen (Cieszyn) 31
Thailand 35, 55
Thailand–Burma Railway 63, 349
Thessalonica 85
Thirty Years War 17
Thomas, Georg 246
Thompson, Frank 376
Tirpitz 136, 156
Tito, Josip Broz 320, 422
Tobruk 89, 131
Todt, Fritz 346
Tojo Hideki 50, 54, 345
Tokyo 71, 72, 324, 325, 326, 410
Tolbukhin, Fedor 287
Tolstoy Conference (Moscow
 Conference) (1944) 197
Tomoyuki Yamashita 202
Tonkin, Indochina 61, 337
Torch, Operation 154, 179, 181,
 184, 190
'total war'
 civilian casualties 293
 demands of 2–3
 experience of civilians 379
 First World War 7
 Japanese 38, 66
 and propaganda 373, 374, 375
 Second Sino-Japanese War 45
totalitarianism
 art and 384, 385
 Communism and 413, 415, 421
 German 50, 201
 Italian 77
 Japanese 50
 and peacetime conscription 274
 post second world war 400
 and propaganda 373, 374
Toulon 154, 164
trade 31
Train Was on Time, The (Der Zug war
 pünktlich, (Böll) 375
training, military 211–12, 274–5,
 272–9
Tran Trong Kim 62
Treaty of Alliance with Iran
 (1942) 416
Treaty for the Limitation and
 Reduction of Naval Armament
 (1930) 145
Trevelyan, Julian 384

490 Index

Trianon, Treaty of 11, 23
Trident Conference (Washington) (1943) 186, 192
Trieste 406
Tripartite Pact (1940) 35, 36, 52, 81, 118
Tripoli 89, 144
Tripolitania (Libya) 418–19
Truman, Harry S. 409
  on atomic bomb 425
  on Byrnes 406
  and Cold War 415, 416
  on peace 402
Truman Doctrine 415
Tsingdao (Qingdao) 37
Tunisia 81, 89, 154, 184, 187
Tunku Abdul Rahman 56
Turin 105
Turkey 81, 124, 416, 417, 418
Turkish–Italian war (1911–1912) 77
Two-Ocean Navy 160, 173
Two-Ocean War 144–50
Typhoon, Operation 126–7, 128
typhus 339, 340, 367

U-Go (Operation C) campaign 67, 68
Ukraine 126, 276, 331
Ultra intelligence 199
Umberto, Prince of Italy 97
United Nations Organization
  on atomic energy 426
  founding of 409, 410
  Italy and 106
  supports South Korea 428
United Service Organizations (USO) 281
UNPA (National Union for Anti-Aircraft Protection) 297
Uranus, Operation 132
US air force (USAAF)
  Battle of Midway 150
  bombing offensives 61, 69, 71, 72, 165, 196, 227, 228, 229
  'Combined Bomber Offensive' 191, 192
  German civilian casualties 129
  increased strength of 172
  long-range bomber development 192
  losses 228
  precision bombing 179, 181
  success over Germany 159
  training 278
  very-long-range aircraft 225
US army
  Army General Classification Test 262
  atrocities against Japanese 291, 292
  class distinction in 266
  demographic of 211
  expansion of 219
  home contact 281, 282
  innovation Western Front 218, 219–20
  losses in battle of the Bulge 199
  Normandy landings 159, 193, 195, 210
  North Africa 131
  production of equipment 219
  propaganda in armed forces 288
  reduction of 192
  Rhineland 196
  and Sherman tanks 248
  specialization of forces 262
  training 212, 276
  Women's Auxiliary Army Corps 271
US Marine Corps 222
US navy 149
  aircraft carriers 146, 160
  amphibious landings 222
  Atlantic convoy protection 222
  attacks Saipan 160
  Battle of the Atlantic 128
  and BPF 165, 166
  and British against Japan 165
  carriers with radar 220
  class distinction in 266, 267
  coastal convoys 147, 148
  and defence of communication 180
  defence of Denmark Strait 147
  entry into war 142
  importance of submarines 161
  increased strength of 180, 181
  invasion of Sicily 155
  Kamikaze losses 166
  Mariana Islands 159
  Normandy landings 158–9
  refusal black recruits 261
  training of pilots 278, 279
  'Two-Ocean Navy' programme 145, 172
USA
  against Japanese war in China 52
  Armed Forces Radio Service 282
  art and propaganda 393–9
  attitude towards Japanese 213
  Congress rejection of League of Nations 11, 17
  conscription 172
  control of information 397, 398
  coordination with Britain 52, 168, 174
  culture, in Europe 284
  defensive measures early years 172
  desire for war with Japan 180–1
  economic sanctions on Japan 53
  effect on supplies of entry into war 176
  entry into war 176
  equipment production 206
  expansion of operations in Pacific 186
  fleet in Hawaii 52, 53
  food consumption and health 303, 304
  'Germany First' strategy 150, 151, 174
  Great Depression 169
  home front 248, 249–50, 313
  importance of technical development 370, 371, 372
  and international economic initiatives 256
  internment 309
  isolationism 31, 169, 393
  and Japanese dollar assets 144
  Korean War 428, 429
  labour force 237, 238, 249
  military deferment 260
  military production 238
  natural resources 237
  Office of Scientific Research and Development (OSRD) 357
  'open door' policy 53
  in opposition to Axis powers 28
  opposition to Soviet influence post war 403, 404
  Pacific War 67, 68, 135, 192
  pre-war economy 237
  propaganda in Cold War 399
  racial prejudice in 249
  racial segregation of forces 260, 261
  relationship with Japan 38, 65, 66
  strategy in Allied debate 178
  strikes 250
  supply of goods to Britain 236
  support troops 209, 210
  troop movements across Atlantic 151
  use of atomic bomb 209
  War Production Board 245
  War Relocation Board 309
  wartime economy 238
  weapons development 357
  and Western Atlantic 142
  women as non-combatants 271
USO (United Service Organizations) 281
USSR 89, 90–2
  Anglo-American aid 144
  Anti-Fascist resistance movements 34, 100
  appeasement with Germany 169
  arts 388–93
  backing for Communist International 43
  blockade West Berlin 412–13
  collectivization of agriculture 22
  conscription 251, 258
  displacement of population 306, 307, 309–10

Eastern Europe post war 403
entry into war on Japan 33, 72, 73
equipment production 206, 257
expansionism 34, 418, 419, 429
Five-Year Plans 172
Formation of 7, 10
food supply 304–5, 306
and Germany 30, 34, 53, 124, 152, 290, 335
home front 251, 253, 313
labour camps 237
League of Nations membership 15
Lend Lease 240, 241, 242
long term effect of war 200
loss of industrial output 237
losses of equipment 243, 244
and Marshall Plan 420
military preparation 171–3, 237, 244
neutrality 171
occupation of Balkans 118
partisans 320
pre-war economy 236
propaganda 388, 392
re-militarization 111
Russian Orthodoxy 287
State Defence Committee 346
supplies from Allies reduced 181
total losses armed forces 199
use of militia 261
'Victory Day' 392
wartime economy 237, 244
weapons development 358
women in armed forces 268–9, 270
USSR air force 126, 189, 200–1, 214
USSR army (Red Army)
advance to Western Ukraine 190
atrocities 290, 291, 335
attack on Berlin 134, 198
Battle of Stalingrad 185, 186
defeat of German troops Eastern front 159
defence of Moscow 131
depletion of 128
German army losses 183
and German attack 126, 174–5
and German extermination camps 133
harsh disciplinary system 212
home contact 282, 283
innovations 216, 217–18
leadership 218
losses 177, 187, 188, 189, 194–5, 217, 218
membership Communist party 288
motor vehicles 189
policy of 'Germany First' 172
prisoners of war 212, 213, 334
propaganda 287, 288
reliance on Allied supplies 156
resistance in 131–2

social structure 265
surrender 289
training 211, 276
Ustaša 332
Ustinov, D. F. 347

V1 'flying bomb' 209, 247, 327
V2 ballistic rocket 209, 247, 327, 358
Vannikov, Boris L. 346
Vasilevskii, Aleksandr M. 188
Versailles, Treaty of (1919) 407–8
disputed by Germany 12, 13
Hitler's response to 111
Italy 77, 78
veterinarians 350
Vichy regime, France
civil defence system 297
clergy and 286
Indochina 52, 53, 61
Japanese pressure on 52, 53
North Africa 138, 154
resistance groups 317
Victor Emmanuel III, King of Italy 93, 94, 97
Vidar, Fred 395
Viet Minh 55
Vietinghoff, Heinrich von 102
Vietnam 5, 52, 55, 60
Vietnamese Revolution (1945) 62
Vistula River 194, 195, 196
Vistula–Oder operation 196
Vittorio Veneto, Battle of (1918) 94
Vladivostok 156
V-mail 281
Volga River 131, 132, 186
Volksgemeinschaft (People's Community) 263, 264, 385
Volkssturm 270, 273
volunteers 259, 262, 267, 268, 274
von dem Bach-Zelewski, Erich 314, 316
Voronezh 178
Voznesensky, Nikolai 244, 245
V-weapons 129
Vyshinsky, Andrei 420

Waffen SS 264, 267, 287, 289
Walcheren 164
Wall Street Crash 24–5
Wallace, Henry A. 345, 348
Wang Jingwei 52
War Artists Advisory Committee (WAAC) 377, 380
war crimes 290
War Department Art Advisory Committee (WDAAC) 395
War of Resistance 44–8, 52, 68, 72
war reparations 12, 29, 411
war trials 410, 411
Warsaw 195, 320, 327
Warsaw Pact 430
Warsaw Uprising (1944) 314

Warship Week (1942) 282
Washington Conference (1921–22) 37, 38
Waugh, Evelyn 375
Wavell, Archibald 337
weapons development 3, 262, 352–8, 364–6
Weimar Republic 12, 24
West Indies 267
West Point 266
West Virginia 146, 147
Westphalia, Treaty of 17
'White Dominions' 33
White, Theodore H. 322
Why We Fight (film)(Capra) 396
Wilkie, Wendell 394
WILPF (Women's International League for Peace and Freedom) 7
Wilson, Woodrow 11, 13, 24, 38, 39
Wolf's Lair 96, 127
women
Allied attitude to 270
in armed forces 268–71
atrocities by Japanese 64
Auxiliary Territorial Service 270–1
British conscription 235
campaign for power post First World War 7, 11
Chinese war effort 47
civil defence 298–300
'comfort women' 64
French resistance and 318, 319
in German art 387
Jewish 127
mobilized in USSR 217
in propaganda films 397
Singapore Overseas Chinese Army 55
in Southern Italy 104
war artists 379
Women's Auxiliary Army Corps 271
workers 249, 250, 251, 253, 254, 302, 394
see also rape
Women's International League for Peace and Freedom (WILPF) 7
Women's Voluntary Services for Air Raid Precautions (WVS) 299
Workers, Farmers and Soldiers (Schmitz-Wiedenbrück) 387, 388
World Economic Conference (1927) 24
Wuhan 46, 47, 59
Württemberg 329

Xuzhou 46, 59

Yakovlev, Alexander 347, 348
Yalta Conference (1945) 106, 198, 402, 404, 411

Yamagata Aritomo 38
Yamamoto Isoroku 145, 150
Yamato 166, 364
Yeager, Chuck 279
Yonai Mitsumasa 52
Yoshihito, Emperor 50
Young, Louise 40
Yuan Shih-kai 37
Yugoslavia
    alliance with France 17
    Anti-Fascist resistance
      85, 100
    claim to Trieste 406
    Dalmatian coast 15
    expulsion from Cominform 422
    German invasion of 84, 124
    German troops replacing
      Italian 187
    resistance 314, 320
    USSR push 195

Zhdanov, Andrei 414, 420, 421
Zhukov, Georgy 33, 188, 196, 197,
    198, 265
Zinkeisen, Doris 381
Zitadelle 155, 187, 189
Zyklon B 367